PELICAN BOOKS

THE PROBLEM OF SLAVERY
IN WESTERN CULTURE

David Brion Davis received his A.B. degree at Dartmouth College and his M.A. and Ph.D. degrees at Harvard University. He is now Ernest I. White Professor of History at Cornell University. Professor Davis is the author of *Homicide in American Fiction, 1798–1860: A Study in Social Values*, and of numerous articles in such journals as the *American Historical Review*, *Journal of American History*, *New England Quarterly*, *American Quarterly*, and the *Journal of Negro History*.

THE PROBLEM OF SLAVERY
IN WESTERN CULTURE

David Brion Davis

PENGUIN BOOKS

Penguin Books Ltd, Harmondsworth, Middlesex, England
Penguin Books Australia Ltd, Ringwood, Victoria, Australia

—

First published by Cornell University Press 1966
Published in Pelican Books 1970

—

Copyright © Cornell University Press, 1966

—

Made and printed in Great Britain
by Cox & Wyman Ltd,
London, Reading and Fakenham
Set in Intertype Plantin

To the memory of my mother,
MARTHA WIRT DAVIS,
and my father,
CLYDE BRION DAVIS

Contents

CONTENTS

Preface

PERHAPS the best way to define the purpose and scope of this book is to give a brief account of its origin. Quite some time ago I began a comparative study of the British and American anti-slavery movements. I was interested in such questions as international influence, the effect of different social and political structures on anti-slavery thought, and the interaction between the changing social role of reformers and their governing beliefs and values. Above all, I was interested in a problem of moral perception. Why was it that at a certain moment of history a small number of men not only saw the full horror of a social evil to which mankind had been blind for centuries, but felt impelled to attack it through personal testimony and cooperative action?

As I pursued these questions in both America and Great Britain, I became convinced that the problem of slavery transcended national boundaries in ways I had not suspected. Unlike representative government or trial by jury, Negro slavery was an institution common to virtually all New World colonies; it was, so to speak, the joint creation of the maritime powers of Europe. Moreover, the nations of Western Europe shared a whole network of beliefs and associations regarding slavery which derived from the Bible, the works of classical antiquity, and actual experience with various kinds of servitude. To a large extent this cultural heritage provided the framework and defined the issues for the public controversies of the late eighteenth and nineteenth centuries. And when anti-slavery movements arose almost simultaneously in Britain, France and North America, the reformers drew on the same accounts of Africa by such travellers as Michel Adanson; they borrowed the same philosophical arguments from Montesquieu and Francis Hutcheson; and they were inspired by the same eighteenth-century ideals of moral progress and disinterested benevolence.

The more I became aware of this cultural and historical dimension of the problem, the more I realized that I could not see abolitionists in proper perspective until I knew whether slavery had long been a source of latent tension in Western culture; whether there had been continuing protests against the institution; whether 'slavery' meant something radically different in ancient Greece and Rome, medieval Europe, and North and South America; whether Christianity had always had the tendency of softening and gradually eroding the institution. Much to my surprise, I found that while there were excellent recent histories of slavery in antiquity, in the Middle Ages and in the United States, there was no modern study of slavery in different periods and nations. And since the publication of Russell P. Jameson's highly informative *Montesquieu et l'esclavage,* in 1911, there has been no systematic attempt to trace the intellectual origins of anti-slavery thought. Any comparative analysis of slave systems must owe much to the questions framed by such original and provocative books as Frank Tannenbaum's *Slave and Citizen* and Stanley M. Elkins's *Slavery: A Problem in American Institutional and Intellectual Life.* Any student of changing attitudes towards slavery must be heavily indebted to such specialized studies as Edward D. Seeber's *Anti-Slavery Opinion in France during the Second Half of the Eighteenth Century* and Wylie Sypher's *Guinea's Captive Kings.* I was unable, however, to find any general history of the intellectual and cultural sources of the great international controversy over Negro slavery.

This book, then, was written as an introductory volume for a projected history, of anti-slavery movements. It makes no pretence of being a history of slavery as such, or even of opinion concerning slavery. Although the scope is broad, I have omitted much that has not seemed relevant to an understanding of the later conflicts over Negro bondage. I have been concerned with the different ways in which men have responded to slavery, on the assumption that this will help us distinguish what was unique in the response of the abolitionist. I have also been concerned with traditions in thought and value from which both opponents and defenders of slavery could draw. I hope to demonstrate that slavery has always been a source of social and psychological tension, but that in Western culture it was associated with certain religious and philosophical doctrines that gave it the highest sanction. The underlying contradiction of slavery became more manifest when the institution was closely linked with American colonization, which was also seen as affording mankind the opportunity to create a more perfect society. After surveying representative attempts to conceptualize this moral and historical problem, we shall turn, in chapter 2, to a comparative analysis of slave systems in the Old World. Chapters 3 and 4 will then deal with the response to slavery in European thought from antiquity to the eighteenth century, excluding, for the most part, the question of Negro bondage in America. Chapters 5 through 9 consider early attitudes towards American slavery, and are particularly concerned with problems and conditions which might aid or impede the rise of anti-slavery thought. Chapters 10 through 15 are devoted to early protests against Negro bondage, and to the religious, literary and philosophical developments that contributed to both sides in the controversies of the late eighteenth century. In sketching certain broad economic and institutional trends, it has sometimes seemed appropriate to include material from the late eighteenth century and even the nineteenth. In general, however, this study extends only to the early 1770s, and does not cover the first organized efforts to abolish the African trade or Negro slavery. The next volume will begin with the reformers in England, France and North America whose writings and correspondence led to the creation of the first anti-slavery societies. And it will be my hope in the succeeding volumes to trace the evolution of the international controversies over Negro slavery, giving particular attention to the growth and implications of anti-slavery thought.

Any broad work of historical synthesis is heavily dependent upon the research, aid and criticism of many people. This is particularly true when a historian strays beyond his own field and ventures into unfamiliar and often forbidding territory at a time when scholars reap the greatest rewards by tending their own gardens. I am all too aware of the risks I have taken by attempting so much, and I would not excuse my inevitable errors by pointing to those who have helped me. Nevertheless, I would have committed many more mistakes of both fact and judgement if portions of the manuscript had not been read by Professors Donald Kagan, Allan Bloom, Denys Hay, Brian

Tierney, Kenneth Stampp, Carl N. Degler, Winthrop D. Jordan, Paul W. Gates, Arthur M. Wilson, Walter LaFeber, Walter Simon and Knight Biggerstaff. For their criticism, advice and generosity I am deeply grateful.

I am also indebted to Dr John Walsh, Dr Robert W. Greaves, and Professors Walter Pintner, Eugene Rice, Magnus Mörner and Richard Graham for guiding me to materials I would otherwise have missed. Dr John A. Woods generously lent me his transcriptions of the Granville Sharp papers, which served as general background for this book and which will be invaluable for the succeeding volume. When I was nearing completion of this manuscript and learned that Professor Winthrop D. Jordan was working on a related topic, he allowed me the extraordinary privilege of reading his excellent study, 'White Over Black: The Development of American Attitudes Toward the Negro, 1550–1812', which will soon be published by the University of North Carolina Press, for the Institute of Early American History and Culture. While Professor Jordan and I found that we had used many of the same sources, we were comforted to discover that our books complemented each other and that we could exchange bits of useful information.

My greatest debt is to Dr Felix Reichmann, Assistant Director of Cornell University Libraries, who not only acquired countless books and microfilms which aided my research, but whose astonishing erudition guided me to numerous discoveries. This book could not have been written without the great collection on slavery and anti-slavery which Cornell has been accumulating since the University's founding. I am most grateful to the entire staff of Cornell University Libraries, and I am also grateful for the help and cooperation I received from the library of the British Museum; the Bodleian Library; the Historical Manuscripts Commission, National Register of Archives; Friends House, London; the Library of Congress; the Henry E. Huntington Library; the Library Company of Philadelphia, Ridgeway Branch; Duke University Library; the British and Foreign Bible Society; the New York Historical Society; the Historical Society of Pennsylvania; the Boston Athenaeum; Boston Public Library; Allegheny College Library; and Harvard University Library.

PREFACE

I am indebted to the John Simon Guggenheim Memorial Foundation for a fellowship which allowed me to begin my researches in England. I am also indebted to the Ernest I. White Professorship at Cornell, which has provided funds for research and clerical assistance. In the later stages of research Miss Jean Laux was an invaluable aid in tracking down books, transcribing material and offering helpful suggestions. I am also most grateful to Professors Jean Parrish and Dalai Brenes for aiding me with French and Spanish translations; to Miss June Hahner, Miss Irene Berkey, Miss Christy Reppert and Mr Philippe Chaudron for checking footnotes; to Mrs Tazu Warner and Mrs Jacqueline Holl for typing different drafts of the manuscript; to Miss Anne Loveland, Miss Marcia Luther and Mr Jack Holl for various bibliographical chores; and to Mrs Catharine McCalmon for helping with the index. An earlier version of chapter 3 was published in *The Anti-Slavery Vanguard: New Essays on the Abolitionists*, edited by Martin Duberman (copyright © 1965); Princeton University Press has kindly granted me permission to reprint this essay. To my students, both graduate and undergraduate, I owe the questions and criticisms which dissolved some of my most dubious theories and helped to clarify the rest. Finally, I can never express sufficient gratitude to my wife and children for their patience and encouragement.

D. B. B.

Ithaca, New York
October 1965

PART I

I

The Historical Problem:
Slavery and the Meaning of America

AMERICANS have often been embarrassed when reminded that the Declaration of Independence was written by a slaveholder and that Negro slavery was a legal institution in all thirteen colonies at the beginning of the Revolution. 'How is it,' asked Samuel Johnson, 'that we hear the loudest *yelps* for liberty among the drivers of Negroes?' The inconsistency was not overlooked by American Tories, who exhibited it as proof of the rebels' hypocrisy. Even English liberals who sympathized with the Revolution were disturbed by a conception of liberty that seemed to exclude the Negro race. During the struggle with Great Britain, American leaders often admitted that slavery was contrary to the principles for which they fought, and a number of reformers warned that the Revolution could be justified only by a decision to rid the land of slavery. In 1775, for example, Deacon Benjamin Colman noted that Boston, the first slave-trading port on the continent, had been the first victim of British oppression, a 're-markable providence' which clearly indicated that Massachusetts could not secure her own freedom until she emancipated her slaves. And towards the end of the war David Cooper observed that 'our rulers have appointed days for humiliation, and offering up of prayer to our common Father to deliver us from *our* oppressors, when sights and groans are piercing his holy ears [*sic*] from oppressions which we commit a thousand fold more grievous.'[1]

But the irony of slaveholders fighting for the natural rights of man

1. James Boswell, *The Life of Samuel Johnson* (Modern Library ed., New York, n.d.), pp. 747–8; George H. Moore, *Notes on the History of Slavery in Massachusetts* (New York, 1866), p. 147; [David Cooper] *A Serious Address to the Rulers of America, on the Inconsistency of Their Conduct Respecting Slavery: Forming a Contrast between the Encroachments of England on American Liberty, and American Injustice in Tolerating Slavery* [Originally published in Trenton, N.J.] (London, 1783), p. 16.

was only part of a larger paradox which has seldom been grasped in its full dimensions.[2] The anti-slavery arguments of the revolutionary period were often grounded upon a belief in America as a liberating and regenerating force – as the world's new hope. This belief had taken various forms and had only recently been directed against slavery. But from the time of the first discoveries Europeans had projected ancient visions of liberation and perfection into the vacant spaces of the New World. Explorers approached the uncharted coasts with vague preconceptions of mythical Atlantis, Antillia and the Saint Brendan Isles. The naked savages, living in apparent freedom and innocence, awakened memories of terrestrial paradise and the Golden Age described by the ancients. Even the practical-minded Columbus fell under the spell of the gentle natives of the Gulf of Paria, who wore golden ornaments and lived in a land of lush vegetation and delicious fruits. He concluded in August 1498 that he had arrived on the 'nipple' of the earth, which reached closer to Heaven than the rest of the globe, and that the original Garden of Eden was near by.[3] Seventeen years later, when Sir Thomas More began writing *Utopia,* he naturally chose the Western Hemisphere as his setting.

Columbus's successors pursued elusive visions of golden cities and fountains of youth; their narratives revived and nourished the utopian dreams of Europe. From antiquity Western thought had been predisposed to look to nature for the universal norms of human life. Since 'nature' carried connotations of origin and birth as well as of intrinsic character, philosophers often associated valid norms with

2. Even Gunnar Myrdal fails to see the importance of the historical dimension of the 'American Dilemma', which he conceives as simply a conflict between 'the American Creed' and social conduct and valuations concerning the Negro. He perceives, however, that 'the Negro problem is an integral part of, or a special phase of the whole complex of problems in the larger civilization. It cannot be treated in isolation.' And he notes the tendency of Americans 'to localize and demarcate the Negro problem'. The same points can be made regarding the history of slavery and anti-slavery. See Myrdal *et al., An American Dilemma: The Negro Problem in Modern America* (New York, 1944), p. liii.

3. Samuel Eliot Morison, *Admiral of the Ocean Sea: A Life of Christopher Columbus* (Boston, 1942), pp. 556–7.

what was original in man's primeval state. They contrasted the restraints, prejudices and corrupting tastes of civilized life with either a former age of virtue or a simpler, more primitive state of society.[4] Many of the explorers and early commentators on America drew upon this philosophic tradition; in the New World they found an Elysium to serve as a standard for criticizing the perverted manners of Europe. Catholic missionaries, being dedicated to ideals of renunciation and asceticism, saw much to admire in the simple contentment of the Indians, whose mode of living seemed to resemble that of the first Christians. As Gilbert Chinard has pointed out, the *voyageurs* and Jesuit priests who compared the evils of Europe with the freedom, equality and felicitous life of the American savages, contributed unwittingly to the revolutionary philosophy of the eighteenth century.[5]

Some writers, to be sure, described the Indians as inferior degenerates or as Satan's children, and presented a contrary image of America as an insalubrious desert. Antonello Gerbi has documented the long dispute over the nature of the New World 'mondo nascente a neonato, mondo deserto e misero.'[6] Howard Mumford Jones has recently shown that America was conceived at once as an idyllic Arcadia and as a land of cannibalism, torture and brutality, where extremities of human greed and cruelty were matched by the unexpected terrors and monstrosities of the wilderness.[7] But in Hebrew and Christian thought the idea of wilderness had long been linked

4. Arthur O. Lovejoy, Gilbert Chinard, George Boas and Ronald S. Crane, *A Documentary History of Primitivism and Related Ideas* (Baltimore, 1935), I, pp. 12–18, 109–11.

5. Gilbert Chinard, *L'Amérique et le rêve exotique dans la littérature française au XVIIᵉ et au XVIIIᵉ siècle* (Paris, 1913), pp. v–vii, 119–50, 431. See also Lois Whitney, *Primitivism and the Idea of Progress in English Popular Literature of the Eighteenth Century* (Baltimore, 1934), pp. 40–48 and *passim*; Maren-Sofie Røstvig, *The Happy Man; Studies in the Metamorphoses of a Classical Ideal, 1600–1700* (Oslo, 1954), pp. 16, 41–6, and *passim*; Hoxie Neale Fairchild, *The Noble Savage: A Study in Romantic Naturalism* (New York, 1928), pp. 10–13 and *passim*.

6. Antonello Gerbi, *La disputa del Nuovo Mondo: storia di una polemica, 1750–1900* (Milano, 1955), *passim*.

7. Howard Mumford Jones, *O Strange New World! American Culture: The Formative Years* (New York, 1963), pp. 35–70.

with rebirth and fulfilment. After being delivered from slavery in Egypt, the children of Israel had crossed the Red Sea and had wandered in the wilderness for forty years before finding the Promised Land. The desert was a place of refuge and purification, of suffering and perseverance; and no matter what hardships it offered, there was the assurance that a fertile paradise would ultimately emerge from its desolate wastes. Thanks to the researches of George H. Williams, we know what an important part such imagery played in Christian ideas of redemption.[8] The wilderness might be thought of as a purely spiritual state, or as the abode of monks, hermits or persecuted sects. But early American colonists could hardly escape the symbolic implications of a baptismal crossing of the Atlantic, or of dwelling in a land which could be seen as either desert or primeval garden. The New World, like the wilderness in both the Old and New Testaments, was a place of extraordinary temptation, obligation and promise.

While a growing literature celebrated America as a symbol of nature, free from the avarice, luxury and materialism of Europe, promoters and colonizers saw the virgin land as a place for solving problems and satisfying desires. This was true of the conquistadores who tried to recreate the age of chivalric romance; it was true of the Jesuits who followed Manuel da Nóbrega to Brazil, determined to purify morals and spread the faith; it was true of the English Puritans who sought to build a New Jerusalem as a model of piety for the rest of the world; it was true of the drifters and ne'er-do-wells, the bankrupts and sleazy gentlemen, who fluttered to the New World like moths drawn to a light. In America things would be better, for America was the Promised Land. It could be said, of course, that America was an asylum for scoundrels, adventurers and religious fanatics. But in time much of the magic of the virgin continent seemed to rub off on its conquerors. French humanitarians, for example, found it easy to shift their enthusiasm from noble savage to peace-loving Quaker. In Saint-John de Crèvecoeur's *Letters from an*

8. George H. Williams, *Wilderness and Paradise in Christian Thought: The Biblical Experience of the Desert in the History of Christianity and the Paradise Theme in the Theological Idea of the University* (New York, 1962), pp. 10–137.

American Farmer we see perhaps the clearest picture of the American idyll, a skilful weaving together of primitivist, pastoral and democratic themes, the portrayal of a land in which individual opportunity and social progress are somehow merged with the simple, self-denying virtues of Seneca and Virgil.

This long tradition, based on a mixture of Biblical and classical sources, helped to shape the American's image of himself as the new Adam of the West, a being unencumbered by the fears and superstitions of a mouldering civilization, a wise innocent dwelling in a terrestrial paradise. He was at once the Happy Husbandman, content to enjoy the serene blessings of a simple, rural life, and an adventurous pioneeer, expansive and supremely confident of his ability to improve the world. Such an image contained an intrinsic contradiction which contributed to severe tensions in the race of rapid social and economic change. But if Americans were often inclined to see Satan fast at work corrupting their new Eden, this only enhanced the moral importance of their mission. And by the time of the Revolution many European liberals looked to America as the hope of mankind, for it was there that institutions seemed most clearly modelled on nature's simple plan. By reconciling nature and human progress, the newly independent states appeared to have fulfilled the ancient dream of a more perfect society.[9]

But what was the meaning of slavery in an earthly paradise? By the time of Columbus involuntary servitude had begun to disappear through much of Western Europe. Two centuries before the discovery of America, Philippe the Fair had written, in an ordinance freeing the serfs of Valois, 'Attendu que toute créature humaine qui

9. For discussions of the themes of innocence, moralism and the American mission, see Charles L. Sanford, *The Quest for Paradise: Europe and the American Moral Imagination* (Urbana, Ill., 1961), pp. 34–55, 86, 106–10, 134; R. W. B. Lewis, *The American Adam: Innocence, Tragedy and Tradition in the Nineteenth Century* (Chicago, 1955), pp. 4–34 and *passim*; Perry Miller, *The New England Mind: The Seventeenth Century* (Cambridge, Mass., 1954), pp. 463–91; Miller, *Errand into the Wilderness* (Cambridge, Mass., 1956), pp. 1–15; Edward McNall Burns, *The American Idea of Mission: Concepts of National Purpose and Destiny* (New Brunswick, N.J., 1957), pp. 61–86; Henry Nash Smith, *Virgin Land: The American West as Symbol and Myth* (Cambridge, Mass., 1950), *passim*.

est formée à l'image de Notre-Seigneur doit généralement être franche par droit naturel.'[10] Henry VII of England was said to have manumitted some of the villeins on his estates 'because in the beginning nature made all men free, and afterwards the law of nations reduced some under the yoke of servitude'.[11] Yet slavery had been linked from the very beginning with what Edmundo O'Gorman has called 'the invention of America'. The African voyages promoted by Prince Henry of Portugal prepared the way for the first crossing of the Atlantic; and when Columbus arrived in Lisbon in 1477 the trade in Negro slaves was a flourishing enterprise. The same Columbus who identified the Gulf of Paria as the gateway to the Garden of Eden had no compunction about sending hundreds of Indians to be sold in the slave marts of Seville, although some two hundred died on the first voyage and had to be thrown into the sea.[12] It was thus the discoverer of America who initiated the transatlantic slave trade, which moved originally from west to east.

It was soon apparent, however, as the Spanish came close to exterminating the native inhabitants of Hispaniola, that successful colonization would require a fresh supply of labourers. Negro slaves arrived in the New World at least as early as 1502, and by 1513 the sale of licences for importing Negroes was a source of profit for the Spanish government.[13] Following the Guinea current and trade winds, Portuguese ships provided the colonists with a mounting supply of slaves, but seldom with enough to meet the insatiable demand. As Negro labour became indispensable for Spanish and then Portuguese colonization, European traders and African chieftains slowly built a vast commercial system which brought a profound transformation in African culture and stunted the growth of other commerce between Europe and the Dark Continent.[14]

10. De Lévis Mirepoix, *Le siècle de Philippe le Bel* (Paris, 1961), p. 147.

11. E. Lipson, *The Economic History of England,* I: *The Middle Ages,* 11th ed. (London, 1956), p. 130.

12. Morison, *Admiral of the Ocean Sea,* pp. 32, 291, 486–93.

13. Elizabeth Donnon (ed.), *Documents Illustrative of the History of the Slave Trade to America* (Washington, 1930–35), I, pp. 14–16.

14. Basil Davidson, *Black Mother: The Years of the African Slave*

For three centuries the principal maritime powers competed with one another in the lucrative slave trade, and carried at least fifteen million Africans to the New World.[15] Historians have long been inclined to regard this vast movement of population as an unfortunate but relatively minor incident in American history. Interest in national and sectional history has often obscured the significance of Negro slavery in the overall development of the Americas. But if the institution was of little economic importance in Massachusetts or Nova Scotia, it nevertheless extended from Rio de la Plata to the Saint Lawrence, and was the basic system of labour in the colonies most valued by Europe. In the most profitable colonies Negro slaves were employed in mines and in clearing virgin land, or on the great plantations which provided Europe with sugar, rice, tobacco, cotton and indigo. The northern colonies that were unsuited for the production of staple crops became dependent, early in their history, on supplying the slave colonies with goods and provisions of various kinds. As a stimulus to shipbuilding, insurance, investment and banking, the slave trade expanded employment in a diversity of occupations and encouraged the growth of seaports on both sides of the Atlantic. Africa became a prized market for iron, textiles, firearms, rum and brandy. Investments in the triangular trade brought dazzling rewards, since profits could be made in exporting consumer goods to Africa, in selling slaves to planters, and especially in transporting sugar and other staples to Europe. By the 1760s a large number of the wealthy merchants in Britain and France were connected in some way with the West Indian trade; and capital accumulated from investment in slaves and their produce helped to finance the building of canals, factories and railroads. Even after the United States had achieved independence and a more diversified economy, her principal export

---

Trade (Boston, 1961), pp. 44–8, 82–112, 117–62; Alexander Marchant, From Barter to Slavery: The Economic Relations of Portuguese and Indians in the Settlement of Brazil, 1500–1580 (Baltimore, 1942), pp. 73–9, 131.

15. It is impossible, of course, to make more than an informed guess, but this estimate is on the conservative side. See Davidson, Black Mother, pp. 79–81, and Frank Tannenbaum, Slave and Citizen: The Negro in the Americas (New York, 1947), pp. 31–2.

was slave-grown cotton, which was the chief raw material for the Industrial Revolution.[16]

Without exaggerating the economic significance of Negro slavery, we may safely conclude that it played a major role in the early development of the New World and in the growth of commercial capitalism. Given the lack of an alternative labour supply, it is difficult to see how European nations could have settled America and exploited its resources without the aid of African slaves. Yet slavery had always been more than an economic institution; in Western culture it had long represented the ultimate limit of dehumanization, of treating and regarding a man as a thing. How was one to reconcile the brute fact that slavery was an intrinsic part of the American experience with the image of the New World as uncorrupted nature, as a source of redemption from the burdens of history, as a paradise which promised fulfilment of man's highest aspirations?

Fore more than two centuries this momentous question was generally ignored. Missionaries and travellers such as Jean-Baptiste Du Tertre, who celebrated the virtues of the American Indian and portrayed the New World as a second Eden, were indifferent to the predicament of the African slave. A double standard in judging Negroes and Indians enabled colonists of various nationalities to channel moral concern towards the aborigine, whose freedom was often essential for commercial and military security, and to screen off the critical centre of the American dilemma.[17] Yet protests against the dispossession and exploitation of innocent Indians often implied that

16. Paul Mantoux, *The Industrial Revolution in the Eighteenth Century* (rev. ed., tr. by Marjorie Vernon, New York, 1929), pp. 105–11; Eric Williams, *Capitalism and Slavery* (Chapel Hill, 1944), pp. 36–8, 46–58, 92–107; Davidson, *Black Mother*, pp. 60–65; Frank W. Pitman, 'Slavery on British West India Plantations in the Eighteenth Century', *Journal of Negro History*, XI (October 1926), 584–7.

17. Chinard, *Amérique*, pp. 20–21, 51–3; Lewis Hanke, *Aristotle and the American Indian: A Study of Race Prejudice in the Modern World* (Chicago, 1959), p. 9. We shall later discuss the question in more detail, but for evidence of the continuation of a double standard in judging Indians and Negroes in the Spanish colonies, see Jaime Jaramillo Uribe, 'Esclavos y señores en la sociedad colombiana del siglo XVIII', *Anuario colombiano de historia social y de la cultura*, I (Bogotá, 1963), pp. 21–5.

America's promise could not be realized without a price of guilt. And in popular literature, at least, the distinction between Indians and Negroes had a tendency to dissolve.

The tale of Inkle and Yarico was one of the first portrayals of American moral experience to attract popular interest on an international scale.[18] Translated into eight languages, this great folk epic inspired some forty separate works during the eighteenth century, and was given form in poems, essays, plays and ballet. The story may be interpreted as merely an early outburst of middle-class sentimentality. But it may also be taken as the first significant attempt to give imaginative expression to the meaning of slavery in America.

In 1657 Richard Ligon told of an Indian woman in Barbados who had been a slave in the house where he had lived. She had been sold by a 'Christian servant' who had brought her from the mainland, where he had been shipwrecked. The lovely maiden had actually saved the Christian's life, had fallen in love with him, and had cared for him in a secluded cave. After becoming pregnant, she had accompanied her lover to Barbados, only to be betrayed: 'And so poor Yarico for her love, lost her liberty.'[19]

This was the nucleus of the story used by Sir Richard Steele's 'Arietta' to prove that women are more faithful than men. But Steele, writing in 1711, gave a softer and more sentimental picture of primi-

18. Lawrence Marsden Price has collected and edited the most important versions of the tale in his fascinating *Inkle and Yarico Album* (Berkeley, 1937). But Gilbert Chinard credits Jean Mocquet, whom Price does not mention, with originating the story. Mocquet, who travelled to America in the first years of the seventeenth century, told of an English sailor who was shipwrecked and cared for by an Indian maiden. After promising to marry her and travelling with her through the wilderness for two or three years, he contemptuously abandoned her as an uncouth savage when they came upon an English ship. The couple had had a child in the wilderness, and the Indian woman, outraged by her betrayal, cut the baby into two pieces and hurled one part towards the departing ship! (Jean Mocquet, *Travels and Voyages into Africa, Asia, and America* . . . [tr. by Nathaniel Pullen, London, 1696], pp. 124–7.) The connexion between this story and Inkle and Yarico would seem to be rather tenuous.

19. Richard Ligon, *A True & Exact History of the Island of Barbadoes* (London, 1673), pp. 54–5.

tive life in America.[20] After being saved by the innocent Yarico, Thomas Inkle, a young English sailor, enjoys an idyllic honeymoon in an Eden-like setting. The couple sport together in moonlit groves, and Yarico brings tropical fruit to their remote cave and plays with Inkle's curly hair while the nightingales sing. Inkle, however, is an ambitious young man who could never be content to waste his life in such a paradise; when he promises to take Yarico to England and to clothe her in fine silks, she signals a ship which eventually carries the couple to Barbados. Regretting the time and profits he has lost, Inkle, who is a 'prudent and frugal young man', decides to sell his mistress as a slave. When he learns that Yarico is pregnant, he simply raises her price.

Steele obviously wished to dramatize the evils of ingratitude and infidelity. For this purpose he chose an exotic setting and a primitivistic scale of values, contrasting the selfishness and cunning of the European with the spontaneous virtues of the American savage. Neither Ligon nor Steele questioned the institution of slavery; the nature of Yarico's misfortune was less important than the fact that she had been spiritually free in a state of nature, whereas Inkle had remained a slave to avarice and ambition. Steele's imitators, however, increasingly dwelt on the cruelty and injustice of selling human beings. In an anonymous poem of 1736, Barbados is 'the sad Place, where Sorrow ever reigns / And hopeless Wretches groan beneath their Chains'.[21] The New World is at once a terrestrial paradise where a European may escape the buffetings of a tempestuous world and enjoy an idyllic love in the state of nature; and it is the scene of heartless exploitation where men disregard the elemental ties of humanity and sell their fellow creatures into perpetual bondage. By 1734, moreover, Yarico has become a Negro virgin, and by the middle of the century the story's setting is expanded to include Africa and Jamaica.[22]

20. *The Spectator: A New Edition, Carefully Revised in Six Volumes, with Prefaces Historical and Biographical by Alexander Chalmers* (New York, 1853), I, pp. 133–8.

21. *Yarico to Inkle: An Epistle* (London, 1736), p. 1, in Price, *Inkle and Yarico Album.*

22. ibid., pp. 10, 18, 35ff; *London Magazine*, XXVII (1758), p. 168.

It is possible that the pathetic figure of Yarico helped to stimulate a general sympathy for American slaves. The tale was eventually appropriated by anti-slavery writers, such as the Abbé Raynal. But the fact remains that the betrayed girl was usually portrayed as an Indian.[23] If the thematic materials of the story provided a means of conceptualizing America's contradiction in the timeless categories of nature and civilization, love and betrayal, innocent contentment and mean ambition, they also raised moral questions which eighteenth-century writers found easier to evade than explore. By 1787, when George Colman the Younger built an opera on the plot of Inkle and Yarico, the tale had become little more than farce and ephemeral entertainment.

As we shall see in subsequent chapters, the legal and moral validity of slavery was a troublesome question in European thought from the time of Aristotle to the time of Locke. It was only in the eighteenth century, however, that discussions of American slavery acquired a prominent place in the standard works of history, jurisprudence, political economy and moral philosophy. Firmly established by Montesquieu, Francis Hutcheson, William Robertson, Blackstone, Adam Smith and Jefferson, the convention was sustained by leading thinkers of the nineteenth century. For as the Western mind increasingly looked to history for moral guidance and self-understanding, it became imperative to reconcile the revival of slavery in modern times with various theories of human progress. Disciples of the Enlightenment, for example, might well ask why the institution had continued to flourish in an age of reason and improved understanding of natural law. In the nineteenth century the persistence of slavery took on new implications as men identified progress with a widening influence of Christian morality, of social science or of popular democracy. Since these four views of progress long governed the dominant interpretations of slavery in modern history, and since they reveal somewhat different contours of the problem, it is well to exam-

---

For a discussion of the literary confusion of Indians and Negroes, see Wylie Sypher, *Guinea's Captive Kings: British Anti-Slavery Literature of the XVIIIth Century* (Chapel Hill, 1942), pp. 105–8.

23. Price, *Inkle and Yarico Album, passim.*

ine four works which are representative of each perspective. In the Abbé Raynal we may see an example of the Enlightenment's faith in reason and nature; Henri Alexandre Wallon and Auguste Comte may stand respectively for belief in the progress of Christian and scientific principles; for an exponent of popular democracy we may turn to George Bancroft.

The Abbé Raynal and his distinguished collaborators, who in 1770 brought out the first edition of the *Histoire des deux Indes,* assumed that the discovery and colonization of America had profoundly influenced the history of the world and all aspects of European civilization.[24] The great question was whether this influence had furthered human progress or had only brought more rapid change.[25] Slavery, quite obviously, could not be excluded from so momentous an evaluation.

Like most *philosophes* of this age, Raynal thought that slavery was contrary to nature and thus universally wrong. He conceded, to be sure, that dependence and authority were necessary as man progressed from the most primitive state of equality. What was more difficult to explain was why a mild domestic slavery had developed into a more brutal system that had spread throughout the ancient world as wealth, power and enlightenment had increased. Raynal did

24. Although the *Histoire des deux Indes* was the work of a large number of writers, including Diderot, Dubreuil, Saint-Lambert and d'Holbach, and although Jean de Pechméja was responsible for some of the sections on colonial slavery, for convenience we may refer to Raynal as the author. See Michèle Duchet, 'Diderot collaborateur de Raynal: à propos des "fragments imprimés" du Fonds Vandeul', *Revue d'histoire littéraire de la France,* LX (1960), pp. 531–56; Anatole Feugère, 'Raynal, Diderot et quelques autres "Historiens des deux Indes",' *Revue d' histoire littéraire de la France,* XX (1913), pp. 343–78. There is no conclusive evidence that Raynal's views on slavery were different from those of his collaborators. Naigeon complained that in one edition Raynal had cut out some of Pechméja's boldest lines on slavery, but Hans Wolpe argues persuasively that the relevant changes in the 1781 edition are stylistic and show no diminution of anti-slavery zeal. See Hans Wolpe, *Raynal et sa machine de guerre* (Stanford, 1957), pp. 177–85.

25. Guillaume-Thomas Raynal, *Histoire philosophique et politique des établissemens et du commerce des Européens dans les deux Indes* (Genève, 1781), I, pp. 1–2.

not attempt to resolve this paradox, as some historians had done, by reference to the moral depravity of the pagan religions. While seeing slavery as evidence of man's greed and selfishness, he indicated that its worst evils had been aggravated by the growth of complex civilization. To Montesquieu's belief that Christianity had ultimately abolished slavery in Europe he gave no credence. If the gradual emancipation of European slaves had produced a more felicitous society, the result should be attributed not to religion, which had done nothing to promote human liberty, but to the political and economic self-interest of kings who had sought to lessen the power of great lords.[26] Raynal did not explain why material progress seemed at times to encourage slavery, as in the ancient world, and at other times to destroy it, as in the late Middle Ages. Like many thinkers of his century he simply assumed a sharp distinction between an unnatural hunger for gold and luxury, which corrupted society and enslaved whole peoples, and a natural expression of self-interest, which led to freedom and genuine wealth.

In any event, domestic liberty was scarcely born in Europe when it was buried in America. In Raynal's eyes European expansion into the New World was characterized from the beginning by unbelievable cruelty, slaughter and despotic slavery.[27] Far from bringing a message of hope and redemption, America provided an unlimited field for the exploitation of man's fellow beings. Although European morals had progressed in the Age of Enlightenment, the slave trade to America gave a constant stimulus to the worst vices and passions of mankind.

Was this a necessary outcome of America's development? Since Raynal believed that slavery was utterly repugnant to nature, he could not easily accept its historical inevitability. He fixed the blame for initiating the French and British slave trade on pirates and freebooters whose insatiable greed had led them, step by step, to the cultivation of sugar and the devastation of Africa. Presumably, if the nations of Europe had understood their true interests and the laws of economics, the history of the New World might have taken a happier course. Yet it had been the initial voyages to America that had

26. ibid., I, pp. 17–18; VI, pp. 117–25.
27. ibid., IV, pp. 213–16; VI, p. 125.

unsettled the European imagination and had produced a new breed of men who, at the expense of health, virtue and ancestral ties, were always roving in search of wealth. If most of the European nations had become stained with the guilt of slave trading, it was America that had led them astray. Nor could Raynal really believe that the tropical and semi-tropical colonies could have been cultivated without slaves. In the first two editions of his work he made a surprising compromise when he objected to the original prohibition against slaves in Georgia as an 'oppression' which prevented the growth of the colony.[28] Somewhat modifying this view in the edition of 1781, he concluded nevertheless that the question of allowing slaves in Georgia should have been decided by asking whether they were required for the better cultivation of land and for the greater security of property. The answer to this question must have been clear in Raynal's mind, since he had already claimed that South Carolina was the richest of the continental colonies and would soon double her population and produce if she were able to beat out the French and Spanish in the markets of the world.[29] As he summed up his thoughts towards the end of the tenth volume, Raynal blurted out, rhetorically, 'But without this labour, these lands, acquired at such a high cost, would remain uncultivated.' To this his only reply, as a committed enemy of bondage, was a flourish of despair 'Well then, let them lie fallow, if it means that to make these lands productive, man must be reduced to brutishness, whether he be the man who buys or he who sells, or he who is sold.'[30]

But though Raynal recognized that slavery was intimately connected with the very meaning of America, he did not abandon the traditional idea of the land of promise. The inhabitants of the New World, though corrupted by slavery, had an opportunity to create a new society based on the principles of reason and nature; if they should succeed one day in throwing off the evil that enveloped them, they might become a great race, enriched by a mixture of diverse peoples, united in their dedication to liberty, science and humanity. After having been devastated by Europe, the New World might rise

28. Wolpe, *Raynal*, p. 158.
29. Raynal, *Histoire*, IX, pp. 74–6.
30. ibid., X, p. 297.

to greatness and liberate the rest of mankind from enslaving customs
and institutions.[31]

For Raynal, then, the great promise of America could not be
fulfilled without the abolition of slavery; but between her potential
mission for saving the world and her actual state of corruption there
was an immeasurable gap. Such a view of the American dilemma
carried overtones of the traditional Christian conception of man's
condition as a sinner potentially capable of regeneration. Yet Raynal
had no faith in the power of Christianity to remove America's burden
of sin, since the Church had openly tolerated the worst forms of
cruelty and inhumanity. His faith in the effectiveness of reason was
only slightly greater, though he took the trouble of suggesting a
rational plan of emancipation to the rulers of Europe. But to talk to
slaveholders of the superiority of free labour was like relying on
rational persuasion to convert hardened sinners. Were there, we
might ask, any inherent forces at work in America that would lead to
the eradication of slavery and thus free the land for its providential
mission? Was slavery in America only a historical accident, or was it
part of the essential being of the New World?

Raynal gave no definite answers, but he had acknowledged that in
the ancient world slavery had co-existed with prosperity, republican
government and advancing civilization; it had been unaffected by
Christianity and had come to an end in Europe only when economic
and political conditions were favourable to freedom; it had been
associated with the development of America from the first Spanish
settlements. Raynal seemed to suggest that slavery was intrinsic to
America, much as orthodox theology has considered original sin to be
intrinsic to man's nature. He indicated that its end would come only
through some cataclysmic unheaval, such as a rebellion of the slaves
led by a black Spartacus, who would be a vehicle for Nature asserting
her rights against the blind avarice of Europeans and American colonists. The good *philosophe*'s enthusiasm for such a blood atonement

31. ibid., VI, pp. 171–2. His faith in America's historical promise was
combined with a belief in the degeneracy of most American species. Like
many European thinkers, Raynal accepted sharply contrasting images of the
New World; slavery was part of the darker side of the dualism. See Gerbi,
Disputa del Nuovo Mondo, pp. 52–7.

showed his lack of faith in any indwelling force for gradual freedom and peaceful salvation. America could not fulfil her promise to mankind without agony.

When the Abbé Raynal raised these disturbing questions Negro slavery extended through most of the settled provinces of the Western Hemisphere, and the slave trade flourished without restraint. Almost eighty years later, when Henri Wallon wrote his three-volume *Histoire de l'esclavage dans l'antiquité*, slavery had been abolished in Canada, the British West Indies, Haiti, Mexico, Central America and many of the independent countries of South America; it had virtually disappeared from the northern section of the United States, and Wallon could assume that Negroes would soon be emancipated in the French West Indies. The Atlantic slave trade, while far from dead, was officially condemned by all civilized nations. American slavery survived as a vital institution only in Cuba, Brazil and the southern United States.

Wallon's work on ancient slavery, which was to have considerable influence on subsequent historical writing, reflected many of the values and assumptions of the international anti-slavery movement of the mid nineteenth century, much as the *Histoire des deux Indes* epitomized the anti-slavery thought of the *philosophes*. In a lengthy introduction he pointed to the connexion between ancient and modern servitude, and placed the contemporary problem within a context of historical progress resulting from the spread and influence of Christianity.

Wallon had far greater faith than Raynal in the power of moral truth to guide the course of history. Since slavery violated eternal moral laws, it was always wrong and could never be a necessary condition of historical development; the struggle between liberty and bondage was as old as human society. Why, then, had slavery persisted so long? Wallon took pains to refute the pro-slavery theorists who argued that what was accepted in antiquity should be at least condoned in the nineteenth century. Slavery in the ancient world had rested on the supremacy of force over moral sensibility. Despite a common recognition that bondage was an unnatural and unsatisfying condition, there had been no moral influence to overcome the specious arguments of Aristotle, who had confused nature with the actual institutions of the city-state, and had provided sophisms for all future apologists for slavery. Even the Stoic conception of freedom had led only to an indifference towards man's external condition.[32] Wallon dissociated slavery from all that was good or admirable in antiquity. It was the radical flaw which had led to the decay of the Greek city-states and to the corruption of Rome.[33] But the introduction of Christianity had brought a profound transformation to the slave-burdened world. The doubts of philosophers had finally been answered by the revealed Word that all men are equal before God. While the Church had accepted the hierarchy of ranks in society, it had expressed solicitude for the slave and had charged masters with the duty of treating their servants as brothers in Christ. After slowly softening the harsh laws and manners of the Roman world, Christianity had improved the condition of slaves until, gently and almost imperceptibly, they had entered a state of freedom.[34]

This widely accepted view of European emancipation conformed with a faith in progress and an aversion to abrupt, revolutionary changes. But it raised perplexing questions with respect to America. As Wallon recognized, his theory implied that the restoration of slavery that accompanied the settlement of America was not only an act of violence against the spirit of the Gospel, but a brusque departure from the normal development of humanity. The inescapable conclusion seemed to be that America was an accidental or extraneous force, which led to a retrogression from the providential course of moral progress. Wallon suggested that the settlement of the New World had provided a small group of selfish merchants and planters with an opportunity to derail the train of historical progress; accordingly, it was necessary for reformers, supported by an enlightened public, to get the train back on the track.[35]

Raynal had considered slavery and the natural order to be mutually exclusive, even though slavery seemed to have been an intrinsic

32. Henri Wallon, *Histoire de l'esclavage dans l'antiquité* (Paris, 1847), I, pp. 356–9, 371–405; III, pp. 36–8.
33. ibid., I, pp. 455–60; II, p. 446.
34. ibid., III, pp. 1–5, 341, 413–66.
35. ibid., III, pp. 466–9.

part of New World history; Wallon held that it was slavery and the progress of Christianity that were mutually exclusive, a view which was shared by many fellow abolitionists. Like Raynal, he perceived a contradiction between human bondage and a system of fundamental values, but his interpretation was even less successful in clarifying the problem of slavery in America. It presupposed a kind of idealistic teleology, since history was conceived as a gradual realization of Christian principles. Retrogressions were explained by reference to a few evil groups, who unaccountably gained sufficient power to thwart the tide of progress. Wallon evaded the question whether slavery had played an essential function in various periods of history. And he seemed to reverse the traditional view of America as a liberating force and stimulus to human progress.

Six years before the publication of the *Histoire de l'esclavage,* Auguste Comte sought to give a scientific explanation of human slavery, and reached conclusions which in some respects were remarkably similar to Wallon's. He greatly simplified the problem of ancient slavery by abandoning the concept of universal moral standards; unlike Raynal and Wallon he saw no absolute contradiction between slavery and nature or slavery and Christianity. Indeed, for Comte human bondage had served an indispensable function in the progress of civilization, since it had replaced cannibalism and human sacrifice, and had enforced the discipline of sustained and regular work on men who would otherwise have been ruled by the most immediate passion or desire.[36] Such arguments could, of course, be used to justify the enslavement of primitive peoples; Comte himself found profound meaning in Aristotle's theory that some men are slaves by nature.

But Comte's philosophic system rested on a rigidly prescribed series of ascending stages of history. If slavery was a normal institution in a polytheistic society, it became a useless vestige as society progressed through monotheistic and metaphysical stages. By the nineteenth century it was a monstrous aberration. It reversed the course of progress and prevented the extension of those general scientific principles that were necessary for the emergence of a rational society. In Africa slavery might well contribute to the progress of the Negroes,

36. Auguste Comte, *Cours de philosophie positive* (Paris, 1840–42), V, pp. 186–93.

as it had contributed to the progress of ancient societies; but en-slavement of primitive peoples by more advanced nations inter-fered with the laws of history and disrupted the whole scheme of gradual progress.[37] Thus Comte substituted a theory of historical stages for the traditional dualism of worldly evil and immutable, higher law; and in the end he agreed with Wallon that slaveholders were pitting themselves against the stream of history. If the insti-tution were not doomed by the eternal principles of nature or by the spread of Christianity, its fate was sealed by the laws of positivistic science.

Yet how had this 'disgraceful anomaly' come into being, and how was it related to the meaning of the New World? Comte was not particularly troubled by the latter question, since America played no important function in his theory of historical progress. Protestant-ism, in his eyes, had led the English colonies in a path contrary to that prescribed by science; the American Revolution was something of an anachronism. To be sure, the Catholic Church, which had originally helped to emancipate Europe, had, in its decadence, sanctioned and promoted colonial slavery. Yet even a debilitated Catholicism tended to mitigate the worst evils of human bondage, whereas the spiritual anarchy of the Protestant colonies left the way open to unlimited private oppression.[38]

Comte's institutional approach had much in common with later studies in comparative slavery. But without the trappings of tele-ological history, his arguments could easily be turned to a defence of servitude as an institution performing necessary functions of dis-cipline and socialization. This was, in effect, the approach of many of the 'scientific' historians of the early twentieth century.

The European thinkers we have discussed thus far had somewhat ambivalent views on the moral influence of the New World. George Bancroft, the most popular and nationalistic of early American his-torians, had not the slightest doubt that the influence had been all for the good. Limiting himself to the area included in the United States, he set out to explain how in only two centuries the happiest and most

37. ibid., VI, pp. 133–6.
38. ibid., VI, p. 134.

enlightened civilization in history had arisen from the wilderness to become a model for the rest of the world. But when he grappled with the problem of slavery – how it was related to the American mission, whether it was integral to American development, and whether its extension to the New World was a retrogression from the course of progress – he resorted to a curious mixture of assumptions which reflected inconsistencies prevalent in American thought from late colonial times to the twentieth century.

As a loyal Democrat and patriotic American, writing at a time when his party supported the expansion of slave territory, Bancroft went out of his way to emphasize the antiquity and universality of an institution which, one might conclude, was not so 'peculiar' after all. Unlike Wallon, he found no continuing contest between liberty and bondage in the ancient world: 'In every Grecian republic, slavery was an indispensable element.' Nor was the practice wholly incompatible with virtue and religion, for 'the light that broke from Sinai scattered the corrupting illusions of polytheism; but slavery planted itself even in the promised land, on the banks of Siloa, near the oracles of God.'[39] It was true that the extreme harshness of the Roman slave law had hastened the Empire's fall; but Bancroft's picture of the ancient world suggested that slavery might be planted in other promised lands without blighting their mission.

He adopted, however, the conventional view of Christianity slowly sapping the foundations of bondage in Europe. If slavery had not detracted from the splendour of Grecian republics, it was still incompatible with human progress, and would have disappeared entirely among civilized nations had not an outside force intervened. In Bancroft's eyes this outside force was not America, but the continuing wars between Islam and Christianity, which had nourished bigotry and revenge. Angered by the raids of Saracen corsairs, Christians had felt justified in capturing any Moor they could lay hands upon, and they had classified all Africans as Moors.[40] In any event, the Negroes themselves had always accepted slavery, and when the Portuguese

39. George Bancroft, *History of the United States, from the Discovery of the American Continent* (14th ed., Boston, 1850–74), I, pp. 159–61. The first volume was originally published in 1834.

40. ibid., I, p. 163–4.

had commenced trading along the western coast of Africa, they had simply appropriated a commercial system which the Moors of the north had established centuries before. Bancroft admitted that the Portuguese were guilty of 'mercantile cupidity',[41] but in a certain sense it was Africa that had corrupted Europe.

The Spanish, who had also been brutalized by wars with the Moslems, had endeavoured to enslave the Indians, or, as Bancroft called them, the 'freemen of the wilderness'. Even Columbus had participated in this unnatural act, though such a lapse was presumably redeemed by his contribution to the advance of liberty; and, as Washington Irving had said, 'the customs of the times . . . must be pleaded in his apology'.[42] Slavery, however, was totally alien to American soil, and in order to rivet the system on their colonies, the Spanish had been forced to import a more docile and submissive race. The significant point about Bancroft's interpretation is that he considered slavery basically extraneous to the New World and contrary to the natural development of Europe. It was thus a kind of abnormal excrescence which had been fastened on America by Europeans whose avarice and brutality had been stimulated by their contact with Africa.

When Bancroft turned to the founding of the North American colonies, he underscored the fundamental conflict between slavery and the very meaning of the New World. 'While Virginia,' he wrote, 'by the concession of a republican government, was constituted the asylum of liberty, by one of the strange contradictions in human affairs, it became the abode of hereditary bondsmen.' Monarchy, aristocracy and priestcraft had no motive to cross the Atlantic:

Nothing came from Europe but a free people. The people, separating itself from all other elements of previous civilization; the people, self-confiding and industrious; the people, wise by all traditions that

41. David Levin has pointed out a significant ambivalence in Bancroft's view of commerce, which he at times associated with greed and materialism, and at other times with progress and natural principles. See Levin, *History as Romantic Art: Bancroft, Prescott, Motley and Parkman* (Stanford, 1959), p. 42.

42. Washington Irving, *The Life and Voyages of Christopher Columbus*, in *The Works of Washington Irving* (New York, 1897), VI, p. 375.

favoured popular happiness – the people alone broke away from European influence, and in the New World laid the foundations of our republic.[43]

As part of this classic picture of American innocence and separateness, Bancroft stressed the original and deep antipathy that the people felt for slavery. His argument that slavery was essentially foreign to America appeared to stumble a bit when, discussing South Carolina, he seemed to adopt Montesquieu's belief in the primacy of climate; he even asserted that the contrast between Carolina and New York was due to climate and not to the superior humanity of the original Dutch colonists.[44] Yet he thought that the people and legislation of every colony had favoured freedom, and that Massachusetts, especially, had opposed the introduction of slaves from the beginning. In Rhode Island, if Providence and Warwick had failed to enforce their law of 1652 against slavery, 'the principle lived among the people'.[45]

How, then, could one account for the survival and growth of an institution so repugnant to the desires of a free people? Bancroft's answer was one which Americans had long resorted to; it was founded on a sharp moral distinction between the original cause of American slavery – the selfish greed of European merchants and governments – and the conditions which led to its perpetuation. If the type of servitude fastened on America had been the same as that which Europeans had long endured, the problem would soon have been solved 'by the benevolent spirit of colonial legislation'. But from the beginning, America had been plagued with racial incompatibility: 'The Negro race, from the first, was regarded with disgust, and its union with the whites forbidden under ignominious penalties.'[46]

Thus racial dissimilarity could be offered as an excuse for laws and practices which simply made the best of an unfortunate situation. And when Bancroft took a larger perspective, he had to admit that America's burden was not, after all, without its rewards. In his native

43. Bancroft, *History*, I, p. 159; II, p. 451.
44. ibid., pp. 170–71; II, p. 303.
45. ibid., I, pp. 175, 190; III, p. 408.
46. ibid., I, p. 177.

continent the African would have remained in 'unproductive servitude'; in America at least his labour contributed greatly to the wealth of nations. Adopting for the moment one of the favourite theories of Southern apologists, Bancroft concluded that 'in the midst of the horrors of slavery and the slave trade, the masters had, in part at least, performed the office of advancing and civilizing the Negro.'[47]

While Bancroft saw a basic contradiction between slavery and America's mission, he resolved the dilemma in a manner that was apparently satisfactory to most of his countrymen. The institution was alien to the true nature of the New World; it had been imposed on the people against their will, and the guilt thus fell upon an already guilt-sickened Europe. Yet in a larger view, even slavery appeared as part of the providential plan for the redemption of the human race. In Bancroft's eyes the first ship that brought Negroes to America was a 'sure pledge' that in due time ships from the New World would carry the blessings of Christianity to Africa. Even selfishness and injustice had a role to play in the historical unfolding of truth and liberty. Americans could comfort themselves with the thought that Negro slavery, a vestige of Old World corruption, was only a temporary irritant which would gradually disappear under the beneficent pressure of democratic institutions. The history of the slavery controversy in the United States well testifies that Bancroft was not alone in this optimistic belief.

We have suggested that Negro slavery, a product of innumerable decisions of self-interest made by traders and princes in Europe and Africa, was an intrinsic part of American development from the first discoveries. The evolution of the institution was also coeval with the creation of the idea of America as a new beginning, a land of promise where men's hopes and aspirations would find fulfilment. The dreams and ideals embodied in various images of the New World would not necessarily conflict with the enslavement of a foreign people unless there were already tensions over slavery in the system of values which Europeans applied to America. That there were such tensions remains to be shown. For the moment it will suffice if we

47. ibid., III, p. 408.

note that the problem of slavery in the New World could be conceptualized as part of a general conflict between ideals and reality in the course of human history. Thus the Abbé Raynal hinted that the discrepancy between natural law and colonial slavery was so great that revolution might be necessary to bring the ideal and reality of America into harmony. For Henri Wallon and Auguste Comte, America itself was something of an anomaly, since it represented a disturbing retrogression from the course of historical progress. Yet Wallon's faith in the power of Christianity and Comte's confidence in the inexorable laws of history led them to expect the imminent triumph of freedom. To some extent all three of these thinkers associated the paradox of modern slavery with America itself, but to George Bancroft servitude was fundamentally extrinsic to the New World, whose very meaning lay in the emancipation of mankind. Although Bancroft recognized that the Negro had played a vital part in the founding of certain colonies, he felt that slavery was so contrary to America's destiny that it would evaporate from the sheer heat of triumphant democracy.

Each of these writers, like an increasing number of men on both sides of the Atlantic, saw modern slavery as a moral contradiction, as a force incompatible with natural law, Christianity, the progress of scientific enlightenment or the mission of American democracy. We may feel that the growth of such anti-slavery opinion was itself evidence of moral progress. But the very recognition of slavery as a moral contradiction raised perplexing questions concerning the history of the institution and the sources of anti-slavery thought. Nineteenth-century writers tended to exaggerate the historical opposition between slavery and Christianity, to disregard the crucial economic function of slavery in American development, and to read history as a struggle between the children of light and the children of darkness, a struggle whose outcome had fortunately been decided beforehand by the Great Contriver of events.

In the cosmic view of Ralph Waldo Emerson, for example, the emancipation of slaves in the British West Indies was 'an event singular in the history of civilization; a day of reason; of the clear light; of that which makes us better than a flock of birds and beasts: a day, which gave the immense fortification of a fact – of gross history

– to ethical abstraction.'[48] It was true, Emerson conceded, that the British moral sense had been supported by self-interest and material advantage – 'Else, I know not how, in our world, any good would ever get done.' The British knew that 'slavery . . . does not love the whistle of the railroad; it does not love the newspaper, the mailbag, a college, a book, or a preacher who has the absurd whim of saying what he thinks.' But if England was a nation of calculating shopkeepers, this only made emancipation the more sublime; in an age of smoking factories and money-grubbing it was a 'stately spectacle'. During the epic conflict all that was wise, noble and generous had been arrayed against the cramped and mean elements of life. Emerson noted that 'other revolutions have been the insurrection of the oppressed; this was the repentance of the tyrant'. Thus British emancipation was both proof of moral progress in history and the harbinger of a new era when the masses would awaken and apply an absolute moral standard to every public question. 'The Power that built this fabric of things,' Emerson concluded, 'has made a sign to the ages, of his will.'[49]

The persuasive force of this optimistic view can be seen in its adoption, on a far more sophisticated level, by Alfred North White-head, who used emancipation as an example of the compelling force of moral ideas in the progress of civilization. The history of ideas, he held, was a history of mistakes, 'but through all mistakes it is also the history of the gradual purification of conduct'.[50] This could be seen in the slow and tortuous evolution of Plato's doctrine of the human soul, which was the ultimate source of the anti-slavery movement. Centuries of rationalizations and social obstacles had repressed the inherent conflict between ancient slavery and Plato's vision of what man can be. Yet general ideas were always a danger to the existing

48. Ralph Waldo Emerson, *An Address in the Court-House in Concord, Massachusetts, on 1st August, 1844, on the Anniversary of the Emancipation of the Negroes in the British West Indies* (Boston, 1844), p. 3. A similar view was taken by William E. H. Lecky, who called the British crusade against slavery one of the three or four 'perfectly virtuous' pages in history. See his *History of European Morals from Augustus to Charlemagne* (3rd ed., New York, 1890), I, p. 153.

49. Emerson, *Address*, pp. 19, 26, 34.

50. Alfred North Whitehead, *Adventures of Ideas* (New York, 1933), p. 30.

order, and as civilization progressed, as Greek and Hebrew glimpses of perfection acquired new force in the Enlightenment and Wesleyan revival, slavery was doomed. Whitehead avoided the common error of supposing that men in one generation are endowed with greater moral insight than those in another. But he was by no means clear on what the 'conditions' were that gave a cutting edge to Plato's doctrine, and his theory seemed to rest on an assumption that historical progress is the result of the gradual realization of general ideas.

The great virtue of such interpretations is that they recognize slavery as a genuine moral problem, and attach importance to moral values as an element in history. Historians who ignore conflicts in moral values, or who attempt to reduce to other categories of explanation moral questions that have an autonomy of their own, can be justly charged with blindness to the facts of life as we experience it.[51] Yet even Whitehead was writing in a happy era when he could say with confidence that anti-slavery reformers 'had produced the final effective force which hereafter made slavery impossible among progressive races'.[52] Belief in the certainty of moral progress is a matter of personal faith, but in the second half of the twentieth century historians have been less inclined to assume that we have been moving irresistibly towards a golden age. Recognition that slavery in America involved a genuine moral problem does not require us to believe that emancipation was preordained by the progressive unfolding of moral truth, or that men in the nineteenth century were morally superior to those in periods when slavery was universally accepted, or that in the contest between slaveholders and abolitionists all virtue and reasonableness were on one side.

In recent decades historians have been less content with theories of progressive currents washing away the dregs of an evil past. Certain sceptics and reductionists have portrayed the entire slavery controversy in terms of contending economic interests, holding that the institution was supported as long as it was profitable to a given group or nation, and was repudiated only when it ceased to pay. As we have

51. For a critique of amoral history, see John Higham, 'Beyond Consensus: The Historian as Moral Critic', *American Historical Review*, LXVII (April 1962), pp. 609–25.

52. Whitehead, *Adventures*, p. 28.

seen, Emerson recognized the economic motive in British emancipation, but the role of the abolitionist was protected by his transcendental scheme of progress. Twentieth-century historians have not been so charitable. They have told us that if the reformers were not hypocrites or a front for economic interests, they were perhaps a displaced elite who sought to retain power and status by mobilizing public opinion. Such lines of investigation, when cautiously pursued, have brought rewarding insights into the relations between ideology and social structure. But while these newer approaches have revealed weaknesses in the traditional teleological view of the anti-slavery crusade, they have tended to divert attention from the fact that Negro slavery in the eighteenth and nineteenth centuries posed a genuine moral problem that reflected deep tensions in Western culture and involved the very meaning of America.

2

Patterns of Continuity in the
History of Servitude

DURING the great slavery controversy of the nineteenth century, abolitionists took pains to emphasize the uniqueness of an institution that subjected one race to the unlimited power of another. Their opponents were equally fond of arguing that Negro slavery was not essentially different from historical varieties of bondage and serfdom. On this issue, at least, modern historians have tended to side with the abolitionists. Particularly since the publication in 1947 of Frank Tannenbaum's *Slave and Citizen*, the most original and thoughtful studies have supported the view that slavery in British America had little in common with previous forms of servitude, and was far harsher than the Negro slavery in Latin America, where Old World customs and institutions preserved a more traditional form of bondage. It has been suggested that as the emerging forces of capitalism and democracy dissolved European notions of social rank, one of the unhappy by-products was an unmitigated form of slavery.[1]

If the salient traits of North American slavery were indeed unprecedented, we might suspect that abolitionist movements were a direct and almost reflexive response to an iniquitous innovation. The absence of such movements in other slave societies would only lend support to this conclusion, and would indicate that Europe's historical experience with slavery had no relevance to the controversies of the late eighteenth and nineteenth centuries. On the other hand, if it could

1. See Frank Tannenbaum, *Slave and Citizen: The Negro in the Americas* (New York, 1947); Oscar Handlin, 'The Origins of Negro Slavery', in *Race and Nationality in American Life* (Anchor paperback ed., Garden City, N.Y., 1957), pp. 4–22; Carl Degler, *Out of Our Past: The Forces That Shaped Modern America* (New York, 1959), pp. 26–39; Stanley M. Elkins, *Slavery: A Problem in American Institutional and Intellectual Life* (Chicago, 1959); Milton R. Konvitz, *A Century of Civil Rights* (New York, 1961), pp. 3–37.

be shown that recent studies have tended to overlook certain continuities and common features in the history of servitude, we should have more difficulty in accounting for the sudden emergence of antislavery thought.

Since the history of slavery is an immense and complex subject, and since the purposes of this chapter are necessarily limited, it is well to begin by summarizing our principal arguments. First of all, we shall not imply that slavery in North America lacked distinctive characteristics, such as its racial basis and its legal barriers against manumission. But because of the number of variables, the conflicting and inadequate evidence, and the lack of rigorous comparative studies, we simply do not know enough about the actual treatment of bondsmen in different societies to warrant precise generalizations on the relative severity of slave systems. This is not to say that all bondage was equally oppressive. No doubt a harsh form of chattel slavery was more likely to appear in expansive, fluid societies, such as the Roman Republic and the United States. But one should not idealize the condition of bondsmen in feudal or patriarchal societies, where there was often a risk of the cruellest punishment and sudden death.

Second, one must make a clear distinction between slavery as an abstract legal status, and as an actual institution involving economic functions and interpersonal relationships. It is the latter aspect of slavery for which we lack satisfactory data, since few slaves recorded their thoughts, and until modern times scholars did not think the subject worthy of study. We know considerably more about slavery as a legal and philosophic concept; and as a result of the generalizing tendency of books and systems of law, the *idea* of slavery was less subject to regional variation and historical change than was the institution itself. The discrepancy between the two should not lead us to conclude that the persistence of the idea of slavery was unimportant. Medieval jurists might fail in their efforts to fit serfdom within the framework of Roman law, but they handed down legal concepts which became more applicable to the African slave trade of the fifteenth century.

Third, there was more institutional continuity between ancient and modern slavery than has generally been supposed. While it has sometimes been recognized that American slavery had much in common with that of Greek and Roman antiquity, the apparent disappearance of chattel servitude in Europe seemed to preclude any theory of direct influence. But the question of continuity assumes new meaning when we learn that true slavery persisted as a viable institution around the edges of medieval Europe – in Spain, in the vast Moslem world, in the Byzantine Empire, in Kievan Russia – and that from the thirteenth century to the late fifteenth century an international slave trade flourished in the Black Sea and the Mediterranean.

Fourth, a comparative analysis of historical forms of servitude reveals precedents for most of the striking traits of American slavery. As we have already suggested, this does not mean that American Negro slavery was the same as earlier varieties of servitude. But although American slavery was shaped into a distinctive pattern, few of its features were unique to the New World. Previous forms of servitude bore enough resemblance to the South's peculiar institution to warrant the main criticisms of the abolitionists. Despite great historical diversity in such matters as employment, manumission and the differentiation of bondsmen from other classes, the very ways of defining and regulating the institution show that slavery has always raised certain fundamental problems that originate in the simple fact that the slave is a man.

In general it has been said that the slave has three defining characteristics: his person is the property of another man, his will is subject to his owner's authority, and his labour or services are obtained through coercion. Since this description could sometimes be applied to wives and children in a patriarchal family, various writers have added that slavery must be 'beyond the limits of the family relations'.[2] Certain other attributes derive from the definition of the

2. H. J. Nieboer defined slavery as 'the fact, that one man is the property or possession of another beyond the limits of the family proper'; (Slavery as an Industrial System [The Hague, 1900], p. 29). For Edward Westermarck it was 'essentially an industrial institution, which implies compulsory labour beyond the limits of the family relations' (The Origin and Development of the Moral Ideas [London, 1906], I, p. 670). I fail to see how either of these definitions distinguishes slavery from various types of serfdom, though Nieboer attempted to do so (pp. 32–8). For an analysis of the difficulties in

slave as movable property. His status does not depend on his relation to a particular owner, and is not limited by time or space. His condition is hereditary and ownership in his person is alienable.

Laws defining and regulating slavery have nearly always come long after the institution has been established. For this reason we cannot assume that slavery did not exist, prior to such laws, as a recognized system of rules, practices and expectations; nor can we assume, without definite evidence, that specific legislation changed the actual status of slaves.[3] Yet even before the Eighteenth Dynasty in Egypt, the slave was legally defined as a thing; and the same conception prevailed in Babylonia, Assyria, Greece, Rome, India, China and parts of medieval Europe. As laws governing chattel property evolved from the earliest civilizations, it was almost universally agreed that a slave could be bought, sold, traded, leased, mortgaged, bequested, presented as a gift, pledged for a debt, included in a dowry or seized in a bankruptcy. For more than three thousand years these legal characteristics of bondage changed very little; and in the Western world it was the Roman law that gave a systematic and enduring form to the rights of masters and slaves.[4]

---

arriving at a satisfactory legal definition, see Willam W. Buckland, *The Roman Law of Slavery: The Condition of the Slave in Private Law from Augustus to Justinian* (Cambridge, England, 1908), pp. 1–11.

3. For the origins and sources of slavery, see Moses I. Finley, *The World of Odysseus* (Meridian paperback ed., New York, 1959), p. 50; William L. Westermann, *The Slave Systems of Greek and Roman Antiquity* (Philadelphia, 1955), p. 7; Isaac Mendelsohn, *Slavery in the Ancient Near East; A Comparative Study of Slavery in Babylonia, Assyria, Syria, and Palestine, from the Middle of the Third Millennium to the End of the First Millennium* (New York, 1949), pp. 1–5; Abd el-Mohsen Bakir, *Slavery in Pharaonic Egypt* (Cairo, 1952), pp. 6, 122; Melville J. Herskovitz, *Dahomey: An Ancient West African Kingdom* (New York, 1938), I, p. 99; C. Martin Wilbur, *Slavery in China during the Former Han Dynasty, 206 B.C. – A.D. 25* (Chicago, 1943), pp. 73, 241; E. G. Pulleyblank, 'The Origins and Nature of Chattel Slavery in China', *Journal of the Economic and Social History of the Orient*, I, pt. 2 (1958), pp. 201–5.

4. Bakir, *Slavery in Pharaonic Egypt*, pp. 8, 53, 66–9; Mendelsohn, *Slavery in Ancient Near East*, pp. 34, 40–42, 50; Dev Raj Chanana, *Slavery in Ancient India, as Depicted in Pali and Sanskrit Texts* (New Delhi, 1960), pp. 32–3, 64; Pulleyblank, 'Origin and Nature of Chattel Slavery in China',

In most respects it was convenient to regard the slave as a *res*, as a being without rights or family or even a name other than the one given him by his owner. The Romans merely systematized the practice of many nations when they ruled that a slave could not make a will or formal accusations in criminal charges, or appear as a witness in most civil cases. But there were times when the law could not ignore the bondsman's human capacities. Slaves were universally punished for delicts, and many nations allowed them certain legal capacities and afforded them at least theoretical protection against murder and severe bodily harm. It was for this reason that the Roman jurists quite openly acknowledged that the slave was both a person and a thing.[5]

The slave's insecurity and rightlessness have customarily been contrasted with the status of the serf, who is bound to a particular lord, attached to a plot of land, and liable only for prescribed dues and services. This sharp distinction has been presupposed in theories of historical progress which trace the European slave's ascent to *colonus*, serf and free peasant.[6] As we shall see, however, the transitions from one stage to another were seldom clear-cut. Not only did slavery and serfdom coexist and overlap, but medieval jurists tended to confuse the two conditions. French legal scholars translated the words *servitus* and *servus* from the Justinian Code as *servage* and *serf*. They regarded the French serf as legally subject to the almost absolute authority of his owner, and as alienable by sale, exchange or gift.[7]

p. 212; George Vernadsky, *A History of Russia*, II; *Kievan Russia* (New Haven, 1948), pp. 150–51; Iris Origo, 'The Domestic Enemy: The Eastern Slaves in Tuscany in the Fourteenth and Fifteenth Centuries', *Speculum*, XXX.(July 1955), p. 334.

5. Buckland, *Roman Law*, pp. 2–11, 83–7; Westermann, *Slave Systems*, pp. 24, 83–4, 107–8; Origo, 'Domestic Enemy', p. 351.

6. As might be expected, Marxist historians have devoted much attention to the periodization of slavery and serfdom, and to revolutionary transitions from slave to feudal societies. For a comparison of China, Persia and Rome, see Ernst Werner, 'De l'esclavage à la féodalité: la périodisation de l'histoire mondiale', *Annales: économies, sociétés, civilisations* (Sept–Oct 1962), pp. 930–39. For a critique of Marxist views of slavery, see A. Kotsevalov, *Soviet Studies of Ancient Slavery and Slave Uprisings* [in Russian, with English summary] (Munich, 1956).

7. Pierre Petot, 'L'Evolution du servage dans la France coutumière du XIe

Similarly, Bracton identified the English villeins with the Roman *servi*, and carefully distinguished them from the *adscripticii* and *coloni*, whose rights had been protected by the State. In theory the villein was a chattel who could be sold apart from the manor and whose labour was unregulated by law. If his life could not be taken with impunity by his master, the same had been true of the Roman slave of the late Empire.[8]

There was, of course, an enormous gap between the legal status of the villein or serf and his actual condition in a feudalistic society. By custom and economic circumstance the serf was in fact bound to the soil. There was no market for a mobile labour force, and no incentive to maximize the production of agricultural commodities. No doubt serfs have generally escaped the worst pressures and insecurities of slavery. But a recognition of the limiting effects of customs and economic conditions only increases the difficulty of arriving at precise definitions of servitude. The word 'slave', even when confined to Negroes, hardly had the same meaning when applied to fieldworkers, drivers and trusted household servants; a similar variation in the condition of individual slaves can be found in most societies. The terms

---

au XIVe siècle', in *Le servage: communications présentées à la Société Jean Bodin* (Bruxelles, 1937), pp. 156–7; Petot, 'L'Evolution numérique de la classe servile en France du IXe siècle', in *Recueils de la Société Jean Bodin*, II: *Le servage* (2nd ed., Bruxelles, 1959), p. 164n.

8. Paul Vinogradoff, *Villainage in England: Essays in English Mediaeval History* (Oxford, 1892), pp. 43–58; Daines Barrington, *Observations on the Statutes, Chiefly the More Ancient, from Magna Charta to the Twenty-First of James the First* . . . (London, 1766), pp. 248–55. Barrington thought that by the time of Henry VIII the idea began to prevail that slavery was contrary to Christianity and hence to common law.

The conviction that villeins were legally bound to the soil was partly the product of a misunderstanding which arose in the sixteenth century and which later supported the belief that England had 'too pure an air for a slave to breathe in'. It came to be assumed that villeins *regardant* to a manor, as opposed to villeins *in gross,* had enjoyed the legal security of being attached to the soil. In practice, however, the two terms had merely indicated the mode by which a lord proved his title to a villein: if he possessed a deed or a confession of status, his villein was said to be *in gross*; otherwise, he would point to the manor and plead prescriptive right. But in either case he was free to convey or sell his villein as he might see fit.

'servant', 'bondsman' and 'slave' have often been accepted as synonyms; without overstatement, Catherine the Great referred to the seigniorial peasantry of Russia as slaves, not serfs.[9] No single definition has succeeded in comprehending the historical varieties of slavery or in clearly distinguishing the institution from other types of involuntary servitude.

In most languages, moreover, the word for slave has been further blurred by metaphorical usage. Thus in Shakespeare: 'Let me be a slave, t'achieve that maid'; 'Purpose is but the slave to memory'; 'But thought's the slave of Life, and Life, Time's fool'. Yet even such figurative meanings suggest that men have always recognized slavery as a kind of ultimate limit in dependence and loss of natural freedom, as that condition in which man most closely approximates the status of a thing.

Though actual slaves never formed a significant percentage of the populations of China or ancient Egypt, in Greece, where they were treated as commodities and put to industrial and commercial employments, the number kept increasing from the Persian Wars to the time of Alexander.[10] Historians disagree on the exact percentage of slaves in the total population of fourth-century Athens, but Moses Finley states that the proportion was as great as in the combined slave states of America in 1860, and that the ownership of slaves in Greece was even more widely distributed among the free population than in America.[11] The Greek economy was not so dependent on slavery as were the economies of the West Indies and the deep South; yet Finley argues persuasively that the institution was an integral element in Hellenic society. Moreover, 'the cities in which individual freedom

9. Jerome Blum, *Lord and Peasant in Russia from the Ninth to the Nineteenth Century* (Princeton, 1961), p. 469.

10. Westermann, *Slave Systems*, pp. 3, 5–7.

11. A. H. M. Jones, 'Slavery in the Ancient World', reprinted in M. I. Finley (ed.), *Slavery in Classical Antiquity: Views and Controversies* (Cambridge, 1960), p. 3; and Moses I. Finley, 'Was Greek Civilization Based on Slave Labour?', reprinted in the same book, pp. 58–9. Finley thinks that there may have been as many as one-hundred-thousand slaves in Athens. Jones estimates the maximum number at twenty thousand.

reached its highest expression – most obviously Athens – were cities in which chattel slavery flourished'.[12] Thus the history of ancient Greece presents the same paradox that has perplexed Americans since the eighteenth century: freedom and slavery seemed to advance together.

The rise and expansion of the Roman Republic was also intimately associated with slavery. Following Roman conquests in the East, a mounting stream of slaves flowed westward from Egypt and Asia, where debtors and children were sold to the invader, and from Greece, which bred slaves for Rome much as Virginia and Maryland were later to do for the lower South. Frequent wars brought Rome additional numbers of prisoners. According to William L. Westermann, the proportion of slaves in the Roman Republic of the second and first centuries B.C. was greater than that in any other nation of antiquity. As in Greece, bondsmen were employed in mining and handicraft manufacturing; and on the *latifundia* of Sicily and southern Italy there developed a system of gang labour, professional management and absentee ownership which in many respects resembled the plantation slavery of the New World. The Roman economy always rested on a mixture of slave and free labour, but this can also be said of the slave states of America. As the number of slaves increased and as bloody revolts broke out periodically, the Republic evinced the pervasive fear and harsh militancy that were later to characterize the West Indies and American South. Moreover, the Romans developed marketing techniques which would have seemed familiar to slave dealers of a later age. Crowds gathered at the slave markets and watched professional traders exhibit their human merchandise on raised platforms, where the miserable beings were handled and forced to display their agility. Each slave wore a placard bearing his price and other specifications.[13]

The problem of the decline of slavery in later Roman history is so entangled with the question of the decline of the Empire itself that one must be suspicious of any simple explanation. It appears that the

12. Finley, 'Was Greek Civilization Based on Slave Labour?', p. 72.
13. Westermann, *Slave Systems*, pp. 9, 29, 34, 63–5, 75, 84, 97–8, 134–5; Mikhail Rostovtzeff, *The Social and Economic History of the Roman Empire* (2nd ed., rev. by P. M. Fraser, Oxford, 1957), I, pp. 17–18.

condition of slaves improved at a time when the liberty of other groups was being eroded by economic hardship and the expanding power of emperors. While the *servi* benefited from legislation restraining their masters from the worst cruelties, the mass of agricultural workers suffered from oppressive fiscal policies and from the absorption of small farms into the great estates of the imperial aristocracy.[14]

Yet the course of evolution from slaves to serfs and from serfs to free peasants was not as direct or invariable as has sometimes been thought. Slaves and *coloni* often worked together on a villa and were hardly distinguishable, but the wars of the fourth and fifth centuries brought fresh supplies of captives. Actual slaves still played an important part in the agriculture of Visigothic Spain, where the entire society was divided into two great classes of the free and unfree. During the Carolingian period Jewish and Syrian merchants guided troops of slaves across Russia, Poland and Germany to the Mediterranean; in the early Middle Ages there were 'manufacturers' of eunuchs in Verdun and Sicily. It is none the less true that in most parts of Western Europe slavery declined and then virtually disappeared with the emergence of the feudal system. According to Marc Bloch, during the slow and profound transformation of the European economy, there was an overlapping and interpenetration of the systems of slavery and serfdom, so that servitude and dependencies of various kinds were modelled on the prototype of hereditary slavery, and such words as *servus*, *Knecht* and *vassus*, which had originally

14. The *coloni*, though attached to the soil, were for a time permitted a certain freedom of movement. Another class, the *coloni servi*, were treated more like slaves, and even came to be called *servi*, but could not be sold apart from the land. The *adscripticii*, who appear by the mid fourth century, may have become assimilated with slaves. Scholars still disagree over the evolutionary ancestry of the medieval serf, but there can be no doubt that through the later Empire the gap continued to narrow between slaves and an ever-expanding class of hereditary serfs (Westermann, *Slave Systems*, pp. 109–13, 120, 140; Rostovtzeff, *Social and Economic History*, I, pp. 192–254; Paul Collinet, 'Le colonat dans l'empire romain', in *Le servage: communications présentées à la Société Jean Bodin*, pp. 85–122; M. Pallasse, 'Note complémentaire', in *Recueils de la Société Jean Bodin*, pp. 212–28).

implied unlimited bondage, acquired new connotations of status, rights and willing service.[15]

But such blurring of distinctions did not always imply an elevation in status. If the French serf was protected by local custom and if there was little incentive to exploit his labour for commercial or industrial profit, he enjoyed few legal rights not possessed by Roman slaves of the late Empire. As we have suggested, the revival of Roman law also revived the concept of chattel slavery, which medieval jurists took as the proper model for serfdom. Defined as movable property, the French serf was in theory subject to the almost unlimited disciplinary power of his owner. In court he could testify only against another serf; except by permission he could not marry the serf of another master. Under Lombard and Frankish law, the child of parents of mixed status inherited the lower condition; but by the thirteenth century French courts, except in Burgundy, had extended the Roman rule of *partus sequitur ventrem* to serfs. And while true serfdom had begun to disappear in western France by the eleventh century, it later spread through most of the regions to the north-east and south-east of Paris, where by the fourteenth century it was the basic system of labour. In such areas as Lombardy and Piedmont domestic slaves persisted as a class distinct from the dependent peasantry; and though serfdom declined in western Germany during the late Middle Ages, it became entrenched east of the Elbe in a form close to slavery.[16]

In Domesday Book approximately 10 per cent of the recorded population were classified as outright slaves. Legally no more than

15. Charles Verlinden, 'Les conditions des populations rurales dans l'Espagne médiévale', in *Recueils de la Société Jean Bodin*, pp. 172–3; Verlinden, *L'Esclavage dans l'Europe médiévale, I: Péninsule Ibérique, France* (Brugge, 1955), pp. 61–3; Origo, 'Domestic Enemy', p. 323; Georges Duby, *L'Economie rurale et la vie des campagnes dans l'occident médiéval* . . . (Paris, 1962), II, p. 403; Marc Bloch, 'Comment et pourquoi finit l'esclavage antique', reprinted in *Slavery in Classical Antiquity*, pp. 219–21.

16. Duby, *L'Economie rurale*, II, pp. 406, 484; Petot, 'L'Evolution numérique de la classe servile', pp. 159–68; Melvin Knight *et al.*, *Economic History of Europe* (Boston, 1928), pp. 458–9. It should be noted that the Church came to recognize the validity of a marriage of serfs contracted without the master's permission.

chattel goods, these people could apparently be killed by their owners without penalty; if a freeman killed someone else's slave, he was liable only for the man's market value. And yet the slaves of Domesday were entitled by Anglo-Saxon law to specified annual rations and by custom were apparently accorded certain rights to property and free time. They were also protected in some instances by the Church, which as a great landowner possessed many bondsmen of its own.[17]

Villeins constituted the major portion of the English population as recorded in Domesday Book. The term *villanus*, however, is clouded with ambiguities. In France the *vilain* was a free commoner. English villeins of the eleventh century still retained certain vestiges of their former liberty, and at times the word referred only to a particular kind of tenure. But gradually *villanus* came to connote a vague status of almost total unfreedom that was easily confused with slavery. Though English society was in fact divided into numerous classes of unfree workers – the *coliberti, coceti, cotarii, bordarii*, and so on – Bracton followed the great Bologna jurist, Azo, in stating that all men are either free or slave.[18]

The discrepancy between English institutions and Roman legal concepts makes it difficult to discuss villeinage with any precision. The difficulty is compounded by the fact that true slavery virtually disappeared in England by the thirteenth century, while villeins continued to lose the remaining remnants of their former liberties. Like the slave, the villein's person was owned by his master, who was theoretically free to use or dispose of his property in any way not specifically prohibited by law. In practice, however, the villein found protection in the economic immobility of the manorial system. Custom ensured

17. Paul Vinogradoff, *The Growth of the Manor* (2nd ed., London, 1951), p. 24; R. Welldon Finn, *An Introduction to Domesday Book* (London, 1963), pp. 118–21.

18. F. Joüon des Longrais, 'Le vilainage anglais et le servage réel et personnel', in *Recueils de la Société Jean Bodin*, pp. 204–6, 227–36; Finn, *Introduction to Domesday*, pp. 122–6; E. Lipson, *The Economic History of England*, I: *The Middle Ages* (11th ed., London, 1956), pp. 28–9; F. M. Stenton, *Anglo-Saxon England* (Oxford, 1943), pp. 463–72; Vinogradoff, *Villainage in England*, pp. 43–8.

him certain privileges and secure expectations. The Church sanctified his marriage and accorded him the dignity of a human soul. The criminal law made few distinctions between freemen and villeins, so that even Bracton affirmed the principle that while a villein was subject to the will of his master, he was free in his relations with the rest of society. This was not strictly true, as Glanvill had observed. To the heirs or creditors of a master, or to the free woman who wanted to marry him, the villein was not a free man. Nevertheless, his servitude was peculiarly confined to the territorial domain of his lord, and limited by the customs and prescriptions of an organic society.[19]

The significant point, however, is that villeinage gave jurists and scholars an opportunity to keep alive Roman concepts of slavery. It was the vehicle, so to speak, which served to transmit legal notions of total subordination to the early modern era. The Dialogus de Scaccario, Glanvill, Bracton and the minor jurists of the late Middle Ages – all tried to apply the Roman law of slavery to medieval serfdom. Glanvill, for example, said that a villein could not buy his freedom, since he could possess no money of his own. Glanvill also made villeinage conform to the Roman rule of *partus sequitur ventrem,* though by the late thirteenth century English common law ruled that the status of servitude passed from the father. In the next century courts decided that bastards must be deemed free since the status of their fathers was unknown. But the same judges who applied the common law principle of *favor libertatis* also continued to think of villeinage as essentially synonymous with Roman slavery.[20] Despite the effects of enclosure, the widening of markets, the Black Death and the Hundred Years' War, the legal condition of villeins remained virtually unchanged. When a shortage of labour and rising wages threatened to undermine the entire manorial system in the late fourteenth century,

19. Sir Frederick Pollock and F. W. Maitland, *The History of English Law* (Cambridge, England, 1898), I, pp. 415–24, 431; Longrais, 'Le vilainage anglais', pp. 227–39; Vinogradoff, *Villainage in England*, pp. 48–58, 64–9, 76, 151–2, 300–313; Vinogradoff, *Growth of the Manor*, pp. 343–8.

20. Vinogradoff, *Villainage in England*, pp. 43–8, 59, 86–7, 129–37. For the legal complexities of writs, and pleas concerning villeinage and freedom see Anthony Fitzherbert, *The New Natura Brevium of the Most Reverend Judge Mr Anthony Fitz-Herbert* (London, 1730), pp. 176–82.

the ancient principles of servitude justified severe laws to keep workers on the land. Laws, of course, could not prevent economic transformation. During the fifteenth and sixteenth centuries feudal services gradually gave way to rents, free contracts and monetary payments. True villeinage became economically absolete. And yet the legal principle of slavery survived as a weapon of social control. In 1547, for example, it was possible to enact a temporary law stating that vagabonds who attempted to escape from enforced service were to be branded on the forehead with the letter 'S', which signified that they would be 'slaves' for the rest of their lives.[21]

There is a striking contrast between the fate of slavery in the insulated parts of medieval Europe and in the limited areas that retained commercial or military contact with the outside world. When the Saracens invaded the Iberian Peninsula the existing system of slavery was much as it had been at the end of the Roman Empire. But the continuing struggle of Christians and Moslems brought a decisive change. For some six centuries both sides enslaved prisoners of the opposing religion. As the servile class of Christians rose gradually to various stages of serfdom, the lowest order of labour was filled by Moslem captives. Throughout the Iberian Peninsula the religious wars kept slavery alive as a vital institution, with an unbroken continuity from Roman times to the revival of Mediterranean trade.[22]

If chattel slavery all but disappeared on the feudal manors of Europe, it flourished at such urban seats of learning and civilization as Cordova and Constantinople, at the extremities of the continent. And it revived and spread with the development of commerce. In the tenth and eleventh centuries Swedish merchants, moving down the Volga and Dnieper valleys, established contact with the Caliphate of Baghdad and the Byzantine Empire; along with wax and furs, they traded Russian slaves for the spices and silks of the East. The mer-

21. Vinogradoff, *Villainage in England*, pp. 215–307; Longrais, 'Le Vilainage anglais', pp. 207–10, 236–41; Lipson, *The Middle Ages*, pp. 88–132; Lipson, *The Economic History of England*, III: *The Age of Mercantilism* (6th ed., London, 1956), p. 423.

22. Verlinden, *L'Esclavage dans l'Europe médiévale*, pp. 61–3, 103–13, 156–7; Verlinden, 'Les conditions des populations rurales', pp. 169–200.

chants and princes of Kievan Russia looked on the export of slaves as one of their principal sources of wealth.[23] At the same time, enterprising Venetians transported slaves, captured or purchased on the Dalmatian coast, to the harems of Syria and Egypt; this trade, according to Henri Pirenne, was as vital to Venetian prosperity as was the later Atlantic slave trade to the economies of Britain and France.[24]

Long before the birth of Columbus, Genoese and Venetian merchants invented the distinctive institutions that would later be applied to the African trade and West Indian colonization. Arriving on the coasts of the Black Sea in the thirteenth century, they ultimately established bases or factories which became thriving markets for the purchase of slaves. Like the later Portuguese who built forts in West Africa, the Italians were not required to seize slaves on their own. Tartar merchants swarmed to such posts as Tana, and eagerly traded their children, neighbours or captives for precious goods. The Italians not only created joint stock companies, commercial bases or *fondachi*, and a highly organized slave trade, but in the colony of Cyprus they established plantations where imported bondsmen were employed in the cultivation of sugar cane. By 1300, indeed, there were Negro slaves on Cyprus, which had become virtually a prototype for the West Indian colonies. In the words of Charles Verlinden, 'L'économie esclavagiste des colonies modernes est purement et

23. Chattel slavery was an important institution in Kievan Russia, but there is disagreement on when it gave way to serfdom. See Vernadsky, *Kievan Russia*, pp. 15–18, 30, 111, 126, 146; Vernadsky, *A History of Russia*, III: *The Mongols and Russia* (New Haven, 1953), pp. 336–7; Vernadsky, *A History of Russia*, IV: *Russia at the Dawn of the Modern Age* (New Haven, 1959), pp. 7–8, 201–2; M. Tikhomirov, *The Towns of Ancient Rus* (Moscow, 1959), pp. 149–62; B. Grekov, *Kiev Rus* (Moscow, 1959), pp. 224–51; Marc Szeftel, 'Note complémentaire sur les études et publications de sources depuis 1936', in *Recueils da la Société Jean Bodin*, pp. 263–74.

24. Henri Pirenne, *Economic and Social History of Medieval Europe* (Harvest paperback ed., New York, n.d.), pp. 17–23; Origo, 'Domestic Enemy', p. 330. The Genoese profited from a trade in Moslem slaves in the western Mediterranean until a treaty with the enemy curtailed the supply.

simplement la continuation de celle des colonies médiévales.' Much is yet to be learned about continuities between trade in the Mediterranean and Atlantic, but it is significant that later colonizing nations looked to the Italians for commercial theory and practices, that there were close trade relations between Venice and England, that certain Genoese merchants who owned slaves on Cyprus played an important role in developing commerce in the Atlantic, and that Italian sailors and merchants who were familiar with the Black Sea and the eastern Mediterranean were attracted to the first Spanish and Portuguese ventures at exploration.[25]

The great Mediterranean slave trade reached its peak in the fourteenth and fifteenth centuries. The tolerant Genoese provided Saracen traders with ships and Christian slaves, and even signed a treaty with the Kamchil khan of Solgat for the return of fugitives. Tartars, Circassians, Armenians, Georgians and Bulgarians flowed into the markets of Italy and Spain. The splendour of Venice and Tuscany, like that of ancient Rome and Athens, was intimately associated with slavery. Iris Origo has discovered that between 1414 and 1423 no fewer than ten thousand slaves were sold in Venice alone. In the fourteenth and fifteenth centuries they formed a significant proportion of Tuscany's population, and in Florence it was common for petty shopkeepers and even nuns and priests to own a slave. And though the sale of Christians was occasionally denounced as impious, and in 1386 the Venetian senate outlawed the marketing of bonds-

25. Vernadsky, *Kievan Russia*, pp. 346–7, 364; Charles Verlinden, 'La colonie vénitienne de Tana, centre de la traité des esclaves au XIVe et au debut du XVe siècle', in *Studi in onore di Gino Luzzatto* (Milano, 1950), II, pp. 1–25; Verlinden, 'Le problème de la continuité en histoire coloniale: de la colonisation médiévale à la colonisation moderne', *Revista de Indias*, (Madrid, 1951), XI, pp. 219–36; Verlinden, 'Les origines coloniales de la civilisation atlantique: antécédents et types de structure', *Cahiers d'histoire mondiale*, I (October 1953), pp. 378–98; Verlinden, 'Aspects de l'esclavage dans les colonies médiévales italiennes', in *Eventail de l'histoire vivante, hommage à Lucien Fabvre* (Paris, 1953), II, pp. 91–103; Verlinden, 'Le influenze italiana nella colonizzazione iberica', *Nuovo revista storica*, XXXVI (May–August 1952), pp. 265–70; Verlinden, *L'Esclavage dans l'Europe médiévale*, pp. 320–21, 330–40, 427. Although there is no evidence of such bases in the pre-Mongol period, Russion slaves were apparently transported to Italy and Spain long before the thirteenth century.

men on the *piazza*, it is clear that merchants disregarded all attempts at regulation. Italians felt no more need to justify the Black Sea trade than did the pagans, Jews and Moslems with whom they mixed in the great markets of the East. In the same period, according to Charles Verlinden, Aragon and Catalonia were slave societies from top to bottom, the supply of Moslem captives from North Africa being augmented by Circassians and Georgians from the Black Sea.[26]

In the late Middle Ages there were thus flourishing slave societies along the main routes of commerce from Russia and Egypt to Venice and the south of France. But by the end of the fifteenth century, as Alberto Tenenti has written, the merchants of Tana were only a memory. After surviving a host of invasions from the east, the slave markets of the Black Sea were finally sealed off by the Turkish capture of Constantinople and the Dardanelles. In Florence the price of slaves rose so prohibitively that they soon became a luxury which only nobles or rich merchants could afford. Negro children would be kept as pets and presented as gifts in the Renaissance courts of Mantua, Milan and Ferrara. Corsairs would continue to supply small numbers of bondsmen, and slaves would toil in the great Renaissance galleys. But with the end of an organized commerce in slaves, the institution became increasingly associated with an extortive system of piracy and ransom. Italian merchants became more concerned with rescuing their friends and relatives from Barbary pirates than with acquiring slaves of their own. By 1600 the commercial slave trade had all but disappeared from the Mediterranean basin, and within the next century slavery itself would nearly die out in Italy, although it would persist in Sicily until 1812.[27]

26. Alberto Tenenti, 'Gli schiavi de Venezia alla fine del cinquecento', *Rivista storica italiana*, LXVII (1955), pp. 52–4, 60; Origo, 'Domestic Enemy', pp. 321–9; Verlinden, 'La colonie venitienne de Tana', pp. 7, 10; Verlinden, *L'Esclavage dans l'Europe médiévale*, *passim*.

27. Alberto Tenenti, 'Schiavi e corsari nel Mediterraneo orientale interno al 1585', in *Miscellanea in onore di Riberto Cessi* (Roma, 1958), II, pp. 184–5; Tenenti, *Cristoforo da Canal: la marine vénitienne avant Lépante* (Paris, 1962), *passim*; Verlinden, *L'Esclavage dans l'Europe médiévale*, pp. 103–11; Origo, 'Domestic Enemy', pp. 354–5; Tenenti, 'Gli schiavi de Venezia alla fine del cinquecento', pp. 52–4. The last-named work presents

But the Turkish conquests failed to have so decisive an effect in the Iberian Peninsula. Parts of Spain had become densely populated with slaves as a result of the Black Sea trade, piracy and expeditions against the Moslems. By the thirteenth century there had also been some Negro bondsmen in Catalonia-Aragon and the realm of Majorca. The number had increased significantly by the end of the following century, although the supply was always limited by the necessity of buying or capturing Negroes from the Moslems. But in the very decades when the Turks were gradually extinguishing the trade of Genoese and Venetian merchants, Portuguese navigators were nosing south along the Atlantic coast of Africa. By establishing direct contact with Negro societies, they broke the monopoly of Arab traders. In the 1440s various expeditions exchanged horses and other merchandise for black slaves and after 1462 the Portuguese were exporting Negroes to Castille. During the following half-century the slave trade slowly shifted from the Mediterranean basin to the coasts and islands of Portugal and West Africa, and then across the Atlantic to the Carribbean. And while new markets for labour were being developed in the New World, the Iberian Peninsula continued to absorb frequent shipments of Negroes, who gradually replaced Arabs and Circassians in the lowest segment of the labour force. The number of slaves in eastern Spain declined in the seventeenth century, but they were still being imported from Portugal as late as 1785 for employment in the mines. It was not until 1836 that Spain prohibited the introduction of bondsmen who had previously lived in the colonies, and it was not until 1869 that slavery was finally abolished in metropolitan Portugal.[28]

Even such a compressed summary suggests important lines of continuity between the history of servitude in Europe and America. We must repeat that there was often a wide difference between the word for 'slave', with all its legal connotations, and conditions of unfreedom which varied according to local custom and economic circumstance. And yet the basic characteristics of chattel slavery were

documents on the manumission and sale of slaves in the sixteenth century (pp. 61–9).

28. Verlinden, *L'Esclavage dans l'Europe médiévale*, pp. 358–9, 619–25, 839–45.

clearly established in antiquity. The institution continued to thrive along the principal routes of trade and in fluid societies that allowed individuals relative freedom in the acquisition and use of property. If the history of American colonization can be said to begin with the revival of commerce in the Mediterranean, American slavery can be traced back to the Italian merchants who followed the example of their Roman forebears and transported foreign captives to the most profitable markets. Even in northern Europe, where true bondage was gradually replaced by other forms of labour, the continuing prestige of Roman law tended to perpetuate a concept of the slave as a personal possession almost totally subject to his owner's will.

But in the Mediterranean world, as in Asia and Africa, human bondage was accepted throughout an entire society. Even when defined as chattels and cruelly treated, slaves were looked upon as a normal class within the body politic. They were as much a part of the social order in Tuscany and Spain, at the beginning of the modern era, as they had been in ancient Greece and Rome. When the Spanish and Portuguese transferred slaves to the New World, the Atlantic formed no barrier between domestic and colonial institutions. Yet by the seventeenth century, when the slave trade became as vital for the expansion of France, Holland and Britain as it had been for Spain and Portugal, bondage had almost disappeared from Northern Europe.

Furthermore, when the bourgeoisie had struggled against the feudal system, they had not only won privileges and personal freedom within the towns, but had established the principle that a degree of liberty was inherent in the very air or soil of a municipality. 'Stadluft,' said the Germans, 'macht frei.'[29] As early as the twelfth century the city of Bremen became a sanctuary for escaped serfs or slaves, who were deemed free after residing for one year and a day within the city's walls. By the next century a similar privilege was given to English chartered towns. And ultimately, the concept was extended to include entire nations. In 1538 a Greek slave brought to France by an Italian merchant was declared free under the common law; and in 1571 the parlement of Guienne, in an attempt to generalize the cus-

29. Pirenne, *Economic and Social History*, pp. 50–51.

tom of Toulouse to the whole realm, ruled that 'la France, mère de la liberté, ne permet aucun esclave'.[30]

In one sense, slavery was more appropriate to an open, commercial society which valued the perpetuity and easy transferability of relationships, than to a feudal society, with its limits of place and tenure. But when the privileges of corporate bodies were extended to entire nations or even empires, they inevitably collided with the principle of slavery. The notion that a slave was instantly liberated if he touched the free soil of France or England would cause considerable difficulty when colonists returned to the mother country with Negro servants. In both countries the courts vacillated in their judgements and endeavoured to find a compromise. But Spain and Portugal were not faced with this troublesome question until late in their imperial history. They were the transitional link between slavery as it had existed throughout history and slavery as it developed in America. In the newer colonies the traditional dualism between the world of slaves and the world of the free, which had always been encompassed within a single state, was made both geographic and racial. The problem of a house divided against itself originated when burghers and merchants used their hard-won liberty to launch expeditions for the enslavement of a different race.

In no ancient society was the distinction between slave and freeman so sharply drawn as in America. Marriages between male slaves and freeborn women were common in ancient Babylonia, and the children of any mixed marriages were apparently considered free.[31] For Homer the contrast between aristocrat and commoner was the vital distinction; he used the word *drester* indiscriminately for servants and labourers, both slave and free. The *thetes*, in the eyes of Achilles, formed the lowest social order, for unlike slaves, these uprooted workers were not true members of a household.[32] The harsh slave

30. Lipson, *The Middle Ages*, pp. 218–19; Verlinden, *L'Esclavage dans l'Europe médiévale*, pp. 848–53.

31. Bakir, *Slavery in Pharaonic Egypt*, pp. 4–7; Mendelsohn, *Slavery in Ancient Near East*, p. 55.

32. Finley, *The World of Odysseus*, pp. 49–50, 70–71. In certain areas of India slaves were considered so superior to the lowest castes of freeman that they could not touch a Niadis or Pariah, for example, without defilement

codes of many societies were mitigated by the fact that masters and bondsmen were of a common race and shared a culture in which permanent social inequalities were accepted as the obvious will of providence.

But precisely because it was difficult to treat men of one's own tribe as no more than animals, the survival of true slavery required some form of social or psychological discrimination. It is not surprising to find that houseborn servants in the ancient Near East enjoyed privileges denied to purchased bondsmen or prisoners of war, though all were legally of the same status. In most primitive societies, slaves born within the tribe fared much better than those bought or captured from foreign groups. In the Sumerian tongue the very words for slave meant 'male (or female) of a foreign country'.[33] This may be taken as evidence both of man's ethno-centrism and of slavery's ultimate dependence on real or simulated ethnic barriers.

The most portentous discrimination, perhaps, was that in Leviticus: Hebrew slaves were to be treated as hired servants until the year of jubilee, when, by the law received on Sinai, they were to be freed; at all times aliens holding Hebrews in bondage were to allow their redemption by relatives; but non-Hebrew slaves were not to benefit from such protective regulations.[34] As the Commandments

---

(William Adam, *The Law and Custom of Slavery in British India* [London, 1840], p. 131).

33. Herskovitz, *Dahomey*, I, pp. 82, 101; Nieboer, *Slavery as Industrial System*, pp. 38–9; Mendelsohn, *Slavery in Ancient Near East*, pp. 1–5.

34. Leviticus xxv 39–55; Mendelsohn, *Slavery in Ancient Near East*, pp. 85–90. Mendelsohn thinks that the law of Leviticus applied to Hebrews who had sold themselves into bondage to escape destitution, and that it had no connexion with the provisions in Exodus and Deuteronomy for freedom on the sabbatic year. These provisions, he argues, were directed against the unscrupulous practices of many creditors, and pertained only to defaulting Jewish debtors, who were not really slaves. This view receives some support from the fact that the Hammurabi Code limited the servitude of defaulting debtors to a term of three years. According to a more traditional interpretation, the sabbatic emancipation applied to all Jewish slaves, but the term of service was lengthened in Leviticus because the earlier provisions could not be enforced (see S. R. Driver, *A Critical and Exegetical Commentary on Deuteronomy* [New York, 1895], p. 185). A more recent view is that of Martin Noth, who points out that the term 'Hebrew', in remote antiquity,

were later interpreted in Rabbinical law, Jews were reminded of their own deliverance from Egyptian bondage, and exhorted to treat their Hebrew slaves as brothers. Yet a rigid distinction persisted between the Israelite and the alien bondsman. Much later the Moslems adopted a similar differentiation. Captives of their own faith were not regarded as true slaves, and except for being barred from holy offices and pilgrimages, enjoyed religious equality with freemen. Infidels, however, were in most respects treated as chattel goods.[35] While Christian practice was complex and must be discussed more fully in subsequent chapters, we may note that paganism and religious infidelity were the prime excuses for enslaving non-Europeans.

Although slaves in most ancient societies were not distinguishable by skin colour or other racial characteristics, their masters often marked them with visible symbols of their lowly status. No doubt the original purposes of such labelling were identification and prevention of escape. Some slaves merely had their heads shorn or wore an identification tablet of clay or metal, which could be broken when they were freed. But more permanent branding or tattooing was also common in Egypt, the Neo-Babylonian Empire, Roman Sicily and even fifteenth-century Tuscany. From the earliest times such skin markings became indelible signs of a servile status, and suggested a deformity of character which deserved contempt. The Chinese, for example, used mutilation and tattooing to mark off their slaves as a

---

referred not to an ethnic or national group, but to an uprooted, wandering people who occupied a subordinate position within the ancient oriental communities. A 'Hebrew slave' was thus a member of this underprivileged class who had sold himself, probably from economic necessity. If a 'Hebrew' sold himself to an Israelite, he was to serve for a period of six years (*Exodus, A Commentary* [Philadelphia, 1962], pp. 177–8). Although this may have been the original meaning of 'Hebrew slave', it is clear that at an early date the Jews drew a sharp distinction between Israelite and 'Canaanite' slaves. And whether the sabbatic law was limited to Jewish debtors or was extended for a time to all Jewish servants, the foreign slaves and their descendants were doomed to perpetual slavery. (Leviticus xxv 39–55).

35. George F. Moore, *Judaism in the First Centuries of the Christian Era: The Age of Tannaim* (Cambridge, Mass., 1927), II, pp. 135–6; R. Brunschvig, 'Abd', in *The Encyclopedia of Islam* (new ed. 1960), I, pp. 26–7. Conversion to Islam did not bring emancipation to a slave.

base and ignoble class, and automatically imposed such stigma on succeeding generations.[36] In later centuries men would come to regard darkness of skin as a brand which God or nature impressed upon an inferior people.

As one might expect, the Greek concept of slavery was more rational and secular than that of previous societies. Instead of marking their bondsmen with physical brands or tattoos, they defined the concept of slave, or *doulos*, with increasing legalistic precision. As the slave became a member of a distinctive class, 'a kind of possession with a soul', in Aristotle's phrase, he was cut off from legal relations with freemen. A slave woman, for example, could not marry a freeman without first being emancipated. Roman law continued the trend towards precise definition of the slave's status and social relationships, further segregating him from ordinary society. Even under Constantine the law ruled that if a freewoman lay with a slave, she would be executed and he would be burned alive.[37]

Yet Roman slaves participated in cult worship and in the general life of the *familia*; during the feasts of the Saturnalia they momentarily joked and caroused with their masters as equals. And if Romans usually showed more sensitivity to social distinctions between slaves and freemen, they seldom appeared conscious of racial differences. As evidence of a lack of racial prejudice, Westermann quotes an inscription in which a Negro slave is praised by his master: 'The darkness of the Negro's skin was caused by the rays of the sun; but his soul bloomed with white blossoms.'[38] This is a remarkable anticipation of William Blake's lines:

> My mother bore me in the southern wild,
> And I am black, but O! my soul is white.[39]

36. Bakir, *Slavery in Pharaonic Egypt*, pp. 68, 112; Mendelsohn, *Slavery in Ancient Near East*, p. 44; Westermann, *Slave Systems*, p. 64; Origo, 'Domestic Enemy', p. 321; Pulleyblank, 'Origin and Nature of Chattel Slavery in China', pp. 205–6.

37. Westermann, *Slave Systems*, pp. 78–9, 113–14; William E. H. Lecky, *History of European Morals from Augustus to Charlemagne* (3rd ed., New York, 1890), I, pp. 63–4.

38. Westermann, *Slave Systems*, p. 104.

39. William Blake, 'The Little Black Boy', in *Poems of Blake* (ed. by Laurence Binyon, London, 1931), p. 32.

Without doubting the general truth of Westermann's argument, we may still observe that Blake's poem can hardly be taken as evidence of a lack of racial consciousness in English society, and that the dominant thought in both cases is that a Negro's soul may be white, in spite of his colour, and that white is somehow better.

Racial distinctions were more important in the Arab world and in Mameluke Egypt, where Negro slaves were far more numerous than in the Roman Empire. Although Moslem jurists regarded slavery as an unnatural condition that could be justified by only exceptional circumstances, they tended to relax their standards as Arab traders moved into the interior of Africa and returned with increasing numbers of Negroes. Moslems not only accepted the legitimacy of Negro enslavement, but were inclined to think of black Africans as a docile race who were born to be slaves. The Arabic word for slaves, *abid*, was increasingly confined to Negroes. The *abid* usually occupy a lowly status in the *Arabian Nights*, and were despised and downtrodden in medieval Egypt. In the fifteenth century, Egyptian *mamluks* were outraged when the sultan gave arquebuses to the Negroes, who had previously been no more than personal servants to *mamluk* knights. In 1498 a virtual race riot erupted in Cairo, after the sultan had married the chief of his arquebusiers to a white Circassian slave girl. The *mamluk* knights, who technically were 'slaves' of the highest order, slaughtered the coloured troops, including the chief of the arquebusiers, and the sultan gave in to their demands.[40]

40. *Encyclopedia of Islam*, I, p. 32; Edward W. Lane (tr.), *The Arabian Nights' Entertainments, or the Thousand and One Nights* (New York, 1944), pp. 987–9, ch, i, n. 13 and *passim*; David Ayalon, *Gunpowder and Firearms in the Mamluk Kingdom: A Challenge to Medieval Society* (London, 1956), pp. 66–70. It should be noted that the *mamluks* were as much opposed to firearms as they were to Negroes being used as combat soldiers. The *mamluks* were often of Turkish, Georgian or Circassian origin, and formed a slave military caste that dominated politics and even supplied Egypt with sovereigns. It was an army of white slaves that crushed Louis IX in the Seventh Crusade, and over five centuries later it was an army of *mamluks* that Napoleon routed at the Battle of the Nile. For accounts of this unique slave system, see William Popper, *Egypt and Syria under the Circassian Sultans, 1382–1468 A.D.* (Berkeley, 1955), pp. 2–3, 87; Sir William Muir, *The Mameluke or Slave Dynasty of Egypt, 1260–1517* (London, 1896), p. 1 n. 3–4; pp. 215–19; Edward W. Lane, *An account of the Manners and*

In general, it would appear that coloured slaves in Algiers, Morocco and Tripoli suffered little discrimination in status or treatment.[41] In China of the T'ang Dynasty, however, there was a definite connexion between slavery and racial prejudice. Bondsmen had long been marked off as a criminal class, sharply differentiated from the 'good' population. To kidnap or wrongfully sell a 'good' person was a serious crime, and the victim was not considered to have been an authentic slave. But since foreigners were thought to be something less than human, the Chinese had no compunction about enslaving Koreans, Turks, Persians and Indonesians. In Chinese eyes even Persians were 'black', but a special contempt was reserved for the dark-skinned barbarians of the southern islands, whose inferiority was abundantly proved by their nakedness and primitive customs. During the seventh and eighth centuries A.D. large numbers of these men were transported to Canton. The Persian Gulf trade brought even a few Negro slaves to the booming southern port, where they were bought as curiosities. Because the Chinese feared pollution from inferior blood, foreign slaves were strictly prohibited from having sexual relations with native women. The slave who committed violence on a freeman was condemned to death.[42]

Customs of the Modern Egyptians ... (5th ed., London, 1871), I, p. 126; Stanley Lane-Poole, *A History of Egypt in the Middle Ages* (London, 1901), pp. 242–74, 641; David Ayalon, *L'Esclavage du mamlouk* (Jerusalem, 1951), pp. 1–34.

41. Norman R. Bennett, 'Christian and Negro Slavery in Eighteenth-Century North Africa', *Journal of African History*, I (1960), pp. 65–82.

42. Edward H. Schafer, *The Golden Peaches of Samarkand: A Study of T'ang Exotics* (Berkeley, 1963), pp. 14, 44–6; Pulleyblank, 'Origins and Nature of Chattel Slavery in China', pp. 205–6, 213, 215. For many centuries the Aryans expressed contempt for the 'noseless', flat-lipped and black-skinned Dasas, whom they had subjugated in India. In the Vedic period the word *dasa* (feminine *dasi*) which has continued to mean 'slave', had strong ethnic connotations. Gradually, however, the concept of slavery was dissociated from racial attributes; in the Buddhist period a *dasa* could have a light skin. As slavery lost its ethnic meaning, there was a relaxation in the traditional restrictions on intermixure. Kautalya provided for the manumission of a *dasi* who bore a son to her master. Nevertheless, if a free woman had sexual relations with a slave, her breasts were to be amputated and both parties were to be killed (see Chanana, *Slavery in Ancient India*, pp. 19, 22, 94, 105–6, 108–9).

It is often assumed that such ethnic and racial distinctions were totally absent from European servitude. During the late Roman Empire differences in status and treatment of *servi* and *mancipia* were largely the result of occupation, local custom and mode of enslavement. As we have seen, the Latin words for servitude, which carried no ethnic connotations, were still in common use in the thirteenth century, and were applied to various classes of serfs and villeins. But for a limited period in the tenth and eleventh centuries, Germans sought to distinguish the *servi* of their own nationality from the captives who arrived from the east, and who were apparently given a far lower status. The foreigners were called *sclavi*. According to Charles Verlinden, the term died out with the trade which brought Slavic prisoners to the west. But in the thirteenth century, when the Genoese and Venetians began bringing cargoes of men out of the Black Sea, the word *sclavus* suddenly came into common usage in Italy. Because there was close communication between clerical scholars in Italy and parts of northern Europe, the word rapidly spread and was adopted in French and English texts as a means of distinguishing unfree foreigners from native serfs.[43]

In the Iberian Peninsula the terms *sarracenus* and *captivus* had gradually replaced the more neutral *servus*, and were still the common expressions for a slave during the thirteenth century. As a result of the Mediterranean slave trade, *sclavus* was increasingly adopted in Spain by the following century. It was not until the fifteenth century, however, that *escravo* won acceptance in Portugal.[44] And if, etymologically, the word was inappropriate for Negro slaves, it is surely significant that a term which originally suggested a foreign bondsman came into common usage in Portugal at the very moment when Negroes were beginning to fill the lowest rank of the servile order.

Compared with the French and English, the Iberians were no doubt tolerant of racial differences, and were eventually able to assimilate much of their coloured populations. Yet from the start, the

43. Charles Verlinden, 'L'Origine de "sclavus" – esclave', *Archivum latinitatis medii aevi*, XVII (1943), pp. 97–128. It would appear that the words 'esclave' and 'slave' soon became interchangeable with *servus*. 'Slave' appeared in English law under Edward II.

44. ibid., pp. 114–28.

Moors and Negroes not only formed the lowest rank of slaves, but had a profound effect on the general character of servitude. Negro slaves in Portugal, for example, were frequently refused burial, and in 1515 the King ordered that their bodies be thrown into a separate common ditch, the *Poço dos Negroes*.[45] In parts of Spain they must have been marked off as a separate group even after emancipation, since free Negroes in Barcelona and Valencia founded religious welfare associations which provided for decent burials. That these brotherhoods showed a sense of group-consciousness is evident from their inclusion, with a master's permission, of Negro slaves. Moreover, legislators in sixteenth-century Spain were much concerned over the supposedly subversive character of free Negroes; and the Cortes went so far as to propose that freedmen be prohibited from living outside the region where they were known and be punished with one hundred lashes if they greeted or fraternized with slaves. In Portugal, freedmen remained a legally separate class until 1878.[46]

Such evidence suggests that while slaves were more sharply differentiated in North America than in other societies, slave systems have often rested on discriminations of various kinds. Indeed, a comparative study of slave societies reveals not only the diverse means by which freemen dissociated themselves from bondsmen, but the essential components of the later American concept of servitude: the primitive effort to mark or brand the slave with some physical emblem of his status; the change from the Greek concept of a *drester*, who was simply one who worked or served, whether slave or free, to a *doulos*, who was a clearly defined slave and the member of a separate class; the attempts in Roman law to deny the manhood of *servi* by refusing to recognize the legality of their human relationships with freemen; the Hebrew and then Christian distinction based on religion and nationality; the shift in usage, in the thirteenth century, from the Latin *servus* to *sclavus* and *esclave*, which signified foreign origin; and finally, the incipient discrimination against Negro slaves in parts

45. Verlinden, *L'Esclavage dans L'Europe médiévale*, pp. 80–84, 631.
46. ibid., pp. 529–30, 631, 840–41. For a critique of the view that there was no colour problem in Portuguese colonies, see C. R. Boxer, 'S. R. Welch and His History of the Portuguese in Africa, 1495–1806', *Journal of African History*, I (1960), pp. 55–63.

of the Arab world and in the Iberian Peninsula, where the institution flourished at the beginning of the modern era.

The ease and frequency of manumission would seem to be the crucial standard in measuring the relative harshness of slave systems. If we had to be slaves and were allowed to choose the time and place of our servitude, we should obviously prefer a society that held out some hope of eventual freedom. And according to this standard, the British West Indies and the Southern states would unquestionably come near the bottom of the scale.[47] Yet one should not assume an invariable correlation between the frequency of emancipation and the overall condition of slaves.

In the nations of remotest antiquity, for example, an extreme rarity of manumissions was coupled with what appears to have been a relatively mild, domestic servitude. In the ancient Near East slaves were members of a household and might enjoy the privilege of marrying freemen and, in the Neo-Babylonian period, of conducting trades and businesses on their own. Since any man might become a slave through economic misfortune, there could be no sharp line separating bondsmen as an inferior caste. Nevertheless, Mendelsohn has observed that 'in view of the large number of slave documents from the Chaldean, the Persian, and the Greek periods, it is indeed very surprising that so few of them relate to manumission'. There was no word for emancipation in Pharaonic Egypt, and not a single manumission contract appears among the documents of the Late Assyrian period.[48]

Yet in Greece and Rome, where slaves suffered from a harsher exploitation, and where their status as a separate class was more sharply defined, manumissions were remarkably common. The ex-slave in fifth century Athens bore no stigma from his servile past, and some rose to positions of political or economic power.

47. According to William Graham Sumner, the Guykurus of Paraguay practised a kind of total slavery: 'Slaves and free do not intermarry, lest marriage be profaned. There is no way in which a slave may become free' (*Folkways* [Mentor paperback ed., New York, 1960], p. 236). The source for this statement is not clear.

48. Bakir, *Slavery in Pharaonic Egypt,* pp. 75–9, 82–3, 123; Chanana, *Slavery in Ancient India,* pp. 80–81; Mendelsohn, *Slavery in Ancient Near East,* pp. 42, 74–90.

And even in Greece and Rome the road to liberty was not without obstructions. As the Greeks developed a clearer conception of personal freedom, it became more difficult for a slave to cast off his disabilities at a single stroke. During the Hellenistic period some Greek communities passed freedmen's laws that provided separate regulations and restrictions for ex-slaves. The Roman Republic collected a 5 per cent tax on manumissions, and in the second century B.C. passed various regulatory laws, including one which confined freedmen to membership in a single tribe. After the death of Julius Caesar, the warring factions violated an ancient Roman principle by enlisting slaves in their armies. This practice, coupled with the increasing numbers of manumissions, aroused deep resentment and nourished a growing prejudice against the *libertini*, who were subjected to various legal disabilities. Octavianus Caesar either killed captive slave soldiers or returned them to their owners for punishment. As Emperor, he secured legislation which strictly limited the number of slaves a master might free by testament, in order to protect the heirs against a heavy loss of property.[49]

For reasons of both economy and religion, manumissions multiplied during the late Empire and early Middle Ages. Christian masters, particularly on their deathbeds, liberated faithful slaves as a pious act that might win atonement for sins. Yet in Spain the slaves of the government and Church, who had little hope of emancipation, enjoyed certain comforts and privileges denied to ordinary bondsmen; and freedmen were subject to so many disabilities that their condition was hardly better than that of slaves. Under Lombard law an enfranchised slave was only half free, and even in Carolingian times the descendants of a freedman could not claim the full rights of the freeborn until three generations had passed. By the thirteenth and fourteenth centuries most Tuscan cities had adopted provisions from the Justinian Code granting full liberty to emancipated slaves. The offspring of masters and female slaves, who were lodged in astonishing numbers in the foundling hospitals, were considered free. Nevertheless, the plight of slaves and freedmen in medieval Tuscany

49. Westermann, *Slave Systems*, pp. 15–18, 23, 35, 42, 63–75, 89–90; A. M. Duff, *Freedmen in the Early Roman Empire* (Oxford, 1928), pp. 12–35, 50, 58.

was little helped by Christian charity and beneficent legislation. A brooding fear of what Petrarch termed the *domestici hostes* was everywhere apparent. Margherita Datini, referring to her own slaves as *femmine bestiali*, complained that 'you cannot trust the house to them: they might at any moment rise up against you'. Such attitudes carried over into a prejudice against freedmen, who were barred from the guilds and subjected to restrictive laws. With few opportunities for legitimate employment, the male freedmen joined the rogues and vagabonds who haunted the Tuscan highways; the females, who as slaves were accused of sexual promiscuity, often became prostitutes. There were so many tramps and homeless waifs in Rome as late as 1545 that Pope Paul III repealed an ancient law which had granted the right to claim freedom to any slave seeking refuge beneath the emperor's statue on the Capitol.[50]

Despite differences in the ease of manumission, slave societies have shown a nearly uniform severity in dealing with bondsmen who sought freedom on their own accord. The Hammurabi Code prescribed death for anyone who sheltered a fugitive or helped a slave to escape. In Rome the efforts of the government were supplemented by private specialists, or *fugitivarii*, who were trained to track down the most elusive slave.[51] Throughout medieval Europe the Church was ready to aid a bondsman who fled from a Jewish master, but other fugitives were punished according to the harsh law of Justinian. Pisa, Bologna, Florence, Lucca and Genoa entered into agreements for the capture and extradition of escaped slaves. In medieval Tuscany officials posted descriptions of runaways in the main squares of the cities; it was the duty of every citizen to join in the search. Any unknown coloured man or woman came immediately under suspicion. A decree of 1452 ruled that any man who concealed a slave for three days or more would be hanged. And when a slave was finally caught, he was tortured and disciplined according to his master's wish.[52] If a

50. Charles Verlinden, 'Les conditions des populations rurales', pp. 173–4; Origo, 'Domestic Enemy', pp. 322, 340–48, 350–54.

51. Mendelsohn, *Slavery in Ancient Near East,* pp. 58–9, 63; Westermann, *Slave Systems,* pp. 107–8.

52. Origo, 'Domestic Enemy', pp. 349–50. In Russia, *The Revised Pravda* prescribed a fine for anyone who gave bread or aid to a runaway slave

few privileged slaves were to be cleansed of the stain of bondage, it was always to be on the terms of the master class.

It is no easy matter to judge the relative severity of slave systems. Since so much depends on local customs, social pressures, economic development, and the extent to which slaves are feared, it would appear that regulatory laws and the ease of emancipation are fallible guides when taken by themselves. Yet these are often the only criteria we have for judging the slavery of antiquity and the Middle Ages. Our picture of North American slavery, on the other hand, rests on a wealth of traveller accounts and evidence accumulated by anti-slavery writers. It is no apology for the cruelty and injustice of American slavery to suggest that if such evidence were available from other societies, the contrast might not seem so great.

The difficulties in evaluating slave codes can be illustrated by an apparent contradiction in the trends of North American law as it evolved from the late seventeenth to the mid nineteenth century. On the one hand, the slave codes reveal a stiffening opposition to emancipations of any form. In 1712 South Carolina not only allowed a master to free his slave, but invited Negroes illegally kept in bondage to present their claims to the governor and council. The Consolidated Slave Act of 1740 continued the provisions for a Negro's appeal for freedom, but added that the presumption would always be against him, and prescribed punishment for making a false claim. It was not until 1800, however, that private manumissions were limited to deeds, and required an examination of the slave's character by a magistrate and freeholders. In 1820 the state tried to prohibit all emancipations except by special acts of the legislature, but it was not until 1841 that a law voided testamentary manumission. The pattern was similar in most of the Southern states; by the 1850s legal enfranchisement was difficult if not impossible, and the Virginia constitution of 1851 went so far as to prohibit the General Assembly from freeing any slave, including those who were yet to be born.[53]

(Medieval Russian Laws [tr. by George Vernadsky, New York, 1947], p. 55).

53. John Codman Hurd, The Law of Freedom and Bondage in the United States (Boston, 1858–62), I, pp. 299, 303; II, pp. 11, 96–7, 99; M. Eugene Sirmans, 'The Legal Status of the Slave in South Carolina,

On the other hand, the same codes of law show an increasing concern for the life and welfare of slaves. Until well into the eighteenth century it was no crime in South Carolina for an owner to kill or mutilate his slave in the ordinary course of chastisement. Until 1788 the laws of Virginia assumed that since no master could destroy part of his estate with malice prepense, the killing of a slave was not felonious. In 1740 South Carolina ruled that a man who wilfully murdered his own or someone else's slave should pay a fine of seven hundred pounds; the amount was cut in half for killing a slave in the sudden heat of passion. Yet the Georgia constitution of 1798 put the killing or maiming of a slave on the same level of criminality as the killing or maiming of a white man. In 1821 South Carolina prescribed death for the deliberate and wilful murder of a slave, and six months' imprisonment and a fine of five hundred dollars for killing one in the sudden heat of passion. By the 1850s most Southern states provided heavy fines for even the cruel treatment of slaves. Of course few Southerners suffered the penalties of these laws, since juries were reluctant to convict, and slaves, who were often the only witnesses to such crimes, were barred from testifying against white men. But it is also true that laws against manumission were often evaded.[54]

The laws and customs of every slave society give evidence of the essential contradiction in thinking of a man as a thing. Despite historical and cultural variations, slaves have generally been defined as chattels personal, incapable of legal marriage, property ownership or judicial testimony; they have been subject to the will and authority of a private or institutional owner; their labour and services have been totally at the disposal of others.[55] Yet unlike a machine or beast of

1670–1740', *Journal of Southern History*, XXVIII (November 1962), pp. 462–72.

54. Hurd, *Law of Freedom and Bondage*, I, pp. 23, 48, 232, 297, 306; II, pp. 97, 100, 103; Kenneth M. Stampp, *The Peculiar Institution: Slavery in the Ante-Bellum South* (New York, 1956), pp. 219, 221.

55. Unlike Rome, Carthage and Hellenistic Greece accepted the validity of slave marriages; but even in medieval Europe, where slave marriages were recognized if approved by a master, the bondsman seldom had any legal

burden, the slave was potentially capable of an infinite number of services, and in many societies, including the United States, his occupations were highly diversified.[56] We have seen that even in antiquity governments were troubled by the problems of devising special criminal codes for slaves, of differentiating them from other social classes, of preventing the escape of fugitives, and of defining and regulating methods of emancipation. Except for certain Arab states, governments have also shown an extreme reluctance to allow slaves the use of arms. Bondwomen have always been the victims of sexual exploitation, which was perhaps the clearest recognition of their

---

claim to his wife and children. From early Babylonian times slaves were occasionally granted the privilege of using and accumulating property, which was legally owned by their masters but might eventually be used for their own redemption. This *peculium*, as it developed in Rome, was a kind of security which permitted the slave to conduct business with freemen; yet it was always the property of the master and could not be conveyed to another person without the master's permission. And the master could revoke such a privilege and recover the *peculium* (see Mendelsohn, *Slavery in Ancient Near East*, pp. 34, 40–42, 50; Westermann, *Slave Systems*, pp. 58–9, 81, 83, 115; Buckland, *The Roman Law of Slavery*, pp. 1, 76–7, 187–8; Origo, 'Domestic Enemy', pp. 344–5).

Among Moslems, the Mālikīs alone allowed slaves the use of a *peculium*; with his master's consent, the slave might even keep the property after manumission (*Encyclopedia of Islam* [new ed.], I, pp. 27–9).

56. While domestic service has often been the dominant function of slaves, in the ancient world they were employed in mines, handicraft industries, commerce, public works, and in field gangs on plantations. The majority of American slaves worked as field hands on plantations, but South Carolina newspapers of the mid eighteenth century mention slave tailors, shoemakers, shipwrights, cabinet-makers, bricklayers, navigators and even silversmiths. In 1820 slaves constituted at least 20 per cent of the populations of the major Southern cities, and though the proportion soon diminished, there were some 500,000 Negro bondsmen by 1860 who were in jobs not connected with agriculture. (See Mendelsohn, *Slavery in Ancient Near East*, pp. 67–8, 121; Westermann, *Slave Systems*, pp. 5, 8, 12–13; Finley, 'Was Greek Civilization Based on Slave Labour?', pp. 53, 56–7; Marcus W. Jernegan, *Laboring and Dependent Classes in Colonial America, 1607–1783; Studies of the Economic, Educational, and Social Significance of Slaves, Servants, Apprentices, and Poor Folk* [Chicago, 1931], pp. 10–11, 13–14, 16–18; Stampp, *Peculiar Institution*, pp. 59–67, 72–3, 259; Richard C. Wade, *Slavery in the Cities; the South: 1820–1860* [New York, 1964], pp. 3–4, 26, 30–54, 244–8).

humanity; and most societies have been highly sensitive to the relations of free women and male slaves Yet the master class has usually responded to the obvious humanity of slaves with contempt and prejudice. The white slaves of antiquity and the Middle Ages were often described in terms that fit the later stereotype of the Negro. Throughout history it has been said that slaves, though occasionally as loyal and faithful as good dogs, were for the most part lazy, irresponsible, cunning, rebellious, untrustworthy and sexually promiscuous.

Let us be entirely clear, however, on the essential point. No slave system in history was quite like that of the West Indies and the Southern states of America. Marked off from the free population by racial and cultural differences, for the most part deprived of the hope of manumission, the Negro slave also found his life regimented in a highly organized system that was geared to maximum production for a market economy. But slavery in America was not unique in its central characteristics or in its underlying contradiction. Because slaves are men who are defined as things, the institution has always generated tension and conflict. In any slave society an apologist could doubtless have pointed to a large number of humane masters and seemingly contented slaves. But if abolitionists had appeared in antiquity, they would have had little difficulty in compiling lists of atrocities that would rival the most grisly tales of the nineteenth century.

Under the Hammurabi Code, a man who killed someone else's slave was merely required to pay compensation to the owner; the same rule appeared in Europe as late as the medieval Russian Law. No Biblical legislation prohibited the beating or maltreatment of bondsmen, though a Jewish owner might be liable to punishment if his slave died within three days of a severe chastisement. A master might kill his slave with impunity, however, in Homeric Greece, ancient India, the Roman Republic, Saxon England, Kievan Russia and, under certain circumstances, in China of the Former Han period. The Pali canon, *Tipitaka*, provided no redress for a bondwoman who, forced to sleep with her master, had her nose and ears cut off by his jealous wife.[57] The criminal law was almost everywhere

57. Mendelsohn, *Slavery in Ancient Near East*, pp. 64–5; Wilbur, *Slavery*

more severe for slaves than freemen. The Roman government tortured bondsmen on the slightest suspicion of wrongdoing, and took over entirely the right of punishment for serious offences. A slave who cohabited with his mistress faced certain death; a lingering death on the cross awaited the one who led or joined a revolt. And while a master's right to kill his slaves was somewhat restricted in 12 A.D. and finally abolished by Hadrian, Rome was notorious for ghastly atrocities; Vedius Pollio, for example, was said to have fed the meat of slaves to his pet fish. The reform legislation of the Empire gives eloquent testimony of the power which masters had hitherto enjoyed: one law required magisterial approval for forcing slaves into deadly combat with animals; others prohibited castration and the killing of slaves who were sick or infirm. And the later imperial laws were not always marked with Christian charity. In the late fourth century Gratian ruled that a slave who accused his master of any offence other than high treason should immediately be burned alive, regardless of the justice of the charge. Even in medieval Italy slaves were tortured by magistrates and whipped without restraint by masters; in Siena a man who damaged another's slave paid the same fine as if he had damaged a cow.[58]

Since there is no evidence that human beings in antiquity or the Middle Ages were better suited than nineteenth-century Americans for the exercise of nearly absolute power over their fellow men, it would appear safe to conclude that the abuses and cruelties exposed by the abolitionists were associated with slavery from its very origin.

---

in China, pp. 152, 164; Westermann, Slave Systems, pp. 3, 17; Chanana, Slavery in Ancient India, pp. 54, 107–8; Vernadsky, Kievan Russia, p. 150. It should be noted that later Hindu law punished the murder of a slave with a small fine (Adam, Law and Custom, p. 62). In Russia, the Charter of Dvina Land ruled that if a master beat a slave to death without intent to kill, he should not be liable to a fine (Medieval Russian Laws, p. 59).

58. Westermann, Slave Systems, pp. 75–6, 91–3, 115; Lecky, History, I, p. 303; II, pp. 64–5; Origo, 'Domestic Enemy', pp. 340–41.

3

Slavery and Sin: The Ancient Legacy

THE inherent contradiction of slavery lay not in its cruelty or economic exploitation, but in the underlying conception of man as a conveyable possession with no more autonomy of will and consciousness than a domestic animal. This conception raised a host of problems and was seldom acted upon without compromise. Occasionally men recognized that the institution was dangerous to the security of the State, that it provided some masters with too much idleness and too much power, that slaves were men and should be treated with consideration. But from the ancient world we find no assertion that slavery was an intolerable evil that should be eradicated by any civilized nation.

Nowhere in the religious literature of the Sumero-Accadian world says Isaac Mendelsohn, was the slightest protest made against slavery, 'nor is there anywhere an expression of the mildest sympathy for the victims of this system. Slavery was simply taken for granted.' Noting that no ancient author wrote specifically on slavery, William Westermann concludes that it was never a 'problem' in antiquity. He rejects as sentimental the traditional belief that Greek writers accepted slavery as a necessity but regarded it with uneasiness. With this judgement Moses Finley completely agrees:

The Greek world was one of endless debate and challenge. Among the intellectuals no belief or idea was self-evident: every conception and every institution sooner or later came under attack – religious beliefs, ethical values, political systems, aspects of the economy, even such bedrock institutions as the family and private property. Slavery, too, up to a point, but that point was invariably a good distance short of abolitionist proposals.

Even in times of rebellion and social upheaval, slavery went unchallenged.[1]

1. Isaac Mendelsohn, *Slavery in the Ancient Near East; Comparative*

But this does not mean that the Bible and classical literature had no bearing on the later anti-slavery movements. From the earliest times slavery was taken as a model for certain religious, philosophic and political dualisms, and was thus implicitly connected with some of the greatest problems in the history of human thought. As a result of these associations and precedents, embodied in Holy Scripture, in the works of philosophers and divines, in the corpora of Jewish and Roman law, any future attack on slavery would be bound to produce reverberations through the vast range of Western culture. Slavery could never be isolated as an objective issue of public policy.

The Hebrew word for slave, '*ebed*', was used in one sense to refer to a righteous punishment sanctioned by the Lord. 'Cursed be Canaan', cried Noah. 'A servant of servants shall he be unto his brethren.' The phrase 'a servant of servants', we are told, meant 'the meanest slave', and the descendants of Canaan were thus condemned to perpetual bondage.[2] Solomon was authorized to raise an annual levy of slaves

---

Study of Slavery in Babylonia, Assyria, Syria, and Palestine, from the Middle of the Third Millennium to the end of the First Millennium (New York, 1949), p. 123; William L. Westermann, 'Between Slavery and Freedom', *American Historical Review*, L (January 1945), pp. 213–16; Westermann, *The Slave Systems of Greek and Roman Antiquity* (Philadelphia, 1955), pp. 1, 26; Moses I. Finley, 'Was Greek Civilization Based on Slave Labour?', reprinted in Finley (ed.), *Slavery in Classical Antiquity: Views and Controversies* (Cambridge, 1960), pp. 61, 63–4. For a quite different view, see Gerhard Kehnscherper, *Die Stellung der Bibel und der alten christlichen Kirche zur Sklaverei* (Halle, 1957).

2. Genesis IX 25; John Skinner, *A Critical and Exegetical Commentary on Genesis* (New York, 1900), p. 184. In view of the significance attached to Noah's curse by later apologists for Negro slavery, we might note that the passage, while giving divine sanction to slavery as a punishment, is filled with complexities and inconsistencies. According to Gerhard Von Rad, the original Yahwistic narrative had nothing to do with Shem, Ham and Japheth, and the ecumenical scheme of nations which follows. It was rather an older story, limited to the Palestinian Shem, Japheth and Canaan, and connected with the horror felt by the newly arrived Israelites at the sexual depravity of the Canaanites. Later on, a redactor inserted the name Ham as the father of Canaan, in an effort to harmonize the narrative with the later table of nations (*Genesis: A Commentary* [tr. by John H. Marks, Philadelphia, 1961] pp. 131–3). This provided the basis for elaborate exegesis

from among the Canaanites not killed in battle; and after the destruction of Babylon by Yahweh, the former oppressors of Israel were to become their slaves.[3]

But slavery was also the clearest example of the total subordination of one individual to another, of the negation of personal choice and desire. It was associated in the Old Testament with religious humility and self-surrender, as when Abraham, Lot, Moses, Job and David were referred to as slaves of the Lord. The Hebrews were perhaps the first people to think of God as a noble master who might be persuaded to give aid and guidance to His lowliest slave.

Moses used the same word to refer both to Israel's slavery in Egypt and, after deliverance, to their bondage to Yahweh.[4] But this new relationship was based on a voluntary convenant in which both parties pledged to abide by their word. In Isaiah, Israel's new Master explicitly acknowledged His children as 'abādīm', and promised them His protection. Moses repeatedly reminded his people of their former slavery and their new obligations: 'And thou shalt remember that thou wast a servant in the land of Egypt.'[5] Thus liberation and purposeful mission were conceived as a transfer of dependence from arbitrary worldly masters to the Lord, who gave assurance of future peace and plenty in return for faith. The promise of God revealing himself to mankind through a chosen people was associated with emancipation from physical slavery and the voluntary acceptance of a higher form of service

These religious connotations of slavery had profound · consequences. On Sinai Moses was told that the Hebrews should buy their slaves from neighbouring nations, and

moreover of the children of the strangers that sojourn among you, of them shall ye buy, and of their families that are with you, which they have begotten in your land: and they shall be your possession. And ye

---

designed to prove that Negroes, being descended from Ham, were meant to be slaves.

3. Isaiah xiv 2; I Kings ix 21.

4. Exodus ii 23; vi 6, 9; xiii 3, 4. Israel's bondage in Egypt was of a special kind, since the Jews were apparently impressed into service for the State.

5. Deuteronomy v 15; xv 15.

shall make them an inheritance of your children after you, to hold for a possession; of them shall ye take your bondmen for ever: but over your brethren the children of Israel ye shall not rule, one over another, with rigour.[6]

As Josephus later noted, explaining Jewish history to the Hellenistic world, it was not reasonable for Hebrews to make slaves from their own people when God had made so many nations subject to Israel.[7] The careful regulations concerning Jewish servants were justified by the memory of bondage in Egypt – by the recognition of a common dependence on Yahweh the emancipator. Thus no Hebrew bondsman was to serve, without his consent, for longer than fifty years; severe punishment awaited the Jew who stole and sold one of his brethren; and Moses received detailed provisions for the redemption of indigent Jews bought by resident aliens.[8] But while Jeremiah condemned his people for re-enslaving Hebrew bondsmen who had been released from service, and while Job tried to prove his righteousness by acknowledging that God would have had reason to punish him if he had despised the cause of his servants, the Old Testament contains no explicit protest against slavery.[9] Of greater significance for the future, however, was the association of religious mission with liberation from bondage to men and with a new bondage to a higher authority. This central conception would ultimately have special meaning for American colonists who thought of their own mission as a deliverance

6. Leviticus xxv 44–6.

7. Josephus, *Jewish Antiquities*, viii, 160.

8. Leviticus xxv 39–55; Exodus xxi 4, 20–26; xxiv 7.

9. Jeremiah xxxiv 8–20; Job xxxi 13–15. I think Kehnscherper greatly exaggerates the significance of the passage from Jeremiah (*Die Stellung der Bibel*, pp. 15–17). It is true that Job recognizes that he and his slaves share a common humanity and owe their origin to the same God, but it is doubtful whether he means anything more than that masters should be humane and considerate. In the Apocrypha, masters are told to treat slaves with kindness, an injunction that is repeated many times in the Talmud. But in Sirach (xxxiii 24–31) it is also said that heavy fetters should be put on bad slaves, and

> Fodder and stick and burdens for an ass,
> Bread and discipline and work for a servant!
> Put thy servant to work, and he will seek rest;
> Leave his hands idle, and he will seek liberty!

from spiritual slavery in Europe, and as adherence to divine law in a New Jerusalem.

The claim has often been made that Plato was at heart an opponent of slavery. There is not the slightest evidence, however, that he found human bondage contrary to the highest good or that he intended to exclude it from his ideal Republic. He wished, it is true, to discontinue the enslavement of Hellenes, but the servitude of foreigners he took for granted.[10] In his *Laws* the departures from Athenian practice were all in the direction of increasing the authority of masters and of widening the distinction between slaves and freemen. His prohibition on bondage as a punishment for citizens implied that slavery would be confined to men of foreign stock. Their permanent inferiority was ensured by making the status of slavery inheritable from a parent of either sex. Even the manumitted slave was obliged to serve his former master, and there were no legal safeguards to prevent his being reduced again to slavery. The freedman had no hope of rising to the rank of citizen, for he was required to leave the state after a limited term of residence. Although slaves were to serve the government as informers, they were otherwise subjected to the full authority of their masters, and had no protection against harsh treatment. Plato would even deny them friendly intimacy with the master class, and would give any free person the right to judge and punish a slave for certain crimes, or to take summary vengeance against insult. No American slave code was so severe.[11]

Plato's view of slavery was related to his general philosophy in certain ways that were of importance for the future. By the fifth century B.C. many Greeks had come to believe that the inferiority of barbarians could be seen in their willingness to submit to despotic and absolutist rulers. According to Herodotus, when two brave Spar-

10. Republic, v, 469.

11. *Laws*, vi, 776E, 777D, 778A; ix, 865, 868, 872, 882; xi, 914, 936; Glenn R. Morrow, *Plato's Law of Slavery in its Relation to Greek Law* (Urbana, 1939), pp. 122–31. Curiously, the Russian Law later held that if a slave struck a freeman and then sought refuge in his master's house, the master must pay compensation to the freeman, who was also permitted to beat the slave whenever he could be found (*Medieval Russian Laws* [tr. by George Vernadsky, New York, 1947], p. 29).

tans were told by a Persian commander that they might expect great rewards if they submitted to Xerxes, they said in defiance: 'A slave's life you understand, but never having tasted liberty, you can not tell whether it be sweet or no.'[12] For certain Greek writers, including Plato, two consequences followed from this popular distinction between Hellene and barbarian.[13] First, bondage was closely associated with tyrannical government and arbitrary power; a people with a capacity and ardent desire for freedom, as evidenced by their political institutions, could not legitimately be slaves. Second, a 'slavish people' lacked the capacity not only for self-government but also for the higher pursuits of virtue and culture. Thus for Plato a slave might hold a true belief but could never know the truth of his belief, since he was inherently deficient in reason. While Plato thought that a similar deficiency was shared by many free subjects, and would have allowed certain barbarians an opportunity to acquire civic virtues, he nevertheless supplied the elements for a theory of intellectual inferiority as the natural basis for slavery.

He also saw the relation of slave to master as a kind of microcosm of the hierarchical pattern that pervaded society and the entire universe.[14] This is not to say that Plato derived his cosmology or political theory from the model of slavery; yet his reference to the body as the slave of the soul, as Gregory Vlastos has pointed out, was meant as a serious philosophic truth.[15] The relations of body and soul, of sovereign and subjects, of master and slave Plato subsumed under a single theory of authority and obedience. Moreover, in his cosmology he perceived a similar dualism of primary cause, which was intelligent and divine, and mechanical or slave cause, which was irrational,

12. *Persian Wars*, vii, 135 (Modern Library ed., tr. by George Rawlinson, New York, 1942).

13. For the development of the Greek concept of barbarian inferiority and its relation to slavery, see Robert Schlaifer, 'Greek Theories of Slavery from Homer to Aristotle', *Harvard Studies in Classical Philology*, XLVII (1936), 166–70.

14. See ibid., p. 190, for a passage from Philemon 'where the entire universe is viewed as a hierarchy of slavery, in which one's place on the scale mattered but little'.

15. Gregory Vlastos, 'Slavery in Plato's Republic', *The Philosophical Review*, L (1941), pp. 289–304.

disorderly, and lacking in both freedom and conscious purpose. Like a wise master, the Demiurge guided the *ananke* of the material universe towards the good.[16] It is of the utmost significance that Plato associated slavery with both the unruly multitude and the chaotic material world devoid of Logos. In effect, he rationalized the contradiction of slavery within a vast cosmic scheme in which irrational nature was ordered and controlled by a divine, intelligent authority. Future apologists for slavery were perhaps indebted to Plato for linking the authority of masters to the cosmic principle of order. On the other hand, when we recall that the Abbé Raynal pictured a slave revolt as Nature vindicating herself against the perversions of society, it is clear that the terms of the dualism could be reversed when 'nature' acquired new meanings.

In one sense Plato's doctrine of ideas was a source for future social criticism, since it implied that the imperfections of this world could be judged in the light of eternal ideals of perfection. This potentiality was largely nullified, however, by what Arthur Lovejoy has termed the 'principle of plenitude'.[17] If God's goodness depended on his unlimited fecundity and the completeness of his creation, then the world was a full replica of the realm of ideas or essences; every link in the great chain of being had a valid and necessary function. With Plato's followers, particularly Plotinus, this best of all possible worlds, emanating as a complete and unbroken chain from the divine One, was thought to contain all possible degrees of evil. Evil, which was simply the privation of some good, had a sufficient reason for existence, and could not be eliminated without destroying the beauty and balance of the whole.[18] While few thinkers accepted this principle of plenitude in its extreme form, which could easily become a kind of pantheism, it was to exercise an enormous influence on Western thought. Thus slavery could be seen not only as exemplifying a cosmic principle of authority and subordination, but as

16. ibid. According to Vlastos, *ananke* was used in Greek to denote both the state of slavery and the constraint and torture to which slaves were subjected.

17. Arthur O. Lovejoy, *The Great Chain of Being: Study of the History of an Idea* (Harper Torchbook ed., New York, 1960), p. 53.

18. ibid., p. 64.

having a necessary place in the ordered structure of being. Like other contradictions, it could be absorbed in higher unities.

According to Plato, Aristotle noted, the same principle governed the rule of slaves, of a household, or of a nation. Yet 'others affirm that the rule of a master over slaves is contrary to nature, and that the distinction between slaves and freemen exists by law only, and not by nature; and being an interference with nature is therefore unjust.'[19] This is the first definite indication that some philosophers had taken the momentous step of associating the contradiction of slavery with the dualism of nature and conventional society, rather than with that of rational order and brute chaos. Aristotle felt the force of this argument, but like Plato he wished to rationalize slavery by showing its relation to the structure and purposes of being. It had emerged, he thought, from the primitive household, or *oikia*, and was as natural as other relationships of superior and inferior, such as soul and body, man and wife, or father and child. By considering slavery as an essentially domestic relationship, Aristotle endowed it with the sanction of paternal authority, and helped to establish a precedent that would govern discussions of political philosophers as late as the eighteenth century.

On one crucial point, however, he disagreed with Plato. Each type of rule had its own characteristics, and one could not say that the master's government of his slaves was the same as the constitutional government of subjects who by nature were free.[20] In fact, if a free people were subjected to the absolute rule of a sovereign who was responsible to no one but himself, they would be the victims of tyranny and would have reason to be the enemies of their government.[21] By drawing this distinction between the authority of masters and the authority of constitutional rulers, Aristotle narrowed the ground on which slavery could be justified. Unlike certain Sophists, he could not simply say that all authority rests on force, which is its own justification. He was certain that slavery had a rational basis

19. *Politics*, i, 1253[b] (*The Student's Oxford Aristotle*, vol. 6, tr. by W. D. Ross, New York, 1942).
20. ibid., i, 1255[b].
21. ibid., iv, 1295[a].

that differentiated it from tyranny. Yet the Greeks had long used the term 'slavery' to describe the tyrannical governments of their neighbours; and a desire for political liberty might easily develop into a hostility to slavery in any form. To reinforce the separation of political freedom and domestic servitude, Aristotle built his entire argument around Plato's theory of natural inferiority. Later apologists for slavery would adopt a similar strategy to meet a similar problem.

Aristotle was obviously attracted by the idea of a social relationship founded on natural differences, analogous to the subordination of body to soul, or of animals to men.[22] Without forced labour there might have been no *polis*, and hence no basis for virtue and wisdom. Living in a society that increasingly dissociated culture and public service from the slightest taint of manual labour, he saw slavery as a necessary means of supplying the wants of life. In an apparent admission, seized upon by nineteenth-century reformers, he said that if the shuttle would weave and the plectrum touch the lyre without a hand to guide them, 'chief workmen would not want servants, nor masters slaves'.[23] We may doubt, however, whether he yearned for the industrial revolution. The illustration was meant to show the complex nature of the slave as both an instrument of action and a conscious agent who must obey and anticipate his master's will.

This ambiguous conception raised many problems and did little more than magnify the basic contradiction of human bondage. For Aristotle true slavery derived from an innate deficiency in the beauty and inner virtue of the soul. 'From the hour of their birth,' he wrote, 'some are marked out for subjection, others for rule.'[24] The natural slave lacked the moral and intellectual freedom to make decisions in the light of deliberative judgement. But just as later Calvinists were to deny that the sinner was capable of righteous action, and yet allow that certain restraining graces enabled him to approximate virtue, so Aristotle admitted that the slave had a partial soul and might at least participate in reason. The bondsman was even capable of a lower form of moral virtue, which arose from the proper fulfilment of his

22. ibid., i, 1254^a, 1254^b; *Ethics*, i, xiii.
23. *Politics*, i, 1253^b.
24. ibid., i, 1254^a.

86

function. Aristotle had no sympathy with Plato's view that masters should only command their slaves and never converse with them in a friendly manner; the relationship was clearly one of mutual benefit. And yet true friendship was impossible, for the slave was incapable of reciprocating genuine goodwill or benevolence. His true interests could never be other than those of his master. Indeed, one could scarcely speak of his having interests, since as a tool or possession he was only an extension of his master's physical nature.[25] The best slave, it would appear, was the one whose humanity had been most nearly effaced.

The difficulties raised by this conception, even in the Hellenic world, can be illustrated by several passages from the plays of Euripides, which were written in the previous century. In *Helen* a slave finds his moral freedom and human identity precisely where Aristotle would obliterate them. Sympathizing with his master's joys and sorrows, this bondsman says that he would not want to suffer the two evils of physical slavery and a corrupt heart.[26] Thus even a born slave could assert his inner freedom by identifying himself with his master. And while Euripides raised no protest against the injustice of slavery, he sensed that its origins were filled with dramatic pathos. Any Greek could admire the spirit of Polyxena, sister of Hector, who was marked, as she said, to be a bride for kings, and who preferred death to degrading slavery.[27] She and Andromache were shadowy prototypes of the royal African slaves of eighteenth-century verse and drama.

It is clear that even Aristotle was bothered by the origin of slavery and by the messiness and ambiguity of social, as opposed to natural, distinctions. The natural slave, having no deliberative faculty, could not be happy with freedom. But obviously some men who by nature were free and virtuous had been enslaved as a result of war. Aristotle acknowledged that such slaves, held by force and mere social convention, could have no common interest with their masters.[28] Pre-

25. ibid., i, 1254ᵃ, 1259ᵇ–60ᵇ; *Ethics*, vii, v, viii, ii, x, vi. For a discussion of the inconsistencies in Aristotle's position, see Schlaifer, 'Greek Theories of Slavery', pp. 192–8.
26. *Helen*, lines 727–34.
27. *Hector*, lines 352–78.
28. *Politics*, i, 1255ᵃ, 1255ᵇ.

sumably, the authority of their masters was no more legitimate than that of political tyrants. Though he was confident that nature would like to make sharp distinctions in the bodies of men, equipping some for a docile acceptance of hard labour, others for politics and the arts of war and peace, he admitted that physical differences were no clear indication of natural status. This admission opened a significant gap between the actual and theoretical slave – a gap that would be widened by Stoics and Christians and not fully closed until later generations invented the theory of racial inferiority.

The difficulty of detecting natural slaves might have led Aristotle to conclude, as did the later Stoics, that external distinctions were of no meaning. But his philosophy presupposed a close harmony between nature and society. Since Hellenes found it unnatural to use the term *doulos* for a man of their own race, and generally reserved the word for a barbarian, this must reveal an awareness of innate differences. It would be best, Aristotle said, if the Greeks acquired their agricultural slaves from a different race, a race lacking the Hellenic spirit of liberty. In various ways he expressed his desire for a neater separation between slaves and freemen. He objected to citizens who practised the crafts of their inferiors, since this would eventually tend to eliminate the distinctions between slaves and freemen. It was dangerous, he said, for children to be much in the company of slaves.[29]

Like Plato, Aristotle associated slavery with an ideal of intelligent and virtuous authority ruling the irrational forces of the world. Apparently troubled by possible injustices in the way slaves were acquired, he searched for an answer in the assumed inferiority of barbarians. But while he favoured increasing the division between slaves and freemen, he said at one point that he would explain why it was expedient to hold out liberty as an ultimate reward for service.[30] This promise he failed to keep, except, perhaps, in the example of emancipating his own slaves.

We do not know the names of Aristotle's opponents who believed that slavery was a violation of nature. Along with the Hebrew concept of

29. ibid., i, 1255ᵃ; iii, 1277ᵇ; vii, 1330ᵃ, 1336ᵃ.
30. ibid., vii, 1330ᵃ.

deliverance, the doctrine was one of the cultural sources of anti-slavery thought, though this potentiality was limited by the fact that it was the product of a developing trend in philosophy which exhibited a profound indifference to worldly problems.[31] Only fragments survive from the writings of Cynics and early Stoics, whose influence for some five centuries was nevertheless greater than that of the Peripatetics. We know that instead of rationalizing the diverse elements of society into a coherent system, in which such institutions as slavery were securely connected to natural principles or to an ideal realm of essences, they perceived an immense gap between objective truth and human conventions. Virtue they conceived as action in accord with nature, as revealed to man through uncorrupted reason. This meant that instead of subordinating himself to an ordered system of social relationships, the individual must liberate himself from the constraint of both institutions and the ideology supporting them. He could work out the meaning of truth only in independent and practical conduct. While such a quest for individual freedom could easily lead to a challenge of accepted norms and institutions, the dissident philosophers were largely unconcerned with questions of social justice; their brave scepticism arose from a desire for truth and inner purity.

The Sophists were apparently the first to conclude that since slavery was a product of human convention, it had no basis in the objective and unchanging law of nature. Alcidamas, when defending the emancipation of the Messenians by the Thebans, argued that the distinction of slave and freeman was unknown to nature.[32] It is

31. Historians who hold that men's response to slavery has always been dominated by economic interest have used the Stoics to illustrate the impotence of philosophic moralizing which can only end in nullifying contradictions and meaningless abstractions. See, for example, E. Ciccotti, *Il tramonto della schiavitù nel mondo antico* (Torino, 1899). For a more balanced view which recognizes the importance of economic interest but also stresses the role of ideas, see Eleuterio Elorduy, *Die Sozialphilosophie der Stoa, Philologus* (Supplementband XXVIII, Heft 3, Leipzig, 1936), pp. 201–6.

Eduard Zeller, *A History of Greek Philosophy from the Earliest Period to the Time of Socrates* (tr. by S. F. Alleyne, London, 1881), II, pp. 476–7.

impossible to tell how far he would have carried the point. Antisthenes, who was the crucial link between Socrates and the Stoics, was said to have written a treatise, 'Of Freedom and Slavery', which may have been a source of later Stoic doctrine.[33] Believing that virtue was a matter of individual commitment and independence, this founder of the Cynic school also strove to shock public opinion in a way that anticipated later reformers. He not only set himself off with a beard and peculiar garb, but attacked the State, marriage and private property. The emblem of the Cynics, who bore a certain resemblance to the bohemians and beatniks of later ages, was the dog.[34]

The pattern of demonstrative contempt for accepted values was most pronounced in Antisthenes's famous pupil, Diogenes of Sinope. Striving for a life of perfect simplicity, he lived in a tub, walked barefoot in snow, and threw his cup away in shame after seeing a child drink from its hands. Though he favoured abolishing marriage and holding wives in common, there is no report of his having denounced slavery. Yet a defiant disregard for the conventional distinction between slave and freeman was part of his quest for virtue as an inner freedom and independence. 'It would be absurd,' he said, when his own slave had run away, 'if Manes can live without Diogenes, but Diogenes cannot get on without Manes.' When he was captured by pirates on a voyage to Aegina and taken to a slave market in Crete, he pointed to a spectator wearing purple robes, and said, 'Sell me to this man; he needs a master.' He called the friends who wished to redeem him simpletons. Lions, he said, were not the slaves of those who fed them, 'for fear is the mark of the slave, whereas wild beasts make men afraid of them'.[35] Whether these tales are true, they illustrate a pattern of thought that gave rise to the first explicit questioning of slavery. For if freedom is conceived as a liberation of the individual from the norms and institutions of society, as well as from the desires of the flesh, external distinctions lose all importance. Ac-

33. Diogenes Laertius, vi, 16.

34. ibid., vi, 7–16; Alfred W. Benn, *The Greek Philosophers* (London, 1882), II, pp. 5–6.

35. Diogenes Laertius, vi, 20–75 (Loeb Classical Library ed., tr. by R. D. Hicks, London, 1925).

cording to Bion, a pupil of Crates, 'Good slaves are free, but evil men are slaves, desiring many things'.[36]

But we must not read too much into these isolated statements. Zeno, who was also a pupil of Crates, is supposed to have said that it was as great a crime to strike a slave as to strike one's father. Yet Diogenes Laertius tells us that when Zeno was chastising a slave who said that it was his fate to steal, the philosopher replied, 'Yes, and to be beaten too.'[37] It has been claimed that Onesicritus, a Cynic philosopher and pupil of Diogenes of Sinope, advocated the abolition of slavery; he has even been called a forerunner of William Lloyd Garrison. Onesicritus was sent to India by Alexander, and his account of his travels was one of the first combinations of historical narrative and utopian fantasy. The land of Musicanus he described as a kind of ideal society in which the people refrained from the use of gold and silver and ate publicly at a common mess. One might assume that a Cynic philosopher would exclude slavery from such a primitivistic utopia. Yet the passage in Strabo which has been taken as evidence of Onesicritus's hostility to slavery has precisely the opposing meaning:

But although Magasthenes says that no Indian uses slaves, Onesicritus declares that slavery is peculiar to the Indians in the country of Musicanus, and tells what a success it is there, just as he mentions many other successes of this country, speaking of it as a country excellently governed.[38]

Whereas Aristotle held that a slave was actually part of his mas-

---

36. Farrand Sayre, *The Greek Cynics* (Baltimore, 1948), p. 33. The quotation is from Stobaeus; the idea, which was expanded by Philo Judaeus, may have come from Crates.

37. Diogenes Laertius, vii, 23.

38. Strabo *Geography*, xv, 54 (Loeb Classical Libarary ed., tr. by Horace Leonard Jones, London, 1923). This is the passage referred to by Schlaifer ('Greek Theories of Slavery', p. 200), who says that Onesicritus favoured the abolition of slavery. Schlaifer has been followed by other writers who have expanded upon the error. Strabo, Plutarch, Lucian, Pliny, Diogenes Laertius and Arrian all provide material on Onesicritus, but none of them mentions his being opposed to slavery. (See also, Pauly-Wissowa, *Real-encyclopädie*, XXXV, pp. 460–67.)

ter's physical being, Zeno and Chrysippus saw his soul as part of the total substance of a universal reason. External distinctions between Greek and barbarian, male and female, or slave and freeman were thus mere accidents that had no relevance to nature. True virtue, which could be achieved only by living in accordance with principles revealed by a common and universal reason, had nothing to do with conventional standards of morality.[39] But as these early Stoics attempted to work out the practical meaning of virtue, they qualified their belief in the universal brotherhood of man with the principle that the majority of men were slaves to desire and prejudice. Only the philosopher, who achieved the power of independent action in the cold light of reason, could be termed truly free. There is a rough analogy between the Stoic and Hebrew conceptions of liberation from human authorities and conformity to the laws of a higher power. From both points of view true freedom was a privilege to be enjoyed by an elite group, and there could be no gradations of relative improvement between the slavish multitude and the Children of Virtue. The Stoics' ethical world was one of stark antithesis. All sins were equally sinful, and from moral slavery there could be no gradual emancipation.[40]

And while the Stoics measured the evils of society against the absolute standard of nature, and held that the philosopher-saint must persevere in exercising his virtue, they found no difficulty in accepting as inevitable the many imperfections of the world. The wise man's virtue lay not in good works but in decisions that revealed an inner purity and self-control. Since the world had fallen irretrievably from a former Golden Age, he could not regard poverty, disgrace, slavery or even death as evils in themselves, any more than he could

39. Diogenes Laertius, vii, 187–8; Eduard Zeller, *The Stoics, Epicureans and Sceptics* (tr. by Oswald J. Reichel, London, 1880), p. 211. Elorduy argues that the Middle Stoa, who thought of equality in terms of subordination to the State, were more inclined to accept slavery than were the Old and New Stoa, represented by Chrysippus and Seneca, for whom equality was an elevation of man's essence in a higher collective spirit (*Die Sozialphilosophie der Stoa*, p. 206).

40. Diogenes Laertius, vii, 121–2, 127–8; C. J. de Vogel, *Greek Philosophy: Collection of Texts with Notes and Explanations* (Leiden, 1959), p. 140.

consider their opposites as intrinsic goods. The only thing that mattered was the way one responded to the vicissitudes of fortune. True freedom meant self-transcendence, a disengagement of the ego from one's surroundings; and thus the environment of the slave was no more dangerous than any other to the well-being of the soul.[41] It might, indeed, afford greater security against distracting stimuli. Epictetus, who had been a slave himself in his early life, used the bondsman's desire for immediate liberty as an example of the illusions of worldly expectations. After describing the plight of the hungry, homeless freedman, Epictetus observed that even if the ex-slave should ultimately enjoy material success, he would have no knowledge of virtue, and would only become a slave to love, to desire or to political faction. The philosopher pictured the disenchanted freedman looking back with nostalgia to a time when his physical needs were limited and cared for by a master.[42]

But the Stoics' indifference to society and history should not blind us to the fact that they associated slavery with the imperfections of the world, and sin with a special kind of slavery. These associations would have a different meaning if combined with the belief that a particular place or a particular time was marked for the redemption of humanity. Even in the Roman world of the first and second centurier A.D. the Stoic doctrines led to what Westermann has aptly termed a 'frigid sympathy' for the slave. Though Cicero believed that subjection was beneficial for some men, he saw slavery as the result of greed and ignorance. Plutarch and Juvenal sharply criticized the cruelty of certain masters.[43] Epictetus suggested that slaveholders

41. Zeller, *Stoics*, pp. 228–32. It should be noted that Aristotle placed more emphasis on the environment and recognized that men would be perverted if subjected to gross indignities from childhood (*Ethics*, vii, v).

42. *Discourses*, iv, i.

43. Plutarch used Cato the Censor's cruelty to his slaves as evidence of a harsh and narrow spirit; the Censor's great grandson, Cato the Younger, who was influenced by the Stoics, owned slaves but was not accused by Plutarch of maltreating them (see the biographies of the two Catos in *Lives*, ii and iii). It might be said that Juvenal anticipated Jefferson on the effect of slavery on free children: 'What is a young man taught by a sire who delights in the clanking of the iron chains, the branded slaves, and the dungeons?' (*Satires* [tr. by Rolfe Humphries, Bloomington, Ind., 1958], p. 162.)

could not attain true freedom and virtue, since the owner of a slave could not help but become a slave himself.[44] And Seneca developed the theory that only the body of the slave was at the mercy of his master, for 'that inner part cannot be delivered into bondage'. Because the slave's soul was untouched by his condition, he had the capacity to do more for his master than required. Such beneficent service might provide the basis for a relationship transcending external condition.[45] The same idea had been rejected by Aristotle but affirmed long before by Euripides. For Seneca, it was essential that masters treat their slaves as they would be treated by their own superiors: ' "They are slaves," people declare. Nay, rather they are men. . . . "Slaves!" No, they are our fellow-slaves, if one reflects that Fortune has equal rights over slaves and free men alike.'[46]

Seneca's eloquent defence of the freedom of the slave's soul has often been contrasted with Aristotle's doctrine of total inferiority. The difference, while significant, can easily be exaggerated. Aristotle had admitted that some slaves had the souls of free men, though of course he had assumed a closer correspondence between inner slavishness and external condition than did Seneca. Yet Seneca had no doubt that some men, as the result of sin and corruption, had the souls of slaves. Moreover, he was far more concerned with the pride of

Aristotle, it will be recalled, was worried about free children being corrupted by *slaves*.

44. *Fragmenta*, xlii–xliii. Doubt has been expressed concerning the authenticity of some of these selections, which appeared first in Stobaeus. Though Epictetus may have been one of the first to say that a man who desires freedom should be careful not to enslave others, I think that it is incorrect to read this as a moral protest against slavery (see Kehnscherper, *Die Stellung der Bibel*, pp. 53–4). Epictetus is clearly concerned about the effect of slaveholding on the master; he likens the free man being served by slaves to the healthy man being ministered to by the sick. In his *Discourses*, however, he plainly states that the physical slave is far better off than many types of freemen, and anticipates some of the favourite arguments of pro-slavery theorists. Like other Stoics, he probably regarded physical slavery as a matter of small importance so long as it did not corrupt the soul of a particular master.

45. *De Beneficiis*, III, xvii–xxviii (Loeb Classical Library ed., tr. by John W. Basore, London, 1935).

46. *Epistulae Morales*, xlvii, 1, 11.

masters than with the sufferings of slaves. He associated the mal-treatment of bondsmen with luxury, arrogance and gluttony. Discussion of slavery was thus a vehicle for preaching simplicity and humility, and for reminding the well-to-do of how much they owed to fortune. When Seneca wanted to give evidence of his own simplicity of life, he told of taking only a few personal slaves on one of his trips.[47]

The Stoics of the Hellenistic age developed a theory of language that derived from both the Greek tradition of rational analysis and the allegorization of the poets. Essentially, they came to believe that by truly understanding a name, apart from the accidents of convention, they could understand the nature of the thing named.[48] The theory led Hellenistic Jews, especially Philo of Alexandria, to an allegorical interpretation of the Pentateuch. Later on, Irenaeus of Lyons searched in the Old Testament for prefigurations of a universal salvation though the divine Logos. Because of their sins, he concluded, the Jews had had to pass through slavery in Egypt and a subordination to Mosaic law as preparations for freedom.[49] Physical slavery thus began to acquire a new meaning in the history of human salvation.

In the Hellenistic period two of the most significant attempts to relate slavery to the progress of the human spirit were those of Philo and Dio Chrysostom, a wandering Greek Sophist who was known for denouncing the immorality of cities and for his idealization of the simple life of the herdsmen of Euboea. Both philosophers endeavoured to distinguish the true from the literal meaning of 'slave'. They agreed that men naturally love liberty and look on slavery as shameful and degrading. The difficulty was that ordinary men had no understanding of what the words really meant.

Two lines of argument exposed the ambiguities of common usage.

47. ibid., ii, lxxxvii, 2.
48. Robert M. Grant, *The Letter and the Spirit* (London, 1957), pp. 6–7.
49. ibid., p. 83. See also Fred L. Polak, *The Image of the Future* . . ., vol. I: *The Promised Land, Source of Living Culture* (Leyden, 1961), pp. 29–33, 95–115.

What do we mean, asked Dio, in the tantalizing spirit of all philosophers, when we say that a man is a slave? It cannot be a lack of freedom to act on his own judgement, for soldiers and sick men and members of choruses are not slaves. It cannot be that money has been paid for a man, since this is done in a ransom. It cannot be a negation of all personal benefit, since wise masters will always look out for the well-being of their property. It cannot be dependence upon another for one's life, since pirates and judges may execute those who come within their power.[50] And is it not possible, Philo asked, for a man to be a slave to vices and passions, to the fear of death or to the opinions of the multitude.[51]

After showing the difficulties in arriving at a satisfactory definition, both philosophers used the traditional Stoic argument that slavery of the body is the result of mere chance and convention. Since this condition had no basis in objective nature, Philo concluded that it was not a proper subject for philosophy, the implication being that the vicissitudes of fortune could not raise moral issues.[52] Apparently Dio would have agreed with this judgement, but in order to show that true slavery and freedom had nothing to do with external conditions, he went on to undermine the entire legal basis of the institution. Prisoners of war, he said, could not be true slaves; held only by force, there was no reason why, if given the power, they should not escape or retaliate by capturing their former masters. If this was true, masters had no better title to the descendants of captives:

Consequently, if this method of gaining possession, from which all the others take their beginning, is not just, it is likely that no other one is

50. Dio Chrysostom, 'The Fourteenth Discourse: On Slavery and Freedom, I' (Loeb Classical Library ed., *Dio Chrysostom*, vol. II, tr. by J. W. Cohoon, Cambridge, Mass., 1939), 1–12.

51. Philo Judaeus, *Quod Omnis Probus Liber Sit* (Loeb Classical Library ed., tr. by F. H. Colson, London, 1941), 11, 17, 23. The argument was a Stoic commonplace; see Epictetus, *Discourses*, iv, i, 6–10, 128–31; Seneca, *Epistulae Morales*, xlvii, 17 (Loeb Classical Library ed., tr. by Richard M. Gummere, London, 1918–25): 'Show me a man who is not a slave; one is a slave to lust, another to greed, another to ambition, and all men are slaves to fear. ... No servitude is more disgraceful than that which is self-imposed.' The thought continually reappears in Western culture, as in *Hamlet* (III, ii, 77): 'Give me that man that is not passion's slave.'

52. *Quod Omnis Probus*, 17–19.

either, and that the term 'slave' does not in reality correspond to the truth.[53]

This argument would seem to come close to the position of later abolitionists who held that slavery had no legal basis whatsoever. The abolitionist would assume that if 'the term "slave" does not in reality correspond to the truth', then freeborn men were being subjected to an oppressive environment and should in all justice be released from illegal coercion. Dio Chrysostom, however, lived in a different intellectual world, and the fact that physical slavery lacked any legitimate basis suggested to him only that one must look beyond literal meanings to understand the true nature of slavery and freedom. He utterly rejected, of course, the Aristotelian distinction between Greek and barbarian, and pointed out that any race would have countless ancestors who were both slaves and freemen. Yet in one sense he and Philo simply reframed the Aristotelian distinction on Stoic principles.

The true slave was a man ignorant of what was allowed and forbidden by natural law. A great king might be a slave, a man in bonds a freeman. For Philo and Dio Chrysostom this was not figurative language but a statement of reality.[54] If a man found himself called a slave and treated like one, this was a matter of no importance so long as he possessed the freedom of all virtuous men to rise above material conditions. Every good man was free. But 'he who with a mean and slavish spirit puts his hand to mean and slavish actions contrary to his own proper judgement is a slave indeed'.[55] Philo said he agreed with Zeno that a true slave had no right to speak to a good man as an equal.[56] The slave was, in short, a sinner.

And despite his indifference to social condition, Philo slipped back into the significant inconsistency of identifying spiritual with physical slavery. To show that good men love freedom and detest slaves, he cited the examples of Athenians excluding bondsmen from the

53. Dio Chrysostom, 'The Fifteenth Discourse: On Slavery and Freedom, II', 25–8.

54. Dio Chrysostom, 'Fourteenth Discourse', 18; 'Fifteenth Discourse', 31–2.

55. *Quod Omnis Probus*, 24.

56. ibid., 53–4.

celebrations of the Venerable Goddesses, and of the Argonauts barring slaves from their crew. Apparently forgetting his distinction between true and apparent slaves, he wrote:

We may well deride the folly of those who think that when they are released from the ownership of their masters they become free. Servants, indeed, they are no longer now that they have been dismissed, but slaves they are and of the vilest kind, not to men, which would not be so grievous, but to the least reputable of inanimate things, to strong drink, to pot-herbs, to baked meats. ... Thus Diogenes the cynic, seeing one of the so-called freedmen pluming himself, while many heartily congratulated him, marvelled at the absence of reason and discernment. 'A man might as well,' he said, 'proclaim that one of his servants became from this day a grammarian, a geometrician, or musician, when he has no idea whatever of the art.' For as the proclamation cannot make them men of knowledge, so neither can it make them free, for that is a state of blessedness.[57]

Philo did not see that a man released from physical bondage might have a greater chance of acquiring spiritual freedom. Environment, he believed, had no bearing on morality. Yet he still thought of the 'slavish character' as that exhibited by physical slaves, and this was a defect that no deed of manumission could remedy.

But when Philo had given examples of groups of men dedicated to a life of virtue, such as the Persian Magi and Indian Gymnosophists, he had allowed himself a long digression on the Essenes of Palestinian Syria. There is no evidence that he had first-hand knowledge of the Essenes, and his picture of them bears a resemblance in tone to the idealization of American Quakers by French *philosophes*. He presented these 'athletes of virtue' as proof of the possibility of a life of true freedom and perfection. Refraining from any association with war or weapons, or from any employment that stimulated vice, they led a frugal and simple existence, sharing houses and property, providing for the sick and aged, and contributing their earnings to a common fund. Moreover,

not a single slave is to be found among them, but all are free, exchanging services with each other, and they denounce the owners of slaves,

57. ibid., 139–42, 156–7.

not merely for their injustice in outraging the law of equality, but also for their impiety in annulling the statute of Nature, who mother-like has born and reared all men alike, and created them genuine brothers ... though this kinship has been put to confusion by the triumph of malignant covetousness, which has wrought estrangement instead of affinity and enmity instead of friendship.[58]

Although this passage is of obvious importance in the history of anti-slavery thought, it raises many problems.[59] Josephus, the other principal source on the Essenes, was also trying to accommodate Judaism to Greek ideas, though he claimed to have lived for a while with the association.[60] In the *Jewish War* he enumerated their distinctive practices: they avoided oaths, believed in the immortality of the soul, and sought to escape from the wantonness of women by leading celibate lives. They had suffered great persecution from the Romans, who had futilely tried to make them violate their principles. But while Josephus mentioned that new members gave their property to the order, he said nothing of slavery. Among the several references to the Essenes in his *Jewish Antiquities*, the only relevant one is a statement that they neither married nor were 'desirous to keep servants', since servants tempted men to be unjust. This scarcely confirms the strong anti-slavery attitude mentioned by Philo. The only certainty is that anti-slavery was part of Philo's idealized picture of the brotherhood.[61]

We should not need to stress that such an unqualified condemnation of slaveholding was unusual, even unprecedented, in

58. ibid., 79. In *Hypothetica*, 11, 14, Philo said that the Essenes avoided marriage.

59. While few scholars would accept the arguments of H. E. Del Medico that the Essenes were invented by Philo and the confirming passages later interpolated into the writings of Josephus, his extreme theory shows how little can be said of the Essenes with any certainty (*The Riddle of the Scrolls* [London, 1958], pp. 64–74).

60. Matthew Black, *The Scrolls and Christian Origins: Studies in the Jewish Background of the New Testament* (London, 1961), pp. 25–6.

61. *Jewish War*, ii, viii, 2–14; *Jewish Antiquities*, xviii, i, 5; Duncan Howlett, *The Essenes and Christianity: An Interpretation of the Dead Sea Scrolls* (New York, 1957), pp. 87–8.

antiquity.[62] It was associated, let us note, with a combination of three elements: first, the primitivistic ideal of liberating the individual from the corrupting influences of society; second, the perfectionist ideal of working out in concrete terms the social meaning of moral freedom; third, the expectation of an apocalyptic fulfilment and judgement of man in history. In the sense that they sought freedom from sin, from society, and from history as mere repetition, the Essenes anticipated the more radical sects of Protestantism, which were the first groups in the modern world to denounce the holding of slaves. We can only surmise that with the Essenes the Hebraic sense of place and promise gave a forward momentum to the Stoic belief that mankind was united through a common reason unaffected by the accidents of time.

According to the jurists Florentinus and Ulpian, slavery was a manifest departure from the *jus naturale*, but was sanctioned by the *jus gentium*. It was the single instance, Ulpian said, of a conflict between the principles of nature and the common law of nations. This sense of tension, inherited from the Stoics, was passed on to the Institutes of Justinian, and thence to the jurisprudence of Western civilization.[63]

62. Glenn Morrow says that slaveholding was forbidden in Locris and Phocis, but that these were remote areas that never would have had many slaves (*Plato's Law of Slavery*, p. 130 n.).

63. R. W. Carlyle and A. J. Carlyle, *A History of Medieval Political Thought in the West* (Edinburgh and London, 1927), I, p. 50. By a remarkable coincidence, a variety of laws designed to protect slaves appeared at about the same time in China, India, Ptolemaic Egypt and Rome. Wang-Mang, whose rule overlapped that of Augustus, tried unsuccessfully to eliminate the institution by indirect means. Without discounting political, military and economic objectives, C. Martin Wilbur has concluded that the spread of humanistic Confucian philosophy probably contributed to the Chinese reform legislation of the first century A.D. (*Slavery in China during the former Han Dynasty, 206 B.C.–A.D. 24* [Chicago, 1943], pp. 237–40). Ptolemaic Egypt prohibited the export of slaves, required legal permission for corporal punishment, and provided minimal standards for the physical welfare of bondsmen; Alexandria, especially, set an example which might have been imitated with advantage by the later colonizing nations of Europe. It is difficult to know how much this legislation drew from the ideals of Hellenistic Philosophy (see Westermann, *Slave Systems*, pp. 30–31, 38, 53, 102–3, 116).

But if slavery was unknown to nature and yet was so universal as to be part of the *jus gentium*, how could one account for the degeneration? And if all good men were free and all bad men slaves, could the bad men become good and so escape their slavery? What would prevent the original causes of slavery from reducing them to their former bondage? These questions the Stoics raised but could not answer. They associated true slavery with a kind of sin, but it was a sin that could be conquered only by man's inner resources.

For Christians, Jesus gave the answer when he spoke to the Pharisees:

If ye abide in my word, then are ye truly my disciples; and ye shall know the truth, and the truth shall make you free. They answered unto him, We are Abraham's seed, and have never yet been in bondage to any man: how sayest thou, Ye shall be made free? Jesus answered them, Verily, verily, I say unto you, Every one that committeth sin is the bondservant [*doulos*] of sin. And the bondservant abideth not in the house for ever: the son abideth for ever.[64]

At first sight this passage resembles the Stoic paradox that true liberty can come only from an inner change in man's nature – that most men who think of themselves as free are really slaves. Yet Jesus preached a profounder conception of man's need for redemption from his slavery to sin. It may be objected (as the Pharisees might well have done) that the word 'slave' was only figuratively applied to the sinner. But as early Christians repeatedly conceived of sin and salvation in terms of slavery and freedom, the words acquired complex layers of meaning that necessarily affected men's response to the institution of slavery. Thus Saint John Chrysostom, commenting on the above passage of Scripture in the fourth century, complained that many people would still prefer to be the slaves of sin rather than the slaves of men.[65] And whereas Plato associated the disorder of the material world with slavery, and the Stoics thought of conventional society as irretrievably fallen, Paul spoke of all creation being delivered from the *douleia* of corruption into the liberty of the children

64. John viii 31–5.
65. Saint John Chrysostom, *Commentary on Saint John the Apostle and Evangelist*, Homily 54 (tr. by Sister Thomas Aquinas Goggin, New York, 1960), p. 66.

of God. Both he and Jude referred to themselves as the slaves of Jesus Christ. And since no servant (*oiketẹs*) could have two masters, men were told that they must choose between God and mammon.[66] The concept of slavery is further widened when we learn that the story of Abraham's sons was an allegory of Christ's liberating mankind from bondage to Mosaic law. Ishmael, born of a slave mother, represented bondage to the flesh and to the old covenant of Sinai; Isaac, born of a free mother, represented the spiritual liberty of the future; thus 'we are as Isaac was, children of promise'. This meant that Christians had been called for a life of freedom, not of the flesh, but as willing slaves to one another.[67]

In the eyes of Christians the independent, natural man, idealized by primitivists in all ages, was a sinner who, lacking the essential capacity for virtue, bore a certain resemblance to Aristotle's natural slave. Even Aristotle had implied that the natural slave, bereft though he was of the highest faculties, had at least the freedom to accept the gift of emancipation. So under Christianity the most hardened sinner could accept the gift of grace. In a rather extravagant analogy, Tertullian said that just as a slave girl who was espoused but not yet married, because not yet freed, should be excused if she committed adultery with another man, so a pagan who was a slave to sin, though pledged to Christ, would be forgiven for his sins.[68] But freedom from the slavery of sin was not freedom from the principle of bondage. If the sinner was free from righteousness, the saint was the slave of righteousness.[69] Perfect liberty, as theologians were long to maintain, lay in absolute conformity to God's will. The result, as Lecky acutely observed, was that Christianity gave a certain moral dignity to servitude. For the Romans the servile character was synonymous with everything lowly and vicious; Christianity raised obedience humility, patience and resignation to the level of high virtues.[70]

66. Romans i 1; viii 20; Jude i; Luke xvi 13.
67. Galatians iii 23–9; iv 1–4.
68. Tertullian, *Treatises on Penance: On Penitence and On Purity* (tr. by William P. Le Saint, Westminster, Md, 1959), p. 280. For other associations of sin and slavery, see pp. 25, 76–7, 118, 160.
69. Romans vi 15–23.
70. William E. H. Lecky, *History of European Morals from Augustus to Charlemagne* (3rd ed., New York, 1890), II, pp. 66–8.

Lecky concluded, with perhaps too much zeal, that Christianity inevitably equalized men and thus led the way to the abolition of slavery. It is true that upon conversion, early Christians sometimes gave up their property and manumitted their slaves.[71] As a priest, the ex-slave saw the greatest nobles kneeling humbly at his feet. The author of Ephesians said that God, no respecter of persons, was the master of masters as well as of slaves. But he also told slaves to be obedient 'unto them that according to the flesh are your masters, with fear and trembling, in a singleness of your heart, as unto Christ'.[72] We thus come to a fundamental duality in the New Testament. As men gathered to prepare for the imminent Kingdom, temporal distinctions were of little importance. Christ's message was universal; all men were brothers in union with God. But for this very reason if a man was called to be a slave, he should not try to become free: 'For he that was called in the Lord being a bondservant, is the Lord's freeman: likewise he that was called being free, is Christ's bondservant.'[73] In the blinding light of the Gospel message, men could both accept and disregard social distinctions.

It is only with this attitude in mind that we can understand the meaning of Paul's Epistle to Philemon, which aroused such wearisome debates during the slavery controversies of the eighteenth and nineteenth centuries. Because the letter pertained to the relations of a particular master and a particular runaway slave, and because the circumstances of the case can only be inferred, we must not read too much into the text. Paul himself drew no general propositions. He simply exhorted Philemon to take back Onesimus, whom Paul had converted to Christianity, 'no longer as a servant, but more than a servant, a brother beloved, specially to me'.[74]

The letter would seem to prove no more than that early Christians were allowed to hold even fellow Christians as slaves, though they were urged to treat such bondsmen more as spiritual brethren.[75] In the

71. Frederick van der Meer, *Augustine the Bishop: The Life and Work of a Father of the Church* (tr. by Brian Battershaw and G. R. Lamb, London, 1962), p. 136.

72. Ephesians vi 5–9.

73. 1 Corinthians vii 20–22; xii 13.

74. Philemon 16.

75. Paul Robinson Coleman-Norton suggests that Onesimus was owned by

fourth century Saint Basil saw in the Epistle no implication that Christian slaves should be freed; on the contrary, Paul had set a precedent for admonishing and returning fugitives to their masters. Even if masters tried to force slaves to break the laws of Christ, there was no excuse for flight.[76] We may assume that the early Christian attitude towards slavery was summarized by Ignatius, Bishop of Antioch, in his epistle to Polycarp:

Despise not men or women slaves. Yet let them not be puffed up, but rather bear their slavery for the glory of God, that they may win from Him thereby a better liberty. Let them not seek to be emancipated at the expense of the common fund, that they may not be found the slaves of desire.[77]

Theologians, it is true, continued to insist on a theoretical distinction between spiritual and physical slaves. Like the earlier Stoics, Saint Ambrose and Ambrosiaster maintained that a slave may in reality be freer than his master. Augustine agreed with Philo of Alex-

---

Archippus and that Paul was writing to Philemon as an intermediary; he also argues that Paul would have liked to keep Onesimus. The evidence for this view does not seem very strong (Coleman-Norton [ed.], *Studies in Roman Economic and Social History, in Honor of Allan Chester Johnson* [Princeton, 1951], pp. 164–9).

76. *The Ascetic Works of Saint Basil* (tr. by W. K. L. Clarke, London, 1925), pp. 172–3. Saint Basil's view that slaves should persevere as Christians and endure whatever punishments they received is remarkably close to the position of the Buddha, who said that if a man was born a slave, it was certain he was being punished for his sins of a previous life, and that he could hope for a better condition in the future only if he resigned himself to his destiny and submitted with calm patience even to the tortures of a cruel master (Dev Raj Chanana, *Slavery in Ancient India, as Depicted in Pali and Sanskrit Texts* [New Delhi, 1960], pp. 7, 53, 61–2). It is also interesting to note that Buddhists, like the early Christians, specifically prohibited the ordination of runaway slaves. On the other hand, Saint John Chrysostom wrote three homilies on the Epistle to Philemon in which he stated that while slavery was the consequence of sin, masters should treat their bondsmen as brethren in Christ and manumit them if at all possible (Johannes Quasten, *Patrology* [Utrecht and Westminster, Md, 1960], II, p. 450).

77. Ernest Barker, *From Alexander to Constantine: Passages and Documents Illustrating the History of Social and Political Ideas, 336 B.C.–A.D. 337* (Oxford, 1956), pp. 406–7.

andria that good men were free and evil men slaves, irrespective of their stations in life.[78] Masters were often charged with the sins of pride and sensuality. Clement of Alexandria saw a connexion between slavery and sexual perversion.[79] Gregory of Nyssa accused the arrogant slaveowner of condemning a man who by nature was free, and thus of setting himself up in rivalry to God.[80] But since the entire drama of sin and salvation was conceived as a spiritual analogy to slavery and emancipation, even to the point of imagining sin as an inherited but deserved defect that one could not escape on one's own volition, it was only natural that physical slavery should be increasingly seen as the consequence of sin.

Saint Ambrose, Saint Isidore of Seville, and especially Saint Augustine thought of slavery, along with all secular instruments of coercion and government, as part of the punishment for man's fall from grace. They recognized, as had Aristotle and the Stoics, that the chances of fortune did not always correspond to the inner condition of an individual's soul. It was inconceivable, however, that injustice should darken God's omnipotent rule of the world. According to Augustine, slavery was a remedy as well as a penalty for sin, and it was God who bore the direct responsibility for appointing both masters and slaves. Though man had originally been free and had been given dominion over only the beasts, his presumptuous violation of the natural order had made bondage a necessary check on the excesses of his own evil will.[81] Thus as Plato had intimated, slavery was part of the grand scheme of divine order and government, a disciplining force restraining subterranean currents of evil and rebellion. If it were objected that military victories were sometimes won by wicked men who enslaved their innocent victims, Augustine's reply was that

78. *City of God*, iv, iii. See also, *Confessions*, vi, xv.

79. Clement of Alexandria, *Christ the Educator* (tr. by Simon P. Wood, New York, 1954), pp. 216–17, 226.

80. Westermann, *Slave Systems*, p. 160. Saint John Chrysostom agreed with Epictetus that a master who could not get along without his servants was the true slave (Homily 77, *Commentary on Saint John the Apostle*, p. 374).

81. *City of God*, xix, xv. He noted that the word 'slave' was not mentioned in Scripture until Noah branded his son's sin with this name.

no men were innocent; even such an apparent injustice should be seen as a divine judgement. All slaves thus deserved to be slaves, and their only comfort might be in the thought that if they served with faithful affection, they might at least make their bondage in some sense free. The only true slave, after all, was the slave to sin.[82] The Christian household should be a sanctuary for the cultivation of piety and discipline; the *paterfamilias* was enjoined to treat his dependants with charity, but he was also obliged to enforce the domestic peace.[83]

As Christians looked less to an imminent millennium and more to the need of accommodating themselves to the world, they tended to accept the institutions of state and society as a necessary framework for controlling sin and allowing the Church to perform its sacramental functions. Slavery was increasingly justified under what Ernst Troeltsch has termed 'das Relative Naturrecht', which was a natural law adapted and modified for sinful man.[84] The Church not only accepted the institution, but made every effort to ensure the security of masters in controlling their property. Thus the Canons of the Church reinforced civil law in protecting owners against the loss of slaves to the Church; no slave could be ordained unless he had first been emancipated.[85] The Fathers exhorted slaves to obey even the harshest masters, and in A.D. 362 the Council of Gangrae laid anathema on 'anyone who under the pretence of godliness should teach a slave to despise his master, or to withdraw himself from his service'.[86]

On the other hand, the Church embodied the principle that all men were equal, not as a positive right but as the dependent children of God. It upheld the ideal of a spiritual world in which all men might

82. ibid. See also the discussion in Carlyle, *History*, I, pp. 113–21. Significantly, Augustine said that the Hebrew precedent of freeing slaves on the seventh year had no application for Christians.

83. *City of God*, xix, xvi. In his *Sermones*, Augustine preached that kindness to slaves was a Christian duty.

84. Ernst Troeltsch, *Die Soziallehren der christlichen Kirchen und Gruppen Gesammelte Schriften* (Erster Band, n.p., 1961), pp. 53–4, 132–4, 144–74, 264.

85. Carlyle, *History*, I, pp. 205–6, 122; Westermann, *Slave Systems*, p. 158.

86. Carlyle, *History*, I, 120–21.

be free. We cannot discuss here the complex question of Christianity's role in ameliorating the condition of European slaves. Despite the Church's unquestioning acceptance of slavery as an institution made necessary by original sin, there can be little doubt that it often lightened the burden of the individual slave. But if Christians preached religious equality and expected pious masters to be kind to their slaves, the same would later be true of the Moslems. In neither instance is there any reason to believe that religious belief promoted the outright abolition of slavery. The fact that Christians accepted the institution until the eighteenth century without marked protest suggests a high degree of tolerance.

Many historians have exaggerated antithesis between slavery and Christian doctrine. The contradiction, as we have tried to show, lay more within the idea of slavery itself. Christianity provided one way of responding to this contradiction, and contained both rationalizations for slavery and ideals that were potentially abolitionist. The significant point, however, is that attitudes towards slavery were interwoven with central religious concepts. This amalgam, which had developed through antiquity, was foreshadowed in Judaism and philosophy.

In one sense slavery was seen as a punishment resulting from sin or from a natural defect of soul that precluded virtuous conduct. The slave was a Canaanite, a man devoid of Logos, or a sinner who scorned the truth. Stoics and Christians endeavoured to distinguish the true from the apparent slave, but physical bondage always suffered from the guilt of association.

In a second sense slavery was seen as a model of dependence and self-surrender. For Plato, Aristotle and Augustine this meant that it was a necessary part of a world that required moral order and discipline; it was the base on which rested an intricate and hierarchical pattern of authority. Yet Jews called themselves the slaves of Yahweh, Christians called themselves the slaves of Christ. No other word so well expressed an ultimate in willing devotion and self-sacrifice.

In a third sense slavery stood as the starting point for a divine quest. It was from slavery that Hebrews were delivered and from which they acquired their unique mission. It was slavery to desire and social convention that Cynics and Stoics sought to overcome by self-discipline and indifference to the world. And it was from slavery to the corrupted flesh of Adam that Christ redeemed mankind.

For some two thousand years men thought of sin as a kind of slavery. One day they would come to think of slavery as sin.

4

The Response to Slavery in
Medieval and Early Modern Thought

As slavery all but disappeared from most parts of Europe, and as discussions of the institution became increasingly theoretical, one might expect to find the Church turning away from its compromises with the Roman world and using its great moral power to hasten a seemingly beneficial change. It is true that for many centuries bishops, popes, churches and monasteries continued to own slaves; but the reforms demanded by the Cluniac Order and Pope Gregory VII in the tenth and eleventh centuries challenged more vital customs and interests of the clergy. How, then, can we account for an almost universal acceptance of the principle of slavery in areas where the institution had become virtually extinct? Why did the rationalizations of the early Church Fathers, who had been forced to adjust their thinking to the realities of the Roman world, exert a profound influence on European attitudes towards slavery for more than a millennium?

The most plausible explanation would seem to lie in the complex network of mental associations, derived from antiquity, which connected slavery with ideas of sin, subordination and the divine order of the world. To question the ethical basis of slavery, even when the institution was disappearing from view, would be to question fundamental conceptions of God's purpose and man's history and destiny. If slavery were an evil and performed no divinely appointed function, then why had God authorized it in Scripture and permitted it to exist in nearly every nation? If slavery violated the natural law of equality and the divine law of human brotherhood, could not the same be said of the family, private property, social orders and government? And if Christianity gave men the freedom to abolish one worldly institution, did this mean they were cleansed of the last stain of sin and might achieve perfection and happiness on earth by throwing off all secular controls. The continuing appearance of certain heretical sects made it clear that Christianity embodied ideas of liberation and perfection that were potentially explosive when torn from their protective casings and ignited in the charged atmosphere of class rivalry and discontent. The most powerful ideological force for containing and harnessing these dynamic ideals was the doctrine of original sin, which, as we have seen, had become closely connected with slavery.

There were times when this linkage seemed to point towards freedom. In the sixth century, after the barbarian invasions had reduced many Christians to slavery, Saint Gregory the Great reasoned that since the purpose of the Incarnation had been to liberate man from his bondage to sin and restore him to his original liberty, it was fitting for masters to emancipate slaves who had been born free and enslaved only by the law of nations.[1] This recommendation was no doubt consistent with the Church's efforts to infuse a spirit of charity in the hearts of kings and masters, and to protect the right of slaves to marry and to enjoy rest on holy days; but the analogy, if consistently pursued as a basis for action, might become revolutionary. Some two centuries later, for example, Archbishop Agobard is supposed to have said it was the duty of any slave or serf to acquire his natural liberty if he were able to do so, which would seem to imply that the slave, like the sinner, had some responsibility for his own deliverance.[2] Abbot Smaragdus not only deemed manumission a meritorious work, but made a bold appeal to Charlemagne (or to his son Louis the Pious) to prohibit his subjects from enslaving one another. In 960 the Patriarch and other bishops of Venice pointed to the tribulations which the city had suffered in former times because of its sin in selling slaves, and attempted to win divine forgiveness by prohibiting residents of the

1. R. W. Carlyle and A. J. Carlyle, *A History of Medieval Political Theory in the West* (Edinburgh and London, 1927), I, p. 208; II, pp. 126, 135; Edward Westermarck, *The Origin and Development of the Moral Ideas* (London, 1906), I, pp. 695–6; R. W. Logan, 'The Attitude of the Church Toward Slavery Prior to 1500', *Journal of Negro History*, XVII (October 1932), pp. 472–3.

2. Paul Allard, *Les origines du servage en France* (Paris, 1913), p. 320. It seems certain that Agobard did not mean that slaves should escape from their masters; the Church regarded this as a mortal sin.

city from engaging in the nefarious trade.[3] Eight hundred years later the same argument would be heard in Boston, Massachusetts.

A collection of such isolated pleas for liberty might lead us to suppose that an incipient stream of anti-slavery thought flowed alongside a 'pro-slavery' stream deriving from Augustine and Aristotle. But while there can be no question that servitude was frequently a source of tension and uneasiness, it would be a mistake to superimpose the divisions of the nineteenth century on earlier history. Augustine urged masters to treat their slaves as brothers in Christ; and there is no indication that Gregory the Great or Smaragdus attacked the ethical basis of slavery. The variations in early Christian opinion on servitude fit comfortably within a framework of thought that would exclude any attempt to abolish slavery as an institution.

Insofar as the Church upheld the belief that men shared a common origin and were free and equal in their natural state, it promoted laws and regulations that acknowledged the bondsman's humanity. The canonists, for example, ruled that a marriage could be legitimate between a male slave and a free woman.[4] Despite his lowly station, the slave retained some irreducible vestige from that state of nature which had antedated sin and society. And even in this fallen world, the Christian master could give evidence of his own charity and humility by showing kindness to individual slaves, who could thus become instruments for his own salvation. But such an impulse towards benevolent action was balanced and kept in check by the two views of God and creation which medieval theology sought to reconcile. When the world was conceived as evil and its values illusory and opposed to the highest and only Good, which was God, then man's destiny could lie only in transcending himself and the world – in finding union with

3. ibid., pp. 323–5; Carlyle, *History*, I, p. 208. Allard thought that Smaragdus advocated the total abolition of slavery, but there seems to be no evidence for this. The Venetian document on the slave trade is printed in Howard L. Adelson, *Medieval Commerce* (Princeton, 1962), pp. 147–50, and its antecedents are discussed by José Antonio Saco, *Historia de la esclavitud desde los tiempos mas remotos hasta nuestros dias* (2nd ed., Habana, 1936–45), III, pp. 179–80. As Saco shows, however, the Venetians continued to trade in slaves and profited especially from supplying Egypt (ibid., pp. 182–7).

4. Carlyle, *History*, II, pp. 118–19.

the One. In this view, the only true slaves would be slaves of the flesh. But when God was conceived as a creative force whose goodness was examplified by the plenitude and harmony of his creation, and when the varieties of being were perceived as a progressive hierarchy of types, each fulfilling a possibility and function, then every institution would have an eternal place in the ordered and purposeful structure of the universe.[5] A concerted attack on the institution of slavery would be most likely to appear only when man's yearning to cross the gulf from finite reality to an infinite good was combined with an interest that endowed this world with primary value. But it was the distinctive characteristic of medieval theology to justify the existing world while providing the means for escaping from it.

No one would expect to find abolitionism in the writings of Saint Thomas Aquinas. Recalling the examples of Plato and Aristotle, we might even suspect that the greatest philosophers have been more inclined than less systematic thinkers to find a reason and purpose for slavery. With Saint Thomas, at any rate, the contradiction of thinking of man as a thing was rationalized within a monumental system of ascending stages in which every type of being and relationship had its own place and end.[6] At times, Aquinas suggested that the principle of slavery was part of the governing pattern of nature. He agreed with Aristotle that the principles of despotic and constitutional rule were exemplified in the human faculties: thus the intellect governed the appetites by a 'politic power', but the soul's relation to the body was like that of master to slave.[7] Yet Aquinas noted that Saint Gregory, among others, had said that slavery was contrary to nature. To deny this judgement, as Aristotle had done, would tend to invalidate the Stoic concept of man's original liberty under natural law, which had become essential in explaining his fall

5. My discussion of the tension between these two views is based on Arthur O. Lovejoy, *The Great Chain of Being: A Study of the History of an Idea* (Torchbook paperback ed., New York, 1960), pp. 64–98.

6. But as Lovejoy notes, while Aquinas tended to identify the goodness of creation with the plenitude and variety of the world, he was usually careful to deny that *all* possibility had been created, as Abelard had claimed (Lovejoy, *Great Chain*, pp. 73–6).

7. *Sum. Theol.*, Part I, Q. 82, Art. 3 [tr. by the Fathers of the English Dominican Province, London, 1911–12].

from grace and need for redemption. If slavery were a positive good and a necessary part of creation, the same might be said of sin itself. It would then become impossible to preserve a sharp distinction between ideal and reality; and one might conclude not only that the existing world was the best of all possible worlds, but that the Creator was indistinguishable from His creation. Saint Thomas avoided this danger by insisting that slavery could not have been present in man's original state. It could not be the true good of any man, since a true good must be desired, and no one would desire slavery, which necessarily inflicts pain by depriving man of the power of disposing of himself. But the use of this hedonistic standard did not mean that Saint Thomas agreed with the Stoics and early Christians who said that men in the state of nature had lived in perfect liberty and equality. Even the angels in heaven were subjected to a hierarchical pattern of rule and authority based on intrinsic differences in merit.[8] Thus despite the fall of man, the contrast between the state of nature and the existing social order was not disturbingly great. The difference between slavery and natural subordination was more of degree than of kind.

This belief made it easier for Saint Thomas to reconcile slavery with natural law without relying entirely on the doctrine of original sin. The canonists maintained that even in man's fallen state no institution could be valid if it violated the law of nature. Roman jurists had ruled unmistakably that slavery was contrary to the *jus naturale*, and in general Christianity had accepted this view. Yet the Canon Law itself sanctioned slavery. Bishops, for example, were not allowed to manumit slaves owned by a church unless they made up the loss from their own property; anathema was pronounced upon anyone who incited slaves to escape or to defy their masters.[9] The canonists attempted to explain this apparent contradiction by arguing that sin had made it necessary to disobey certain *demonstrationes* of natural law, as opposed to explicit commands or prohibitions, in order to carry out the true intentions of the law.[10] In other words, slavery was

8. ibid., Part I of 2nd Part, Q. 96, Art. 4.
9. Carlyle, *History*, II, pp. 117–22.
10. ibid., II, p. 117; V, p. 21. Hostiensis, the author of the canonistic *Commentaria*, went so far as to say that slavery was the result of divine law.

consistent with that part of the natural law which was still applicable to sinful man. In Aquinas's terms it was contrary only to the first intention of nature, but not to the second intention, which was adjusted to man's limited capacities. He compared bondage with the impediment of old age. Although the first intention of nature would be to preserve the perfection of each being forever, this was impossible in the world that exists, and accordingly the second intention of nature was to preserve being in successive generations. Like the physical degeneration of old age, slavery was a useful and necessary, if somewhat painful, means of fulfilling the purposes of nature. It was agreeable to man's natural reason, which determined the specific meaning and consequences of natural law in the world of nations. Saint Thomas still thought of slavery as occasioned by sin, but he made it seem more natural and tolerable by identifying it with the rational structure of being, which required each individual to accept, along with old age and death, the necessity of subordination to higher authority.[11]

This tendency brought him perilously close to a belief in the natural inferiority of slaves. To be sure, he upheld the view that 'a slave is his master's chattel in matters superadded to nature, but in natural things all are equal'. But rather different conclusions might be drawn from Aquinas's attempt to reconcile the Roman rule of *partus sequitur ventrem* with the scholastic notions of form and substance. It was accepted doctrine that in physical generation the father supplied the form and the mother provided the matter; and since the being of a thing depended primarily on its form, how could it be held that the son of a free man and a bondwoman should be a slave?

We observe (answered Saint Thomas) that in animals born from different species the offspring follows the mother rather than the father;

According to Archbishop Antonius, 'Slavery was instituted by divine law, and confirmed by customary law and canon law' (Iris Origo, 'The Domestic Enemy: the Eastern Slaves in Tuscany in the Fourteenth and Fifteenth Centuries', *Speculum*, XXX [July 1955], pp. 334–5). For the revival of legal studies after the medieval rediscovery of the Justinian Code, and for the development of social theory in the Canon Law, see Brian Tierney, *Medieval Poor Law: A sketch of Canonical Theory and Its Application in England* (Berkeley, Calif., 1959).

11. *Sum. Theol.*, 3rd Part, Supplement [London, 1922], Q. 52, Art. 1.

wherefore mules born of a mare and an ass are more like mares than those born of a she-ass and a horse. Therefore it should be the same with men.

Moreover, the woman's womb had the same relation to a man's seed as a plot of land to a sower; hence the owner of the woman, like the owner of land, had claim to all produce. Finally, bondage was a condition of the body, and since the mother provided the substance of the body, it was she who transmitted the condition of slavery. While these arguments did not add up to a theory of inherent inferiority, it is not surprising that Aquinas's followers, Ptolemy of Lucca and especially Egidius Colonna, appeared to accept the Aristotelian view that some men were slaves by nature.[12]

It is interesting to find this belief strongly implied in the eccentric *Mirror of Justices*, which is thought to have been written or edited in the late thirteenth century by Andrew Horn, chamberlain of London. Contrary to all legal precedent, Horn advanced the radical doctrine that there could be no right of prescription against free blood. To keep a man of free ancestry as a slave was a personal trespass. Yet

serfage in the case of a man is a subjection issuing from so high an antiquity that no free stock can be found within human memory. And this serfage, according to some, comes from the curse which Noah pronounced against Canaan, the son of his son Ham, and against his issue; or, according to others, from the Philistines. ... And thus are men serfs by divine law, and this is accepted by human law and confirmed by canon law.[13]

Horn sharply differentiated serfs from villeins, although this distinction was unknown in English law and practice. Villeins he re-

12. ibid., 3rd Part, Supplement, Q. 52, Art. 4; Carlyle, *History*, V, pp. 23–4. It should be noted that the continuing rediscovery of Aristotle and the availability of fresh translations reinforced traditional justifications for slavery. According to Charles H. McIlwain, the Aristotelian belief that the subjection of the slave was as natural and advantageous as the subjection of the body or the subjection of beasts was one of the main sources of the medieval theory of dominion (*The Growth of Political Thought in the West: From the Greeks to the End of the Middle Ages* [New York, 1932], p. 70).

13. [Andrew Horn], *The Mirror of Justices* (ed. by William Joseph Whittaker, introd. by Frederic William Maitland, London, 1895), p. 77.

garded as essentially free men, protected by law, while serfs 'do not know in the evening what service they will do in the morning, and there is nothing certain in their services. The lords may put them in fetters and in the stocks, may imprison, beat and chastise them at will, saving their lives and limbs.' It is clear he associated serfdom with the slavery of infidels who had been captured or purchased beyond the 'Grecian sea'. Whereas Gentile Christians were descended from Shem and Japheth, serfs were the sons of Ham 'whom the Christians can give and sell like their other chattels'. This separate ancestry could not, of course, be kept distinct. But for all his bias in favour of freedom, Horn thought servile blood carried a nearly indelible stain:

They are serfs who are engendered by a serf and born of a serf, and whether they be born in or out of wedlock. And one who is begotten by a serf and born of a free woman in wedlock is a serf. And one who is begotten of a free man but born of a bondwoman out of wedlock is a serf.[14]

Since medieval Christianity accepted slavery in principle, the questions of controversy were largely of a practical nature. The most ominous of these pertained to infidels and the effects of baptism. Had all masters and slaves been faithful Christians, the Church could have arrived at a simple and consistent position. The early church Fathers had ruled that baptism had no effect on the status of a slave, and that a slave must be manumitted before being admitted to orders. In general, the canonists endorsed this traditional stand, and held that a slave or serf who had been ordained, because his status was unknown, must be returned to his master. But what should be the status of a baptized slave owned by an infidel living in a Christian land? If he remained a slave his faith might be corrupted by his unbelieving master; but if he were freed by the mere fact of baptism, the security of all slave property might be endangered.

A tradition that baptism automatically liberated the slave of a Jew or heretic found sanction in the Canon Law, the Third Lateran Council and the *Code de Tortosa*. A Jew might keep his slaves, of course, by accepting baptism himself; yet it was obvious that the

14. ibid., pp. 77–9.

official policy, if rigorously enforced, might have the effect of impeding conversions. Archbishop Agobard implied that some of the clergy had denied baptism to the pagan slaves of Jews on the ground that baptism would lead to freedom. Such hesitancy Agobard condemned as impious; he reminded the clergy of the brotherhood and natural equality of man. But Louis the Pious found it convenient to make various concessions to Jewish slaveowners.[15] And some four centuries later Saint Thomas gave expediency a philosophical justification. Ideally, he admitted, unbelievers should not have dominion over the faithful. But the distinction between unbelievers and the faithful was derived from divine law, which did not abrogate dominion established by natural reason as it worked through human law. Hence the authority of Jewish masters was legitimate; the principle of slavery was secure. The Church, carrying the authority of God and mediating between the divine law and the sinful world, could of course prohibit infidels from possessing Christian slaves, if such a policy seemed to promote the cause of religion. The Church had decreed that a Jew might purchase Christian slaves for trade, so long as they were sold within a period of three months. Otherwise, the bondsmen were to be released without compensation to the owner. Saint Thomas noted, however, that in the interest of spreading the faith the Church had made no attempt to enforce such laws against unbelievers who were not subject to her temporal authority. A contrary course might give Christianity a bad name.[16]

During the fourteenth and fifteenth centuries the Church became

15. Allard, *Origines du servage*, pp. 317, 325.
16. *Sum. Theol.*, Part II of 2nd Part, Q. 10, Art. 10. The policy of the Church in the Middle Ages considerably reduced the number of Jewish slaveholders even in Spain, where slavery flourished. While the few Jewish masters continued in general to treat their non-Hebrew slaves as Canaanites, who were not entitled to the benefits of Mosaic and Talmudic regulations, there were occasional protests against chattel slavery. In a treatise on the rights of servants, Maimonides said that men who owned large numbers of slaves added daily to the sum of their sins. Instead of buying slaves, wealthy men should give employment as servants to the orphans and poor who roamed the streets. While Maimonides did not advocate the abolition of slavery, his position is in marked contrast to that of Saint Thomas Aquinas (see Charles Verlinden, *L'Esclavage dans l'Europe médiévale, I: Péninsule Ibérique, France* [Brugge, 1955], pp. 243–7).

more militant in its efforts to keep Christians from becoming the slaves of infidels.[17] Two popes accused the Genoese slave traders of contributing to the power of unbelievers. In 1425 a papal Bull threatened Christian slave dealers with excommunication and ordered Jews to wear a badge of infamy on their clothing, in part to prevent them from buying Christians. But merchants who handled thousands of slaves paid little attention to the religion or origin of their commodities; and, in the Black Sea trade, the Christian slave who was seized or purchased from a Jewish master was simply sold to a man who professed to share his faith.[18]

Nevertheless, by the fifteenth century Europeans had become increasingly prejudiced against the enslavement of men from Christian countries. The Church denounced and threatened to punish her subjects who kidnapped or forcibly enslaved their fellow Christians. These scruples, however, did not extend to unbelievers, who were usually thought to be undeserving of freedom. When Europeans seized or purchased infidels, they saw themselves as dealing a blow to infidelity in general as well as procuring new souls for the Church to win. These were the assumptions that guided the Church when Europeans first came into contact with Negro Africa. In 1452 Pope

17. For Christian attempts to cut off all trade and contact with the Moslem world, see Norman Daniel, *Islam and the West: The Making of an Image* (Edinburgh, 1960), p. 115 and *passim*.

18. George Scelle, *La traite négrière aux Indes de Castille: contrats et traités d'assiento* (Paris, 1906), I, pp. 86–8; Saco, *Historia de la esclavitud*, III, p. 192; Origo, 'Domestic Enemy', pp. 327–8. The futile moves by John XXII and Martin V against the slave trade were obviously motivated by a fear of infidel power and had nothing to do with a hostility to slavery as such. The Genoese economy was partly dependent on supplying Egypt and Syria with slaves from the Black Sea, and in 1466 this trade won the full approval of Emperor Frederick III (Azis S. Atiya, *Crusade, Commerce and Culture* [Bloomington, Ind., 1962], pp, 183–4). The Bulls of the earlier popes have sometimes been misleadingly associated with the appeal of Pope Urban VIII, who in 1639 tried to outlaw the Atlantic slave trade; but it is doubtful whether Urban VIII was more of an abolitionist than his predecessors. As Charles Verlinden points out, his denunciation of the slave trade came just two years after the heretical Dutch had captured the strategic fort of Saint George of Elmina, and had thus won temporary control of the Guinea trade (*L'Esclavage dans l'Europe médiévale*, p. 838).

Nicholas V authorized the king of Portugal to deprive Moors and pagans of their liberty.[19] In 1488 Pope Innocent VIII accepted a gift of one hundred Moors from Ferdinand of Spain, and distributed them among the cardinals and nobility.[20]

But if slavery was thought of both as a weapon for extending Christianity and as a deserved punishment for pagans and heretics, what was the fate of the Turk or Moor who accepted the true faith? Should such a convert be put on equal footing with men born in Christian countries? Did not baptism cleanse him of sin and endow him with at least a capacity for freedom? Franco Sacchetti, in his *Sermoni evangelici*, went so far as to say that the baptism of slaves was no more valid than the baptism of oxen, for a slave was utterly lacking in free will. Lest someone conclude that this was an excuse for manumission, Sacchetti hastened to say that freedom would only lead the ex-slave to commit greater sins and could thus never promote his spiritual welfare.[21] Few Christians, however, could accept the harsh implications of an argument that would undercut all belief in the spiritual unity and equality of mankind. In 1366 the Priors of Florence, who had previously given their sanction to the import and sale of infidel slaves, explained that by 'infidel' they had meant 'all slaves of infidel *origin*, even if at the time of their arrival they belong to the Catholic faith'; and 'infidel origin' meant simply 'from the land and race of the infidels'.[22] With this subtle change in definition the Priors of Florence by-passed the dilemma of baptism by shifting the basis of slavery from religious difference to ethnic origin.

It may not be out of place to note the striking similarity between

19. Carlyle, *History*, II, pp. 126, 134; Origo, 'Domestic Enemy', pp. 334–5; Elizabeth Donnan (ed.), *Documents Illustrative of the History of the Slave Trade to America* (Washington, 1930–35), I, p. 5. A Bull of 1454 also alluded to the happy consequences of enslaving pagans (see Verlinden, *L'Esclavage dans l'Europe médiévale*, p. 838).

20. In Italy the Negro slave was usually referred to as a *moro nero;* the slaves of Innocent VIII were called *mori*. For these and other references to Negro slavery in Italy, see Jacob Burckhardt, *Die Cultur der Renaissance in Italien* (Leipzig, 1869), pp. 231–2, n. 3; and Scelle, *Traite négrière*, I, pp. 86–8.

21. Origo, 'Domestic Enemy', p. 335.

22. ibid., pp. 334–5.

these medieval positions regarding infidels and baptism, and certain laws of colonial America which dealt with the same problems. A law of colonial Virginia, for example, ruled that any Christian white servant was automatically free if purchased by a Negro, Indian, Jew, Mohammedan or 'other infidel'. Yet at least six colonies passed acts from 1664 to 1706 proclaiming that unless a man had been a Christian in his native country, or had been free in some Christian country before being imported to America, baptism did not affect his status as a slave. The Virginia law of 1682, which was designed to counteract apprehensions similar to those expressed by Franco Sacchetti before the discovery of America, and to encourage the conversion of slaves 'borne of and in heathenish, idollatrous, pagan, and Mahometan parentage and country', stated that all servants imported by land or sea,

whether Negroes, Moors, mullatoes, or Indians, who and whose parentage and native country are not Christian at the time of their first purchase ... by some Christian, though afterwards and before ... their importation ... they shall be converted to the Christian faith ... shall be adjudged, deemed, and taken to be slaves, to all intents and purposes.[23]

As in fourteenth-century Tuscany, conversion to Christianity was to have no effect on a status associated primarily with ethnic origin.

The humane provisions of *las Siete Partidas*, the great thirteenth-century codification of law sponsored by Alfonso the Wise, have been seen by some historians as characteristic of the Catholic approach to slavery. Accordingly, the Negro slaves of Latin America have been described as the beneficiaries of a long tradition of legislation designed to make the best of a necessary evil.[24] It is therefore worth

23. Marcus W. Jernegan, 'Slavery and Conversion in the American Colonies', *American Historical Review*, XXI (April 1916), pp. 506–7; John Codman Hurd, *The Law of Freedom and Bondage in the United States* (Boston, 1858–62), I, pp. 234–40. The provisions in the Virginia law respecting Turks and Moors were not to apply if their nations were at peace with England.

24. Frank Tannenbaum, *Slave and Citizen: The Negro in the Americas* (New York, 1947), pp. 45–6.

asking whether the legislation of medieval Iberia embodied a spirit essentially hostile to chattel slavery, and thus at variance with such authorities as Augustine and Aquinas.

Las Siete Partidas followed the Justinian Code in recognizing war, birth and self-sale as valid grounds for human bondage. The definition of the slaveholder's power echoed ancient Roman law: 'The master has full power over his slave [*siervo*] to do with him as he wishes. . . . Everything that the slave in any way earns, should belong to his master.'[25] But *las Siete Partidas* was a theoretical work aimed at synthesizing the best elements of Roman and Canon Law. It affirmed that by nature men were free, and that no master could violate the principles of natural reason. A slave might marry even against his owner's will; if tortured or cruelly treated he might complain to a judge, who could have him sold to a more humane master. Certain provisions increased his chances for manumission. No Jew, Moor or heretic was to own a Christian slave. It is important to note, however, that as a body of ideal law, *las Siete Partidas* had little relation to the living law of Castille. The learned intellectuals who compiled it were under no illusions about the discrepancy between their ideal picture of human bondage and the actual condition of Moorish slaves in Spain, which was 'the most miserable that men could have in this world'. Even in their model law they drew a sharp distinction betwen Christian bondsmen and non-Christian captives. And their conception of justice was not altogether humane. The slave who violated a woman of good reputation or who committed adultery with his master's wife was to be burned alive.[26] The *Code de Tortosa*, which was compiled in 1272, about a decade after *las Siete Partidas*, prescribed the harshest punishments for slaves, and allowed them to appear before a magistrate only when they had a legitimate claim to freedom. A mere chattel in the eyes of the law, the slave

25. *Las Siete Partidas de Rey don Alfonso el Sabio* . . . (Madrid, 1807), III, pp. 117, 120.

26. ibid., III, pp. 117–28; Verlinden, *L'Esclavage dans l'Europe médiévale*, pp. 593–5; Scelle, *Traite négrière*, I, p. 94; Saco, *Historia de la esclavitud*, III, pp. 270–76. But as Saco pointed out, while a slave was to be burned alive for seducing a virgin, a nun or a widow, his own wife was to be protected from the lusts of his master.

could not give testimony in court except in rare instances, when it was received by torture, 'because what their servants say on such things should not be believed unless they are tormented'. In general, the Spanish law limited the master's punitive power only by denying him the right to kill his slaves. But in Portugal, some two centuries later, even such murder was easily absolved under Manueline legislation, which also required death for the slave who struck his owner.[27] While the treatment of Moorish and Negro slaves was probably better than such laws implied, there is no evidence that the legislation of Iberia tended to undermine the institution by curbing the power of masters.

In theory, however, medieval Christianity acknowledged the slave's legal and moral capacity for marriage. On this question the position of Saint Thomas was almost identical with that of *las Siete Partidas*. And since acceptance of the bondsman's right to marry would seem to imply a repudiation of chattel slavery, it is well to examine the question with some care.

Probably no society has attempted to prohibit slaves from having sexual intercourse with members of their own class, or even from living in more or less monogamous or polygamous units; but marriage leads to a contractual relationship of authority and obedience, of reciprocal rights and obligations within a family, which is clearly incompatible with the concept of a master's absolute ownership of his slaves. One should not confuse this basic incompatibility with the various restraints that have usually modified even chattel slavery, such as a denial of the master's right to exterminate his living property. In many modern societies it is against the law to torture domestic animals, and the owners of such property must necessarily make concessions to the temperament and natural instincts of their living possessions; yet their power of ownership, however limited in practice, is in theory as absolute as the health and safety of the community will permit. This was the kind of power that slaveowners were traditionally said to possess. It was a power that could not be divided and given over in part to the slaves without destroying the very concept of slavery. It was for this reason that Roman masters retained

27. Verlinden, *L'Esclavage dans l'Europe médiévale*, pp. 290–95, 315, 631.

full legal ownership of a slave's *peculium,* and that Roman law refused to recognize a slave's capacity for marriage. It was for this reason that Canon Law prohibited the slave from being ordained, which would require the freedom to accept obligations that would, in effect, nullify a master's authority. The obligations of baptism were spiritual and in no way infringed upon a master's authority. But if at times it was difficult to reconcile slavery even with baptism, how could one begin to reconcile the institution with the tangible loyalties and obligations of marriage?

When Saint Thomas spoke of the slave as the physical instrument of his owner, who had full claim to everything the slave possessed or produced, including children, he would seem to have ruled out the possibility of marriage. It was, however, a primary goal of Aquinas to locate functioning points of accommodation between the claims of nature and the restraints of authority. While the master had nearly absolute power over his slave instrument by virtue of the secondary or relative law of nature, the bondsman was still subject to the primary law of nature insofar as it had not been modified by sin. Slavery, then, was a physical impediment to marriage, comparable to impotence, and the marriage of a slave and free person could be valid only if the latter had knowledge of the impediment, as was the case with impotence.[28] Yet only the marriage rite could sanctify the mating of human beings, which was as natural and inevitable as the mating of animals. Like eating and sleeping, marriage could not be prohibited by a master's authority. By identifying marriage with the natural union of the sexes, Aquinas made it appear outside the range of authority derived from the social needs of a sinful world.

But to what extent did the 'impediment' of slavery, as justified by the secondary intent of nature, limit the primary law of conjugal union? How were the sanctified unions of slaves to differ from the casual breeding of livestock? It is at this crucial point that the synthesis of nature and authority appears to weaken. For a slave's right to marry amounts to no more than a right to escape the guilt of fornication unless the unity and integrity of his family are guaranteed. Aquinas assumed that a stable and non-speculative economy

28. *Sum. Theol.,* 3rd Part, Supplement, Q. 52, Art. 1.

would always allow an owner to receive a just price for his slaves, and that therefore no owner should be obliged to separate slave families in a sale. He could not, however, question the owner's right to separate members of a family, since he had accepted the owner's absolute claim to the offspring of female slaves. Thus the slave husband and father had no power to protect his family, and no sphere of authority that might not be invaded by the overriding commands of his master. It is true that an owner who had consented to the marriage of his slaves was bound, in Saint Thomas's view, to respect the obligations of the contract. This, of course, would hardly be chattel slavery. But when a slave had married without his master's permission, Aquinas admitted that the commands of the master should ordinarily take precedence over marital duty.[29]

No doubt the Catholic recognition of a slave's right to marry represents a moral position considerably in advance of Roman or Protestant American law. In practice, the Church urged masters to consent to such unions and to respect the sanctity of all marriages. But it is also true that the marriage of slaves was often accepted in practice in both ancient Rome and nineteenth-century America. And if the Church's foremost philosopher endowed slave marriages with the high justification of natural law, he was careful to prevent this law from undermining the supreme authority of masters, or from modifying the essential character of chattel slavery. In so doing, he deprived slave marriage of its essential meaning.

In subsequent chapters we shall have occasion to discuss Protestant sources of anti-slavery thought, as well as early Catholic protests against the African trade. For our present discussion, however, it is sufficient to note that the Reformation brought no immediate change in the traditional ideas of servitude. When Swabian serfs appealed for emancipation in 1525, holding that Christ had died to set men free, Martin Luther was as horrified as any orthodox Catholic. Such a total distortion of Scripture would make Christian liberty 'gantz fleisschlich'. The peasants' demands would make all men equal and convert Christ's spiritual kingdom into a worldly, external thing. As Saint Paul had shown, masters and slaves must accept their present

29. ibid., Q. 52, Art. 2.

stations, for the earthly kingdom could not survive unless some men were free and some were slaves.[30]

But if Luther's traditionalism is hardly surprising, we might well expect to find a growing hostility to perpetual bondage in the writings of jurists and humanists of the Renaissance, who took an increasingly secular view of human institutions, and who arrived at an enlarged estimate of man's creative powers and inherent nobility. Such a trend towards liberalism would have been in conformity with the actual erosion of slavery and serfdom in Western Europe. As early as the fourteenth century an eminent Italian jurist, Bartolo de Sassoferrato, noted that Europeans had long since abandoned the custom of enslaving one another in war. By 1608 Antoine Loisel could say that in France all men were free.[31] One might suppose that this progress in the accepted rules of warfare had discredited the leading justification of slavery inherited from the Justinian Code. From the perspective of the nineteenth century, it would have been only natural if such beneficent changes had been accompanied by stirring protests against human bondage in any form.

Yet one could not lightly challenge an institution approved not only by the Fathers and canons of the Church, but by the most illustrious writers of antiquity. Men who showed increasing respect for Plato, Aristotle and Roman law would not be likely to condemn slavery as an intrinsic evil. Hence the revival of classical learning, which may have helped to liberate the mind of Europe from bondage to ignorance and superstition, only reinforced the traditional justifications for human slavery.

Consider, for example, the *Utopia* of Thomas More. Because More permitted both war and slavery in his imaginary society, scholars have long debated whether he proposed an ideal of true social perfection. Certainly More was bold enough to criticize many in-

---

30. Martin Luther, 'Ermahnung zum Frieden auf die zwölf Artikel der Bauerschaft in Schwaben', *Werke* (Weimer, 1908), XVIII, pp. 326–7.

31. Paul Viollet, *Histoire du droit civil français; accompagnée de notions de droit canonique et d'indications bibliographiques* (3rd ed., Paris, 1905), p. 362; Russell P. Jameson, *Montesquieu et l'esclavage: étude sur les origines de l'opinion antiesclavagiste en France au XVIIIe siècle* (Paris, 1911), p. 84.

justices, such as enclosure and a barbarous penal code. If he felt that man could never achieve absolute perfection on earth, he suggested that natural reason could create a society in which the individual and common good would merge to produce the maximum possible happiness. In the words of R. P. Adams, his utopia offered 'a concrete vision of a good life perhaps attainable'.[32] And yet he would allow the 'vyle drudge' who was 'a poore labourer in an other cowntreye' to become a bondsman in utopia. Persons convicted of atrocious crimes would be excommunicated from society and would be enslaved, 'For there commeth more profite of theire laboure, then of theire deathe'. Like later Americans, More showed faith in the criminal justice of less perfect countries, since utopia's slaves would include those who 'in the Cytyes of other landes for great trespasses be condemned to deathe'. And while the foreign perpetrators of wars would be killed, their troops would be captured and enslaved. The stigma of bondage would not be passed on to subsequent generations, but the fact remains that More embraced a fully developed slave system. In part this was a logical extension of his sharp dichotomy between the children of virtue and the criminals and aliens who refused to live by the highest standards of reason. But it was also a reflection of his dependence upon previous thinkers, such as Duns Scotus, Plato and the Stoics.[33] The problem of slavery in *Utopia* is put in better perspective when we note that no protest against the traditional theory emerged from the great seventeenth-century authorities on law, or from such philosophers and men-of-letters as Descartes, Malebranche, Spinoza, Pascal, Bayle or Fontenelle.[34]

But the fact that slavery had declined in Europe and yet was being

32. R. P. Adams, *The Better Part of Valor: More, Erasmus, Colet and Vives, on Humanism, War and Peace, 1496–1535* (Seattle 1962), p. 157.

33. Thomas More, *The Utopia of Sir Thomas More* (ed. by J. H. Lupton, Oxford, 1895), pp. 221–2, 230–31, 263; Edward Surtz, *The Praise of Wisdom: A Commentary on the Religious and Moral Problems and Backgrounds of Sir Thomas More's Utopia* (Chicago, 1957), pp. 258–69; Shlomo Avineri, 'War and Slavery in More's *Utopia*', *International Review of Social History*, VII (1962), pp. 260–90; Adams, *Better Part of Valor*, pp. 133–42.

34. Jameson, *Montesquieu et l'esclavage*, pp. 100, 137–8, 154–6.

revived in a deadly form in America gave a peculiarly abstract character to discussions governed by the Justinian Code. Throughout Europe scholars debated the relation of slavery to divine and natural law as an exercise in dialectic; it was as if the learned volumes on law and statecraft had been produced in a different world from that which contained the Negro captives awaiting shipment at Elmina Castle, the disease of sickening stench of the slave ships, and the regimented labour of colonial plantations. Even in sixteenth-century Spain the theories of such imposing figures as Covarruvias and Luis Molina regarding legal enslavement of prisoners of war had little relevance to the actual slaving raids of African chieftains.[35] The inherent contradiction of human slavery had always generated dualisms in thought, but by the sixteenth and seventeenth centuries Europeans had arrived at the greatest dualism of all – the momentous division between an increasing devotion to liberty in Europe and an expanding mercantile system based on Negro labour in America. For a time most jurists and philosophers met this discrepancy simply by ignoring it, and by adhering to classical theories of slavery that were thought to have universal application.

Nevertheless, the polarities of geography and race were matched by a widening division in the jurisprudence of slavery which arose from changing attitudes towards natural law. Traditionally, philosophers had assumed a direct correspondence between human institutions, the law of nations, and the fundamental rules of equity as established by nature and right reason. Jurists searched for the concrete applications of a law that was at once transcendent and written on the hearts of in the consciences of men. In the fifteenth century Bartolomeno Coepolla could assume that slavery was authorized not only by civil law and the *jus gentium*, but by natural and divine law

35. ibid., pp. 85–6, 134. Molina at times criticized the cruelty and violence practised against slaves, but the Abbé Grégoire was quite incorrect in classing him as an opponent of the slave trade (Saco, *Historia de la esclavitud*, V, p. 44). Despite the reputation given him by Grégoire and others, Molina believed that in a just war even the innocent members of an enemy population might legitimately be enslaved as a way of punishing the entire State. Their children might also be enslaved in order to punish the parents, according to Johann Kleinhappl, *Der Staat bei Ludwig Molina* (Innsbruck, 1935), pp. 145–6.

as well.[36] But increasingly there was a weakening of the link of relative natural law that had connected the world of human institutions with the ideal realm of nature. This was particularly true in Protestantism. Luther's profound separation of inner liberty from outward obedience to established authority transformed every subject into a divided being who resembled, to some extent, the Stoic picture of the slave. For Melanchthon, as for the Stoics, there was no incompatibility between bondage and true liberty.[37] By shifting the ground of religion from meritorious works to an inward faith, Protestantism moved away from the idea of an organic society in which rights and duties are intricately balanced, and tended to free worldly authority from the restraints of natural law.

But even Francisco Suarez, who followed Saint Thomas in many respects, accepted a sharp dualism between the eternal law of nature and a law of nations governed by expediency and conditioned by circumstance. Slavery, like private property, could not be justified by the highest moral law; yet its *expediency* had been revealed by the almost universal practice of nations. According to Suarez, it was unnecessary that an institution sanctioned by utility and common practice be shown as conformable to the absolute ideal of nature.[38] Similarly, when the Protestant Pierre Jurieu used the traditional Christian argument that slavery, though a consequence of sin, was contrary to nature, Jacques Bossuet based his reply on the practical ground that one could not reject the institution without rejecting both war and the law of nations. Citing slavery as an example of a dominion unlimited by compact, Bossuet argued that all authority, regardless of its origin, became legitimate with time and common acceptance. Anarchy was the worst of all evils, for it made everyone both master and slave.[39] And if slavery was often seen as a necessary

36. Jameson, *Montesquieu et l'esclavage*, pp. 85–6. Coepolla found the divine law origin in Adam's sin, the natural law sanction in Noah's curse, and the justification of the *jus gentium* in war.

37. William Archibald Dunning, *A History of Political Theories: From Luther to Montesquieu* (New York, 1928), p. 18.

38. ibid., pp. 139–41.

39. Jameson, *Montesquieu et l'esclavage*, pp. 127–8; Henri Sée, *Les idées politiques en France au XVII siècle* (Paris, 1923), pp. 154–7, 200–206.

instrument for discipline and secular statecraft, needing no further
sanction of natural or divine law, circumstances might justify it in one
country and not in another. François Delaunay, whom Louis XIV
appointed to the chair of French law at Paris, could affirm that colonial slavery was in no way contrary to Christianity, and yet take
satisfaction from the fact that in France all men were free.[40]

The inclination to discuss slavery as a matter of public policy was
of course strengthened in the seventeenth century, when the slave
trade and colonial plantations became increasingly important in the
international contest for economic and military power. As attention
shifted from original sin and natural rights to more practical questions of national self-interest and the best means of procuring and
governing a colonial labour force, the moral grounds of slavery re-
ceded from view. We shall treat these questions in some detail later
on, but first we need to ask whether the trends in secular political
thought, at the highest level, provided an intellectual basis for challenging the decisions of judges and statesmen, and for demanding a
reversal in the policy of nations.

That Jean Bodin should show a marked hostility to human bondage, and originate what may properly be called an anti-slavery

Like other French Huguenots of the late seventeenth century, Jurieu used the
traditional Christian mistrust of unlimited power in any worldly form as a
weapon against absolutism and the theory of divine right of kings (see Guy
Howard Dodge, *The Political Theory of the Huguenots of the Dispersion,
with Special Reference to the Thought and Influence of Pierre Jurieu* [New
York, 1947], pp. 52–6, 86).

40. Jameson, *Montesquieu et l'esclavage*, pp. 95–8. While Delaunay
attacked the Aristotelian belief in natural slaves, he thought that the
authority of masters over slaves was parallel to that of king over subjects. It
is perhaps significant that new justifications of slavery, including that of
racial inferiority, were arising at a time when the medieval notion of kingship
as a power conferred by an act of consecration was giving way to a theory of
sovereignty transmitted by royal blood. The new mystique of royal blood
reached its culmination when Louis XIV extended the idea to include his
bastard children (see Ralph E. Giesey, 'The Juristic Basis of Dynastic Right
to the French Throne', *Transactions of the American Philosophical Society*,
LI [September 1961], pp. 3–42; and Giesey, *The Royal Funeral Ceremony
in Renaissance France* [Geneva, 1960], pref.).

philosophy, presents a perplexing problem. His mind was medieval enough to be obsessed with witches and demons. He so exalted the rights of private property that he would require the consent of owners to all taxation. He would give to fathers, in the interest of proper discipline, the rights of life and death over their children. But of all Renaissance political thinkers he was in some ways the most original and modern. He did much to create the idea of sovereignty as a supreme political authority which responded to change by constructive legislation. His views on slavery were no more anomalous than were his views on the State, and in the last analysis must be regarded as the product of a uniquely independent mind.[41]

Bodin's mind, however, did not work in a historical vacuum. Apparently while he was a student of civil law at the University of Toulouse, a Genoese merchant visited the province with a slave. When the merchant's host persuaded the slave to demand his freedom, the magistrates discovered records proving that any slave who entered Toulouse was automatically free. The merchant, who was on his way from Spain to Genoa, could not see why he should be bound by French law, but he reluctantly manumitted his slave after making a contract for lifetime service. Bodin was impressed by the incident, and used it as evidence that the laws of France did not permit slavery.[42] And for Bodin such legal precedent was vaguely associated with a higher law which guided and limited even the sovereign, free as he might be from all human authority.

We should note that in the 1570s, when the *Republic* was written, France had not yet committed herself to the slave trade, and a supporter of Henry III would not lose favour by exposing the barbarity of the Spanish. Bodin's religious unorthodoxy, which verged on Protestantism, had caused him to be imprisoned for a year and a half. In an age of the cruellest religious warfare, he looked to an all-powerful sovereign as the best means for fashioning a rational social order. If his independence of mind and religious unorthodoxy equipped him to perceive the injustice of widely accepted institutions, he did not ar-

41. Jean Bodin, *The Six Bookes of a Commonweale* (ed. with introd. by Kenneth Douglas McRae, Cambridge, Mass., 1962), introd., pp. A14–16; Dunning, *From Luther to Montesquieu*, pp. 87–91.
42. Bodin, *Six Bookes*, p. 42.

rive at his anti-slavery position through a belief in the natural equality of mankind. His chief disciple in England was not John Locke, but Sir Robert Filmer. For Bodin it was unthinkable that any group of men, no matter how base or degraded, should be excluded from the body politic and thus deprived of being subjects of an absolute sovereign. His concept of an organic state would not permit the dualism of slavery and freedom. One of his analogies was given heightened significance by the traditional association between slaves and sex:

There be in mans bodie [he discreetly suggested] some members, I may not call them filthie (for that nothing can so be which is naturall) but yet so shamefull, as that no man except he be past all shame, can without blushing reveale or discover the same: and doe they for that cease to be members of the whole bodie?[43]

But what of the opinions of philosophers and the precedents of antiquity? Bodin took obvious delight in assaulting Aristotle and the entire tradition of scholastic reasoning, and his key weapon in this demolition was the logic of Petrus Ramus. The disciples of Ramus assumed that truth, which was eternal but frequently obscured by fallacious reasoning, could be revealed most simply and directly by reducing a question to one or more dichotomies, and discarding those parts which seemed to violate common sense. As applied to the problem of slavery the process appears obviously simple, but it represented a radical departure from the traditional discussions of natural law and the law of nations. Bodin was content to summarize arguments for and against slavery, and to ask which of the two was the better. In each argument the final test was expediency and common sense. Hence the Aristotelian case for natural slavery would hold only if the brutal rich and ignorant obeyed the wise, prudent and humble. The

43. ibid., introd., pp. A3–9, A35, A64, 387. McRae places the date of composition at approximately 1574–6; it should be noted that the Latin version, which appeared in 1586, was more strongly anti-slavery than was the original French edition. The Latin version was more outspoken against the Spanish and also condemned the pirates and brigands who, even if they posed as princes, waged war for the purpose of seizing slaves.

Augustinian theory of slavery as punishment for sin would be valid only if masters were agents of the divine will and invariably obeyed God's laws. The provisions of the *jus gentium* for enslaving prisoners of war were impractical as well as inhumane, for it was no charity to spare a man's life only to exploit his labour; and if examples were wanted to deter future aggressors, it would be more effective to kill all captives. The appeal to precedent and to the common practice of nations was groundless, since every kind of wickedness, including human sacrifice, had been regarded as virtuous at some time in history.[44]

Of cardinal importance was Bodin's belief that mankind could err through centuries in both thought and practice, but that social and political truths were knowable if one used the correct process of reasoning. While this implied a rejection of historical precedent, the gravamen of his case against slavery rested on historical evidence. With great learning he showed that slavery had always brought cruelty, corruption, conspiracy and rebellion. Even the mitigating regulations of Jews, Moslems and Christians had seldom been observed. It was a catastrophe that slavery had ever been introduced into the world, let alone reintroduced into America after Europe had progressed so long towards freedom. Yet bondage seemed to be creeping back into the continent from its outer boundaries. The Tartars had enslaved many Christians in eastern Europe; bondsmen had appeared again in Italy; in Spain and Portugal they were openly sold as if they were beasts. Though Bodin placed considerable blame on the latter two countries, he did not really explain how this retrogression had come about. He implied that it was simply the result of a spirit of boldness and insubordination which could not be controlled even by benevolent monarchs like Charles V. Bodin was more interested in positive legislation that would prevent slavery from spreading across Europe, or that would modify it for the good of the commonwealth. The wise legislator, who could anticipate problems, would destroy a possible source of bondage by providing public houses where the poor could learn useful trades. In nations where slavery already existed, it could best be eradicated by a very gradual process of emancipation, 'having before their enfranchisement taught them some occupation

44. ibid., introd., pp. A3, A25–7, 33–5.

whereby to releeve themselves'. Unless they were 'strangers', by which Bodin apparently meant men of different nationality, the liberated slaves should become full citizens.[45] To many ears these cautious arguments and proposals would still sound radical after some two centuries had passed.

If Bodin has often been pictured as a defender of absolute power and hence as an enemy of freedom, Hugo Grotius has been classed as a liberal humanist who, along with Jacobus Arminius, helped free the human will from a theoretical bondage imposed by Augustine and revived by Calvin. It was Grotius who also loosened natural law from the confining web of theology and raised it as a supreme authority above not only the will of every earthly sovereign but above the will of God. Ernst Cassirer has said that Grotius accomplished for law what Galileo did for natural science. By making law independent of both divine revelation and the transitory conditions of life, and thus as autonomous and self-evident as mathematics, he created a standard which might at once bind the capricious will of tyrants and help shape the world of men into a more rational and purposeful order.[46]

But did this transcendent law, revealed to man by natural reason, secularized by its divorce from the doctrine of sin, necessarily exclude the practice of slavery? Was it legal for Dutch captains, sailing in increasing numbers while Grotius wrote, to purchase Negroes on the coast of Africa and transport them to the New World? Here we arrive at a seeming paradox. Where Bodin would use the will of the sovereign to abolish slavery in the most expedient fashion, Grotius, who would subordinate all sovereign power to the rules of reason, saw slavery as harmonious with natural justice. His intimate knowledge of classical authorities could be used to create a secular philosophy of law and constitutional power; but it could also be turned to a secular defence of slavery at a time when the prosperity of Holland was closely linked to the African trade.

Few of his contemporaries could have possessed so wide a know-

45. ibid., pp. 36–48, 388.
46. Ernst Cassirer, *The Philosophy of the Enlightenment* (tr. by Fritz C. A. Koelln and James P. Pettegrove, Beacon paperback ed., Boston, 1951), pp. 236–8.

ledge of the history of slavery. His discussion was studded with references to the views of Aristotle, Philemon, Seneca, Saint Paul, Gaius, Ulpian, Augustine and Clement of Alexandria. He gave lip-service to the traditional belief that slavery, being unknown in man's primeval state, was not a product of nature. But Grotius made no attempt to bridge the gap between slavery and nature by appealing to original sin or to man's fall from a better condition. For how could an institution supported by so many authorities and sanctioned by the general custom of nations be intrinsically unjust or repugnant to natural reason?[47]

In attempting to construct a rational and secular defence of slavery Grotius betrayed at moments a profound uncertainty. If one chose as a criterion the actual practice of nations, he must conclude that the subjects of an enemy could be enslaved, even when they had committed no delict. The utility of slavery as a means of sparing the lives of prisoners seemed self-evident; a soldier would be more likely to preserve the life of a captive if he knew that he could later sell such property or claim the progeny that would never have been born had he killed a female prisoner. Yet Grotius had to admit that Christians and Moslems did not enslave members of their own faiths. The example of Christians in ransoming captives showed that slavery was not always necessary to prevent wholesale slaughter. Grotius appeared to feel more confident in arguing that masters who provided sustenance to the children of slaves had a right to their perpetual service; there could be nothing shocking, he said, about such an exchange of bondage for a perpetual certainty of food. Parents, after all, had a natural right to sell children who could be provided for in no other way.[48] But it was precisely when Grotius turned to the rights of masters that his assumed harmony between general custom and natural reason broke down. The custom of endowing a master with absolute power could be justified on the utilitarian ground that a more limited power might not have been sufficient inducement for sparing the life of the original captive. Yet absolute power was repugnant to Grotius's entire philosophy of law, and accordingly he drew

47. Hugo Grotius, *De Jure Belli et Pacis* ... *Accompanied by an Abridged Translation by William Whewell* (London, 1853), III, p. 148.

48. ibid., I, pp. 334–6; III, pp. 148–52.

a distinction between external right, derived from utility, and intrinsic justice as revealed by natural reason. And since a slaveowner might have a legal right to do that which was intrinsically unjust, there were certain limits to the slave's duty of obedience. It was Grotius's 'probable opinion' that it was lawful for a slave subjected to extreme cruelty to seek refuge in flight. Similarly, the slave or the descendant of a slave who had been unjustly captured would not be morally guilty of theft if he should escape, provided that he did not owe anything to his master.[49]

Despite these reservations, which were necessary to preserve the supremacy of a higher law, Grotius tended to associate slavery with the entire fabric of social discipline and authority. Without reference to original sin, he quoted Augustine on the necessity of people bearing with their princes, and of slaves submitting to their masters. The most telling reason why slaves could not disobey or resist their masters was that the latter's external rights, though originating in utility and only *permitted* by natural reason, were protected and supported by judicial tribunals. Thus to resist the master was to challenge the authority of the magistrate. While Grotius helped to free the subject of slavery from the doctrine of original sin, he saw it as an integral part of a system of authority and discipline that was an expression of the world's rational order.[50]

The lingering uncertainties which Grotius felt over intrinsic justice and external right disappear entirely in the writings of Thomas Hobbes. For Hobbes slavery was an inevitable part of the logic of power. It raised no questions of sin or natural inferiority, except in the sense that all authority rested on a natural force restraining man from his anarchic and aggressive individualism. While Hobbes retained the traditional view that slavery was a component in the world's system of subordination and authority, he felt no sense of tension between this worldly state of obedience and discipline and an ideal state of natural freedom. He also abandoned completely the Stoic and Christian distinction between external bondage of the flesh and internal liberty of the soul. Indeed, for Hobbes the slave's will was so utterly subordinated to that of his master that he could only

49. ibid., I, pp. 336–7; III, p. 151, 155–6, 256.
50. ibid., III, pp. 150–51.

will whatever his master willed. It was therefore impossible for an owner to do injury to his slave.[51]

It is true that Hobbes recognized, as had Dio Chrysostom many centuries before, that when a man was captured in war there was nothing to prevent him from attempting to escape or from continuing the war by trying to kill his captor. Presumably, such a prisoner would be physically bound, which for Hobbes was the only true meaning of deprivation of liberty. Up to this point the relation of captor to captive was purely one of physical power. But when the bonds were broken and the prisoner accepted obedience in return for corporal freedom, the dominion of the master was sanctioned by compact. This model of slave-making resembled in many respects Hobbes's concept of the social compact. Hobbes stated quite explicitly that the only difference between the free subject and the 'servant' was that one served the city and the other served a fellow subject. Hence the 'servant' had no cause to complain of oppression or lack of liberty, when he was only kept from hurting himself and was provided with sustenance in exchange for being governed. By 'compact', however, Hobbes did not imply reciprocal rights and obligations. The 'servant' had no rights whatsoever and was obliged to obey every command of his lord. For disobedience he might even be killed with impunity. He could be sold or conveyed as his master wished.[52]

Since the time of Plato and Aristotle there had been few justifications of such unmitigated power of one man over another. Nevertheless, it was precisely this unmitigated power that made the 'compact' between master and slave a meaningless fiction, and opened the way for the bondsman's legitimate escape or rebellion. The master could use all the power at his command to prevent such resistance from a slave who felt that continued bondage was not in his own self-interest, but in Hobbes's theory there was no legal basis for challenging successful revolt.[53] Indeed, in a paradoxical way Hobbes may be seen as one of the prime sources of anti-slavery thought. By

51. Hobbes, *De Cive, or the Citizen* (ed. with introd. by Sterling P. Lamprecht, New York, 1949), pp. ii, viii.

52. ibid.; Hobbes, *Leviathan*, chs 2, 20.

53. George H. Sabine, *A History of Political Theory* (3rd ed., New York, 1961), pp. 470–71.

sweeping away traditional distinctions based on supposedly natural merit and wisdom, and by reducing all social relations to fear and self-interest, he undermined both the classical and Christian justifications for human bondage.

Insofar as Hobbes linked the defence of slavery with the defence of an absolutist state, departing from the Hellenic distinction between domestic bondage and constitutional government, he also made it easier for future writers to move from an attack on absolutism to an attack on slavery. In France, the same can be said of Bossuet. Yet Hobbes's views on servitude were adopted at least in part by men like Samuel Pufendorf, whose philosophies of natural law and social compact inspired eighteenth-century defenders of liberty. Though Pufendorf did not follow Hobbes to the extreme of maintaining that a master could do no injury to his slave, he agreed that the institution was founded on compact and was in accord with natural law. Moreover, since the majority of men lived by selfish impulse, he thought that slavery was highly useful as an instrument of social discipline, comparable to monogamous marriage or to the coercive functions of the state. Believing that it would reduce the number of idlers, thieves and vagabonds, Pufendorf had no objections to its being revived in Europe.[54]

For John Locke, on the other hand, 'Slavery is so vile and miserable an estate of Man, and so directly opposite to the generous Temper and Courage of our Nation; that 'tis hardly to be conceived, that an *Englishman*, much less a *Gentleman*, should plead for 't.'[55] This ringing challenge was directed to Sir Robert Filmer's contention that all authority was like that of master over slave, and that regal power, beginning with Adam, was absolute, arbitrary and unlimited. Yet John Locke, who was certainly an Englishman and a gentleman, had in 1669 transcribed, as secretary to Lord Ashley, the Fundamental Constitutions of Carolina, which provided that church membership would have no effect whatever on the status of slaves,

54. Jameson, *Montesquieu et l'esclavage*, p. 160; Dunning, *From Luther to Montesquieu*, pp. 320–22.

55. John Locke, *Two Treatises of Government, a Critical Edition with an Introduction and Apparatus Criticus*, by *Peter Laslett* (Cambridge, England, 1960), p. 159.

and that 'every freeman of Carolina, shall have absolute power and authority over his Negro slaves'. There is no evidence that he found these provisions objectionable; indeed, he was to become an investor in the Royal African Company, and clearly regarded Negro slavery as a justifiable institution.[56]

But how can it be that so great a defender of the inalienable rights of man was not at heart a determined enemy of slavery? It was Locke, after all, who sought to free the individual from authority based on revelation, precedent or sheer might. It was Locke who held that even after an individual had voluntarily subjected himself to the social compact, his fundamental rights should always be protected from 'the inconstant, uncertain, unknown, Arbitrary Will of another Man'.[57] It was of the very essence of Locke's philosophy of inalienable rights that no man could sell himself to another. And regardless of his station in life, every man, in Locke's eyes, should have a right to his own person and labour, and to the property which resulted from mixing his labour with nature. Surely this is the very antithesis of the pro-slavery views of Pufendorf, Hobbes and Grotius. Since slavery was so utterly repugnant to the spirit of Locke's social contract, there could be no question of its being justified as a useful or necessary link in society's chain of authority.

But we have already noted the curious capacity of slavery for generating or accommodating itself to dualisms in thought. We have seen that American colonists were not the first to combine a love of political liberty with an acceptance of chattel slavery. And ironically, it

56. ibid., pp. 29–30, 43, 302–3 n.; 'The Fundamental Constitutions of Carolina – 1669', in Benjamin Perley Poore (comp.), *The Federal and State Constitutions, Colonial Charters, and Other Organic Laws of the United States*, part 2 (Washington, 1877), pp. 407–8; Maurice Cranston, *John Locke: A Biography* (London, 1957), pp. 119–20; Caroline Robbins, *The Eighteenth-Century Commonwealthman: Studies in the Transmission, Development and Circumstance of English Liberal Thought from the Restoration of Charles II until the War with the Thirteen Colonies* (Cambridge, Mass., 1959), p. 59. Locke had been in correspondence with Sir Peter Colleton, a resident of Barbados and a proprietor of Carolina, and may have acquired from him knowledge of Barbadian slave laws (M. Eugene Sirmans, 'The Legal Status of the Slave in South Carolina, 1670–1740', *Journal of Southern History*, XXVIII [November 1962], p. 463).

57. Locke, *Two Treatises*, p. 302.

was precisely the same opening in Locke's theory of social contract that allowed both a justification of slavery and the preservation of natural rights. For in Locke's view, the origin of slavery, like the origin of liberty and property, was entirely outside the social contract. When any man, by fault or act, forfeited his life to another, he could not complain of injustice if his punishment was postponed by his being enslaved. If the hardships of bondage should at any time outweigh the value of life, he could commit suicide by resisting his master and receiving the death which he had all along deserved: 'This is the perfect condition of *Slavery*,' Locke wrote, 'which *is* nothing else, but *the state of War continued, between a lawful Conquerour, and a Captive*.'[58] Hence the relationship was one in which the obligations of the social compact were entirely suspended. Like the murderer, the slave had abrogated the compact and forfeited his natural rights. But whereas the relatives of the murderer's victim were required to surrender to the State their natural right of retaliation, the continuing war between master and slave carried over into society, and was presumably outside the jurisdiction of the State.

Though it may be objected that these views had little subsequent influence, they raise a number of interesting implications. First of all, in Locke's world men would be either entirely free or entirely slave, and the condition of the latter would not be mitigated by the influence of natural reason or intrinsic justice. The master's authority would be as unlimited as it had been for Hobbes, but even Hobbes thought of slavery as part of the social order and as having at least the form of a compact; in theory it could be regulated or abolished by the sovereign. But the elemental struggle between two enemies – which Hobbes took as only the natural condition which made slavery necessary as a social institution – Locke took as slavery's continuing and essential character. This meant that he had turned the traditional Stoic and Christian conception of slavery upside down, for instead of picturing bondage as a product of sinful society, he found its origins and justification outside the limits of a free and rational society. It followed, though Locke did not press the point, that slavery was in conformity with natural law and was as universally valid as private

58. ibid., pp. 297–302.

property. And since slaves were private property, and the title of owners was based on natural right, it would presumably be the duty of any state to protect the rights of slaveholders.

Locke's entire argument was highly legalistic and abstract. Unlike Bodin and Grotius, he generally ignored historical precedent. Unlike Suarez, he appealed to principle rather than to expediency or the common practice of nations. He wrote as if no one had ever questioned the right to enslave prisoners of war. And whereas servants were subject only to limited and contractual duties, slaves, 'being Captives taken in a just War, are by the Right of Nature subjected to the Absolute Dominion and Arbitrary Power of their Masters'.[59] Locke assumed that the authority of West Indian planters was like that of the Biblical patriarchs, but argued that in both cases dominion derived from the purchase of legitimate captives rather than from the inheritance of divinely instituted rights. Like Hobbes, Locke narrowed the ground on which slavery could be justified; and obviously his theory of natural liberty could become a vital component of abolitionist thought. But his unquestioning acceptance of colonial slavery shows how remote abolitionism was from even the more liberal minds of the late seventeenth century.

We must conclude, then, that the thought of Grotius, Hobbes, Pufendorf and Locke, while preparing the way for the secular theories of the Enlightenment, provided little basis for criticizing Europe's policy of supporting and extending slavery in the New World. The ancient Stoic dualism of slavery and nature, which had been embodied in Christian doctrine, might have served as a foundation for anti-slavery thought as soon as men sought to develop a theory of politics on natural principles. But despite the early lead of Jean Bodin, political thought in the seventeenth century did not move in the direction of abolitionism. To be sure, the most original minds no longer justified human bondage as the dark fruit of sin or as a disciplinary force in the divine government of the world. But for Grotius, Hobbes and Pufendorf the divine order had been at least partly replaced by a system of law or power in which slavery was a rational and harmonious element. This, after all, was in the great tradition of Plato, Aristotle and Aquinas. For Locke, on the other

59. ibid., p. 341.

hand, original sin had been replaced by a supposedly wilful act which required that the slave be forever excluded from the paradisial compact and worked, in the sweat of his brow, for the benefit of others. And from this secular hell there was apparently no redemption.

PART II

5

Changing Views on the Value and Dangers of American Slavery

IN 1688 Governor Denonville of Canada wrote to Louis XIV and begged him to end the manpower shortage of New France by authorizing direct shipments of Negro slaves. The Canadian case for slavery was presented more fully to the king by Ruette d'Auteuil, the attorney-general, who argued that the northern colony could never hope to prosper until enterprises were assured a reliable supply of slave labour. D'Auteuil did his best to prove that Negroes could thrive in the frigid wilds. Their presence in New England and New Holland showed they could endure harsh winters. In Canada, no doubt, they would have to be warmly clad, but this apparent expense simply opened the way to greater profits. Indians, he pointed out, seasoned beaver skins by wearing them until they were saturated in sweat and oil, which made the long hair fall off and thereby doubled the price. A Canadian slaveowner could thus keep his Negroes warm in winter and at the same time double the price of his beaver skins! Could any West Indian planter claim so much? The king was apparently persuaded that Canadians needed slaves for agriculture and clearing new ground, and although he continued to fear large financial losses if the Negroes should die from the cold climate, he gave his consent to Governor Denonville's proposal.

But despite the renewal of such authorization in 1701 and the legal establishment of slavery in 1709, Canada was spectacularly unsuccessful in her effort to become a second Brazil. This was largely because she could not compete with the richer colonies of the south for a supply of labour that was never able to meet the demand. Nevertheless, Canadian officials were reluctant to give up their visions of converting New France into a thriving slave colony. In 1716 the intendant attributed the success of New York and New England to Negro labour, and predicted that Canada could produce wheat and other commodities for the West Indian markets if she were given sufficient credit to buy slaves. The continuing pleas to France pictured Negro slavery as the cure for all Canada's economic and social ills.[1]

Canadian officials greatly exaggerated New England's dependence on slave labour, but the general assumptions of Governor Denonville and Ruette d'Auteuil were not totally foreign to the New England mind. Forty-three years before Denonville's appeal to Louis XIV, Emanuel Downing had expressed an ardent hope to his brother-in-law, John Winthrop, that Indians captured in 'just wars' might be exchanged in the West Indies for Negro slaves,

for I doe not see how wee can thrive untill wee get into a stock of slaves sufficient to doe all our business, for our children's children will hardly see this great Continent filled with people, soe that our servants will still desire freedome to plant for them-selves, and not stay but for verie great wages.[2]

For at least some New Englanders, as their northern neighbours, the West Indies presented a model for solving the problem of a chronic shortage of labour.

Since it has often been assumed that slavery was morally repugnant to most Americans, and that its tragic introduction was the response of commercial avarice to a tropical climate, such views raise disturbing questions. Was the 'peculiar' institution truly an aber-

1. Marcel Trudel, *L'Esclavage au Canada français: histoire et conditions de l'esclavage* (Québec, 1960), pp. 20–35; Francis Parkman, *The Old Régime in Canada* (Boston, 1901), p. 454. The intendant, Bégon, compiled a list of some hundred people in Canada willing to buy slaves, but the Company of the Indies was apparently unimpressed by so small and uncertain a market. According to Trudel, only a few hundred Negroes appeared in Canada during the entire French régime, and most of these were taken by capture or as contraband from the English colonies; there was never a genuine slave trade to Canada (pp. 89–93). Canadian Indian slavery will be discussed later. For the problem French authorities faced in securing a labour force, see Sigmund Diamond, 'An Experiment in "Feudalism": French Canada in the Seventeenth Century', *William and Mary Quarterly*, 3rd ser., XVIII (January 1961), pp. 11–19.
2. Elizabeth Donnan (ed.), *Documents Illustrative of the History of the Slave Trade to America* (Washington, 1930–35), III. p. 8.

ration whose baneful effects were confined to certain regions, or was it accepted by all colonizing states alike as a vital and necessary part of American expansion? Was slavery morally and economically uncongenial to the northern colonies, or was it simply that the West Indies and Southern colonies were better equipped to buy cheap labour with needed commodities, and hence became the engines that developed America's economic power? Is it possible that the slave system provided the initial thrust to an economy that could later rely on immigration, technology and expanding domestic markets?

Although we have already touched on such questions in chapter 1, thus far we have been primarily concerned with slavery as a moral problem in the culture and thought of Western Europe. We now need to turn to the assumptions, attitudes and circumstances which governed the development of the institution in the New World. We shall not attempt to present a full account of the early history of American slavery; we should, however, look at certain forces that favoured the expansion of Negro bondage in America, as well as at conflicts of interest and changing historical conditions that could produce a climate hospitable to anti-slavery thought.

Here, briefly, are the points to be elaborated in this chapter. Although northern colonists sometimes looked enviously at the West Indians' armies of labour and fabled wealth, the American demand for slaves was not a constant or universal force. In most colonies the institution developed slowly and as a result of the uncoordinated decisions and preferences of many people. If a demand for cheap labour was nearly universal throughout the Americas, the motives of planters, merchants and legislators were complicated by problems of credit and payments, by a need for revenue, by the mercantilist policies of mother countries, by a desire for immigration from Europe, and by a widespread fear of servile insurrections. It was possible for the same colonists to call in one breath for more slaves at cheaper prices, and in the next to deplore the growing disproportion between the Negro and white races. For some two and a half centuries the policies of most New World colonies were dominated by two seemingly contradictory views of Negro slavery: according to the first, the institution was the base on which the entire economy rested, and was the main route to individual wealth and imperial grandeur; it was therefore essential that the government ensure a continuing supply of Africans and protect slaveholders in the free enjoyment of their property. According to the second, Negro slaves endangered public security, and it was therefore the duty of the government to limit their numbers, control their activities, and encourage the introduction of white servants and artisans. While these divergent views might co-exist in the same colony, the emphasis given to one or the other depended on a variety of circumstances. With very few exceptions, however, it was not until the second half of the eighteenth century that public policy was influenced by a belief that slavery was incompatible with basic ideals or institutions.

A conflict between the colonist's desire for labour and his fear of the Negro slave was apparent from the very beginning. The Negroes whom Governor Ovando had been authorized to transport to Hispaniola in 1502 were born in Iberia and were thus presumably Christian; yet Ovando soon became alarmed at the danger of Negroes inciting Indians to revolt, and he asked that the slave trade, then in its infancy, be suspended. In 1514, after King Ferdinand had revived the traffic, the royal treasurer said that the number of Negroes should be kept to a minimum in the interest of security; but despite an original order that the proportion of Negroes to Spaniards be limited to one to three, it was estimated by 1560 that the Negroes in Hispaniola outnumbered the Europeans fifteen to one.[3]

According to Fernando Romero, the Negro slave made it possible for the Spanish to colonize America, for by nature the conquistadores were slow to learn the necessity of working themselves, and the Indians' mortality was too great to ensure an adequate supply of labour.[4] It has often been forgotten that there were fewer whites than Negro

---

3. ibid., I, pp. 14–15; Lewis Hanke, *The Spanish Struggle for Justice in the Conquest of America* (Philadelphia, 1949), p. 60; Arthur Helps, *The Spanish Conquest in America, and its Relation to the History of Slavery and to the Government of Colonies* (London, 1900), III, p. 153 n.; C. H. Haring, *The Spanish Empire in America* (New York, 1947), p. 221.

4. Fernando Romero, 'El negro en tierra firme durante el siglo XVI', in *Actas y trabajos científicos del XXVII° Congreso Internacional de Americanistas* (Lima, 1939–42), II, p. 441.

slaves in colonial Lima and Mexico City. In Mexico imported Negroes outnumbered white immigrants for more than a century, and helped provide the labour which made the colony one of the richest countries in the world. But while the Negroes toiled in the mines and on the *latifundia* that supported the mines, they also broke into open revolt as early as 1537. In 1553 Luis de Velasco warned the king that the country might face disaster if the number of licences to import slaves were not curtailed.[5]

The slave trade, however, was becoming a prodigious enterprise which could not easily be regulated or shut off at will. The Portuguese, as leaders of what they took to be a new crusade, built numerous establishments on the African coast for the combined purposes of spreading their faith and reaping commercial profit. Among their most important customers were the merchants and speculators of Europe who had acquired the privilege of supplying the Spanish Empire with slaves. After 1518, when Charles V rewarded one of his favourites with a licence to furnish the colonies with four thousand Negroes, this supposedly exclusive right was divided and sold, and was then followed by additional licences and contracts which soon became a vital source of revenue for the Spanish throne.[6] In the New World, Cartagena emerged as a booming slave entrepôt which distributed Negroes to the eager proprietors of mines and sugar fields. Negro slavery had seemed to develop almost fortuitously in Latin America, but after a century of colonial history it had become a basic

5. Gonzalo Aguirre Beltrán, 'The Slave Trade in Mexico', *Hispanic American Historical Review*, XXIV (1944), pp. 413–14; Oriol Pi-Sunyer, 'Historical Background to the Negro in Mexico', *Journal of Negro History*, XLII (October 1957), pp. 239–42; James F. King, 'The Negro in Continental Spanish America: A Select Bibliography', *Hispanic American Historical Review*, XXIV (1944), p. 548.

6. Donnan (ed.), *Documents*, I, pp. 1–7; H. A. Wyndham, *Problems of Imperial Trusteeship: The Atlantic and Slavery* (London, 1935), pp. 8–10. For the meaning and origin of the *assientos*, see Georges Scelle, *La traite négrière aux Indes de Castille: contrats et traités d'assiento* (Paris, 1906), I, pp. 24–34, and the documents themselves (I, pp. 755–836). A convenient chart of the assientists can be found in Elena Fanny Scheuss de Studer, *La trata de negros en el Rio de la Plata durante el siglo XVIII* (Buenos Aires, 1958), pp. 58–60.

system of labour from Peru to Puerto Rico. In Brazil priests as well as planters acknowledged that without African labour, Portuguese America would be an impossibility.[7]

It was this realization, which became increasingly prevalent in Latin America, that made the slave trade and then slavery itself so important for the commercial expansion of Western Europe. The nearly unlimited demand for slaves in the Spanish Empire might provide the opening wedge for an even more profitable commerce; and in the eyes of European expansionists who looked with awe at mountains of Spanish bullion and tropical produce, Latin America exemplified the value of overseas colonies. During the sixteenth century France and Britain had little opportunity to exploit the connexion between slavery and American expansion, since they lacked colonies of their own and were jealously excluded from Spanish ports. To be sure, John Hawkins dazzled the world by forcibly crashing the Spanish markets and selling slaves at enormous profit. But the utter failure of Hawkins's third slaving voyage proved that such rich profits could be secured only by acquiring bases on the African coast and in the Caribbean.[8]

As early as the 1590s the Dutch had begun to undermine Port-

---

7. While in most parts of Latin America, Indian workers greatly outnumbered Negro slaves, the significance of the latter has often been underestimated. For the introduction of Negroes into various colonies, see Alexander Marchant, *From Barter to Slavery: The Economic Relations of Portuguese and Indians in the Settlement of Brazil, 1500–1580* (Baltimore, 1942), pp. 15, 51, 73–9, 131; Maurilio de Gouveia, *História da escravidão* (Rio de Janeiro, 1955), pp. 67–8; Instituto Panamericano de Geografía e Historia Comisión de Historia, *El mestizaje en la historia de Ibero-América* (México, D.F., 1961), p. 66; Celso Furtado, *The Economic Growth of Brazil: A Survey from Colonial to Modern Times* (Berkeley, 1963), pp. 50–58; Ildefenso Pereda Valdés, 'Negros esclavos, pardos libres y negros libres en Uruguay', *Estudios afrocubanos*, IV (1940), pp. 121–7; Rollando Mellafe, *La introducción de la esclavitud negra en Chile* (Santiago de Chile, 1959), *passim*; Jaime Jaramillo Uribe, 'Esclavos y señores en la sociedad colombiana del siglo XVIII', *Anuario colombiano de historia social y de la cultura*, I (Bogotá, 1963), pp. 3, 5, 14; C. R. Boxer, *The Golden Age of Brazil, 1695–1750: Growing Pains of a Colonial Society* (Berkeley, 1962), pp. 1–2.

8. Donnan (ed.), *Documents*, I, pp. 9–10, 44–65.

uguese power on the Guinea coast; and by 1637, when they won
dominance by capturing the strategic fortress of Elmina, they had also
established a considerable beachhead in Brazil and had seized
Curaçao and Saint Eustatius, from which slaves could conveniently
be smuggled into the Spanish colonies. Their timing proved to be
most fortunate, for in 1640 Portugal rose in arms against sixty years
of Spanish domination, and for the next twenty-two years Spain altogether suspended the *assiento*, or slave contract, which had been in
Portuguese hands since the beginning of the century.

In 1662, when Spain finally moved once again to meet her colonists' demand for slaves, her choices were limited by the changing
balance of power. France had already won supremacy over Spain on
the continent, and it was the determined policy of Colbert, who took
office in 1662, to encourage the slave trade as part of a vast mercantilist system. England had already deprived Spain of Jamaica, and
had emerged from a period of civil war and political upheaval with a
fresh appetite for commercial power. In 1663 the Duke of York and a
group of prominent shareholders, including the king himself, would
launch the Company of Royal Adventurers Trading to Africa, which
nine years later would be reorganized as the powerful Royal African
Company. Before the end of the seventeenth century the African
coast was dotted with slave-trading posts which flew the flags of
Portugal, France, England, Holland, Denmark and Brandenburg.
While the Germans would eventually sell out to the Dutch, even the
Danes acquired an entrepôt at St Thomas from which they profitably
smuggled slaves to the Spanish. Thus no matter who received the
assiento, a large proportion of the slaves purchased by Spanish col-
onists would come from illegal sources. In 1662 Spain granted the
assiento to Genoese merchants who in turn bargained with the Eng-
lish Company of Royal Adventurers and with the Dutch West India
Company. After considerable vacillation and soul-searching, the
Spanish finally turned directly to the Dutch, and eventually to the
French.[9]

9. ibid., I, 73–9, 107–8, 169–70; Scelle, *La traite négrière*, I, pp. 473–81;
II, pp. 3–174; Scheuss de Studer, *La trata de negros*, pp. 74–9. It should be
noted that the earliest English company, which was chartered in 1618,
suffered heavy losses in trying to develop an African trade in other com-

Largely in the hope of monopolizing a hitherto irregular and competitive trade, the British began negotiations early in the eighteenth century which culminated in the well-known article of the Treaty of Utrecht. But though the award of the *assiento* to the South Sea Company was celebrated in London by a torchlight procession, there was soon conflict between that ill-fated company and its supplier, the Royal African Company. And Jamaicans, who had done well by smuggling when the *assiento* had been held by France, now resented the loss of prime slaves to foreign competitors, and tried unsuccessfully to impose a duty on the re-export of the South Sea Company's Negroes, who were shipped initially to their island. By the 1730s England was ready to admit that the *assiento* was a losing business. It had been the markets and produce of the Spanish colonies that had originally lured the maritime powers into the slave trade, but the profits anticipated from monopolizing the Spanish trade proved to be illusory. Eventually, Spanish policy was forced to move towards the principle of free commerce in slaves. But meanwhile, British planters might well question the wisdom of stocking Cuba with 10,700 Negroes during a brief nine months of military occupation. Conflicts of interest might provide the ground for general dissatisfaction with a trade that augmented the labour force of rival colonies.[10]

By the mid seventeenth century the tropical colonies of Britain and France had begun to produce sugar, which required for its cultivation a substantial amount of labour. A shortage of labour was the complaint of every colony from Canada to Barbados, but especially of areas rich in fertile land and dependent on the exportation of tobacco, rice or sugar. For the small planter who lacked capital and who could

---

modities than slaves. The slave trade was apparently taken for granted by an exclusive company chartered in 1631 by Charles I, but even by the 1660s it was not clear to merchants that commerce with Africa would increasingly be limited to the purchase of slaves.

10. Donnan (ed.), *Documents,* I, pp. 120–21; II, pp. xxxiv–xxxix; Scelle, *La traite négrière,* II, pp. 455–630; Eric Williams, *Capitalism and Slavery* (Chapel Hill, 1944), p. 33; James F. King, 'The Evolution of the Free Slave Trade Principle in Spanish Colonial Administration', *Hispanic American Historical Review,* XXII (February 1942), pp. 34–56.

not plan far into the future, the need for labour was well met by indentured servants. It has been estimated that such unfree workers formed more than half of all white immigration to the continental colonies south of New England; yet even when supplemented by convicts and political prisoners, the number was never equal to the demand. It was, moreover, the considered opinion of the governor of Barbados that three Negroes could do more work at cheaper cost than one white servant.[11] But regardless of the possible economic merits of slave labour, few planters, even in the Caribbean, possessed sufficient capital to contract in advance for the minimum quantities of Negroes initially offered by the monopolistic companies.[12] Hence in 1663 Governor Charles Calvert confessed to Lord Baltimore that Maryland, though eager to receive Negroes, was not rich enough to guarantee a profitable annual market to the Company of Royal Adventurers.[13]

Cheaper slaves meant reduced costs of production, and colonial legislators were alert to the fact that a predictable influx of slaves would be a predictable source of revenue. Britain was determined, however, to control the slave trade for her own advantage, and for this purpose her rulers favoured a monopolistic company powerful enough to amass capital and specialized knowledge, maintain forts and installations on the African coast, and eclipse the efforts of rival nations. Such ambitious designs were not easy to execute. Despite impressive profits from the slave trade, the British companies suffered losses in the wars with Holland, their monopoly was infringed

11. Abbot Emerson Smith, *Colonists in Bondage: White Servitude and Convict Labor in America, 1607–1776* (Chapel Hill, 1947), pp. 3–4, 30.

12. C. S. S. Higham, *The Development of the Leeward Islands under the Restoration, 1660–1688: A Study of the Foundations of the Old Colonial System* (Cambridge, England, 1921), p. 151. The Dutch West India Company, which was heavily involved in the slave trade, discovered that few of its settlers in New Netherlands were able to purchase Negroes, but under British rule the number increased with a general rise in prosperity (Ulrich B. Phillips, *American Negro Slavery: A Survey of the Supply, Employment and Control of Negro Labor as Determined by the Plantation Regime* [reprint ed., Gloucester, Mass., 1959], pp. 107–8).

13. George Louis Beer, *The Old Colonial System, 1660–1754* (New York, 1912), I, p. 331 n.

upon by interlopers, including a few New Englanders, and they were plagued by problems of credit, payments and organization.[14] It was, after all, no small matter to undertake the competitive marketing of quantities of goods in a totally alien Africa, or to supply large numbers of labourers to distant purchasers whose optimism usually transcended their ability to pay. And though the Royal Adventurers enjoyed the direct support of the royal family and of men deeply involved in colonial expansion, such as Lord Berkeley and Sir George Carteret, the colonists themselves remained unsatisfied. In 1662 Barbados petitioned the king to allow a free trade in slaves; Governor Willoughby later predicted that the island's economy would be ruined if the monopoly were continued. The Jamaican council and assembly pleaded with the Duke of York to induce the Royal African Company to furnish a cheaper and more plentiful supply of slaves. And the Leeward Islands, chafing under the necessity of buying their slaves from Nevis, which was the official depot of the Royal African Company, were further outraged in 1682 when the Company shut off their supply altogether as retaliation against local laws which made it difficult to recover debts incurred from the purchase of Negroes. King Charles, however, publicly defended the privileges of the Company, and warned his American subjects not to incur his wrath by trying to crash the gates of Africa on their own.[15]

In the 1680s the colonial demands for a free slave trade were reinforced by the arguments of British merchants and investors who accused the Company of complacent inefficiency. In defence, the Company pointed to its heavy expenses in maintaining posts in Africa, and charged that the interlopers, who were often encouraged by colonial officials, had injured the trade by kidnapping prominent Africans and arousing the revenge of their fellow tribesmen.[16] But

14. For the problems faced by the Royal African Company, see Kenneth G. Davies, *The Royal African Company* (London, 1957), and Donnan (ed.), *Documents*, I, pp. 87–92, 167 n.

15. Beer, *Old Colonial System*, I, pp. 331, 354; *Journals of the Assembly of Jamaica*, I (Jamaica, 1811), pp. 9–10; Higham, *Development of Leeward Islands*, pp. 151–5; Donnan (ed.), *Documents*, I, pp. 194–5.

16. Donnan (ed.), *Documents*, I, pp. 267–84. For evidence of the abuses, crimes and sharp practices of the 'separate traders' on the African coast in

Parliament, convinced that the slave trade was 'highly beneficial and advantagious to this kingdom, and to the Plantations and Colonies', gave way in 1698 and opened the trade to private traders willing to pay a 10 per cent duty, which went to the Royal African Company as compensation for the upkeep of forts. Almost immediately the African coast swarmed with independent traders. For a time, the French Guinea Company tried to cooperate with the Royal African Company in maintaining prices and standards, but the pattern which the large companies had imposed on the African trade slowly disintegrated.[17] In the eighteenth century the only regulative forces in this violent and intensely competitive commerce would be the pressures of supply and demand.

By the time of the American Revolution it was morally reassuring to think of Negro slavery as a burden forced by a tyrannical government on an unwilling people. But Britain never required her colonists to buy slaves, and in truth the original and essential grievance of the colonists who cared about the matter was that they could not buy enough slaves at a reasonable price. In every colony there was at least a small market for domestic servants, and in New England, New York, New Jersey and Pennsylvania, slave labour was applied to

---

the years immediately following the legal opening of the trade, see Charles Davenant, *The Political and Commercial Works of that Celebrated Writer Charles D'Avenant ... Collected and Revised by Sir Charles Whitworth* (London, 1771), V, pp. 179–98.

17. Donnan (ed.), *Documents*, I, pp. 421–2; II, pp. xxx, xli–xlii; Thomas Astley (ed.), *A New General Collection of Voyages and Travels ...* (London, 1745–7), II, pp. 78–9. French planters had also complained of high prices and too few slaves. In 1713 France followed England's lead and opened the trade to all citizens, though a duty was imposed on every Negro transported to the colonies and in 1716 the trade was confined to ships of the five ports. A monopolistic company was reorganized by John Law in 1720, and the French slave trade remained restricted until 1767. Unlike England, France paid a bounty on every Negro imported into the colonies. This aroused the envy of the British merchants, but the French colonists remained discontent over the monopoly enjoyed by the Company of the Indies (Pierre François Xavier de Charlevoix, *Histoire de l'Isle Espagnole ou de Saint-Domingue ...* [Amsterdam, 1733], IV, p. 221; Gaston Martin, *Histoire de l'esclavage dans les colonies françaises* [Paris, 1948], p. 130; Donnan (ed.), *Documents*, I, pp. 101–2; II, pp. xxiii–xxviii).

farming and to a variety of trades and productive industries. Since the slave trade tended to deposit numbers of Negroes at the ports from which it was carried on, it is not surprising that the activities of the Pepperrells, Saffins, Cabots, Faneuils, Belchers and Browns left a scattering of slaves along the New England coast from Kittery to Newport. By 1756 they constituted some 16 per cent of the population of both Newport and New York City. The great landed proprietors of the fertile stock-farming region of southern Rhode Island depended on slave labour. And while the proportion of Negroes remained very small in other parts of New England, the Yankees who moved to Westchester and Long Island were quick to purchase slaves. Ulrich B. Phillips has estimated that by 1750 slaves were owned by one-tenth of the householders in the province of New York.[18]

No matter what their potential demand might have been, the Northern colonies were not ordinarily in a position to compete for slaves with the West Indies, where increased numbers of labourers were required to extract sugar from the depleted soil of the Leeward Islands, to develop new plantations in Jamaica, and to fill the ranks that were constantly cut down by a ghastly rate of mortality. It is significant that the small slave trade to Pennsylvania hit its peak during the Seven Years' War, which disrupted markets in the West Indies.[19] Even the planters of Virginia, who thought that slaves

18. Carl Bridenbaugh, *Cities in Revolt: Urban Life in America, 1743–1776* (New York, 1955), p. 88; Lorenzo J. Greene, *The Negro in Colonial New England, 1620–1776* (New York, 1942), p. 103; Edward R. Turner, *The Negro in Pennsylvania: Slavery, Servitude, Freedom, 1639–1861* (Washington, 1911), p. 3; Donnan (ed.), *Documents*, III, pp. 9–16; Joseph Williamson, 'Slavery in Maine', *Collections of Maine Historical Society*, 1st ser., VII (Bath, Maine, 1876), pp. 213–14; Greene, *Negro in Colonial New England*, pp. 28–9, 74, 76, 99; Edward Channing, *The Narragansett Planters* (Baltimore, 1886), pp. 8–10; Phillips, *American Negro Slavery*, pp. 108–10; Arthur Zilversmit, 'Slavery and its Abolition in the Northern States' (Ph.D. dissertation, University of California, Berkeley, 1962), pp. 45–61. Although there were only a few thousand slaves in Connecticut, a pro-slavery sentiment persisted even after the Revolution (see Bernard C. Steiner, *A History of Slavery in Connecticut* [Baltimore, 1893], p. 69).

19. Frank Wesley Pitman, *The Development of the British West Indies, 1700–1763* (New Haven, 1917), pp. 73–9; Beer, *Old Colonial System*, I,

would enable them to compete on a better footing with the Spanish tobacco colonies, found it difficult to pay the price for substantial shipments of Negroes. Although the assembly had earlier tried to encourage the importation of slaves, in 1670 the proportion in Virginia was less than that in Rhode Island a century later; it was only in the 1680s and 1690s that the example of large planters, such as William Byrd and William Fitzhugh, pointed the way to reduced production costs and thus to fortune. But despite a vast increase in slaves during the early decades of the eighteenth century, the demand in Virginia was stabilized by a fear of debt in the face of overproduction and an uncertain tobacco market.[20] And if the rice planters of Carolina were generally more confident of the future, Henry Laurens confessed in 1768 that selling slaves was a risky business, since a ship could not move on to the most favourable market, as in the West Indies, and the prices tended to be too high or too low to make a profit. After deciding to abandon a trade which he found distasteful, Laurens was again attracted by the prospect of a good market with the lifting of the pre-Revolution non-importation agreement. In 1773, however, he feared that South Carolina was overstocked with Negroes, especially in light of her mounting debts and hard times. As a good patriot he tended by 1776 to think of the slave trade as a British iniquity.[21]

We have noticed that even in the sixteenth century the demand for slaves in the Spanish colonies was tempered by a fear that excessive numbers of Negroes would endanger security. This fear of servile revolt would be intrinsic to American slavery, no matter what later apologists for the institution might say of the Negro's docility. West Indian planters who clamoured for more Negroes were well aware of the risks they took, especially during war, in stocking vulnerable

pp. 331, 354; Darold D. Wax, 'Quaker Merchants and the Slave Trade in Colonial Pennsylvania', *Pennsylvania Magazine of History and Biography*, LXXXVI (April 1962), pp. 144–59.

20. Beer, *Old Colonial System*, I, p. 367; Thomas J. Wertenbaker, *The Shaping of Colonial Virginia: The Planters of Colonial Virginia* (New York, 1958), pp. 108, 125–32; James Curtis Ballagh, *A History of Slavery in Virginia* (Baltimore, 1902), pp. 9–10; Donnan (ed.), *Documents*, IV, p. 241.

21. Donnan (ed.), *Documents*, IV, pp. 424–71.

islands with what amounted to captured foreign armies. In the last quarter of the seventeenth century the legislatures of Barbados, Jamaica, the Leeward Islands, South Carolina – wherever the proportion of slaves rose rapidly – made every effort to increase security by attracting white settlers or by requiring planters to maintain a prescribed number of white servants capable of bearing arms.[22] But the laws requiring a fixed proportion of whites to Negroes were no more effective than had been the similar efforts of the Spanish. In Jamaica the so-called deficiency laws, which allowed a planter to pay a tax in lieu of supporting white servants, simply became measures for increasing revenue. By 1773 a joint committee of the Jamaican council and assembly could point to the dangers faced by an island whose white population had risen in eighty years from 7,768 to only 16,000, while the slave population had shot from 9,504 to some two hundred thousand.[23]

22. *Acts of Assembly, Passed in the Charibbee Leeward Islands from 1690 to 1730* (London, 1732), pp. 159–63; *The Laws of the Island of Saint Vincent, and its Dependencies, from the First Establishment of a Legislature to the End of the Year, 1809* (Bridgnorth, England, 1811), p. 66; *The Statutes and Laws of the Island of Jamaica* (rev. ed., Jamaica, 1889), I, pp. 22–3; *Journals of the Assembly of Jamaica*, III (London, 1827), p. 337; Higham, *Development of Leeward Islands*, pp. 165–8; Smith, *Colonists in Bondage*, pp. 27–36. During the late seventeenth century Bermuda tried to prohibit the further importation of slaves, though apparently without much success (J. H. Lefroy, *Memorials of the Discovery and Early Settlement of the Bermudas or Somers Islands, 1515–1685, Compiled from the Colonial Records and Other Original Sources* [reprinted ed., n.p., 1932], II, pp. 461, 506).

23. Charlevoix, *Histoire de l'Isle Espagnole*, III, p. 259; *Journals of Assembly of Jamaica*, III, p. 337; IV (London, 1827), p. 221; Lowell Joseph Ragatz, *The Fall of the Planter Class in the British Caribbean, 1763–1833* (New York, 1928), p. 9; Pitman, *Development of British West Indies*, pp. 372–4, 380–84; W. E. B. DuBois, *The Suppression of the African Slave Trade to the United States of America, 1638–1870* (reprint ed., New York, 1954), p. 209; *Journals of Assembly of Jamaica*, VI (Jamaica, 1800), p. 486. The population figures are taken from the joint committee's report. Stephen Fuller, Jamaica's official agent in England, listed the population in 1773 as 202,787 slaves, 12,737 whites and 4,093 free Negroes and mulattoes (Stephen Fuller papers, Duke University Library). But Frank Wesley Pitman records the 1778 population as 205,261 Negroes and 18,420 whites (*Development of British West Indies*, p. 374).

Nor were such fears imaginary. During the eighteenth century there were more than a dozen slave revolts in Jamaica alone, and in many colonies escaped Negroes, or maroons, carried on sporadic and unnerving guerilla warfare. In 1712 a slave insurrection and pitched battle brought hysteria to New York City and gave proof that such phenomena would not necessarily be confined to the Caribbean.[24] In the 1730s and 1740s the British colonies were rocked by successive waves of panic. A Spanish royal decree of 1733 confirmed earlier rulings that slaves of Protestant colonies would be considered free if they escaped to Spanish territory. Since a small boat could reach Cuba from Jamaica, and since northern Florida was a short distance from South Carolina, this policy provoked considerable anxiety. Soon afterwards Jamaica exploded with several bloody insurrections. Similar uprisings occurred in other islands, which were suffering from a fall in sugar prices and hence from reduced rations of food. In 1739 a large group of South Carolina slaves seized arms and began marching southwards, killing people and burning houses on the way. A detected conspiracy of Negroes in Charles Town in 1740 was followed the next year by mass hysteria in New York City, where as punishment for an alleged plot eighteen slaves were hanged

24. Ragatz, *Fall of the Planter Class*, pp. 31, 225 ff, 330; [Edward Long], *The History of Jamaica; or, General Survey of the Antient and Modern State of that Island* ... (London, 1744), II, pp. 338–48; Kenneth Scott, 'The Slave Insurrection in New York in 1712', *New York Historical Society Quarterly*, XLV (January 1961), pp. 43–74; Herbert Aptheker, *American Negro Slave Revolts* (New York, 1943), pp. 104–49, 162–208. In 1708 there was also an uprising in Long Island. Various historians, including Phillips, have minimized the importance of slave resistance; in redressing the balance, Aptheker may well exaggerate the tendency to open rebellion and revolution. But the statutes, court records and newspapers of the West Indies and Southern colonies and states are filled with evidence of active and passive resistance, as well as of a pervasive fear of slave insurrection. A most valuable discussion of the subject for a later period is found in Kenneth M. Stampp, *The Peculiar Institution: Slavery in the Ante-Bellum South* (New York, 1956), pp. 86–140. His conclusions would seem to apply for the most part to the colonial period, except that Negroes born in Africa, who were often warriors with combat experience, were more inclined to direct violence.

and thirteen burned alive.[25] In England the news of such repeated violence focused attention on the dangers of American slavery; throughout the colonies it accentuated a desire for a higher ratio of whites to Negroes, and also reinforced an inclination to blame outsiders for the multiplying problems of Negro bondage.[26]

Colonel William Byrd, whose father had been part owner of a slave ship and whose family wealth had grown from dealing in slaves as well as from slave labour, wrote in 1736 that Virginia was in danger of becoming a 'New Guinea' and of being convulsed by servile war. Confident that in Virginia the necessary severities of bondage were less extreme than in the West Indies, he nevertheless feared that maroons would flee to the mountains, and turn the Old Dominion into another Jamaica. This dismal crisis might be averted by stopping the importation of Negroes, for Byrd now saw the source of Virginia's woes in the 'few ravenous Traders' who would willingly sell their own wives and fathers 'if they could black their faces and get anything by them'.[27] A West Indian correspondent, whose report of thirty slave executions appeared in the *London Magazine*, insisted that planters would really like to be rid of all their Negroes.

25. Scelle, *La traite négrière*, I, pp. 714–15; Aptheker, *American Negro Slave Revolts*, pp. 162–208; M. Eugene Sirmans, 'The Legal Status of the Slave in South Carolina, 1670–1740', *Journal of Southern History*, XXVIII (November 1962), pp. 470–71; Pitman, *Development of British West Indies*, p. 621. The 1730s were years of acute crisis in the Caribbean. Beginning in 1734 there was almost continuing warfare with the maroons of Jamaica; in 1736 there were mass executions of slaves on both Jamaica and Antigua after the discovery of planned revolts. This incidence of violence was not matched again until the 1760s. It should be noted that there was a direct correspondence between slave violence in the Caribbean and the number of published articles and pamphlets dealing with the problem of slavery.

26. Accounts in British periodicals were often written by colonial correspondents who expressed no sympathy for the Negroes and who blamed the evil consequences of the slave trade on the mother country (see the *London Magazine*, VI [April 1737], pp. 190–91; the *Gentleman's Magazine*, VII [1737], pp. 187, 215–17; *Gentleman's Magazine*, XI [1741], pp. 145–57, 186).

27. Donnan (ed.), *Documents*, IV, pp. 131–2. The quotation is from a letter to the Earl of Egmont, one of the Georgia Trustees, approving of the prohibition of slavery in that province.

England had forced an excess of slaves upon the helpless sugar-growers. Jamaicans thought the villains were absentee proprietors who hired cruel overseers and who refused to balance their purchases of slaves by encouraging white immigration. According to Governor Edward Trelawny, the island's preservation depended on increasing the number of white settlers, and yet Britain opposed extra taxes on absentee owners who failed to provide one white inhabitant for every thirty slaves.[28] Later in the century Cuban slave holders at once called for cheaper slaves and blamed the *assiento* system for the problems arising from a growing Negro population.[29]

Such a mixture of fears and rationalizations helps us to understand the motives behind the various taxes which colonies imposed on the importation of slaves. Because these duties were often disallowed by England, it was easy for Thomas Jefferson and later historians to picture the continental colonies as the innocent victims of British avarice. But the colonists' intentions seem more questionable when we note, first, that increased duties frequently followed periods of slave unrest and insurrection. Second, even when such taxes were not disallowed by England, they were easily evaded. Negroes destined for New York and Pennsylvania, for example, were often landed in New Jersey, where there were no duties for a period of nearly fifty years. Third, duties were imposed by such colonies as Jamaica, which no one could accuse of being hostile to slavery. Fourth, the restrictive measures were often associated with harsh discriminatory laws against all Negroes. In Massachusetts, for instance, a restrictive duty of four pounds on every imported Negro was part of a 1705 law 'for the Better Preventing of a Spurious and Mixt Issue', which was clearly designed to preserve the 'purity' of white servants and to encourage their immigration. That the law was not intended to injure the slave trade is seen in a provision offering a rebate of the whole

28. *Journals of Assembly of Jamaica*, IV, pp. 181, 221–2. In 1749 the assembly pointed out that the first great revolt in the island originated on the estate of an absentee owner whose overseer had been extremely cruel (see also, Pitman, *Development of British West Indies*, pp. 33–6, 50–51; *London Magazine*, VI [April 1737], p. 191; Ragatz, *Fall of the Planter Class*, pp. 44–7).

29. Hubert T. S. Aimes, *A History of Slavery in Cuba, 1511–1868* ([New York, 1907], pp. 32–3, 52–6, 71).

duty on Negroes re-exported within a year. When British authorities finally gave in to Jamaica's demands for a duty, they suggested that the island's white population might be increased by excluding Negroes from all trades and crafts. The colony responded with a law prohibiting the employment or hiring out of Negro tradesmen or artisans, but it was as unenforceable as a similar measure adopted in 1751 by South Carolina. Much earlier, the Pennsylvania assembly had decided that such a law, though strongly desired by white workers, would be unjust to the owners and employers of slaves.[30]

We may conclude that the colonial demand for cheap labour was often restrained by a fear that excessive numbers of Negroes would inhibit white immigration and endanger public security. In some areas, such as Virginia, an additional motive for restrictive duties can be found in the desire of large planters to increase the value of their slaves and to limit the production of tobacco at a time of surplus crops and low prices.[31] A revenue measure which increased the price of all slaves was naturally preferred to direct poll taxes paid in commodities of declining value. And from Jamaica to Virginia many planters realized that heavy purchases of slaves simply added to colonial debts and hence to the precariousness of the economy. But despite examples of occasional moral protest, there is little evidence, prior to the great conflict between Britain and her colonies, that restrictive duties implied a hostility to slavery itself. It is true that in

30. Donnan (ed.), *Documents*, III, pp. 20, 35, 123, 408; Henry Scofield Cooley, *A Study of Slavery in New Jersey* (Baltimore, 1896), pp. 15–16; Simeon F. Moss, 'The Persistence of Slavery and Involuntary Servitude in a Free State, 1685–1866', *Journal of Negro History*, XXV (January 1950), p. 295; John Codman Hurd, *The Law of Freedom and Bondage in the United States* (Boston, 1858–62), I, p. 284; *Journals of Assembly of Jamaica*, III, pp. 72–3, 335, 337; Bridenbaugh, *Cities in Revolt*, p. 88; Turner, *Negro in Pennsylvania*, p. 5. The Board of Trade was unsympathetic, however, to Virginia's requests for additional duties (Leonard Woods Labaree, *Royal Government in America: A Study of the British Colonial System before 1783* [New Haven, 1930], pp. 62–3).

31. Donnan (ed.), *Documents*, IV, pp. 104–7; Wertenbaker, *Planters of Colonial Virginia*, pp. 129, 131. The traditional view that Virginians were hostile to Negro slavery but were powerless to resist the slave traders, who controlled British colonial policy, is presented by James Ballagh, *History of Slavery in Virginia*, pp. 11–26.

Pennsylvania many Germans and Quakers opposed the introduction of slaves on moral as well as economic grounds. But before 1730, Quaker merchants were actively engaged in importing Negroes from the West Indies, and much of the sluggishness of the market seems to have arisen from the fact that these were often 'refuse' Negroes who proved of little value to their buyers.[32] As late as 1761, when Pennsylvania set the duty at ten pounds, the law exempted new settlers who brought Negroes into the colony. Nor on the surface was Pennsylvania in advance of South Carolina, where an act of 1760 was apparently intended to bring a temporary halt to all importation of slaves. Yet by the 1760s and early 1770s the motives of colonists were beginning to diverge. In Jamaica as well as Massachusetts, legislators pressed for additional duties on Negroes.[33] But while the Jamaicans had no thought of stopping the flood of Negroes from Africa, the northern colonists were beginning to see a fundamental contradiction between slavery and their sense of national purpose. Later on we shall explore some of the cultural and intellectual sources of this divergence.

It is important to note, however, that even the conflict between fear and avarice brought occasional glimpses of the larger moral dilemma of slavery. In 1716 a tract written in Massachusetts on the question of banks and economic growth made the conventional charge that Negro slaves were an obstacle to white immigration, but then went on to cite the proverb that the receiver is as bad as the thief, and to ask, 'Are not we of this Country guilty of that Violence, Treachery

32. The Quakers will be discussed in detail later. For the difficulties in assessing the motives behind Pennsylvania's restrictive duties, see DuBois, *Suppression of African Slave Trade*, pp. 25–6; Turner, *Negro in Pennsylvania*, pp. 3–6, 8–15, 68–70; Wax, 'Quaker Merchants and the Slave Trade', pp. 144–8; Moss, 'Persistence of Slavery', pp. 291–3; Zilversmit, 'Slavery and its Abolition', p. 67. Some Quaker merchants were still selling slaves in Philadelphia in the 1750s.

33. Turner, *Negro in Pennsylvania*, p. 6; DuBois, *Suppression of African Slave Trade*, p. 219; *Journals of Assembly of Jamaica*, VI, p. 504; Ragatz, *Fall of the Planter Class*, p. 242. A bill to prohibit the importation of slaves failed to pass in Rhode Island in 1770, and a similar bill was rejected by the governor of Massachusetts in 1771. In 1774 Britain disallowed an additional Jamaican duty of two pounds per head, but in that year Rhode Island and Connecticut both prohibited slave imports.

and Bloodshed, that is daily made use of to obtain them?' The author even suggested that the colony would benefit more from a law abolishing slavery over the next twenty years than from police regulations designed to protect the public security.[34] Peter Fontaine, rector of Westover parish in Virginia, also moved beyond the usual complaint that slavery discouraged the settlement of white merchants and artisans. Though he blamed the slave trade on England, he recognized that the purchase of Negroes drew Virginians 'into the original sin and curse of the country'. And yet life in the colony would be impossible without slaves. Fontaine could conclude only that poverty was Virginia's best protection, since profits always led to increased demands for slaves. He must have known, however, that America had not been founded on ascetic ideals.[35]

One of the most curious expressions of mixed anxieties appeared in an anonymous *Essay Concerning Slavery, and the Danger Jamaica is Expos'd to from the Too Great Number of Slaves*, which was published sometime in the mid eighteenth century. The author was chiefly alarmed over repeated insurrections and the certainty of disaster if slaves were not more carefully managed. He appealed to Parliament to stop the importation of slaves, in the interest of imperial security. He was as hostile towards Negroes as towards the rich planters who greedily yelped for greater supplies of cheap labour. It was because Negroes had been allowed to practise honourable trades that the white population had diminished. If the lazy household Negroes were turned out to the fields and replaced by free white men, the island would be much better off. And there would be no need for the African trade if masters would beat their barren Negro women once a year, and offer small rewards to those who bore children. Despite such prejudices, the author presents an imaginary debate between a planter and an army officer who admits to being a madman, visionary and enthusiast. The officer refutes certain philosophical justifications for slavery with the delight of a self-taught man, paying particular attention to the absurdity of Locke's theory of

34. Albert Matthews, 'Protests against Slavery in Massachusetts', *Publications of the Colonial Society of Massachusetts* (VIII, *Transactions*, 1902–4, Boston, 1906), p. 288.

35. Donnan (ed.), *Documents*, IV, pp. 142–3.

bondage as a continuation of war. And if the author himself accepts the necessity of Negro labour in tropical colonies, he is uneasily aware that 'whatever Nation in *America* declares first for Liberty, and absolutely abolishes Slavery, must be Masters of the whole Continent, or as much of it as they please'.[36]

Of all the French, British, Dutch, Spanish and Portuguese colonies in the New World, only Georgia, the refuge for debtors and orphans, attempted to avoid the stain of Negro slavery. A possible exception can be made for another refuge, Rhode Island, where the General Court at Warwick, meeting on 19 May 1652, ordered that no 'blacke mankind or white' were to serve longer than ten years 'from the time of their cominge within the liberties of this Collonie'. But there is no evidence that this remarkable law, framed when the commissioners of Newport and Portsmouth were absent, was ever seriously enforced.[37] If Georgia and Rhode Island were envisioned for a time as sanctuaries for the oppressed, the one became the original seat of the Cotton Kingdom, and the other the capital of North America's trade in slaves.

Most of the problems and conflicting desires raised by American slavery were concentrated explosively in a brief fourteen years of Georgia's history. The promoters of the colony had been moved by that English blend of utilitarian shrewdness and concern for human suffering which was ultimately based on a conviction that practical philanthropy furthered both profit and the best interest of the empire. By 1730 various benevolent groups in Britain had established tra-

36. *An Essay Concerning Slavery, and the Danger Jamaica is Expos'd to from the Too Great Number of Slaves, and the Too Little Care that is Taken to Manage Them* (London, n.d.), introd., pp. 2–3, 5, 9–10, 17–24, 34–6, 42–4, 60. George Metcalf gives the publication date as 1757 (*Royal Government and Political Conflict in Jamaica, 1729–1783* [London, 1965], p. 5). The date 1745 is suggested by the New York Public Library card.

37. Donnan (ed.), *Documents*, III, pp. 108–9; Winthrop D. Jordan, 'The Influence of the West Indies on the Origins of New England Slavery', *William and Mary Quarterly*, 3rd ser., XVIII (April 1961), pp. 343–50. The law provided that children under fourteen at the time of their arrival in the colony were to serve to the age of twenty-four.

ditions and lines of communication which enabled men of different background to cooperate in projects extending far beyond the limits of local charity.[38] Whether concerned with converting Indians and Negroes to Christianity, or with the plight of imprisoned debtors and European refugees, these philanthropists could draw on the practical experience of missionaries, soldiers and statesmen. Hard-headed and well-informed, they could not sympathize with the suffering debtor without also recognizing that when imprisoned, he was utterly useless to the State. In a colony south of the Savannah River, the unproductive classes might furnish Britain with silk and wine, for which she depended on Catholic Europe; and they would also erect a buffer state between Carolina and Spanish Florida. Founded on the principles of strict mercantilism, such a colony could avoid the shortcomings of Jamaica, where unequal distribution kept land unproductive; and of New England, whose interests were often at odds with the mother country. Indeed, as a promotional tract suggested, Georgia would be absolutely dependent on England for supplies and credit, and would thus serve as a counterweight to other colonies which might tend towards independence.[39] And as a stabilizing force and buffer zone, Georgia would obviously be more effective if she were free from the danger of slave revolt.

It has been said that James Oglethorpe, who was Deputy Governor of the Royal African Company and who owned slaves on a Carolina plantation, was an abolitionist at heart. It is true that he said, during the later controversy over admitting slaves to Georgia, that a colony founded to bring relief to the distressed of Europe should not be the cause of enslaving thousands of free Africans.[40] And among the

---

38. Edgar L. Pennington, *Thomas Bray's Associates and Their Work Among the Negroes* (Worcester, Mass., 1939); J. Harry Bennett, Jr, *Bondsmen and Bishops: Slavery and Apprenticeship on the Codrington Plantation of Barbados, 1710–1838* (Berkeley, 1958), *passim.*

39. 'Reasons for Establishing the Colony of Georgia, with Regard to the Trade of Great Britain' (London, 1733), printed in *Collections of Georgia Historical Society,* I (Savannah, 1840), pp. 204–38.

40. Donnan (ed.), *Documents,* IV, p. 592; see also Ruth Scarborough, *The Opposition to Slavery in Georgia prior to 1860* (Nashville, Tenn., 1933), pp. 59–62. In 1776, long after his part in founding Georgia, Oglethorpe

groups contributing knowledge and organization to the Georgia project, there was a tradition of interest in educating and Christianizing Negro slaves. Yet slaves were not excluded from Georgia by the charter of 1732, but by a special law of 1735 'for rendering the Colony of Georgia more Defencible'. The most powerful argument behind this prohibitive act, which was stoutly opposed by upholders of the slave trade, such as the Earl of Dartmouth, was that Georgia would lose its strategic military value if the Spanish in Saint Augustine could incite slaves to desert or revolt.[41] Later, after he had failed to capture Saint Augustine, Oglethorpe thought this view was dramatically confirmed by the success of the Spanish in fomenting slave insurrections in Carolina and New York, and a 'mutinous temper' among the inhabitants of Savannah. He was certain it was the plot of the Spanish to undermine Georgia with slaves and liquor.

In 1732, however, there were other weighty reasons for making Georgia the first non-slaveholding colony. As we have seen, the West Indies and South Carolina had been unsuccessful in their efforts to attract white settlers, and if the presence of Negroes should deter white immigration to Georgia, the colony would lose its very purpose. Moreover, the British market had been flooded with tropical produce, and it was undesirable that a new colony add to the surfeit. Experience had shown that slavery produced an idle class of wealthy but debt-ridden planters, who aroused the envy and hostility of those who could not afford to purchase Negroes. Such a society obviously conflicted with the vision of a frugal and gratefully dependent peasantry whose steady labour would furnish Britain with silk and wine.[42]

But we should not allow these practical considerations to obscure

---

wrote to Granville Sharp that slavery was contrary to the Gospel as well as to the fundamental law of England.

41. *The Colonial Records of the State of Georgia*, III (Atlanta, 1905), p. 410; Donnan (ed.), *Documents*, IV, pp. 587–8; Scarborough, *Opposition to Slavery*, pp. 1–19. There was some question whether the law excluded Negroes who were not slaves. For the views of the Trustees, see *Colonial Records of Georgia*, V (Atlanta, 1913), pp. 378–9; *Collections of Georgia Historical Society*, II (Savannah, 1842), pp. 279–81.

42. Donnan (ed.), *Documents*, IV, pp. 587–92; *Collections of Georgia Historical Society*, III (Savannah, 1873), pp. 120–22.

the central point. Slavery had not been excluded from the ideal societies of Plato and Thomas More, nor from the social experiments of Las Casas, the English Puritans or William Penn. The founders of Georgia not only envisioned a state whose economic, social and military purposes would be defeated by slavery, but they thought it practicable to build such a state on the border of South Carolina. This is not to say that they sought to undermine the social system of the older colony. One of the backers of Georgia praised the 'excellent laws' drafted by Locke and Shaftesbury, which had of course provided for slaves in Carolina. The prohibition act of 1735 allowed Carolinians to reclaim Negroes who escaped into Georgia. Other Negroes found in the colony were to be seized and sold, and the Trustees were to receive the proceeds.[43] But although these measures hardly suggested hostility to the principle of human bondage, the fact remains that in 1735 some Englishmen saw slavery as basically incompatible with one of the potentialities of America. If courts of law had not yet found the air of England too pure for slaves to breathe, the soil of Georgia would be free.

Unfortunately, even by 1735 some of the inhabitants of Georgia had decided that the soil could never be productive unless tilled by slaves. The demand increased in succeeding years. Prominent citizens, such as Robert Williams and Thomas Stephens, felt that the colony would sink into ruin if not supplied with Negroes. The eighteen illiterates who put their marks on a petition to the Trustees in 1738 apparently thought that their lives would be happier if they could acquire slaves.[44] But this rising clamour also brought dissent, and thus provoked one of the first public controversies in America over the expediency and justice of Negro slavery. Later controversies would often centre on the means of reforming or abolishing slave systems originating in the past; but in America the great debate would begin and end with essentially the same momentous question: should individuals be allowed to bring slaves into areas which had not had slaves before?

43. *Collections of Georgia Historical Society*, I, p. 231; Scarborough, *Opposition to Slavery*, p. 9; Donnan (ed.), *Documents*, IV, p. 588.
44. *Collections of Georgia Historical Society*, II, pp. 262–3; *Colonial Records of Georgia*, III, pp. 424–6.

The sturdy Germans of Ebenezer did not want slavery because, as they said in a petition, Negroes would rob their houses and fruitful gardens. Eighteen Scots of Darien assured the Trustees in 1739 that, contrary to the claims of an earlier petition from Savannah, slaves would endanger the colony's security, bring mounting debts, and burden the inhabitants with guard duty. But by now the examination of slavery's inconveniences had led to a new angle of vision, for the Highlanders reinforced their case by adding:

It's shocking to human Nature, that any Race of Mankind, and their Posterity, should be sentenced to perpetual Slavery; nor in Justice can we think otherwise of it, than they are thrown amongst us to be our Scourge one Day or another for our sins; and as Freedom to them must be as dear as to us, what a Scene of Horror must it bring about! And the longer it is unexecuted, the bloody Scene must be the greater.[45]

Various inhabitants of Darien later swore that this petition had been written by one of Oglethorpe's officers to lend support to the Trustees' position, and that the signers had been bribed by promises of cattle and servants.[46] The number of Georgians who opposed slavery was admittedly small, and in the last analysis it does not really matter how many of the eighteen Scots believed in the sentiments of the above passage. There is no reason to doubt the author's sincerity in writing two sentences that went far beyond the position of the Trustees. By combining the ideal of natural rights with Biblical guilt and catastrophism, he struck a chord that would reverberate through the anti-slavery movements and culminate in Lincoln's Second Inaugural Address.

But the controversy in Georgia seldom rose above the level of expediency. George Whitefield was certain that neither the colony nor his beloved Orphan House could succeed without the labour of Negro slaves. He acknowledged that the slave trade was conducted 'in a wrong way', but since there was nothing he could do about that, he would be most fortunate, he said, if he could purchase a good number of Negroes and make their lives comfortable. If the great revivalist considered cruelty to slaves to be unchristian, he confessed in 1751

45. *Colonial Records of Georgia*, III, pp. 427–31.
46. *Collections of Georgia Historical Society*, II, pp. 113–20.

that he had no doubts on the lawfulness of slaveholding. Indeed, the providence of God had appointed certain climates, such as Georgia, for the labour of Negroes, who could thus be brought under the paternal care of Christian masters. After criticizing the Trustees for their ignorance of God's designs, Whitefield finally realized his ambition and acquired a plantation and some seventy-five slaves.[47]

His views, however, were vigorously contested by the Reverend John Martin Bolzius, of Ebenezer, who was deeply shocked when he heard of Whitefield's pro-slavery petition. It would be better, Bolzius said, to abandon the Orphan House entirely than to use it as an excuse for Negro slaves. And if Whitefield was sincere in his longing to convert the heathen, which Bolzius doubted, there was room for considerable effort in South Carolina. But although Bolzius predicted that slavery would add to the sins of the land, his opposition was rooted in a conviction that Negroes would endanger the colony and corrupt or impoverish the whites. In Charles Town, he said, white labourers were unable to compete with slaves. Forced to migrate to remote areas, they soon found their agricultural produce was undersold by that of slaveholders who were closer to markets, and whose production costs were lower. In order to survive, the Carolinian yeoman was obliged to buy slaves on credit or seek employment as an overseer. And Bolzius added: 'I hear the Negroes in Carolina learn all Sorts of trade, which takes away the bread of a poor white trades'man Like wise.' Still clinging to the original ideal of a refuge for the industrious poor and the persecuted Protestants of Europe, the good minister insisted that Georgia summers were no hotter than those in parts of Germany, and that his diligent Salzburgers could help support the colony by producing hoops, staves and shingles for the West Indian market. But even John Martin Bolzius finally gave in, and accepted Negro slavery as a necessity.[48]

By 1748 the utlilitarian arguments for prohibition had lost their force. The colony's economic development had failed to meet original expectations. Little effort had been made to prevent Carolina

47. *Colonial Records of Georgia*, XXIV (Atlanta, 1915), pp. 436–7; Scarborough, *Opposition to Slavery*, pp. 69–71.

48. *Colonial Records of Georgia*, XXIV, pp. 434–43; Scarborough, *Opposition to Slavery*, pp. 64–7.

planters from bringing slaves across the Savannah River, or to stop
the institution from creeping southwards. Indeed, Savannah was receiving shipments of Negroes directly from Africa.[49] On 16 May
1719 the Trustees finally recognized the hopelessness of their stand.
A petition from President William Stephens and his Assistants admitted that the law of 1735 had not been enforced; and after noting
that many Carolinians had applied for grants of land, on the condition that they be permitted to bring their slaves, the petitioners
concluded that any further efforts to observe the law would depopulate the colony. Aware that continuing prohibition was opposed
by the Board of Trade, by Horace Walpole and by a growing number
in Parliament, the Trustees decided to ask for repeal.[50]

The new act, which received the royal assent in 1750, anticipated
measures demanded some seventy years later by British reformers.
There was to be a registry of all Negroes born, sold or imported;
slaves were to be instructed in Christianity and protected from inhumane treatment. The original purposes of the colony were supposedly preserved by requiring slaveholders to maintain one white
worker for every four Negroes, and by forbidding racial inter-
marriage and the hiring out of slaves. But British authorities were no
more able to regulate colonial slavery than to prohibit its spread. The
New World might offer opportunities to the debtor or persecuted
Protestant, but the experience of Georgia seemed to suggest that
slavery and opportunity often advanced together.

'The Negroe-Trade,' wrote Malachy Postlethwayt, 'and the natural

49. Hurd, *Law and Freedom*, I, pp. 309–10; Scarborough, *Opposition to
Slavery*, pp. 45–50.
50. *Colonial Records of Georgia*, I, 530–31; Donnan (ed.), *Documents*,
IV, pp. 608–11. While Walpole favoured admitting slaves to Georgia, he
wrote to Horace Mann in 1750 that 'it chills one's blood' to think of the
number of wretches sold in the British colonies alone; and that Parliament
had been 'pondering methods to make more effectual that horrid traffic of
selling Negroes'. This vague and essentially meaningless protest acquired
more point four years later when he criticized the supposedly Christian charity of Christopher Codrington, who had bequeathed plantations and hundreds of slaves to the Society for the Propagation of the Gospel (*The Letters
of Horace Walpole* [Oxford, 1903], II, pp. 432–3; III, p. 349).

Consequences resulting from it, may be justly esteemed an inexhaustible Fund of Wealth and Naval Power to this Nation.'[51] This dictum of an eminent political economist scarcely needed demonstration in the mid eighteenth century, when Britain's attention was focused on the Caribbean. Yet the economic value of colonial slavery had not always appeared so obvious. In 1624, for example, William Usselinx had advised the king of Sweden that his colonies would provide better markets and produce more for the mother country if they were settled with free Europeans.[52] By 1668, however, Josiah Child, the mercantilist and future governor of the East India Company, could answer such views by observing that the emigration of white labourers only deprived a nation of workers and consumers; in the West Indies, on the other hand, a small number of Englishmen controlled an enormous force of Negroes whose labour stimulated trade with England and hence increased domestic wealth, employment and population. Despite his changing opinions on the questions of monopoly and free trade, Charles Davenant remained unshaken in his conviction that of all branches of foreign commerce, the slave trade was the one most 'naturally adapted' to the interests of Britain and her colonies.[53]

For Postlethwayt, as for Davenant and other influential economists, the African trade had those characteristics of the divinely contrived system which so appealed to the eighteenth-century mind.

51. [Malachy Postlethwayt], *The National and Private Advantages of the African Trade Considered: Being an Enquiry how far it Concerns the Trading Interest of Great Britain, Effectually to Support and Maintain the Forts and Settlements in Africa; Belonging to the Royal African Company of England* ... (London, 1746), pp. 1–2.

52. Lorenzo D. Turner, 'Anti-Slavery Sentiment in American Literature Prior to 1865', *Journal of Negro History*, XIV (October 1929), p. 385 n.; Mary S. Locke, *Anti-Slavery in America from the Introduction of the African Slaves to the Prohibition of the Slave Trade* (Boston, 1901), pp. 9–10.

53. Josiah Child, *A New Discourse of Trade, Wherein is Recommended Several Weighty Points Relating to Companies of Merchants* ... (2nd ed., London, 1694), pp. 191, 215–16; Davenant, *Political and Commercial Works*, II, pp. 37–8; V, pp. 73–88, 138. Child observed that slavery had not had similarly beneficial consequences for the Spanish, who had destroyed large numbers of Negroes by concentrating on gold and silver mining, to the neglect of agriculture and commerce (pp. 203–4).

It not only provided Britain with a favourable balance of trade, but surplus Negroes could be sold to the Spanish in exchange for bullion. The African markets stimulated both shipping and manufactures. And where the loss of white labourers would weaken the British economy, an increase of slaves in the plantations simply added to total capital. Davenant took pains to answer the argument that monopolies were inconsistent with the natural rights and common liberties of mankind; he felt no need to consider the relevance of these ideals to slavery. It was a system, then, from which everyone benefited. And precisely because of its supreme value, the traffic was the testing point in the world struggle for empire. France had shown her wisdom in giving the slave trade a direct subsidy.[54]

In France Jean-François Melon, a pioneer economist who was highly praised by Voltaire, had gone even further in his defence of slavery. He conceded that to non-philosophical minds the institution might well appear as an evil. But just as the perfections of the universe justified evils that outraged men incapable of comprehending the whole, so the good of the nation justified apparent injustices. Making use of Locke's principle of the association of ideas, Melon showed how slavery had acquired a bad name. Because slavery originated in the violence of war, it had been associated with barbarism. But when considered as a social and economic institution, regulated by laws and conventions such as the *Code Noir*, it was clearly superior to free labour. It conformed, indeed, to the natural structure of the universe, which evidenced an infinity of gradations and subordinations, of which slavery was only a part. Since true principles were uniform in application, Melon acknowledged that even in Europe slavery would be preferable to a system which deprived the worker of economic and social security. But the prejudices of education would prevent Europeans from enslaving their neighbours, and to Melon, who considered mulattoes a dangerous deformity, the

54. [Postlethwayt], *National and Private Advantages*, pp. 3–7, 20–39; Postlethwayt, *Britain's Commercial Interest Explained and Improved; in a Series of Dissertations on Several Branches of Her Trade and Commerce; Containing a Candid Enquiry into the Secret Causes of the Present Misfortunes of the Nation* (London, 1757), I, p. 437; II, pp. 112–13, 148, 211–12; Davenant, *Political and Commercial Works*, V, p. 148. Postlethwayt's reservations on the slave trade will be discussed later.

introduction of Negroes was out of the question. Perhaps no thinker so well demonstrated how the principles of the early Enlightenment could be applied to a defence of human bondage.[55]

One may assume that, when profits from the slave trade were reputed to run as high as 300 per cent, it was relatively easy to associate the system with the beneficent order of the universe. The merchants of Havre, Nantes, Saint-Malo and Bordeaux, who aspired to culture and who patronized the French Enlightenment, could not forget that the prosperity of these booming ports rested on sugar and slaves. This raises the question whether the colonial labour system would seem less in harmony with the laws of nature if its economic value appeared to diminish. It has been persuasively argued that Britain became disenchanted with the slave trade only when her own Caribbean colonies were on the decline, and when it was very much in the interest of France to increase the labour force in Saint Domingue.[56] There can be little doubt that colonial slavery was of greater importance to the British economy in 1750 than in 1789, or that the reverse was true of France. Yet we should greatly oversimplify the problem if we were to see too close a correlation between economic profit and social values, or to conclude that anti-slavery attitudes were a direct response to economic change. Since men tended to associate slavery with the functioning of a vast system of production and exchange we need rather to ask what elements of strength or weakness in the system might affect the image of slavery held by an essentially non-slaveholding society?

In the eighteenth century Europe was in search of foreign markets, and the African princes and traders showed considerable ingenuity in

55. Jean-François Melon, 'Essai politique sur le commerce', in *Economistes financiers du XVIIIe siècle* (Paris, 1851), pp. 680–82.

56. Martin, *Histoire de l'esclavage dans les colonies françaises*, pp. 140–42; Williams, *Capitalism and Slavery, passim*. Various historians, in attempting to refute Williams's sweeping thesis that colonial slavery was an inevitable phase of commercial capitalism which aroused opposition only when it had served its function, have shown that he exaggerates the role of the slave trade and slavery in accumulating capital for the industrial revolution, and that he is unfair to William Pitt and the abolitionists; it is more difficult, however, to get around the simple fact that no country thought of abolishing the slave trade until its economic value had considerably declined

devising ways to maximize the inflow of European goods. A slaving captain was often obliged not only to pay anchorage fees and taxes to the king, but to hire interpreters, butlers, messengers, gong beaters, trunk keepers and washerwomen at various points along a single coast or river. The special fees and required presents multiplied during long weeks of haggling and negotiation. Unfortunately, while African tribal power came ever more to depend on European goods, particularly on firearms, slaves were the only commodity greatly desired by Europeans. This incessant demand and competition, coupled with the evolution of a highly specialized system, led naturally to an increase in the price of slaves. European traders found it difficult to pass on these mounting prices to their American customers. Though they tended to move south and east in their search for more and cheaper Negroes, only the most prosperous American agriculture could continue to subsidize, as it were, the export of European goods to Africa.[57]

Nevertheless, from 1730 to 1775 the value of British exports to Africa increased by some 400 per cent. Birmingham iron manufacturers, Liverpool gunmakers, refiners, cutlers, dyers, weavers, packers, coopers, fishers, shipwrights, ropemakers and sailmakers felt that their interests were sufficiently identified with the slave trade to petition at various times in its favour. Before the American Revolution approximately one third of the British merchant fleet was engaged in transporting fifty thousand Negroes a year to the New World. Closely linked with the high realms of insurance and banking, the trade rested on a wide base of speculative investment involving large and petty capitalists, and the holders of annuities and mortgages. In the England of George II, with its latitudinarian temper of compromise and worldly wisdom, the slave trader was not only socially respectable, but his business was a recognized route to gentility, and was officially approved by the Board of Trade, the navy and the nobility. Money accumulated from the African trade or from

57. Donnan (ed.), *Documents*, II, pp. 593–6; *Gentleman's Magazine*, XXXIII (1763), pp. 330–31; *The New Cambridge History: VII, The Old Régime, 1713–1763* (ed. by J. O. Lindsay, Cambridge, 1957), pp. 514–28, 567–73; J. D. Fage, *An Introduction to the History of West Africa* (Cambridge, 1955), pp. 77–80.

West Indian plantations bought peerages and political power; and before the mid eighteenth century the men whose income was derived from the slave system had become a formidable pressure group in British politics.[58]

The effects of a system which ramified throughout the British economy were felt scarcely less in North America. Apart from the exports of slave-grown rice, tobacco and indigo, on which the economies of the Southern colonies depended, and apart from the slave ships of Rhode Island and Massachusetts, the North American colonies sent to the West Indies a large proportion of their exports of fish, oats, corn, flour and lumber, and virtually all of their exported peas, beans, hogs and horses. The trade contributed greatly to the prosperity of New England and the Middle colonies, and without it the expansion of the slave trade and West Indian plantations would hardly have been possible. It was, indeed, an illicit trade with North America that enabled the French colonies to expand production until, by 1789, the exports of Saint Domingue alone were more than one-third greater than those of the combined British West Indies. For their part, the assembly of Rhode Island claimed in 1764 that the colony was utterly dependent on molasses from the French and Dutch colonies; when distilled into rum, it had furthered Britain's interests by replacing French brandy in the slave markets of Africa.[59]

58. *New Cambridge History*, VII, pp. 25–32, 572–3; Donnan (ed.), *Documents*, II, pp. 96–8, 602–12; Pitman, *Development of British West Indies*, p. 66; Williams, *Capitalism and Slavery*, pp. 34–7, 92–5, 104–5; James High, 'The African Gentleman: A Chapter in the Slave Trade', *Journal of Negro History*, XLIV (October 1959), pp. 287–307; Lillian M. Penson, 'The London West India Interest in the Eighteenth Century', *English Historical Review*, XXXVI (July 1921), pp. 373–82. The West Indian bloc, which met for a time at the Jamaica Coffee House in London, achieved notable success with the Molasses Act of 1733 and the Sugar Acts of 1739 and 1764.

59. Ragatz, *Fall of the Planter Class*, pp. 82–9; Pitman, *Development of British West Indies*, pp. vii, 124–6; [Long], *History of Jamaica*, I, 491–3; Ludwell L. Montague, *Haiti and the United States, 1714–1938* (Durham, N.C., 1940), pp. 29–30; Williams, *Capitalism and Slavery*, pp. 108–11; Donnan (ed.), *Documents*, II, p. xxxiii; III, pp. 203–5. France was eager to sell molasses to North America because rum was excluded from the home market in order to protect the brandy industry.

But this system which seemed of equal benefit to New England fisherman, to Pennsylvania farmer, to Jamaican planter and to British manufacturer, and so to be in conformity with the delicately balanced laws of nature, was in reality built on precarious ground. Negro slaves might well have been the cheapest labour available in large quantities, but notwithstanding occasional spectacular profits, the slave trade was not always a route to wealth.[60] From the beginning, it involved awesome risks. It was often difficult to procure a cargo of slaves without protracted delays, which meant a waste of provisions, sickness and mortality. Ship captains tended to disregard frightful lessons from the past, and to gamble on losing a large proportion of their cargoes by overcrowding.[61] In addition to the frequent losses of the Middle Passage, there were innumerable difficulties arising from a cumbersome system of credit and exchange. Initially, the greatest profits had come from the return voyage from the West Indies, when ships had been laden with rich tropical produce. But as West Indian planters grew wealthy enough to hire their own agents and factors in England, and as the marketing of sugar on commission became a specialized business in London, the slave ships increasingly returned in ballast.[62] The legendary riches of the triangular trade could prove to be an illusion.

60. Basil Davidson states that French merchants received from the Great Circuit trade 'a regular profit' of 300 per cent (*Black Mother: The Years of the African Slave Trade* [Boston, 1961], p. 63), and J. Gallacher mentions a Liverpool ship earning a 300 per cent profit on a single voyage (*New Cambridge History*, VII, p. 573). Williams says that profits of 100 per cent were not uncommon (*Capitalism and Slavery*, pp. 34–5); Frank J. Klingberg has estimated that the annual profit from the slave trade averaged 24 per cent ('The Evolution of the Humanitarian Spirit in Eighteenth-Century England', *Pennsylvania Magazine of History and Biography*, LXVI [1942], pp. 264–5). The risks and difficulties of the trade are stressed by Davies (*Royal African Company*), and by C. H. Wilson (*New Cambridge History*, VII, pp. 25–32).

61. Donnan (ed.), *Documents*, I, p. 272. The Royal African Company factors at Cape Coast Castle reported to the Company in 1681 that if Captain Woodfin had been content with 400 slaves, he might not have lost 160.

62. R. B. Sheridan, 'The Commercial and Financial Organization of the British Slave Trade, 1750–1807', *Economic History Review*, 2nd ser., XV (December 1958), pp. 249–52; Richard Pares, *War and Trade in the West Indies, 1739–1763* (London, 1963), pp. 10, 123.

The very existence of the slave trade depended, of course, on the prosperity of the West Indies, and this, in turn, depended on the capacity of European markets to absorb tropical produce. To those who have considered slavery in any society as a kind of economic cancer leading inevitably to a depletion of soil and capital, the progressive decline of the British West Indies from the time of the American Revolution to the 1820s has appeared as a natural pattern, later repeated in the American South.[63] It is certainly true that, in both the West Indies and American South, Negro slavery made possible a system of speculative agriculture which led to wasteful exhaustion of soil, to rapid development of new lands, to mounting debts, to a restriction of local markets, and to a lack of capital formation. One may note that these symptoms have not been confined to slave societies. But for our purposes the important point is that Negro slavery has been associated with systems whose tempting profits have been accompanied by slow economic and cultural stagnation. In

63. See especially Herman Merivale, *Lectures on Colonization and Colonies* (London, 1861), pp. 305–9; Phillips, *American Negro Slavery*, pp. 65–6, 344–401. There is, of course, an extensive literature on the profitability of slave labour. For a general survey, see Harold D. Woodman, 'The Profitability of Slavery: A Historical Perennial', *Journal of Southern History*, XXIX (August 1963), pp. 303–25. Phillips summarizes the views of J. E. Cairnes, Arthur H. Gibson and Achille Loria, and for himself concludes: 'The slaveholding regime kept money scarce, population sparse and land values accordingly low; it restricted the opportunities of men of both races, and it kept many of the natural resources of the Southern country neglected. But it kept the main body of labour controlled, provisioned and mobile' (p. 401). For modern arguments that slavery was profitable in itself, at least in certain situations, see Stampp, *Peculiar Institution*, pp. 383–418; Alfred H. Conrad and John R. Meyer, 'The Economics of Slavery in the Ante-Bellum South', *Journal of Political Economy*, LXVI (April 1958), pp. 95–130; Paul W. Gates, *The Farmer's Age: Agriculture, 1815–1860* (New York, 1960), pp. 154–5. But Eugene D. Genovese has recently challenged the Stampp and Conrad-Meyer arguments, and has offered persuasive evidence for the older thesis that slavery impeded the development of capitalism in the South and was responsible for a low productivity of labour, exhaustion of the soil, restricted markets and a retarded development of technology (*The Political Economy of Slavery* [New York, 1965]). Although slavery may well have been profitable for individual planters, it would appear that the system helped to prevent the growth of a balanced and healthy economy.

no country was this more the case than in the British West Indies, where, according to a leading authority, fabulous wealth depended on curtailed production for an artificially protected market.[64]

Richard Pares, in his chronicle of the Pinney family, has revealed both the weaknesses and contributions of the West Indian economy. The sugar plantation was first of all the way to wealth for the self-made man. In a sense, the planter was the prototype for future speculators and industrialists. And like the industrialist who had little desire to become a permanent resident of the mill town he had created, the successful planter lost no time in retreating to England, where he might adopt the life of a west-country squire. If he lived pretentiously, as he often did, he would contribute to the growing prejudice against 'Nabobs' whose astonishing wealth had not been sanctioned by generations of noblesse oblige. Nevertheless, with time a family acquired the manners of polite society, and came to look with considerable distaste on the boorish habits of the managerial society left behind in the colonies, where men cared only for money, duels, lawsuits and cockfighting, and where children were hopelessly spoiled. Unfortunately, it was usually necessary to return temporarily to America if one's estates, and thus one's income, were not to be lost.

Absenteeism has usually been cited as a principal cause of the decline of the West Indies; and yet the separation of ownership and management has come to characterize modern industry. No doubt many of the attorneys, as they were called, who were left in charge of West Indian estates, were either incompetent or were interested only in returning to England after squeezing sufficient income from a plantation. But the chief cause of difficulty would seem to have been that many plantation owners expected to live the serene life of country nobles, aloof from the cares of the speculative, capitalistic environment which gave them their wealth. Confident that the West Indian goose would continue to lay golden eggs, they gave little thought to the need for expanding markets, for technological innovation, or for overcoming wasteful practices. When profits declined as a result of falling prices and mounting costs, they speculated in shipping, the sugar commission business or West Indian mortgages. Finally, when

64. Ragatz, *Fall of the Planter Class*, p. viii.

plantations could scarcely pay interest charges on swollen debts, the successful proprietors, such as the Pinneys, transferred their capital to industry and railroads.[65]

If the system provided an initial thrust for the economies of Europe and North America, the society it left behind was a burnt-out shell. The profits taken from tropical agriculture had gone either to Britain or of the purchase of additional slaves. Of schools, roads and welfare institutions the West Indies were virtually destitute.[66] Unlike the American South, they even lacked a substantial population of poor and middle-class whites. Here, one might conclude, was the pure form of American speculative exploitation, unmitigated by the American ideal of creating a more perfect society. And yet many boom areas, many mining and factory towns, have shared a similar fate. The visitor to Barbados or Guadeloupe would find it difficult to believe that they were once fountains of the wealth of nations; but the same would be true of dozens of forgotten shabby towns in Pennsylvania, Colorado and California. Overvalued at first, it was the misfortune of such areas to be finally abandoned as decayed wastelands. And if in the West Indies and American South the slave was not the prime cause of such misfortune, as has often been claimed, he was certainly its victim.

The rise and fall of the American slave colonies in the eighteenth century was closely related to the international struggle for power.

65. Richard Pares, *A West-India Fortune* (London, 1950), pp. 19–20, 70–77, 111–19, 141; Ragatz, *Fall of the Planter Class*, pp. 54–8, 65–6; W. L. Burn, *Emancipation and Apprenticeship in the British West Indies* (London, 1937), pp. 28–9, 36–7, 46–7. The Hibberts were another family whose wealth, made originally from the slave trade and Jamaican plantations, went into the London sugar commission business and Manchester cotton manufacturing (Sheridan, 'Commercial and Financial Organization', pp. 253–63). While it would be an exaggeration to see the slave trade as furnishing the principal source of capital for the industrial revolution, Paul Mantoux concludes: 'The growth of Lancashire, of all English counties the one most deserving to be called the cradle of the factory system, depended first of all on the development of Liverpool and of her trade' (*The Industrial Revolution in the Eighteenth Century* [rev. ed., tr. by Marjorie Vernon, New York, 1929], p. 111).

66. Ragatz, *Fall of the Planter Class*, pp. 9–36.

We can give only scant attention to this infinitely complex subject, hoping simply to identify the principal turning points and directions of change. We may confine our attention largely to Britain and France, since the Dutch Republic, which once had more than held her own against both countries, was seriously weakened by the War of the League of Augsburg and the War of the Spanish Succession; and on the African coast the Dutch made the mistake of allying themselves with the enemies of the powerful Ashantis.

In the great contest between Britain and France each side possessed certain advantages. The British Caribbean islands enjoyed direct commerce with the continental colonies, and British ships took the lead in the slave trade. As we have seen, however, the French were able to exchange molasses for supplies from North America, and when the need arose, they nearly doubled the number of slaves in Saint Domingue in the space of a decade.[67] British capitalists, attracted after 1713 by a great increase in the domestic demand for sugar, invested heavily in West Indian properties and thus stimulated a rapid expansion of sugar production and the slave trade. But this expansion soon revealed two weaknesses from which the British islands would never recover. Continuing investment led to a rising burden of debt and hence to heavy interest charges and higher costs of production. But from 1728 to 1739 expanded production brought a slump in sugar prices which undermined planters operating on a narrow margin of profit. Given a protected and therefore limited domestic market, it was increasingly essential to sell surplus sugar in Europe. But here the British planters and merchants faced another difficulty. Costs of production were lower in the French colonies, party because French planters, who often remained in the islands, could not rely on investment from abroad and were accordingly obliged to draw on surplus for the purchase of lands and slaves. Unburdened by heavy debts, the French were able to undersell the British in continental markets, where sugar prices by mid-century were little more than half those in England. And though some British planters grew rich from selling sugar at high prices in the home market, they recognized that such wealth depended on keeping supply

67. William Law Mathieson, *British Slavery and its Abolition, 1823–1838* (London, 1926), p. 7.

somewhat short of demand. Despite frequent criticism from British consumers, Jamaican planters were not eager to increase the relatively small proportion of land under cultivation; and in the wars with Spain and France, it was Britain's policy to injure foreign competition without acquiring new territories which might glut the domestic market.[68]

By the 1750s it was apparent to some observers that the system of slave trade and West Indian sugar was an inadequate weapon in the economic contest for world power. This was especially true as Anglo-French rivalry intensified in India and North America. Malachy Postlethwayt, whose views provide a significant index to changing conditions, was extremely pessimistic over the apparent failure of Britain's loose and undisciplined colonial régime. Still bitter over Parliament's abandonment of the Royal African Company, he attributed France's improving position in part to the initiative and wise policies of her government, which had provided the slave trade with both regulation and fiscal encouragement. The consequences were cheaper slaves, more land under cultivation and lower sugar prices.[69] But while the slave trade was the basis of French colonial power, it had fallen to a ruinous state in the hands of British 'separate traders', and might collapse entirely unless put on a better foundation.

Without giving specific reasons, Postlethwayt now felt free to profess a personal dislike for the trade and a wish that it might be stopped. This glimmer of latent humanitarianism he quickly extinguished by affirming that 'we shall take things as they are, and reason from them in their present state, and not from that wherein we

68. Pitman, *Development of British West Indies*, pp. 124–6, 132–3; Mathieson, *British Slavery*, pp. 3–6; Ragatz, *Fall of the Planter Class*, pp. 4, 112. In the Stephen Fuller papers at Duke University, tables of the importation of slaves into Jamaica show a great increase in 1725–6, followed by a period of fluctuation; a great expansion occurred, however, from 1741 to 1775, when Jamaica alone imported 262,169 slaves and exported 43,123.

69. Postlethwayt, *Britain's Commercial Interest*, I, pp. 437; II, pp. 110–13, 148–64, 211–12. It should be noted that Postlethwayt was also scornful of the British colonists' spirit of independence and selfish disregard of the good of the empire. His theme was that Britain could not survive without a tighter ship.

could hope them to be'.[70] He acknowledged that it would be absurd to think of giving up the slave trade as long as Negroes were needed to produce sugar that could compete with that of rival colonies. Nevertheless, Postlethwayt's principal interest had shifted from the triangular trade to a grandiose vision of developing markets for British goods in the interior of Africa. Thus far Britain had enjoyed 'the mere skimming of the coasting trade', and was ignorant of the vast natural resources of the continent. Confident that human nature was the same throughout the world, he suggested that Negroes could be brought to see the propriety of decent clothing, to build substantial houses that would require good furniture, and in short to 'live something in the European way', which would clearly be to the advantage of European traders and manufacturers. A similar vision of civilizing Africa would be popularized by William Pitt and effectively linked with the movement to abolish the slave trade. But Postlethwayt saw no necessary conflict between a continuing slave trade and a new inland commerce monopolized by the East India Company. The important point was that Britain's economic future did not lie in sugar and slaves, but in beating France to the interior of Africa.[71]

Postlethwayt's view that the Caribbean was more vital to France than to Britain was confirmed, rather ironically, by the Seven Years' War. England's decision to keep Canada and to restore Guadeloupe and Martinique to France showed that statesmen were becoming aware of the value of North American markets, and also that British planters were powerful enough to block the acquisition of territories which would flood England with tropical produce. When it is recalled that from 1763 to 1773 British imports from the tiny island of Grenada, which was retained, were worth eight times as much as those from Canada, one can appreciate the threat presented by so rich a colony as Guadeloupe. But this triumph of British West Indian interests served only to stimulate an intensive expansion in the French Caribbean which soon left the British colonies far behind. And

70. ibid., II, p. 217.

71. ibid., II, pp. 214–32. The *Monthly Review* (XVII [July–December 1757], p. 312) approved both of Postlethwayt's dislike of the slave trade and his view that it could not be abandoned unless some other means were found of supplying the sugar plantations.

because this French expansion depended in part on an illicit trade with North America, it contributed, as we well know, to increasing strains within the British Empire.[72]

The relative importance of the slave system to France was reinforced by the American Revolution, which deprived England of colonies whose Negro population, by 1790, would be around 65 per cent greater than that of the entire British West Indies. By that date Virginia alone had nearly forty thousand more slaves than Jamaica, though roughly one hundred and sixty thousand less than Saint Domingue.[73] The Revolution also brought famine and acute shortages of supplies in the British Caribbean, as well as widespread unemployment in Liverpool, where the slave ships were forced to rest at their moorings. The Liverpool trade would rapidly revive in the 1780s, but the islands would continue to suffer from the loss of direct commerce with North America. On the other hand, both Saint Domingue and Cuba began to look to the United States as their chief supplier.[74]

In spite of these growing weaknesses, British interests in the Caribbean were superficially stimulated by the acquisition of Grenada, Tobago, Saint Vincent, Dominica and the Grenadines in the Seven Years' War, and Saint Lucia, Berbice, Demerara, Essequibo and Trin-

72. Pitman, *Development of British West Indies*, pp. 334–60; Ragatz, *Fall of the Planter Class*, pp. 111, 125; Williams, *Capitalism and Slavery*, pp. 114–18; Martin, *Histoire de l'esclavage dans les colonies françaises*, pp. 135–9.

73. Estimates of early Negro populations must be treated with even more caution than other population statistics. A comparison of estimates for the years 1789 to 1791 would suggest the following: there were 757,000 Negroes in the United States, at least 92 per cent of whom were slaves; Negroes formed approximately 19.3 per cent of the nation's total population. The 305,000 Negroes in Virginia made up about 40 per cent of that state's population. There were about 455,000 Negroes in the British West Indies, comprising some 86 per cent of the total population. The 260,000 Negroes in Jamaica, of whom some 97.5 per cent were slaves, made up at least 95 per cent of that island's population. Perhaps 6 per cent of Saint Domingue's Negroes were free, but the 450,000 slaves formed well over 90 per cent of the colony's poplation.

74. Donnan (ed.), *Documents*, II, pp. xlvi–lii, 548–57.

idad in the later wars with France, Spain and Holland.[75] From 1763 to the 1820s these new colonies presented successive frontiers for development, and thus tended to resuscitate a declining system. It was the demand for labour in the ceded islands that brought the British slave trade to its peak just before the American Revolution.[76] And yet the speculative development of new territory only aggravated the endemic problems of debt and agricultural surplus. By 1790 George Hibbert estimated the West Indian debt as at least twenty million out of a total capital investment of seventy million pounds. In the face of national war debts and increasing investment in industry, this put a heavy strain on London financial resources. Bankruptcies multiplied in the 1780s as planters suffered from falling sugar prices, rising costs of production and an unprecedented succession of hurricanes. Squeezed from every side, the entire system was threatened with ruin when the revolution in Saint Domingue shut off Europe's leading supply of sugar.[77]

While this destruction of the most profitable Caribbean colony put slavery on the defensive throughout the Western Hemisphere, the initial effect was a world shortage of sugar which stimulated expanded production in the British islands, and in Cuba and Brazil as well. The supply was further augmented when Caribbean planters introduced new and more productive canes. In 1799 the boom came to an abrupt and devastating end. Before the market collapsed, British plantations earned profits of some 10 per cent on investment; by 1807, without even counting interest on capital investment, British sugar sold at a

75. The Caribbean islands actually changed hands many times during the Anglo-French wars from 1756 to 1815; Saint Lucia, for example, was captured by the British no less than four times before being officially added to the empire in 1814.

76. Bryan Edwards, *The History, Civil and Commercial, of the British Colonies in the West Indies* (Philadelphia, 1806), II, p. 258; Pitman, *Development of British West Indies*, p. 70.

77. Sheridan, 'Commercial and Financial Organization', pp. 253–63; Ragatz, *Fall of the Planter Class*, pp. 189–91. In 1789 the Jamaican assembly even used the planters' great debts as evidence of Britain's moral commitment to continue supporting the slave system (*Journals of the Assembly of Jamaica*, VIII [Jamaica, 1804], p. 455).

loss.[78] And though conditions were to improve for a time after 1814, the decline of the British West Indies was irreversible. Their slow descent from riches to poverty could of course be seen as the inevitable result of a sinful system; and yet the rising areas of sugar production – Cuba, Brazil, Louisiana, Mauritius – depended on Negro slaves for their labour.

Along with the great revolutions and wars of the period from 1776 to 1815, the world witnessed a momentous shift in the equilibrium of the American slave system. Before 1776 it had centred in the Leeward and Windward Islands, Jamaica and Saint Domingue, drawing into orbit, as it were, the rice and tobacco colonies of North America. Sustained by European capital and North American provisions, the system had provided Europe with a wealth of tropical produce and had supported both shipping and the marketing of goods in Africa. The 1780s saw acute distress in the British West Indies, and depression in the American South. The latter area would continue to suffer from a long period of low tobacco prices and difficult adjustments to new techniques of rice cultivation.[79] But the revolution in Saint Domingue, which shattered French power in the Caribbean, also opened the way for the expansion of American slavery into Louisiana and, ultimately, Texas. Even by 1815 use of the new cotton gin had led to the extensive cultivation of cotton in the Georgia–Carolina Piedmont and on westward into Mississippi Territory. New links were being formed between an American slave system and the rising textile industries of Europe and New England. And at the same time, slave labour enabled Cuba and Brazil to supply the world with increasing quantities of sugar, coffee and cotton. For nearly three hundred years American Negro slavery had generated images of easy wealth and social decay, of national power and explosive insurrection. By the early nineteenth century one might associate the institution with the violent ruin of Saint Domingue, the debts and depleted soil of Barbados and Virginia; or one might see in the great plantations of Brazil and Mississippi the indispensable foundations of modern industry.

78. Ragatz, *Fall of the Planter Class*, pp. 205 ff, 307.
79. Phillips, *American Negro Slavery*, pp. 150–53.

6

The Legitimacy of Enslavement
and the Ideal of the Christian Servant:
Moral Doubts and Rationalizations

HAVING discussed certain conflicts of interest that were potentially conducive to anti-slavery thought, we may now turn to the field of practical ethics, and ask how American slavery was actually reconciled with the legal and moral values of Christian civilization. As we have seen in chapters 3 and 4, jurists and theologians could rely on a long duration of justifying human bondage; and yet there had been a continuing tension between slavery and Christian ideals. To what extent, then, was this tension aggravated by the violent and brutal character of New World bondage?

At the time of America's conquest, the Christian view of slavery accommodated a series of balanced dualisms. Slavery was contrary to the ideal realm of nature, but was a necessary part of the world of sin; the bondsman was inwardly free and spiritually equal to his master, in things external he was a mere chattel; Christians were brothers, whether slave or free, but pagans deserved in some sense to be slaves. There was a further division in thought between the troublesome question of the origin and legitimacy of a slaveholder's power, and the ideal of the servant in a Christian family where spiritual equality harmonized with outward obedience and authority to provide a model of the fraternal relationship of unequals. Such amiable servitude, originating perhaps in a benign serfdom, could easily be dissociated from the violent act of enslavement. Jurists and theologians might continue to endorse the abstract theory of enslaving prisoners of war, but the crime of man-stealing they universally condemned. To make a man a slave always involved the possibility of sin, especially if the act seemed to break the order and balance of nature; but to hold a bondservant was to exercise an ordinance that was part of the governing structures of the world.

A good example of this compromise can be seen in the revised edition of Polydore Vergil's immensely popular *De inventoribus rerum*, which was published in 1521. Polydore described with approval an English custom which gave symbolic recognition to the underlying equality of men, and which resembled the Roman practice at Saturnalia; at Christmas time it was traditional to elect a servant to preside temporarily over an entire household. But the name *servus*, he tells us, meant something very different when men were enslaved in war. 'By the grace of God' he concludes

we are now nearly all brothers in Christ and citizens of the kingdom of God. While we have servants [*ministros*] in our houses they are not to be called slaves [*servi*]. Still less should slaves be possessed, though many shamelessly do so.[1]

Polydore wished to dissociate Christian servitude from the barbarous slavery of antiquity; but in 1521 Hernándo Cortés was conquering and enslaving Aztecs in Mexico, and Bartolomé de Las Casas was attempting to establish a utopian colony at Cuman, where Indians and Europeans might live together in harmony. The crucial question, then, was whether the enslavement of men of different races in a wild and distant land could be made to conform to the Christian ideal of a household where human inequalities were at once sustained and melted away in a hallowed crucible of love.

In the present chapter we shall be concerned with the application of these traditional dualisms to the new problems of American slavery. We shall see that differing conditions in Africa and America favoured a double standard in judging the enslavement of Negroes and Indians; and that while a small number of Catholic writers questioned the legitimacy of Negro bondage, their acceptance of traditional assumptions and values narrowed the scope of their criticism and precluded any collective efforts to eradicate the institution. Then, in the next chapter, we shall see that Protestants and Catholics

1. Polydore Vergil, *De inventoribus rerum* (Paris, 1528), V, 2, pp. lvi–lvii. The date of the first revised edition was 1521. I am indebted to Denys Hay, of the University of Edinburgh, for supplying me with this passage, which so well illustrates the ambiguities surrounding the word *servus*, which, as we have seen, had been used for 'serf' and 'villein'.

shared many assumptions in their attempts to make American servitude compatible with Christian ideals, but that Protestants encountered greater difficulties in reconciling external subordination with their expanded notions of religious liberty. We shall also find that the Protestants' failure to Christianize Negro bondage brought great internal strains in the equilibrium of values which had long given sanction to human slavery.

The balanced dualisms of which we have spoken were severely taxed by the enslavement of American Indians. We have already mentioned the inclination of explorers and missionaries to see in the New World the ancient ideal of uncorrupted nature, which might be used as a standard for judging the manners and customs of Europe. Whether pictured as a self-denying Stoic, undistracted from truth by vain desires and superfluities, or as a serenely happy Epicurean, content with the ripe abundance of a tropical Eden, the native American appeared to enjoy the innocence and felicity of an era before the fall of man. He at once represented the simple and the exotic, the outlandish custom and the universal virtue. He appealed to the yearning for retirement and repose, and to the desire for a sensuous life uninhibited by clothes, laws and conventions. Above all, this primeval man was seen to be free from distinctions of rank and wealth, and from the avarice that led Europeans to claim gold and land as their private possessions.[2] If slavery was commensurate with sinful society and could never touch the inner freedom of man's soul, how could one legitimately enslave these children of paradise whose external lives seemed to be the spontaneous expression of man's pristine nature?

In actuality, of course, the American Indian fell short of this idealized image, and even the most fervent missionaries stopped short of Rousseau. Domestic slavery was nearly universal among these sup-

2. Gilbert Chinard, *L'Amérique et le rêve exotique dans la littérature française au XVII siècle* (Paris, 1913), pp. v–vii, 1–20; Maren-Sofie Røstvig, *The Happy Man: Studies in the Metamorphoses of a Classical Ideal, 1600–1700* (Oslo, 1954), pp. 41–7, 71, 174; Hoxie Neale Fairchild, *The Noble Savage: A Study in Romantic Naturalism* (New York, 1928), pp. 1–35.

posed freemen of the wilderness, who sold bondsmen to one another and eventually to the Europeans; and the Dominican friars who were reminded by the Indians of Virgil and Horace, or of the simplicity of the primitive church, could not forget that the most philosophical savage was a heathen living in spiritual darkness.[3] Nevertheless, to Christianize natural man did not necessarily require his enslavement. In 1511 Antonio de Montesinos delivered a fiery sermon in Hispaniola in which he denounced the enslaving of Indians as a wicked sin. His language approached the vehemence of later abolitionists, and he was rebuked for his indiscretion by the Dominican Superior in Spain. In a calmer spirit, the theologian Matías de Paz argued that Indians could be classed neither with Aristotle's natural slaves nor with the Jews and Saracens, who had been exposed to the true faith and had rejected it. But in 1510 John Major concluded that the native American did meet Aristotle's definition of the natural slave; and many soldiers and administrators were convinced that only coercion could protect the savage from his native idleness and gluttony. Thus the American Indian, as Antonello Gerbi has observed, presented Europe with a radically new problem; he did not conform to the traditional antitheses of Christian and infidel, freeman and slave, and man and beast.[4] To a people who valued the disciplines necessary for wealth and power, he appeared as a contemptible travesty of human nature; but to a people whose impulse to civilization was balanced by a longing for the simple and spontaneous, he also appeared as the noble vestige of a lost golden age, when men's acts and ideals were not separated by the shadow of sin.

3. For substantial evidence of slavery among American Indian tribes, see Almon W. Lauber, *Indian Slavery in Colonial Times within the Present Limits of the United States* (New York, 1913), pp. 25–46. Although Indian bondage was often of a mild, domestic nature, slaves were employed in mining, fishing and agriculture, and were sometimes subjected to great cruelty. Occasionally their masters would cut a foot or ankle to prevent escape.

4. Lewis Hanke, *The Spanish Struggle for Justice in the Conquest of America* (Philadelphia, 1949), pp. 11–18, 28; Hanke, *Aristotle and the American Indian: A Study in Race Prejudice in the Modern World* (Chicago, 1959), p. 14; Lauber, *Indian Slavery*, pp. 48–56; Antonello Gerbi, *La disputa del Nuovo Mondo: storia di una polemica, 1750–1900* (Milan, 1955), pp. 77–85.

Prior to 1514, Bartolomé de Las Casas had worked Indian slaves on his estates in Hispaniola, but in that year he experienced one of those crises of conscience that are so indefinable and yet so common in the history of religion. The lives of many future abolitionists would be transformed by a similar upheaval of soul and change of vision. Henceforth, Las Casas's religious life would be given new meaning and direction by his crusade to protect the native American from bondage and extermination. As an alternative to the harsh *encomienda* system, which gave Spanish *encomenderos* rights to the labour and produce of entire Indian villages, he suggested that Indians and Europeans be settled in model communities that would provide the basis for a peaceful Christianization of the New World. If Christian civilization could not establish such harmonious points of contact with American nature, it would fail in its supreme test. Las Casas did fail in his efforts to plant a utopian colony on the coast of South America, but he later succeeded, in his *Very Brief Account of the Destruction of the Indies*, in providing Europe with an enduring image of Spanish cruelty and the rape of innocent America.[5]

But meanwhile Las Casas himself had become involved in the moral ambiguities of America's conquest. Along with his orginal plan for model Christian communities, he had recommended that forced labour in the mines be confined to Negro slaves, who could tolerate such rigorous conditions better than the Indians. About the year 1518 he made his famous proposal to the Spanish Crown for replacing Indian labourers with Negroes purchased in Iberia.[6] In his *Historia*

5. Hanke, *Spanish Struggle for Justice*, pp. 21, 54; Hanke, *Bartolomé de las Casas: An Interpretation of his Life and Writings* (The Hague, 1951), pp. 56–7; Hanke, *Bartolomé de las Casas, Historian: An Essay in Spanish Historiography* (Gainesville, Fla, 1952), p. 4.

6. Hanke, *Spanish Struggle for Justice*, p. 60. Abolitionists and others were influenced by the picture of Las Casas in William Robertson's famous *History of America*. According to Robertson, Las Casas was carried away by rash zeal, and his proposal was rejected by Cardinal Ximenes, who said that he would not reduce one race to slavery in order to save another ([Vienna ed., 1787], I, pp. 289–314). José Antonio Saco, who had seen the manuscript of Las Casas's *Historia*, emphasized the Dominican's repentance; and he argued that Robertson's judgement had been unfair, but that the Abbé Grégoire had erred just as much in attempting to show that Las Casas had never favoured introducing Negro slaves (Saco, *Historia de la esclavitud*

de las Indias, which was not published for more than three hundred years, Las Casas said that 'not long afterwards' he discovered that the enslavement of Negroes was apparently as unjust as that of Indians; and he confessed he was not certain whether his ignorance and good intention of liberating the Indians would excuse him before the bar of divine justice.[7] But beyond this brief acknowledgement of guilt, there is no indication that the 'protector of the Indians' publicly condemned the enslavement of Negroes or advocated their emancipation. He apparently owned slaves himself as late as 1544.[8]

The changing policies of the Spanish and Portuguese governments revealed a similar double standard with respect to Indians and Negroes, which derived in part from the traditional inclination to associate the Africans with Moors, and thus with a menacing infidelity. Even when Negroes had not been tainted by Islam, they were of the Old World, the world of antiquity and of the Bible, which at least had been exposed for many centuries to the word of God. But when Spanish explorers and conquistadores enslaved thousands of helpless Indians, it was difficult to say this was a vindication of the true faith. Hence in 1537 Pope Paul III declared that the sacraments should be withheld from any colonist who, disregarding the truth that Indians were rational beings capable of Christianity, deprived them of their natural liberty.[9] On various occasions the rulers of Spain and Portugal forbade the enslavement of native Americans, even in a

desde los tiempos mas remotos hasta nuestros dias [2nd ed., Habana, 1936–45], IV, pp. 94–111). Arthur Helps also stressed the importance of Las Casas's repentance, and rejected Robertson's image of Ximenes, who, according to Helps, had been interested only in questions of revenue, licensing and the domestic labour supply (Helps, *The Spanish Conquest in America, and its Relation to the History of Slavery and to the Government of Colonies* [rev. ed., London, 1900], I, pp. 349–50; III, p. 153). It should be mentioned that a group of Hieronymite fathers also petitioned Spain for Negro slaves.

7. Bartolomé de Las Casas, *Historia de las Indias* (edición de Agustín Millares Carlo y estudio preliminar de Lewis Hanke) (México, D.F., 1951), III, pp. 274–5. Las Casas asked his Dominican brothers not to publish the work for at least forty years after his death.

8. Hanke, *Aristotle and the Indian*, p. 9. It is perhaps significant that Las Casas devotes very little attention to Negroes in his *Historia de las Indias*.

9. *C. H. Haring, The Spanish Empire in America* (New York, 1947), pp.

supposedly just war. In 1542 the *Nuevas Leyes de las Indias* ruled that owners who lacked proof of a just title must liberate their Indian slaves.

Slaveholders have never taken kindly to moralistic interference, and such laws and edicts provoked colonial insurrections in New Spain, Peru and New Granada. On various occasions Brazilian colonists expelled the Jesuits for their activities in favour of Indian workers, and in 1652 the inhabitants of Maranhão revolted when a governor arrived with orders from the king of Portugal to emancipate Indian slaves. Paulo da Silva Nunes, who represented Maranhão in Lisbon early in the eighteenth century, argued that Indians were more like beasts than human beings; constructing a defence of slavery from Biblical and classical sources, he also suggested the possibility that Indians bore the curse of Cain. Such views were common among slaveholding colonists throughout Latin America, where a humane Indian policy continued to be vitiated by stubborn resistance, jurisdictional disputes and a recognized need for forced labour.[10]

But despite the cruelties of the *encomienda* system, despite the slaving raids into the interior, the separation of families and the frightful mortality in the mines, Spanish and Portuguese authorities succeeded in liberating thousands of Indian slaves and in preventing the enslavement of thousands more. Over a period of three centuries a vast body of legislation was created to segregate and protect the native American from the exploitive forces of colonization. Unfortunately, the erosion of Indian slavery simply contributed to the growing demand for Negroes, who were often regarded as a *mala raza*, and who were not protected by a great network of imperial edicts and laws. And some of the leading advocates of the Indian, such as Bishop Landa of Mexico, were the strongest defenders of Negro slavery. This discrimination between the two coloured races led quite naturally to a view that Negroes were born to be slaves and were inherently inferior to both Indians and whites. In 1771, for

---

55–6. Because of a jurisdictional dispute with the Spanish crown, the pope revoked the penalties in the following year.

10. ibid., pp. 53–7; Robert Southey, *History of Brazil* (London, 1817–22), II, pp. 453–5; C. R. Boxer, *Race Relations in the Portuguese Empire, 1415–1825* (Oxford, 1963), pp. 87, 93, 95–102.

example, the viceroy of Brazil ordered the degradation of an Indian chief who had 'sunk so low as to marry a Negress, staining his blood with this alliance'.[11]

It is significant that the first great debate on the legitimacy of American slavery centred almost exclusively on the nature of the Indian, although by 1550, when Las Casas and Sepúlveda began their momentous controversy at Valladolid, Negro slavery had been well established in the New World. There are certain interesting parallels, however, between the debates at Valladolid and the debates on the slave trade in the British Parliament some two hundred and forty years later. Just as British abolitionists chose to attack the sources of the slave system rather than the system itself, so Las Casas, having been unsuccessful in his attempts to outlaw the *encomienda* system, had launched a campaign to end the brutal wars which supplied Spanish colonists with Indian slaves. Here he encountered the opposition of the learned Sepúlveda, who wrote a treatise, blessed by the president of the Council of the Indies, defending the justice of such wars. If the later champions of the slave trade invoked the principles of mercantilism and the climatic theories of Montesquieu, Sepúlveda opposed religious zeal with the erudite humanism of the Renaissance. In the 1790s proponents of the slave trade sought to link

11. Jaime Jaramillo Uribe, 'Esclavos y señores en la sociedad colombiana del siglo XVIII', *Anuario colombiano de historia social y de la cultura* (Bogotá 1963), I, p. 21; Maurilio de Gouveia, *Historia da escravidão* (Rio de Janeiro, 1955), pp. 53–6, 60, 63, 68; Magnus Mörner, 'The Theory and Practice of Racial Segregation in Colonial Spanish America', *Proceedings of the Thirty-Second International Congress of Americanists* (Copenhagen, 1958), pp. 708–13; Hubert Herring, *A History of Latin America from the Beginnings to the Present* (New York, 1955), pp. 190–91; Haring, *Spanish Empire*, pp. 57–8; Helps, *Spanish Conquest*, III, p. 87; IV, pp. 241–8; Oriol Pi-Sunyer, 'Historical Background to the Negro in Mexico', *Journal of Negro History*, XLII (October 1957), p. 240; Raúl Carrancá y Trujillo, 'El estatuto jurídico de los esclavos en las postrimerías de la colonización española', *Revista de historia de América* (México, D.F.), no. 3 (September 1938), pp. 22–4; Boxer, *Race Relations*, p. 121. It is interesting to note that while free Negroes and mulattoes were often forbidden to have Indian servants, as in colonial Mexico, some Indian tribes that had not previously owned slaves, such as the Creeks, purchased Negroes from the whites (H. J. Nieboer, *Slavery as an Industrial System* [The Hague, 1900], pp. 45, 70–71).

the cause of abolition with the heresies of revolutionary France; at Valladolid, Sepúlveda portrayed an imaginary debate between a wise Democrates and a hare-brained German, Leopoldo, whose pro-Indian views were contaminated with Lutheran errors. Moreover, Sepúlveda's principal arguments would later be used to justify the African slave trade. Exploiting the traditional link between sin and slavery, he held that Indians were guilty of idolatry and of sins against nature, and accordingly deserved to be slaves. In contrast to the enlightened Spanish, their minds were barbarous and darkened by vile superstitions; they were, in short, inferior beings who conformed to Aristotle's definition of the natural slave. The enslavement would promote the spread of Christianity and also protect the weak from being killed or devoured by the strong.[12]

Curiously enough, Las Casas accepted the Aristotelian view that some men were slaves by nature. But for Las Casas, the contrast between natural man and civilized man did not suggest a need for harsh repression and discipline. He argued that Indians were equal to the primitive Europeans of antiquity, and could thus be considered raw material for a Christian civilization. In his faith in the potentialities of all rational beings and in his moral outrage at a brutal violation of human liberty and dignity, Las Casas pointed the way to later abolitionists.[13] Yet his moral vision rested on an assumed dualism between Europe and America, between civilization and innocent nature. Such a dialectic left out the third essential element which Las Casas himself had helped to introduce.

Even Las Casas could not rival Jean-Baptiste Du Tertre, a fellow Dominican of the seventeenth century, in celebrating the natural virtues of the Indian. As a missionary with many years of experience in the French Caribbean, Du Tertre had detailed knowledge of the aborigines' customs and superstitions, which he sometimes saw as the products of sin or at least of religious ignorance. He was also quite frank in admitting that French missionaries had failed dismally in

12. Hanke, *Spanish Struggle for Justice*, pp. 109–24; Hanke, *Aristotle and the Indian*, pp. 12–73; Gerbi, *Disputa del Nuovo Mondo*, pp. 77–9.
13. Hanke, *Aristotle and the Indian*, pp. 56–9; Hanke, *Spanish Struggle for Justice*, pp. 123–6.

their efforts to Christianize the American heathen.[14] Nevertheless, he strove to invert the image traditionally suggested by the word *sauvage*. The American tropics were not a sterile desert inhabited by barbarous creatures who lacked reason and moral sensibility. In a remarkable passage, he exclaimed:

Therefore, since I have shown the air in the Torrid Zone to be the purest, the healthiest, and the most temperate of all, and the land to be a kind of miniature Paradise, always green and watered by the purest streams: it follows that I must show in this treatise that the natives of these Islands are the most contented, the happiest, the least corrupt, the most sociable, the least deceitful, the healthiest of all peoples in the world.

Moreover, precisely because the Indians were the products of an uncultivated nature,

All are equal, with hardly any sort of superiority or servitude being known; and one scarcely finds any form of deference such as exists between relatives, for instance, between father and son. No one is richer or poorer than his neighbour.[15]

But this paradise soon decayed when touched by European greed and artifice. As early as 1636 Gabriel Sagard had portrayed the corruption of the noble savage in Canada, and the theme would be exploited by numerous Jesuits and Jansenists, partly as a means for enlisting financial support for their missions, which would presumably protect the Indians' innocence by reinforcing it with Christianity. Yet according to Baron de Lahontan, the priests and their religion also contaminated natural man; Europeans were the slaves of irrational custom and prejudice, whereas the American savage had been truly free.[16]

14. Jean-Baptiste Du Tertre, *Histoire générale des Antilles habitées par les François* (Paris, 1667–71), II, pp. 364–419, 501. Du Tertre first went to the West Indies in 1640, and the first edition of his work appeared in 1654. It is curious that his enthusiasm for the Indian and his indifference towards the Negro were not reversed by the fact that he and his fellow missionaries claimed to have converted some fifteen thousand Negro slaves but only about twenty Indians in a period of thirty-five years.

15. ibid., II, pp. 356–7.

16. Chinard, *L'Amérique et le rêve exotique*, pp. 119–86. Robert Beverley, the early Virginia historian, thought that Lahontan went too far in

But if the Indian represented at once a victim and an ideal, what of the Negro? Du Tertre summarized the difference when he repeated, with apparent approval, a proverb of the French West Indies: '*To look askance at an Indian is to beat him; to beat him is to kill him; to beat a Negro is to nourish him.*'[17] The Dominican's admiration and sympathy for the noble savage did not extend to the Negro, whom he regarded with that curious mixture of inconsistent attitudes that were to become so characteristic of American slaveholders.[18] He admitted that most Negro slaves had been captured in war and that some, including princes and queens, had been kidnapped or unjustly seized. And yet he observed, without either protesting or stating his own views, that Negroes in the West Indies conformed to Aristotle's definition of a slave as the instrument of his master; that they were treated like animals, as if the blackness of their skins were a mark of their misfortune; and that if physical labour was the penalty for man's rebellion against God, the most severe form of this punishment had been inflicted upon the Africans.[19] Du Tertre did not say that Negroes should be regarded as mere instruments or animals, or that their sin was proportionate to their suffering. On this subject, at least, he adopted the mantle of the objective historian, and announced that he would avoid the knotty question of slavery's ultimate legality. And yet he wanted to vindicate the colonists' reputation, which had been unjustly damaged by pious but ignorant men who had assumed that the laws protecting human liberty in France could be applied to all parts of the world.[20]

---

idealizing the noble savage, but exclaimed himself over the Indians' beauty and morality, which were corrupted by contact with Europeans. He obviously considered Indians vastly superior to Negroes, of whom he had little to say (*The History and Present State of Virginia* [ed. by Louis B. Wright, Chapel Hill, 1947], pp. 159, 162–70, 233).

17. Du Terte, *Histoire générale*, II, p. 490.

18. ibid., II, pp. 483–98; Chinard, *L'Amérique et le rêve exotique*, pp. 53–4. Various references in Du Tertre indicate that the French missionaries owned Negro slaves.

19. Du Tertre, *Histoire générale*, II, pp. 493–5, 523–4.

20. ibid., II, p. 483. Du Tertre's views were translated and printed verbatim, without acknowledgement, by Thomas Jefferys (*The Natural and Civil History of the French Dominions in North and South America* [London, 1760], pp. 186–93).

Du Tertre assured his readers that Negro slaves, when well fed and gently treated, were the happiest people in the world. Charles de Rochefort, who had also been in the West Indies and whom Du Tertre accused of plagiarism, was confident that Negroes preferred a kind European master to their original liberty in Africa.[21] But the Indian, they agreed, could never reconcile himself to bondage, and haughtily refused to associate in any way with the Negro. Unlike the complaisant African, the American savage was quick to defend the honour of his women; unless treated with respect, he often languished and died from a profound melancholy. These were the elements for the later stereotypes of the proud, freedom-loving Indian and the humble Negro who was born for slavery. But in neither Du Tertre nor de Rochefort is the contrast so complete and so free of ambiguities. Both emphasized the necessity of governing Negroes with firmness and strict discipline. Basically arrogant and untrustworthy, the African would exploit the slightest weakness or leniency of his master, and unless kept in due submission, would rise in armed revolt. Excessive severity might also provoke insurrection, but only the constant fear of punishment would induce slaves to labour in the fields under a hot sun. Hence the dualism of Indian and African was matched by a divided image of Negro slavery itself. One has the impression that these missionaries wanted to think of the Negro as a natural servant who could find true happiness only in loyalty and obedience to a kindly Christian master. But the picture they presented was one of fear, violent brutality, and unrelieved drudgery for the benefit of a class whose sole interest lay in the rapid accumulation of wealth.[22]

In spite of a widespread tendency to differentiate the Negro from the Indian and to associate the latter with the freedom of nature, Negro slavery was in actuality imposed on top of a pre-existing Indian slavery; in North America, at least, the two never diverged as

21. Du Tertre, *Histoire générale*, I, preface; II, p. 497; Charles de Rochefort, *Histoire naturelle des Iles Antilles de l'Amérique* (Lyon, 1667), II, p. 136. The second volume is entitled *Histoire morale des Iles Antilles de L'Amérique*.

22. Du Tertre, *Histoire générale*, I, p. 500; II, pp. 484–93, 497–9, 524–5; de Rochefort, *Histoire naturelle*, II, p. 136–8.

distinct institutions.[23] Nevertheless the practical circumstances of colonial settlement afforded the Indian some protection. From Canada to South America colonists took the enslavement of hostile savages as a matter of course; but they knew that their trade, and sometimes their very survival, depended on alliances with friendly tribes.

During the Pequoit War and King Philip's War, New Englanders shipped captured Indians to Bermuda and the West Indies, and at other times used the same punishment as a means of disciplining neighbouring tribes. But this meant that 'praying Indians', and those who cooperated with the colonists, were usually exempt from the danger of enslavement. A few colonists, such as John Eliot and Roger Williams, who had established intimate relations with the natives, were willing to question the wisdom or justice of condemning even hostile savages to perpetual bondage.[24] In Virginia, on the other hand, Nathaniel Bacon bitterly attacked Governor Berkeley's policy of protecting friendly tribes, and in 1676 the rebel leader secured a law authorizing the enslavement of all Indians captured in war. But notwithstanding Bacon's success in arousing racial hatred and in plundering and enslaving friendly tribes, Virginians tended to make a

23. No distinction was made between the two races in most of the early colonial legislation pertaining to slaves, or in intercolonial agreements for the return of fugitives (George H. Moore, *Notes on the History of Slavery in Massachusetts* [New York, 1866], pp. 15–41; Bernard C. Steiner, *A History of Slavery in Connecticut* [Baltimore, 1893], pp. 9–10; Lauber, *Indian Slavery*, pp. 48–102, 105–17, 211–16, 222–9, 250–82).

24. Ulrich Bonnell Phillips, *American Negro Slavery: A Survey of the Supply, Employment and Control of Negro Labor as Determined by the Plantation Regime* (reprint ed., Gloucester, Mass., 1959), p. 101; Lauber, *Indian Slavery*, pp. 118–52, 174–5, 197–202, 305; Moore, *Notes on History of Slavery*, pp. 34–7; *Collections of Massachusetts Historical Society*, 4th ser., VI (Boston, 1863), pp. 195–6. Although Williams suggested to John Winthrop that it might be better policy not to condemn to perpetual slavery captives taken in the Pequoit War, he also wrote that since God had been pleased to give Winthrop 'another miserable droue of Adams degenerate seede, & our brethren by nature, I am bold ... to request the keeping & bringing up of one of the children'. In 1675 Eliot argued that selling Indians to the West Indies was 'a dangerous merchandize' which might prolong the war and bring a judgement on the land.

sharp distinction between domestic allies and foreign enemies.[25] Yet to the purchaser of Negroes, there was no political difference between Mandigo and Dahomean. Removed from the sources of African slavery, he was concerned with tribal origin only as an indication of probable character and stamina.

While North American colonists continued to hold Indian slaves through the eighteenth century, they at least assumed that the majority of Indians were rightfully free and that every bondsman was a legitimate captive, or the descendant of such a captive. They were also alert to the dangers of antagonizing neighbouring tribes or of filling the near-by forests. As a consequence, colonial legislation gradually revealed a double standard towards Indians and Negroes which was analogous to the distinctions made by Spanish law and by such writers as Las Casas and Du Tertre.

For reasons of expediency, a number of colonies flatly prohibited the importation of Indian slaves. From 1712 to 1714 this was done by Massachusetts, Connecticut and Rhode Island, in order to stop the influx of large numbers of captives taken in the Tuscarora War in Carolina.[26] Fearing that the shipment of Indian slaves from the continent was detrimental to other commerce, Jamaica passed a law in 1741 which forbade all future purchases of imported Indians, and which granted liberty to those brought illegally into the island. The law did not affect Indians already in the colony, but it is significant that an attempt was made to outlaw the Indian slave trade at a time when Negroes were demanded in ever-increasing numbers.[27]

25. Wilcomb E. Washburn, *The Governor and the Rebel: A History of Bacon's Rebellion in Virginia* (Chapel Hill, 1957), pp. 38, 58, 123; Wesley Frank Craven, *The Southern Colonies in the Seventeenth Century, 1607–1689* (Baton Rouge, 1949), pp. 366, 368, 385; Helen T. Catterall (ed.), *Judicial Cases Concerning American Slavery and the Negro* (Washington, 1926–37), I, pp. 68–9.

26. Lauber, *Indian Slavery*, pp. 187–90. In 1679 New York drew a legal distinction between native Indians, who were free, and imported foreign Indians, who were slaves. But in 1688 the council decided to liberate and return all Indians who were subjects of the king of Spain. In 1746 Rhode Island took a similar action (ibid., pp. 317–18).

27. Frank Wesley Pitman, 'Slavery on British West India Plantations in the Eighteenth Century', *Journal of Negro History*, XI (October 1926), p. 589.

Although the British and French colonies gave the same legal status to Indian and Negro slaves, they showed a marked tendency, by the eighteenth century, to restrict the bondage of Indians to certain tribes. In South Carolina, Indian slavery was closely linked with the western fur trade; and in the struggle with France and Spain for control of the south-west, the institution became an important weapon for securing alliances and punishing enemies. Carolina traders had no scruples about buying Indians from the *coureurs de bois* at the mouth of the Mississippi, and selling them ultimately in the West Indies. But the proprietors of the colony always promised protection to their Indian allies. And after 1740, the courts of South Carolina held that the colour of an Indian, unlike that of a Negro, was not *prima facie* evidence of slavery, since it could not be presumed that any given Indian or his ancestors had been legitimately captured in war. The distinction would appear to have been an outgrowth of the practical demands of trade and diplomacy.[28]

The French Canadians adopted a somewhat similar policy. From the late seventeenth century the settlements in the Saint Lawrence valley had provided a regular market for Pawnee slaves who were captured in the West by other Indians and eventually sold to the French. But by a law of 1709 all *Panis* and Negroes were legally classed as slaves, and in 1760, in the Treaty of Montreal, England formally recognized the legitimacy of Negro and Pawnee slavery in Canada.[29] If it was extraordinary to single out a particular western

28. Lauber, *Indian Slavery*, pp. 168–75, 315. The 1740 slave code of Carolina ruled that 'all negroes and Indians (free Indians in amity with this government, and Negroes, mulattoes or mustezoes, who are now free, excepted) mulattoes or mustezoes who now are, or shall hereafter be in this province, and all their issue and offspring . . . shall be and they are hereby declared to be, and remain forever hereafter absolute slaves' (John Codman Hurd, *The Law of Freedom and Bondage in the United States* [Boston, 1858–62], I, p. 303). But while this act gave the same status to Indian and Negro slaves, in practice Indians were regarded as in amity with the government unless the contrary could be proved.

29. Marcel Trudel, *L'Esclavage au Canada français, histoire et conditions de l'esclavage* (Quebec, 1960), pp. 41–2, 55. Out of some 2,472 Indian slaves, Trudel estimates that about 68 per cent were *Panis*. The French Canadians had only the vaguest notion of where the *Panis* originated, and

tribe for enslavement, it is all the more significant that the French called the Pawnees 'the Negroes of America'. Like the Africans, the Pawnees came from an area so remote that one could ignore the mode and justice of their enslavement. And as Governor La Jonquière ruled, with respect to Negroes who escaped to Canada from the British colonies, 'tout nègre est esclave, quelque part qu'il se trouve'.[30] But since the ordinance of 1709 confined slavery to these two groups, the question soon arose whether other Indians could legitimately be held as slaves. It was the judgement of Louis XV that the matter should be determined by the established usage of the colony, which gave full rights of French citizenship to converted Indians, with the exception of the unfortunate Pawnees. Although Indians from various western tribes were sometimes classed as *Panis*, which justified their being held as slaves, the French colonists had no wish to jeopardize vital commercial relationships by enslaving Indians from the lake and forest regions. They did seize or purchase a number of Eskimos, but Eskimos proved to be very poor slaves.[31]

The ambiguities of Indian bondage were especially evident in Virginia. An act of 1670 stated that 'all servants not being Christians, imported into this colony by shipping, shall be slaves for their lives; but what shall come by land shall serve, if boys or girls until thirty years of age, if men or women, twelve years and no longer.'[32] This law has sometimes been interpreted simply as a step towards differentiating Indians from Negroes, but since Indian slaves were occasionally imported by sea, the fundamental distinction would seem to have been between heathen from distant areas and those from the surrounding country. This distinction was soon effaced by a number of statutes, most notably by an act of 1682 that put Indians and

used the term loosely for various Indians from the Arkansas and Missouri valleys.

30. ibid., pp. 42, 55, 64.

31. ibid., pp. 80–81. It is probable that cultural differences made Indians or Negroes from certain tribes more or less adaptable to slavery; it is significant, however, that the French classed all Africans as *Nègres*, and most Indian slaves from the West as *Panis*, regardless of actual tribal origins.

32. Hurd, *Law of Freedom*, I, p. 233.

Negroes on the same footing and authorized the purchase of slaves captured or otherwise acquired by neighbouring tribes. A law of 1691 for promoting free trade with Indians apparently withdrew the right to purchase slaves, and in 1705, when part of the law of 1682 was re-enacted, Indians were specifically omitted from the class of imported servants who were judged to be slaves.[33]

Indian bondage persisted in Virginia, but the institution brought increasing confusion and litigation. By the mid eighteenth century virtually all Indians were free, while the vast majority of Negroes were slaves. The final resolution came in 1806, with the crucial case of Hudgins *v.* Wrights, which involved the nearly white descendants of an Indian slave. Drawing on the doctrine of natural liberty embodied in the Virginia Bill of Rights, Chancellor George Wythe held that whenever one person claimed to hold another in bondage, the *onus probandi* lay with the claimant. Saint George Tucker, alarmed by a construction that would apply with equal force to Negroes and Indians, argued that the Bill of Rights 'was notoriously framed with a cautious eye to this subject, and was meant to embrace the case of free citizens, or aliens only; and not by a side wind to overturn the rights of property'. Basing his position on historical precedent rather than abstract principle, Tucker first appealed to an earlier decision that had accorded freedom to all Indians and their descendants who had entered Virginia after 1705, and then noted that the decisive date should be pushed back to 1691, when the importation of Indian slaves had in effect been made illegal. The final decree of the Supreme Court of the State concurred with Chancellor Wythe's principles only so far as they related to white persons and American Indians, 'but entirely disapproving thereof, so far as the same relates to native Africans and their descendants'.[34] After a slow and

---

33. ibid., I, pp. 234–41; John H. Russell, *The Free Negro in Virginia, 1619–1865* (Baltimore, 1913), pp. 39–40; Lauber, *Indian Slavery*, pp. 186, 312–13; Catterall (ed.), *Judicial Cases*, I, pp. 61–5.

34. Catterall (ed.), *Judicial Cases*, I, pp. 112–13. In New Jersey, on the other hand, the chief justice ruled in 1797 that Indians had been recognized as slaves for so long that any contrary view would violate fundamental rights of property (Henry Scofield Cooley, *A Study of Slavery in New Jersey* [Baltimore, 1896], pp. 12–13).

confused development, the distinction between Indian and Negro was now clear-cut; only the aborigine, who had been pictured by Du Tertre and Lahontan as the innocent child of nature, could share the Virginians' natural rights and liberties.

Although Indians and Negroes were both cruelly exploited and often reduced to the same status as chattel slaves, it is undeniable that the European conscience was more troubled by the plight of the native American. We have suggested that this moral sensitivity towards the Indian was the product of an interaction between the conditions of American settlement and certain traditional views of human bondage. On the level of expediency, colonists were reluctant to seize neighbouring savages who provided them with markets and produce. And since it was hardly possible in America to dissociate even the mildest Indian servitude from the violence of enslavement, judges and missionaries were sensitive to the traditional opposition between natural liberty and an act of force that could be justified only by tangible proof of the victim's crime.

It was otherwise in Africa. Because Negroes lived for the most part in populous and highly organized societies, they were able to deal on nearly equal terms with the early Portuguese traders, who respected both the wealth and power of their kings. There was little reason to associate the African with a primitive or uncorrupted nature. He was known from the Bible and from the writers of antiquity, and he often bore the influence of Moslem culture. It was sometimes said that he had once been exposed to the true faith, but had either rejected or forgotten it. He was, in any event, too advanced in culture to be styled as an innocent savage dispossessed of his land and freedom by the avaricious European. He was not overwhelmed by armies or by a mass of colonists spreading through his country. His contact with Europeans was confined to small groups of professional traders who clustered in vulnerable forts along the coast and who were subject to the rules and restrictions of a well-developed commercial system. When the chieftain of a semi-feudalistic society sold bondsmen to a Portuguese trader, he merely followed a practice long established among his own people and further stimulated by Arab merchants. He could not foresee that the settlement of America would revolutionize the character of this trade, or that its evil consequences would be obscured by the apparent power and independence of his people.[35]

The most gradual changes are often the most destructive. If Europe and Africa began their ill-fated relationship as near equals, the influx of European goods, particularly of firearms, slowly disrupted the equilibrium of West African cultures. To Europe improved technology brought power and wealth, but to Africa it brought only more efficient means to capture slaves for the American market. The religious and political power-structure of West African states was peculiarly susceptible to the corrosive effects of the slave system. In the Niger delta, where priests had traditionally imposed heavy fines on men who offended an oracle, it was relatively easy to discover an increasing number of offences which could be expiated only by a payment in slaves, who could then be sold profitably to European traders. Believing in divine kingship and divided by intense religious loyalties, the forest peoples of Guinea looked upon one another as contemptible heretics who deserved death or slavery; accordingly, their religious wars were well adapted for procuring captives who could be exchanged for guns. And since the tribes which captured the most slaves received the most European goods, and were thus best equipped in the struggle for survival, it was only natural that certain groups in the interior, such as the Ashantis and Dahomeans, should rise to power as specialists in the art of enslaving. Initially cut off from the Europeans by coastal tribes who were able to act as middlemen, these forest kingdoms eventually pushed towards the sea, extending the zone of terror as their power increased.[36] Hence in 1727 John Atkins complained that the triumph

35. Basil Davidson, *Black Mother: The Years of the African Slave Trade* (Boston, 1961), pp. 18–24. For an excellent analysis of one of the West African cultures, see Melville J. Herskovits, *Dahomey: An Ancient West African Kingdom* (New York, 1938), and Melville J. Herskovits and Frances S. Herskovits, *Dahomean Narrative: A Cross-Cultural Analysis* (Evanston, Ill., 1958). Davidson describes the disastrous effects of the Portuguese slave trade in the Congo and East Africa, as well as in Guinea (pp. 153–94).

36. Davidson, *Black Mother*, pp. 82–90, 110–62, 224–35, 251–3, 273–85; H. A. Wyndham, *Problems of Imperial Trusteeship: The Atlantic and Slavery* (London, 1935), pp. 3–7, 28–9; W. E. F. Ward, *A History of Ghana*

of Dahomey had destroyed the orderly pattern of the slave trade; the Negro who sold you slaves on one day might be sold himself a few days later. And the chaos brought by the emergence of specialized slaving states was matched, on the side of the Europeans, by the arrival of independent traders who looked only for quick profit. Unrestrained by the long-term interests of the major companies, these merchants cared little how slaves were acquired, and did not scruple at kidnapping or inciting raids on peaceful villages.[37]

In general, however, the system was so institutionalized that Europeans had little contact with the actual process of enslavement. As late as 1721 the Royal African Company asked its agents to investigate the modes of enslavement in the interior and to discover whether there was any source besides 'that of being taken Prisoners in War time?'[38] William Smith showed the dependence of traders on African conditions when he blamed the relative absence of native quarrels for the shortage of slaves along the Quaqua and Grain coasts. Some traders knew that defaulting debtors and tribesmen guilty of the slightest offences were sold as slaves, and that kings sent troops at night to raid distant villages, where defenceless men and women were gagged and bound and infants were thrown in sacks. But this knowledge was usually vague, and since it was also known that Negroes often sacrificed their victims, a European might plausibly conclude that his sole influence in Africa was to spare lives.[39]

(rev. ed., London, 1958), pp. 102–3, 142–3; Elizabeth Donnan (ed.), *Documents Illustrative of the History of the Slave Trade to America* (Washington, 1930–35), II, pp. 342–61.

37. John Atkins, *A Voyage to Guinea, Brazil, and the West-Indies, in his Majesty's Ships, the Swallow and Weymouth* (London, 1735) pp. 119, 151; Donnan (ed.), *Documents*, II, pp. xlii, 342–61.

38. Donnan (ed.), *Documents*, II, pp. 254–5.

39. ibid., II, pp. 330–32; John Barbot, *A Description of the Coasts of North and South-Guinea ...,* in John Churchill, *A Collection of Voyages and Travels* (London, 1732), V, pp. 47, 110; Thomas Astley, *A New General Collection of Voyages and Travels ...* (London, 1745–7), II, p. 268; Davidson, *Black Mother*, pp. 217–21. European traders had little knowledge of the commercial networks in the African interior; William Smith was astonished when some captured Malayans turned up for sale in Accra, after crossing the entire continent!

In the mid fifteenth century, Gomes Eannes de Azurara was an eye-witness to a Portuguese slaving raid and to the subsequent sale of the captives. He was deeply moved by the spectacle of human beings killing themselves to avoid capture, by the brutal separation of families, by the whipping of mothers who futilely clung to their husbands or children. He could not keep from weeping, in spite of his realization that these pagans deserved to be slaved, and he prayed that God might excuse his tears. His response of sympathy, as opposed to his belief that Christianization justified inhumanity, was the reaction of a normal man of any age.[40] Even the slave-ship captains of later centuries were not immune to such feelings, although their sensitivity was blunted by a system that fostered rationalization. Jean Barbot felt that the slave trade should be conducted according to the Golden Rule: Europeans should treat Negroes as they themselves would be treated if they had the misfortune of being captured by Algerines (the same parallel suggested a different answer to the Quakers of Germantown in 1688). Barbot congratulated himself on his own humanity. When by accident he bought members of a family who had been separated when enslaved, he was so touched by their joy at reuniting that he ordered his sailors to treat them better than usual, and he sacrificed profit by selling them to a single buyer in Martinique.[41] He described the Middle Passage on his own ship as a virtual pleasure cruise, with happy Negroes smoking pipes on deck and dancing and singing through the evenings. That many slaves attempted suicide or refused to eat he attributed to their childish fear of being devoured by European cannibals. Barbot said that since he was a naturally compassionate man and could not let them starve, he found it necessary to smash out their teeth and feed them by force.[42] William Snelgrave gave his slaves an orientation programme before departure, assuring them they would not be eaten and describing to them the joys of plantation life in the West Indies. But despite this, and despite his idyllic picture of the Middle Passage, he admitted that his slaves had frequently mutinied.[43] Thomas Phillips, who was

40. Donnan (ed.), *Documents*, I, pp. 25–8.
41. Barbot, *Description*, pp. 271, 548.
42. ibid., pp. 272, 547.
43. Astley, *Voyages*, II, pp. 505–7.

also disheartened by slaves refusing to eat and jumping overboard, confessed that he was too humane to cut off the arms and legs of a few Negroes, as some captains had done, to terrify the rest; as a good Christian he had no doubt that Negroes were as dear to God as white men. But as a practical man he knew that when slaves were fed on board his men must stand by with loaded guns and lighted matches.[44]

In various ways the traders and captains attempted to make the best of their grim business. The agents of the Royal African Company were not supposed to buy Negroes who had been kidnapped, and when in doubt, they were to consult the native Alkade. Frances Moore, who was a factor of the Company, told of freeing a man who had been enslaved for stealing a pipe, although the owner of the pipe had frowned upon such charity.[45] The traders associated with the large companies were unanimous in condemning the cruelty and treachery of the independent merchants. They also knew that regular profits depending on cultivating the goodwill of certain tribes, on providing for speedy and efficient transactions and on keeping their ships as clean and orderly as possible. But this increasing preoccupation with perfecting the details of the system obscured the central problem of what slavery meant for Africa. For most Europeans it was sufficient to know that merchants bought Negroes who had been condemned to slavery by the laws of their own country, and that these bondsmen would lead safer and happier lives in the Christian communities of the New World. At a time when Englishmen considered it humane to ship chained convicts to America under conditions that approximated those of the African trade, few men could appreciate the point made by the publisher, Thomas Astley, in commenting on Snelgrave's argument that Negroes benefited from American slavery. If this were so, said Astley, it should be left to the Negroes to make the choice.[46]

44. ibid., II, pp. 407–8; Donnan (ed.), *Documents*, I, pp. 406–7.

45. Astley, *Voyages*, II, pp. 242, 244; Donnan (ed.), *Documents*, II, p. 396.

46. Donnan (ed.), *Documents*, II, pp. 327–8; Atkins, *Voyage*, pp. 156 ff; Barbot, *Description*, pp. 270–72, 545–6; Abbot Emerson Smith, *Colonists in Bondage: White Servitude and Convict Labor in America, 1607–1776* (Chapel Hill, 1947), pp. 125, 128–9; Astley, *Voyages*, II, pp. 505–7.

The remoteness of Africa and the fact that captives were generally derived from the forest regions behind the coast made it easier to dissociate Negro servitude from the violent act of enslavement. And because the Dark Continent defied penetration, Europeans pictured it as a hostile world of disease, dangerous animals and formidable warriors. Until the eighteenth century, the image of Africa was sharply differentiated from that of peaceful, unspoiled America. If it was a crime, as many writers asserted, to deprive native Americans of their natural liberty, it was actually an act of liberation to remove Negroes from their harsh world of sin and dark superstition.[47] Thus the very conditions of the African trade reinforced the more repressive side of the traditional dualisms regarding slavery. The ideal of the happy servant in a Christian society justified a trade that was vital to the economies of Europe and America. 'Though the odious Appellation of *Slaves* is annexed to this Trade' wrote a leading economist . . .

they are certainly treated with great Lenity and Humanity: and as the Improvement of the Planter's Estates depends upon due Care being taken of their Healths and Lives, I cannot but think their Condition is much bettered to what it was in their own Country.[48]

But the plantation was more easily idealized than the African slave market. If for some two centuries no Las Casas actively fought for

47. Bryan Edwards, *The History, Civil and Commercial, of the British Colonies in the West Indies* (Philadelphia, 1806), II, pp. 237–41; Malachy Postlethwayt, *Britain's Commercial Interest Explained and Improved* . . . (London, 1757), I, pp. 430–32. While Edwards admitted that abuses had crept into the slave trade, he defended Las Casas against the charges of William Robertson, who, he said, ignored the fact that Negroes were used to slavery whereas Indians were born free. Postlethwayt, the great defender of the slave trade, eulogized the Indians in terms reminiscent of Du Tertre. In chapter 15 we shall discuss the discovery of 'primitive' Africa and the noble Negro savage.

48. [Malachy Postlethwayt], *The National and Private Advantages of the African Trade Considered* . . . (London, 1746), p. 4. The same point was frequently made by French writers, who also held that Negroes in the West Indies were better off than peasants in Europe (Lucien Peytraud, *L'Esclavage aux Antilles françaises avant 1789* [Paris, 1897], p. 238).

the Negro's liberty and no Du Tertre celebrated his virtues, there were at least a few men who questioned the legitimacy of the African trade. As we have seen, servitude had long been a source of tension in Christian thought, and there was no lack of precedent for censuring the purchase of men who had been reduced to bondage without just provocation. Such protests would require considerable independence of mind, since the Portuguese slave posts were closely connected with missionary establishments, and criticism of the African trade might challenge the very ideal of spreading the faith.[49] Nevertheless, by the mid sixteenth century Fray Domingo de Soto, who was a friend of Las Casas, took note of rumours that Negroes were being seized by illicit means. While there would be nothing wrong, he said, with buying men who sold themselves into slavery, one could not in good conscience keep a man who had been born free and enslaved by fraud or violence, even if he had been purchased in good faith. De Soto doubted whether there was any justice in Negro slavery.[50]

In 1571 the question was explored more fully by a noted Sevillian theologian, Tomás de Mercado, whose *Suma de tratos y contratos* provided a critical scrutiny of the disruptive effects of American colonization on prices, contracts and business ethics. Mercado's remarks on slavery have sometimes been quoted out of context, and it is important to realize that he worked from thoroughly conventional premises.[51] He recognized the authority of the king of Portugal on

49. Ruth D. Wilson, 'Justifications of Slavery, Past and Present', *Phylon*, 4th Quarter (1958), pp. 408–9; Boxer, *Race Relations*, pp. 8–9.

50. *Biblioteca de autores españoles, desde la formación del lenguaje hasta nuestros dias*, LXV (Madrid, 1873), p. xlvi.

51. Tomás de Mercado, *Summa de tratos y contratos* . . . (Sevilla, 1587), ch. 20. This enlarged edition first appeared in 1571; the first edition, entitled *Tratos y contratos de mercaderes y tratantes* . . . , was published in 1569. Both José Saco and Georges Scelle quoted some of Mercado's attacks on Negro slavery, but by ignoring his positive justifications of the institution made him seem more radical than he really was (Saco, *Historia de la esclavitud*, III, p. 361; Scelle, *La traite négrière aux Indes de Castille: contrats et traités d'assiento* [Paris, 1906] I, pp. 716–21). It is important to note that Mercado had been in America and had first-hand knowledge of slavery (*Enciclopedia universal ilustrada, Europeo-Americana* [Barcelona, n.d.], XXXIV, p. 801).

the coast of Africa. He assumed the legality of slavery as an institution, accepting the traditional rounds of war, crime and self-sale. Though he considered Africans barbarians who committed enormous and detestable crimes, he accepted the justice of their laws condemning offenders to perpetual bondage. Divided into petty states with little sense of order or obligation to a sovereign, the Negroes also engaged in continual warfare and hence took many captives. This was justified by the law of nations, even if the merciful influence of Christianity had led Europeans to ransom prisoners of their own faith. Mercado appeared somewhat more doubtful when he turned to the right of African parents to sell their own children. But while the practice had been prohibited in ancient Greece and Rome and was obviously subject to perversion, it derived ultimately from paternal authority and its legality could not be questioned.[52]

If Negro slavery had rested only on these foundations, Mercado would presumably have had no objections. He found, however, that a large number of slaves were being obtained by trickery, force and robbery. Because the Africans were wild savages, their actions were governed by passion rather than reason. The Portuguese and Spanish offered such high prices for slaves that the Negroes hunted each other like deer, raiding villages and kidnapping unprotected persons, even when they lacked the excuse of war. Incited by greed, princes and judges condemned their rivals and convicted countless others on trumped-up charges. Fathers sold their children out of spite or for the slightest disobedience. Mercado went on to describe the cruelty and oppression of the slave ships, where the smell alone was sufficient to kill a large number of the captives. Only recently, he charged, a ship had left Cape Verde bound for New Spain with five hundred slaves. Jammed under the deck like hogs, one hundred and twenty had died the first night. Only two hundred had survived the voyage.

Mercado anticipated eighteenth-century abolitionists in his conclusions as well as in his descriptions of slaving raids and the Middle Passage. While emphasizing that buying and selling Negroes was not in itself illegal, he asserted that the facts of the situation made it impossible to engage in the African trade without incurring deadly sin. A buyer of any commodity was guilty of sin if he had reason to

52. Mercado, *Summa de tratos*, ch. 20.

suspect that the commodity was stolen property or that the seller lacked a legal title. And since it was common knowledge that a large proportion of Negroes had been obtained unlawfully, no one could enter into the commerce with a clear conscience. Mercado considered the possibility of having royal officials oversee the marketing of slaves and require all traders to prove the legality of their transactions. But he rejected this as infeasible. The inspection would become a meaningless formality; American colonists had already shown how the will of kings could be defied or misconstrued. Mercado feared that it was impossible to remedy the Negro's plight, though he observed that profits from the slave trade were uncertain and of short duration, which was a sign of divine displeasure. With respect to the Negro trade in Seville, he suggested that each man consult his confessor.[53]

An even more radical attack on Negro slavery appeared in 1573, from the hand of Bartolomé de Albornoz, who had become a professor of law at the University of Mexico at the time of its founding, and who had later been called to study at Talavera. Like Mercado, Albornoz challenged both the methods by which Africans were captured and the legality of their subsequent sale. He went beyond the theologian, however, in his contempt for sophistry and rationalization. In the ironic tone of a *philosophe*, Albornoz said that purchase of Negroes from the Portuguese *must* be in conformity with both statute law and the law of conscience, since it was accepted by kings and public opinion; no member of a religious order had spoken out against the trade, and indeed the clergy were as active as other people in buying and selling slaves. Commenting on Mercado's theoretical justifications for slavery, Albornoz thought the reasons must be good since he could not understand them. But when he became serious, he found the arguments which had satisfied Mercado even less convincing than those that the theologian had rejected. Even Aristotle had not stated that prisoners of war should be enslaved; and certainly such a practice was not sanctioned by the law of Christ. How could a purchaser possibly know whether a bondsman had been justly captured? What of women and children who could not be guilty of aggression? By natural law the presumption was always in

53. ibid.

favour of liberty, and men were obligated to help the victims of oppression rather than becoming accomplices in the oppressive acts.[54]

Yet it was commonly said that Negroes were better off in a Christian land, even as slaves, than in living like beasts in Africa. Albornoz approached this argument with cautious scepticism. He suggested that the European might not be the proper one to determine such a matter; and, in any event, improving the welfare of the Negro hardly sanctioned injustice. Judas had won no benefit from the good his evil act produced. No one had proved that Africans must lose their natural liberty in order to become Christians. Did the law of Christ state that liberty of the soul must be paid for by slavery of the body? The truth was that the clergy were too fond of their comforts to go to Africa, to bear the cross, and to work for genuine conversions. Albornoz knew these remarks would be condemned by many. But for his own benefit, and out of love of his fellow beings, he felt the duty of warning merchants that there were better things than this bloodthirsty trade in which to invest their wealth. While Bartolomé de Albornoz did not demand a general emancipation of slaves, he had the outlook of a genuine abolitionist. It would appear that no one else attacked Negro slavery with such uncompromising boldness until the late seventeenth century. And one may note that Albornoz's book, which is now exceedingly rare, was placed upon the Index.[55]

But the questions raised by Mercado and Albornoz continued to trouble a few Catholic writers. Tomás Sanchez, the Jesuit casuist, appeared to agree with the two critics when he ruled that it was illegal to buy Negroes seized by fraud or unjust violence. This meant, as Sanchez knew, that the African trade was largely illegitimate. Yet he provided traders and planters with an enormous door for escape: it was up to the original buyer, in most cases a Negro merchant, to determine the legitimacy of title. All later purchasers could sleep with clear consciences.[56]

54. Bartolomé de Albornoz, 'De la esclavitud', reprinted from *Arte de los contractos*, in *Biblioteca de autores españoles*, LXV, pp. 232–3; *Enciclopedia universal*, IV, p. 175.

55. Albornoz, 'De la esclavitud', pp. 232–3.

56. Russell P. Jameson, *Montesquieu et l'esclavage: étude sur les origines*

Alonso de Sandoval was not sure the problem could be disposed of so neatly. Like Mercado and Albornoz, he knew that Africans were condemned to bondage for the pettiest offences, and he borrowed the very language of Mercado to attack the crimes of European traders. After citing Euripides and Philo of Alexandria, he termed slavery 'una junta de todos los males'.[57] Not all the gold and possessions of the world were a sufficient price for human freedom. But these bold words were balanced by Sandoval's belief that slavery was sometimes justified. In 1610 he wrote to Luis Brandão, rector of the Jesuit college in Loanda, for specific information on the sources of Negro slavery. Brandão explained that it would be impossible to find among the thousands of exported slaves the few who had been illicitly seized or unjustly seized or condemned for trifling offences. No Negro would admit that he was legally a slave. And to say that thousands of souls should be lost to Christ merely because a few slaves had been taken unlawfully would be of no service to God. In any event, Brandão found comfort in the fact that the trade had never been questioned by the Board of Conscience in Lisbon or by the Jesuit fathers in Brazil. And this letter, which appeared in a later book by Sandoval, was accepted as conclusive by the Jesuit Order. In 1685 the Spanish Council of the Indies cited Sandoval, along with Sanchez and Luis Molina, in defence of the legitimacy of the African trade.[58]

But the issue of legitimacy had previously brought conflicts of

---

de l'opinion antiesclavagiste en France au XVIIIᵉ siècle (Paris, 1911), p. 124.

57. Saco, *Histoire de la esclavitud*, IV, pp. 254–7. Saco apparently failed to notice that the passage he quoted from Sandoval used the same phrases that had appeared in a passage he had quoted earlier from Mercado (III, p. 361). C. R. Boxer, apparently thinking largely of this blistering indictment of the slave traders, has pictured Sandoval as one of the most eloquent critics of slavery prior to the British abolitionists of the late eighteenth century (*Four Centuries of Portuguese Expansion, 1415–1825: A Succinct Survey* [Johannesburg, 1961], p. 69). But Georges Scelle stresses the fact that Sandoval attacked only the abuses of the slave trade, and not the trade itself (*La traite négrière*, I, pp. 712, 718–19, 719 n.).

58. Saco, *Historia de la esclavitud*, IV, pp. 254–7; Scelle, *La traite négrière*, I, p. 712; Donnan (ed.), *Documents*, I, pp. 123–4, 124 n.

conscience to the western side of the Atlantic. When the Jesuit Miguel Garcia arrived in Brazil in the 1580s, he was shocked to discover that even his Order's college at Bahia owned Negroes who had been illicitly enslaved. Repudiating the usual rationalizations he went so far as to refuse to hear confession from anyone involved in the injustice of slaveholding. Garcia was clearly a disrupting influence, and he soon encountered the indignant opposition of men who knew their position was not quite morally secure. Neither he nor Gonçalo Leite, the first professor of arts in Brazil, could stomach a country that claimed its survival depended on necessary injustice, and both returned to Europe – perhaps the first but certainly not the last of such émigrés from an American slave society.[59]

More typical was the great Jesuit pioneer, Manuel da Nóbrega, who, upon arriving at Bahia in 1549, courageously denounced the settlers for their mistreatment of the Indians, and whose subsequent pleas to the Board of Conscience in Lisbon helped to bring laws prohibiting the enslavement of Indians except in wars authorized by the king or governor.[60] Almost immediately after his arrival in Brazil, Nóbrega unhesitatingly accepted the necessity of Negro slavery for both the colony and his own Order. In a letter of 1557 to a Jesuit official in Portugal, he spoke of the need for more Negroes to maintain his religious establishment, after referring to the death of some slaves who had been contributed by the king.[61] Miguel Garcia publicly disputed Nóbrega's view that the legality of Negro slavery had been carefully weighed in the consciences of the people; but in 1583, when the question was referred to a body of European jurists and moralists, it was Nóbrega's view that won assent. Serefim Leite, the modern authority on the Jesuits in Brazil, has argued that it is

59. Serafim Leite, *História da Companhia de Jesus no Brasil* (Rio de Janeiro and Lisboã, 1938–50), II, pp. 227–8.

60. Leite, *História da Companhia de Jesus*, II, p. 347; Serafim Leite, *Breve itinerário para una biografia do P. Manuel da Nóbrega, fundador da província do Brasil e da cidade de São Paulo, 1517–1570* (Lisboã and Rio de Janeiro, 1955), pp. 195–6; Southey, *History of Brazil*, I, p. 300; II, p. 453.

61. Leite, *História da Companhia de Jesus*, II, pp. 347, 350–52; Manuel da Nóbrega, *Cartas do Brasil e mais escritos do P. Manuel da Nóbrega, com introdução e notas históricas e críticas de Serafim Leite* (Coimbra, 1955), p. 267.

unhistorical to blame Nóbrega or other Jesuits for not acting like nineteenth-century abolitionists; to accuse them of injustice for favouring the Indians, Leite says, is like condemning a man for founding a hospital for tuberculosis while ignoring the victims of leprosy.[62] But even if one agrees with Leite that the alternatives were to condemn slavery and hence to renounce all efforts at colonization, or to accept slavery, as Nóbrega did, in the hope that it might be mitigated by Christianity, one is bothered by the thought that the most respected and morally influential men lent their voices so easily to endorse what was most profitable.

This is all the more perplexing in light of the moral courage of men like António Vieira, who carried on in the seventeenth century the reforming spirit of Montesinos and Las Casas. Vieira bravely fought for the rights of Indians in Brazil, and argued his case in the courts of Lisbon and Rome. In 1640, when the Portuguese in Brazil were hard pressed by the Dutch, Vieira preached a jeremiad sermon which developed the classic theme of the colonists' betrayal of their original high purpose, and of the need for reform and purification. The source of Brazil's evils, Vieira said, was the same sin that had corrupted mankind: just as Adam had taken something to which he had no right, so the covetous Brazilians had disregarded justice and had seized the possessions of others. The great Jesuit was more explicit in a flaming sermon delivered upon his arrival in Maranhão in 1653, after he had enjoyed a period of political influence in Portugal. Comparing the past calamities of war, disease and famine to the punishments of the Pharaoh for refusing to release the Israel-

62. Leite, *História da Companhia de Jesus*, II, pp. 227, 346–7; VI, pp. 350–51. It is curious that Leite should have chosen turberculosis and leprosy for his analogy; Indians were often pictured as the victims of consumptive physical or social diseases introduced by the white man; the Negro's dark skin and physiognomy were sometimes seen as a kind of leprosy, or as the result of a leprous disease, for which the European, of course, bore no responsibility. Leite seems to accept the traditional distinction between the free Indian and the African who was used to bondage. He shows that the Jesuits often treated their slaves with sympathy and charity, but his defence of their large-scale slaveholding is not altogether convincing. It has been estimated that Jesuits owned 1,200 Negro slaves in Chile alone (Hubert Herring, *History of Latin America*, p. 192).

ites, Vieira approached the vehemence of the radical abolitionist:

Every man who holds another unjustly in servitude, being able to release him, is certainly in a state of condemnation. All men, or almost all men in Maranham [sic], hold others unjustly in servitude; all, therefore, or almost all, are in a state of condemnation.[63]

In former times the devil had had to offer all the kingdoms of earth to purchase a single soul, but in Maranhão the price had been reduced: 'A Negro for a Soul, and the Soul the blacker of the two! This Negro shall be your slave for the few days that you may have to live, and your Soul shall be my slave through all eternity.'[64]

The denunciatory spirit, the device of projecting the blackness of the Negro on the soul of the slaveholder, the image of slavery as the original sin destroying America's innocence and mission – all these anticipate the abolitionist frame of mind and suggest that its components were not dependent on evangelical Protestantism. But though Vieira drew on the Hebraic themes of deliverance and communal guilt, he also accepted the Stoic and early Christian view that slaves, while free in soul and equal before God, should acquiesce in their external fate. Vieira did not acquiesce himself in the fate of the Indians, for though he admitted that Brazil could not exist without their forced labour, he boldly opposed the interests of the colonists in his crusade for protective legislation. By winning for the Jesuits a relatively free hand in Indian affairs, he did much to limit and regulate the future enslavement of aborigines.[65] But these efforts did not

63. Leite, *História da Companhia de Jesus*, VII, p. 81; Southey, *History of Brazil*, I, p. 663; II, pp. 474–8; Richard Graham, 'The Jesuit Antonio Vieira and his Plans for the Economic Rehabilitation of Seventeenth-Century Portugal' (M.A. thesis, University of Texas, August, 1957), p. 10; Boxer, *Race Relations*, p. 87.

64. Southey, *History of Brazil*, II, pp. 474–6. The sermon was more concerned with the enslavement of Tapuya Indians than with Negroes.

65. Leite, *História da Companhia de Jesus*, VI, p. 351; VII, p. 81; Graham, 'Jesuite Antonio Vieira', pp. 15, 17–21. I cannot agree with Leite that Vieira's statement – that all men are descended from Adam, that they are saved by the blood of the same Christ, and that only the body of a slave is captive, his nobler soul being free – is a vehement outcry scarcely equalled by the abolitionists of the nineteenth century. This would seem to be traditional Christian doctrine.

extend to the African. Vieira told Negro slaves that he knew of their wounds and scourgings, their hunger and fatigue and revilings; but if they endured these sufferings with patience, following the example of the blessed Redeemer, they would have the merit as well as the torment of martyrdom. Their bondage might become a new Calvary, but they must not, merely because their labour was hard, shirk their duty. Almost two centuries later an Episcopal bishop would give the same comforting message to Negroes in Virginia.[66]

The fact that the clergy in the Spanish and Portuguese colonies owned thousands of slaves was proof, according to the Council of the Indies, that the African trade was legitimate. This religious sanction was crucial in 1685, when the Council of the Inquisition opposed the grant of the Spanish *assiento* to a Dutch heretic, Balthazar Coymans. The slave trade had traditionally been justified by the argument that it promoted the spread of Catholic Christianity; it was for this reason that Moslem slaves had been barred from the Spanish colonies. The Council of the Inquisition feared that Negroes would now be contaminated with Dutch Protestantism, and would spread the disease through Spanish America. This objection led Charles II to order a full-scale investigation of the African trade.[67]

The campaign against Balthazar Coymans succeeded in raising as a by-product certain questions regarding the legitimacy of African enslavement. It was at this time that the Council of the Indies appealed to the earlier opinions of Molina, Sanchez and Sandoval, as well as to classical authorities. In addition to being infidels, the Negroes were, according to some of the pro-slavery theorists, born and predestined for bondage, and conformed to Aristotle's conception of the natural slave. And even if the origins of Negro servitude were not strictly legitimate, the Council of the Indies held that the slave trade could not be stopped without endangering the survival of the colonies and hence the propagation of the true faith. All the devices

66. António Vieira, *Obras escolhidas com prefácios a notas de António Sergio e Hernâni Cidade*, xi: *Sermões* (ii) (Lisboa, 1954), pp. 30–32; Boxer, *Race Relations*, pp. 40, 102; Southey, *History of Brazil*, II, pp. 675–6. The Episcopal bishop was William Meade.

67. Donnan (ed.), *Documents*, I, pp. 357–9; Scelle, *La traite négrière*, I, pp. 708–11, 738–42.

of casuistry were employed to show that the souls of Negroes might safely survive a transatlantic voyage with a heretic captain. Ultimately, Coymans agreed to equip his ships with Capuchin monks. The first serious examination of the legitimacy and expediency of the slave trade resulted in its thorough vindication.[68]

In the Catholic colonies what concern there was for the Negro was largely channelled towards the salvation of his soul. His greatest champions were men like San Pedro Claver, who met the slave ships when they arrived at Cartagena, who baptized the occupants as they disembarked, and who sought to ease their sufferings with acts of kindness and charity. But though Claver was a dedicated, saintly man, and called himself 'the slave of the Negroes', he did not develop the anti-slavery arguments that had been outlined by Mercado and Albornoz. The rare individuals who did revive the early doubts on the legitimacy of African enslavement were held in disrepute and even banished from the colonies.

As late as 1794, for example, a Capuchin friar, José de Bolonha, was expelled from Bahia for maintaining that the buyers of slaves were responsible for determining the legitimacy of title, and for arguing that because this was not done, the African trade was unlawful. The governor discovered that Bolonha had acquired his radical ideas from some Italian priests, who were also ordered to leave the province. Much earlier, in 1758, Manuel Ribeiro Rocha had published a discourse on slavery after returning to Lisbon from Bahia. Instead of challenging the legality of slavery as an institution, Rocha had focused his attention on the sadistic cruelties which Brazilian masters inflicted upon their slaves. Affirming that Negroes should be treated as brothers in Christ, Rocha recommended that they be permitted to have families, be given adequate food and religious instruction, and be prepared for eventual freedom. But this modst proposal was regarded as highly subversive. When the anti-slavery spirit finally began to emerge in Brazil early in the nineteenth century, it was not nourished by a continuing tradition of protest. The first anti-slavery leaders were not inspired by such isolated figures from the past as

68. Scelle, *La traite négrière*, I, pp. 708–11, 723–45 (for many of the documents, in Spanish, see pp. 836–40).

Sandoval, Rocha and Bolonha, but by the ideas of the Enlightenment and the example of British reformers.[69]

69. Octávio Tarquinio de Sousa, *História dos fundadores do Império do Brasil* (Rio de Janeiro, 1957–8), IX, pp. 68–73; Afostinho Marques Perdigão Malhiro, *A escravidão no Brasil: ensaio historico-juridico-social* (Rio de Janeiro, 1866–7), pt III, p. 90.

7

The Legitimacy of Enslavement
and the Ideal of the Christian Servant:
The Failure of Christianization

IN 1698 Germain Fromageau, who presided at the tribunal for cases of conscience at the Sorbonne, ruled that any buyer of a slave must make certain that his property was originally acquired by legitimate means. Conceding that slavery was permitted by the Bible, the Canon Law and the *jus gentium*, Fromageau went on to observe that Negroes were commonly enslaved by fraud or tyrannical laws. The opinion, which was essentially the same as the one which brought José de Bolonha's expulsion from Bahia, was reported to have caused sharp discontent in the French colonies.[1]

Curiously enough, similar scruples were expressed in Puritan Massachusetts, a fact which shows the persistence in Christianity, both Catholic and Protestant, of the ancient legalistic distinction between lawful captives and the victims of unjust violence. The slavery of the former was authorized in 1641 by the Massachusetts Body of Liberties. But four years later when a New England ship returned from Africa with two slaves, a legal squabble between the captain and mate brought out the fact that the Yankees had seized the Negroes by treachery and violence. Fearing divine retribution, the Puritan authorities extended their jurisdiction to acts committed on the coast of Africa, and ordered the arrest of both captain and mate. It was solemnly determined that the two Negroes should be returned to their native land.[2]

1. Russell P. Jameson, *Montesquieu et l'esclavage: étude sur les origines de l'opinion antiesclavagiste en France au XVIIIe siècle* (Paris, 1911), pp. 131–4.
2. Elizabeth Donnan (ed.), *Documents Illustrative of the History of the Slave Trade to America* (Washington, 1930–35), III, pp. 4–9; John Winthrop, *Winthrop's Journal 'History of New England', 1630–1649* (ed. by

But while Protestant theologians condemned treachery, deceit and man-stealing, their views on the legitimacy of slavery were necessarily coloured by traditional Christian doctrine and by their direct experience, which was generally more limited than that of Catholics in Iberia and Latin America, with various forms of servitude. In England the controversies beginning in the 1660s over kidnapping children and other defenceless people for shipment as servants to America may have led to a greater awareness of unscrupulous modes of procuring slaves; but the increase in convicts transported to America may also have fortified the belief that many African slaves had been similarly spared a deserved punishment of death. William Ames, whom the Puritans looked to as a seminal thinker, had doubted whether a master could hold an innocent servant in absolute bondage without violating the Golden Rule; but even he had admitted that a crime deserving death might be legitimately punished by perpetual slavery.[3]

In general, British theologians accepted the traditional Christian dualisms regarding slavery, which they tended to associate with milder forms of domestic servitude and with the Hebrew bondage of the Old Testament. William Perkins and Samuel Willard, who may be taken as representative of English and American Puritanism, agreed that Aristotle had been wrong in thinking of slavery as a

---

James K. Hosmer, New York, 1908), II, pp. 251–3. There seems to be no basis for the argument that the General Court showed a bias against slavery in the case of Captain James Smith and his mate, Thomas Keyser. The question of the Negroes arose only after a complicated legal dispute between Smith and Keyser, and their respective backers in Massachusetts. The mate, apparently doubting Smith's honesty, had refused to unload a cargo of wine at Barbados, and had sailed to Boston, leaving the captain behind. When Smith arrived home he brought action against Keyser and the crew for taking the ship away from Barbados. It was at this point that some of the sailors told dark rumours about Smith seizing innocent Negroes and helping some Englishmen assault a town and slaughter its people. The case involved much besides the origin of the slaves.

3. William Ames, *De conscientia, et eius iure, vel casibus* (Amsterdam, 1654), V, xxiii, 3 (p. 326). Ames said, however, that liberty was so naturally dear to men that some preferred death to bondage. I use 'innocent servant' to convey Ames's meaning of a voluntary servant who was guilty of no crime.

product of nature.[4] According to Williard, the pagan philosophers had been ignorant of man's primitive state of perfection, and had erroneously identified the law of nature with what they observed in the sinful world. Since all bondage had arisen from man's universal corruption, and since all men owed their primary allegiance to God, no master could claim the right of absolute dominion, and no servant could forfeit his entire liberty. On this crucial point of limiting all worldly power the Puritans were at one with Robert Sanderson, a conservative Anglican, who maintained that we 'must not acknowledge any our *supreme Master,* nor yield our selves to be *wholly* and *absolutely* ruled by the will of any . . . but only *Christ* our Lord and Master in Heaven'. William Ames, like Epictetus, feared that 'perfect' servitude would corrupt a master. Perkins held that the institution of slavery, where established by positive law, might 'stand with good conscience, if it be used with moderation'. But no master had the right to separate families, to command what was forbidden by God, or even to bind servants 'to perpetuall slaverie, and never make them free'. Willard said a master must recognize that the soul of his slave was worth as much as his own, and forbear from cruel punishments, 'scurrilous and undue threatenings', or from giving his servants scornful titles as if they were creatures of another species.[5]

But this preference for limited servitude and for charitable relations between master and slave was more than offset by a fear that the wrong kind of liberty would lead to a forgetfulness of sin and to an overturning of social order. William Gouge, attacking what he took to be the Anabaptist position that all men were equal and that bond service was contrary to nature, said the servant must acquiesce even in unjust beatings, in the knowledge that he would ultimately be

---

4. William Perkins, *The Works of That Famous and Worthy Minister of Christ in the Universitie of Cambridge, Mr W. Perkins* (Cambridge, 1618), III, p. 698; Samuel Willard, *A Compleat Body of Divinity in Two Hundred and Fifty Expository Lectures on the Assembly's Shorter Catechism* (Boston, 1726), p. 613.

5. Willard, *Compleat Body of Divinity,* pp. 613, 615–16, 649; Perkins, *Works,* III, pp. 697–8; Robert Sanderson, *XXXIV Sermons* (6th ed., London, 1674), pp. 290–92; Ames, *De conscientia,* V, xxiii, 3 (p. 326).

vindicated by divine justice.[6] Sanderson was similarly outraged by the Anabaptist view of Christian liberty,

as if *Christ* or his *Apostle* had any purpose ... to slacken those *sinews* and *ligaments*, and to dissolve those *joynts* and *contignations,* which tie into *one body* ... those many little members and parts, whereof all *humane Societies* consist.[7]

Perkins assured his readers that in this life Christian liberty extended only to the spirit; Ames conceded that it was legitimate for a *servant* to accept total bondage out of necessity. Willard explained that though slavery had been brought into the world by sin, 'right reason' showed that the institution was a proper part of the worldly orders of subjection and authority, as well as being profitable and beneficial to mankind. Gabriel Towerson was not even pleased by the gradual abolition of slavery in Eruope, since 'it was neither founded upon any just reason, nor hath prov'd much for the conveniency of the world'. Discussing the Decalogue in 1676, Towerson pointed out that there were many poor men, 'not unlike to certain beasts', who could not govern themselves; slavery would give such a man subsistence and would restrain him from 'those exorbitances, to which either his ignorance or the pravity of his nature may incline him'. And while Towerson would hold masters responsible for providing adequate food and clothing, he told servants that their work was done for God, Who had assigned them to their lowly position.[8] Associating slavery with the image of a stable Christian household ruled by the Bible and right reason, these British Protestants exhorted all bondsmen to revere their masters and to be patient, obedient and diligent. If a

6. Charles H. George and Katherine George, *The Protestant Mind of the English Reformation, 1570–1640* (Princeton, 1961), pp. 298–300.

7. Sanderson, *Sermons,* p. 289.

8. Perkins, *Works,* III, p. 698; Ames, *De conscientia,* V, xxiii, 3 (p. 326); Willard, *Compleat Body of Divinity,* pp. 613–16, 643. Richard B. Schlatter, *Social Ideas of Religious Leaders, 1660–1688* (London, 1940), pp. 66–9. Willard also made it clear that while all men shared a common origin, Providence made distinctions in rank at birth which men were bound to observe. Perkins used the example of Sara and Hagar to show that subjects, like slaves, must bear with unjust punishment from their superiors (Perkins, *Cases of Conscience* [title page missing], III, vi, p. 371).

servant were allowed to question his fate, he would undermine the very foundations of social order.

We have, then, a view of bondage as a reciprocal relationship between loving master and loyal servant, instituted by God for the better ordering of a sinful world, but limited by the rational terms of the social covenant. George Fitzhugh, the most extreme of Southern apologists, would see slavery in the nineteenth century as the ideal form of social order and as the universal bulwark against anarchy; William Lloyd Garrison would conclude that government and law, as well as slavery, were sinful infringements upon Christian liberty. But in the seventeenth century, when there were few hints of this future bifurcation, servitude appeared to balance natural freedom and worldly fate, human authority and the equality of men under the supreme rule of God. Despite a tendency to use the infidelity of Negroes as an excuse for the African trade, Protestant thinkers were usually as wary as their Catholic counterparts in considering the legality of original enslavement.[9] Human bondage they pictured not so much as a righteous punishment as a model of man's dependence on higher authority. By concentrating on the idealized picture of a dutiful servant in a Christian family, it was relatively easy to ignore the violence that produced America's slaves.

It is true that a few Protestant writers continued to raise embarrassing questions. In 1637 the Protestant Synod at Rouen felt it necessary to cite the law of nations in reply to 'overscrupulous persons who thought it unlawful for Protestant merchants to deal in slaves'. In 1704 Jacques Bernard, a Huguenot refugee in Holland, analysed the recently published account of the Guinea trade by William Bosman, a Dutch factor, and found support for his earlier belief in an eternal contradiction between slaveholding and the Golden Rule. A Lutheran divine, Johann Buddeus, asserted that even if some Negroes had been legally captured or convicted of crime, their children should not inherit the penalty of bondage. But this latter objection could be met by the argument of Gabriel Towerson, Samuel

9. Perkins, who once stated that servants should not be 'procured and retained by force; for it is a more grievous crime to spoil a man of his liberties, than of his riches', went on to justify the enslavement of prisoners of war (*Works*, III, p. 698).

Pufendorf and the great jurist, Johann Heineccius, that some men were by nature incapable of maintaining or governing themselves.[10]

Hence Cotton Mather told Negroes in Massachusetts that they should give up their 'fondness for freedom', and recognize that as slaves they lived better than they would as freemen.[11] A number of British writers claimed that the Negro slave, whose 'moderate labour' was unaccompanied by the wretched insecurity of the English lower class, enjoyed 'a state of comparative felicity'; and that, at any rate, 'men in savage life have no incentive to emulation: persuasion is lost on such men, and compulsion to a certain degree, is humanity and charity'.[12] When a young squire from Dorset was confronted for the first time with a West Indian slave market, he soothed his conscience by reflecting that 'surely God ordained 'em for the use and benefit of us: otherwise his Divine Will would have been made manifest by particular sign or token'. And as an absentee planter the same squire later did his best to reinforce the image of a happy Negro peasantry: he instructed his manager to point out to visitors how much better the slaves lived than the poor in England, and to keep such guests at all times away from the sound of the whip.[13]

Regardless, then, of the justice of original enslavement, American slavery, in its functions and blessings, furnished its own vindication. American slaveholders, even in Jamaica, took comfort in the thought

10. H. A. Wyndham, *Problems of Imperial Trusteeship: The Atlantic and Slavery* (London, 1935), p. 234; Jameson, *Montesquieu et l'esclavage*, pp. 102, 186–7, 202–5.

11. Lawrence W. Towner, ' "A Fondness for Freedom": Servant Protest in Puritan Society', *William and Mary Quarterly*, 2nd ser., XIX (April 1962), pp. 201–2. Mather's assumptions can be found as late as 1768 in Aaron Hutchinson, *Iniquity Purged by Mercy and Truth: A Sermon Preached at Grafton . . . after the Execution of Arthur, a Negro Man, at Worcester, Aged about 21, for a Rape* (Boston, 1769), pp. 19–22.

12. Donnan (ed.), *Documents*, II, pp. 469–70; Bryan Edwards, *The History, Civil and Commercial, of the British Colonies in the West Indies* (Philadelphia, 1806), II, pp. 236–8. It should be noted that this line of argument tended to supplement or to replace the more legalistic view that the children of slaves owed perpetual service to their parents' master in return for years of unproductive maintenance.

13. Richard Pares, *A West-India Fortune* (London, 1950), pp. 121–2.

they had simply received their bond servants from others, and bore no moral responsibility for what might have happened in Africa or on the high seas. In 1788, indeed, a committee of the Jamaican assembly had the audacity to state that the slave trade was purely a British affair for which West Indians bore no responsibility'.[14] But this dissociation of American slavery from the legitimacy of African enslavement, while giving planters a sense of moral security, left the foundations of the system highly vulnerable to attack.

To make American slavery conform to the ancient Christian ideal of servitude not only meant that Negroes should be baptized and instructed in the faith, but that they should be brought to internalize those precepts of humility, patience and willing obedience which would allow masters to rule by love instead of force. But how was this to be done? Jean-Baptiste Du Tertre thought Negroes in the West Indies confirmed Plato's observation that God had deprived slaves of half their reason in order to keep them from reflecting upon their wrongs. The missionary noted that the Negroes were lighthearted and apparently oblivious of their sufferings; yet their arrogant, unpredictable temper obliged masters to punish them for the least fault. What if religious instruction succeeded in restoring that part of reason which understood injustice, but failed to replace pagan boldness with Christian humility? Du Tertre skirted around this question, and concluded that missionaries at least provided slaves with the only protection they would receive: 'If interest alone were ever to rule in the Islands, it is certain there would no longer be any relief.'[15] He saw little value in the perfunctory baptisms that the Portuguese gave their Negroes before shipment to Africa, but above all, he held up for scorn the British and Dutch planters who, following a principle of their 'so-called Reformation' that prohibited Christians from holding their brethren in captivity, refused even to baptize their slaves.[16]

14. *Journals of the Assembly of Jamaica*, VIII (Jamaica, 1804), p. 410.
15. Jean-Baptiste Du Tertre, *Histoire générale des Antilles habitées par les François* (Paris, 1667–71), II, pp. 526, 529–34, 538. For the Jesuits' heroic efforts to convert slaves in Saint Domingue, against strong planter resistance, see George Breathett, 'The Jesuits in Colonial Haiti', *Historian*, XXIV (February 1962), pp. 153–71.
16. Du Tertre, *Histoire générale*, II, pp. 502–3. The fear that baptism

Du Tertre pointed to a fundamental difference between the Catholic and Protestant Churches which was bound to affect their relationship with American slavery. Catholics might be very slow in providing slaves with meaningful religious lives, and might long discriminate against even freedmen of the proscribed race. But in time, the Catholic emphasis on universality would remove most of the distinctions that barred the descendants of slaves from spiritual equality. The relative exclusiveness of the Protestants, which was associated with their emphasis on individual responsibility, presented an additional barrier to the Christianization of Negro bondage.

Nevertheless, Du Tertre's challenge was taken up by a number of eminent British Protestants, the most notable of whom were Richard Baxter and Morgan Godwyn. Although Baxter praised rulers who enacted laws making baptism equivalent to emancipation, because this might induce infidels to seek Christianity, he adhered to the traditional view that faith affected the soul rather than external condition. Accordingly, he told servants to *'reverence that providence of God which calleth you to a servant's life, and murmur not at your labour, or your low condition; but know your mercies, and be thankful for them'*. Masters, on the other hand, held their power as Christ's trustees, and were obliged to lead even Negro slaves towards a Christian life, or risk being convicted of open rebellion against God.[17]

Godwyn, who had lived for a time in Virginia and Barbados, was even more emphatic in defending the compatibility of slavery and Christianity:

would emancipate a slave was widespread in the British colonies and long persisted in Surinam, according to Philippe Fermin, no slave could be baptized until his master had purchased letters of franchise (*Déscription générale, historique, géographique et physique de la colonie de Surinam* [Amsterdam, 1769], p. 136). The origin of the belief would seem to be the ancient Hebrew distinction between Jews and Canaanites; but as we have seen, the early Fathers of the Church specifically denied that baptism freed a slave.

17. Richard Baxter, *Chapters from a Christian Directory, or a Summ of Practical Theology and Cases of Conscience* (ed. by Jeannette Tawney, London, 1925), pp. 15, 27–30. Baxter drew a sharp contrast between the sins of Barbados and the virtues of New England, where Eliot had converted the natives and where, he erroneously thought, none had been enslaved. The original edition was printed in 1673.

It [Christianity] establisheth the Authority of *Masters*, over their Servants and Slaves, in as high a measure, as even themselves could have prescribed ... exacting the strictest *Fidelity* ... *requiring service with singleness of heart, as unto the Lord*, and not unto men. ... And so far it is from encouraging Resistance, that it allows them not the *liberty* of *Gainsaying*, or making undutiful replys to their Masters. And referring them to *future recompence in Heaven*, for their *faithful* services done to them upon *Earth* ...[18]

In addition to making slaves better workers, Christianity was the best security against disloyalty and insurrection. Nor was there any ground for the belief that baptism entailed liberation. Abraham's slaves had not been freed by circumcision. Onesimus had not been freed by baptism, except in the sense that counted most, for as a Christian he was free from the law of Judaism, free from the lusts of the flesh, and free to serve Christ, which was the most perfect freedom of all. About 1680 Godwyn had heard on good authority that the late Lord Chancellor had once declared he knew of no law in England whereby baptism would release a slave from service, 'and certainly he, if any Man, must have known it'. Colonists, therefore, had no excuse for withholding religion from their slaves. If there were any laws, originally enacted to make Christianity more appealing, which might be construed as prejudicial to slavery, this danger could easily be removed by legislative authority. And if colonists were uncertain of the validity of their own laws, they could appeal to the king and Parliament – without being bound by 'that over-proud fear of thereby acknowledging *what they cannot possibly avoid*, their dependence upon *England*'. In any event, American masters could enjoy clear consciences only if they knew they had not condemned their Negroes to an eternal slavery in hell.[19]

18. Morgan Godwyn, *The Negro's and Indians Advocate, Suing for Their Admission into the Church: or a Persuasive to the Instructing and Baptizing of the 'Negro's' and Indians in Our Plantations. Shewing, that as the Compliance herewith Can Prejudice No Mans Just Interest; so the Wilful Neglecting and Opposing of It, Is No Less than a Manifest Apostacy from the Christian Faith* ... (London, 1680), p. 112. We shall discuss the anti-slavery potentialities of both Baxter and Godwyn in chapter 11.

19. ibid., pp. 7, 54, 109–12, 141–6; Godwyn, *Trade Preferr'd Before Religion, and 'Christ' Made to Give Place to 'Mammon'* ... (London, 1685), preface, p. 6.

In 1680 Godwyn offered a fairly comprehensive plan for the Christianization of American slaves. Anglican ministers sent out to the colonies should be economically independent of their planter parishioners, and should be duly rewarded upon their return to England. Unswayed by colonial prejudice, they would have the power to protect Negroes from Sunday labour, restrain them from 'polygamy', and force masters to allow them religious instruction.[20]

Masters, of course, did not look kindly upon such meddling proposals, nor were they convinced that slaves would correctly understand the subtleties of Christian liberty. In the 1630s the Puritan officials of Old Providence Island had rebuked Samuel Rishworth for preaching to Negro slaves; in 1680, the very year Godwyn wrote, the crown's committee of trade and plantations, having heard some Barbadians argue that the chief security of their island lay in keeping the Negroes ignorant and separated by a diversity of languages, decided to leave the question of religion to the colonists.[21] Edward Long, the eighteenth-century Jamaican historian, explained that the planters would be delighted to have their Negroes Christianized if this were practicable. But even Portuguese missionaries had found that Africans had no relish for a religion inculcating precepts of honesty, self-denial and sexual abstinence, and had had to content themselves with meaningless collective baptisms. Negroes might look with awe at the 'mummery' and superstitious ceremonies of the Catholics. Long conceded that on the French islands an authoritarian religion reinforced state policy and helped to keep bondsmen in 'peaceable subjection'. Slaves were aroused, of course, by 'those systems, which are set off with abundance of enthusiastic rant and gesticulation ... such as Quakerism, Methodism and the Moravian rites.' But the Church of England, being founded on principles of reason and liberty, was hardly suited for Negro slaves.[22]

Yet even in the French West Indies the status of baptized Negroes

20. Godwyn, Negro's and Indians Advocate, pp. 153–5.

21. Ulrich B. Phillips, American Negro Slavery: A Survey of the Supply, Employment and Control of Negro Labor as Determined by the Plantation Regime (reprint ed., Gloucester, Mass., 1959), pp. 48, 99.

22. [Edward Long], The History of Jamaica; or, General Survey of the Antient and Modern State of that Island ... (London, 1774), II, pp. 428–31.

was not settled definitely until 1685, and until 1709 there was confusion on the matter in Canada.[23] The *Code Noir* of 1685, which was strongly influenced by Canon Law, came close to Godwyn's ideal (with the important exception of excluding Godwyn's religion from the French islands). Though Negroes were defined as chattels, they were to be baptized and instructed in the true faith, and were not to work on Sundays or religious holidays.[24] But French planters stubbornly resisted the enforcement of these provisions, believing, as did the Barbadians, that their only protection lay in the Negroes' ignorance. An entire century passed after the enactment of the *Code Noir* before plantation attorneys were required to keep records of Negro births and deaths.[25]

Appeals for the Christianization of American slaves raised two problems which were frequently intertwined but which were ultimately the product of a growing incompatibility between chattel slavery and two quite separate traditions of liberty. In spite of ancient precedents for Godwyn's opinion that baptism did not free a slave, there was an equally ancient tradition that no Christian could validly be held in a state of bondage that interfered with his performance of religious duties. As Protestants like William Ames and William Perkins expanded the limits of religious obligation, there was an increasing conflict between slavery and the ideal of Christian service.[26] In addition, as we have already seen, there was a striking discrepancy between colonial slavery and the civil freedom which had become identified with the very soil of England and France. While the concept of chattel slavery had been accepted by medieval jurists and had persisted in law as a form of labour discipline as late as the sixteenth century, the actual condition of English villeins had been greatly ameliorated before the discovery of America. The continuing resistance and open rebellion of peasants, the extension of municipal liberties, the appeals to common law and Magna Charta, and, most of all,

23. Marcel Trudel, *L'Esclavage au Canada française; histoire et conditions de l'esclavage* (Quebec, 1960), pp. 38–41.
24. Lucien Peytraud, *L'Esclavage aux Antilles françaises avant 1789* (Paris, 1897), p. 155 (for the text of the *Code Noir*, see pp. 158–66).
25. ibid., pp. 193–4, 243.
26. For the argument that Christian duty conflicted with the status of slavery, see Chamberline *v.* Harvey, 5 *Mod.* 182, 87 *Eng. Rep.* 596.

the disintegration of the manorial economy, had constantly widened the gap between the basic rights which Englishmen took for granted and the total bondage still sanctioned by the law of nations.

Sir Edward Coke was reported to have ruled that infidels, being perpetual enemies, might legitimately be enslaved by Christians; this was, of course, the position of the Catholic Church, and was endorsed by such authorities as Christian Thomasius, a discipline of Pufendorf and a professor at Halle.[27] As there appeared to be no basis for chattel slavery in English common law, seventeenth-century courts upheld the rights of owners to claim Negroes as property, that is, to maintain an action of trover, by citing the fact of the Negroes' infidelity, and by appealing to the common practice of merchants, whose trade in slaves was presumably sanctioned by the *jus gentium*.[28] In Chambers *v.* Warkhouse (1693), for example, Negroes were termed merchandise and compared with musk cats and monkeys. In Gelly *v.* Cleve (1694) it was decided that trover would lie for a Negro boy because he was a heathen. In 1706, however, in Smith *v* Gould, Chief Justice John Holt ruled that trover would not lie for a Negro, after hearing arguments that in common law no man could have property in another except in the special cases of villeinage, and that the law took no notice of Negroes being different from other men.[29] In Smith *v.* Brown & Cooper (date uncertain), Holt was reported to have said that a Negro became free as soon as he came into England.[30]

27. The precedent of Coke's reasoning with respect to infidels is discussed by W. S. Holdsworth, *A History of English Law*, VII (London, n.d.), p. 484; for Thomasius, see Jameson, *Montesquieu et l'esclavage*, p. 102.

28. See, for example, Butts *v.* Penny (1677), 2 *Lev.* 201, 83 *Eng. Rep.* 518; in this case, however, one Thompson argued that there could not be sufficient property in a man to maintain trover.

29. Smith *v.* Gould (1706), 2 *Salk.* 666, 92 *Eng. Rep.* 338. In addition to the cited reports, I have drawn on the discussions and abstracts in Helen T. Catterall (ed.), *Judicial Cases Concerning American Slavery and the Negro* (Washington, 1926–37), I, pp. 1–12, 55–8; John Codman Hurd, *The Law of Freedom and Bondage in the United States* (Boston, 1858–62), I, pp. 179–83; Thomas R. R. Cobb, *An Inquiry into the Law of Negro Slavery in the United States of America* (Philadelphia and Savannah, 1858), pp. 156–61.

30. Smith *v.* Brown & Cooper, 2 *Ld. Raym.* 1274 (?), 91 *Eng. Rep.* 566. The facts of this case, however, are unclear.

And what if a Negro became a Christian and lived under the jurisdiction of the common law? The problem of the effects of baptism arose in the case of Chamberline v. Harvey (1696–7), but the point was left without decision.[31] A number of other judicial cases added to the complexity of the problem until, in 1729, the attorney-general and solicitor-general gave their formal opinions that baptism could not alter the temporal condition of a slave within the British kingdoms, and that a slave was not freed by the mere fact of being brought to England.[32]

This judgement was accepted by a writer in the *Gentleman's*

31. The case was exceedingly complex. The plaintiff was the son of a deceased Barbadian planter, whose wife, the plaintiff's mother, had remarried and moved to England, taking with her a Negro boy. She and her new husband had died, and the boy, who had been baptized without the consent of the plaintiff, had served various people for wages before being employed by the defendant. The plaintiff, who had inherited part of his father's property and who had reversion rights to the rest, brought an action of trespass. It was argued on behalf of the plaintiff that 'perfect bondage' had been allowed in free, Christian countries, that the laws of Barbados had the same force there that acts of Parliament did in Britain, that the status of the Negro slave was analogous to that of the villein *regardant*, and that such a slave could be freed neither by baptism nor by coming to England. For the defendant it was argued that while the 'constitution of nations' permitted the enslavement of prisoners of war, the institution was contrary to nature; when the origins of servitude were in doubt, liberty must be presumed. In any event, baptism should bring 'immediate enfranchisement'. And if a master in England claimed to have absolute property in his servant, this would be contrary to the common law and Magna Charta; but if a master claimed to have only a qualified property, as in villeinage, an action of trespass would not lie. The court agreed that no trespass would lie for taking away a man generally, and termed the Negro as only a 'slavish servant'. In another account, Holt, C. J. said that trover would not lie for a Negro. But the court side-stepped the issue of baptism (see 1 Ld. Raym. 146, 92 Eng. Rep. 603; and 5 Mod. 182, 87 Eng. Rep. 596. Discussions can be found in Hurd, *Law of Freedom*, I, pp. 181–2; Cobb, *Law of Negro Slavery*, pp. 158–9.)

32. Catterall (ed.), *Judicial Cases*, I, p. 12. The opinion was confirmed by the judgement of Lord Hardwicke (who as Sir Philip Yorke had been attorney-general in 1729), in the case of Pearne v. Lisle (1749), *Amb.* 75, 27 *Eng. Rep.* 47. Since the problem of the Negro slave's legal status in Great Britain was to become a central concern of Granville Sharp and was closely related to the early anti-slavery movement, we shall postpone a fuller discussion of the question to the succeeding volume.

Magazine who had been under the erroneous impression that any slave who set foot on England, France, Spain, Portugal, Holland or Denmark was automatically free. England was filled, he said, with 'daring dogmatizing People' who were continually preaching about liberty and the natural rights of mankind, and maintaining that 'to have any Hand in bringing any of the Human Species into *Bondage*, is justly execrable, and that all who partake in the Sweets of *Liberty* shou'd spare for no Cost to procure the same . . . for the rest of Mankind every where'. But when one mentioned the African trade to these people, they were struck dumb. Who among the boldest partisans of liberty 'hath once publickly opened his Mouth before the Court or any where else, on the Subject of the *Slave*-Trade . . . or so much as attempted in any printed Sermon, Speech, or Pamphlet, to consider the Justice or Legality of it?'[33]

It was certainly true that the Church of England overlooked whatever incompatibility there might have been between Negro slavery and English notions of liberty. Godwyn's thesis that Christianity posed no threat to the slaveholder was taken up in 1711 by William Fleetwood, Bishop of St Asaph, in a sermon delivered before the Society for the Propagation of the Gospel in Foreign Parts.[34] In 1727 the Bishop of London told American masters that conversion would place their slaves 'under stronger Obligations to perform those Duties with the greatest Diligence and Fidelity, not only from the Fear of Men, but from a Sense of Duty to God'. Nor would baptism have the slightest effect on the outward condition of slaves: 'The

33. *Gentleman's Magazine*, XI (1741), pp. 186–7. While the writer in general defended colonial planters and accused Britons of hypocrisy, he forecast the appearance of *A Treatise Proving the Absolute Unlawfulness of the Slave-Trade.*

34. Frank J. Klingberg, *An Appraisal of the Negro in Colonial South Carolina; A Study in Americanization* (Washington, 1941), pp. 35–7; Marcus W. Jernegan, 'Slavery and Conversion in the American Colonies', *American Historical Review*, XXI (April 1916), p. 511; Faith Vibert, 'The Society for the Propagation of the Gospel in Foreign Parts: Its Work for the Negroes in North America before 1783', *Journal of Negro History*, XVIII (April 1933), pp. 190–91; William S. Jenkins, *Pro-Slavery Thought in the Old South* (Chapel Hill, 1935), pp. 19–20. Like Godwyn before him, Fleetwood held that Negroes were not inherently inferior, and that religious duty must have precedence over economic interest.

Freedom which Christianity gives, is a Freedom from the Bondage of Sin and Satan, and from the Dominion of Mens Lusts and Passions and inordinate Desires.'[35]

The colonists, however, had not waited for these classical reassurances, but beginning with Maryland, in 1664, had enacted laws stating that baptism did not free a slave.[36] Perhaps the last colony to take such a precaution was, of all places, Prince Edward Island, the Canadian maritime province, whose legislature ruled in 1781 that 'all Negro and Mulatto servants' then on the island or afterwards imported should be slaves, and that baptism should have no effect on their status.[37] Yet the continuing insistence of such legislation revealed a deep-seated doubt which was to remain the greatest obstacle to the Christianization of Anglo-American slavery. And the growing contradiction between colonial slavery and British ideals of liberty was exposed with unconscious irony by the Englishmen of the 1760s who complained that Negroes in the London area 'cease to consider themselves as slaves in this free country ... nor more willingly perform the laborious offices of servitude than our own people, and if put to do it, are generally sullen, spiteful, treacherous, and revengeful.'[38]

Morgan Godwyn had foreshadowed a mood and concern which would stir the Church of England at the beginning of the eighteenth century and give birth to a number of ambitious programmes for the

35. Edward Gibson, *Two Letters of the Lord Bishop of London . . .* (London, 1727), pp. 10–11.

36. I am indebted to Winthrop D. Jordan for the information about the Maryland law, which is found in *Archives of Maryland*, I, pp. 526; II, p. 272; chapter 5 of his study, 'White Over Black', provides the best discussion of slave conversion I have seen, though unfortunately I had written this chapter before reading it. A Virginia law of 1670 exempted from slavery those servants who were Christians at the time of their importation; in 1682 the exemption was narrowed to 'Negroes, Moors, mullatoes or Indians, who and whose parentage and native country are not Christian at the time of their first purchase . . . by some Christian' (Hurd, *Law of Freedom*, I, pp. 323–35).

37. William R. Riddell, 'The Baptism of Slaves in Prince Edward Island', *Journal of Negro History*, VI (July 1921), p. 308.

38. *Gentleman's Magazine*, XXXIV (1764), p. 493.

Christianization of American slavery. We cannot discuss this rising missionary movement in detail, but may note that it was in part a direct response to the sudden burgeoning of the African trade. Six years after Parliament had opened the slave trade to independent merchants, Gilbert Burnet, Bishop of Sarum, reflected that if Britain were to receive so much wealth from the labour of Negroes, the least she could do in return was to save their souls.[39] But this direct response, which evidenced a slightly uneasy state of conscience, drew upon a more general impulse to Christianize the social order that blended British traditions of philanthropy with a kind of benevolistic pietism whose influence extended from Germany to Massachusetts.

During the seventeenth century the wealthy classes of Britain, particularly the rising mercantile aristocracy, had increasingly identified a pious life with munificent gifts or bequests designed to improve the condition of the poor or to promote religion, education or public health.[40] Though mostly directed towards local problems of poverty and social disorganization, these benefactions had included funds for the redemption of Englishmen enslaved by Barbary corsairs.[41] By the early eighteenth century a new spirit of religious tolerance and cosmopolitanism induced philanthropists to look beyond the needs of their countrymen and also to borrow from the thought and practice of foreign reformers. If German Pietists, such as Philipp Jakob Spener, were inspired partly by British Protestantism, the debt was repaid when the German home mission movements and the celebrated orphan house at Halle made a profound impression on the English-speaking world. Cotton Mather eagerly read the 'Devout Spener' on 'the distinguishing Acts of true, real, vital Piety', and corresponded with August Herman Francke.[42] The Germans' interest in reforming society through groups of 'earnest Christians'

39. Klingberg, *Appraisal of the Negro*, pp. 36–7.

40. Wilbur K. Jordan, *Philanthropy in England, 1480–1600: A Study of the Changing Pattern of English Social Aspirations* (London, 1959), pp. 15–18, 56–76, 143–7, 215, 361.

41. C. W. W. Greenidge, *Slavery* (London, 1958), pp. 119–26.

42. Cotton Mather, *Diary of Cotton Mather* (reprinted., New York, n.d.), II, pp. 23, 74, 193, 315, 332, 348, 364, 400, 406, 456, 490, 497, 524, 534, 734. Mather sent some gold as a donation for the orphan house.

was echoed in Massachusetts by Mather's Societies for the Suppression of Disorders and by his *Essays to Do Good*, which exhorted masters to treat servants 'in some sense' like their own children, and which animated the young Benjamin Franklin with a zeal for good works.[43]

A similar frame of mind can be seen in Thomas Bray, who was one of the founders of the Anglican Society for Promoting Christian Knowledge, and whose experience in Maryland as Commissary for the Bishop of London led directly, in 1701, to the formation of the SPG. Interested in all branches of missionary work, Bray was pleased to encounter in Holland one Abel Tassin, Sieur d'Allone, who contributed nine hundred pounds for the aid and instruction of American Negroes.[44] This fund, supplemented by a bequest intended to support a school for Negro children and those parents who were 'inclineable' to Christianity, was administered after 1723 by another organization, 'Doctor Bray's Associates', whose members were soon to play a dual role as Trustees for the Colony of Georgia.[45] Meanwhile, the sympathy of Englishmen had been aroused by the plight of Protestant emigrés from Germany and by the efforts of a godson of Spener's, Count Ludwig Zinzendorf, to build a refuge on his estates for the persecuted Moravian Brethren. Zinzendorf sent a group of his Moravians to Georgia, and on the westward voyage their piety and serene faith made the deepest impression on a fellow traveller, a young SPG missionary named John Wesley. Even by 1732 the Moravians had acted upon their conviction that it was a positive duty to convert all heathen to Christianity, and had sent out missionaries from their isolated asylum at Herrnhut. Within a few decades these brave representatives of a sect that had been nearly exterminated during the Thirty Years' War would be preaching the word of God to

43. Cotton Mather, *Essays to Do Good, Addressed to all Christians Whether in Public or Private Capacities* (Boston, 1808), pp. 58–60; *The Papers of Benjamin Franklin* (ed. by Leonard W. Labaree *et al.*, New Haven, 1959), I, p. 255.

44. Edgar L. Pennington, *Thomas Bray's Associates and Their Work Among the Negroes* (Worcester, Mass., 1939), pp. 3–7.

45. ibid., pp. 7–17, 63–7; Verner W. Crane, 'The Philanthropists and the Genesis of Georgia', *American Historical Review*, XXVII (October 1921), pp. 63–7.

Negroes, both in the West Indies and on the North American continent.[46]

It is perhaps not remarkable that a tradition of persecution should make men concerned with at least the spiritual fate of slaves. The first missionaries of the SPG to work for the conversion of Negroes, Elias Neau and Francis Le Jau, were former Huguenots. A generation later, when George Whitefield tried unsuccessfully to establish a Negro school in Pennsylvania, his chief supporters were Gilbert Tennent, an evangelistic leader of the Great Awakening, John Stephen Benezet, a former Huguenot refugee, and Benjamin Franklin.[47] Benezet, as a Quaker convert, provides a link with another minority sect whose traditions of persecution and resistance to absolute power were similar to those of Huguenots and Moravians.[48] For three years after the Conventicle Act of 1664, English Quakers were themselves threatened with the punishment of being shipped to America as temporary slaves, and some members of the Society were still in prison in 1671, when George Fox told the Negroes in Barbados that Christ had also died for them.[49] We must postpone a fuller discussion of Quakerism to a later chapter, but it should be noted that Friends provided English Protestants with the first examples of evangelizing Negro slaves. Morgan Godwyn had been a violent anti-Quaker, but he had also witnessed the activities of George Fox in Barbados.[50] Quaker

46. J. H. Buchner, *The Moravians in Jamaica* (London, 1845), pp. 16–36; Lowell Joseph Ragatz, *The Fall of the Planter Class in the British Caribbean, 1763–1833* (New York, 1928), pp. 28–9; Edward R. Turner, *The Negro in Pennsylvania: Slavery, Servitude, Freedom, 1639–1861* (Washington, 1911), pp. 43–4. The first Moravian missionary in the British West Indies, Zacharias G. Carries, arrived in Jamaica in 1754.

47. *Papers of Benjamin Franklin*, II (New Haven, 1960), pp. 285, 291.

48. For Huguenot theories on the limitation of power, see Guy Howard Dodge, *The Political Theory of the Huguenots of the Dispersion, with Special Reference to the Thought and Influence of Pierre Jurieu* (New York, 1947), pp. 52–65, 132–3.

49. Abbot Emerson Smith, *Colonists in Bondage: White Servitude and Convict Labor in America, 1607–1776* (Chapel Hill, 1947), pp. 175–9.

50. Godwyn, *Negro's and Indian's Advocate*, p. 4; Thomas Drake, *Quakers and Slavery in America* (New Haven, 1950), pp. 5–7; George Fox, *Journal* (ed. by Ernest Rhys, London, 1944), p. 277.

missionary efforts were severely shaken when William Edmundson's programmes for the religious instruction of slaves raised a storm of protest in Barbados and resulted, in 1676 and 1680, in harsh restrictive laws.[51] In later years, as the Society of Friends won acceptance as a dissenting sect, it tended to lose its original missionary zeal. But the precedents remained.

The missionary movements backed by the S PG and Bray's Associates could draw on resources that dwarfed those of Quakers and Moravians. Officially supported by the Church of England, these philanthropists could also count on the cooperation of the government, which regularly sent instructions to colonial governors asking them to encourage the conversion of Indians and Negroes, and to seek laws protecting slaves from inhuman cruelty.[52] Throughout the parishes of England men were becoming more concerned with the spiritual life of white colonists as well as of pagans, and contributed freely to support missionaries, schools, and the distribution of Bibles and religious tracts. But even if American colonists had welcomed it, there were insuperable obstacles to the mass conversion of Negro slaves. At a time when the majority of the British poor was without church or minister, and when colonial planters were dispersed over immense areas, living often beyond the reach of organized religion or communal discipline, it was quite out of the question to bring a meaningful Christian life to hundreds of thousands of slaves. And the sheer physical difficulties of numbers and distances were more than equalled by the problem of communicating with men of a radically different culture, whose knowledge of English was at best imperfect, and who were shrewd enough to suspect, as the Reverend James Blair admitted, that pronouncements that baptism did not bring emancipation were part of a colonial conspiracy to block the benign intentions of the English king. Blair went on to say that when Negroes had misconstrued the sincere efforts of missionaries, it had been necessary

51. Drake, *Quakers and Slavery*, p. 8.
52. Leonard W. Labaree, *Royal Government in America: A Study of the British Colonial System before 1783* (New Haven, 1930), pp. 118–19; Frank J. Klingberg, 'The evolution of the Humanitarian Spirit in Eighteenth-Century England', *Pennsylvania Magazine of History and Biography*, LXVI (1942), pp. 265–7.

to hang a few troublemakers who had rebelled against the view that Christianity brought no change in status.[53]

But the greatest obstacle lay in the indifference or open hostility of the American colonists. Missionaries and catechists assured planters that Christian Negroes would be more loyal and diligent; they often required their new converts to promise, before being baptized, not to seek freedom.[54] Yet most slaveholders were unconvinced, and were quick to blame disturbances or insurrections on ministers who had allegedly filled the minds of slaves with dangerous notions of liberty. And quite apart from the fear that religion would awaken a yearning for freedom, most planters were unwilling to allow religious instruction to break the continuity of the working week, even for children. Those Negroes who were not required to labour in gangs on Sunday were usually expected, in Pennsylvania as well as in the West Indies, to spend the day tending their own provision gardens.[55] The entire routine of the semi-autonomous plantation might be upset by the arrival of an itinerant minister, whose presence would be especially unwelcome if he happened to represent a denomination alien to the surrounding country. Religious rivalry made even so ardent a proponent of Negro conversion as Cotton Mather look with suspicion on the missionary activities of the SPG.[56]

Notwithstanding these formidable difficulties, a number of dedicated missionaries went out to the colonies and did their best to transform the sullen slave into a cheerfully compliant Onesimus. After 1705, when Elias Neau won the SPG's approval for his pre-

53. Pennington, *Thomas Bray's Associates*, pp. 42–3. Blair was writing to the Bishop of London from Virginia.

54. Jernegan, 'Slavery and Conversion', p. 511; Pennington, *Thomas Bray's Associates*, pp. 24–5, 40, 56–7; Vibert, 'Society for the Propagation of the Gospel', pp. 179–85. By 1776, however, even a committee of the Jamaican assembly agreed that religious instruction of slaves would promote morality and prevent future rebellion (*Journals of the Assembly of Jamaica*, VI [Jamaica, 1800], p. 655).

55. Jernegan, 'Slavery and Conversion', pp. 516–20; Vibert 'Society for the Propagation of the Gospel', p. 189; Pennington, *Thomas Bray's Associates*, pp. 50, 56–7, 63.

56. Mather, *Diary*, II, p. 410. For the controversy over Jamaica's laws restricting dissenting missionaries, see *Slave Law of Jamaica: With Proceedings and Documents Relative Thereto* (London, 1828), pp. 230–63.

vious instruction of slaves in New York, they built schools, visited Negroes in hovels and garrets, taught children to read and to recite Scripture, and remonstrated with stubborn masters. In South Carolina, Brian Hunt suggested that if every tenth Negro were taught to read, the precious skill would soon germinate through the plantation shanties. South Carolinians received this thought with something less than enthusiasm, and the Reverend Hunt despondently returned to England. But despite a law of 1740 which forbade teaching Negroes to write, Alexander Garden, who represented the SPG and Bray's Associates, founded a Negro school at Charles Town which functioned successfully for twenty years. Believing that the children of slaves could transmit literacy and religion to their parents, Garden also employed his earliest pupils to instruct their successors. Occasionally, masters cooperated with these reformers, or initiated their own experiments in slave education.[57]

The SPG achieved its greatest successes in South Carolina, Philadelphia and New York, where Anglican strength was reinforced by the institutional resources of urban societies. Except for the small-scale activities of the Moravians, the movement to Christianize slaves hardly touched the West Indies, and it languished in Maryland and Virginia.[58] In New England, as we have seen, Cotton Mather warmly endorsed the cause. His morbidly sensitive conscience was responsive to the communal guilt which he knew was in some way involved with Negro slavery (one may note that the witch-seeing girls of Salem had been originally inspired by a Negro servant). Owners of Negroes might become the happy instruments for converting 'the *Blackest* Instances of *Blindness* and *Baseness,* into admirable *Candidates* of Eternal Blessedness'. Admitting that Africans were 'the most Brutish of Creatures upon Earth', and that they might be the offspring of Ham, Mather was scornful of those who whispered that they lacked

57. Klingberg, *Appraisal of the Negro,* pp. 4–13, 44–5, 51–9, 70, 101–22; Pennington, *Thomas Bray's Associates,* pp. 24–32. Bray's Associates hired two Moravian missionaries who had been procured for James Oglethorpe by Count Zinzendorf, a fact which shows the interrelationship of benevolistic reformers.

58. Carter G. Woodson, *The Education of the Negro Prior to 1861* (New York, 1915), pp. 26–50; Jernegan, 'Slavery and Conversion', pp. 514–16; Pennington, *Thomas Bray's Associates,* pp. 46, 52–7, 63–81.

rational souls. Since some of Christ's chosen might be found among them, Mather appealed, 'Let us make a Trial, Whether they that have being Scorched and Blacken'd by the Sun of *Africa*, may not come to have Minds Healed by the more Benign *Beams* of the *Sun of Righteousness*'.[59] Mather was certain that his essay, *The Negro Christianized*, would enrage the devil, and that he would 'immediately be buffeted, in some singular manner, by that revengeful Adversary'. But he was equally confident that national calamities could be prevented if a copy of this pamphlet were placed in every house in New England and the West Indies. Mather named his own Negro boy Onesimus (he was highly incensed when a worldly navy lieutenant named *his* slave Cotton Mather), and for some years he maintained a charity school for the religious instruction of Negroes.[60]

But hostility to the Church of England prevented New England leaders from cooperating with the SPG; the exclusiveness and decentralized character of Congregationalism were obstacles to well-organized missionary effort. Relatively few Negroes were accepted into eighteenth-century New England churches, and those few were often segregated both in worship and burial.[61] Although the Great Awakening gave a slight impetus to the cause of slave conversion throughout the colonies, the zeal of the earlier missionaries did not stimulate an expanding crusade. By the 1760s a number of Negro schools were still in operation, and the movement initiated by the SPG and Bray's Associates had succeeded in bringing perhaps a few thousand Negroes to Christianity and to a rudimentary literacy. It had not, however, laid the foundations for the Christianization of American slavery.[62]

In any event, one should not exaggerate the novelty of these efforts

59. [Cotton Mather], *The Negro Christianized: An Essay to Excite and Assist that Good Work, the Instruction of Negro-Servants in Christianity* (Boston, 1706), pp. 2–3, 23.

60. Mather, *Diary*, I, pp. 176–7, 564–5, 579; II, pp. 532, 663.

61. Lorenzo J. Greene, 'Slave-Holding New England and Its Awakening', *Journal of Negro History*, XIII (October, 1928), pp. 505–8; Lorenzo Greene, *The Negro in Colonial New England, 1620–1776* (New York, 1942), pp. 266–84; Pennington, *Thomas Bray's Associates*, p. 89.

62. For the Great Awakening and, especially, the work of Samuel Davies, see Jernegan, 'Slavery and Conversion', pp. 514, 523–5.

which were so similar in aim and expectation to the programmes of Catholic missionaries and to the traditional policies of the Church. British missionaries and philanthropists regarded the Negro slave as a man possessing an immortal soul, but the institution of slavery they accepted without question. In practice, indeed, their labours were designed to impose restrictive controls over the few areas of the Negro's life which remained undisciplined. They pointed with horror at the slaves' irregular sexual lives and at evenings and Sabbaths spent in merrymaking and licentious dancing. Accepting the necessity of forced labour, they strove to make the slaves' leisure time and social relationships conform to the standards of Protestant morality.[63] It is understandable why some Negroes saw little benefit in a religion which sanctioned their masters' authority, which enjoined them to avoid idleness and to toil more diligently, and which promised to deprive them of their few pleasures and liberties. Yet one cannot doubt the sincerity or courage of reformers like Francis Le Jau and Alexander Garden, who devoted years to the struggle against colonial prejudice and to the often disheartening task of educating and disciplining men of a totally alien culture.

The most dramatic failure of the ideology represented by Godwyn, Mather and Bray's Associates came with the attempt of the SPG to build two model plantations in Barbados. In 1710 Colonel Christopher Codrington bequeathed the Society two Barbadian estates equipped with over three hundred Negro slaves. His request that missionaries be sent to live a monastic life on the estates, and that a college be founded for the instruction, conversion and uplift of the Negroes, seemed to offer a perfect opportunity to demonstrate that Christianity and slavery were compatible. When West Indian planters saw that Christian slaves on the Codrington plantations were more faithful and diligent than any others, they would realize that their true interest lay in converting their own plantations into model

63. Klingberg, *Appraisal of the Negro*, pp. 14–17; Pennington, *Thomas Bray's Associates*, pp. 24–5; Mather, *Diary*, I, pp. 176–7. My conclusion is different from that of Klingberg, who in various studies has pictured antislavery and efforts to Christianize and ameliorate the condition of slaves as parts of a single, swelling current of humanitarianism.

estates where masters and servants would be bound by ties of mutual affection and obligation. Not, perhaps, since Las Casas's experiments at Cumaná had there been such a vision of building a community where separate races might live together harmoniously in the light of Christian ideals.[64]

From the start, however, there were two sobering restraints on such designs for a model slave commonwealth. First, the S PG had no thought of sacrificing the rich profits which the Codrington estates had been earning from the cultivation of sugar. Second, if Barbadian planters were to be shown that slaves could safely be Christianized, it would not do to ignore their prejudices against allowing Negroes undue freedom or privileges. As a result of these practical considerations, the S PG hired agents to manage the estates, and decided not to meddle with a profit-making enterprise by imposing unconventional rules and regulations.[65]

From 1717 to 1726 the S PG failed to make a single convert among its slaves in Barbados. By 1725 the housing for the college had been nearly completed, but financial reverses interrupted the project, and for twenty years the building stood unused. When a school finally did begin to function, it was restricted to white children. Whatever interest the S PG had in the spiritual welfare of its slaves was damped down by the contagious fear of the colonists that literate slaves and public security were irreconcilable. In 1768 the Society's officials in London, who had fallen out of touch with Barbadian affairs, asked the chaplain at Codrington what progress had been made in Negro education. Apparently astonished at such a question, he patiently explained why nothing at all had been done: like Du Tertre, he observed that Negroes were generally perverse and intractable, and

64. J. Harry Bennett, Jr, 'The Society for the Propagation of the Gospel's Plantations and the Emancipation Crisis', in *British Humanitarianism: Essays Honoring Frank J. Klingberg* (ed. by Samuel Clyde McCulloch, Philadelphia, 1950), pp. 16–18; J. Harry Bennett, Jr, *Bondsmen and Bishops: Slavery and Apprenticeship on the Codrington Plantation of Barbados, 1710–1838* (Berkeley, 1958), pp. 1–3. Codrington's wish that missionary teachers and scholars live under monastic vows of poverty, chastity and obedience was disregarded by the S PG.

65. Bennett, *Bondsmen and Bishops*, pp. 3–5, 82–5; Bennett, 'Society for the Propagation of the Gospel's Plantations', p. 18.

that they were really much happier being ignorant. As late as 1793 it was reported that only three of the Codrington Negroes could read, and they were elderly and scarcely literate. In the end, it took one hundred and twenty years for the 'college' to begin its assigned work of instructing and converting slaves.[66]

But what of the model Christian society which would point the way to a general reform of slavery's worst abuses? The ironies generated by the discrepancy between ideal and reality were perhaps best illustrated in 1732, when a Codrington attorney suggested that the SPG might discourage the practice of branding the chests of newly purchased Negroes with the letters 'S-O-C-I-E-T-Y'.[67] A few years later the slaves protested in a group against harsh treatment and excessive labour, an act which resulted in an immediate tightening of discipline. The SPG even failed in its desultory efforts to preserve the Sabbath as a day of rest and worship, since profitable management required a six-day week of labour, and on Sundays Negroes were accustomed to grow their own provisions and to entertain themselves with dancing and trading. On the subject of marriage the Society remained, as one historian has said, 'discreetly silent'.[68] With the exception of half-hearted moves towards a perfunctory conversion of Negroes, the day-to-day practices of the Codrington plantations were much the same as on less hallowed estates. Instead of providing a model for others to follow, the agents of the SPG conformed to whatever local policies and usages seemed to promise the greatest profits.

By the 1760s, however, it was difficult to decide which policies would bring continuing profits. From 1712 to 1761 the Codrington estates had been stocked with some four hundred and fifty new slaves from Africa. This number had been greatly reduced by disease, suicide, accident, and the usual mortality incident to 'seasoning'. Since males outnumbered females, and miscarriages, as well as infant deaths, were common, the death rate had been more than six times

66. Bennett, *Bondsmen and Bishops*, pp. 4–9, 75–86, 98. In 1795 the SPG opened a Sunday school for Negro children, who, of course, were required to work during the week (pp. 106–7).

67. ibid., p. 27.

68. ibid., pp. 22–9, 35.

greater than the rate of births. The fact that the total population of slaves had declined by about one-third in fifty years was damaging both to profits and to the popular image of a happy and well-treated Negro peasantry. After experimenting with hiring slaves from other owners, and with buying a heavily mortgaged estate in order to obtain its seasoned slaves, the managers pondered the economic benefits which might result from encouraging Negro births and from reducing the rate of mortality.[69]

It is difficult to see how this search for alternatives to importing slaves from Africa can be pictured as a trend towards amelioration which would have led inevitably to a kind of humane serfdom.[70] Certainly this was not the case in the United States, where from 1808 to 1860 the slave population increased spectacularly without much benefit from the African trade, and where the burdens of the Negro were not lightened. And if economic pressure led the SPG to abandon its part in the slave trade and to take measures to prolong the lives of its Negroes, one may observe that in 1827, four years after the British government had called for the amelioration and eventual end of slavery, Codrington Negroes, including women, were still driven in the fields by whips, no records were kept of their punishments, their marriages were as yet unsanctified, and they could not look forward, even with good behaviour, to a possible reward of manumission. Without the mounting pressure of a powerful anti-slavery movement, it is questionable whether the SPG would have been shaken from its easy compromises with the American slave system. But even by 1766 the Codrington plantations were an ideal target for men like Bishop William Warburton, who were beginning to doubt that slavery could be made compatible with Christian duty.[71]

We have seen that for some three centuries both Catholics and

69. ibid., pp. 44–74.

70. While I have leaned heavily on Bennett's excellent detailed study of the Codrington plantations, I cannot altogether agree with his optimistic view of the trend towards amelioration (ibid., pp. 136–41). But Bennett does not go nearly so far as Klingberg in stressing the SPG's 'contribution' to progress.

71. Bennett, 'Society for the Propagation of the Gospel's Plantations', pp. 22–6; Bennett, *Bondsmen and Bishops*, pp. 89–90, 116–22.

Protestants found ways of reconciling their beliefs in natural liberty and limited worldly power to the harsh realities of Negro slavery. There were two sides to the conventional rationalization. Glossing over the question of the legality of original enslavement, which was partly obscured by a misunderstanding of Africa, men envisioned the slave trade as a useful instrument for the conversion of pagans, who even as chattel slaves were much better off than their brothers trapped in the dark hell of Africa. But this view of the African side of the system could ultimately be justified only if slavery in America appeared to conform to that happy Christian servitude which had traditionally been seen as a model of the fraternal relationship of unequals. By 1770 it was evident that, in the British colonies at least, hopes for the Christianization of slavery had been ill-founded. When Anthony Benezet denounced the SPG for owning slaves, the society proudly pointed to its evangelizing efforts in Barbados, only to discover that its claims could not be substantiated. The Society's agents concluded that Negroes could not live meaningful Christian lives unless they had first been civilized; and yet their access to civilization was barred by white colonists who feared that nothing was more dangerous than civilized slaves. It was, in the last analysis, the Negro's cultural difference that justified his being held as a slave. Paradoxically, the same cultural gap that impeded Christianization, and thus weakened the American side of the great rationalization, carried implications which would one day undermine the African side. If the Negro could be fitted within the classic framework of primitivism and civilization, which had previously been applied to the American Indian, he would not appear as a pagan rescued from the violence and superstition of a half-civilized barbarism, but as an innocent child of nature ruthlessly seized from his native forests to satisfy the greed of merchants and planters. By the 1760s, quite apart from external influences of anti-slavery thought, there were severe internal strains in the balanced dualisms which for centuries had shaped Christianity's response to slavery.

8

The Continuing Contradiction of Slavery:
A Comparison of British America
and Latin America

WAS anti-slavery, then, a direct outgrowth of slavery itself? We have maintained that the concept of man as a material possession has always led to contradictions in law and custom. In the ancient world these contradictions did not give rise to abolitionism; but in the historical development of American slavery there were deep strains that made the institution a source of dissonance and discontent. Even men whose interests were closely tied to the system expressed occasional misgivings over mounting debts and economic decay, the rising proportion of Negroes to whites, the haunting threat of insurrection, the failure to infuse masters and slaves with a spirit of Christian love, and the growing discrepancy between American servitude and European ideals of liberty. It remains to be asked whether the evolution of colonial laws and customs provided a basis for believing that the worst evils of slavery could be gradually eliminated through wise legislation, or for concluding that slavery by its very nature was beyond reform.

Such a question poses many problems. As a result of differences in economy, social and political institutions, and the ratio of Negroes to whites, the actual status and condition of colonial slaves varied considerably from one region to another. Yet no slave colony had a monopoly on either kindness or cruelty. Slave codes were often enacted with a view to quieting local fears or appeasing a church or government. Travellers were sometimes biased or quick to generalize from a few fleeting impressions. Since we still seriously lack a thorough comparative study of Negro slavery in the various colonies, we must be content with fragmentary evidence and with extremely tentative conclusions. There would seem to be some basis, however, for questioning two assumptions which have been widely accepted by modern historians.

The first is that Negro slavery in the British colonies and Southern United Sates was of a nearly uniform severity, the slave being legally deprived of all rights of person, property and family, and subjected to the will of his owner and the police power of the state, which barred his way to education, free movement or emancipation. The second assumption is that the French, and especially the Spanish and Portuguese, were far more liberal in their treatment of slaves, whom they considered as human beings who had merely lost a portion of their external freedom. Untainted by racial prejudice and free from the pressures of a fluid, capitalistic economy, these easy going colonists are supposed to have protected the human rights of the slave and to have facilitated his manumission. Some historians have simply held that slavery in North America was much harsher than that in Latin America, but Stanley M. Elkins has argued more persuasively that the great contrast was not in the bondsman's physical well-being but in the recognition of his basic humanity.[1] As a methodological device,

1. Stanley M. Elkins, *Slavery: A Problem in American Institutional and Intellectual Life* (Chicago, 1959), pp. 27–80. It is not my purpose to question all of Elkins's highly imaginative insights, or to attempt to prove that differences in religion, economy and social structure had no bearing on the institution of Negro slavery. My aim is simply to show that the importance of such national and cultural differences has been exaggerated, and that all American slaveholding colonies shared certain central assumptions and problems. I do not believe that the modern historian can escape what Elkins terms the moral 'coercions' of the great nineteenth-century controversies by portraying both American slavery and anti-slavery as the pathological results of 'the dynamics of unopposed capitalism'. It should be noted that Elkins borrowed much of his conceptual framework from Frank Tannenbaum's enormously influential *Slave and Citizen: The Negro in the Americas* (New York, 1947). Though Tannenbaum was one of the first historians to emphasize the importance of Negro slavery in the overall development of the Americas, it seems to me that his comparison of Latin and Anglo-American slavery suffers from three basic weaknesses. First, he assumes that North American law, unlike that of Latin America, refused to recognize the slave as a moral personality. But this is an error, as we shall see. Second, he ignores the fact that the 'classical' view of slavery, as embodied in Latin culture, drew as much from Plato and Aristotle as from Cicero and Seneca. Nineteenth-century Brazilian reformers, such as José Bonifácio, found it necessary to counter their opponents' use of classical authorities by arguing that Greeks and Romans had been ignorant of divine religion, and that, in any

this distinction has obvious merit, since a master might look upon his slaves as subhuman animals and still provide them with comfortable maintenance. On the other hand, it would be unrealistic to draw too sharp a line between moral status and physical treatment. It is difficult to see how a society could have much respect for the value of slaves as human personalities if it sanctioned their torture and mutilation, the selling of their small children, the unmitigated exploitation of their labour, and the drastic shortening of their lives through overwork and inadequate nourishment. While a few isolated instances of sadistic cruelty would reveal little about the legal or moral status of slaves, we should not exclude physical treatment when it is part of a pattern of systematic oppression which is fully sanctioned by the laws and customs of a society. We shall find, however, that there is other evidence than physical treatment for challenging the assumption that Latin Americans were more sensitive than Anglo-Americans to the essential humanity of their slaves.

This assumption has important implications for a history of anti-slavery thought. If servitude under the Spanish and Portuguese was generally mild and humane, and if the institution itself tended to promote a gradual achievement of freedom, then we should not be surprised by the fact that anti-slavery agitation began in Britain and

---

event, slavery in antiquity had not been so severe as that in Brazil, where racial and cultural differences deprived the bondsman of opportunities for equality (José Bonifácio de Andrada e Silva, *Memoir Addressed to the General, Constituent and Legislative Assembly of the Empire of Brazil . . .* [tr. by William Walton, London, 1826], pp. 20–22). As in Roman and North American law, the slave in Latin America was conceived at once as a chattel or instrument, and as a man with a soul. Third, Tannenbaum seems to think of Negro slavery in Latin America as a relatively unchanging institution, and assumes that certain humane laws of the late eighteenth and nineteenth centuries were typical of bondage in all Latin America throughout its long history. Even more questionable is his assumption that the admirable laws of European governments were obeyed by colonial slaveholders. For a thoughtful discussion of the Tannenbaum–Elkins thesis, see Sidney Mintz's long review of Elkins's book in *American Anthropologist,* LXIII (June 1961), pp. 579–87. An article which appeared after this chapter was written, and which presents a similar thesis, is Arnold A. Sio, 'Interpretations of Slavery: The Slave Status in the Americas', *Comparative Studies in Society and History,* VII (April 1965), pp. 289–308.

British America. The peculiar severities of British colonial slavery would appear to have arisen from local economic or social conditions, and we should have reason to suspect that anti-slavery movements were a direct response to an unprecedented evil. And while the extremes of both slavery and anti-slavery could be explained by the absence of a stable social structure, we could conclude that the Anglo-American reformer might well have looked to Latin America for a rational model. By gradually imposing the institutional protections of Latin American slavery on the formless and unregulated slavery of the north, he might have removed the evils from a necessary system of labour. But if the contrast between slavery in the various American colonies was not so clear-cut as has generally been supposed, we are left with a different set of implications. It would be likely that the appearance of anti-slavery agitation was less a direct response to a unique evil than a result of particular cultural and religious developments in the English-speaking world. And if both the evils of slavery and the attempts to ameliorate them were fairly pervasive throughout the Americas, we should look more sceptically at programmes for slow and gradual reform. We should expect to find general emancipation often associated with revolutions and civil wars, as was the case in Saint Domingue, the United States and several of the Spanish colonies, or with political upheaval and the fall of a government, as in Brazil.[2]

A word of explanation is in order regarding the chronological range of selected examples and illustrations. If we are to judge the

2. The violence of the American Civil War has led some historians to assume that other nations abolished Negro slavery without bitter conflict. Yet even in Brazil, where Dom Pedro II strove consciously to avoid the bloody course taken by the United States, there was a radical abolitionist movement, an underground railroad and sectional cleavage; the stormy conflict played an important part in bringing the downfall of the monarchy (see especially, Percy A. Martin, 'Slavery and Abolition in Brazil', *Hispanic American Historical Review*, XIII [May 1933], pp. 151–96). British planters in the Caribbean frequently threatened secession, and finally submitted to the superior force of the British government only because they were too weak, economically and politically, to resist. They might have acted differently, as did the planters of Saint Domingue during the French Revolution, if Britain had moved to abolish slavery at the time of their greatest power.

influence of traditional Catholic culture, the crucial period in Latin American slavery is the early colonial era, before the full impact of the Enlightenment, the American and French Revolutions, and the wars of independence. But when we test the assumption that slavery in the British colonies and Southern United States was of a mono-lithic character, unmitigated by any recognition of the Negro's rights of personality, it is appropriate to select examples from the nine-teenth century, when laws and customs had hardened to form a self-contained system of values and precedents. If some of the ameliorative elements we usually associate with Latin American sla-very were common in North America, even at a time when bondage had grown more formalized and severe, then we should have less reason to suppose that the basic evils of the institution could have been eliminated by mere palliative reforms.

By the late eighteenth century most travellers agreed that in Brazil and the Spanish colonies the condition of slaves was considerably better than in British America.[3] Any comparison must consider Negro slavery as a system of forced labour, of social organization, and of class and racial discipline. Numerous accounts from the late eighteenth and nineteenth centuries tell us that the Latin American slave enjoyed frequent hours of leisure and was seldom subjected to

3. Sir Harry Johnston, *The Negro in the New World* (New York, 1910), pp. 42–7, 87–94; Henry Koster, *Travels in Brazil* (London, 1816), pp. 385–6, 390, 444; Mary M. Williams, 'The Treatment of Negro Slaves in the Brazilian Empire: a Comparison with the United States', *Journal of Negro History*, XV (1930), pp. 313–36; Donald Pierson, *Negroes in Brazil* (Chicago, 1942), pp. 45–6; H. B. Alexander, 'Brazilian and United States Slavery Compared', *Journal of Negro History*, VII (1922), pp. 349–64; Gilberto Freyre, *The Masters and the Slaves: A Study in the Development of Brazilian Civilization* (tr. by Samuel Putnam, New York, 1946), pp. 7–11, 40–41, 369 ff. and *passim*; Tannenbaum, *Slave and Citizen*, pp. 56, 100–105. An occasional traveller, such as Alexander Marjoribanks, observed that if Brazilian slaves were as well treated as those in the United States, there would have been no need to rely so heavily on the African trade as an answer to slave mortality (*Travels in South and North America* [London, 1853], p. 60). Freyre, Johnston and Pierson have balanced a generally favourable picture of Latin American slavery with references to extreme cruelty and suffering.

the factory-like regimentation that characterized the capitalistic plantations of the north; that he faced no legal bars to marriage, education or eventual freedom; that he was legally protected from cruelty and oppression, and was not stigmatized on account of his race. This relative felicity has quite plausibly been attributed to a culture that de-emphasized the pursuit of private profit, to the Catholic Church's insistence on the slave's right to marry and worship and to what Gilberto Freyre has termed the 'miscibility' of the Portuguese, which submerged sensitivity to racial difference in a frank acceptance of sexual desire.[4]

No doubt there is much truth in even the idyllic picture of the Brazilian 'Big House', where slaves and freemen pray and loaf together, and where masters shrug their shoulders at account books and prefer to frolic with slave girls in shaded hammocks. But we should not forget that West Indian and North American planters were fond of idealizing their own 'Big Houses' as patriarchal manors, of portraying their Negroes as carefree and indolent, and of proudly displaying humane slave laws which they knew to be unenforceable. Their propaganda, which was supported by travellers' accounts and which long seemed persuasive to many Northerners and Englishmen, has largely been discredited by numerous critical studies based on a wealth of surviving evidence. Many of the records of Brazilian slavery were destroyed in the 1890s, in a fit of abolitionist enthusiasm, and the subject has never received the careful scrutiny it deserves.[5] Only in recent years have such historians as Octávio Ianni, Fernando Henrique Cardoso, Jaime Jaramillo Uribe and C. R. Boxer begun to challenge the stereotyped images of mild servitude and racial harmony.

There is little reason to doubt that slavery in Latin America, compared with that in North America, was less subject to the pressures of competitive capitalism and was closer to a system of patriarchal rights and semi-feudalistic services. But after granting this, we must

4. Freyre, *Masters and Slaves*, pp. 7–11, and *passim*. But Freyre also maintains that the sexual relations of masters and slaves were authoritarian in character, and often led to sadistic cruelty.

5. Arthur Ramos, *The Negro in Brazil* (tr. by Richard Pattee, Washington, 1951), pp. 19–20.

recognize the inadequacy of thinking in terms of idealized models of patriarchal and capitalistic societies. Presumably an exploitive, capitalistic form of servitude could not exist within a patriarchal society. The lord of a manor, unlike the entrepreneur who might play the role of lord of a manor, would be incapable of treating men as mere units of labour in a speculative enterprise. But neither would he think of exploring new lands, discovering gold mines, or developing new plantations for the production of sugar and coffee. It is perhaps significant that accounts of Latin American slavery often picture the relaxed life on sugar plantations after their decline in economic importance, and ignore conditions that prevailed during the Brazilian sugar boom of the seventeenth century, the mining boom of the early eighteenth century, and the coffee boom of the nineteenth century. Similarly, Southern apologists tended to overlook the human effects of high-pressure agriculture in the south-west, and focus their attention on the easygoing and semi-patriarchal societies of tidewater Maryland and Virginia. Eugene D. Genovese has recently suggested that while the North American slave system was stimulated and exploited by the capitalist world market, it retained many pre-capitalistic features, such as a lack of innovation, restricted markets and low productivity of labour, and actually gravitated towards an uneconomical paternalism that was basically antithetical to capitalistic values.

Although a particular instance of oppression or well-being, can always be dismissed as an exception, it is important to know what range of variation a system permitted. If an exploitive, capitalistic form of servitude was at times common in Brazil and Spanish America, and if North Americans conformed at times to a paternalistic model and openly acknowledged the humanity of their slaves, it may be that differences between slavery in Latin America and the United States were no greater than regional or temporal differences within the countries themselves. And such a conclusion would lead us to suspect that Negro bondage was a single phenomenon, or *Gestalt*, whose variations were less significant than underlying patterns of unity.

Simon Gray, a Natchez river boatman, provides us with an example of the flexibility of the North American slave system. During the 1850s, most Southern states tightened their laws and to all appearances erected an impassable barrier between the worlds of slave and freeman. But the intent of legislators was often offset by powerful forces of economic interest and personality. Simon Gray was an intelligent slave whose superior abilities were recognized by both his master and the lumber company which hired his services. In the 1850s this lowly slave became the captain of a flatboat on the Mississippi, supervising and paying wages to a crew that included white men. In defiance of law, Gray was permitted to carry firearms, to travel freely on his own, to build and run sawmills, and to conduct commercial transactions as his company's agent. Entrusted with large sums of money for business purposes, Gray also drew a regular salary, rented a house where his family lived in privacy, and took a vacation to Hot Springs, Arkansas, when his health declined. Although there is evidence that in Southern industry and commerce such privileges were not as uncommon as has been assumed, we may be sure that Simon Gray was a very exceptional slave.[6] He might well have been less exceptional in Cuba or Brazil. The essential point, however, is that regardless of restrictive laws, the Southern slave system had room for a few Simon Grays. The flatboat captain could not have acted as he did if the society had demanded a rigorous enforcement of the law.

By the time Simon Gray was beginning to enjoy relative freedom, Portugal and Brazil were the only civilized nations that openly resisted attempts to suppress the African slave trade. It has been estimated that by 1853 Britain had paid Portugal some £2,850,965 in bribes intended to stop a commerce whose horrors had multiplied as a result of efforts to escape detection and capture. But despite British bribes and seizures, the trade continued, and was countenanced by the society which has been most praised for its humane treatment of slaves. One of the boats captured by the British, in 1842, was a tiny vessel of eighteen tons, whose crew consisted of six Portuguese. Between decks, in a space only eighteen inches high, they had intended to stow two hundred and fifty African children of about seven years

6. John H. Moore, 'Simon Gray, Riverman: a Slave Who was Almost Free', *Mississippi Valley Historical Review*, XLIX (December 1962), pp. 472–84.

of age.[7] Suspicion of Britain's motives probably prevented more outspoken attacks on a trade that outraged most of the civilized world. But the fact remains that Brazilian society not only permitted the slave trade to continue for nearly half a century after it had been outlawed by Britain and the United States, but provided a flourishing market for Negroes fresh from Africa. During the 1830s Brazil imported more than four hundred thousand slaves; in the single year of 1848 the nation absorbed some sixty thousand more. That the reception of these newcomers was not so humane as might be imagined is suggested by a law of 1869, six years after Lincoln's Emancipation Proclamation, which forbade the separate sale of husband and wife, or of children under fifteen. Not long before, even children under ten had been separated from their parents and sent to the coffee plantations of the south.[8]

These examples are intended only to illustrate the range of variation that could occur in any slave society, and hence the difficulties in comparing the relative severity of slave systems. Barbados and Jamaica were notorious for their harsh laws and regimentation, but occasional proprietors like Josiah Steele or Matthew Lewis succeeded in creating model plantations where Negroes were accorded most of the privileges of white servants. John Stedman, who provided

7. Christopher Lloyd, *The Navy and the Slave Trade: The Suppression of the African Slave Trade in the Nineteenth Century* (London, 1949), pp. 34, 45. The United States showed laxness in suppressing the African trade, and American ships and capital helped to supply slaves to the chief nineteenth century markets, Cuba and Brazil. But this laxness was quite a different thing from the open approval of the slave trade by Brazilians. And a recent study which takes a more favourable view of the American attempts to suppress the slave trade points out that between 1837 and 1862 American ships captured at least 107 slavers (Peter Duignan and Clarence Clendenen, *The United States and the African Slave Trade, 1619–1862* [n.p. (Stanford University), 1963], p. 54).

8. Octávio Tarquinio de Sousa, *História dos fundadores do Império do Brasil* (Rio de Janeiro, 1957–8), IX, p. 74; Stanley J. Stein, *Vassouras: A Brazilian Coffee County, 1850–1900* (Cambridge, Mass., 1957), p. 20; Williams, 'Treatment of Negro Slaves in the Brazilian Empire', p. 325. Not only did laws protecting the unity of slave families come surprisingly late, but they were for the most part unenforceable. See Stein, *Vassouras*, pp. 155–9; Martin, 'Slavery and Abolition in Brazil', *passim*.

Europe with ghastly pictures of the cruelty of Dutch masters in Surinam, also maintained that humanity and gentleness coexisted with the worst barbarity. The well-being of any group of slaves was subject to many variables. It seems certain that the few Negroes in eighteenth-century Quebec lived a freer and richer life than hundreds of thousands of slaves in nineteenth-century Brazil and Cuba, despite the fact that the latter were technically guarded by certain legal protections, and the former were defined as chattels completely subject to their owners' authority. Islands like Dominica and Saint Lucia, which were disorganized by war and a transfer from one nation to another, had few social resources for restraining the unscrupulous master or curbing slave resistance. In the newly developed lands of captured or ceded colonies, such as Berbice, Demerara, Trinidad and Louisiana, there were few effective checks on the speculative planter bent on reaping maximum profit in the shortest possible time. And whereas the North American slave frequently lived in a land of peace and plentiful food, his West Indian brother was the first to feel the pinch of famine when war cut off essential supplies, or when his master was burdened by debt and declining profits. On the small tobacco farms of colonial Virginia and Maryland the physical condition of slaves was surely better than in the mines of Minas Gerais or on the great plantations of Bahia, where a Capuchin missionary was told in 1682 that a Negro who endured for seven years was considered to have lived very long.[9]

9. Lowell Joseph Ragatz, *The Fall of the Planter Class in the British Caribbean, 1763–1833* (New York, 1928), pp. 66–7, 70–71; John Gabriel Stedman, *Narrative of a Five Years' Expedition, Against the Revolted Negroes of Surinam* ... (London, 1796), I, pp. 201–7; Marcel Trudel, *L'Esclavage au Canada française: histoire et conditions de l'esclavage* (Quebec, 1960), pp. 160–92, 232–56; C. R. Boxer, *The Golden Age of Brazil, 1695–1750: Growing Pains of a Colonial Society* (Berkeley, 1962), p. 174; *Acts of the Assembly, Passed in the Charibbee Leeward Islands from 1690 to 1730* (London, 1732), *passim*; W. L. Burn, *Emancipation and Apprenticeship in the British West Indies* (London, 1937), pp. 64–70. Jean F. Dauxion-Lavaysse, who had travelled widely in the Spanish, French and British colonies, said that the slaves on Sir William Young's model plantation at Saint Vincent were treated better than any he had seen (*A Statistical, Commercial, and Political Description of Venezuela, Trinidad, Margarita, and Tobago* [tr. by E. Blaquière, London, 1820], p. 390).

North American planters were fond of comparing the fertility of their own slaves with the high mortality and low birth rate of those in the West Indies and Latin America, and of concluding that theirs was the milder and more humane system. Such reasoning failed to take account of the low proportion of female slaves in the West Indies, the communicable diseases transmitted by the African trade, and the high incidence of tetanus and other maladies that were particularly lethal to infants in the Caribbean. No doubt differences in sanitation and nutrition, rather than in physical treatment, explain the fact that while Brazil and the United States each entered the nineteenth century with about a million slaves, and subsequent importations into Brazil were three times greater than those into the United States, by the Civil War there were nearly four million slaves in the United States and only one and one-half million in Brazil.[10] But after all such allowances are made, it still seems probable that planters in Brazil and the West Indies, who were totally dependent on fresh supplies of labour from Africa, were less sensitive than North Americans to the value of human life. When a slave's life expectancy was a few years at most, and when each slave could easily be replaced, there was little incentive to improve conditions or limit hours of work. According to both C. R. Boxer and Celso Furtado, Brazilian sugar planters took a short-term view of their labour needs, and accepted the axiom, which spread to the British Caribbean, that it was good economy to work one's slaves to death and then purchase more. In colonial Brazil, Jesuit priests felt it necessary to admonish overseers not to kick pregnant women in the stomach or beat them

10. Gaston Martin, *Histoire de l'esclavage dans les colonies françaises* (Paris, 1948), pp. 124–35; Ragatz, *Fall of Planter Class*, pp. 34–5; Frank W. Pitman, 'Slavery on British West India Plantations in the Eighteenth Century', *Journal of Negro History*, XI (October 1962), pp. 610–17; Celso Furtado, *The Economic Growth of Brazil: A Survey from Colonial to Modern Times* (Berkeley, 1963), pp. 127–8. There is a certain irony in the fact that pro-slavery Southerners like Thomas R. R. Cobb accepted the conventional anti-slavery view of the West Indies. In contrast with the cruelty, impersonality and despotism of the islands, North American masters and slaves worked side by side in clearing forests, building new homes and hunting game; consequently, there developed a sense of cooperation and mutual sympathy which was unknown in the Caribbean, or so Cobb claimed in his *Inquiry into the Law of Negro Slavery* (Savannah, 1858), pp. clvii–clix.

with clubs, since this brought a considerable loss in slave property.[11]

But what of the benevolent laws of Latin America which allowed a slave to marry, to seek relief from a cruel master, and even to purchase his own freedom? It must be confessed that on this crucial subject historians have been overly quick to believe what travellers passed on from conversations with slaveholders, and to make glowing generalizations on the basis of one-sided evidence.

Much has been made of the fact that the Spanish model law, *las Siete Partidas*, recognized freedom as man's natural state, and granted the slave certain legal protections. But the argument loses some of its point when we learn that the same principles were accepted in North American law, and that *las Siete Partidas* not only made the person and possessions of the bondsman totally subject to his master's will, but even gave owners the right to kill their slaves in certain circumstances.[12] Some of the early Spanish and Portuguese legislation protecting Indians has erroneously been thought to have extended to Negroes as well. In actuality, the first laws pertaining to Negroes in such colonies as Chile, Panama and New Granada were designed to prohibit them from carrying arms, from moving about at

11. Furtado, *Economic Growth of Brazil*, pp. 51, n. 129; C. R. Boxer, *Race Relations in the Portuguese Colonial Empire, 1415–1825* (Oxford, 1963), p. 101; Boxer, *Golden Age of Brazil*, pp. 7–9; Maurilio de Gouveia, *História da escravidão* (Rio de Janeiro, 1955), p. 68. In 1823 José Bonifácio noted that while Brazil had been importing some 40,000 slaves a year, the increase in the total slave population was hardly perceptible. Like British and North American reformers of a generation earlier, he was confident that the abolition of the trade would force masters to take better care of their human property (*Memoir Addressed to the General, Constituent and Legislative Assembly*, pp. 26–8).

12. *Las Siete Partidas de Rey don Alfonso el Sabio . . .* (Madrid, 1807), III, pp. 117–28. Even Elsa V. Goveia exaggerates the liberality of Spanish law, although she rightly emphasizes the importance of an authoritarian government in checking the worst inclinations of slaveholding colonists. In the British West Indies, where the colonists long had a relatively free hand in framing their own laws, slaves were for a time deprived of virtually any legal protection. But given the loopholes and ambiguities in the Spanish law, one suspects that any difference in actual protection was more a result of differences in administrative machinery than in legal traditions (see Goveia, 'The West Indian Slave Laws of the Eighteenth Century', *Revista de ciencias sociales*, IV [March 1960], pp. 75–105).

night and, above all, from fraternizing with Indians.[13] It is true that in the late seventeenth and early eighteenth centuries the Portuguese crown issued edicts intended to prevent the gross mistreatment of Negro slaves. But as C. R. Boxer has pointed out, Brazilian law was a chaotic tangle of Manueline and Filipine codes, encrusted by numerous decrees which often contradicted one another, and which were interpreted by lawyers and magistrates notorious for their dishonesty. Even if this had not been true, slaves were dispersed over immense areas where there were few towns and where justice was administered by local magnates whose power lay in land and slaves. It is not surprising that in one of the few recorded cases of the Portuguese crown intervening to investigate the torture of a slave, nothing was done to the accused owner. This revisionist view receives support from Jaime Jaramillo Uribe's conclusion that the judicial system of New Granada was so ineffective that even the reform legislation of the late eighteenth century did little to change the oppressive life of Negro slaves.[14]

In theory, of course, the Portuguese or Spanish slave possessed an immortal soul that entitled him to respect as a human personality. But though perfunctorily baptized in Angola or on the Guinea coast, he was appraised and sold like any merchandise upon his arrival in America. Often slaves were herded in mass, stark naked, into large warehouses where they were examined and marketed like animals. As

13. Rollando Mellafe, *La introducción de la esclavitud negra en Chile: tráfico y rutas* (Santiago de Chile, 1959), pp. 76–82; Richard Konetzke (ed.), *Colección de documentos para la historia de la formación social de Hispanoamérica, 1493–1810* (Madrid, 1962), II, pp. 280, 427–8; Magnus Mörner, 'Los esfuerzos realizados por la Corona para separar negrese indies en Hispano-américa durante el siglo XVI' (unpublished paper); Jaime Jaramillo Uribe, 'Esclavos y señores en la sociedad colombiana del siglo XVIII', *Anuario colombiano de historia social y de la cultura*, I (Bogotá, 1963), pp. 5, 21.

14. Boxer, *Race Relations in Portuguese Colonial Empire*, p. 103; Gouveia, *História da escravidão*, p. 69; Boxer, *Golden Age of Brazil*, pp. 7, 138–9, 306–7; Uribe, 'Esclavos y señores en la sociedad colombiana', pp. 22–5. In 1710 the king of Spain, hearing of the extremely cruel treatment of slaves in Peru and New Spain, issued orders allowing the governors to intervene and sell slaves who had been abused to kinder masters (Konetzke [ed.], *Colección de documentos*, III, pt 1, pp. 113–14).

late as the mid nineteenth century the spread of disease among newly arrived Negroes who were crowded into the warehouses of Rio de Janeiro brought widespread fears of epidemic. The Spanish, who ordinarily sold horses and cows individually, purchased Negroes in lots, or *piezas de Indias*; which were sorted according to age and size. There is abundant evidence that Brazilians were little troubled by the separation of Negro families; in the 1850s coffee planters in the rich Parahyba valley thought nothing of selling their own illegitimate children to passing traders. Despite protests from priests and governors, it was also common practice for Brazilians to purchase attractive girls who could profitably be let out as prostitutes.[15]

In Brazil, as in other slave societies, there were apparently authentic reports of bondsmen being boiled alive, roasted in furnaces, or subjected to other fiendish punishments. More significant than such extreme cases of sadism is the evidence that planters who were successful and were accepted as social leaders equipped their estates with the chambers and instruments of torture; that it was common custom to punish a recalcitrant slave with *novenas*, which meant that he would be tied down and flogged for nine to thirteen consecutive nights, his cuts sometimes being teased with a razor and rubbed with salt and urine. In the mid eighteenth century Manuel Ribeiro Rocha attacked the Brazilian 'rural theology' which allowed masters to welcome their new slaves with a vicious whipping, to work them in the fields without rest, and to inflict one hundred or more lashes without cause. A century later planters in the Parahyba valley taught their sons that Negroes were not true men but inferior beings who could only be controlled by continued punishment; and some of the clergy maintained that Africans were the condemned sons of Cain. This widespread conviction of racial inferiority justified a regime of hatred and brutality in which the slave had no right of appeal and even fatal beatings went unpunished.[16]

15. Boxer, *Golden Age of Brazil*, pp. 2–7, 138, 165; Robert Southey, *History of Brazil* (London, 1817–22), II, pp. 644, 674–5; Georges Scelle, *La traite négrière aux Indes de Castille: contrats et traités d'assiento* (Paris, 1906), I, pp. 504–5; Stein, *Vassouras*, pp. 64, 156–9.

16. Boxer, *Golden Age of Brazil*, pp. 8–9, 45–7; Williams, 'Treatment of Negro Slaves in the Brazilian Empire', p. 326; Ramos, *Negro in Brazil*, pp.

Obviously much depended on regional differences in economy and social tradition. The recent studies of the extreme southern provinces of Brazil by Octávio Ianni and Fernando Cardoso reveal a picture of harsh chattel slavery and racial prejudice which stands in marked contrast to the familiar images of benign servitude in the north. During the last third of the eighteenth century the southern states developed a capitalistic economy which was initially stimulated by the export of wheat, but which came to rely heavily on the production of jerked beef. Whether engaged in agriculture, stock raising, or the processing of meat or leather, the slaveholding capitalists were bent on maximizing production for commercial profit. Because the economy rested on slave labour and because physical labour was largely associated with the African race, Negroes and mulattoes were regarded as mere instruments of production, wholly lacking in human personality. According to Ianni, the slave was a totally alienated being; able to express himself only through the intermediary of his owner, he was under the complete dominion of a master class which rigidly controlled his movements and held power over his life and death. Though kind and paternalistic masters were to be found in Paraná, Santa Catarina and Rio Grande do Sul, as elsewhere in the Americas, the overriding fact is that the ideology and judicial framework of southern Brazil were geared to the maintenance of an exploitive system of labour, to the preservation of public security, and to the perpetuation of power in the hands of a white ruling caste. At every point the Negro was forced to shape his behaviour in accordance with the actions and expectations of the white man.[17]

Conditions were undoubtedly better in the cities, where protective laws were more often enforced and where Negroes had at least a

34–6; Koster, *Travels in Brazil*, pp. 429, 444–55; Boxer, *Race Relations in Portuguese Colonial Empire*, pp. 27, 101, 112; Tarquinio de Sousa, *História dos fundadores do Império do Brasil*, IX, p. 70; Stein, *Vassouras*, pp. 132–9.

17. Octávio Ianni, *As metamorfoses do escravo* (São Paulo, 1962), pp. 82, 134–49, 282–5; Fernando Henrique Cardoso, *Capitalismo e escravidão no Brasil meridional* (São Paulo, 1962), pp. 35–81, 133–67, 310–13; Cardoso and Ianni, *Côr e mobilidade social em Florianopólis: aspectos das relações entre negros e brancos numa comunidade do Brasil meridional* (São Paulo, 1960), pp. 125–35.

chance of acquiring money that could purchase freedom. But in colonial Cartagena Negro slaves were subject to the most repressive police regulations, and to punishments which ranged from death to the cutting off of hands, ears or the penis. In Mariana the city councillors demanded in 1755 that the right to purchase freedom be withdrawn and that slaves who tried to escape be crippled for life. While both proposals aroused the indignation of the viceroy at Bahia, they indicate the state of mind of a master class which, in Minas Gerais, posted the heads of fugitive slaves along the roadsides. And men who accepted such brutality as a necessary part of life could not always be expected to abandon their fields or shut down their sugar mills on thirty-five religious holidays, in addition to fifty-two Sundays.[18] It was not an idyllic, semi-feudal servitude that made colonial Brazil widely known as 'the hell for Negroes', and as a place where their lives would be 'nasty, brutish and short'; or that drove countless bondsmen to suicide or revolt, and reduced others to a state of psychic shock, of flat apathy and depression, which was common enough in Brazil to acquire the special name of *banzo*.[19]

18. Southey, *History of Brazil*, III, pp. 780–84; Uribe, 'Esclavos y señores en la sociedad colombiana', pp. 21–3; Boxer, *Golden Age of Brazil*, pp. 171–2. According to Boxer, in Brazil's 'Golden Age' slaves on sugar plantations were worked around the clock when the mills were grinding cane, and some planters successfully evaded the rules against work on Sundays and religious holidays (*Golden Age of Brazil*, p. 7). In the nineteenth century slaves worked on Sundays and saints' days in the Parahyba valley (Stein, *Vassouras*, p. 75). Obviously there was more incentive to observe such rules when there were fewer pressures to maximize production. But the laws of many British colonies prohibited Sunday work and provided for religious holidays. Edward Long claimed that Jamaican slaves enjoyed about eighty-six days of leisure a year, counting Sundays and Saturday afternoons. The Jamaican slave code of 1816 prohibited Sunday work and ruled that at least twenty-six extra days a year should be given to slaves to cultivate their own gardens. There is evidence, however, that these regulations were disregarded, especially during crop time ([Edward Long], *The History of Jamaica; or, General Survey of the Antient and Modern State of that Island* ... [London, 1774], II, p. 491; *Slave Law of Jamaica: with Proceedings and Documents Relative Thereto* [London, 1828], pp. 2, 63–5, 145–58; Burn, *Emancipation and Apprenticeship*, pp. 44–5).

19. Boxer, *Golden Age of Brazil*, pp. 7–9; Boxer, *Race Relations in*

In the second half of the eighteenth century Spain and Portugal, like Britain and France, became intensely concerned with the reform of imperial administration. Severe losses in the Seven Years' War forced Spain to re-examine her colonial policy and to consider the best means for increasing the labour force, especially in Cuba. Ideas derived in part from the French Enlightenment encouraged statesmen to centralize administration, draft vast systems of law, and experiment with plans for social and economic progress. In Portugal the Marquis de Pombal initiated colonial reforms that included a tightening of administration and the enactment of laws for the protection of slaves and the greater equalization of races. It is important to note, however, that Pombal's legislation affirming the civil rights of Indian and Asiatic subjects did not, in the words of C. R. Boxer, extend 'in anything like the same measure to persons of Negro blood'. And even in Asia there was such racial prejudice among the Portuguese that colonists long resisted the decrees, though they dreaded Pombal's dictatorial methods and usually carried out his orders without delay.[20]

Portuguese Colonial Empire, p. 101; Stein, *Vassouras*, pp. 139–41; Pierson, *Negroes in Brazil*, pp. 3–7; Ramos, *Negro in Brazil*, p. 36. It is interesting to note that, according to Elkins, slavery in the United States was so severe and absolute that it moulded the Negro's character into a submissive, child-like 'Sambo', whose traits resembled those of the victims of Nazi concentration camps. Elkins could find no 'Sambos' in Latin America, and concludes that the character type was unique to the United States (*Slavery*, pp. 81–139). Without debating the merits of this intriguing thesis, we should point out that one source of 'Sambo', which Elkins ignores, can be found in eighteenth-century English literature. In chapter 15 we shall consider how this fictional stereotype suited the tastes of a sentimental age. In actuality, ship captains and planters of various nationalities agreed that when Negroes were subjected to the harshest treatment, their usual responses were revolt, suicide, flight, or a sullen withdrawal and mental depression. The state which the Portuguese described as *banzo* was clearly the result of severe shock which altered the entire personality.

20. Raúl Carrancá y Trujillo, 'El estatuto jurídico de los esclavos en las postrimerías de la colonización española', in *Revista de historia de América* (México, D.F.), no. 3 (September 1938), 28–33; Agostinho Marques Perdigão Malheiro, *A escravidão no Brasil; ensaio historico-juridico-social* (Rio de Janeiro 1866–7), pt 3, pp. 32, 89–129; James Ferguson King, 'The Evolution of the Free Slave Trade Principle in Spanish Colonial Admin-

Inspired by French ideals and administrative techniques, Charles III of Spain also supported a series of enlightened reforms that were intended to increase the force of reason and humanity in the Spanish Empire. Since Spain intended to stock Cuba with prodigious numbers of new slaves, and since the existing laws were a confused patchwork of ancient statutes and ordinances, it was obviously essential to follow the example of Colbert, and construct a code that would ensure a profitable use of labour without wholly subverting the cardinal precepts of religion and morality. Because the *Real Cédula* was drafted in 1789 and bore the influence of the Enlightenment as well as of Spanish-Catholic tradition, it was an improvement over the *Code Noir* of 1685. Mostly notably, it included provisions for registering and keeping records of slaves, and machinery for securing information and punishing masters who denied their slaves adequate food or religious instruction. In 1784 a royal edict had also prohibited the branding of Negroes, a protection which had been given to Indians long before. But in spite of laws and traditions in the Spanish colonies that permitted slaves to buy their own freedom, the *Real Cédula* was silent on the subject of manumission. And it not only ruled that every slave was to work from dawn to dusk, but made clear that his employment should be confined to agriculture alone.[21] There

---

istration', *Hispanic American Historical Review*; XXII (February 1942), pp. 34–56; Boxer, *Race Relations in Portuguese Colonial Empire*; pp. 73–4, 98–100. In 1761 Portugal prohibited the introduction of Negro slaves and ruled that all slaves brought to Portugal, the Azores or Madeira would be emancipated. This law has sometimes been interpreted as humanitarian in motive and has been credited with having abolished slavery in metropolitan Portugal. According to Charles Verlinden, however, slavery remained legal in Portugal, and such legislation was an answer to the protests of free labourers against slave competition. A law of 1773 which provided for the emancipation of imported slaves also prohibited the importation of free coloured labourers from Brazil, and in some ways resembled a French law of 1777 excluding all Negroes (see José Antonio Saco, *Historia de la esclavitud desde los tiempos mas remotos hasta nuestros dias* [2nd ed., Habana, 1936–45], III, p. 345; Charles Verlinden, *L'Esclavage dans l'Europe médiévale*, I: *Péninsule Ibérique, France* [Brugge, 1955], p. 839; Boxer, *Race Relations in Portuguese Colonial Empire*, p. 100).

21. The text of the *Real Cédula* is in Carrancá, 'Estatuto jurídico de los esclavos', pp. 51–9; for a detailed discussion of the law, see pp. 34–49.

are many indications, moreover, that Spanish planters paid little attention to the law. Certainly the Negro slaves who revolted in Venezuela in 1795 did not think their grievances could be expressed through appeals to kindly priests and judges.[22] Without minimizing the importance of the *Real Cédula* as an advance in humane legislation, one may observe that by 1789 there were far more enlightened proposals being discussed in Britain, France and the United States, and that even British and American slaveholders were suggesting reforms that went beyond the Spanish law.

Furthermore, to round out one's picture of Spanish attitudes towards slavery it is well to look at other colonial slave codes, such as the one written for Santo Domingo in 1785, which claimed to be in accordance with a recent royal ordinance. The chief purposes of this detailed code were to reinvigorate a declining economy, to prevent insurrection, to put an end to the growing idleness, pride and thievery of Negroes, and to preserve a clear-cut division between the white race and 'las clases infimas'. Since slaves were regarded as indispensable instruments for the public welfare, their owners were obliged to provide adequate food and clothing. Yet slaves were incapable of acting in their own behalf in court, and could acquire no property except for the benefit and by the permission of their masters. All Negroes, whether slave or free, were barred from public and religious elementary schools; their movements and employment were placed under the strictest regulations; they were required at all times to be submissive and respectful to all white persons, and to treat each one like a master. Any Negro or mulatto who contradicted a white man, or who spoke in a loud or haughty voice, was to be severely whipped. The penalties increased for raising a hand against a white person, but diminished in accordance with the lightness of the offender's skin. The stigma of slavish origin extended even to occupation and dress: Negroes were not to deprive white men of jobs by working in artisan trades, nor were they to wear fine clothes, gold or precious jewels.[23]

22. Uribe, 'Esclavos y señores en la sociedad colombiana', pp. 22–35, 42 ff.; Federico Brito Figueroa, *Las insurrecciónes de los esclavos negros en la sociedad colonial Venezolana* (Caracas, 1901), pp. xii–xiii, 15–17, 41–2.

23. Konetzke (ed.), *Colección de documentos*; III, pp. 553–73. If a

There is evidence that, beginning in the late eighteenth century, Negro bondage became milder and better regulated in certain parts of Latin America. In such areas as New Granada the very survival of the institution was jeopardized by the revolutionary example of Saint Domingue, the outbreak of rebellions and continuing raids by fugitive *cimarrons*, the uncertainty of the African trade in the face of war and British humanitarianism, and the unsettling effects of war on markets and credit. The tumultuous period from the French Revolution to the Spanish American wars for independence brought abrupt changes in economic and political interests which often favoured the Negro slave. But even Cuba, which had a long tradition of encouraging manumissions, was the scene of gross cruelty and heavy slave mortality through much of the nineteenth century; and critics of the régime, like the reformer José Antonio Saco, were either silenced or banished from the island.[24]

In 1823, when the British government pledged itself to the amelioration and eventual eradication of colonial slavery, José Bonifácio de Andrada hoped to persuade his fellow Brazilians that the success of their independence and new constitution depended on making a similar commitment. Although Portugal, he charged, was guilty of the initial sin, 'we tyrannize over our slaves and reduce them to the state of brutish animals, and they, in return, initiate us in their immorality and teach us all their vices'. Calling on Brazil to follow the lead of Wilberforce and Buxton, José Bonifácio's words approached the violence of a Garrison: 'Riches, and more riches, do our pseudo-statesmen cry out, and their call is re-echoed by the buyers and sellers of human flesh, by our ecclesiastical blood hounds, by our magis-

---

Negro raised his hand against a white man, the penalty was one hundred lashes and two years in jail. In the next chapter we shall discuss the parts of this code pertaining to manumissions.

24. Uribe, 'Esclavos y señores en la sociedad colombiana', pp. 21–5; 42–51; Figueroa, *Las insurrecciónes de los esclavos negros*, pp. 41–2; Goveia, 'West Indian Slave Laws', p. 79; Friedrich Heinrich Alexander von Humboldt, *The Island of Cuba* (tr. by J. S. Thrasher, New York, 1856), pp. 211–28, and *passim*; Hubert H. S. Aimes, 'Coartación: A Spanish Institution for the Advancement of Slaves into Freedom', *Yale Review*, XVII (February 1909), p. 421; Augustin Cochin, *The Results of Slavery* (tr. by Mary L. Booth, Boston, 1863), pp. 159–85.

trates.' His proposals included the abolition of the African trade, the creation of special councils for the protection of bondsmen, the encouragement of marriage and religious instruction, and the transfer to a new master of any slave who could prove he had been the victim of cruelty or injustice. While we have been told that these moderate provisions were always characteristic of Brazilian slavery, they received no hearing after the General Constituent Assembly was dissolved and José Bonifácio was arrested and banished. His proposal that the sale of slaves be registered so that a price could be fixed for the eventual purchase of freedom was not guaranteed by statute until 1871, although judges in some areas often enforced such a rule.[25]

In conclusion, it would appear that the image of the warmly human Big House must be balanced by a counter-image of the brutal society of the coffee barons, who even in the 1870s and 1880s governed a world in which there were no gradations between slavery and freedom. In their deep-rooted racial prejudice, their military-like discipline, their bitter resistance to any restrictions on a slave-owner's will, their constant fear of insurrection, and their hostility towards meaningful religious instruction of their Negroes, these planters were hardly superior to their brothers in Mississippi. Even with the approach of inevitable emancipation, they made no effort to prepare their slaves for freedom. It was in the face of this 'slave power' that the Brazilian abolitionists resorted to the familiar demands for 'immediate' and 'unconditional' emancipation, and modelled themselves on the champions of British and American reform. Joaquim Nabuco,

---

25. José Bonifácio de Andrada, *Memoir Addressed to the General, Constituent and Legislative Assembly*, pp. 14–23, 38–53; José Bonifácio de Andrada, *O patriarcha da independencia* (São Paulo, 1939), pp. 288–316; Tarquinio de Sousa, *História dos fundadores do Império do Brasil*, I, pp. 129–30, 247–9; IX, 71–2. The English translator of José Bonifácio's address wrote a preface presenting a more favourable view of Brazilian slavery; but this was in line with British anti-slavery doctrine, which held that British slavery was much worse than that in either Latin America or the United States. José Bonifácio, on the other hand, said his reforms had been drawn from Danish, Spanish and Mosaic legislation, and clearly thought Brazil was lagging behind the more enlightened nations. He was particularly harsh on the clergy, whom he accused of oppressing slaves for profit and sexual gratification.

the great leader of the Brazilian anti-slavery movement, adopted the pen name of 'Garrison'.[26]

With the exception of legal barriers to manumission, which we shall discuss in the next chapter, the salient traits of North American slavery were to be found among the Spanish and Portuguese. Notwithstanding variations within every colony as a result of environment, economic conditions, social institutions and the personality of owners, the Negro was everywhere a mobile and transferable possession whose labour and well-being were controlled by another man. Any comparison of slavery in North and South America should take account of the fact that Brazil alone had an area and variety comparable to all British America, and that the privileged artisans, porters and domestic servants of colonial Brazilian cities can be compared only with their counterparts in New York and Philadelphia. Similarly, conditions in nineteenth-century Alabama and Mississippi must be held against those in the interior coffee-growing areas of south-central Brazil. Given the lack of detailed statistical information, we can only conclude that the subject is too complex and the evidence too contradictory for us to assume that the treatment of slaves was substantially better in Latin America than in the British colonies, taken as a whole.

The slave trade itself was a powerful agent of acculturation – one might say, of Americanization – which tended to blur distinctions in custom and give a more uniform character to Negro slavery than would have been found among earlier forms of European serfdom and villeinage. With the acquisition of important Caribbean islands by Holland, Britain and France, and with the development of sugar

26. Stein, *Vassouras*, pp. 67, 132–45, 155–60, 196–9, 290; Ianni, *As metamorfoses do escravo*, pp. 144–9; Cardoso, *Capitalismo e escravidão no Brasil meridional*, pp. 133–67; Carolina Nabuco, *The Life of Joaquim Nabuco* (tr. and ed. by Ronald Hilton, Stanford, 1950), pp. 108–13. One complex question which we cannot begin to consider is whether the survival of African cultural patterns in Brazil was the result of a less rigorous system of slavery. It seems possible that this persistence of culture was partly a product of heavy slave mortality and a continuing reliance on the African trade. By 1850 most slaves in the United States were removed by many generations from their African origins; this was certainly not the case in Brazil.

planting in the 1640s, the mounting demand for slaves made it impossible for mercantilist governments to prevent the growth of a vast system of smuggling and illicit trade. The same slave ships brought cargoes to mainland and island colonies, and competed with one another in supplying the Spanish. Planters of various nationalities bought slaves at reduced prices at the great Dutch entrepôts at Saint Eustatius and Curaçao. From their forts on the African coast to their colonies in America, the Dutch, French, English, Danes and Portuguese were thrown together in a common enterprise that doubtless produced some blending of customs and attitudes towards the Negro slave.[27] Barbadians not only studied and imitated Brazilian methods of sugar cultivation, but possessed slaves by the 1650s who knew the language and customs of Brazil. In Guadeloupe and Martinique, Dutch émigrés from Brazil introduced the Portuguese practice of allowing slaves to grow their own provisions. During the seventeenth century there were close ties between Barbados and the mainland colonies of North America; and many of the Negroes in the continental colonies had lived for a time in the West Indies. Some of them spoke French, Dutch or Spanish.[28]

27. Evidence of the mixing of nationalities in the slave trade, and of the frequent contact between Dutch, English, French, Spanish, Portuguese, Danes and Swedes, can be found throughout Elizabeth Donnan's *Documents Illustrative of the History of the Slave Trade to America* (Washington, 1930–35). Fernando Romero stresses that the entire slave trade was a single process divided into various branches (Romero, 'The Slave Trade and the Negro in South America', *Hispanic American Historical Review*, XXIV [August 1944], p. 371. See also, Scelle, *Traite négriére*, I, p. 707; Basil Davidson, *Black Mother: The Years of the African Slave Trade* [Boston, 1961], *passim*; Daniel P. Mannix and Malcolm Cowley, *Black Cargoes: A History of the Atlantic Slave Trade, 1518–1865* [New York, 1962], *passim*).

28. Richard Ligon, *A True and Exact History of the Island of Barbados* (London, 1673), pp. 52, 85; Vincent T. Harlow, *A History of Barbados, 1625–1685* (Oxford, 1962), pp. 268–91; Jean-Baptiste Du Tertre, *Histoire générale des Antilles habitées par les François* (Paris, 1667–71), II, p. 515; Frank Wesley Pitman, *The Development of the British West Indies, 1700–1763* (New Haven, 1917), pp. 6–15; Wesley Frank Craven, *The Southern Colonies in the Seventeenth Century, 1607–1689* (Baton Rouge, 1949), pp. 18, 25; 'Eighteenth-Century Slaves as Advertised by Their Masters', *Journal of Negro History*, I (April 1916), pp. 163–216; Pierre-

Much is yet to be learned about this process of cultural exchange and its possible influence on the evolution of systems of slavery in the various colonies. Few questions in American history have been so controversial or so charged with moral significance as the origin of chattel slavery and its relation to racial prejudice. The most convincing recent studies suggest that the mainland colonists adopted from Barbados the view that Negroes were especially suited for perpetual slavery; and that while the early status of some Negroes was close to that of white servants, an increasingly degraded position was both a source and result of racial prejudice.[29] But however unfamiliar perpetual servitude may have been to most Elizabethan Englishmen, as early as 1617 a noted Puritan writer could assume that 'slavish' servants were 'perpetually put under the power of the master, as blackamores with us'.[30] The problem is considerably complicated by the ambiguity of seventeenth-century terms. Some historians have assumed that a 'servant' was not a slave, and yet Samuel Purchas and Thomas Hobbes, to mention only two writers of that century, used the word 'servant' to refer to the most absolute

---

François-Xavier de Charlevoix, *Histoire de l'Isle Espagnole ou de Saint-Domingue* ... (Amsterdam, 1733), III, pp. 162–3; Winthrop D. Jordan, 'The Influence of the West Indies on the Origins of New England Slavery', *William and Mary Quarterly*, 3rd ser., XVIII (April 1961), pp. 248–9.

29. See especially the following articles: Winthrop Jordan, 'Influence of West Indies', pp. 243–50; Jordan, 'American Chiaroscuro: The Status and Definition of Mulattoes in the British Colonies', *William and Mary Quarterly*, 2nd ser., XIX (April 1962), pp. 183–200; Jordan, 'Modern Tensions and the Origins of American Slavery', *Journal of Southern History*, XXVIII (February 1962), pp. 18–30; M. Eugene Sirmans, 'The Legal Status of the Slave in South Carolina, 1670–1740', *Journal of Southern History*, XXVIII (November 1962), pp. 462–73; Carl N. Degler, 'Slavery and the Genesis of American Race Prejudice', *Comparative Studies in Society and History*, II (October 1959), pp. 49–67. The seminal study which raised issues that have not yet been resolved is Oscar and Mary Handlin, 'Origins of the Southern Labour System', *William and Mary Quarterly*, 3rd ser., VII (April 1950), pp. 199–222.

30. Paul Baynes, *An Entire Commentary upon the Whole Epistle of the Apostle Paul to the Ephesians*, reprinted in *Nichol's Series of Commentaries*; XI (Edinburgh, 1865), pp. 365–9. Although this work was not published until 1643, Baynes died in 1617. I am indebted to Lawrence W. Towner for supplying me with a copy of this document.

slaves.[31] In the French and Spanish colonies, as well as in the English, the word for 'Negro' was frequently used as a synonym for 'slave'. But Richard Ligon considered the condition of white servants in Barbados worse than that of the Negroes. Although white men were not subject to perpetual and inheritable servitude, it would be a mistake to think they were free from all burdens of slavery. In many colonies white servants could be sold, inherited, wagered or recovered for a debt; Gabriel Towerson, an eminent English divine, complained that too many servants confused service with a profession and thought they needed to obey only when assigned a specific task.[32]

There were two historical circumstances, however, which differentiated the white from the Negro servant. As Oscar and Mary Handlin have observed, the emigration of white labourers was in large part voluntary, and the demand for their services was great enough to induce colonial legislators to offer them various protections and rewards; this was not only true on the mainland, but also in the West Indies, where there was the additional incentive of increasing public safety and avoiding a rebellious union of Negroes and lowly whites. We should also remember that white servitude was based on the customs and laws of particular countries. The English servant was not ordinarily an article of international commerce, nor was he subject to the ancient laws of slavery, as incorporated in the *jus gentium*.[33] Yet it was a general belief that Christianity permitted the

31. Thomas Hobbes, *De Cive, or the Citizen* (ed. and with introd. by Sterling P. Lamprecht, New York, 1949), pp. ii, viii; Samuel Purchas, *Purchas His Pilgrimes in Five Bookes* (London, 1625), III, p. 419 (Purchas refers to the 'cholopey' of Novograde both as 'bondslaves' and 'servants').

32. Ligon, *True and Exact History*, pp. 43–4; Abbot Emerson Smith, *Colonists in Bondage: White Servitude and Convict Labor in America, 1607–1776* (Chapel Hill, 1947), pp. 224, 233; Richard B. Schlatter, *The Social Ideas of Religious Leaders, 1660–1688* (Oxford, 1940), p. 66.

33. Oscar and Mary Handlin, 'Origins of the Southern Labor System', pp. 210–21; *Acts of Assembly ... Charibbee Leeward Islands*, pp. 159–63; Harlow, *History of Barbados*, pp. 303–5; *Journals of the Assembly of Jamaica*, I (Jamaica, 1811), pp. 120–1, 125; Smith, *Colonists in Bondage*, pp. 227–38. The servitude of English and Irish convicts and prisoners was not, of course, contractual in character; it was mitigated only by the traditional belief that 'Christians', meaning men who were not of 'infidel' origin, should not be held in perpetual slavery. My interpretation differs from that of the

enslavement of men 'of infidel origin', and that Negroes purchased on the African coast had either been convicted of crime or captured, hopefully in a just war, and were therefore slaves by virtue of the law of nations. Hence Sir Edward Coke could affirm, in *Calvin's Case*, that infidels could either be put to death or enslaved; and Cotton Mather, doubtless drawing on Aristotle, could tell Massachusetts Negroes that they were 'the *Animate, Separate, Active Instruments* of other men'.[34]

Even if colonists were inclined to apply ancient concepts of slavery to the Negro, there was nothing, of course, to prevent individual masters from evolving their own rules and practices. First in Barbados and the Leeward Islands, then in Virginia and Maryland, and finally in Pennsylvania, New York, New England and French Canada, societies accepted the perpetual slavery of Indians and Negroes without specific legislative sanction. In some areas the actual status of Negroes differed little from that of white servants; in New England, where the Confederation of 1643 recognized the slavery of captives, bondsmen were considered for a time to be under the protective regulations of the Old Testament. But the fact that stands out from all the variations in temporary custom is the cumulative debasement of the Negro in every British and French colony. Whether he served the Puritans of Old Providence Island or the French of Martinique, the Jamaica overseer or the Virginia farmer, the Pennsylvania Quaker or the Canadian convent, his person was the property of his owner, and he and his progeny, if they were born of a slave woman, were condemned to eternal bondage.[35]

Handlins with respect to the origins of chattel slavery and the degree of similarity between West Indian and mainland colonies.

34. W. S. Holdsworth, *A History of English Law*, VII (London, n.d.), p. 484; Lawrence W. Towner, ' "A Fondness for Freedom": Servant Protest in Puritan Society', *William and Mary Quarterly*, 2nd ser., XIX (April 1962), p. 210.

35. J. H. Lefroy, *Memorials of the Discovery and Early Settlement of the Bermudas or Somers Islands, 1515–1685, Compiled from the Colonial Records and Other Original Sources* (n.p., 1932 reprint ed.), I, pp. 526–7; II, pp. 70, 166; Degler, 'Slavery and the Genesis of American Race Prejudice', pp. 49–67; Ligon, *True and Exact History*, pp. 22–37; Lucien Peytraud, *L'Esclavage aux Antilles françaises avant 1789* (Paris, 1897), pp. 144–5;

From 1680 to 1710 virtually every English and French colony from the Saint Lawrence to South America acquired laws that attempted to define the slave's peculiar position as conveyable property, subject to rules respecting debt, descent and taxation; and as a man who might be protected, punished, or prevented from exercising human capacities. Given the wide range of differences in colonial societies, the surprising fact about these laws is their underlying similarity. Everywhere they embodied ambiguities and compromises that arose from the impossibility of acting consistently on the premise that men were things. The basic contradiction was elucidated much later by a Virginia court, which echoed the doctrine of Seneca:

Slaves are not only property, but they are rational beings, and entitled to the humanity of the Court, when it can be exercised without invading the rights of property; and as regards the owner, their value is much enhanced by the mutual attachment of master and slave; a value which cannot enter into the calculation of damages by a jury.[36]

Both French and English colonial law assumed that the slave had essentially the attributes of personal property, and like a horse or cow

---

Ulrich Bonnell Phillips, *American Negro Slavery: A Survey of the Supply, Employment and Control of Negro Labor as Determined by the Plantation Régime* (reprint ed., Gloucester, Mass., 1959), pp. 46, 52, 98–9; Trudel, *L'Esclavage au Canada français*, pp. 99–100; Almon W. Lauber, *Indian Slavery in Colonial Times within the Present Limits of the United States* (New York, 1913), pp. 214–16; Susie M. Ames, *Studies of the Virginia Eastern Shore in the Seventeenth Century* (Richmond, 1940), pp. 101–6; Towner, 'Fondness for Freedom', pp. 201–19; Lorenzo J. Greene, *The Negro in Colonial New England, 1620–1776* (New York, 1942), pp. 124–6, 167–90; Edward R. Turner, *The Negro in Pennsylvania: Slavery, Servitude, Freedom, 1639–1861* (Washington, 1911), pp. 18–26; Jordan, 'Influence of West Indies', pp. 243–50; Jordan, 'Modern Tensions', pp. 23–30. For interpretations which place more emphasis on local conditions and differences, see Handlin, 'Origins of Southern Labor System', pp. 199–222; John M. Mecklin. 'The Evolution of the Slave Status in American Democracy', *Journal of Negro History*, II (April 1917), pp. 105–25; (July 1917), pp. 229–51; James C. Ballagh, *History of Slavery in Virginia* (Baltimore, 1902), *passim*. Stanley Elkins provides an excellent summary and discussion of the entire question in *Slavery*, pp. 37–52.

36. Helen T. Catterall (ed.), *Judicial Cases Concerning American Slavery and the Negro* (Washington, 1926–37), I, pp. 142 , 144.

could be moved, sold or rented out at the will of his owner. In several colonies, however, there was doubt whether for purposes of taxation slaves should be rated as persons, personal property or real estate. And while no colony presumed to infringe upon the slaveholder's rights to move or sell his property, it was widely recognized that, in the interests of both the slave and society, there would be special rules regarding debt and inheritance.[37]

As early as the 1660s planters in the Leeward Islands were disturbed by the fact that merchant creditors could force the sale of Negroes and other chattels at auction, and thus deprive an estate of its productive capacity. In addition, the death of a planter sometimes resulted in the ruin of his estate when executors or minor heirs needlessly disposed of slaves. To prevent these evils, colonial legislators tried to invest bondsmen with some of the attributes of real estate, and thus provided lawyers with a subject for endless debate and confused litigation. In 1669 an Antigua law ruled that if a debtor's chattels, including white servants, were insufficient to satisfy a claim, the creditor must accept slaves as 'estates of inheritance', attached to the freehold, and assume management of the plantation. In the previous year Barbados had defined slaves as freehold property, although in 1672 they were deemed chattels for the payment of an owner's debts. For more than a century legislators in Jamaica and the Leeward Islands sought to make the descent of slaves conform to the law for freehold property, and to prevent Negroes from being seized for debt when claims could be satisfied by other means. But in all other respects, as a Nevis statute of 1705 made clear, there was no question that slaves were chattels.[38]

The French islands, Virginia and South Carolina all experienced

37. Peytraud, *L'Esclavage aux Antilles françaises,* pp. 144–5, 213–41, 253–65; Trudel, *L'Esclavage au Canada français,* pp. 99–102; Lauber, *Indian Slavery,* pp. 216–17, 226–9; Greene, *Negro in Colonial New England,* p. 126; George H. Moore, *Notes on the History of Slavery in Massachusetts* (New York, 1866), pp. 62–5.

38. *Acts of Assembly ... Charibbee Leeward Islands,* pp. 18–19, 82; *The Laws of the Island of Saint Vincent, and Its Dependencies, from the First Establishment of a Legislature to the End of the Year, 1809* (Bridgnorth, England, 1811), pp. 24–29; C. S. S. Higham, *The Development of the Leeward Islands under the Restoration, 1606–1688: A Study of the Foundations*

the same difficulties in trying to reconcile the notion of a slave as personal property with the desire to protect the integrity of estates. Under the *Code Noir* the slave was unmistakably a chattel; but a royal decree of 1721 prohibited heirs under the age of twenty-five from selling slaves from their estates.[39] After 1705 bondsmen in Virginia were accounted real estate for purposes of descent, but chattels, by an act of 1727, with respect to gifts and devises. Three years later a court decided that, regardless of previous statutes, executors were to consider slave property as no different from horses or cattle, a view which the assembly endorsed in 1748, when it was decided that

---

of the Old Colonial System (Cambridge, England, 1921), pp. 157–9; *Journals of the Assembly of Jamaica*, II (London, 1824), pp. 16–17, 30–31; *The Statutes and Laws of the Island of Jamaica* (rev. ed., Jamaica, 1889), pp. 115–16; Lawrence Henry Gipson, *The Triumphant Empire: New Responsibilities within the Enlarged Empire, 1763–1766* (New York, 1956), p. 259. There was considerable conflict between British and colonial governments on the precise legal character of slave property. This was especially true after 1732, when Parliament enacted a law to facilitate the recovery of colonial debts. Although British law defined slaves as real estate, and the government disallowed a Virginia statute classing them as personal goods, the dispute involved the interests of debtors and creditors and had nothing to do with the general status of slaves as conveyable property. For this reason I think that M. Eugene Sirmans exaggerates the moral significance of slaves being defined as freehold property for purposes of descent in Barbados and South Carolina ('The Legal Status of the Slave in South Carolina, 1670–1740', *Journal of Negro History*, XXVIII [November 1962], pp. 462–73). Even in Louisiana, where slaves were long classed as real estate, they retained most of the characteristics of chattels personal (Kenneth M. Stampp, *The Peculiar Institution: Slavery in the Ante-Bellum South* [New York, 1956], p. 197). I have seen no evidence to show that a definition of slaves as freehold property implied that an owner had a right only to the services of his slave and not to the slave himself. Regardless of rules on descent and seizure for debt, slaves in both British and French colonies could be sold or otherwise conveyed apart from the land on which they worked.

39. *Le Code Noir, ou recueil des reglemens rendus jusqu'à présent. Concernant le gouvernement, l'administration de la justice, la police, la discipline et le commerce des nègres dans les colonies françoises* (Paris, 1742), pp. 308–9; Peytraud, *L'Esclarage aux Antilles françoises*, pp. 247–64. Article 44 of the *Code Noir* classed slaves as *meubles*, but the law prohibited seizure and separate sale of husbands and wives, or of children under the age of puberty.

confusion could be lessened by reducing bondsmen to their 'natural condition' as personal goods. This new law was nullified, however, by the Crown. There is evidence that Negroes in Virginia were sometimes annexed to the land and entailed, and were considered by courts as in some sense bound to the soil in inheritance. But in 1794 it was held, in Walden v. Payne, that though the law had protected bondsmen from unnecessary sale for the payment of debts and levies, they were chattels by nature. We might note that the confusion was carried across the mountains into Kentucky, which adopted the Virginia law of 1705 defining slaves as real estate for certain purposes. In colonial South Carolina bondsmen were regarded as chattels personal, notwithstanding an attempt in 1690 to class them as real estate; and yet as late as 1837 a court upheld an action of trespass against the captain of a patrol who had whipped a slave belonging to the plaintiff, but hired out to another man, on the ground that a slave was more analogous to land than to personal property. In addition to appealing to the analogy of an easement, the court maintained that a master possessed all the legal means of protecting his slave that the slave himself would have, had he been a freeman.[40]

It is not quite accurate, then, to think of chattel slavery as a well-defined status which put the Negro on precisely the same footing as other personal property. In no American colony was he attached to the soil in the sense of the *colonus*, or in a way that limited the freedom of his owner. But for both economic and humanitarian reasons, judges and lawmakers recognized that the slave was something more than a private and expendable possession.

The ambiguity was more pronounced when it came to regulating the bondsman's daily life and defining his relations with other people. If we think of freedom as a power to act or cause others to act, then it is clear that even the most authoritarian master, supported by the most oppressive laws, was to some extent limited by the will of his slaves, who had the power to appeal, flatter, humiliate; disobey, sab-

---

40. John Codman Hurd, *The Law of Freedom and Bondage in the United States* (Boston, 1858–62), I, pp. 239, 242–3, 297, 303; II, pp. 15–16; Sirmans, 'Legal Status of the Slave in South Carolina', pp. 462–73; Catterall (ed.), *Judicial Cases*, I, pp. 83–6, 99–103, 269, 312, 318; II, pp. 365, 393–6.

otage or rebel. Richard Ligon reported that Barbadian Negroes not only persuaded planters to improve their diet but complained so long about a shortage of women that their owners felt obliged to purchase more, the coveted females being apportioned by the slaves themselves in accordance with their own social hierarchies.[41] Courts and legislatures were farther removed from the direct influence of slaves, and had, besides, the mission of maintaining the standards and morale of slaveholders; yet in few instances could the law ignore the human capacities of slaves.

We have already seen that there were formidable obstacles to the religious conversion of slaves. By and large, Catholics showed far more concern for the souls of Negroes than did Protestants; and yet a number of British colonies, including New York, Jamaica and South Carolina, gave official encouragement to such missionary work. If this amounted to little more than pious lip-service, the same could be said of the religous provisions in the *Code Noir*. The Spanish and Portuguese were more successful in winning converts, but it is doubtful whether the mass of slaves in any colony enjoyed a meaningful religious life.[42]

Whether a Negro worked on Sunday or had an opportunity to marry were largely matters of local custom and circumstance. An article in the *Code Noir* forbidding Sunday work was apparently no better enforced than similar laws in colonial Georgia and South Carolina. But in many British colonies it was customary to reserve Sundays for leisure and marketing, and to grant days of respite at Christmas, Easter and Whitsuntide.[43] Since even Pennsylvania pro-

41. Ligon, *True and Exact History*, pp. 43, 47–8. A thoughtful discussion of the meanings and complexities of liberty is Oscar and Mary Handlin, *The Dimensions of Liberty* (Cambridge, Mass., 1961), pp. 18–20.

42. Hurd, *Law of Freedom*, I, pp. 232, 281, 297, 400; *Journals of the Assembly of Jamaica*, I, pp. 120–25; Peytraud, *L'Esclavage aux Antilles françaises*, pp. 243–5; Martin, 'Slavery and Abolition in Brazil', p. 168; Stein, *Vassouras*, pp. 196–9. In some English colonies, such as Pennsylvania, the proportion of converted Negroes may have been as high as that in any of the Spanish and Portuguese colonies (Turner, *Negro in Pennsylvania*, pp. 43–5).

43. See p. 263, note 18; Peytraud, *L'Esclavage aux Antilles françaises*, pp. 213–14; Hurd, *Law of Freedom*, I. pp. 306–7; Ruth Scarborough, *The

hibited the marriage of white servants without their masters' consent, it is not surprising that this was a minimal restriction for slaves under both English and French law. A Massachusetts statute said that so long as servants were of the same 'nation', their marriage should not be unreasonably denied. But in French Canada, where slave marriages were legally valid when permitted by a master, infants were disposed of at the will of the mother's owner, and when they died, were listed only as the property of a master, with no indication of their parentage. In the British West Indies and Southern mainland colonies, slave marriages were no more legal than under Roman law. But as in Roman law, nineteenth-century Louisiana courts acknowledged that such a *contubernium* had legal consequences, and could become valid as a contract after manumission. In 1871 a judge of the supreme court of Tennessee delivered the opinion that slave marriages had always been valid in that state, though not followed by all the legal consequences of a marriage between freemen. This somewhat questionable view simply underlines the essential point: it was impossible to ignore the fact that slaves could and did marry; but even where given legal sanction, such marriages were radically altered by the effects of bondage.[44]

Opposition to Slavery in Georgia Prior to 1860 (Nashville, Tenn., 1933), p. 84; *Laws of Island of Saint Vincent*, p. 46; [Long], *History of Jamaica*, II, p. 491. Unlike the *Code Noir*, the laws of many of the British colonies, both on the mainland and in the West Indies, attempted to limit the number of hours a slave could work each day.

44. Smith, *Colonists in Bondage*, p. 271; Peytraud, *L'Esclavage aux Antilles françaises*, pp. 244–5; Turner, *Negro in Pennsylvania*, pp. 45–6; Hurd, *Law of Freedom*, I, p. 263; Trudel, *L'Esclavage au Canada français*, pp. 267–73; Cobb, *Law of Negro Slavery*, p. 243; Catterall (ed.), *Judicial Cases*, II, 479, 592. Although the Catholic Church had long accepted the right of slaves to marry even without their masters' permission, this measure was still being demanded by Brazilian reformers of the nineteenth century (José Bonifácio, *Memoir Addressed to the General, Constituent and Legislative Assembly*, pp. 45–6. There is considerable evidence to suggest that slaves benefited very little from having their marriages recognized by law. In Brazil, Saint Domingue, Quebec and Massachusetts such legal sanction did not prevent the separation of families or the independent sale of small children (Williams, 'Treatment of Negro Slaves in Brazilian Empire', p. 325; Greene, *Negro in Colonial New England*, p. 211). William Huskisson, as

The capacity to marry was closely related to the capacity to make contracts, own property and hold offices or commissions, all of which were specifically denied by the *Code Noir*. As early as 1623 Bermuda prohibited Negroes from exchanging goods for tobacco without consent of their owners; and within a century British colonies from Connecticut to Barbados had evolved an elaborate system of police regulations which required Negroes to have a pass or ticket, signed by their masters, for the buying or selling of goods. These measures, which were designed to curtail theft, were a tacit admission that a slave might act as his master's agent. There is substantial evidence that bondsmen in the English colonies were often permitted to own horses, mules and cattle, and to trade in a variety of merchandise. Moreover, in the nineteenth century some courts and legislative bodies were inclined to accept the fact that 'a slave, although a chattel, is also a person, and, to some extent, capable of the acquisition of property for the benefit of the master'. This meant that when he acted, for example, as a purchasing agent for his master, the latter might be held liable for any debts incurred. But though courts often acknowledged that slaves might acquire and hold personal property, at law such property vested with the master.[45] This was a principle, as we have seen, which appeared in Spanish law from *las Siete Partidas* to the code of 1785 for Santo Domingo.

Secretary of State for the British Colonial Office, pointed out that a Jamaican law of 1826 permitting slave marriages was largely meaningless because it required baptism and permission from masters, and because, in any event, the integrity of slave families was unprotected. And yet in certain regions of the South, Christian marriages of slaves were widely sanctioned by public opinion even if not by law (*Slave Law of Jamaica*, pp. 62, 145–58; Edward W. Phifer, 'Slavery in Microcosm: Burke County, North Carolina', *Journal of Southern History*, XXVIII [May 1962], p. 148).

45. Peytraud, *L'Esclavage aux Antilles françaises*, pp. 158–66; Lefroy, *Memorials of Discovery*, I, pp. 308–9; Bernard C. Steiner, *A History of Slavery in Connecticut* (Baltimore, 1893), pp. 12–13; *Laws of Island of Saint Vincent*, pp. 34–6, 41; Hurd, *Law of Freedom*, I, p. 306; *Journals of the Assembly of Jamaica*, V (Jamaica, 1798), pp. 124–5, 203, 245; Cobb, *Law of Negro Slavery*, pp. 240–42, 261; Catterall (ed.), *Judicial Cases*, II, pp. 383, 422. One of José Bonifácio's proposals of 1823 was that Brazilian slaves be allowed to own property in their own right (*Memoir Addressed to the General, Constituent and Legislative Assembly*, pp. 43, 48).

Men who thought the evils of slavery could be gradually abolished by humane laws were much impressed by the fact that the *Code Noir* and *Real Cédula* set minimal standards for food. Yet a leading authority on French slavery concluded that the regulations regarding food, clothing and care of the sick and aged had been largely ineffective. This judgement was confirmed by Pierre Charlevoix, who in the 1720s saw slaves in Saint Domingue living on roots, dwelling in what seemed to be bear cages, and being driven by the lash to almost unceasing work. A royal ordinance of 1786 raised and extended the minimal standards of welfare, anticipating in some respects the *Real Cédula*; but in a few years the French colonies were racked by war and revolution, and it is questionable whether the provisions were ever seriously enforced.

While Jamaican law set standards for slave food and clothing, and by 1792 required masters to support disabled slaves, one may doubt Bryan Edwards's picture of a kind of welfare state, where 'many' bondsmen lived in large houses with boarded floors, slept on linen sheets, and ate off Staffordshire ware. As early as 1740 South Carolina law decreed that owners must supply slaves with sufficient food and clothing, but there is no evidence that enforcement was any more effective than in Jamaica or Saint Domingue. Even when a slave had suffered from famine and frostbite, a South Carolina court found it necessary to justify its authority: 'Instances do sometimes, though rarely, occur, in which it is necessary to interfere in behalf of the slave against the avarice of his master.' Of all colonizing peoples the British were undoubtedly the most jealous of the rights of private property and the least inclined to welcome the State's intervention in the management of slaves. But we must qualify this generalization by emphasizing that the *principle* of intervention was accepted by courts in the British colonies and the United States, and that even more-authoritarian governments were generally unsuccessful in their efforts to promote the welfare of slaves.[46]

46. Peytraud, *L'Esclavage aux Antilles françaises*, pp. 213–41; Charlevoix, *Histoire de l'Ile Espagnole*, IV, p. 360; [Long], *History of Jamaica*, II, p. 490; Bryan Edwards, *The History, Civil and Commercial, of the British Colonies in the West Indies* (Philadelphia, 1806), II, pp. 349–53; 371 ff.; *Laws of Island of Saint Vincent*, p. 47; Hurd, *Law of Freedom*, I, pp.

No aspect of American slavery was more disturbing to men's consciences than the Negro's lack of protection from murder and physical assault. In 1683, two years before French Negroes were given some physical security by the *Code Noir*, the English Committee for Trade and Plantations strongly objected to a Jamaican law that would have punished the wilful killing of a slave with only a fine. For many decades Britain brought pressure on colonial governments to enact stricter penalties for crimes against the persons of slaves. In a few colonies, such as Pennsylvania, there were no forces to check the public's sense of justice, and slaves enjoyed many of the legal protections of freemen. But the legislators of Antigua gave voice to the fear that was dominant wherever the proportion of Negroes was large; admitting that the killing and mutilation of human beings were contrary to the laws of God, they also observed that it would be dangerous 'to set slaves so far upon an equality with the Free Inhabitants, as to try those that kill them for their Lives'. In the British West Indies even the most wanton murder of a bondsman was long thought to deserve but a small fine; for a time the laws of Virginia refused to admit that such an act could be a crime.[47]

Nevertheless, both on the mainland and in the Caribbean, eighteenth-century legislatures gradually stiffened the penalty for killing a slave, and sometimes provided rewards for informers. Except in a few recalcitrant colonies, such as Barbados, American lawmaking bodies were willing by the early nineteenth century to enact statutes that made the wilful killing of a slave a felony punishable by death. As early as 1791 North Carolina was ready to call the crime 'murder'; by 1816 the law of Georgia held that the killing or maiming of a

---

306–7; Catterall (ed.), *Judicial Cases*, II, pp. 412–13; Goveia, 'West Indian Slave Laws', pp. 96, 99–105. Edward Long, who translated the *Code Noir* in his *History*, and recommended that Jamaicans imitate some of its measures, thought the French food allowance was too scanty.

47. *Journals of the Assembly of Jamaica*, I, pp. 67, 120–21; Leonard Woods Labaree, *Royal Government in America: A Study of the British Colonial System before 1783* (New Haven, 1930), pp. 118–20; Turner, *Negro in Pennsylvania*, p. 36; *Acts of Assembly ... Charibbee Leeward Islands*, p. 216; Hurd, *Law of Freedom*, I, p. 232.

slave was on the same level of criminality as the killing or maiming of a white man. Under abolitionist pressure, Jamaica went so far as to make the rape of a slave woman punishable by death.[48]

More significant than a gradual hardening of penalties was a view endorsed by a committee of the Jamaican assembly, at a time when the islanders were first being stung by abolitionist attacks. The committee held that slaves had always been under the protection of the common law except where it was limited, for the public good, by definite statutes.[49] This doctrine would seem to imply that, so far as criminal law was concerned, the rights of slave and freeman were roughly the same, and that the status of slavery involved only limited and express disabilities which had been imposed by specific legislation. While such a view would appear to run counter to all conceptions of chattel slavery, it won the acceptance of certain American judges. In 1823 the highest court of North Carolina ruled that an indictment for murder or for unprovoked battery on a slave was sufficient under the common law. Later on, courts in the same state said that a bondsman had the right to resist or to escape from cruel or excessive assaults, and that even the insolence of a slave could not justify a felonious attack upon his person. One such decision brought a bitter dissent on the ground that Negroes, being an inferior race, were insensitive to the provocation of assault; but in general, this view did not win judicial support.[50]

The doctrine of the Jamaican assembly committee appeared somewhat negatively in a Virginia decision of 1827, which ruled that specific statutes prevented the jurisdiction of common law from extending so far as to protect slaves against minor injuries at the hands of their owners. But this verdict aroused a vigorous dissenting opinion which maintained that until 1669 slaves had been protected

---

48. Hurd, *Law of Freedom*, I, pp. 296–7, 304–6; II, pp. 5, 83, 85, 97, 103; Catterall (ed.), *Judicial Cases*, II, p. 277; III, pp. 283–4; Cobb, *Law of Negro Slavery*, pp. 82–5, 99–100; [Long], *History of Jamaica*, II, pp. 492–7; *Slave Law of Jamaica*, pp. 12–15, 76–7.

49. *Journals of the Assembly of Jamaica*, VII (Jamaica, 1804), p. 410.

50. Catterall (ed.), *Judicial Cases*, II, pp. 1–3; Ernest James Clark, Jr, 'Aspects of the North Carolina Slave Code, 1715–1860', *North Carolina Historical Review*, XXXIX (April 1962), pp. 160–62.

by common law, and that since later 'ferocious and sanguinary' statutes had been repealed in 1788, the common law had been revived in all its force. This assumption seemed to underlie the decision in Souther *v.* Commonwealth (1851), in which the court said that a master might punish his slave to ensure obedience, but that he did so at his own peril; for if death ensued, the principles of common law relating to homicide applied without qualification or exception. In this particular case, the master was deemed guilty of murder.[51]

But one reason why planters were gradually willing to accept more stringent laws protecting their slaves can be seen in the admission of Bryan Edwards, the Jamaican pro-slavery apologist, who noted that the great and 'incurable' defect of the system was that the testimony of slaves could never be accepted against white men, even in cases of the most atrocious injury. Hence when a judge in Virginia made an appeal to his colleagues on the bench, asking them to extend protections of the common law to slaves, it was with the reassurance that there could be no danger so long as courts and juries were composed of men who owned slaves.[52] Under the *Code Noir,* slaves had the privilege of appealing to the attorney-general, who might act as their legal agent. But as Elsa V. Goveia has observed, the attorney-general was more preoccupied with prosecuting slaves than with protecting them; and there is apparently no record of a French master being executed for killing a slave. In Grenada and other British colonies Negroes had a similar right to report grievances to a guardian or justice of the peace, but since these men were largely sympathetic to slaveholders, and since the slaves themselves could not give evidence, the meanest planter had little to fear.[53] It was common for courts to

51. ibid., I, pp. 150–51, 223–5. Although a South Carolina court said in 1794 that Negroes had personal rights and were under the protection of the laws, a half century later a judge proclaimed, though not without bringing dissent, that they could invoke neither Magna Charta nor the common law. In 1820 a Mississippi court was of the opinion that slaves were 'reasonable and accountable beings' whose live could not be taken with impunity, and it accordingly sentenced a white man to be hanged for murdering a Negro (ibid., II, pp. 277, 403; III, pp. 283–4).

52. Edwards, *History, Civil and Commercial,* II, pp. 356–7; Catterall (ed.), *Judicial Cases,* I, p. 151.

53. Peytraud, *L'Esclavage aux Antilles françaises,* pp. 213–35; Goveia,

admit the testimony of one slave against another in criminal cases, but this was usually to a master's advantage; it not only furnished intelligence of plots and insurrections, but served to keep Negroes suspicious of one another.

Even in colonial Pennsylvania slaves were denied a jury trial and were relegated to special courts which lacked the procedural protections guaranteed to freemen. In the Leeward Islands, during most of the eighteenth century, a Negro might be condemned to death or dismemberment at the discretion of any two justices. The most advanced position was that taken by Georgia and North Carolina, both of which granted slaves the right to jury trial; in 1816 the latter state extended their procedural rights so that a bondsman might, through the agency of his owner, make pre-emptory challenges of jurors.[54] But while slaveholders in both the West Indies and the Southern states showed increasing inclination after the 1780s to soften the barbarous codes of the past and to provide Negroes with a somewhat fairer mode of trial, they stood firm in refusing to place in the bondsman's hands the full power of the law. To do so, they felt, would subvert the very foundations of their authority. And yet it was impossible, at times, to deny the legal capacities of the slave. As a South Carolina justice explained, in 1845: 'The words of a Negro are at least as significant as the cry of a brute animal . . . and if any sound whatever, contemporaneous with an act . . . might serve to give meaning to the act, it would be admissible.'[55]

It is a curious fact that both abolitionists and apologists for slavery argued that the existing laws were meaningless. The former contended that the slave's legal protections were mere window dressing,

---

'West Indian Slave Laws', pp. 99–101; Edwards, *History, Civil and Commercial*, II, pp. 356–7; *Slave Law of Jamaica*, pp. 14–15, 134–5, 145–58.

54. Turner, *Negro in Pennsylvania*, pp. 26–9; *Acts of Assembly . . . Charibbee Leeward Islands*, pp. 135–9; *Laws of Island of Saint Vincent*, pp. 26–49; *An Abridgement of the Acts of Assembly, Passed in the Island of St Christopher, from 1711 to 1740, Inclusive* (London, 1740), pp. 191–4; Scarborough, *Opposition to Slavery in Georgia*, p. 85; Catterall (ed.), *Judicial Cases*, II, pp. 1–2.

55. Catteral (ed.), *Judicial Cases*, II, p. 396.

which was largely true; and slaveholders replied that the worst features of the law of bondage were mere vestiges of a barbarous era when men had not learned that slavery and benevolence were compatible. According to Edward Long, the sanguinary slave codes of Jamaica had been borrowed from Barbados, which in turn had copied the savage laws of England regarding villeins and seamen; in no case had they been rigorously enforced.[56] According to patriotic Americans, slavery was a creation of British avarice and intrigue, and the most shocking laws were either anachronisms or should be interpreted as security measures which had never been intended to be enforced. Hence it was unjust for zealous critics to use these ancient or forgotten statutes as evidence that Negroes were still being mutilated or burned alive at the whim of any justice of the peace. In both the West Indies and the American South, apologists could quite plausibly point to a steady growth in the slave's substantive and procedural rights, and conclude that slavery, like any other institution, was subject to the inexorable laws of human progress.[57]

We should not dismiss these efforts of slaveholders at self-reform as sheer hypocrisy and propaganda There can be no doubt that enlightened men in Jamaica and Antigua, as well as in Virginia and South Carolina, were often deeply disturbed by the grosser defects and injustices of slavery. In the 1780s, for example, Jamaica made a concerted effort to repeal sanguinary laws and to enact a code which would at once be more in conformity with actual conditions and serve as a minimal standard for the less charitable managers. Edward Long, who had no admiration for the Negro and who stoutly opposed the abolition of the African trade, was nevertheless in favour of promoting the health and welfare of slaves, of lightening their punishments, of preserving the integrity of their families, and of taking steps to attach them to the soil. As early as 1740 South Carolina

---

56. [Long], *History of Jamaica*, II, pp. 493–6. Like most defenders of slavery, Long maintained that it was as unfair to judge the institution by the few exceptional cases of cruelty and barbarism as it would be to judge a non-slaveholding society by newspaper accounts of crime and brutality (ibid., II, p. 442).

57. Edwards, *History, Civil and Commercial*, II, pp. 371–406; Cobb, *Law of Negro Slavery*, pp. 82–94, 269–70.

lawmakers condemned cruelty to slaves as 'odious in the eyes of all men who have any sense of virtue or humanity'.[58]

Yet even if one conceded that reform was possible, there were formidable problems of jurisdiction, inspection and enforcement. The *Code Noir*, which failed to provide adequate measures for inspection and enforcement, could at least be repealed or modified by the central government that drafted it. After the British government had once consented to colonial laws, its powers were considerably more limited. In the 1670s there was some feeling in Britain that the interests of the nation, and of the Royal African Company, would be advanced by a more centralized administration of colonial slavery. It was pointed out that the only way to prevent smuggling or an eventual rebellion of Negroes would be to require a uniform branding and registry of British slaves, administered by a major general who would be independent of the planters and colonial governments. There was not the slightest trace of anti-slavery feeling in this proposal, but if it had been put into effect, the later task of British abolitionists would have been infinitely easier.[59] As it was, Britain

58. *Journals of the Assembly of Jamaica*, IV (London, 1827), pp. 119–21; VI (Jamaica, 1800), p. 148; VIII, pp. 404, 420; Edwards, *History, Civil and Commercial*, II, pp. 369–70; [Long], *History of Jamaica*, II, pp. 405–7, 437–41, 485–7, 492–3; III, pp. 429–32; Hurd, *Law of Freedom*, I, p. 306. If all of the reforms proposed by Long had been put into effect, the British West Indies would have moved far beyond even the most idyllic picture of slavery in the Spanish and Portuguese colonies. Yet Long acknowledged that French protective laws had not been enforced, and his own vagueness on enforcement machinery meant that his programme came down to a pious wish that slaveowners and overseers live by the Golden Rule (p. 407). For all his humanitarian yearnings Long, who was a judge in Jamaica, bitterly attacked Lord Mansfield's decision in the Somerset case, which deprived slavery in England of legal sanction; and he argued that Negroes were inherently inferior and were intended by divine will to be slaves (*Candid Reflections upon the Judgment Lately Awarded by the Court of King's Bench* ... [London, 1772], pp. 46–7. Long was by no means the only writer who combined a dedicated defence of slavery with proposals for reforms that would improve the institution's public image without altering its essential character.

59. Donnan (ed.), *Documents*, I, pp. 173–4. It was the principal aim of British abolitionists from 1814 to the early 1820s to obtain a very similar system of centralized registration.

could not rely on an established system of courts and administrators independent of slaveholder influence. And the American Revolution not only removed the largest portion of slaves from the jurisdiction of the British crown and Parliament, but vindicated principles which sanctioned the right of all slaveholders to self-government.

There is no evidence that the irrevocable forces of history worked to guide American slavery gently and peacefully towards ascending phases of serfdom and liberty.[60] If the institution was sometimes eroded by economic change or by the necessities of war, there is no reason to think that the Negro's position was improved by a gold rush in Minas Gerais, by an expansion of Brazilian coffee plantations, or by a development of new lands in Jamaica, Trinidad or Mississippi. And yet in no country was it possible to ignore the bondsman's essential humanity, or to deny him, however inconsistently with the law, certain rights and privileges. Everywhere the more thoughtful masters had cautious hopes of augmenting these rights and privileges until, by some miracle of evolution, the obvious evils of slavery would wither away and the grateful Negro would willingly give his service without coercion. But all such dreams and hopes ran aground on the simple and solid fact, which for centuries had been obscured by philosophy and law, that a slave was not a piece of property, nor a half-human instrument, but a man held down by force.

60. For the continuing defects and failure of amelioriative reforms in the British West Indies, see H. A. Wyndham, *Problems of Imperial Trusteeship: The Atlantic and Emancipation* (London, 1937), pp. 101–10; Ragatz, *Fall of the Planter Class*, p. 267; *Slave Law of Jamaica*, pp. 145–58; James Stephen, *The Slavery of the British West India Colonies Delineated, As It Exists both in Law and Practice* ... (London, 1824–30), *passim*. Augustin Cochin described a similar history of useless and unenforceable laws in Dutch Guiana (*Results of Slavery*, pp. 209–12).

9

The Continuing Contradiction of Slavery: Emancipation, Intermixture and Prejudice

IT is an incontestable fact that slaves in Latin America had more opportunities for manumission than did those in the British colonies or the United States. This acceptance of individual emancipation, coupled with a growing tolerance of racial diversity, probably helped Latin Americans to avoid the tragic hatreds, the malignant fears and the unjust discriminations that followed the abolition of slavery in North America. When one looks at the striking contrast between American and Brazilian experience in the late nineteenth century and the twentieth century, it is only natural to presume that attitudes towards race and freedom were always so sharply differentiated. On the other hand, it is theoretically possible that the divergence had less to do with the character of slavery in the two countries than with economic and social structures which defined the relations between coloured freedmen and the dominant white society.

Thus far we have tried to show that throughout the Americas Negro slavery presented more significant similarities than differences. To acknowledge that manumissions were more common in Cuba and Brazil than in the United States, and that in the former countries the descendants of slaves came to be integrated into the rest of the society, does not necessarily mean that we must concede this central point. Unless the Latin American bondsman always had a reasonable chance of becoming free and of being accepted as an equal of the white man, and unless North Americans were always consistently opposed to the principle of manumission, refusing to grant the freedman even the most elemental rights and protections, the difference could well be more of a degree than of kind. While we should avoid giving the erroneous impression that there were no national differences in racial prejudice and attitudes towards manumission, it is necessary to correct certain exaggerated but widely held beliefs concerning the expectations of the ordinary Negro slave in Latin América and North America.

The strongest evidence of a radical and fundamental difference regarding manumission is the restrictive legislation of the British West Indies and mainland colonies. From the late seventeenth century to the time of the American Revolution, virtually every British colony enacted laws which in some way limited the master's power to free his slaves. Sometimes he was merely required to provide security against the freedman's becoming a public burden; sometimes he was obliged to prove that his slave, by meritorious service, deserved freedom. As early as 1691 Virginia anticipated the common nineteenth-century policy of holding masters responsible for transporting manumitted slaves out of the state. Despite a tendency to liberalize these restrictions in the period immediately after the American Revolution, slaveholding states showed an unmistakable trend toward limiting the number of manumissions. By the mid nineteenth century the American master who wished to free his slaves was forced to rely on legal ingenuity and subterfuge. And while the *Code Noir* placed no restrictions on emancipation, the French colonies followed a similar pattern of development. In Guadeloupe no slave could be liberated without specific authorization from the government. A French ordinance of 1713 required masters in the Leeward Islands to have written permission from the governor-general before manumitting a slave, and on occasion authorities in France went so far as to annul testamentary emancipations. In both British and French colonies the chief motives behind such restrictions were the beliefs that free Negroes were an unassimilable element, and that they contributed to crime, prostitution, public disorder and, above all, discontent among the slaves.[1]

1. James M. Wright, *The Free Negro in Maryland, 1634–1860* (New York, 1921), pp. 23–6, 36–9, 261–315; John H. Russell, *The Free Negro in Virginia, 1619–1865* (Baltimore, 1913), pp. 22–3, 46–53; George H. Moore, *Notes on the History of Slavery in Massachusetts* (New York, 1866), p. 53; John Codman Hurd, *The Law of Freedom and Bondage in the United States* (Boston, 1858–62), I, pp. 240, 263, 281, 284, 289, 293; Ernest J. Clark, Jr, 'Aspects of the North Carolina Slave Code, 1715–1860',

Since the Spanish and Portuguese colonies were generally free from such legal restraints, and at times even encouraged the manumission of slaves, it would appear that national attitudes towards race and the capacity for freedom were radically different even in colonial times. Yet we should not assume that restrictive laws tell the whole story. In every slaveholding colony and state there were considerable numbers of freedmen, but only in parts of New England did private manumissions, aided by the action of courts, lead progressively to the actual eradication of slavery. If national differences were as great as the laws suggest, there would have been few free Negroes in North America and few slaves in Cuba or Brazil.[2] In order to gain a somewhat clearer picture of attitudes towards manumission, it is well to examine the means by which a slave could obtain liberty, and the disabilities he might suffer as a freedman.

From ancient times judges and lawmakers had recognized that a man might be unjustly held in bondage, and that slaves should therefore be allowed the right to plead for freedom. And because servitude was often considered as a kind of merited punishment, it was recognized that a slave might win atonement by some extraordinary deed of loyalty or courage. In 1540 a Spanish law required the royal *Audiencias* to hear the plea of any Negro claiming a right to freedom, and

---

North Carolina Historical Review (April 1962), pp. 156–7; Helen T. Catterall (ed.), *Judicial Cases concerning American Slavery and the Negro* (Washington, 1926–37), I, pp. 109–10, 161; II, pp. 4–6, 267–8, 392–3, 423, 442; III, pp. 1–3, 126; William Law Mathieson, *British Slavery and its Abolition, 1823–1838* (London, 1926), pp. 38–9; *Journals of the Assembly of Jamaica*, VI (Jamaica, 1800), pp. 530–38; Lucien Peytraud, *L'Esclavage aux Antilles françaises avant 1789* (Paris, 1897), pp. 407–10.

2. In 1860 there were approximately 58,000 free Negroes in Virginia, or about one-eighth the number of slaves. The number of free Negroes had increased from about 2,000 in 1782 to 30,500 in 1810, which was a faster rate of growth than that of the slave population. From 1790 to 1860 the number of free Negroes in Maryland had grown from 8,000 to nearly 84,000. In 1860 free Negroes in Delaware outnumbered slaves nearly ten to one. While this high proportion in the border states can be partly explained by the migration of manumitted slaves from the lower South, the fact remains that there were over 250,000 free Negroes in the slaveholding states on the eve of the Civil War. In 1888, after seventeen years of government-sponsored emancipation, there were still some 600,000 slaves in Brazil.

a similar provision was incorporated in a Spanish code of 1680. But the same principle was embodied in a South Carolina statute of 1712, and was accepted even by nineteenth-century courts in American slaveholding states. Many Latin American slaves won their freedom as a result of military service, especially in the wars for independence. Yet this practice, which could arise from expediency as well as from a traditional sense of justice, was not confined to one region. In Virginia and Jamaica, for example, Negroes were officially awarded freedom for reporting slave conspiracies or for helping in the pursuit and capture of runaways. The Jamaican government supplemented the main reward with a badge which on one side read, 'Freedom, for being honest', and on the other, 'By the country'. It has been estimated that after the American Revolution the number of free Negroes in Virginia doubled in the space of two years, partly as the result of manumissions for service in the war.[3] Obviously more slaves would benefit from this policy in regions where their military assistance was indispensable and where, once armed, they might determine the balance of power. In the American Revolution, unlike the wars for liberation in the Spanish colonies, it was not necessary to issue edicts of general emancipation in order to mobilize an adequate army. But the principle of using freedom to reward public service won widespread acceptance.

A far more distinctive feature of Latin American slavery was the well-known provision allowing a bondsman to purchase his own freedom. Recalling the traditional links between slavery and sin, one is tempted to see in the gradual purchase of freedom some parallel with

3. Arthur Helps, *The Spanish Conquest in America, and its Relation to the History of Slavery and to the Government of the Colonies* (London, 1900), IV, p. 250; Elsa V. Goveia, 'The West Indian Slave Laws of the Eighteenth Century', *Revista de ciencias sociales*, IV (March 1960), p. 78; Hurd, *Law of Freedom*, I, p. 299; James Curtis Ballagh, *History of Slavery in Virginia* (Baltimore, 1902), pp. 123–4; Russell, *Free Negro in Virginia*, pp. 52, 56–61; Henry Scofield Cooley, *A Study of Slavery in New Jersey* (Baltimore, 1896), pp. 46–9; Ruth Scarborough, *The Opposition to Slavery in Georgia prior to 1860* (Nashville, Tenn., 1933), p. 79; Thomas R. R. Cobb, *Inquiry into the Law of Negro Slavery* (Savannah, 1858), p. 311; *Journals of the Assembly of Jamaica*, III (London, 1827), pp. 51–3, 82; V, pp. 234–5; IX (Jamaica, 1805), p. 324.

Catholic penances and indulgences, which were wholly alien to the Protestant mind. The custom, however, was not established in the French colonies, and as we shall discover, it was not unknown to the North American law of slavery. Its origins, development and effectiveness in Latin America are also somewhat obscure.

In the 1520s there was a proposal, apparently originating in New Spain, that slaves should be permitted to pay a fixed sum to secure their freedom. The purpose of the plan was to reduce the danger of insurrection and to make Negroes more manageable, but it seems to have been without effect.[4] Yet by the mid eighteenth century the practice of *coartación* had long been established in Cuba, which up to that time had a relatively small population of slaves. Under the system of *coartación* a slave could make his master agree on a fixed price, which might be set through the arbitration of a local court or official, and the slave might then purchase his liberty in instalments. After he had paid a certain portion of the total price, he could not be sold, though he might at his own will arrange to be transferred to a different master. The system varied in technical details from one period to another, and from one part of the island to another, and its success depended less on law than on the force of public opinion. It was often customary, for example, to regard a slave who had paid one-half of his price as one-half free and accordingly entitled to one-half of his time; but the law held that a master had an absolute right to all his slave's time until the last instalment was paid. It is also worth noting that, at least after 1789, *coartación* was not transmissible to children, so that a child born while a mother was purchasing her own freedom was still the absolute property of the mother's owner.[5] In other words, the right of self-purchase was not

4. Helps, *Spanish Conquest in America*, III, p. 86; José Antonio Saco, *Historia de la esclavitud desde los tiempos mas remotos hasta nuestros dias* (2nd ed., Habana, 1936–45), IV, p. 140.

5. Hubert H. S. Aimes, 'Coartación: A Spanish Institution for the Advancement of Slaves into Freedom', *Yale Review*, XVII (February 1909), pp. 412–31; Richard Konetzke (ed.), *Colección de documentos para la historia de la formación social de Hispano-américa, 1493–1810* (Madrid, 1962), III, pp. 337–40. Roman law furnished some precedent for the purchase of freedom, but the Roman slave had only a limited right to his

allowed to infringe upon the concept of personal property, which was still the central element in defining the status of the slave.

The practice of *coartación* seems to have spread from Cuba to other Spanish colonies, but there was considerable variation in its application. In New Granada it was apparently not authorized by law until the late eighteenth century. The royal governor of Louisiana opposed its introduction to that province, claiming that what was proper for Cuba was not necessarily suitable for other Spanish possessions.[6] What is most remarkable is that the Santo Domingo code of 1785 allowed *coartación* but placed severe restrictions on private manumissions. In the supposed interest of preventing robbery and other crimes, this law denied masters the unlimited power of liberating their Negroes. No slave could request his liberty unless he could give satisfactory proof of his good character and conduct; no master could accept payment for freedom from a Negro who could not prove that he had acquired the money by legitimate means. Furthermore, in order to manumit a slave it was necessary to obtain a licence from the government.[7] Since this code was obviously designed to discipline and limit the size of the free Negro population, it would appear that *coartación* was regarded as an unusual transaction in which a master voluntarily agreed to sell liberty to a highly superior slave.

In Brazil, even in the early colonial period, it was customary for some masters to free slaves upon payment of the original purchase price. There are records of Negroes acquiring gold from placer

---

peculium, and could not, like some Spanish slaves, force his master to accept payment for freedom. But it should be emphasized that *coartación* was a custom and was not, for example, mentioned in the *Real Cédula*.

6. Aimes, 'Coartación', pp. 412–17; Herbert Aptheker, *To Be Free: Studies in American Negro History* (New York, 1948), p. 196 n.; Catterall (ed.), *Judicial Cases*, III, pp. 427, 440; Jaime Jaramillo Uribe, 'Esclavos y señores en la sociedad colombiana del siglo XVIII', *Anuario colombiano de historia social y de la cultura* (Bogotá, 1963), I, pp. 50–51. According to Aimes, Venezuela adopted a fixed tariff of prices for redemption from slavery, a practice which would have soon abolished slavery in Cuba, where slave prices increased at a rapid rate. Despite the governor's opposition, Louisiana courts upheld slaves' pleas for appraisal and the right to purchase freedom, at least by the 1770s.

7. Konetzke (ed.), *Colección de documentos*, III, pp. 565–8.

mining and buying their freedom, and of organized brotherhoods, often religious in character, which pooled resources for the purpose of emancipation. But however beneficial the custom may have been for skilled labourers, we should not exaggerate its effectiveness in giving most slaves a realistic hope of freedom. Octávio Ianni has shown that in southern Brazil masters sometimes relieved the tensions of slavery by granting special favours to domestic servants; yet manumissions could never be allowed to weaken a system that required absolute authority and submission. Until the late nineteenth century, emancipations in the south were not frequent enough to be socially or economically significant. As late as 1871 Brazilian reformers, aided by considerable diplomatic pressure from Great Britain, secured a law compelling masters to emancipate any slave who could pay his market price, a measure which would not have been thought necessary if the practice had been as universal as has been supposed.[8] The so-called Rio Branco Law of 1871 also provided special taxes and a national lottery to pay for emancipations, and gave masters the option of accepting indemnification from the State for freeing all children born of slave mothers, or of enjoying the services of such children up to the age of twenty-one. Yet slaveholders found so many ways of ignoring or evading the law that reformers were forced to admit in a few years that it was totally unenforceable. The campaign of the radical abolitionists was based on the utter failure of such ameliorative measures. This suggests that earlier and much milder laws and customs were not particularly effective in forcing masters to part unwillingly with their slaves. Moreover, the reformers' ultimate

8. Donald Pierson, *Negroes in Brazil* (Chicago, 1942), p. 51; Robert Southey, *History of Brazil* (London, 1817–22), III, p. 781; C. R. Boxer, *The Golden Age of Brazil, 1695–1750: Growing Pains of a Colonial Society* (Berkeley, 1962), p. 177; Hubert Herring, *A History of Latin America from the Beginnings to the Present* (New York, 1955), p. 113; Octávio Ianni, *As metamorfoses do escravo* (São Paulo, 1962), pp. 169–76. The practice of allowing slaves to buy their own freedom was apparently not established by law until 1871, and even then few slaves were able to benefit from the opportunity (see Mary W. Williams, 'The Treatment of Negro Slaves in the Brazilian Empire: A Comparison with the United States', *Journal of Negro History*, XV (1930), pp. 332–3; Percy A. Martin, 'Slavery and Abolition in Brazil', *Hispanic American Historical Review*, XIII (May 1933), p. 170.

triumph was not the result of a new national unity or of a gradual amelioration of slavery. Brazilian emancipation was made possible only by the growing militancy of urban industrialists, bureaucrats, engineers and military officers, who saw the slave system as a primary obstacle to economic progress, and who openly encouraged Negroes to desert the plantations and flee to the cities.[9]

If it is answered that Brazilian courts at least upheld contracts for the purchase of freedom, the same can be said of certain courts in North America. In South Carolina, for example, a Negro woman named Sally was given permission by her master to live in town and work independently, on the condition that she pay him a stipulated portion of her wages. Sally was industrious and succeeded in saving enough extra money to buy the freedom of her daughter. After being paid, however, the master refused to release the child, on the ground that any money earned by Sally was rightfully his. In 1792 the chief justice of the state ruled that the master had no claim to what Sally earned, over and above the amount agreed upon, and that Sally had a perfect right to purchase her child's freedom. The jury found that Sally's daughter was free.[10]

One cannot dismiss this case as a product of liberalism still lingering from the Revolution. In 1828 a Virginia judge asserted that the laws of all civilized nations favoured liberty, and quoted Ulpian (which shows that traditions of Roman law were not confined to Latin America): 'In obscura voluntate manumittentis, favendum est libertati.' In 1844 the highest court of the same state held that when a master agreed to manumit a slave on the condition that the slave serve for six years and pay a stipulated sum, the deed should be

9. Richard Graham, 'Action and Ideas in the Abolition Movement of Brazil', unpublished paper read at the Conference on Race and Class in Latin America during the National Period, Columbia University, 16–18 December 1965; Martin, 'Slavery and Abolition in Brazil', pp. 170, 176–83. Many Brazilian slaves had been freed for military service in the Paraguayan War (1865–70), and the nation was strongly influenced by French abolitionists, as well as by the example of the United States. Nevertheless, the programme of gradual emancipation was a total failure. The most radical and devastating attack on the institution, Joaquim Nabuco's O obolicionismo, was published twenty years after Lincoln's Emancipation Proclamation.

10. Catterall (ed.), Judicial Cases, II, pp. 275–6.

interpreted as an immediate emancipation, since in cases of doubt, the construction should be favourable to freedom.[11] Tennessee courts repeatedly denied slave-owners the right to break a contract with a slave for freedom, and recognized a status of quasi servitude in which a Negro was no longer under the dominion of his master, but was not yet free under the laws of the State. In 1846 a Kentucky judge made this astonishing declaration:

A slave is not in the condition of a horse. . . . He is made after the image of the Creator. He has mental capacities, and an immortal principle in his nature, that constitute him equal to his own, but for the accidental position in which fortune has placed him. . . . The law . . . cannot extinguish his high born nature, nor deprive him of many rights which are inherent in man. . . . He can make a contract for his freedom, which our laws recognize, and he can take a bequest of his freedom, and by the same will he can take personal or real estate.[12]

If this doctrine seems utterly contrary to the statutes which defined the slave as chattel property and prohibited manumissions, it is because there was a very great difference between statute law and judicial interpretation. The whole tendency of statute law was to inhibit emancipations in the supposed interest of public safety and welfare. But this bias frequently clashed with the benevolent will of masters and with judicial precedent. In order to avoid overstating the point, let us emphasize that while thousands of North American Negroes were permitted to purchase their freedom, the practice was much more widely accepted in Latin America. But the legal principles and traditions were not so strikingly different as has been supposed. In North America emancipation was sometimes deemed to be *implied* by certain acts of a master, such as abandoning a sick slave, giving a slave a legacy, or living in open concubinage with a female slave.[13] The growing conflict between restrictive statutes and judicial precedent brought confusion and complexity to the law, especially with respect to wills. But even in the nineteenth century, American courts

11. ibid., I, pp. 157–8, 208.
12. ibid., II, pp. 479, 530.
13. Aptheker, *To Be Free*, pp. 31–40; Scarborough, *Opposition to Slavery in Georgia*, pp. 124–70.

occasionally recognized a slave's rights to promised freedom.

One of the most troublesome questions was whether children born of a female slave who had been promised freedom were entitled to the same benefit. The will of Jonathan Pleasants, drawn in 1776, contained a strong indictment of slavery and ordered that, whenever the laws of Virginia made it possible, his slaves and their offspring should be given absolute freedom at the age of thirty, 'which I desire they may enjoy in as full and ample a manner as if they had never been in bondage' In Pleasants v. Pleasants (1799) it was not only decided that slaves over the age of thirty should be free, as a result of a law of 1782 authorizing manumission, but Judge Roane advanced the opinion that since a mother under the age of thirty had a positive right to future freedom, her condition was that of a free person held to service for a term, and accordingly her children were *born* free and were beyond the power of the testator.[14] This view, which was more liberal than the rule of *coartación* in Cuba, was repudiated in 1824 in the case of Maria v. Surbaugh. Judge Green's opinion was based on the argument that if a promise to emancipate a female slave automatically freed children born during her remaining period of service, the owner could not be held responsible for supporting these children, and the burden would inevitably fall on the public.[15] Other slaveholding states followed the precedent set by Maria v. Surbaugh, and yet the Virginia code of 1849 ruled that when a female slave had been emancipated by deed or will, her issue born between the recording of the deed (or the death of the testator) and the time of her actual manumission were to be considered free. And in Parks v. Hewlett (1838), Henry Saint George Tucker modified the judgement in Maria v. Surbaugh by holding that creditors had no claim to either a woman or her children who had been emancipated *after* their owner had contracted a debt; and that any qualifications attached to a

14. Catterall (ed.), *Judicial Cases*, I, pp. 105–6. The actual decision accorded freedom only to those slaves over the age of thirty, and to the issue of those over the age of forty-five, whose mothers had been more than thirty at the time of their birth. Slaves under the age of thirty whose mothers had been under thirty at the time of their birth were to serve until *they* were thirty. It was on this point that Judge Roane differed with President Pendleton.

15. ibid., I, pp. 138–9.

mother's emancipation could not carry over to her children.[16]

The law of slavery in the United States was filled with ambiguities and compromises which resulted from an underlying assumption that, in the words of Henry Saint George Tucker, 'emancipation is not strictly a gift of property. It is the exoneration of a human being from the bonds which our institutions have fastened upon him, and which the beneficence of our times has authorized the master to remove.'[17] Increasingly, the fear of social and economic problems created by a growing class of free Negroes brought restrictive laws that implied that bondage was a permanent and unalterable condition. But a judicial bias in favour of freedom was never entirely extinguished.

In order to safeguard testamentary manumissions, for instance, slave-owners were generally permitted to specify in their wills that debts were to be discharged through the sale of real estate. In the absence of such an expression of intent, state law differed regarding the effect of testamentary manumission on the sale of property to satisfy claims. Nevertheless, if an executor wrongfully sold Negroes who had been emancipated by will, when there were sufficient assets to pay all debts, the sale was invalid even though the purchaser had acted in good faith.[18] When in 1844 a Virginia court was confronted by the conflicting wills of John Randolph, who had first provided for the emancipation of his hundreds of slaves, and had then revoked the gift, it was decided that his sudden change of heart was the result of insanity Courts held that the status of a fugitive could not be

16. ibid., I, pp. 75 n., 192–3. The Alabama supreme court took a similar view that not all the incidents of a mother's condition at the birth of her child attached to the offspring, and that while a Negro mother, even after being emancipated, might be subject to antecedent claims against her former owner, her offspring could not be touched. In one particular case the court ruled that even the mother must be regarded as free to all the world (ibid., III, pp. 127–38).

17. ibid., I, pp. 192–3.

18. Cobb, *Law of Slavery*, pp. 299–300. In the Virginia case of Dunn *v.* Amey (1829), the court held that if there were insufficient assets to pay debts of a deceased slaveholder who had emancipated bondsmen by testament, the slaves were to be sold for a term of years in order to earn a sufficient fund to pay the debts (Catterall [ed.], *Judicial Cases, I*, pp. 159–60).

inherited, and that children born of a slave mother after her flight to freedom could not be recovered. As late as 1836 a distinguished Virginia judge could proclaim, with the assent of the entire court, that

a slave, who is capable of nothing else, is at least capable to take his freedom, and that the grant of it is just as susceptible of gradations in its progress to perfection, as a bargain and sale of land. ... It is clear, that not only will an inchoate and imperfect right to freedom in a slave be recognized, but even a modified *quasi* state of freedom is sanctioned by this court; a state in which an emancipated female is held in unqualified slavery, yet is deemed capable of having freeborn issue; a state, therefore, in which the party is half free, half slave, with the mingled rights of each state.[19]

What differences there were in national attitudes towards manumission can partly be attributed to changing views on racial intermixture. White men had sexual intercourse with Negro bondwomen through the Americas. But such relations were naturally more common and acceptable in regions where there were relatively few white women. In colonial Brazil, the French West Indies, and even Barbados and Jamaica, planters and administrators met the need for female companionship, as well as for sexual gratification, by living openly with Negro mistresses who were often accorded many of the privileges of legitimate wives.[20] The governors of the Spanish prov-

19. Catterall (ed.), *Judicial Cases*, I, pp. 184–5, 204–6; III, p. 128. There was, of course, contrary judicial opinion; but as late as the 1850s courts in Alabama and Virginia upheld the validity of emancipations outside the state, even when the former slaves had returned (ibid., I, pp. 227–9; III, p. 126).

20. Boxer, *Golden Age of Brazil*, pp. 15–17, 166; Lowell J. Ragatz, *The Fall of the Planter Class in the British Caribbean, 1763–1833* (New York, 1928), p. 33; Frank W. Pitman, *The Development of the British West Indies, 1700–1763* (New Haven, 1917), p. 28. By far the most thoughtful study of this question is Winthrop Jordan's 'American Chiaroscuro: The Status and Definition of Mulattoes in the British Colonies', *William and Mary Quarterly*, 2nd ser., XIX (April 1962), pp. 183–200, which seeks to relate acceptance of miscegenation to sex ratio and the proportion of Negroes in a total population. While Pitman tells of one governor of Barbados letting his coloured mistress reign at the official mansion, Jordan shows that of all the British islands, Barbados was the most prejudiced against racial inter-

inces, being forbidden to marry, had no compunctions about living with slave mistresses, and accordingly set an example for men of less exalted rank in Louisiana as well as South America. It was a universal judgement that the Portuguese, who had been the first to intermix with Negroes on the African coast, excelled all other peoples in their tolerance of racial blending.[21]

But no matter how much love and respect an individual master might feel for his slave concubine, it took centuries, even in Brazil, for the power of sex to dissolve the colour line. As C. R. Boxer has bluntly said, 'it did not follow from this readiness to mate with coloured women, that the Portuguese male had no racial prejudice'.[22] Nor did the long warfare between Portuguese and Moors result in a spirit of racial toleration. In colonial Brazil so much prestige was attached to a relative whiteness of skin that Negro and mulatto mothers thought themselves blessed by fortune when their children's complexion appeared lighter than their own. As a popular Brazilian adage put it, 'White women are for marriage, mulattoes for fornification, and Negresses for work'. Even in the mid nineteenth century, coffee planters in the Parahyba valley treated Negroes as mere brutes whose marital ties deserved no respect; and mulatto children were often unrecognized by their fathers or persecuted by the planters' jealous wives.[23]

Nor was it an absence of racial consciousness that led the Spanish

---

mixture, and also had a sex ratio of about eighty white males to one hundred white females (pp. 197–8). But Jamaica, whose white males continued to outnumber females by nearly two to one, was far more liberal towards mulatto offspring. Jordan tends to underestimate the importance of racial discrimination even in Jamaica, but it seems probable that sex ratio and the proportion of slaves were at least as important as nationality in shaping attitudes towards the manumission and treatment of mulattoes.

21. Catterall (ed.), *Judicial Cases*, III, pp. 392–3; Maurilio de Gouveia, *História da escravidão* (Rio de Janeiro 1955), p. 94. It is significant that the mulattoes in British and American territory who enjoyed relatively high status were in precisely those areas that had been governed by Spain in the late eighteenth century, such as Trinidad and Louisiana.

22. C. R. Boxer, *Race Relations in the Portuguese Colonial Empire, 1415–1825* (Oxford, 1963), p. 40.

23. ibid., pp. 6, 29; Stanley J. Stein, *Vassouras: A Brazilian Coffee County, 1850–1900* (Cambridge, Mass., 1957), pp. 132–5, 155–9; Boxer,

to devise an elaborate system which classed the child of a Negro and white as a *mulato* (the term being derived, apparently, from the word for 'mule'), and which supplied a complex terminology to describe every conceivable mixture of white and Negro blood. Throughout the Spanish colonies authorities tried to prevent the cohabitation of Negroes and Indians. In Venezuela eighteenth-century laws flatly prohibited the marriage of whites and free Negroes. According to Richard Konetzke, the Spanish concern for purity of blood developed in the colonies into a widespread racial prejudice which found expression in discriminatory laws. Yet for all their racial consciousness, the Spanish and Portuguese were distinctive in their final acceptance of the inevitability of intermixture. Latin American society increasingly took concubinage as a matter of course; and instead of concealing their liaisons, masters felt free to acknowledge their mistresses and to accord them special privileges. This fact, coupled with the view that each step towards whiteness was a progression in status, and each infusion of Negro blood a retrogression, made possible a slow assimilation which, in time, brought a relative tolerance of racial diversity.[24]

But in spite of the frequency of intermixture in the French,

Golden Age of Brazil, pp. 3–4, 17, 42; Boxer, *Four Centuries of Portuguese Expansion, 1415–1825: A Succinct Survey* (Johannesburg, 1961), *passim*; Boxer, 'S. R. Welch and his History of the Portuguese in Africa, 1495–1806', *Journal of African History*, I (1960), pp. 55–63; Pierson, *Negroes in Brazil*, pp. 120–21. The adage comes from Heinrich Handelmann, *História do Brazil*, as quoted by George P. Browne in a paper written at the College of Wooster, 'The Black Hand: A study of the Negro and his Contribution to Brazil, 1530–1900'. Browne also shows that racial prejudice was present during the latter period of Brazilian slavery, and was one of the themes of a novel by Aluizio de Azevedo, *O mulato* (pp. 33–5).

24. Raúl Carrancá y Trujillo, 'El estatuto jurídico de los esclavos en las postrimerías de la colonización española', *Revista de historia de América* (México, D.F.), no. 3 (September 1938), pp. 22–5; Ferando Romero, 'El negro en tierra firme durante el siglo XVI', in *Actas y trabajos científicos del XXVIIº Congreso Internacional de Americanistas* (Lima, 1939–42), II, pp. 441–61; Romero, 'The Slave Trade and the Negro in South America', *Hispanic American Historical Review*, XXIV (August 1944), pp. 374; Oriol Pi-Sunyer, 'Historical Background to the Negro in Mexico', *Journal of Negro History*, XLII (October 1957), pp. 243–4; Magnus M. Mörner, 'Los

Dutch and British colonies, the practice was severely condemned. If this suggests that social values were different from those in Latin America, it would be hazardous to base an explanation on a simple contrast between Catholic and Protestant cultures. A seventeenth-century Catholic missionary, expressing horror over sexual irregularities in the French West Indies, showed that he was not merely troubled by the sin of fornication:

Our French colonists . . . allow themselves to love their Negro slaves, in spite of their black faces which make them hideous and in spite of the stench they give off – two qualities which should, in my opinion, extinguish the ardour of their masters' criminal passion.[25]

The *Code Noir*, to be sure, permitted a master to liberate and marry a female slave, but most French colonists considered Negroes fit only

esfuerzos realizados por la Corona para separar negrese indies en Hispano-américa durante el siglo XXVI' (unpublished paper); Instituto Panaméricano de Geografía e Historia Comisión de Historia, *E mestizaje en la historia de Ibero-América* (México, D.F., 1961), pp. 59–60; Gouveia, *História da escravidão*, pp. 69–70; Uribe, 'Esclavos y señores en la sociedad colombiana', pp. 36–7; Federico Brito Figueroa, *Las insurrecciónes de los esclavos negros en la sociedad colonial Venezolana* (Caracas, 1961), p. 20; Boxer, *Race Relations in the Portuguese Colonial Empire*, pp. 30–32, 114–18. Romero advances the plausible thesis that prejudice actually accelerated racial integration in the Spanish colonies; and Pi-Sunyer states that the only way persons of Negro descent could enter the higher *castes* in Mexico was by the long process of racial dilution. It is an open question whether a society that sees every addition of white blood as a step towards purification is more, or less, prejudiced than a society that sees any appreciable trace of Negro blood as a mark of degradation. Certainly the Spanish and Portuguese had more faith than the French or North Americans in the dissolving power of white blood, a fact which must have been related to their acceptance of intermixture.

25. Jean-Baptiste Du Tertre, *Histoire générale des Antilles habitées par les François* (Paris, 1667–71), II, pp. 511–12. According to Du Tertre, the 'crime' of intermixture was far more common among the Portuguese than among the French. Though he compared the offspring to mules, which were also produced by the mating of two different species, he approved of the rule of certain French governors which declared mulattoes to be free. It was enough, he said, that they must carry on their faces the opprobrium of their birth, without adding slavery to punish a crime of which they were innocent.

for illicit connexions. In Louisiana a law of 1724 forbade the marriage of whites and Negroes. In the West Indies the French planter who had sexual relations with a slave faced the threat of fines and other penalties. And while French planters were deterred neither by law nor public opinion, they made some effort to conceal their illicit connexions, and prided themselves on their superiority to the Spanish and Portuguese, who were lascivious without shame.[26]

An eighteenth-century Jamaican judge was similarly contemptuous of the Latin Americans, but confessed that his own countrymen were all too prone to unite 'two tinctures which nature has dissociated, like oil and vinegar'. The underlying cause, he felt, was not the shortage of white women, or the supposed burdens and expenses of marriage, but rather the sexual attractiveness of Negro women: 'Many are the men, of every rank, quality and degree here, who would much rather riot in these goatish embraces, than share the pure and lawful bliss derived from matrimonial, mutual love.' He hinted, as did other British and French writers, that the judgement of many planters had been warped by the influence of concubines, who obtained jewels and riches as well as great privileges, and who used their sexual charms to exhaust and finally kill their generous masters. In Maryland seventeenth-century legislators were particularly concerned by the fact that women servants of English origin enjoyed connexions with Negro slaves, 'always to the satisfaction of their lascivious and lustful desires'.[27]

Since intermixture occurred in every colony, regardless of laws

26. ibid., II, p. 512; Peytraud, *L'Esclavage aux Antilles françaises*, pp. 155–7, 195–212, 426–7.

27. [Edward Long], *The History of Jamaica; or, General Survey of the Antient and Modern State of that Island* ... (London, 1774), II, pp. 327–32; Philippe Fermin, *Description générale, historique, géographique et physique de la colonie de Surinam* ... (Amsterdam, 1769), I, pp. 127–8; Hurd, *Law of Freedom*, I, pp. 249–50. Long shared the fear of the Maryland legislators: 'The lower class of women in *England* are remarkably fond of the blacks, for reasons too brutal to mention; they would connect themselves with horses and asses, if the law permitted them. By these ladies they generally have a numerous brood' (*Candid Reflections upon the Judgment Lately Awarded by the Court of King's Bench ... on What is Commonly Called the Negro Cause* ... [London, 1772], pp. 48–9). He predicted that the blood of the entire English nation would soon be contaminated, until

and prejudice, it was essential to determine whether the ancient rule of *partus sequitur ventrem* applied to mulattoes. For a time Maryland adopted a reverse standard in order to inhibit the 'lustful desires' of white women. But even when a child inherited his mother's status, it was only natural for a master to feel a sense of responsibility towards his own illegitimate children, especially if he had been living in intimate concubinage with their mother. The dilemma presented by this situation, which was a product of the universal contradiction of slavery, was much the same whether an owner lived under the laws of Britain, France or Portugal. In Brazil and the Spanish colonies the child of a slave mother inherited her status. But inasmuch as these societies accepted open concubinage, and slave mistresses often occupied positions of privilege and power, it is not surprising that mulatto children were often regarded as free. Prior to the *Code Noir*, French planters in Martinique customarily freed their mulatto children at the age of maturity. The *Code Noir*, however, made the rule of *partus sequitur ventrem* universal in the French West Indies, and also held that if an owner had a child by his own female slave, he was to be fined and the child removed to a poorhouse or asylum; all such children were to remain slaves for the rest of their lives. Notwithstanding this severe restriction, which was supplemented by an ordinance prohibiting the emancipation of children whose mothers were not definitely free, French planters continued to liberate their own mulatto children, who in time formed a significant element in the colonial populations. The Dutch planters of Surinam showed a similar inclination to spare their children from the burdens of servitude. But while free mulattoes came to form a large class in both Dutch and French colonies, they could not look forward to a steady progression towards the status of whites. Unlike the Spanish and Portuguese, the Dutch and French attached the stigma of slave descent to any man with the slightest trace of Negro ancestry.[28]

Englishmen became like the Portuguese 'in complexion of skin and baseness of mind'. Virginia, South Carolina, Delaware, Pennsylvania, Massachusetts and other mainland colonies had harsh penalties for whites who had sexual relations with Negroes; and the punishments were usually more severe for white women.

28. Hurd, *Law of Freedom*, p. 249; Jordan, 'American Chiaroscuro', p.

In Jamaica, on the other hand, a man was considered legally the same as a white if he was removed by more than three generations from a Negro ancestor. As late as 1835 a South Carolina judge argued that the problem should be dealt with in a flexible and pragmatic manner:

> We cannot say what admixture . . . will make a colored person. . . . The condition . . . is not to be determined solely by . . . visible mixture . . . but by reputation . . . and it may be . . . proper, that a man of worth . . . should have the rank of a white man, while a vagabond of the same degree should be confined to the inferior caste.[29]

This statement, which shows that even Southern courts might sanction the passage from one caste to another, also reveals one of the distinguishing marks of slavery in North America. As Winthrop Jordan has pointed out, there were no gradations between the status of

184; Boxer, *Golden Age of Brazil*, p. 17; Peytraud, *L'Esclavage aux Antilles françaises*, pp. 152, 156–66, 195–212, 401–11, 422–3; Fermin, *Description générale*, I, pp. 120–21; [Long], *History of Jamaica*, II, p. 261. Fermin said that most mulattoes in Surinam were emancipated by their white fathers, but John Stedman recorded a case of a Dutch captain selling his own offspring (*Narrative of Five Years' Expedition against the Revolted Negroes of Surinam* . . . [London, 1796], p. 206).

29. [Long], *History of Jamaica*, II, p. 261; Pitman, *Development of British West Indies*, p. 28; Catterall (ed.), *Judicial Cases*, II, pp. 269, 358–9. The laws of American states differed considerably on the degree of Negro ancestry required for legal disabilities. Keeping in mind that the French thought the stain of Negro ancestry could never be effaced, that the Spanish imposed disabilities through the fifth generation, and that Jamaicans made no legal distinctions after the third generation, we may note that less than one-fourth part of Negro blood was *prima facie* evidence of freedom in Virginia and Kentucky. In Louisiana, any 'person of colour', whether part white or Indian, was presumed free. In some states, as little as one-sixteenth Negro ancestry classed a man as 'mulatto', though in Alabama a person of mixed blood was not deemed a mulatto if he was removed by more than three generations from a Negro ancestor. In most cases, visible 'colour' was the most important test; but in South Carolina, juries were warned that visibility was sometimes misleading, and that reputation and character were of more importance than a trace of visible colour (Catterall [ed.], *Judicial Cases*, I, p. 330; II, pp. 269, 346–59, 385–6; III, pp. 392–3; Kenneth M. Stampp, *The Peculiar Institution: Slavery in the Ante-Bellum South* [New York, 1956], pp. 195–6).

Negro and white; the mulatto did not occupy a halfway position, but was seen as essentially a Negro. This bias may well have been the result of a moral indignation at racial intermixture, which was more intense where large numbers of white women and a high valuation of marriage made illicit sexual relations less tolerable.

Yet even here we run the risk of exaggerating and oversimplifying national differences. Jamaicans borrowed the Spanish gradations of mulatto, sambo, quadroon and mestize, but their law regarded all these classes as 'mulatto'.[30] Edward Long, the Jamaican judge and historian, favoured a law that would liberate every mulatto child. But Long was violently prejudiced against the mulatto class, and also advocated laws restricting the amount of real and personal estate that a white man could bequeath to a man of colour. His motive for desiring the emancipation of mulatto children was to penalize masters who cohabited with their female slaves. He would not have admired the Kentucky judge who said, with respect to a master's intention to free and marry his slave concubine, *'de gustibus non disputandum'*, and who upheld the validity of the master's will involving the woman and her children.[31] In North America there were numerous cases of slave-owners acknowledging and freeing their mulatto children, and such intentions were sanctioned by courts. While men and women of mixed ancestry were frequently kept in bondage, there were reports of such slaves being allowed to work for wages, and of eventually passing as white freemen. Southern juries sometimes ruled that men who were visibly coloured were legally white because of their character and reputation. In South Carolina, as well as Jamaica, a few men

30. Jordan, 'American Chiaroscuro', pp. 184–9, 192; Ragatz, *Fall of Planter Class*, p. 33; Bryan Edwards, *The History, Civil and Commercial, of the British Colonies in the West Indies* (Philadelphia, 1806), II, pp. 215–18. Although it is generally true, as Jordan maintains, that the colour line was less rigid in Jamaica than on the mainland, it should be noted that prominent Jamaicans like Edward Long and Bryan Edwards condemned racial intermixture, and that mulattoes, quadroons and mestizes (the offspring of a white man and quadroon woman) suffered from the same severe legal discriminations. Early in Jamaica's history there were differences in disabilities, but these were governed by the mode of emancipation and not by the proportion of Negro blood.

31. [Long], *History of Jamaica*, II, pp. 323–33; Catterall (ed.), *Judicial Cases*, I, p. 318.

with Negro blood in their veins rose to positions of power and prestige.[32]

But after every allowance is made for such flexibility, there can be little doubt that it was more likely for people of racially mixed ancestry to be emancipated and eventually to rise to the status of whites in Latin America than in the British colonies, and that it was similarly more likely in the British West Indies than in the mainland colonies and states. That this difference was largely the result of a willingness to accept the consequences of illicit sexual relations is suggested by a succession of eighteenth-century petitions to the Jamaican assembly. These petitions, which began in the 1730s and 1740s and reached flood stage by the 1790s, convey a general picture of ageing planters surrounded by families of mulattoes and quadroons, who, in the absence of legitimate families, were the only objects of their fathers' love and solicitude. It is perhaps significant that these planters, whose livelihood had rested on the labour of slaves in a bleak and often isolated environment, were particularly concerned with the fate of their coloured grandchildren. One has the image of an austere master whose position and sense of shame had stiffened all relationships with concubines and even children, but whose 'parental bent', to use Veblen's phrase, was awakened by the sight of grandchildren, who may have reflected his features, slightly tinted, but who were condemned, because of his youthful passions, to a life of perpetual inferiority.

Such masters were unmoved by the plight of slaves or by the degraded positions of other mulattoes. Always one's own children or grandchildren deserved special consideration, for they were far superior to others of their class; they were of good character and had benefited from Christian training. John Clifford, having no legitimate family, wished to leave his fortune to his natural children and grandchildren, 'which will enable them to support themselves in a manner far above others within their own degree'. George Bedward complained that a law of 1761 to prevent 'inconveniences' arising from exorbitant devises to mulattoes kept him from bequeathing his

32. Catterall (ed.), *Judicial Cases*, II, pp. 269, 385–6, 449, 514–15; III, p. 129; Jordan 'American Chiaroscuro', pp. 189–91; Stampp, *Peculiar Institution*, pp. 195–6, 350–61.

estate and fortune to his natural grandson, a free quadroon, who was a fine, upstanding young man. And the assembly was increasingly sympathetic to such pleas, since its members could comprehend the underlying motives. A succession of special acts granted to hundreds of mulattoes most of the rights and privileges of freeborn Englishmen. Despite frequent condemnations of racial intermixture, legislators knew that the loneliness and isolation that made such relationships inevitable also made a man solicitous about the welfare of his own progeny. There was no need, as in the northern mainland colonies, to conceal the facts of life, or to suppress life's emotions.[33]

In referring to relations between the Portuguese and Negroes, C. R. Boxer has observed that one race cannot systematically enslave another for more than three centuries without acquiring feelings of racial superiority. But to see slavery as the only source of racial prejudice is to oversimplify one of the most complex and troublesome questions in modern history. In this study we can hardly begin to consider such an enormous subject as the origins of racial prejudice. We need to note that there is evidence of such prejudice in eighteenth-century Europe, where slavery could not have been a direct cause. The fact that Africans had traditionally been associated with Moorish infidelity and with Noah's curse of Canaan may have disposed some Europeans to regard them as fit for bondage. Our information is still highly fragmentary, but it is possible there was something in the culture of Western Europe that inclined white men to look with contempt on the physical and cultural traits of the African. Yet we should remember that European slave traders initially dealt as equals with African princes and merchants, and Negroes of royal blood who travelled to Europe were received with respect and honour. In many societies, moreover, a stigma of slavish origin had been fastened on freedmen and their descendants, even when slavery was not racial in character. This was true, in fact, even among the West Africans. It would appear that racial differences reinforced this common tendency to attach some of the burdens and disabilities of slavery to the free offspring of slaves. In any event, for the purposes

33. *Journals of the Assembly of Jamaica*, IV (London, 1827), pp. 45–6, 69, 71, 92, 98–9; VI, pp. 595, 606–8; VIII (Jamaica, 1804), p. 586.

of this inquiry it is sufficient to show that racial discrimination was coextensive with American Negro slavery, and that the divergence between British and Latin America in the treatment of the coloured race was a slow and gradual phenomenon, and not the result of original differences in their systems of slavery and caste.

Even a relative acceptance of racial blending did not mean an absence of racial prejudice. In time, racial prejudice was probably eroded in certain colonies by the militancy of mulattoes and quadroons, who resented and struggled against the restraints which attached to their condition, but who could take pride in their white blood, which placed them in a position above the Negro. In North America, where mulattoes were generally classed as Negroes, the gate to equality was too heavy to force. But racial prejudice long persisted in Latin America, despite the frequency of intermixture. Spanish colonial law barred a freeman of Negro descent from bearing arms, holding public office, entering craft guilds, appearing on the streets after dark, or associating with Indians. In the seventeenth century the viceroy of Peru prohibited Negroes, mulattoes, quadroons or sambos from entering the university; and persons of Negro blood were similarly excluded from higher education in colonial Mexico.[34] These disabilities were not of short duration. José Manuel Valdés, a Peruvian mulatto who was sent to his nation's congress in 1831 and who received honours as a poet and physician, had been barred from the university in his youth, despite his light complexion and obvious intelligence. Until 1812 even the Church refused to admit to orders men of Valdés's condition. His only access to the professions was through the practice of medical quackery.[35]

34. C. H. Haring, *The Spanish Empire in America* (New York, 1947), pp. 218, 231; Carrancá, 'Estatuto jurídico de los esclavos', pp. 22–5; Pi-Sunyer, 'Historical Background to the Negro in Mexico', pp. 243–5; Rollando Mellafe, *La introducción de la esclavitud negra en Chile: tráfico y rutas* (Santiago de Chile, 1959), pp. 76–82; Uribe, 'Esclavos y señores en la sociedad colombiana', pp. 5, 22–3, 40–44; Konetzke (ed.), *Colección de documentos*, II, pp. 427–8; III, pp. 553–73.

35. Fernando Romero, 'José Manuel Valdés, Great Peruvian Mulatto', *Phylon*, III (3rd quart., 1942), pp. 297–319. Religious orders in both Portuguese and Spanish colonies long excluded persons of Negro descent. Even after racial barriers were removed, there was much discrimination (Boxer, *Golden Age of Brazil*, p. 42).

Men of Valdés's generation benefited from the impact of the European Enlightenment and from the ideals propagated by the wars of liberation. Earlier, free Negroes or mulattoes in the Spanish colonies had been required to live with an employer or be bound by contract to work in the fields or mines. In such colonies as Mexico, as in the British provinces, the full force of the law was directed against the alleged danger of mulatto crime, disorder and vagabondage. Even whites who intermarried with descendants of Negroes were subjected to the legal disabilities of the supposedly infamous class.[36]

Until the late eighteenth century conditions were not essentially different in Brazil, where white men, thinking it degrading to work with their hands, repeated an ancient saying that 'work is for a cur or a nigger'. Mulattoes in colonial Brazil suffered far more discrimination than did the *mamelucos* and *coboclos*, who were the offspring of Indians and whites. They were prevented by law from carrying arms, wearing clothes inappropriate to their class, or taking official positions in Church or State. Penal law for persons of Negro descent reflected a pervasive fear that men who were at once unemployed and barred from the most promising opportunities would resort to crime or rebellion. Hence the law threatened a mulatto found with a lethal weapon with one hundred lashes. But as the free coloured class increased in size and power, and struggled for such symbols of prestige as the wearing of a sword, it became impossible to enforce discriminatory laws. By the late eighteenth century this internal pressure was supplemented by the enlightened reforms of the Portuguese Crown. Henry Koster, who visited Brazil early in the nineteenth century, found that mixed castes had gained in rights and status as a result of liberal laws; even then, however, coloured citizens were ineligible for some high offices, and there was a lingering of social prejudice.[37] José Bonifácio, like Manuel Rocha before him, found it necessary to argue that Negroes were true human beings. In 1839 a

36. Haring, *Spanish Empire*, p. 218; Carrancá, 'Estatuto jurídico de los esclavos', pp. 22–5; Pi-Sunyer, 'Historical Background to Negro in Mexico', pp. 243–5.

37. Boxer, *Golden Age of Brazil*, pp. 17, 170–71; Pierson, *Negroes in Brazil*, pp. 69–70; Koster, *Travels in Brazil*, pp. 385–6; Boxer, *Race Relations in Portuguese Colonial Empire*, pp. 114–18.

French immigrant, Charles Taunay, published a *Manual do agricultor Brasileiro*, which maintained that Negroes were so inferior to whites that they were incapable of the responsibilities of freedom. For at least a generation more, this view was widely accepted among the slaveholders of the southern states and interior valleys. In southern Brazil, indeed, a racial ideology and unfavourable stereotypes of the Negro persisted well into the twentieth century.[38]

Such prejudice was also strongly pronounced in the French West Indies, where it was official policy to regard slavery as an ineffaceable stain that contaminated a slave's entire posterity. When some free people of colour asked the superior council of Saint Domingue to register their titles to nobility, as had been done for Indians who claimed descent from French lords, they were told that Indians were born free and always had a right to the privileges of freedom; Negroes, on the other hand, had been introduced to the colonies as slaves, and the brand could never be removed. The French justified harsh discriminatory laws by the theory that a debasement of the free coloured population would ensure the subordination of slaves. Accordingly persons of Negro descent were barred from holding office, carrying arms, taking the names of white men, or wearing clothing unbefitting their rank. If a free mulatto struck a white man, he was to be whipped, branded and sold for the profit of the Crown. Members of this degraded class were constantly threatened with re-enslavement, legal or otherwise, and were required at all times to be able to prove their title to liberty. The mulattoes of Saint Domingue were persecuted and treated with severe brutality to the time of the French Revolution. Even then the provincial assembly of the north, which supported the French National Assembly, sent a strongly worded protest against the Assembly's warm reception of mulatto delegates. In language similar to that of later South Carolinians, the French colonists demanded that the Assembly renounce any intention

38. Octávio Tarquinio de Sousa, *História dos fundadores do Império do Brasil* (Rio de Janeiro, 1957–8), IX, p. 73; Stein, *Vassouras*, p. 132; Fernando Cardoso and Octávio Ianni, *Côr e mobilidade social em Florianópolis: aspectos das relações entre negros e brancos numa comunidade do Brasil meridional* (São Paulo, 1960), pp. 125–35, 191–210; Cardoso, *Capitalismo e escravidão no Brasil meridional* (São, 1962), p. 316.

of interfering with slavery or the colour line; even a delay in such reassurance, they hinted, would strengthen motives for secession. But by 1790 there were enough mulattoes with education and wealth to thwart such efforts to combine revolution with a preservation of racial inequality.[39]

The role of mulatto officers and soldiers in the Saint Domingue revolution may well have contributed to a tightening of restrictions in North America. In colonial Virginia free Negroes had been entitled to jury trial and bail on criminal charges, and had been little restricted in movement or activity. When the British Board of Trade questioned a Virginia act of 1723 depriving free Negroes of suffrage, Lieutenant-Governor William Gooch did not defend the law on the basis of alleged racial differences, but argued instead that most free Negroes were 'the bastards of some of the worst of our imported Servants and Convicts', and that they were a dangerous influence on the slaves. It was therefore well 'to preserve a decent Distinction between them and their Betters ... until time and Education has changed the Indication of their Spurious Extraction, and made some Alteration in their Morals'. But by 1800 such expectations seem to have vanished, for Virginia now required the registration of free Negroes and mulattoes, and a few years later ruled that an emancipated slave would forfeit his freedom if he remained in the state for more than a year without obtaining a certificate of good character, indicating that he was regularly employed and settled in a given county.[40]

We cannot begin to consider why legal discriminations increased in the United States and gradually disappeared in the West Indies and Latin America. It is surely of the utmost significance that free Negroes in the Southern United States were subjected to the harshest restrictions at precisely the time when Jamaica and Barbados were

39. Peytraud, *L'Esclavage aux Antilles françaises*, pp. 420–34; Theodore Lothrop Stoddard, *The French Revolution in San Domingo* (Boston, 1914), pp. 41–2, 90–99, 115–23.

40. Russell, *Free Negro in Virginia*, pp. 103–19, 137; Hurd, *Law of Freedom*, II, pp. 6–9; Emory G. Evans (ed.), 'A Question of Complexion: Documents Concerning the Negro and the Franchise in Eighteenth-Century Viriginia', *Virginia Magazine of History and Biography*, LXI (October 1963), pp. 411–15.

removing legal disabilities from their free coloured populations. In the British West Indies, as well as in Brazil, free Negroes had achieved legal equality before the enactment of general emancipation. This progress may not have hastened the end of slavery, but it certainly had a profound effect on the consequences of abolition. Well before the Civil War the entire society of the United States became permeated with a deep racial prejudice that far exceeded that of any other nation in the New World. There is considerable evidence that this growing fear and scorn of the Negro was a product of what has vaguely been termed 'Jacksonian democracy' and 'the rise of the common man'. For our purposes, however, the important point is that the disabilities suffered by freedmen and their descendants were roughly similar in most American colonies before the Age of Revolution.

In Dutch Surinam, as well as in Brazil, New York and Saint Domingue, it was sometimes said that the condition of free Negroes was worse than that of slaves.[41] Colonial New York, New Jersey and Pennsylvania prohibited free Negroes from holding real estate in their own right. After 1702 they could not be freeholders in the British Leeward Islands, and if any Negro or mulatto acquired more than eight acres of land, the 'overplus' was to be sold within six months or be forfeited to the Crown. Virginia law permitted free Negroes to own real and personal property, including slaves, to the time of the Civil War.[42] But in most British colonies coloured men

41. Albert Baron von Sack, *Beschreibung einer Reise nach Surinam und des Aufenthaltes daselbst in den Jahren, 1805, 1806, 1807* ... (Berlin, 1821), p. 85. Sack also said that a Dutch master could not punish his slave more severely than by selling him to a free Negro (p. 79), an observation to which Bryan Edwards would have assented (*History, Civil and Commercial*, II, p. 221).

42. Hurd, *Law of Freedom*, I, pp. 281, 284, 289–90; *Acts of the Assembly, Passed in the Charibbee Leeward Islands from 1690 to 1730* (London, 1732), pp. 135–9; Russell, *Free Negro in Virginia*, pp. 89–91. According to Stampp, only Delaware and Arkansas prohibited 'free persons of colour' from owning slaves; in the United States in 1830 more than 3,600 free Negroes or mulattoes owned slaves: 'The great majority of these coloured slaveholders had merely purchased husbands, wives or children and were unable to emancipate them under existing laws' (*Peculiar Institution*, p. 194). But as in the British and French West Indies there were some free Negroes who worked slaves on large plantations.

were legally barred from civil and ecclesiastical office, and could not appear as witnesses against whites in criminal cases. In Jamaica, according to Bryan Edwards, the lowest white man considered himself infinitely superior to the richest and best-educated man of colour.[43] Even Pennsylvania legislators voted for the enslavement of any free Negro found living in marriage with a white, and referred to the entire class as 'an idle, sloathful people . . . who often prove burthensom to the neighbourhood, and afford ill examples to other Negroes'. And if in practice free Negroes and mulattoes were frequently allowed to own property, make and enforce contracts and testify in court against men of their own race, the statutes of British colonies were filled with police regulations restricting their movement, employment and possession of arms, dogs and liquor.[44]

The grim and overriding fact is that in every colony free Negroes and mulattoes suffered from legal and social discrimination, and were at once condemned for idleness and prevented from enjoying economic opportunity, accused of being disorderly, and deprived of equal justice. Variations in detail and terminology are less impressive when we learn, for example, that even in colonial Brazil free mulattoes were often legally associated with slaves.[45] This uniform discrimination must have been related to a fairly uniform conception of slavery as a state of absolute subjection and degradation. Like sovereignty, which more than liberty was its polar opposite, slavery

43. Edwards, *History, Civil and Commercial*, II, p. 219. This judgement was confirmed by a petition from some free quadroons, mulattoes and Negroes who complained in 1773 that the law requiring planters to employ a certain number of white men or pay a 'deficiency tax' was particularly burdensome, since they were 'obliged to submit themselves to the humour of every white man they so employ, who oftentimes take advantage of the situation of the petitioners, not being on an equal footing with them, and treat the petitioners with great incivility' (*Journals of the Assembly of Jamaica*, VI, p. 467). In general, however, Jamaica lacked a substantial class of yeomen or poor whites, a fact which may have contributed to the ultimate erosion of legal discriminations.

44. Hurd, *Law of Freedom*, I, p. 289; Arthur Zilversmit, 'Slavery and its Abolition in the Northern States' (Ph.D. dissertation, University of California, Berkeley, 1962), p. 21. This thesis provides an excellent summary of Northern slave codes.

45. Boxer, *Golden Age of Brazil*, p. 17.

could be circumscribed and its limits set by law and custom. In most colonies, courts made efforts to recognize the basic humanity of slaves. But within the encircling limits and modifications, which varied from region to region, the hard core of slavery was much the same. As with sovereignty, there was a resistant, indivisible element that could not be changed without destroying the condition itself. And even when a slave was emancipated, his previous subjugation had been so extreme that he carried the mark of permanent degradation. A king does not lose his aura of privilege with abdication, and no difference in complexion distinguishes kings from other men.

PART III

10

Religious Sources of Anti-Slavery Thought: Quakers and the Sectarian Tradition

'I NEVER read in History of the *Waldenses*, our first Reformers from Popery, that they kept any Slaves.' Thus wrote the Quaker Benjamin Lay, who was determined in 1736 to prove that anti-slavery was the crucial test of religious purity. For according to this 'irrepressible prophet', as Whittier called him, 'As God gave his only begotten Son, that whosoever believed in him might have everlasting Life; so the Devil gives his only begotten Child, the Merchandize of Slaves and Souls of Men, that whosoever believes and trades in it might have everlasting Damnation.' Slavery, in Lay's eyes, was not only a 'Hellish Practice' but a 'filthy sin', 'the Capital Sin', indeed, 'the greatest Sin in the World, of the very Nature of Hell itself, and is the Belly of Hell'. It was Baal and Sodom and the black Dragon all rolled into one putrid mass of evil: 'The very worst part of the old Whores Merchandize, nasty filthy Whore of Whores, *Babilon's Bastards*'.[1]

As this violent language suggests, the key to the religious origins of anti-slavery thought is the idea of sin. There were profound egalitarian implications in the Christian belief that God, being no respecter

1. Benjamin Lay, *All Slave-keepers that Keep the Innocent in Bondage, Apostates Pretending to Lay Claim to the Pure Holy Christian Religion; of What Congregation so Ever; but Especially in Their Ministers, by Whose Example the Fillthy Leprosy and Apostacy is Spread Far and Near; It is a Notorious Sin, Which Many of the True Friends of Christ, and His Pure Truth, Called Quakers, Has been for Many Years and Still Are Concern'd to Write and Bear Testimony Against; as a Practice so Gross and Hurtful to Religion, and Destructive to Government, Beyond What Words Ever Set Forth, or Can be Declared of by Men or Angels, and Yet Lived in by Ministers and Magistrates in America. . . . Written for a General Service, by Him that Truly and Sincerely Desires the Present and Eternal Welfare and Happiness of all Mankind, all the World Over, of all Colours, and Nations, as His Own Soul* (Philadelphia, 1737), pp. 10–13, 18, 27, 46, 59, 61, 88, 104.

of persons, might give His blessings to the lowliest servant. Yet it was also a traditional belief that total subordination was man's natural and legal condition after the Fall of Adam. If the absolute sovereignty of God stood behind all legitimate power, the completeness of creation, as well as divine justice, demanded an absolute subjection – in a spiritual sense, of all Christians; in a worldly sense, of the lowest ranks on the social scale. The essence of both sin and slavery was a denial of self-sovereignty, a negation of the natural ability to will that which was just and lawful. All men were condemned by Adam's sin to sweat for their bread; and some men, as Jean-Baptiste Du Tertre observed, were required to sweat more than others. Sin and the necessities of Providence qualified the belief in the equality of men before God, and sanctioned the enslavement and transportation to America of millions of Africans. Man's debt to God, like more worldly debts, could be put to productive use.

Since sin was traditionally thought of as a kind of slavery, and external bondage was justified as a product of sin, any change in the meaning of sin would be likely to affect attitudes towards slavery. This is not to say that men who rejected the dogma of original sin would perforce be abolitionists; or that abolitionists could not believe in man's depravity. The point is that men could not fully perceive the moral contradictions of slavery until a major religious transformation had changed their ideas of sin and spiritual freedom; they would not feel it a duty to combat slavery as a positive evil until its existence seemed to threaten the moral security provided by a system of values that harmonized individual desires with socially defined goals and sanctions.

We may recall that the Essenes were supposed to have repudiated slaveholding along with other worldly compromises that prevented the soul from achieving perfection. They not only sought to escape from sin by withdrawing to a primitive refuge, but attempted, in the expectation of an apocalyptic judgement, to realize the social meaning of moral freedom. It would be a gross oversimplification to categorize such a response to sin and salvation as Hebraic, as opposed to a Hellenistic disengagement and elevation of the soul, and to a Roman reliance on the institutional mediation of the Church. But the fact remains that the Hebraic tradition of prophecy, millennialism and deliverance from bondage gave a temporal and social dimension to man's struggle with sin. In so far as this tradition was incorporated by the early Christian Church, it profoundly altered the meaning of slavery. Some Christian masters felt it a duty to manumit their bondsmen; some former bondsmen rose to high ecclesiastical positions; and servitude itself was expected to disappear with the imminent coming of the millennium, when creation would be restored to its pristine state. In time, however, the Biblical prophecies were interpreted as allegories, Origen described the Kingdom of God as a spiritual event in the individual soul, and Augustine helped to channel men's hopes and aspirations away from millennial expectation and towards the Church as an extension of the Incarnation. The bondsman might be liberated from the sins of the flesh, but he could not look forward to a moment in history when cruel masters would tremble and slaves rejoice as the Lord appeared against a flaming sky.[2]

Yet Christianity continued to embody a latent egalitarianism that was linked with dreams of prophetic fulfilment and freedom from the necessities of sin. Sometimes the impulse was sublimated in the form

2. My discussion of sectarianism and millennialism draws particularly on Ernst Troeltsch, *Die Soziallehren der christlichen Kirchen und Gruppen* (*Gesammelte Schriften*, Erster Band, n.p., 1961); Karl Mannheim, *Ideology and Utopia: An Introduction to the Sociology of Knowledge* (tr. by Louis Wirth and Edward Shils, New York, n.d.); H. Richard Niebuhr, *The Social Sources of Denominationalism* (New York, 1957); Norman Cohn, *The Pursuit of the Millennium* (London, 1957); Ernest Lee Tuveson, *Millennium and Utopia: A Study in the Background of the Idea of Progress* (Berkeley, 1959); Fred L. Polak, *The Image of the Future: Enlightening the Past, Orienting the Present, Forecasting the Future* (tr. by Elise Boulding, Leyden, 1961); Rufus M. Jones, *Spiritual Reformers in the 16th and 17th Centuries* (Boston, 1959); W. H. G. Armytage, *Heavens Below: Utopian Experiments in England, 1560–1960* (Toronto, 1961); Ronald A. Knox, *Enthusiasm: A Chapter in the History of Religion, with Special Reference to the Seventeenth and Eighteenth Centuries* (Oxford, 1950). My assumptions regarding the role of social values are derived in part from Florence R. Kluckhohn and Fred L. Strotbeck, *Variations in Value Orientations* (Evanston, Ill., 1961); Talcott Parsons and Edward A. Shils (eds), *Toward a General Theory of Action* (Cambridge, Mass., 1952); and A. L. Kroeber (ed.), *Anthropology Today: An Encyclopedic Inventory* (Chicago, 1953).

of monastic or missionary activity, or in movements for purification and ascetic reform. Sometimes it erupted in the frenzied efforts of perfectionist sects to purge themselves of sin. The relation of these sects to the moderate reform movements within the Church was roughly analogous to the relation of later abolitionists to groups working for the Christianization and amelioration of slavery. But while the first uncompromising attacks on Negro slavery came from men who were heirs of the sectarian and perfectionist traditions, the relevance of these traditions to anti-slavery is not to be found in a direct transmission of ideas. Even if one could show that Gnostics, Albigensians, Waldensians, Hussites, Taborites, Ranters and Quakers were parts of a continuous development, we must recognize that such groups were concerned with their own freedom from sin and not with the freedom of slaves.

The relation of the sectarian tradition to anti-slavery thought goes deeper than a simple transmission of ideas. If we are to understand the frame of mind of a Benjamin Lay or the religious tensions which led a small number of Quakers to see slavery as the very epitome of sin, when the institution had been condoned by the dominant religions and philosophies of the West, we must first look briefly at the aspirations and behaviour of certain sectarians who had no contact with the institution of slavery. For the history of sects shows that the doctrine of original sin, which had proved to be a powerful instrument of social control, was the centre of severe and continuing strains in the value systems of Western culture. By picturing God as a revolutionary, transforming force, rather than a fixed Good to which man aspires, some of the sectarians undermined the ideology which rationalized the existing social order as a necessary compromise with sin. In so doing, they anticipated the patterns of thought and action of the more extreme abolitionists, as well as of other secular reformers and revolutionaries who would measure human institutions against moral absolutes. The main point, then, is that the religious and philosophical compromises which had been used to justify slavery for two thousand years also shaped a mode of protest that would ultimately appear in the abolitionist movements.

Even the more radical sects differed in their views on the necessity of violence and the time and nature of the millennium. Some of the sectarian movements were the products of social or economic dislocations, and embodied the concrete grievances of oppressed groups. Some leaders, like Thomas Müntzer, seized upon chiliasm after a period of religious scepticism and uncertainty. The image of an imminent Kingdom of God could revive an expiring faith and give new meaning to doctrines that had become overly abstract and irrelevant to the lives of ordinary men. But here we must disregard questions of origin and emphasis, and confine our attention to general traits and tendencies associated with the sectarian's assault on sin.

Inspired by the apocalyptic fantasies of Hellenistic Judaism, especially the Sibylline and Johannine prophecies, the millennial sects discovered that history might replace the rituals and sacraments of the Church as man's hope for salvation. This dramatic shift in the meaning of history foreshadowed the transition in eighteenth-century secular thought from the idea of nature as a fixed and complete chain of being to the idea of history as a creative process leading to perfection. To Joachim of Fiore, a twelfth-century Calabrian abbot, was attributed an eschatology that exerted continuing influence on European thought. From an epoch of slave-like submission to an authoritiarian God, man had progressed to a Second Age of filial obedience to Christ, a relationship resembling the Christian ideal of servitude. In the Third Age, which was near at hand, there would be neither servitude nor institutional authority. Emancipated from sin and presided over by the Holy Spirit, men might live as brothers in absolute freedom and love, without need of restraint. Such an ideal of the world as a New Eden fulfilled the projected wishes of most millenarians.

But if the central turning point of history lay in the immediate future rather than in the distant past, it followed that the laws and principles of the existing social order did not have prescriptive sanction, and could not be associated with the immutable structure of nature. The ideals of absolute liberty, equality and brotherhood, which the ancients had confined to a lost Golden Age, and which Christians had relegated to the realm of spirit, acquired destructive power when fused with a changed perception of time. Some millenarians had sufficient faith in the rightness of the social order to imagine that perfection would arrive through gradual transformation, and that a direct confrontation of the worldly and divine would come only at the distant terminus of history. But others expected an explosive contest between the powers of light and darkness, a violent purging of sin and error, and a final triumph of freedom and goodness.

Possibly the millenarian indulged in fantasies of persecution and suffering in order to justify his ultimate victory over original sin and social restraint. It has been said that masochists achieve a forbidden pleasure by anticipating and controlling the punishment that expiates their guilt.[3] When sectarians went out of their way to provoke the wrath of secular and ecclesiastical authorities, they may have wished to bring on the inevitable retribution and to release a powerful tension generated by a new vision of time and salvation. But actual conflict between religious groups undoubtedly nourished desires for revenge and intensified the violence of apocalyptic imagery. Millennialism had a strong appeal to early Protestants who, facing the awesome might of the Church, sought reassurance in the design of history. Such men saw the pope as Antichrist and the Reformation as the fulfilment of prophecy; but defeat might also show that the Last Days had arrived, and that goodness could triumph only by annihilating the world. History could lead to both exultation and despair.

Traditionally, sin had been identified with the individual's desires and impulses which society repressed in the supposed interests of peace and harmony. Thus even John Wyclif had agreed with Augustine that bondage to sin was the only servitude that mattered, and that physical slavery, being a consequence of sin, was of no concern to the elect.[4] But a changed view of history made it possible to identify

3. Recognizing that Theodor Reik's theories are disputed by some psychiatrists, I think that his *Masochism in Modern Man* (New York, 1941) has important implications for the study of certain social movements. Evidence of the sado-masochistic fantasies and actions of the millenarians can be found in Cohn, *Pursuit of the Millennium, passim.*

4. William A. Dunning, *A History of Political Theories: Ancient and Mediaeval* (New York, 1921), p. 262. But though Wyclif connected *dominium* with sin, he maintained that it could be validly exercised only by just men, and he placed particular emphasis on the duties of masters as well as of servants (*The English Works of Wyclif* [ed. by Frederick D. Matthew, Lon-

virtue with man's deepest desires, and sin with the inhibiting and repressive forces blocking the path to the millennium. Instead of thinking of sin as a principle of corruption diffused through nature and transmitted by generation, the millenarian hypostasized it in the person of an Antichrist who represented, significantly, an absolute power and sovereignty. In the eyes of the more radical millenarians, the universe was suddenly transformed from a fixed hierarchy of moral gradations into an irreconcilable division of evil and righteousness, of darkness and light, of freedom and slavery. In so far as all Protestants rebelled against the Church as a symbol of temporal authority which kept men's souls in bondage, they shared in the transvaluation of values which dethroned the collective superego. But unlike the radical sectarians, the great Reformers knew that a dethroned authority must be replaced; and they never doubted that the roots of sin lay in man's nature, which could never be purified by history.

For Thomas Müntzer, on the other hand, the great moment had arrived when, inspired by the Holy Spirit, man could liberate himself from sin, annihilate evil and establish the Kingdom of God. The time had come when all human institutions could be judged by the absolute law of God. Men like Luther, who made compromises with human authority on the ground that sinners required restraint, were in fact surrendering to sin. According to Müntzer, all masters and princes had lost their rights of dominion; all servants were released from their obligations. Confident that symbolic acts of violence would break the binding cords of an evil society and release the pent-up forces of righteousness, this John Brown of the Peasants' War led raiding parties to destroy monasteries and convents. Other radical chiliasts attempted at times to fulfil apocalyptic fantasies by slaughtering the children of darkness. Such outward aggression was balanced, however, by a kind of social masochism that took the forms of mutual flagellation or of demonstrative acts that invited persecution. Freedom from the bondage to sin could not be won without suffering.

---

don, 1880], pp. 227–34; L. J. Daly, *The Political Theory of John Wyclif* [Chicago, 1962], pp. 68–72).

When hard pressed, the millenarian summoned the wrathful God of the Old Testament to judge and punish his enemies. But millennialism was often combined with a kind of perfectionism which substituted a compassionate and forgiving spirit for the image of the deity as an avenging master. The Holy Spirit has been associated historically with a universal power of love which dissolves human forms and distinctions. For the mystic, union with the Divine Spirit is so subjective and intensely personal that the restraints of the external world lose all significance. The perfectionist sects drew upon the mystic tradition, with its emphasis on direct experience, on an 'opening' of the soul to a ravishing power, and on the cultivation of potential divinity within man. They were primarily concerned, however, with the social consequences of moral freedom. The adepts of the Free Spirit, for example, claimed that when man had been liberated from the dominion of sin, he was morally sovereign and could do no wrong. Since the principle of divine authority had been introjected within the saint's personality, every act he committed was a sacrament. The Holy Spirit wiped out all human distinctions of law, status and morality; between the divine and the worldly there were no gradations, no compromises and no agents of mediation. The bondage of sin was abolished immediately and totally, or not at all.

In attempting to affirm his moral freedom, his independence from worldly standards and conventions, the perfectionist resembled the ancient Cynics who considered all other men slaves. The English Ranter, Lawrence Claxton (or Clarkson), maintained that no man was truly emancipated from sin until he could commit adultery without a twinge of conscience. Various sects tried to demonstrate their moral kinship with Adam by symbolically stripping off their clothes in a secluded 'Eden', or by encouraging sexual promiscuity within the brotherhood. Occasional repudiations of monogamous marriage were only the extreme expression of a more widespread tendency to place men and women on an equal footing. For if sin, as the Ranters claimed, was not a reality but only a name that could be made meaningless by an act of will, there could be no justification for inequalities of sex and property which violated the law of spontaneous love. The Münster Anabaptists made the immediate surrender of personal property a test of faith. No man, they said, had a right to live off the toil of others.[5]

When changing social and economic conditions brought a convergence of millennialism, perfectionism and primitivism, the entire social order was seen to be based on a principle of slavery. There is a wide difference, of course, between identifying sin with a single institution and with the entire social order. But in their faith in man's will and the power of love, in their hostility to all compromise and rationalization, and in their determination to wage unremitting war against the forces of darkness, the radical sectarians were, in a sense, the first abolitionists. By affirming man's freedom to overcome all restraints and dominion, and by shifting the locus of fundamental value from external authority to internal impulse, they pointed the way to both reform and revolution. Later abolitionists would frequently fall into the role and pattern of thought of the radical sectarians; and occasionally they would find it impossible to contain their social protest within a narrow channel. An attack on slavery could easily develop into a challenge to law, government and institutional restraints of every kind.

During the civil wars of the mid seventeenth century British Protestantism fluctuated between spasms of uncertainty and ecstatic moments when truth and holiness seemed to have been found at last. Once the fabric of political and ecclesiastical authority began to unravel, men's aspirations were left without guides or limits. To the horror of the more orthodox Presbyterians and Independents, the wars spawned a host of 'gangrena' whose millennial prophecies were coupled with defiance of the law and demands for political and agrarian reform. For these sectarians the essence of religion was a rapturous experience that had nothing to do with creeds, churches or covenants; in a searing flash the Divine Spirit annihilated man's sinful nature, his creaturehood, and freed him from obligations to the external law. The fundamental question was whether this rebirth required violent action to institute a social order harmonious with the law of love, or a gathering of the saints and a separation from sinful society. One road would lead to martyrdom, the other to sterility and gradual extinction.

5. Cohn, *Pursuit of Millennum*, pp. 188–90, 288, 345–8.

Of the multitude of sects that arose during the civil wars, only the Quakers found a way of meeting this dilemma. That the Society of Friends was able to preserve and perpetuate sectarian ideals had an important bearing on the origins of anti-slavery thought; but even more significant was the particular way in which Quakers sublimated their radical impulse to perfection, and reconciled the absolute law of love with the realities of life. This gift for pragmatic adjustment not only guaranteed survival, but served to direct moral energies towards concrete objectives instead of diffusing them in a general attack upon the social order.

The original Quaker leaders had no intention of founding another sect or church. Their Society, as Rufus Jones has written, was 'a little visible part of the whole family of God, a tiny fragment of the invisible Church. It had no constitution, no creed, no sacraments, no clergy, no ordained officials, no infallibilities, except the infallibility of the guiding Spirit.'[6] As missionaries carried the message of George Fox to the Turks, the Vatican and the Massachusetts Puritans, they expected to emancipate men from enslaving creeds and institutions, and to unite them in Christian fellowship. The universality of the Quaker mission was complemented by the radical effects of personal regeneration. When a man assented to a mystical union with Christ, his soul received a divine seed which brought rebirth, freedom from sin and a resurrection of the inward image of God. And while the religious drama was enacted within the interior of the human soul, the external world caught its shadowy reflections. Quaker converts demonstrated their spiritual liberty by refusing to pay tithes, to take oaths before magistrates or to bow or doff their hats to superiors. Sometimes servants and apprentices denounced the impiety of their masters; a few Quaker enthusiasts paraded naked in the streets. George Fox, who considered himself as sinless as Adam before the Fall, was unsparing in his attacks on the 'hireling' ministry. James Naylor, his schismatic follower, claimed to be Christ manifest. If the Society of Friends had been unable to discipline this impulse towards personal perfection and social regeneration, they would

6. Rufus Jones, introd. to William C. Braithwaite, *The Second Period of Quakerism* (London, 1919), pp. xxix–xxx.

doubtless have been destroyed by internal disunity if not by persecution.[7]

It is not easy to account for the Quakers' self-discipline and capacity for compromise. George Fox was remarkably successful in converting men of unusual ability and experience, as well as entire groups, such as the Westmorland Seekers, who had already acquired a tradition of Biblical scholarship, techniques or organization, and methods of accommodating themselves to an unrighteous society. The principle of non-resistance was itself an effective agent of social control. It differentiated Friends from more radical groups, such as the Fifth Monarchy Men; it precluded violent attempts to transform the basic structure of society; and it united men in the sense of purity that comes from mutual renunciation and suffering.

Robert Barclay, who systematized Quaker theology, by no means agreed with the Ranters and Anabaptists who held that sin was but a name, and that man was free to build an egalitarian utopia. Barclay did place the inward testimony of the Spirit above the authority of Scripture, reason or external law, and thus tended to undermine the traditional foundations of social discipline. He maintained, furthermore, that Adam's sin could not be imputed to newborn infants. But if sin was supposedly the result of voluntary choice, it was not the less

7. My discussion of Quakerism draws on the following secondary works, in addition to primary sources which have a direct bearing on slavery and which will be cited subsequently: William C. Braithwaite, *The Beginnings of Quakerism* (London, 1912); and Braithwaite, *Second Period of Quakerism* (London, 1919); Rufus M. Jones, *The Later Periods of Quakerism* (London, 1921); Elbert Russell, *The History of Quakerism* (New York, 1942); [Nathan Kite], *A Brief Statement of the Rise and Progress of the Testimony of the Religious Society of Friends, against Slavery and the Slave Trade* (Philadelpha, 1843); Thomas Drake, *Quakers and Slavery in America* (New Haven, 1950); Edwin B. Bronner, *William Penn's 'Holy Experiment': The Founding of Pennsylvania, 1681–1701* (New York, 1962); Arthur Raistrick, *Quakers in Science and Industry; Being an Account of the Quaker Contributions to Science and Industry during the 17th and 18th Centuries* (London, 1950); Frederick B. Tolles, *Meeting House and Counting House: The Quaker Merchants of Colonial Philadelphia, 1682–1763* (Chapel Hill, 1948); Sydney V. James, *A People among Peoples: Quaker Benevolence in Eighteenth-Century America* (Cambridge, Mass., 1963); Anne T. Gary, 'The Political and Economic Relations of English and American Quakers' (D. Phil. thesis, Oxford University, 1935).

inevitable. It was as if the child of bondsmen, though not inheriting the punishment of his parents, became legally enslaved as soon as he acted within the narrow limits of his condition. By nature man possessed no ability for righteous action. Until his soul was 'disjoined' from the evil seed and united with the Divine Light, he could not escape from sin. While Barclay emphasized the importance of personal responsibility, he did not challenge the traditional view of a corrupt world requiring discipline and authority. The magistrate, to be sure, had no right or power to force men's consciences, for as well might he 'seek to wash the black-moor white'. But liberty of conscience could not be extended to 'such wild notions' as those of the Münster Anabaptists, who would 'seek to make all things *common*, and would force their neighbours to share their estates with them'. If the Quakers' personal ethics were close to Anabaptism, their views on property and government resembled those of the English Puritans.[8]

It was the Quaker genius, then, to achieve a dynamic balance between an impulse to perfection and a way of life tending to crystallize the impulse in forms that could meet the demands of reality. Expectations of both individual perfection and social regeneration shrank markedly when, well before the end of the seventeenth century, Quakers accepted their position as a minor sect, and assumed a posture of detachment and circumspection.[9] As Friends came to confine their demonstrative protests to such questions as oaths, tithes and bearing arms, and otherwise adjusted themselves to the institutions of society, they developed their own distinctive psychology, a state of mind acutely sensitized to the dangers of both fanaticism and worldly compromise. This internal watchfulness was reinforced by a growing sense of their own peculiarity, a common memory of persecution, and an inclination to separate themselves, so far as possible, from an unfriendly world.

But the necessity of maintaining an equilibrium between moral principles and daily life resulted in constant tension and soul-search-

8. Robert Barclay, *An Apology for the True Christian Divinity: Being an Explanation and Vindication of the Principles and Doctrines of the People Called Quakers* (Providence, 1843), pp. 94–5, 102–3, 497; Tolles, *Meeting House and Counting House*, p. 53.

9. James, *People Among Peoples*, pp. 29–31.

ing. Precisely because Quaker organization and discipline served to fix the radical sectarian impulse at a particular stage, minute points of controversy, such as the exact wording of oaths, were charged with intense emotional significance. Each generation was put to the test of divided loyalties, knowing that refusal to obey the State might result in imprisonment or confiscation of property, but that betrayal of principle could lead to disownment. Only constant surveillance and the systematic cultivation of charity could keep the clear springs of Quaker experience from becoming polluted. The merchant or proprietor must show that neither wealth nor the press of business had dimmed the Inner Light; the reformer must prove that his schemes for human betterment in no way promoted worldly licence. John Bellers, whose radical plans for penal reform were ultimately to influence Francis Place and Robert Owen, could still draw on the original missionary zeal of the fathers of Quakerism. Yet Bellers's proposals were as much for social control as for liberation. Distressed by the vices of the idle poor, he envisioned highly ordered communities where industrial discipline would bring the regularity of habits essential for a life of obedience to Christ. Anthony Benezet, whose life of benevolent activity did much to initiate the great age of Quaker philanthropy, could affirm that 'the only end for which thou wast created in this world is, that by living in a state of obedience, by constant watching and prayer, thy soul may, with the assistance of divine grace, become so purified, as to be fitted to dwell with God for ever.'[10]

Now perfectionists who thought it possible to live in absolute conformity with the law of love would presumably refrain from slaveholding as well as from war. Quakers condemned war; and yet they recognized the power and persistence of sin, they respected the authority of government and the inviolability of private property, and they viewed labour as at once a duty and a necessary discipline. How far would they follow the Catholic and Protestant Churches in reconciling conflicts between worldly interests and transcendent standards of the Gospel? Would the fellowship of the meeting and the formalized positions on war and oaths take the place of Catholic

10. Braithwaite, *Second Period of Quakerism*, pp. 568–78; George S. Brookes, *Friend Anthony Benezet* (Philadelphia, 1937), p. 210.

reliance on sacraments and meritorious works, or of Protestant dependence on inner grace and forensic theology, so that mundane questions like slavery would appear irrelevant to man's quest for salvation?

For most sectarians, of course, slavery presented no problem. But by a remarkable coincidence, the growth of the Society of Friends was closely tied to British expansion in the North Atlantic and Caribbean, and hence, either directly or indirectly, to the African slave trade. Indeed, the destiny of the Society of Friends was intertwined with American slavery in an almost providential design. In 1655, at the time of the earliest Quaker missionary work, William Penn's father captured Jamaica from Spain, and thus gave a major impetus to British sugar cultivation and the African trade. Admiral Penn was not a Quaker, but it was his fortune, coupled with an immense debt owed to him by the Duke of York, that made possible the Holy Experiment of Pennsylvania. Before the founding of Pennsylvania, Quaker missionaries had won many converts in Barbados, which George Rolfe called 'the nursery of truth', but which was also the nursery of British slavery. Among the converts were wealthy sugar planters and slaveholders, some of whom entertained George Fox during his first American visit.[11] And a second base of American Quakerism was Rhode Island, the future capital of the North American slave trade. Inevitably, Quaker merchants in Rhode Island, the Jerseys and Pennsylvania looked to the West Indies as their principal market. The prosperity of Quaker communities in the New World depended, to a large extent, on slave labour in the Caribbean.

George Fox was by no means blind to the problems raised by American slavery. In his famous letter of 1657 'To Friends Beyond Sea That Have Blacks and Indian Slaves', he gave new force to the traditional doctrines of Christian mercy and brotherhood. Fourteen years later he preached to slaves in Barbados and, developing upon the ideal of Christian servitude, went so far as to suggest that terms of bondage be limited to thirty years.[12] But there can be no doubt that

11. Braithwaite, *Beginnings of Quakerism*, p. 402.

12. George Fox, *Journal* (ed. by Ernest Rhys, rev. by Norman Penney, London, 1944), p. 277. The recommendation for a term of thirty years was changed to 'certain years' in the 1694 English edition.

Fox accepted Negro slavery as an institution which could be rationalized by the ancient dualisms of body and soul, matter and spirit. In his faith that the relations of master and slave could be imbued with a spirit of love, he was not in advance of many orthodox Catholics and Protestants of earlier and later times.

We should not be surprised, therefore, to learn that William Penn bought and owned Negro slaves, that a Quaker-dominated government of Pennsylvania enacted a harsh slave code, or that as late as 1730 Quaker merchants in Philadelphia were importing and selling West Indian Negroes.[13] The Rhode Island slave trade of the 1760s involved leading Quaker families.[14] And those who refrained from slave-dealing had no scruples about dealing in rum, molasses, sugar and rice. In England, where Quaker economic power was initially based on commerce, and centred in such ports as Bristol, Liverpool and London, connexions with the African trade were inevitable. Active and powerful Friends like David Barclay, Alexander Barclay and Thomas Mildred were members of the Royal African Company.[15] As Quaker merchant princes moved into banking, textiles and iron, they were still tied to African markets and West Indian investments. Nor should one forget the small but important part played by Friends in developing the American South. George Fox himself organized Quaker communities in Virginia and Carolina; one of his converts, John Archdale, became governor-general of Carolina, and encouraged the spread of his faith in Charles Town. During the eighteenth century Quaker families moved southwards from Pennsylvania into Maryland, Virginia and North Carolina. And, as successful farmers, many acquired slaves.[16]

Quaker masters may have been more humane than average, but they did not Christianize the institution of slavery. It was not until

13. William Penn to James Harrison, 4 December 1685, Penn Domestic and Misc. Letters (Penn MSS, Pennsylvania Historical Society); Drake, *Quakers and Slavery*, pp. 23–4; Harold D. Wax, 'Quaker Merchants and the Slave Trade in Colonial Pennsylvania', *Pennsylvania Magazine of History and Biography*, LXXXVI (April 1962), pp. 144–59.

14. Gary, 'Political and Economic Relations', p. 197.

15. ibid., pp. 194–5.

16. Stephen B. Weeks, *Southern Quakers and Slavery: A Study in Institutional History* (Baltimore, 1896), pp. 40–70.

1756 that the Society of Friends took serious steps to induce owners to provide their slaves with religious instruction. Even then Negroes were not accepted as brethren entitled to equal membership or to Quaker burial.[17] The very exclusiveness of the Society, reinforced by the rigorous obligations of membership, made it difficult to consider bondsmen as spiritual equals. Protected by this wall of separation, many Friends found it easy to exclude the problem of slavery from consciousness. A Quaker woman in Charles Town could condemn luxury, music, great wealth and cruelty to children, and yet say nothing about the labourers of her city.[18] Joseph Wanton, a Rhode Islander who stood on principle in his refusal to take an oath, could engage in the slave trade between 1769 and 1775 both as a captain and merchant.[19] William Dillwyn, a pupil of Anthony Benezet and a future leader of the British anti-slavery movement, could write from Charles Town in 1773, discussing his success in exchanging West Indian rum for Carolina rice, and ignore the institution which made his transactions possible.[20]

But there is a mass of evidence to suggest that slaveholding provoked far more tension among Quakers than among Catholics, Anglicans or Congregationalists. For reasons that should now be clear, the Society of Friends had a limited power to assimilate compromises with Christian ideals, and was more inclined than were the orthodox churches to associate moral evil with institutions of the external world. Unhampered by dogmatic theology, guided by the continuing revelations of the Inner Light, Friends were partly immune from rationalizations which identified ancient custom with natural

17. James, *People Among Peoples*, pp. 112–114.

18. Herbert Aptheker, 'The Quakers and Negro Slavery', *Journal of Negro History*, XXV (July 1940), pp. 340–41. While both Herbert Aptheker and Anne Gary bring out the Quakers' economic involvement in slavery, they avoid the untenable position of Eric Williams, who argues that Quaker attitudes towards bondage were determined by economic interest ('The Golden Age of the Slave System in Britain', *Journal of Negro History*, XXV [January 1940], p. 97).

19. Gary, 'Political and Economic Relations', p. 197.

20. William Dillwyn to James Pemberton, 27 January 1773, Pemberton Papers, XXIV (Pennsylvania Historical Society).

law. In America, where there was opportunity to build a society consonant with emergent Truth, no makeshift controls could stifle individual moral inquiry. There were, of course, economic or psychological conditions which favoured the questioning of slavery. Some Quakers became 'concerned' about the problem as a result of petty inconveniences or of fears that they would be unable to discipline Negro bond servants.[21] Small farmers, used to a life of simplicity and hard work, could express contempt for the piety of urban merchants who sported a retinue of domestic slaves. Quaker converts, such as the Nantucket carpenter, Elihu Coleman, who had become convinced that their relatives and former associates were blinded by false education and custom, might apply the same critical spirit to the failings of their new brethren.[22] But whatever the occasions for individual protest, it was the Quaker frame of mind that enabled men to disregard law and precedent, and to judge slavery by the Inner Light.

William Edmundson, who accompanied George Fox to Barbados in 1651, was one of the first to move beyond the conventional faith that Christianity would soften the hearts of masters. Like many later critics of slavery, Edmundson was a man of humble origins and wide experience. He had been a carpenter's apprentice in Yorkshire, a combat veteran under Cromwell, and a Quaker missionary in Ireland. During a second visit to Barbados, when his religious instruction of slaves aroused the intense hostility of planters, he felt it necessary to assure the governor that he was interested only in saving the Negroes' souls.[23] But in 1676 Edmundson sent out from Newport, Rhode Island, a general letter to Quakers in slaveholding colonies. Reflecting upon the ancient linkage between sin and bondage, he observed that Barbadian masters allowed slaves the unlawful liberty to act in accordance with their own corrupt natures, but denied them

21. This appears to have been the origin of Cadwalader Morgan's questioning of slavery in 1696. See Wax, 'Quaker Merchants', p. 148.
22. Elihu Coleman, *A Testimony against that Antichristian Practice of Making Slaves of Men, Wherein it is Shewed to be Contrary to the Dispensation of the Law and Time of the Gospel, and Very Opposite both to Grace and Nature* (n.p., 1733), p. i.
23. Drake, *Quakers and Slavery*, pp. 7–8.

the freedom to be servants of Christ. If they were to obey the command to 'make their condition your own', Quakers would have to enable their Negroes to fulfil the law of Christ. By suggesting that physical slavery and Christian liberty were incompatible, Edmundson inverted the traditional dualisms. Negroes were slaves to sin because they were slaves of men. From this position it was but a short step to the conclusion that slavery itself was sin.[24]

William Edmundson not only dissociated Negro slavery from the Christian ideal of servitude but held that perpetual bondage was 'an oppression on the mind' which could not be justified by God's curse on the children of Canaan. Even if it could be shown that Africans were the descendants of Ham, had not Christ removed the 'wall of partition' that separated peoples? The only differences that mattered were those of sincerity and purity of faith. Ironically, the Quaker slaveholder could prove his own moral superiority, and thus erect a different kind of partition, by emancipating his servants, so that his 'self-denial may be known to all'.

It seems probable that men who had suffered from religious persecution were more likely to see a connexion between bodily and spritual liberty. Edmundson knew the mental and physical anguish of imprisonment. The Dutch-speaking Quakers who emigrated from Krefeld to Germantown, and who signed the famous anti-slavery petition of 1688, could never forget the bloody tortures and executions of their Mennonite ancestors.[25] Comparing the suffering of

24. The letter is reprinted in *The Friend*, LXI (1887), p. 68, where it is wrongly attributed to George Fox. Sydney James provides by far the most illuminating discussion of Edmundson in *People Among Peoples*, p. 106.

25. For the origins of the Germantown petitioners, see J. Herbert Fretz, 'The Germantown Anti-Slavery Petition of 1688', *Mennonite Quarterly Review*, XXXIII (January 1959), pp. 42–59. The text of the petition can be found in Samuel W. Pennypacker, 'The Settlement of Germantown, and the Causes Which Led to It', *Pennsylvania Magazine of History and Biography*, IV (1880), pp. 28–30; and in William Hull, *William Penn and the Dutch Quaker Migration to Pennsylvania* (n.p., 1935), pp. 297–9. The best-known of the petitioners was the German Pietist, Francis Daniel Pastorius, but there is no reason to believe that the anti-slavery protest was primarily his work. Although the other petitioners were Quakers before they migrated to America, it is possible that their Mennonite background, coupled with later

slaves with their own religious persecution, they could flatly declare that liberty of conscience should bring liberty of the body. The eyes of Europe were directed towards the Quaker experiment in religious freedom. What would happen to the cause of Truth if it were discovered that Friends profited from a form of slavery more brutal than that of the Turks or Barbary pirates?[26]

We have seen that both Catholics and Protestants were able to reconcile slavery with the Golden Rule by piously affirming that masters should treat their bondsmen as they themselves would be treated, should they have the misfortune of becoming slaves. For the Germantown Quakers, enslavement was not a question of fate. The Africans had been criminally seized and shipped off to America without their consent. To purchase them was to purchase stolen goods. Because Negroes had a perfect right to liberty, they might resort to armed rebellion, which Friends could not resist without violating pacifist principles. Slaveholding, then, was based on sheer physical force, and involved infringements of divine law, as when families were separated and adultery encouraged. The origins and consequences of Negro slavery made the institution absolutely incompatible with the Golden Rule.

We should not think of Edmundson's letter and the Germantown petition as parts of a continuous and progressive evolution of antislavery doctrine. By associating physical with spiritual liberty, and consequently expanding the scope of individual moral responsibility, they brought out one of the potentialities of Quaker thought. But Edmundson's letter was without effect. The Dublin Monthly Meeting, to which the Germantown petition was referred, considered the matter too 'weighty' for action. Philadelphia Quarterly Meeting quickly passed the petition on to the Yearly Meeting, which quietly

---

Mennonite influence in Germantown, made them particularly sensitive to the problems of slavery.

26. The comparison of Negro slavery with the enslavement of Europeans by Turks and Barbary pirates became a stock theme of anti-slavery literature. Quakers in both England and America had raised funds in the late seventeenth century for the ransom of Europeans captured in the Mediterranean. The publicity given to the outrages of the Barbary pirates undoubtedly aided the anti-slavery cause.

buried it.[27] Unknown to Benjamin Lay and Anthony Benezet, to John Woolman and Thomas Clarkson, the Germantown protest was not rediscovered until well into the nineteenth century.

And yet a protest had been made, a protest which forced a response from the highest official bodies of the Society of Friends. Though Quaker leaders were no more disposed to condemn slavery than had been the Spanish Council of the Indies a few years before, they could not defend their position by citing noted theologians and classical authorities.[28] Their extreme caution and secretiveness suggest a realization that Quakers would be hard put to justify the institution. The moral vulnerability of slaveholding Friends was soon to be revealed in the hot crossfire of religious schism.

George Keith arrived in East Jersey three years before the Germantown petition was written, having first stopped off at Barbados on his way from Europe. Like Edmundson, he had personally observed West Indian slavery; and since he had visited Quaker groups through Holland and Germany in 1677, it is possible that he knew some of the Germantown petitioners even before their migration. In general background Keith was altogether different from such men as Fox and Edmundson. A student of philosophy, mathematics and modern languages, he had received a master of arts degree at Aberdeen, and had read Descartes with Gilbert Burnet. Keith's scholarship was balanced by a flaming religious zeal which in some respects anticipated the evangelical emphasis on personal choice and purity of life which transformed Quakerism in the latter part of the eighteenth century. It appeared to Keith that the leading Quaker ministers and magistrates in America had lost sight of Christ the Saviour, and, by disregarding the imperatives of 'immediate revelation', had compromised themselves with a sinful world. Such attacks on the elite of American Quakerism brought swift retaliation. When, in 1691 and 1692, Keith was disowned, publicly condemned and even fined, he defiantly formed his own sect of 'Christian Quakers'.[29]

Without doubting the sincerity of his opinions, we may suspect

27. Drake, *Quakers and Slavery*, pp. 12–13.
28. See above, pp. 214, 218–19.
29. Ethyn Williams Kirby, *George Keith* (New York, 1942), pp. 1–7, 35–6, 60–88.

that George Keith seized upon the issue of slavery as a convenient means of embarrassing his persecutors, who included wealthy merchants and some of the powerful leaders who had suppressed the Germantown petition. After inducing his followers to sign, in 1693, *An Exhortation and Caution to Friends Concerning Buying or Keeping of Negroes,* Keith apparently gave no further thought to the matter. Returning to Britain, he became an Anglican convert and, ultimately, a missionary for the slaveholding SPG.[30] But even if Keith embraced anti-slavery as a means of exposing the inconsistency of Quakers, and of proving the virtue of his own sect, the fact remains that religious schism released deep-seated tensions and provided an angle of vision undistorted by traditional rationalizations. Later opponents of slavery, such as John Hepburn and Benjamin Lay, were aware of Keith's challenge.[31]

Keith's *Exhortation* was similar to the Germantown petition in its application of the Golden Rule and in its argument that Negroes were stolen goods. The latter point was made more forceful by invoking the Biblical condemnation of manstealers and by associating prisoners of war with prize goods, which the pacifist Quakers were forbidden to buy.[32] But Keith went well beyond the Germantown petitioners in foreshadowing the major religious themes of nineteenth-century abolitionism. His emphasis on the Atonement, as applying universally to all mankind, was clearly an expression of his central belief in Christ the Redeemer. Christ had died not only to save souls, but to deliver the oppressed, to bring 'Liberty both inward and outward.'[33] It was the duty of Christians to show compassion towards anyone in misery; the choice between keeping or manumitting a slave was a test of true virtue. Since the guilt of manstealing carried over to the buyers of slaves, masters must expect the

30. ibid., pp. 113 ff. Keith became a violent anti-Quaker.

31. John Hepburn, *The American Defence of the Christian Golden Rule, or an Essay to Prove the Unlawfulness of Making Slaves of Men, By Him Who Loves the Freedom of the Souls and Bodies of All Men* (n.p., 1715), p. 2; Lay, *All Slave-keepers ... Apostates ...,* p. 69.

32. Keith, 'An Exhortation and Caution to Friends Concerning Buying or Keeping of Negroes', reprinted in *Pennsylvania Magazine of History and Biography,* XIII (1889), pp. 267-9.

33. ibid., pp. 265-6.

full wrath of God's judgement if they failed to repent and reform. They must sacrifice their riches, come out of Babylon, and not be partakers of her sins. But though the salvation of slave-owners depended on an immediate repentance and decision to act, Keith recognized that it would be impossible to liberate all slaves at once. Bondsmen must be prepared for freedom by Christian education. It was only reasonable that they should pay for their maintenance by a limited period of 'moderate service'.[34] By combining expediency with an absolute condemnation of the very principle of slavery, Keith announced the central doctrines of future abolitionism. One should note that he arrived at this position after a search for religious truth which led him through painful conflicts with his brethren, and that his views on slavery were, in a sense, an externalization of his religious beliefs.

For more than a generation after Keith's *Exhortation*, no Quaker wrote on the issue with such uncompromising boldness. Yet a few isolated individuals came to see the slave system as a threat to religious purity, and bore testimony against it in Meeting or in unauthorized preaching and writing. Robert Pyle, a well-to-do farmer and prominent citizen of Chester County, gives us a rare insight into the deep tensions that might lead to a conviction that slavery was sinful. Having experienced great difficulty in retaining English servants, Pyle felt a strong 'motion' within himself to purchase a Negro, apparently a woman with small children. Then he dreamed that he and a friend were walking down a road. They came upon a black pot, which was lying by the roadside. When Pyle picked it up, his friend wanted part of it. Pyle refused to surrender the pot, but soon came to an enormous ladder, which, he tells us three times, was standing 'exact upright'. The ladder led, of course, to heaven, and Pyle realized that he would have to climb it with the black pot in his hand. He soon discovered, however, that it was hard enough work to climb the ladder with both hands, and that he would have to leave the pot at the base of the ladder. Upon awaking, he instantly grasped the religious, if not the Freudian, symbolism of this remarkable dream, and decided 'to lett black negroes or pots alone'. Moreover, he concluded that if slavery were unlawful in 'this gospel time', it would be

34. ibid., pp. 266–7.

expedient for Quaker Monthly Meetings to encourage manumissions by judging whether owners could bear the financial loss and whether slaves were prepared for freedom. Evidently a Negro's right to liberty would depend on his piety and willingness to obey God.[35]

During the early eighteenth century a number of Quaker meetings in America were stirred by anti-slavery agitation, but we know the names of only a few of the more outspoken abolitionists. William Southeby, who had quarrelled publicly with George Keith, helped to promote in 1698 an official letter to Barbadian Friends, requesting them to end shipments of Negroes to Pennsylvania. Some years later, Southeby's persistent attacks on slavery apparently resulted in his disownment.[36] William Burling provoked a flurry of debate in Long Island, until he was silenced by the Quakers' subtle disciplinary machinery. More intractable was John Farmer, an Englishman who denounced slavery in Nantucket, and then defied the warnings and remonstrances of the Rhode Island Yearly Meeting. Disowned in New England, Farmer moved on to Philadelphia where, though he met with a chilly reception, he continued his lonely crusade.[37] While conservative Friends were generally successful in quieting or isolating anti-slavery agitators, a questioning spirit developed in a number of local meetings, such as Flushing, Long Island, Dartmouth, Massachusetts; and Chester, Pennsylvania.

Even the cautious merchants who dominated Philadelphia Yearly Meeting found it impossible to ignore the sentiments of vocal Friends

35. Henry J. Cadbury, 'An Early Quaker Anti-Slavery Statement', *Journal of Negro History*, XXII (October 1937), pp. 492–3. Pyle wrote in 1698. For other Quaker dreams pertaining to slavery, see Cadbury, 'Negro Membership in the Society of Friends', *Journal of Negro History*, XXI (April 1936), p. 182 n.

36. Drake, *Quakers and Slavery*, pp. 19–29, 34–5; Henry J. Cadbury, 'Another Early Quaker Anti-Slavery Document', *Journal of Negro History*, XXVII (April 1942), pp. 210–15. The anti-slavery writings of Southeby, Burling and Farmer have not survived. Benjamin Lay reprinted an extract of one of Burling's writings in *All Slave-keepers ... Apostates ...* (pp. 9 ff); but Lay's tract is so disordered and his own mind was so clearly unbalanced that little trust can be placed in the text.

37. Drake, *Quakers and Slavery*, pp. 29–33; James, *People Among Peoples*, p. 123; Kite, *Brief Statement*, p. 43.

who were 'straightened in their minds' against holding slaves. A number of circumstances contributed to a guarded shift from the official policy of inaction. In the late 1690s, with the prospect of a vastly enlarged African trade, men might well wonder, on purely economic grounds, whether an influx of Negroes would be advantageous to Pennsylvania. There is evidence that many independent farmers and artisans, regardless of their views on the morality of slaveholding, were opposed to heavy importations of Negro labourers. In addition, the same racial prejudice and fear of insurrection which were expressed in acts 'for the better regulating of Negroes' could strengthen the desire to limit or prohibit the inflow of slaves. As we have seen, such motives contributed in the early eighteenth century to restrictive laws in a number of colonies. And despite the inclination of many Quakers to justify the simple ownership of Negroes, the institution would obviously be more palatable if it were further removed from the wars of Africa and the violence of the slave ship. As Philadelphia attracted an increasing number of non-Quaker merchants, who had no scruples about profiting from war or prize goods, the distinction between slavery and the slave trade acquired still greater significance. Men who were threatening the Quakers' economic and political dominance, and who were outside the reach of religious controls, could at least be scorned as the importers of human flesh. It would be a triumph of power as well as of morality if Quakers succeeded in persuading their own people to avoid the trade, and then exerted influence to secure its legal prohibition.[38]

As early as 1696 Philadelphia Yearly Meeting defined the broad principles that would govern official policy for more than half a century. Owners were charged with the moral welfare of their bondsmen, but were tacitly assured that their property rights did not conflict with religious purity. To purchase slaves for private use was permissible; but Friends were cautioned against trading in Negroes as a business or being involved in their further importation. Since even this compromising position carried no sanctions, there was con-

38. Gary, 'Political and Economic Relations', p. 181; Tolles, *Meeting House and Counting House*, pp. 48–9, 51 ff; Hepburn, *American Defence*, pp. 15–18; Ralph Sandiford, *The Mystery of Iniquity, in a Brief Examination of the Practice of the Times* (n.p., 1730), p. 5.

siderable room for further steps which would not menace the profits or security of slaveholders. Many prominent Quakers were willing to encourage the Pennsylvania Assembly to restrict or prohibit the importation of Negroes. Knowing the opposition of the Privy Council to such measures, they realized that their best hope lay in enlisting the aid of powerful British Friends, who might bring pressure on the central government. Over the strenuous protests of William Southeby, who thought that a moral decision required no outside support, Philadelphia Yearly Meeting appealed in 1712 to London Yearly Meeting, observing that 'some' Friends had been morally troubled by slavery, and that previous efforts had failed to block an influx of Negroes into Pennsylvania. The timing of this message was inopportune, for Britain was about to secure the coveted *assiento*; London Yearly Meeting was influenced by conservative mercantile thought, and was rendered still more cautious by its campaign for greater religious toleration in a period of rising High Church sentiment. London Friends not only dismissed the question as being 'too weighty' for an immediate decision, but rebuked Philadelphia for writing without first consulting the other groups of American Quakers. In this reply and in later epistles, London Yearly Meeting strongly disapproved of Quakers engaging in the African slave trade. But as Sydney James has written, 'The crisis had arrived, and the Quakers had not been able to cope with it. Instead of decision there had been paralysis in the highest institutions of the church.'[39]

In some respects the Quaker psychology was remarkably similar to that which later characterized many Americans. Lacking the guidance of established tradition or philosophic doctrine, Friends devised subtle mechanisms for creating and assessing group consensus. One congregation could not take a position far in advance of the others, as was discovered by the Germantown petitioners and by Philadelphia

39. James, *People Among Peoples*, pp. 118–19. James, who gives by far the most perceptive account of the crisis from 1711 to 1716, also points out that in 1712 William Penn came down with the apoplexy, which removed a source of Quaker influence at court and stopped negotiations to sell the government of Pennsylvania to the crown (p. 118). Anne Gary brings out the conservative economic interests of London Yearly Meeting ('Political and Economic Relations', pp. 181–5).

Yearly Meeting, when it appealed to London. 'Religious Truth might grow,' writes Sydney James, 'but not in different directions.'[40] When Quakers in Newport asked their Monthly Meeting in 1715 whether it was 'agreeable to Truth' to brand a slave on the cheek, they were told that it was not. But when doubts arose regarding the lawfulness of perpetual bondage in Dartmouth, Massachusetts, where a Quaker woman had been temporarily disowned for beating her slave to death, the question was finally evaded.[41] Men like Southeby, who in 1712 openly petitioned the Pennsylvania Assembly for the abolition of slavery, were clearly threatening a religious unity which depended upon a finely tuned sensitivity and an unquestioning response to the norms of the group.[42] If the most admired and influential Friends ever accepted anti-slavery as a test of religious purity, their opinions would spread with rapidity and would be backed by the most powerful forces of conformity. But in the meantime, dissenters risked the danger of appearing, as it were, 'un-Quaker'. Philadelphia Yearly Meeting continued to affirm, and even to strengthen, its policy of 1696; encouraged by London's growing disapproval of the African trade, it advised Friends in 1730 not to buy Negroes imported by others.[43] Yet in 1715 Philadelphia had warned Chester Quarterly Meeting against judging brethren who happened to own slaves. A few years later the most outspoken rebels had been silenced, and the Society of Friends entered a period of uneasy compromise. But as the United States was to learn in future years, no compromise could conceal the fact that disturbing questions had been raised.

40. James, *People Among Peoples*, p. 117.

41. Drake, *Quakers and Slavery*, pp. 29–30. Rhode Island Quarterly Meeting referred the question back to its various subordinate meetings, which replied with different answers. No decision was reached.

42. ibid., p. 28; Edward R. Turner, *The Negro in Pennsylvania: Slavery, Servitude, Freedom, 1639–1861* (Washington, 1911), p. 70.

43. In answer to queries from Philadelphia, London Yearly Meeting spoke out against the African slave trade in 1715, 1720 and 1727. But while Friends were told that even the importation of slaves from Africa was not commendable or allowable, the question was not made a part of church discipline: Gary, 'Political and Economic Relations', pp. 184–5; Drake, *Quakers and Slavery*, p. 41; Michael Kraus, *The Atlantic Civilization: Eighteenth-Century Origins* (Ithaca, N.Y., 1949), p. 146.

A period of eighteen years intervened between the publication of John Hepburn's *The American Defence of the Christian Golden Rule*, in 1715, and Elihu Coleman's *A Testimony against that Antichristian Practice of Making Slaves of Men*, which was the first attack on slavery to receive official approval from a Quaker meeting.[44] The two pamphlets are, however, strikingly similar in tone and approach. They give the impression of having been written by temperate-minded mechanics, whose independent reading and serious reflection made up for lack of formal education. Both men were obviously devout Quakers, but they had assimilated, to some degree, the ideas and mood of the early Enlightenment. Whereas Edmundson had seen slavery as an obstacle to conversion and the exercise of Christian liberty, and Keith had emphasized the liberating effect of the Atonement, Hepburn and Coleman virtually ignored the implications of original sin. They built their cases on the argument that man was created with a free will, with a capacity to choose the Good and even to conform to the attributes of God. And since moral perfectibility was the proper end of man, and could be achieved only through freedom of choice, even the most beneficent slavery was a 'manifest Robbery of that noble Gift'. Coleman explicitly maintained that bondage was contrary to nature as well as to Scripture.[45]

There is no hint that either writer questioned the dogmas of revealed religion. Yet the issue of slavery provided a framework for developing secular moral arguments and for applying the critical method to Scripture. In 1676 Edmundson had felt it necessary to attack the assumption that Negro slavery was a fulfilment of the curse of Canaan. The great attention Coleman devoted to this question may have indicated an increasing tendency of Americans to identify Negroes with the children of Ham. But it also showed the writer's willingness to examine Biblical texts in the light of reason and human standards of justice.[46] For Coleman, who said that he

44. Henry J. Cadbury, 'Quaker Bibliographical Notes', *Friends' Historical Association Bulletin*, XXVI (1937), p. 43.

45. Hepburn, *American Defence*, pp. 1–2; Coleman, *Testimony*, p. 6.

46. Coleman, *Testimony*, pp. 9–10. He also tried to answer the argument that blackness of skin was the mark which God had placed on the posterity of Cain.

himself would not be guilty of slaveholding for all the riches and glory in the world, it was inconceivable that the Divine Goodness had condemned a class of men to perpetual misery. Deists and sceptics took a similar view of original sin and reprobation.

Rational analysis was particularly evident in two articles which Hepburn added to his text. The first, 'Arguments against Making Slaves of Men', was written by an American, probably a Quaker, in 1713. The second was taken indirectly from *The Athenian Oracle* of London, a few pages of which had been reprinted in Boston in 1705.[47] Taken together, these remarkable essays answered virtually every pro-slavery argument that would appear during the next century and a half. By 1713 it had already been said that the slave trade encouraged wars and crimes in Africa, that enslavement was not the necessary consequence of sparing a captive's life, that it was unlawful to punish without a reason or to profit from labour without recompense, that bondage defaced the image of God, that it compelled men to act in ways that brought cruel punishment, that it led to the separation of families, to adultery, and to the violation of all the Commandments. Both writers took special pains to discredit the significantly secular argument that Negroes were far *happier* as American slaves than as African savages. And the American author anticipated the warning, dramatized by Hinton Rowan Helper in 1857, that Negro bondage would lead to a growing divergence and conflict between rich slaveholders and poor whites. Yet even in 1713 an anti-slavery writer could affirm an axiom later accepted by Thomas Jefferson and countless other Americans: it was unthinkable that Negroes and whites should live together in freedom. His proposed solution was essentially that of the later colonizationists. Before being

47. Hepburn, *American Defence*, pp. 23–43. It is possible that William Southeby was the 'native of America' referred to by Hepburn as the first author. The second selection had appeared in the first edition of *The Athenian Oracle: Being an Entire Collection of All the Valuable Questions and Answers in the Old Athenian Mercuries* (London, 1703), I, pp. 529–32 (because of errors in pagination, the numbers should read 545–8). Internal evidence shows that Hepburn had copied the four-page reprint, entitled *The Athenian Oracle* ... (Boston, 1705). We shall later discuss John Dunton, the editor of the *Oracle*, and the use which Samuel Sewall made of his work in Massachusetts.

emancipated, Negroes should be given a Christian education. Then subscriptions should be raised to send all manumitted slaves back to Africa, where they could further the cause of religion and civilization.[48]

A taste for irony and satire was as much a part of the enlightened mind as was an enthusiasm for social planning. To those who maintained that the Negro's ignorance and wickedness were sufficient reason for his enslavement, Coleman replied with the spirit of a born *philosophe*: 'If that Plea would do, I do believe they need not go so far for Slaves as now they do.'[49] Both Hepburn and Coleman compared Turks with Christians, to the latter's disadvantage. And Hepburn even adopted the mode of what Paul Hazard calls 'the ubiquitous critic', who sought a new objectivity by viewing the follies of his society through the eyes of a Persian or Chinese traveller.[50] In Hepburn's rather clumsily contrived dialogue, a Turk exposes the inconsistencies of an American slave-owner. When it begins to appear that Islam is at least free from the hypocrisy of Christianity, an apologist arrives who tries to show that the slaveholder is not a true Christian. But the slaveholder dryly observes that the English bishops have accepted the ownership of slaves; the houses of SPG missionaries are 'crawling black with them'. Presbyterians, who claimed to be zealous followers of the Reformation, engage actively in the enslavement of Africans. The Baptists, for all their piety and reputed simplicity of life, 'lovingly embrace' slavery. The American master concludes with some glee: 'Now if the *Church*, and *Presbyterians*, and *Baptists* did but agree so lovingly in other Points as they do in making Slaves of Negroes, I think they might be stiled *One Community*.' The apologist replies somewhat lamely to this point, and suggests that only pacifists can be consistent Christians. When the

48. Hepburn, *American Defence*, pp. 23–43. The author also said that any Negroes who chose not to return to Africa might remain in America, but only as bondsmen. Hence 'voluntary' slavery was justified on the basis of racial prejudice by a writer who otherwise embraced the leading principles of later abolitionists.

49. Coleman, *Testimony*, p. 9.

50. Paul Hazard, *European Thought in the Eighteenth Century: From Montesquieu to Lessing* (tr. by J. Lewis May, Meridian paperback ed., Cleveland, 1963), pp. 3–13.

master maintains that no group is more 'forward' in making slaves than the Quakers, the Christian can only answer that it is 'the greatest wonder' to see such a people 'embrace an inriching Sin'.[51]

For Hepburn and Coleman, as indeed for the *philosophes*, the ultimate problem was how evil had become entrenched as custom and accepted as universal practice. Since Quakers could assume that other churches still lived in the shadow of apostasy, the question narrowed to an explanation of their own sect's impurity.[52] The Old Testament gave examples of a chosen people suffering for the cause of Truth, and then, in a time of ease, becoming forgetful of their mission. Friends had once been subjected to the bitterest hardships; now wives painted their faces, powdered their hair and adorned themselves with ruffles, ribbands and lace. These luxuries, and the idleness of Quaker children, were made possible by Negro slavery. It was not Friends but the servants of Friends who lived like dogs and walked barefoot in the snow. Hepburn and Coleman were confident that George Fox and the Quaker fathers had opposed slavery. Always a few conscientious men had remained pure and had even spoken out against the creeping pollution. But the change had come almost imperceptibly. The slaveholders had succeeded in suppressing antislavery writings until, according to Hepburn, copies were as scarce 'as a Phenix egg'. Hepburn confessed that he himself had brooded in silence for thirty years, and hoped he would be forgiven.[53] The effects of lost innocence could now be seen in the Quakers' involvement in political affairs, and in their cowardly acceptance of war-time taxes. What was needed, perhaps, was a new era of persecution, which would awaken Friends to their senses. For Negro

---

51. Hepburn, *American Defence*, pp. 9–15.

52. But in qualification it needs to be said that both Hepburn and Coleman thought that a few Christians of most denominations had always been opposed to slavery. This was in keeping with the Quaker view that the true Church contained men of different persuasions.

53. Hepburn, *American Defence*, preface, pp. 18–19; Coleman, *Testimony*, pp. 1–6, 16. Hepburn was by no means consistent in his memory. He claimed to have been disturbed for thirty years, that is, since 1685; and yet he said that Quakers had been 'clean' of slaveholding, except for one miscreant, in 1692. We may recall that George Keith, whom Hepburn mentioned, wrote in 1693.

slavery was a symbol of the Quakers' own spiritual bondage, which blocked the way to restoration and redemption.

These latter themes were developed far more stridently by Ralph Sandiford and Benjamin Lay, neither of whom betrayed the slightest awareness of living in the Age of Enlightenment. Unlike Hepburn and Coleman, these men made abolitionism the core of their religion and the centre of their existence. Both were ready to be ostracized or even to die for the cause; and their works drip with blood and smell of the smoke and ash of hell.

Sandiford was born in Liverpool in 1693, the year of Keith's *Exhortation*, and was converted to Quakerism early in life. There is a chiliastic note in his writing that suggests a certain affinity with the radical reformers of the English civil wars. He could not conceal his sympathy for the soldiers who, prior to their conversion to Quakerism, had been willing to fight to liberate men from the oppression of priests, physicians and lawyers.[54] Perceiving the world in the lurid colours of the Book of Revelation, Sandiford was prepared to find evil in high places and in the most hallowed traditions. He was enough of a Biblicist to say that he himself would 'lay out his interest' in the slave trade if it had been ordained by God; he had not learned, however, that Christ's Atonement 'should allow his Followers in the most arbitrary and Tyrannical Oppression that Hell has invented on this Globe'.[55] Therefore, when Sandiford was employed for a while by a planter in South Carolina, after being shipwrecked and marooned in the Bahamas, he was afflicted by the thought of his own involvement in sin. He tried to escape the taint of evil by refusing to share his employer's riches.

Sandiford was noted for his extreme simplicity of life, but he apparently prospered as a Philadelphia merchant. Because his shop looked out upon a market where slaves were auctioned, he was burdened night and day by the thought that Christians of his own sect

54. Ralph Sandiford, *A Brief Examination of the Practice of the Times* (n.p. [Philadelphia], 1729), preface; Roberts Vaux, *Memoirs of the Lives of Benjamin Lay and Ralph Sandiford: Two of the Earliest of the Public Advocates of the Emancipation of the Enslaved Africans* (Philadelphia, 1815), p. 59.

55. Sandiford, *Brief Examination*, pp. 27–8.

saw no harm in selling men like beasts. He carried his concern to Philadelphia Yearly Meeting, where his accusations aroused a storm of controversy. In 1729 he persuaded Benjamin Franklin to print *A Brief Examination of the Practice of the Times*, a work which brought him persecution and disownment. Ill and at bay, he retired to the country, and died in 1733, at the age of forty. Possibly he received some solace from the visits of a little hunchbacked sailor and merchant named Benjamin Lay.[56]

If Benjamin Lay was not quite sane, one should remember that the sanest minds found excuses for Negro slavery. In an earlier age Lay might have founded a religious sect. He dreamed of a millennium when men might unite in loving fellowship, when the entire earth would become a new Eden, cleansed of sin, deformity and ugliness.[57] But he knew from bitter experience that the world was full of hatred and persecution. He struck back by denouncing the unrighteous and by seizing opportunities to assert his own moral freedom.

Benjamin Lay had long been a troublemaker and a man in search of a cause. It was quite by accident that he came to see Negro slavery as the epitome of sin. He was born in 1681/2, in Colchester, England. His parents were poor Quakers, who bound out the deformed lad to a glovemaker. By 1710 he had become a sailor. On a voyage to Turkey he learned of the relative mildness of Moslem slavery. He also listened in disgust to the boastful stories of some of his shipmates who, loosened by alcohol, described scenes of lust and cruelty in the African slave trade. But Lay could not have been much concerned over the question, for he had no qualms about moving later in life to Barbados. After his experiences at sea he returned to England, married a hunchbacked woman named Sarah, and settled down as a glovemaker and draper. His mind, however, could never be settled, and he soon developed an obsession that provided an outlet for his

56. ibid., pp. 71–2; Lay, *All Slave-keepers ... Apostates ...*, pp. 18–19, 21–2; Vaux, *Memoirs of Lay and Sandiford*, pp. 64–8; Drake, *Quakers and Slavery*, pp. 39–41. In 1730 Sandiford brought out a revised edition, entitled *The Mystery of Iniquity*, which appealed to London Yearly Meeting for support. Vaux claimed that the Chief Justice of Pennsylvania threatened Sandiford with severe penalties if he circulated this latter work. Lay said that he had been censured for visiting Sandiford.

57. Lay, *All Slave-keepers ... Apostates ...*, pp. 192–3.

smouldering discontent. It appeared to Lay that the Society of Friends had been corrupted by the practice of allowing ministers to speak when they had not been directly prompted by God. This was simply an extreme application of the views of George Fox, but when Lay incited public disturbances in a number of meetings, he was summarily disowned. Undaunted, the reformer began disrupting the services of Baptists and Presbyterians, and even secured a private audience with George II, to whom he presented Milton's tract on removing hirelings from the church. He continued to attend the Quaker meetings at Colchester, sometimes offering apologies and asking forgiveness. When he finally decided to emigrate to America, the Colchester Monthly Meeting, obviously grateful for good riddance, gave him a membership certificate to present at Philadelphia. But after being censured by the Quarterly Meeting for unfaithfulness to the Philadelphians, Colchester Meeting then sent a full report to America which warned that Lay had been disowned for contentious conduct, and that he had continued to cause trouble up to the time he left England.[58]

We cannot be certain when Benjamin and Sarah Lay lived in Barbados, but it was probably soon before they arrived in Philadelphia in 1731.[59] Because they ran a store and sold food, they were made acutely aware of the near famine of neighbouring slaves. Negroes

58. C. Brightwen Rowntree, 'Benjamin Lay', *Journal of the Friends' Historical Society*, XXXIII (1936), pp. 3–13; Vaux, *Memoirs of Lay and Sandiford*, pp. 13–21.

59. Roberts Vaux claimed that Lay had gone to Barbados in 1718 and had lived there until 1731, when he moved to Philadelphia (*Memoirs of Lay and Sandiford*, pp. 17–20). But Rowntree found that Vaux had been in error on the year of Lay's birth, and had also not known of Lay's residence in England during the 1720s. He was disowned in 1720 by Devonshire House Monthly Meeting, and was in Colchester during most of the decade. Rowntree concluded that Lay could not have lived in Barbados for more than a year ('Benjamin Lay', p. 12). Thomas Drake agrees with Rowntree, and says that Lay went from Barbados back to England, and then to Philadelphia (*Quakers and Slavery*, p. 44). Yet Lay himself implied that he had been in Barbados in 1718 (*All Slave-keepers ... Apostates ...*, pp. 9–10). It is possible that he went there more than once. The question is of some significance, since one would like to know whether he became concerned with slavery before or after his difficulties in England.

rushed for the garbage that Sarah threw into the street, although it was too rotten for the dogs to touch. On market days, when the slaves crowded into the shop, Sarah would sometimes give them decayed fish or cockroach-infested biscuits, but even this could not prevent the Negroes from stealing food. Benjamin became seasoned enough to the ways of Barbados to whip those thieves he caught. He felt remorse, however, and worried over the corrupting influence of a slave society. This fear became overwhelming when Sarah saw a naked slave hanging in front of a Quaker's house, a pool of blood under his feet. The Quaker master explained that the ungrateful creature had been punished for running away. But the Lays decided that they themselves must escape from Barbados. When they arrived in Philadelphia and discovered that even there the evil had taken root, it was only natural that Benjamin should find in Ralph Sandiford a kindred spirit.[60]

Thomas Clarkson, who must have received his information from American Quakers, admitted that Lay had been an eccentric who 'was apt to go out of the due bounds'. J. F. Watson called him 'the singular Pythagorean, cynical, Christian philosopher'.[61] Perhaps Lay is best thought of as the Quaker Diogenes. Like Diogenes, he was remembered by legends of his spectacular nonconformity. When a man routinely referred to himself as Lay's humble servant, Benjamin was supposed to have snapped back, 'if thou art my humble servant, clean my shoes'. No doubt his shoes were dirty, for he refused to travel by horse or any vehicle. He wore clothes of his own making, to avoid materials produced by slave labour or by the killing of animals. He was a strict vegetarian, and once put on a public exhibition of smashing a set of Sarah's tea cups, in order to discourage the use of sugar, which Lay said was mixed with the chopped-up limbs, bowels and excrement of poor slaves. According to one account, the crowd succeeded in rescuing and running off with much of Sarah's china.[62]

60. Lay, *All Slave-keepers ... Apostates ...* , pp. 33–44.
61. Thomas Clarkson, *The History of the Rise, Progress and Accomplishment of the Abolition of the African Slave-Trade by the British Parliament* (London, 1808), I, p. 102; John F. Watson, *Annals of Philadelphia* (Philadelphia, 1830), I, p. 552.
62. Watson, *Annals*, I, p. 552; Vaux, *Memoirs of Lay and Sandiford*, pp. 35–6; Drake, *Quakers and Slavery*, p. 45.

His demonstrative protests against slavery were much in the style of a Cynic philosopher or radical perfectionist. He went to a Quaker meeting clothed in sackcloth, and denounced the wealthy slave masters. In winter he sat outside a meeting-house, one leg and foot bare in the snow; and when people expressed concern for his health, he asked them why they were blind to the sufferings of their scantily clad Negroes. When ejected from a meeting-house, he lay in front of the door in the rain, and made the congregation step over his body. He supposedly kidnapped the child of a slave-owner, in order to show the father, if only for a few hours, how it felt to have a child taken away. His most famous exploit occurred at the Quaker meeting in Burlington. To dramatize the coercive basis of slavery, Lay put on a military uniform, complete with sword, which he disguised under the conventional Quaker cloak. Then he enclosed a bladder filled with pokeberry juice within the empty covers of a folio volume, which presumably represented the Bible. After rising in meeting to castigate the slave-owners, he finally told his enemies that they might as well throw off the plain coat of Quakerism, as he himself now did, standing forth in the dress of war. Men who forcibly held their brothers in bondage, he cried, would be no less justified in the eyes of God if they plunged a sword into the hearts of their slaves. At this point Lay thrust his sword into his 'Bible', and the red juice gushed out, spattering the horrified Friends who sat near by.[63]

After Sarah's death in 1735 Benjamin Lay became increasingly isolated. Cut off from all religious fellowship, he lived in a cave-like dwelling in the country, cultivating his garden and writing tracts against slavery, alcohol and capital punishment. Lay admitted that Ralph Sandiford had become mentally deranged, and there can be no doubt that the little hunchback suffered from a similar malady. The patient reader of *All Slave-Keepers . . . Apostates* can well believe the story that the original manuscript was completely lacking in order of pagination, and that when Benjamin Franklin pointed this out to the author, he was told that he could print the pages in any order he chose.[64] The significant point, however, is not that Lay and

63. Vaux, *Memoirs of Lay and Sandiford*, pp. 25–7.
64. Rowntree, 'Benjamin Lay', p. 16. Rowntree thought that the disorderly manuscript had been written earlier than *All Slave-Keepers . . . Apostates . . .*

Sandiford became alienated and unbalanced, but that anti-slavery served as an outlet for deviant personalities.

The writings of Lay and Sandiford are charged with feelings of anguish and persecution; they preach the necessity of moral purification and the inevitability of divine judgement. Both men expressed a longing for love and fellowship, and occasionally fell into despair over their own unworthiness. Lay, especially, who called himself 'a poor common Sailor, and an illiterate Man', said he felt mean and contemptible in the sight of other men. But this tension between the desire to be and belong and a crushing sense of self-hatred could be resolved by marching to Armageddon with the forces of the Lord. The founders of Quakerism had not put love of unity above devotion to Truth. Modelling themselves on Isaiah and Jeremiah, the anti-slavery prophets knew that the devil could not be intimidated by sweet language. To speak the truth would, of course, bring a furious backlash from the powers of darkness. Satan's conspirators threatened Lay with the stocks and removed him bodily from Quaker meetings; they were responsible, he thought, for Sandiford's insanity and early death. They had even plotted to separate Benjamin from his wife Sarah, and after bringing on her death, had sought to shift the blame to her husband. But the anti-slavery martyrs took courage in thought that they stood with such men of the past as Fox and Keith, and were supported by hidden Quaker illuminati in Nantucket, Long Island and Jersey.[65]

While Lay and Sandiford could draw on personal experience with plantation slavery, they devoted remarkably little attention to the Negro. Their long digressions on seemingly extraneous subjects are puzzling until one grasps the fact that anti-slavery was a vehicle for

---

He had not, however, been able to locate a copy of the latter work, which actually fits the description very well. For a suggestion of Lay's financial irregularities, see the letter from John Pemberton to Elizabeth Kendal, 29 April 1754, Pemberton Papers, X (Pennsylvania Historical Society).

65. Sandiford, *Brief Examination*, pp. 71–2; *Mystery of Iniquity*, subtitle; Lay, *All Slave-Keepers ... Apostates ...*, pp. 19, 21–2, 48–9, 56–8, 67–8, 84. Apparently Sarah was acceptable to the Quakers in Pennsylvania, who wrote to England requesting a separate certificate of membership for her. Lay said that he had been publicly accused of causing her death.

attacking a multitude of evils. It provided a way of exposing the hypocrisy of a fallen ministry, which performed the devil's work by making preaching a trade and an instrument of compromise. It was a medium of moral purification, since slavery had long been associated with luxury, idleness and sexual immorality, as well as with social discipline. In their diatribes against whoredom, divorce and lazy women, the two writers seemed to lose all sight of their central subject. But slavery for them was not simply one of various unrelated evils, but the source of all iniquity. Indeed, the validity of religious truth, and of man's ability to know right from wrong, depended upon a perception of slavery as sin. Deism or atheism were the only alternatives to a religion based on anti-slavery. As Sandiford put it, 'if this is not an Evil there is no Evil in the World but what Tradition and Custom makes such'. According to Lay, an acceptance of slavery invalidated all religious activities.[66] For slavery had come to symbolize not only sin and death, but every violation of the Christian ideal of love and brotherhood. It was a concrete model of selfishness, greed and man's cruelty to man. All the tyranny and corruption that perfectionists like Thomas Müntzer had seen in the social order, men like Lay and Sandiford saw in Negro slavery.

And anti-slavery gave an order and pattern to history, as well as to moral experience. Sandiford posed the central question:

And has not the Lord, by his extraordinary Providence, opened this *America* before the *Europeans,* and given us Peace and Plenty among the Natives? and shall we go to *Africa* for Bread, and lay the Burden which appertains to our Bodily Support on their Shoulders?[67]

The Quakers had arrived in the New World, according to Lay, as 'poor, vile, miserable wretches, destitute and forlorn'. As long as they had been disciplined by hard work, they had lived with a sense of their 'filthy, abominable, undone, and woful cursed condition'. Because of their piety and humility they had prospered, and for a time had been true to their great mission. But blinded by custom and

66. Sandiford, *Brief Examination,* pp. 22, 27, 40, 68, 72; Sandiford, *Mystery of Iniquity,* pp. 5–8; Lay, *All Slave-Keepers . . . Apostates . . . ,* pp. 17, 27–32, 64, 98, 124–5.

67. Sandiford, *Brief Examination,* dedication.

convenience, they had allowed Negro slavery to seep in like a black poison. Their fall from virtue gave a new meaning to Biblical prophecy. If Negroes were not the descendants of Cain, their bondage was most certainly the fruit of Cain's rebellion. American slavery was the Antichrist and the seven-headed dragon of Revelation. The Lord was whetting his glittering sword, and his vengeance was certain, unless the new Children of Israel separated themselves from the filthiness of the Heathen, and came away from Babylon. In America, where the millennium had seemed so imminent and where Satan had committed his force, God would show no mercy to the betrayers of righteousness.[68]

In the mid nineteenth century a few radical Quakers such as William Edward Forster came to see the mass poverty of Ireland and the English cities as a national sin. Unless the entire social system was transformed, Forster said, the guilt would fall on everyone.[69] This critical vision, while no doubt an authentic outgrowth of the Quaker social conscience, was a far cry from the Society's traditional acceptance of economic inequalities. It was one thing to preserve the original testimonies against war, oaths or using such words as 'you' and 'February'; it was quite another to risk upsetting the founding fathers' delicate equilibrium between conscience and authority, individualism and conformity. And yet the living faith of the fathers could not be perpetuated by mere words and formalized acts. Like Americans in the Age of Jackson, eighteenth-century Quakers assumed that the central turning-point of history had come in the recent past. Much as the American Revolution had culminated a century of Enlightenment, George Fox had fulfilled the promise of the Reformation. The task of Friends, as a chosen people, was to maintain

68. Sandiford, *Brief Examination*, preface, pp. 1–4, 36; Lay, *All Slave-Keepers . . . Apostates . . .*, pp. 16, 32–3, 51, 55, 69, 80–84, 118–19. Sandiford proposed sending all slaves back to Africa who were willing to go; the others, he said, should be educated, freed and integrated into white society (*Mystery of Iniquity*, p. 97). Lay offered no plans, but was contemptuous of slave-owners who promised to free their Negroes by testament or after a term of years. According to Lay, 'God will not be mocked so' (*All Slave-Keepers . . .*, p. 87).

69. Jones, *Later Periods of Quakerism*, I, p. 369.

the purity of a discovered Truth by re-experiencing it in their daily lives. But as Quakers lost their status as rebellious outlaws and acquired relative security, it became increasingly difficult to re-experience, with any conviction, the selfless courage of the fathers. The fear of declining zeal and corruption from the outside world might have been overcome by an extended attack on the existing social order. But the Quaker mind, as we have seen, had been thoroughly immunized against the virus of radical Anabaptism. The social protest of a William Forster would require a long development of reform consciousness.

In the early eighteenth century Quakers began developing new means of combating the sins of pride, sloth and sensuality. Because they conceived the world as a testing-ground and man's life as a continuing quest for Truth, they were free from the prejudices which assigned a higher virtue to the nobler or more refined occupations. The important question was whether a man was honest and diligent in his calling, not whether he was a prince or a carpenter. Barred in England from the professions and government, Quakers rapidly acquired a reputation as shrewd and incredibly successful businessmen. On both sides of the Atlantic Friends prospered as merchants, bankers and manufacturers. But while hard work was associated with mental discipline and sobriety of temper, wealth itself brought spasms of anxiety. Precepts regarding diligence and concentration were coupled with the gravest warnings. Economic activity was perhaps an aid to religious purity, but wealth could be a sign of decay.[70]

The softening influence of wealth was offset in part by a tightening of organization and discipline. By the second quarter of the eighteenth century Quaker leaders were much alarmed by the threat of worldliness, religious apathy, immorality and even deism. In time of war they were particularly concerned over a laxness in discipline which led many Friends to compromise traditional standards. In reponse to these pressures, Quaker meetings became increasingly specialized in function. Elders and local groups of overseers acquired wider powers. Through regular correspondence and travelling

70. Tolles, *Meeting House and Counting House*, pp. 48–51, 97–100; Gary, 'Political and Economic Relations', pp. 4–5.

missionaries, closer communications were established among the various meetings in America, and between America and Great Britain. In addition to providing regular channels for the exchange of information and opinion, the communications network enabled Friends to enlarge and institutionalize charitable activities. The developing patterns of mutual aid, which extended across the Atlantic, would have a profound relevance for the future anti-slavery movement.[71]

Moreover, by the mid eighteenth century the Quaker International had devised effective mechanisms for political action. Originally designed to aid Quaker victims of persecution, the London meetings for Sufferings had developed into an executive committee dealing with important questions between Yearly Meetings. Long accustomed to the need for lobbying against discriminatory laws in England, the Meeting for Sufferings became increasingly preoccupied with colonial laws which infringed upon the interests of American Friends. By mid century the Meeting had appointed a Parliamentary agent and a standing sub-committee for Parliamentary and colonial affairs. Knowledge of American affairs was kept up to date by the presence in London of Quaker colonial correspondents.[72]

The rise of the Society of Friends as an international pressure-group was paralleled by the Quakers' growing sense of separate identity. Rules against marriage with outsiders, a new emphasis on wearing distinctive dress, and the inauguration, in 1737, of birthright

71. For an excellent discussion of Quaker organizational activity, see James, *People Among Peoples*, pp. 1–22. I have also drawn on 'London Yearly Meeting, Epistles Sent' (1683–1934) and 'Epistles Received' (1683–1916); 'London Yearly Meeting, Christian and Brotherly Advices' (1738); 'Letters Which Passed betwixt the Meeting for Sufferings in London, and the Meeting for Sufferings in Philadelphia; Also Letters to & from Governors &c. of the Different Provinces in America, 1757–1816' (all in M S, Friends House, London); and on Jones, *Later Periods of Quakerism*, I, pp. 104–45; and Braithwaite, *Second Period of Quakerism*, p. 377, and *passim*.

72. Gary, 'Political and Economic Relations', pp. 27–8, 35–6; N. C. Hunt, *Two Early Political Associations: The Quakers and the Dissenting Deputies in the Age of Sir Robert Walpole* (New York, 1961), pp. xiv–xv, and *passim*.

membership, served to insulate Friends from the corruptions of the world. Like a black skin, the peculiar garb and speech marked Quakers as a people apart. Yet their survival would depend, in large measure, on their ability to transcend symbols of separateness and establish fruitful contacts with the children of the world.[73]

Along with economic and organizational activity came a growing spirit of otherworldliness, a renewed conviction of man's depravity and utter dependence on the will of God. This movement may have been influenced by the writings of European Quietists, and it was probably in part a reaction against rationalism and religious uncertainty.[74] In any event, many Quakers came to feel an overpowering sense of guilt which could be overcome only by self-crucifixion, or by what John Woolman called 'daily dying'. By dissociating one's-self from the distractions of the world, it was possible to concentrate one's life in a series of expectations and fulfilments, in which the soul would be purified by the inner movings of the Spirit. This orientation could lead to obsessive introspection and withdrawal. And yet Quakers had long been conditioned to seek the social correlatives of inward purity. The moral 'exercises' of the ideal Christian could be seen only in his way of life. Religious truth, which would not be discovered by rational analysis, might best be known by observing and imitating the actions of obvious saints.

Whether a man is considered a saint or a trouble-making eccentric depends largely on circumstance. Down to the mid eighteenth century Quaker abolitionists were isolated and forced into extreme positions. There were no channels through which they could exert a positive influence on Quaker leaders, or receive moderating pressures from a receptive audience. It was otherwise with John Woolman and Anthony Benezet, who were instrumental in convincing the Society of Friends that anti-slavery was a test of religious truth. Since the activities of Woolman and Benezet were closely connected with the rise of anti-slavery movements in Britain and America, we shall

73. Jones, *Later Periods of Quakerism*, I, pp. 170–77, 178–9.
74. ibid., I, pp. 34–6, 83, 93; James, *People Among Peoples*, p. 157. According to Tolles, the more literate Quakers of Philadelphia showed great interest in the deist controversy (*Meeting House and Counting House*, pp. 172–4).

not discuss them here. The important point is that by the mid eighteenth century Quakerism provided a cultural setting in which hostility to slavery could become something more than individual dissent.

But while Quakerism furnished a complex set of conditions which made an anti-slavery movement possible, it was essential that there be some triggering force to set off a cumulative reaction. Despite continuing advice from the various Yearly Meetings against buying or selling slaves, there is little evidence of a gradual evolution towards abolitionism. The change was sudden, when it came. In 1757 London Yearly Meeting became alarmed over the involvement of Friends in the slave trade; in the same year, the London Meetings for Sufferings appointed a committee to investigate the problem. The next year saw Philadelphia Yearly Meeting alter its traditional policy. Henceforth, all members who bought or sold Negroes were to be excluded from business meetings or from making financial contributions to the Society. In 1760 New England Quakers made the importation of slaves an offence subject to discipline. This flurry of legislation culminated in 1761, when London Yearly Meeting announced that slave dealers merited disownment.[75] It is clear that this sudden stiffening of official policy was the direct response to a crisis brought on by the Seven Years' War. There were a number of reasons why the war strained the Quaker conscience. The British and colonial governments, recognizing the grim seriousness of the conflict, were understandably impatient over the Quakers' refusal to fight or pay taxes. Both in England and America, Friends endured the unpleasant experience of being branded as traitors and fanatics. The era of persecution, which John Hepburn almost hoped for, had arrived. A strengthening of in-group discipline was accompanied by despair, by yearnings for withdrawal from evil, and by millennial prophecies. The crisis was most acute in Pennsylvania, where the presence of Friends in the colonial government forced a decision on the compatibility of politics and morality. For the Quaker members of the assembly, there could be no middle ground between compromise and withdrawal. To remain in office and to obstruct the war effort would be disastrous for the

75. Gary, 'Political and Economic Relations', pp. 191–200; James, *People Among Peoples*, pp. 129–30.

Quakers' reputation, and might conceivably prevent a victory which even pacifists could consider essential.[76] Subjected to heavy pressure from English Friends, who feared retaliatory measures from their own government, the Pennsylvanians resigned from office and surrendered their original idea of a Holy Experiment. This decision for withdrawal and self-purification led to a significant linkage of ideas: Quakers who continued to hold public office were subject to the same disciplinary rules as slaveholders.

In addition, the frontier warfare seemed to annihilate the Quakers' traditional hopes for a just Indian policy. In many respects the Indian problem had paralleled that of slavery. The Quaker demand that settlers prove a just title to land purchased from the Indians could be related to questions regarding the legitimacy of slave property. The view that Indian raids were *prima facie* evidence of injustice was similar to the argument that the coercion required by slavery was proof of the institution's unlawfulness.[77] When hostilities broke out in 1755 on the Pennsylvanian frontier, and were interpreted as deserved retribution for generations of injustice, the lesson had obvious relevance for the holders of slaves. The point was pressed home by a special committee, appointed by Philadelphia Yearly Meeting in 1758, to visit neighbouring slaveowners. The very forces that led to a disengagement from politics intensified a sense of obligation to other victims of hatred and persecution.

It was, then, in a time of severe crisis that the Society of Friends took the first significant steps of commitment to anti-slavery principles. In a period of intense soul-searching, of desire for self-purification, and of concern over their image in the eyes of others, a decision to refrain from dealing in slaves was a means of reasserting the perfectionist content of their faith. It was a way of proscribing a form of selfish economic activity without repudiating the pursuit of

76. Anne Gary holds that many British Friends were aware that their fortunes depended on a decisive victory over France ('Political and Economic Relations', pp. 91–7). There is some controversy over the importance of pressure of British Friends in influencing the withdrawal from government by the Pennsylvanians.

77. James, *People Among Peoples*, pp. 89–90, 102. James does not bring out this parallel.

wealth; a way of tightening discipline and organization without severing all ties with outsiders; a way of affirming the individual's moral will, and the historic mission of the church, without challenging the basic structure of the social order.

II

Religious Sources of Anti-Slavery Thought:
The 'Man of Feeling' in the
Best of Worlds

ALTHOUGH the Quakers' particular needs and beliefs may help explain their growing uneasiness over Negro slavery, we should not forget that most of the early non-Quaker opponents of slavery were devout British Protestants.[1] Were there, then, broader developments in British religion which tended to change men's perception of human bondage? Were there more general counterparts to the Quakers' belief in the continuing inward revelation of Truth, and to their need for preserving the purity of Testimony in the face of a rapidly changing society?

The simplest explanation is that anti-slavery was an extension of a noble philanthropic tradition. Early in its history British Protestantism was forced to adjust traditional Christian doctrines to meet problems raised by enclosure, an uprooted peasantry, urban growth and new forms of poverty. The disintegration of medieval patterns of charity and social responsibility led, even in the sixteenth century, to a spectacular rise of private philanthropy, which received the warm encouragement of the clergy. It was not that bequests for education or hospitals earned merits for eventual salvation; rather, as William Ames said, one could not love God without showing charity towards one's neighbours. The new ideal of individual responsibility appealed particularly to the merchant elite who, though lacking inherited

1. Wylie Sypher has argued persuasively that the Church of England remained indifferent to the slavery question, but this leads him to the dubious conclusion that eighteenth-century anti-slavery was not primarily religious in character (*Guinea's Captive Kings: British Anti-Slavery Literature of the Eighteenth Century* [Chapel Hill, 1942], pp. 64–5). One cannot overlook the essentially religious motivation of Granville Sharp, James Ramsay, Thomas Clarkson, William Wilberforce, Samuel Hopkins, Benjamin Rush, Theodore Dwight, Jonathan Edwards, Jr, and a host of others.

status, could at least prove their moral worth by increasing the security or opportunities of the less fortunate.[2] In the seventeenth century such aspirations stimulated a prodigious growth of private and institutionalized philanthropy. And some historians have reasonably concluded that anti-slavery was simply a late product of this expanding spirit of benevolence, which turned inevitably from local good works to free the suffering slave.[3]

There were doubtless continuities of various kinds between traditional domestic philanthropy and the anti-slavery movement. But the theory that abolitionism was the natural outgrowth of a continuously swelling social consciousness fails to explain the long period when Negro slavery aroused virtually no protest, and was accepted or regarded with indifference by the most benevolent of men. Britain's great expansion of the slave trade was not mitigated by centuries of developing domestic philanthropy, nor could intelligent men plead ignorance of a form of commerce and labour so central to the imperial economy. The philanthropy theory does not account for the continuing tendency to associate bondage with legitimate subordination and social discipline, or for the sudden indignation and crusading fervour of abolitionists in the 1780s and 1790s, who even then met an equally passionate resistance. The main stream of traditional philanthropy would seem to have flowed less into anti-slavery than into the missionary efforts of the Society for the Propagation of the Gospel, which presupposed the compatibility of temporal bondage and spiritual freedom. Even such potentially radical sects as the Baptists showed little indication of allowing charity to infringe on the rights of property or the apparent ordinances of

2. Wilbur K. Jordan, *Philanthropy in England, 1480–1660: A Study of the Changing Pattern of English Social Aspirations* (London, 1959); and also *The Charities of London: 1480–1660; The Aspirations and the Achievements of the Urban Society* (London, 1960). For the development of charity as a theme in sermons, see Richard B. Schlatter, *The Social Ideas of Religious Leaders, 1660–1688* (London, 1940), pp. 124–45.

3. This is, for example, the assumption of Frank J. Klingberg in 'The Evolution of the Humanitarian Spirit in Eighteenth-Century England', *Pennsylvania Magazine of History and Biography*, LXVI (1942), pp. 206–78; and *The Anti-Slavery Movement in England: A Study in English Humanitarianism* (New Haven, 1926).

God. In 1711, for example, when some South Carolina Baptists requested advice from the English brethren concerning a fellow member, who in compliance with a law respecting habitual runaways, had castrated his Negro slave, they were told that they should not risk dissension over 'light or Indifferent Causes'. The English Baptists affirmed that since slavery was authorized by Scripture, was part of the governing structure of the world, and could not be maintained without social discipline, the law was a rational necessity and the master was innocent of crime.[4] There is no reason to think that such views would have disturbed the kindly men of the same period who left fortunes for hospitals or the support of orphans.

But this very respect for property and social order suggests a possible alternative to the theory of continuously expanding benevolence. British philanthropy, as one of the expressions of an emerging capitalist ethic, embodied the values of individual effort and responsibility. Yet if philanthropists went too far in their attempts to widen opportunities and promote self-reliance at home, they would undermine not only the old regime but the prevailing justifications for inequality and social rank. They might, however, experiment with liberal values by focusing their attention on a distant symbol of patriarchal society. We have seen that even in the eighteenth century British clergymen as well as colonial planters rationalized slavery by invoking the ancient idea of a patriarchal family in which the master's authority and the servant's subordination were softened by Christian love.[5] An attack on colonial slaveholders could also be a repudiation of prescriptive authority and paternalistic responsibility. It is conceivable that the image of feudal servitude, which long lent sanction to colonial slavery, became in a time a hidden liability.

Moreover, British philanthropy was at once an expression of the capitalist ethic and a moral response to problems created by economic

4. William G. McLoughlin and Winthrop D. Jordan (eds.), 'Baptists Face the Barbarities of Slavery in 1710', *Journal of Southern History*, XXIX (November 1963), pp. 495–7.

5. Richard B. Schlatter provides an interesting discussion of the mercantilist theory of labour and religious views of servitude in *Social Ideas of Religious Leaders*, pp. 82–4.

change. And here again, domestic philanthropists could not move beyond certain limits in aiding the victims of social upheaval without endangering the entire system of values which linked individual incentive with social rewards and punishments. Whenever these limits were approached, it would be far safer to channel benevolent emotions towards remote symbols of suffering and exploitation, which would provide a secure ground for testing and developing new attitudes. As soon as the rationalizations were stripped away, the African trade and colonial plantation presented heightened analogies to the most disturbing trends in Britain, such as the uprooting of peasants, the separation of families, absentee ownership, and the systematizing of work discipline. The slave system could stand for the insecurity and mobility of labour in a profit-oriented society; and yet the injustice of slavery could be identified with individuals rather than with impersonal forces.[6] And whatever hardships the Negro might suffer, he was free from the guilt of economic failure. His emancipation would not be like the elevation of a worker to an undeserved station; it would substitute the fear of hunger for the fear of the whip. And according to the Reverend Joseph Townsend, who defended laissez-faire at the very moment British abolitionism was gaining momentum, hunger was the most 'natural' motive to industry; the poor laws, said Townsend, were founded on the principle of slavery.[7] Then, too, freedom would open the worker's soul to those inner controls and moral restraints which were, according to Hannah More and the Reverend Thomas Malthus, essential to industry and social subordination.

We might conjecture that anti-slavery performed the dual function of associating inhumanity with a pre-capitalistic system, and of displacing fears and emotions engendered by the vast social changes of

6. These overtones are particularly evident in one of the few classics of anti-slavery literature, James Stephen's *The Slavery of the British West India Colonies Delineated* (London, 1824–30). For a discussion of British compassion for victims of individual injustice and indifference towards victims of social injustice, see Georg Simmel, *The Sociology of Georg Simmel* (ed. and tr. by Kurt H. Wolff, Glencoe, Ill., 1950), pp. 225–6.

7. [Joseph Townsend], *A Dissertation on the Poor Laws, by a Well-Wisher to Mankind* (1786), in J. R. McCulloch (ed.), *A Select Collection of Scarce and Valuable Economical Tracts* (London, 1859), p. 404.

the eighteenth century. This would not mean that the problem of slavery was less real than any other, or that the response of abolitionists was essentially irrational. The central question is: What led men to see the problem? But when one considers the broader implications of the subject, and perceives the anti-slavery movement as one of the first modern testing grounds of Christianity, as a vital bridge from the saving of souls to the quest for social justice, it becomes apparent that we must first look more deeply into sources of religious transformation. For there would have been no need or inclination to see the Negro slave as a symbol of dehumanization if British Protestants had continued to believe that natural man was totally corrupt, that suffering and subordination were necessary parts of life, and that the only true freedom lay in salvation from the world.

Although many English Protestants of the early seventeenth century accepted Calvin's grim views on predestination as well as Luther's treatise *On the Enslaved Will*, they adhered to a number of beliefs which were to become essential ingredients of the anti-slavery mind. Puritanism was strongly tinged with the sectarian's sense of moral self-assurance. If the majority of men were condemned to sin and were incapable of moral freedom, the saints might know God in their hearts and live by a higher law.[8] 'This infallible assurance,' writes H. N. Fairchild, 'could easily become identified with the Inner Light of the antinomian enthusiast, the universal reason of the rationalist, the natural goodness of the sentimentalist.'[9] It could also provide a basis for judging the immoral compromises in human laws and institutions. And if saints enjoyed spiritual equality and their outward acts were but reflections of an inward purity, external distinctions were of

8. William Haller, *The Rise of Puritanism, or, the Way to the New Jerusalem as Set Forth in Pulpit and Press from Thomas Cartwright to John Lilburne and John Milton, 1570–1643* (New York, 1938), pp. 82–90, 180–81; Ernst Troeltsch, *Die Soziallehren der christlichen Kirchen und Gruppen (Gesammelte Schriften*, Erster Band, n.p., 1961), pp. 605–794; Charles H. George and Katherine George, *The Protestant Mind of the English Reformation, 1570–1640* (Princeton, 1961), pp. 103–5, 162–93.

9. Hoxie N. Fairchild, *Religious Trends in English Poetry* (New York, 1939–49), III (*Romantic Faith, 1780–1830*), p. 23.

limited and temporary importance; a white soul might be found in the blackest body. Conversely, there were no kings, judges or masters who might not be corrupted by self-will, or led to abuse their power. Though British Protestants accepted the ancient belief that women were destined to lives of perpetual inferiority and subordination, they pictured marriage as a contractual relationship which imposed limits on the arbitrary power of husbands.[10] Such suspicion of unlimited power, indifference towards external distinctions, and faith in individual moral judgement, were not diminished by the turmoil of the civil wars and a growing desire for toleration and social harmony.

We have already presented Richard Baxter as a leading exponent of the Christianization of Negro slavery. In one sense his view of the subject was thoroughly conventional, and differed little from the position of Catholic writers of the previous century. Never doubting that slavery was a legitimate consequence of war, crime or poverty, he urged masters to be merciful, and to accept the obligations of guarding their slaves' souls.[11] Baxter's ideals of limited power and moral trusteeship were ultimately adopted by the Church of England and were even embodied in colonial law; but slavery, as we have seen, continued to be slavery.

There was, however, another side to Richard Baxter. *A Christian Directory*, written in 1664-5, was designed to bring theology down to earth and to show the practical consequences of particular beliefs. Baxter knew how slaves were obtained in Africa, and he called their procurers the 'common enemies of mankind'. It was a 'heynous sin' to buy such bondsmen, except for the purpose of freeing them. Colonial planters who reduced their Negroes to the level of beasts were 'incarnate Devils'. As Baxter likened British slaveholders to the Spanish conquistadors, and interpreted West Indian plagues and hurricanes as deserved retribution, his rhetoric approached the vehemence of the most militant abolitionists.[12]

10. George, *Protestant Mind*, pp. 277–85.

11. Richard Baxter, *Chapters from a Christian Directory, or a Summ of Practical Theology and Cases of Conscience* (ed. by Jeannette Tawney, London, 1925), pp. 15–18, 26–7, 31–2.

12. ibid., pp. 28–35.

A mild Puritan, influenced by the austere William Ames but also by the moderating doctrines of Benjamin Whichcote, Baxter sought above all to find a middle course between warring theologies, and to distinguish the vital core of Christian morality.[13] He was also eager to vindicate the reputation of British Protestantism, which had been debased by years of civil strife. While mainly concerned with saving the souls of Negro servants, he found that an attack on colonial slavery could be a way of affirming and clarifying traditional values, and of identifying greed and covetousness with an un-Christian innovation.

This purpose is even more apparent in the writings of Morgan Godwyn, whose angry outbursts reveal the intensity of religious strains in the 1680s, and provide insight into early sources of anti-slavery sentiment. Godwyn, like Baxter, was bitterly opposed to the Quakers, and it was George Fox, 'an *officious* FRIEND', who first directed his attention to Negro slavery. When Godwyn was visiting Barbados, Fox had given him a pamphlet attacking the Church of England for its refusal to minister to slaves. In the eyes of the good Anglican, this was like Judas being a spokesman for the poor. Since the true Church was now threatened not only by its traditional Catholic foe, but by mad Quakers, Commonwealthmen and rank atheists, there could be no delay in self-purification. Indeed, Godwyn suspected that the neglect of heathens' souls had been the prime cause of creeping infidelity and anti-religious conspiracy.[14]

Godwyn's crusade against West Indian planters was clearly a way of externalizing religious tensions. This can be seen in his obsession with the purity of faith and in his lack of interest in the Negro. Slavery was first of all a model of atheistic Mammonism, which had been alarmingly promoted by the discovery and exploitation of America. Troubled by the quickening drive for wealth in England, Godwyn saw America as the very source of the heresy that everything profitable was legal. And slavery epitomized the new commercial

13. Hugh Martin, *Puritanism and Richard Baxter* (London, 1954), pp. 73, 170.

14. Morgan Godwyn, *The Negro's and Indian's Advocate, Suing for their Admission into the Church* ... (London, 1680), dedication, preface, pp. 4–6.

spirit.[15] The planters' greed also led to a false idea of liberty and to a materialistic philosophy whose counterparts had already thrown England into turmoil. Whereas Christianity had always supported the absolute authority of rulers and masters, the Americans had insisted that religion would be dangerous for slaves. This betrayed their affinities with the licentious Commonwealthmen, who confused spiritual liberty with a total freedom from duty and external restraint. And in addition to holding infidel notions of liberty, the slaveholders had blurred distinctions between soul and body, between substance and accident. Slavery, a mere accident, could not affect the soul or alter the substance of manhood. Yet by exaggerating accidental qualities and treating men as mere mechanisms, the Americans had fragmented the essential unity of being. Negro slavery was a paradigm of libertinism, nominalism and materialism.[16]

Moreover, the growing belief in Negro inferiority contained two of the most dangerous threats to true religion. Godwyn pointedly observed that while contemporary Englishmen had little stomach for the severe doctrine of reprobation, they were quick to apply it to the supposed posterity of Ham, as if mere man could know and execute God's judgements. More ominous still was the attempt of certain infidels to undermine the Bible by suggesting the separate creation of the Negro race.[17] In Godwyn's mind the West Indian planters and their English allies stood for all the secular, materialistic forces, the subversive notions of political liberty, the religious heterodoxy and abuse of Scripture, which were destroying the old world of faith,

15. Morgan Godwyn, *Trade Preferr'd before Religion, and Christ Made to Give Place to Mammon: Represented in a Sermon Relating to the Plantations . . .* (London, 1685), pp. 1–2, 6.

16. Godwyn, *Negro's and Indian's Advocate*, pp. 10, 27, 31, 106–12.

17. ibid., pp. 14–17, 46, 54. It is probable that the learned doctor whom Godwyn accused (pp. 16–17) of holding pre-Adamite theories was Peter Heylyn (referred to on p. 46). Heylyn was High Anglican, an arch-foe of Baxter, and had written some gross passages implying that Negroes were inferior (ΜΙΚΡΟΚΟΣΜΟΣ, *A Little Description of the Great World* [5th ed., Oxford, 1631], p. 719; and *Cosmographie in Foure Books . . .* [3rd ed., London, 1667], pp. 44–5). He had not, however, suggested that Negroes were descended from a pre-Adamite race, but had worked out a complex theory of the planting of the world by the sons of Noah.

obedience and contentment. As a defender of imperilled tradition, he assumed the role of a Christian warrior bravely exposing the sins and conspiracies of slaveholders. Like later abolitionists, he made much of his willingness to face censure and persecution in the interest of truth. It is curious that a man who actually *upheld* the institution of slavery and who demanded no more than the baptism and religious instruction of Negroes should have fallen into so many of the patterns of later anti-slavery thought. This was, one suspects, about as far as traditional Protestant culture could go.

There were men who went beyond the positions of Baxter and Godwyn, but in these rare cases there is evidence that religious tensions, compounded by personal and social strains, had already brought a subtle transformation in the Protestant world view.

Early in the seventeenth century a Puritan writer named Paul Baynes drew a highly conventional analogy between sin and slavery.[18] Holiness, he wrote, derived neither from good nature nor from moral justice, but rather from a renunciation of the will and a liberation from 'brutish bondage' to the flesh. Men, however, were so evil that they imagined themselves to be free when they were really Satan's slaves and could only be emancipated by Christ's ransom. For Adam's sin had condemned all his posterity to perpetual slavery, and 'the children you know of persons in bondage, are all bondmen likewise; *portus sequitur ventrem*'.[19] Although Baynes was primarily concerned with the bondage of the human soul, he went on to describe servitude, in an expanded edition of his work, as 'a miserable condition, which entereth through sin'. The bodies of 'slavish' servants

18. Baynes was William Perkins's successor at St Andrew's, Cambridge. He died in 1617, and his works, which were published posthumously, were highly regarded by the New England Puritans.

19. Paul Baynes, *A Commentarie upon the First Chapter of the Epistle of Saint Paul, Written to the Ephesians* (London, 1618), pp. 167–78, 184–5, 385. I am much indebted to Lawrence W. Towner for calling my attention to Baynes's *An Entire Commentary upon the Whole Epistle of the Apostle Paul to the Ephesians*, which was not published until 1643. Mr Towner kindly furnished me with a copy of portions of this latter work, which was reprinted in *Nichol's Series of Commentaries*, XI (Edinburgh, 1865).

were 'perpetually put under the power of the master, as blackamores with us'. And though masters were limited by certain duties, their authority was as absolute as that of kings over 'the flesh, or outward man'. A servant must walk in fear and trembling towards his master; he 'must not do his own will, but his master's whom he serveth'; he must obey even an evil master, and be silent and humble when punished, knowing that he serves 'not man so much as God in man ... And the reason of all followeth, from God's recompense'.[20]

In 1700 Samuel Sewall, the Massachusetts jurist, was inspired by Baynes to denounce Negro slavery. Sewall was a good Puritan who should have been more preoccupied than Baynes with the outward conditions of wordly life. He believed in original sin and in the necessity of grace for 'bettering Mens Estates, respecting God and themselves. ... Yet,' he went on, 'through the Indulgence of God to our First Parents after the Fall, the outward Estate of all and every of their Children, remains the same, as to one another. So that Originally, and Naturally, there is no such thing as Slavery.'[21] Somehow, the traditional Christian distinction between inner and outer states had become blurred, and the effects of sin had all but disappeared. Paul Baynes notwithstanding, 'good nature' and 'moral justice' had assumed some of the aspects of holiness.

Before turning to a further analysis of Sewall's writing and the controversy it provoked, it is well to consider the circumstances which must have influenced his thought. In the first place, Massachusetts in 1700 was receiving a rather sudden influx of Negro slaves. Even John Saffin, Sewall's pro-slavery opponent, admitted that this was undesirable, since white servants were infinitely preferable; the Boston News-letter would soon point with alarm at Negro crime and disorder, and there was a flurry of agitation for regulatory

20. Baynes, *Entire Commentary*, in Nichol's, pp. 365–9.

21. Samuel Sewall, *Diary of Samuel Sewall*, in *Collections of Massachusetts Historical Society*, 5th ser., VI (Boston, 1879), II, p. 16; Sewall, *The Selling of Joseph, a Memorial*, in *Proceedings of Massachusetts Historical Society, 1863–1864*, VII, p. 161–2. Lawrence Towner has shown that it was Baynes's *Entire Commentary* which Sewall read ('The Sewall-Saffin Dialogue on Slavery,' *William and Mary Quarterley*, 3rd ser., XXI [January 1964], p. 41).

laws and restrictions on importation.[22] We have already seen how Cotton Mather tried to use conversion as an instrument of social control.

It is doubtful, however, whether a modest increase in Negro slaves would have provoked moral protest if Massachusetts had not been, like Pennsylvania, in the grip of severe religious and cultural tensions. Perry Miller has said that if one begins with the original New England conception of a unified culture, 'what happened between 1698 and 1701 would seem a convergence of devilish, and disruptive forces beyond the ability of man to subdue.'[23] On the frontier Solomon Stoddard openly defied traditional rules confining church membership to the visible saints; in Boston itself prosperous merchants founded a new church where Benjamin Colman, fresh from England in 1700, preached a tolerant, reassuring religion in the elegant style of the English 'Men of Latitude'; in Harvard, the very seat of Puritan learning, the Mather dynasty was further undermined by the introduction of Descartes and a new spirit of religious rationalism. The older leaders, such as Samuel Sewall, looked on with anguish as their holy commonwealth fell apart.[24]

In his *Phaenomena Quaedam Apocalyptica,* written in 1697, Sewall had celebrated America as the theatre of a cosmic moral drama. He was convinced of the superiority of the American environment, and imagined that the New World had been a virtual Garden of Eden at the time of discovery. But from Las Casas he had learned that paradise could be the scene of the most dreadful sins and retributions. In America the consequences of vice and virtue were magnified, and it was there that the Antichrist would make his final stand.[25]

Such beliefs, which entailed an awesome sense of personal responsibility, gave an added poignancy to Sewall's own tragedy. He had been, in 1692, one of the judges of the Court of Oyer and Terminer

22. *Collections of Massachusetts Historical Society,* 5th ser., VI (Sewall *Diary,* II), p. 16; George H. Moore, *Notes on the History of Slavery in Massachusetts* (New York, 1866), pp. 107–8, 252.

23. Perry Miller, *The New England Mind: From Colony to Province* (Cambridge, Mass., 1953), p. 242.

24. ibid., pp. 237–48.

25. Charles L. Sanford, *The Quest for Paradise: Europe and the American Moral Imagination* (Urbana, 1961), pp. 90, 112.

which had condemned the Salem witches. This grisly affair, as Perry Miller has remarked, gradually ate into the New England conscience. Sewall publicly confessed his guilt in 1697, and asked for pardon. He knew that his sins had been responsible for the deaths and afflictions of his family and friends, which continued through the decade. God's controversy with New England was amply illustrated by a succession of bad harvests and the prolonged war in Europe. Samuel Sewall needed no further proofs that public opinion, as well as the best of men, could be grievously wrong.[26]

In June of 1700, when Sewall was pondering Paul Baynes, 'in came Bror Belknap to shew me a Petition he intended to present . . . for the freeing a Negro and his wife, who were unjustly held in Bondage'. It seems probable that this slave was named Adam, and belonged to John Saffin, a prosperous merchant, landowner, and former deputy to the General Court.[27] In 1694 Saffin had decided to place Adam in the employment of a tenant farmer, and had written an instrument to free the Negro in seven years if he proved obedient and industrious. The tenant, however, claimed that Adam was insolent and even dangerous, and gave him back to Saffin. After further disciplinary troubles, Adam demanded his freedom, and told Saffin 'in a sawcy and surly manner . . . that I must go to Captain *Sewall*'.[28] Judge Sewall upheld Adam's claim and rebuked Saffin, who was obviously not pleased and who marshalled all his political power for

26. Miller, *From Colony to Province*, pp. 206–8; *Collections of Massachusetts Historical Society*, 5th ser., V (Sewall *Diary*, I), p. 445; 6th ser., I (Sewall *Letter-Book*), pp. 214–15.

27. *Collections of Massachusetts Historical Society*, 5th ser., VI (Sewall *Diary*, II), p. 16. Lawrence Towner doubts whether this first Negro was the Adam of later court records, since there is no evidence that Adam had a wife, and the case of Adam did not come before Judge Sewall until March 1701 ('Sewall–Saffin Dialogue', pp. 46–7). However, Saffin was having difficulties with Adam by June 1700, and the Negro may well have had a wife at that time. The delay might have been occasioned by the need for waiting until the seven-year contract with Saffin had expired.

28. Abner C. Goodell, Jr, 'John Saffin and his Slave Adam', Colonial Society of Massachusetts *Transactions*, I (Boston, 1895), pp. 85–92; John Saffin, *A True and Particular Narrative by Way of Vindication of the Author's Dealing with and Prosecution of his Negro Man Servant . . .* (Boston, 1701), reprinted in above, pp. 103–12.

battle. Since Saffin was at times a judge himself, the contest was long and bitter – Sewall accused him of jury-tampering – but towards the end of 1703 the Superior Court, of which Sewall was one of the four justices, declared that Adam was free.[29]

Meanwhile, on 24 June 1700 Sewall had published his famous tract, *The Selling of Joseph*, which was answered by Saffin the following year. Emphasizing that all men were sons of Adam (and he seemed to play upon the name), Sewall went on to develop Baynes's argument, taken from the Epistle of Paul to the Ephesians, that Christ had broken the wall of partition between Jews and Gentiles, and had united all men under the law of love.[30] At moments he was more eloquent than Godwyn or Baxter: 'There is no proportion between Twenty Pieces of Silver, and LIBERTY. The Commodity itself is the Claimer.'[31] And yet the most striking characteristic of Sewall's writing was its mood of doubt and uncertainty. The judge of the Salem witches shrank from being 'Executioner of the Vindictive Wrath of God'. For New England Puritans the Bible was presumably a clear and authoritative guide, but Sewall wondered whether the curse of Canaan was now out of date, or whether there had been a misreading of the original text.[32] Such questions might easily be pursued to the conclusions of men like John Locke and John Toland. Sewall also had doubts on the legitimacy of African wars and enslavement; he suspected that holiness was 'rarely engraven' on this kind of servitude. And yet he knew that few of his countrymen would accept the emancipation of Negroes, for 'indeed they can seldom use their freedom well'. Racial difference would be an added threat to the unity of Puritan culture: 'They can never embody with us, and grow up into orderly Families, to the Peopling of the Land: but still remain in our Body Politick as a kind of extravasat Blood.' The only solution Sewall suggested, was to stop the further importation of slaves.[33]

29. ibid., p. 100; *Collections of Massachusetts Historical Society*, 5th ser., VI (Sewall *Diary*, II), p. 41.

30. Towner, 'Sewall-Saffin Dialogue', p. 45; Sewall, *Selling of Joseph*, p. 165.

31. Sewall, *Selling of Joseph*, p. 162.

32. ibid., pp. 162–3.

33. ibid., p. 162.

John Saffin took advantage of Sewall's equivocations, and exposed the latent subversiveness of his arguments. By ignoring Biblical sanctions for perpetual slavery and by falsely invoking the Hebrews' rules against selling their own brethren, Sewall had, in effect, undermined the authority of Scripture. While carefully conceding that not all slavery was unlawful, he inconsistently called the sons of Adam co-heirs, with *equal* rights to liberty, love and respect. This was to challenge the entire structure of orders and degrees which God had established for men. For if kings and slaves had equal rights to liberty and respect, God's 'ordinary providences' in governing the world were clearly unjust and wrong. Sewall was, then, well on the road to blasphemy and infidelity. But even Saffin sensed that the ancient theory of fixed social orders could not be pushed too far. What was proper for captive heathens was not necessarily proper for European Christians. Africans, he hinted, were really unfit for freedom, and since it would be difficult to remove them from the country, they would have to remain as slaves.[34] For all their violent conflict in principle, Sewall and Saffin were remarkably close in their conviction that Negro slavery was undesirable, but that emancipation and racial integration would be disastrous.

What distinguished Samuel Sewall was a conscience sensitized to human injustice and to the woeful fate of an unrepentant America. The fact that his protest was a single-shot affair suggests that his concern was the product of a critical and temporary convergence of pressures, in which the plea of the enslaved Adam was a catalysing agent. Weary of contention on a number of other fronts, Sewall soon wrote a friend that he had declined to trouble the province with a reply to John Saffin.[35] He had already contributed, however, to an intercolonial and transatlantic transmission of ideas which faintly anticipated the later exchanges of Benezet, Sharp and Wesley. It is doubtful whether Benjamin Lay had many readers, but the intrepid little Quaker embedded *The Selling of Joseph* within his own wild

34. John Saffin, *A Brief and Candid Answer to a Late Printed Sheet, Entitled The Selling of Joseph.* .. (Boston, 1701), reprinted as appendix in Moore, *Notes on History of Slavery*, pp. 251–6.

35. *Collections of Massachusetts Historical Society*, 6th ser., I (Sewall Letter-Book), pp. 325–6.

prose. And as we have seen, John Hepburn reprinted material from a pamphlet, *The Athenian Oracle*, which Sewall had published in 1705.

The Athenian Oracle was actually an English periodical edited by John Dunton, an eccentric bookseller and publisher who had ties with the literary world of Swift and Defoe, and who was aided as editor by his brother-in-law, Samuel Wesley, the father of the great Methodist. It is possible that Dunton had met Sewall in 1685, when he had visited Boston on a bookselling trip and had acquired a high respect for John Eliot.[36] But it is difficult to imagine the Puritan fathers warming to a man who made studies of London prostitutes and whose Athenian Society was dedicated to the re-birth of ancient civilization. *The Athenian Oracle* was a curious blend of rational analysis, sentimentalism and sensationalism, and in its exploitation of the device of startling questions and glib answers was not unlike the popular advice columns in modern newspapers. Its readers were enlightened on such fascinating questions as 'Was Adam a Giant?' and 'Can a Man Commit Adultery with his own Wife?'

Some insubstantial evidence suggests that Sewall may have written to Dunton, at the time of the legal controversy with Saffin, asking whether the slave trade was unlawful in itself.[37] In any event, in December 1705 Sewall was browsing in a bookshop and discovered the *Oracle*'s answer to this question, which he immediately asked Bartholomew Green to reprint as an anonymous reply to John Saffin.[38] This piece was considerably stronger than Sewall's own

36. Peter Murray Hill, *Two Augustan Booksellers: John Dunton and Edmund Curll* (Lawrence, Kans., 1958), *passim*; John Dunton, *Letters Written from New-England, A.D. 1686* (ed. by W. H. Whitmore, Boston, 1867), *passim*; Dunton, *The Life and Errors of John Dunton, Citizen of London* (London, 1818), *passim*. Dunton saw a good bit of Major Stephen Sewall of Salem, a relative of Samuel's, and Samuel himself was in London in 1688 and might have called on Dunton, who had been so recently in New England.

37. The editor of Sewall's *Letter-Book* said that a copy of *The Athenian Oracle* owned by the Massachusetts Historical Society had the following words written above the title: 'Cap. Sewall sent the following question to the Athenian Society' (*Collections of Massachusetts Historical Society*, 6th ser., I, pp. 545–8).

38. *Collections of Massachusetts Historical Society*, 6th ser., I (Sewall

pamphlet. It branded the slave trade as a sin against the very laws of nature, and specifically answered six pro-slavery arguments. Thinking perhaps of the recent case of Chamberline *v.* Harvey, the author held that as soon as an infidel was baptized in England, he enjoyed equal protection of laws. He praised New England for its success in Christianizing Indians, and said that were it not for the slave trade, similar results might have been achieved in Africa. This gesture of goodwill towards the Puritans did not prevent the pamphlet from bringing frowns and hard words in Boston.[39]

But consistency was not one of Dunton's virtues, and if John Saffin had cared, he could have reprinted his own *Oracle.* In the same edition which Sewall had used, the editor considered the obligation of colonial masters to baptize their slaves. And here he defended all the arguments that the other essay had refuted. Baptism had no effect on man's civil state. Some nations, such as the barbarous Africans, seemed to be born for slavery, and had known no other condition through history. And they certainly fared much better as the slaves of Christians than as cut-throats and cannibals at home, 'especially when by the Slavery of their Bodies, they are brought to a Capacity of Freeing their Souls from a much more unsupportable Bondage'.[40] John Saffin could have asked for no more.

While Samuel Sewall did little more than raise doubts and questions, he wrote at a time of great cultural transformation in the English-speaking world. The growth of anti-slavery thought, as the pioneering work of Wylie Sypher has shown, was dependent upon the emergence of a new ethic of benevolence.[41] It is a mistake, however, to

---

Letter-Book), pp. 322–3, 325–6. The article had appeared in the 1st ed. of *The Athenian Oracle* (London, 1703), I. p. 545–58, but was not listed in the index and the pagination was scrambled. Sewall used the 2nd ed. (London, 1704). It is curious that the piece was omitted entirely from certain copies of the 3rd ed. (London, 1728), but not from all.

39. *The Athenian Oracle* (Boston, 1705), pp. 1–4.

40. *The Athenian Oracle* (2nd ed., London, 1704), II, pp. 460–63. George Moore erroneously reprinted this piece, thinking it was the one which Sewall had used (*Notes on History of Slavery*, pp. 91–4).

41. Sypher's brilliant article, 'Hutcheson and the "Classical" Theory of Slavery', *Journal of Negro History,* XXIV (July 1939), pp. 263–80, is a

picture this momentous shift in values as a secular movement originating with Shaftesbury and Francis Hutcheson.[42] The philosophy of benevolence was a product of the seventeenth century, when certain British Protestants, shaken by theological controversy and the implications of modern science, looked increasingly to human nature and conduct as a basis for faith. In their impatience with theological dogma, their distaste for the doctrine of original sin, their appreciation for human feeling and sentiment, and their confidence in man's capacity for moral improvement, these latitudinarians,[43] as they were called, anticipated the main concerns of the Enlightenment, and laid an indispensable foundation for social reform.[44]

Interest in English Puritanism has often diverted attention from a liberal tradition that runs from the nature philosophers of the Italian Renaissance, from the Neoplatonism of the Florentine Academy, through John Colet, Erasmus, Thomas More and, finally,

refreshing contrast to the simplistic theories of converging 'streams' of Enlightenment and philanthropic religion. But Sypher overlooks the religious meaning of the ethic of benevolence, and also minimizes the tension which slavery had always occasioned in Western culture.

42. Ronald S. Crane, review of W. E. Alderman, 'Shaftesbury and the Doctrine of Benevolence in the Eighteenth Century', *Philological Quarterly*, XI (1932), pp. 204–6; Ernst Cassirer, *The Platonic Renaissance in England* (tr. by James P. Pettegrove, Edinburgh, 1953), pp. 159–60; John Herman Randall, Jr, *The Career of Philosophy: From the Middle Ages to the Enlightenment* (New York, 1962), pp. 466, 709–10; G. R. Cragg, *From Puritanism to the Age of Reason; A Study of Changes in Religious Thought within the Church of England, 1660–1700* (Cambridge, England, 1950), pp. 60–61.

43. Like most labels, 'latitudinarian' has been subject to multiple uses. After first being applied to the Cambridge Platonists, it was extended to include such liberal ministers as John Tillotson; in the eighteenth century it was applied to almost anyone who was not a Calvinist or Evangelical. For our purposes, the description of views just given will serve as a crude definition.

44. For parallels between English rational religion and the Enlightenment, and for differences between England and France in the reconciliation of religion and philosophy, see Ernst Cassirer, *The Philosophy of the Enlightenment* (tr. by F. C. A. Koelln and James P. Pettegrove, Beacon paperback ed., Boston, 1951), pp. 105–7, 137–8, 141, 159–60, 174–96; Leslie Stephen, *History of English Thought in the Eighteenth Century* (3rd ed., New York, 1949), I, pp. 89–91.

Benjamin Whichcote, who brought to Emmanuel College, the very citadel of Puritanism, a religion of sweetness and light.[45] Even before the pilgrim fathers had departed from Holland, other Englishmen had been stirred by the hopeful doctrines of the Dutch Arminians, and had, like John Hales, 'bid Calvin good night'. These men not only shook off beliefs in predestination and total depravity, but began to think of redemption as an historical process, in which man gradually came to know and live by the laws of eternal reason.[46] It was possible, they believed, to break through the barriers which had separated the depraved present from the sacred past, and the estranged soul from the harmonies of universal being. There was no need for conflict between religion and humanistic philosophy, since true religion was not a set of beliefs or prescribed ceremonies, but a way of life and a new relationship with the world. This basic assumption was nourished by a reaction to Puritanism and religious war, and passed from Whichcote and the Cambridge Platonists to the most influential clergymen of the Church of England. In 1663 Henry More claimed that the majority of English divines had become Arminians. Within a generation the Church would be dominated by men who preached of reason and human ability, whose 'notions of morality', as was said at the funeral sermon for Archbishop John Tillotson, 'were fine and sublime', and who were religious without 'affectation, bigotry or superstition'.[47]

45. Arthur C. McGiffert, *Protestant Thought before Kant* (New York, 1961), pp. 107–8; Cassirer, *Platonic Renaissance*, pp. 8, 18–24; Randall, *Career of Philosophy*, pp. 173–4, 219, 468–72.

46. Rosalie L. Colie, *Light and Enlightenment: A Study of the Cambridge Platonists and the Dutch Arminians* (Cambridge, England, 1957), pp. ix–x, 3–23; Edward A. George, *Seventeenth Century Men of Latitude* (New York, 1908), pp. 39–40, 69–71.

47. George, *Men of Latitude*, pp. 169–72; Franklin L. Baumer, *Religion and the Rise of Skepticism* (New York, 1960), p. 109; Preserved Smith, *A History of Modern Culture* (reprint ed., Gloucester, Mass., 1957), I, p. 383; Gilbert Burnet, *Bishop Burnet's History of His Own Time* ... (Oxford, 1833), IV, p. 242. While men like Tillotson and Burnet differed on many political and philosophical points from the Cambridge Platonists, for the purposes of this discussion they may be considered as parts of a continuing tradition.

Such a thorough repudiation of Calvinism was bound to change beliefs about nature and the meaning of evil. According to Benjamin Whichcote, 'Nothing of the natural state is base or vile.' Man was alone responsible for his alienation from God, and could at any time achieve reunion, 'For a man cannot open his eye, nor lend his ear, but everything will declare more or less of God.'[48] In France, Diderot would later give the same thought a sharper edge: 'Liberate God; see Him everywhere where He actually is, or else say that He does not exist at all.'[49] But in England there was no cause for such a defiant tone. Revealed religion did not seem threatened by saying that heaven was a 'temper of spirit' before it was a place, that the soul of man was 'the Candle of the Lord' or a 'little medal of God'.[50] And yet the bland optimism of the Men of Latitude reactivated an ancient problem. If right and wrong were defined by the eternal order of nature, and not by God's inscrutable will; if human reason was a divine light that provided access to moral truth and to immediate union with the Good, then what was evil? Perhaps, after all, the apparent opposition between grace and nature was only a result of distorted perception. Seen in the proper light, everything had a place and function, and it was really the best of all possible worlds. On the other hand, if one could find an ideal in nature from which a portion of mankind had fallen, there would still be a ground for discontent and aspiration.

When the latitudinarian clergy became disturbed by the vices and luxuries of Restoration England, they turned to more primitive societies for models of natural virtue. Their efforts to bridge the gap between human reason and nature came at a time when Europe was still engaged in the self-discovery that accompanies the discovery of different races and cultures. What was the meaning of the astounding diversity in human laws and customs? Were hundreds of millions of heathen living in a state of perdition through ignorance of the Gospel, or were they enjoying a natural felicity which had long been lost to Europe? As seventeenth-century Europeans pondered Virgil's *Georgics* and Horace's *Odes* and *Epodes*, they found striking parallels

48. George, *Men of Latitude*, pp. 77–84.
49. Quoted in Cassirer, *Philosophy of the Enlightenment*, p. 166.
50. George, *Men of Latitude*, p. 126; Cassirer, *Platonic Renaissance*, p. 40.

between primitive life and the classic pastoral tradition.[51] Here, surely, was an answer to the senseless struggles over religious dogma, and to the spirit of greed which had led to plunder and a ruthless pursuit of wealth. For beneath a superficial diversity of cultures one might find a universal capacity for happiness and contentment, so long as man's natural faculties had not been perverted by error and artificial desire. We must look to primitive man, said Benjamin Whichcote, if we would seek man's moral sense in its pristine stage. Natural law, said Nathaniel Culverwel, is truly recognized and practised only by men who have escaped the corruptions of civilization.[52] If traditionalists objected that savages were ignorant of the Gospel, the answer was that heathen might carry within them the true spirit of Christ, and hence be better Christians than hypocrites who knew and professed all the articles of faith.[53]

This primitivistic strain in English theology was always balanced by a respect for common sense and civilized manners. It did not, as in France, play into the hands of enemies of religion and social inequality. But if Baron de Lahontan could picture a Huron sage proclaiming that all Europeans were slaves, and that private property was the source of their ills, John Dennis could write an immensely popular play, in 1704, in which a noble savage symbolized the natural love of liberty, and denounced the French as despicable slaves.[54]

51. Gilbert Chinard, *L'Amérique et le rêve exotique lans la littérature française au XVIIe et au XVIIIe siècle* (Paris, 1913), *passim*; Maren-Sofie Røstvig, *The Happy Man: Studies in the Metamorphoses of a Classical Idea, 1600–1700* (Oslo, 1954), pp. 16, 41–7; Hoxie N. Fairchild, *The Noble Savage: A Study in Romantic Naturalism* (New York, 1928), pp. 1–13.

52. Lois Whitney, *Primitivism and the Idea of Progress in English Popular Literature of the Eighteenth Century* (Baltimore, 1934), pp. 13–19, 23–4.

53. Cassirer, *Platonic Renaissance*, p. 35.

54. Chinard, *L'Amérique et le rêve exotique*, pp. 167–85; John Dennis, *Liberty Asserted; A Tragedy as It is Acted at the New Theatre in Little Lincoln's Inn-Fields* (London, 1704), pp. 16, 40, 52. When Vlamar, the Indian, says 'Tyrant and Slave at once thou'dst have me turn,/ And weaken and debase my free-born Mind . . .', Frontenac replies, 'Thou hast a noble Soul, by Heav'n' (p. 52). Dennis, as we shall see, was one of the early theorists on 'the sublime'.

More significant was the way in which primitivism reinforced Christian asceticism, and provided a means of discharging anxieties generated by commercial prosperity. Poets like James Thomson, who reflected much of the spirit of latitudinarian theology, tended to celebrate economic progress and especially commercial expansion, which they associated with the beneficent laws of Newtonian science; but they were also enchanted by the swains and bowers of the pastoral tradition, by the simple innocence of children and untutored men, by the serenity of the Golden Age.[55] It was essential to keep commercial greatness distinct from false refinements, self-seeking, and artificial cravings which brought the degeneracy and fall of nations. Defoe, who created the most memorable picture of the sufficiency of simple life, classed the African trade with whoring and drunkenness in his *Reformation of Manners*:

> The harmless Natives basely they trepan,
> And barter Baubles for the *Souls of Men*:
> The Wretches they to Christian Climes bring o'er,
> To serve worse Heathens than they did before.

The cruelties and debaucheries of American slavery were a reproach to Christianity; the despairing slaves

> ... look for Famines, Plagues, Disease, and Death,
> Blasts from above, and Earthquakes from beneath:
> But when they see regardless Heaven looks on,
> They curse our Gods, or think that we have none.[56]

Yet retributive justice could be as much a part of nature as of God. In Thomson's vivid image, a shark following a ship 'of that cruel trade,/ Which spoils unhappy Guinea of her sons,/Demands his share of

55. Marjorie H. Nicolson, *Newton Demands the Muse: Newton's Opticks and the Eighteenth-Century Poets* (Princeton, 1946), pp. 149–50; James Thomson, *Seasons* (London, 1730), pp. 13, 88–9, 131–2; Hoxie N. Fairchild, *Religious Trends in English Poetry*, I, *Protestantism and the Cult of Sentiment, 1700–1740*, p. 526. Thomson came from an orthodox Calvinist background, like so many Latitudinarians, and acquired his liberal theology at the University of Edinburgh.

56. Daniel Defoe, *Reformation of Manners, a Satyr* (London, 1702), pp. 17–18.

prey'. And when a storm dashes the ship to pieces, the sharks riot in a 'vengeful meal' of tyrants and slaves.[57] Neither Thomson nor Defoe had any thought of becoming abolitionists, but they represented a tendency, which would become far more apparent in sermons and literature of the mid eighteenth century, to associate luxury, corruption and materialism with certain kinds of 'unnatural' commerce.[58]

It may appear that the latitudinarian clergy pointed the way to secular rationalism. Their humanistic leanings made them trust reason above tradition. The new Cartesian philosophy was embraced by Dutch Arminians and was spread in England by Henry More. Like Hobbes, the liberal clergy looked for first principles in the nature of man, and subjected Scripture to rational standards of interpretation which would have horrified Samuel Sewall. Tillotson used arguments against Transubstantiation which Hume would later turn against all miracles.[59] And when Newton uncovered the secrets of the heavens, and Lock deduced the attributes of God from man's idea of himself, it remained only for divines like Samuel Clarke to show that religion, like any other science, was a rational system of propositions.

But despite such confidence in the reasonableness of both Christianity and the universe, there was a growing shadow of doubt which

57. This passage appeared first in the rev. ed. of 1744, and later inspired Turner's famous painting of the slave ship (Alan D. McKillop, *The Background of Thomson's Seasons* [Minneapolis, 1942], pp. 129, 165).

58. Defoe, for example, gave strong support to the slave trade in his political writings (Sypher, *Guinea's Captive Kings*, p. 158). For anti-commercialism, see Whitney, *Primitivism and the Idea of Progress*, pp. 42–51. In an anonymous dialogue of 1765, 'Agriculture' accuses 'Commerce' of corrupting simple nature and arousing a taste for luxury; 'Commerce', who says there is nothing wrong with dealing with slave traders as long as they pay their bills, tells 'Agriculture' to go 'starve on philosophic plan,/ With Rousseau in the Valaisan' (Fairchild, *Religious Trends in English Poetry*, II: *Religious Sentimentalism in the Age of Johnson, 1740–1780*, p. 4). The trend culminated with Thomas Day, who dedicated the 2nd ed. of his *The Dying Negro* (London, 1774) to Rousseau.

59. Colie, *Light and Enlightenment*, pp. 49–59; Basil Willey, *The Seventeenth-Century Background* (Anchor paperback ed., Garden City, N.Y., 1953), pp. 78–9; Stephen, *History of English Thought*, I, pp. 76–9.

was crucial for the development of the philosophy of benevolence and, indeed, for the entire romantic movement. Even in the seventeenth century a few men began to sense the point which Shelley made when he said that science, enlarging the empire of man over the external world, 'proportionately circumscribe those of the internal world; and man, having enslaved the elements, remains himself a slave'.[60] If humanists and Latitudinarians had narrowed the cleavage between the realms of nature and grace, Descartes, as his Arminian supporters were to discover, had unleashed new sources of despair by severing the human soul from a mechanistic world of motion and substance.[61] Long before the emergence of romanticism, religious poets like Edward Young, who was greatly admired by later evangelical reformers, experienced a dread of meaninglessness in an inanimate world, and turned inward, to the feelings and passions, to find the voice of eternity.[62] The actual world was cold and colourless; and man was thrown back upon himself:

> *Helpless* Immortal! Insect *infinite*.
> A worm! a God! I tremble at myself,
> And in myself am lost! At home a stranger . . .[63]

It was Thomas Hobbes who largely turned the attention of British theologians to man's capacity for subjective feeling. Philipp Jakob Spener, the German Pietist, won his master's degree by disputing Hobbes; Whichcote, Isaac Barrow, Henry More, Tillotson and a host of others joined the crusade against the great symbol of atheism. The

60. From 'The Defense of Poetry', quoted in Fairchild, *Religious Trends*, II, p. 6.

61. For the controversy over Descartes in Holland, see Colie, *Light and Enlightenment*, pp. 49–59.

62. In his M S Memoirs (British Museum, Add. M S S 46443–4), James Stephen tells what powerful effect Young's *Night Thoughts* had upon him as a youth; the experience was shared by other British abolitionists, as well as by John Wesley and John Newton. Sir Leslie Stephen, knowing of his grandfather's opinion, judged that Young was shallow and insincere, but that his 'affectation of religious unction' had misled 'serious minds' (*History of English Thought*, II, pp. 362–3).

63. Edward Young, *The Complaint, Or, Night-Thoughts on Life, Death, and Immortality* (London, 1755), pp. 2–3, 109. Young was, it should be said, an ardent Newtonian, and called God 'the great Philanthropist'.

most shocking thing about Hobbes was his contention that man was nothing but an engine of egoism, dominated by fear, greed and lust. Divines who had rebelled against Calvin's conceptions of man's depravity and God's unlimited sovereignty were even more outraged by this secular philosophy which identified law with the will of a worldly sovereign and held that man's only salvation lay in his becoming a slave to the state.

The way to counter Hobbes was to show that men were not discrete particles of self-interest, requiring, for harmonious union, a coercive external will. 'Nature has endu'd us,' said Knightly Chetwood, 'with the tenderest Passions: We are all counterparts one of another. . . . The doleful Cry of one in extreme Distress, makes the strings to tremble at our very Hearts.'[64] Hobbes had ignored man's capacity for moral feeling, his instinctive responses of sympathy, approbation and disapproval, which had nothing to do with calculated self-interest. Intellect, according to Henry More, could apprehend goodness, but only the 'boniform faculty' could taste its sweetness. Before the end of the seventeenth century, the idea of an inherent moral sense had become a commonplace in English sermons.[65]

But to say that doing good was rewarded by a 'delicious relish upon the mind', or by 'a sort of pleasing Anguish, that sweetly melts the Mind, and terminates in a Self-approving Joy', was to be as hedonistic as Hobbes.[66] And, as Shaftesbury was to show, the cultivation of sensibility could become an exclusive affair, confined to men of aristocratic tastes. It is true that, as early as the 1670s, Isaac Barrow

64. Quoted in Ronald S. Crane, 'Suggestions Toward a Genealogy of the "Man of Feeling",' *Journal of English Literary History*, I (1934), p. 225. For a brilliant study of this continuing effort to overcome man's sense of alienation from the material and mechanical universe of the philosophers, see M. H. Abrams, *The Mirror and the Lamp: Romantic Theory and the Critical Tradition* (New York, 1953).

65. Crane, 'Suggestions Toward a Genealogy of the "Man of Feeling",' pp. 225–30. Ernest Tuveson, 'The Origins of the "Moral Sense",' *Huntington Library Quarterly*, XI (May 1948), p. 241; Samuel Mintz, *The Hunting of Leviathan; Seventeenth-Century Reactions to the Materialism and Moral Philosophy of Thomas Hobbes* (Cambridge, England, 1962), *passim*.

66. Isaac Barrow and David Fordyce, as quoted in Crane, 'Suggestions Toward a Genealogy of the "Man of Feeling",' pp. 205–6, 227.

and Richard Cumberland were emphasizing that the subjective
pleasure of the spectator was not enough. Like grace, the moral sensibility was inseparable from social duty. If man was, in a sense,
justified by his benevolent soul, and hence cleared from the accusations of Hobbes, his nobility must find expression in useful
works. The public welfare was served by each individual's 'Self-
approving Joy'.[67] But this utilitarian argument again seemed to lead
towards the enemy's position of fusing private and public interests.
And it was opposed to the inclinations towards introspection and self-
cultivation, which were so much a part of the latitudinarian temper.
The 'man of feeling' would long be torn between the ideal of medi-
tative passivity and an ultimate need to make disinterested contact
with the bewildering world of cause and effect.

The posture of the sensitive spectator was encouraged by a new
literary mode which was closely related to latitudinarian religion. In
1696 Colley Cibber's *Love's Last Shift* began its half-century of
success on the English stage, and instead of laughing at the plight of
fools or rejoicing in the fate of villains, audiences learned to weep
over the misfortunes of the innocent. While the sentimental drama
made slow headway against the reigning style of neo-classicism, it
enjoyed increasing popularity by the 1720s, and was a prevailing
vogue by the 1760s.[68] Poets, novelists and essayists paid homage to
the cult of sensibility; the result of their collective efforts was a profound though immeasurable transformation in public values.
H. N. Fairchild has maintained that sentimentalism in religion and
literature was a single movement whose psychological root was a
repudiation of sin and an expansion of the ego. The Christian has lost
most of his faith, but

67. ibid., p. 211; Whitney, *Primitivism and the Idea of Progress*, pp.
24–5.

68. Ernest Bernbaum (ed.), *Anthology of Romanticism*, II: *Selections
from the Pre-Romantic Movement* (New York, 1929), *passim;* Bernbaum,
*The Drama of Sensibility: A Sketch of the History of English Sentimental
Comedy and Domestic Tragedy, 1696–1780* (Boston, 1915), pp. 2–10, 76,
94–5, 139–40; Bernbaum, *Guide through the Romantic Movement* (2nd
ed., New York, 1949), pp. 9–16; Walter Jackson Bate, *From Classic to
Romantic: Premises of Taste in Eighteenth-Century England* (Cambridge,
Mass., 1946), pp. 35, 43–7, 49–53; Fairchild, *Religious Trends*, II, pp. 365–8.

he retains, in a blurred and softened form, the emotions which his creed had both reflected and fostered. The God above him becomes more shadowy than the God within him, until at last he is left with the basic attitude of sentimentalism – a sense of inward virtue and freedom which must somehow find corroboration in the nature of the universe. Just enough brimstone remains to tinge his optimism with melancholy, just enough otherworldiness to make him shrink at times from the civilization which he has built.[69]

The dominant characteristic of the new literature was a juxtaposition of two opposing worlds of value: the world of sin was hard-boiled, cynical, self-seeking, licentious, and wholly preoccupied with luxury and power; the world of virtue rested on human relationships of sympathy and genuine emotion. And since the moral faculty was often associated with man's original innocence, and was increasingly conceived as something independent of reason and civilization, one might achieve a sense of communion with universal goodness by sympathizing with the moral feeling of a primitive subject. The ideal, perhaps, was discovered by Herbert Croft in 1776, when he had the 'luxury' of watching a Negro stop on a London street, and give three half-pence and a farthing, 'his little all', to a weeping sailor with one arm and two wooden legs.[70] By this time the suffering of Negro slaves had become a popular theme in verse and drama, and within a decade the heartless master and lamenting slave would be accepted as conventional symbols of the two worlds of value. No doubt this flood of anti-slavery literature conditioned many people to an active support of abolition, and attitudes which had first been learned in the theatre or in an idle hour of reading were transferred to the grim stage of reality. Nevertheless, there was an immense gulf between literary pathos and dedicated reform, between the ideal of moral refinement and a willingness to liberate the uncultivated forces of nature. Hannah More, who used the plight of slaves to soften the hearts of women of rank, preached a different morality in her tales for the common people.[71]

69. Fairchild, *Religious Trends*, I, pp. 545–6. A similar interpretation is presented by Stephen, *History of English Thought*, II, pp. 333–4;
70. Whitney, *Primitivism and the Idea of Progress*, p. 88.
71. ibid., pp. 100, 104. Henry Mackenzie and Bryan Edwards are

But the distance between spectator and actor was somewhat narrowed by the theory of the sublime. Interest in the sublime developed concurrently with interest in the moral sense – Boileau's revival of Longinus coincided with the sermons of latitudinarians on man's natural sense of virtue; the writings of John Dennis on the sublime overlapped Shaftesbury's *Inquiry Concerning Virtue or Merit*; Burke's treatise on the sublime followed by two years the publication of Hutcheson's *System of Moral Philosophy*.[72] And like the moral sense, man's response to the sublime was subjective, non-intellectual, and was supposedly derived from inborn taste and emotion. In Dennis's words, sublimity evoked 'a delightful Horrour, a terrible Joy'.[73] These powerful emotions might arise from a direct confrontation with nature in its most frightening manifestations, such as storms, earthquakes or volcanic eruptions. But it was essential that the fear of pain and death be mitigated by a sense of personal security, since terror, as Burke put it, 'is a passion which always produces delight when it does not press too close, and pity is a passion accompanied with pleasure, because it rises from love and social affection'.[74] In other words, the Creator had implanted in man a capacity for delighting in 'the real misfortunes and pains of others', and it was this pleasure which made benevolence possible, for 'if this passion was simply painful, we would shun with the greatest care all persons and places that could excite such a passion; as, some who are so far gone in indolence as not to endure any strong impression actually do'.[75]

Religious subjects were said to evoke the loftiest emotions, and indeed, the cult of the sublime has aptly been called 'a sort of

---

examples of writers who indulged in sentimentality over Negro slaves but who openly supported the African trade.

72. Samuel H. Monk, *The Sublime: A Study of Critical Theories in Eighteenth-Century England* (New York, 1935), pp. 29–32, 45–51, 59–60, 87. Both Thomson and Young consciously strove for the sublime in their poetry, and Thomson's famous image of the slave ship was one of the passages added in later editions to heighten this effect.

73. Quoted by J. T. Boulton, in introd. to Edmund Burke, *A Philosophical Enquiry into the Origin of our Ideas of the Sublime and Beautiful* (London, 1958), p. lvii.

74. Burke, *Philosophical Enquiry*, p. 46.

75. ibid.

Methodist revival in art'.[76] There would appear to be more than a tenuous connexion between the terrifying images in Jonathan Edwards's sermons, which were designed to strike through the senses of the most indolent of sinners, and the succession of tempests, corpses and beasts of prey in the works of Thomson and Savage. John Wesley would not have believed that any true Christian could delight in the sufferings of others, let alone that such delight could serve as a basis for compassion; but in his *Thoughts upon Slavery* he made effective use of images of the most sadistic torture. And slavery in fact, conformed almost perfectly to Burke's requirements for the sublime. Where else could pain and death be found on so vast a scale, from the bloody wars which drove innocent men from their Eden-like garden, from the fateful crossing of the Atlantic-Styx, to the Dante-esque horrors of the colonial plantation? And it was all as remote as the deists' God, though far more terrifying. The response to slavery, then, could be disinterested, since the pain did not press too close. In the final analysis it was the response itself that counted for sublimity, as Longinus had said, 'is the echo of a great soul'. Yet slavery was 'the prison of the soul' which extinguished all that was noble in the human mind. England would never be so thrilled by the struggling African as by the man who descended from exalted rank to plead his cause.

The trends we have been describing can be interpreted as reactions to religious controversy, decaying faith, and the hard-boiled realism and sophistication of England's ruling classes in the Age of Walpole. By the early eighteenth century the aristocracy was strongly tinged with scepticism, which reinforced a traditional distaste for religious enthusiasm and nonconformity. Men like John Sheffield, Earl of Mulgrave, easily reconciled a Hobbesian materialism with support of the High Church party; and through the century the boldest wits and scoffers would be good Tories.[77] It was Lord Macclesfield's friend, Bernard de Mandeville, who took up Hobbes's role of shocking public opinion, and who maintained that benevolence was a sham, that men were and should be self-interested, and that private vices were public benefits. The 1723 edition of Mandeville's *Fable of the Bees* brought a much wider appreciation of his opponent, Shaftesbury, who had

76. Monk, *Sublime*, p. 235.
77. Fairchild, *Religious Trends*, I, pp. 3–4, 96; II, pp. 13–14, 50.

earlier popularized and developed the moral insights of the Cambridge Platonists.[78] The belief in man's natural benevolence won its way in England as an answer to infidelity. Even the orthodox clergy, who mounted an overwhelming offensive against the challenge of deism, found themselves compelled to convince the reading public of the morality or reasonableness of revelation. By the 1730s, when the battle subsided, mystery and emotion had virtually been drained from English theology. God was to be known chiefly through the amazing ingenuity of His works; the best religion was that which promoted a moral life.[79] In marked contrast to France, religion in England absorbed and softened much of the rationalist attack; and out of the latitudinarian past, encouraged by the Great Whig families, there emerged in both the established and dissenting churches a kind of pragmatic middle way, which found proof of the moral order of creation in man's capacity for virtue, liberty and happiness. The architects of this compromise, such as Francis Hutcheson and James Foster, shifted attention from man's necessary subjection to the will of God to his natural place in a harmonious and benevolent universe.[80] And these same writers, as we shall see, were also the first to give anti-slavery a basis in moral philosophy.

But secularization did not necessarily lead towards humanitarian reform. The great moral crisis of the eighteenth century, which preoccupied the keenest minds from Leibniz and Voltaire to Jonathan Edwards, revolved around two related points. First, the triumph of

78. Randall, *Career of Philosophy*, pp. 159–60, 742–61; C. A. Moore, 'Shaftesbury and the Ethical Poets in England, 1700–1760', *Publications of the Modern Language Association*, XXXI (1916), pp. 264–74, 280–82; Crane, review of Alderman, *Philological Quarterly*, pp. 204–6. Shaftesbury wrote the introduction for the 1st ed. of Whichcote's *Sermons*. It should be noted, however, that Samuel Clarke developed the rationalistic tendency of the Cambridge Platonists, which meant that there was a divided stream of influence.

79. Mark Pattison, 'Tendencies of Religious Thought in England, 1688–1740', in *Essays and Reviews* (2nd ed., London, 1860), pp. 254–329; Stephen, *History of English Thought*, I, pp. 83–91, 271–2.

80. Caroline Robbins, *The Eighteenth-Century Commonwealthman: Studies in the Transmission, Development and Circumstance of English Liberal Thought from the Restoration of Charles II until the War with the Thirteen Colonies* (Cambridge, Mass., 1959), pp. 7–10.

reason appeared to have liberated man from enslavement to original sin. But as philosophers pursued the implications of Lockean psychology, it seemed that man was imprisoned within the walls of sensory experience, and subjected to the tyranny of pleasure and pain. Hume's conclusion was that reason 'is and only ought to be the slave of the passions'. As we have seen, one might try to ennoble pleasure by associating it with an instinctive and disinterested response to suffering. But a second problem was implicit in the view that man's tender passions were part of the universal harmony of creation. For if nature was a unified whole and conformed to invariable laws, as Newtonian science had shown; and if nature was not a dark and soulless mechanism, then human suffering must serve a necessary moral function. Evil, as William King and numerous divines maintained, was simply a privation of perfection, and was part of the necessary plenitude of the best of all possible worlds.[81] The idea was popularized by Pope, who could not, however, quite decide whether the world was a harmonious chain of being, or a brutal arena where 'all subsists by elemental strife'. But Soame Jenyns had no doubt 'that the sufferings of individuals are absolutely necessary to universal happiness', or that

the Universe is a system whose very essence consists in subordination; a scale of Beings descending by insensible degrees from infinite perfection to absolute nothing: in which ... the beauty and happiness of the whole depend altogether on the just inferiority of its parts, that is, on the comparative imperfections of the several Beings of which it is composed.[82]

As an alternative to this self-justifying universe one might accept

81. Arthur O. Lovejoy, *The Great Chain of Being: A Study of the History of an Idea* (Harper Torchbook ed., New York, 1960), pp. 212–22; Cassirer, *Philosophy of Enlightenment*, pp. 35–6, 148–9; Stephen, *History of English Thought*, I, pp. 119–34, 168–73; Paul Hazard, *European Thought in the Eighteenth Century, from Montesquieu to Lessing* (Meridian paperback ed., New York, 1963), pp. 60–61, 284–324.

82. Soame Jenyns, *A Free Inquiry into the Nature and Origin of Evil* (London, 1757), pp. 28–9. By the mid eighteenth century, the view that 'THAT WHICH IS, IS BEST' was supported by both deists and defenders of original sin. See, for example, *Monthly Review*, VI (January–June 1752), p. 226.

Daniel Waterland's tough and self-justifying God, who sanctioned lying, cheating, death and slavery whenever He pleased, and whose standards were not to be measured by sentimental men. But either way the reformer must focus his energies on individual moral failings, and not tamper with the ordained structure of things.

And yet Christian morality had always depended upon a sense of incompleteness, upon a tension between the world as it is and the world as it ought to be. If deists were horrified by the barbarities of the Old Testament, which Waterland was so eager to justify, Joseph Butler was prepared to show that nature itself was no more humane. The talk of nicely balanced forces of perfection and imperfection, of suffering and happiness, was sheer illusion. The world was so full of misery and injustice that only an after-life could possibly redress the imbalance.[83]

There was, however, another answer to Butler's frank realism. Some of the early Latitudinarians had held that men could only gradually understand the full meaning of God's revealed law; the moral sense, like the seed of a flower, grew slowly to fruition. In response to the deists' arguments that Christianity was as old as creation, and that nature was always governed by the same laws, Anglican clergymen began to find in the idea of moral progress a substitute for revelation. They believed, to be sure, in a fixed and eternal law; but it was a law revealed to man only in successive stages. Hence most of the ordinances of the Old Testament were marks of a primitive age, when the moral sense was still in an undeveloped state.[84] As King and the numerous theodicies had said, evil was necessary for the existence of good; but as the chain of being was stretched out on a frame of time, the imperfections faded slowly into the past. From the 1740s to the 1760s Anglican apologists met the two crucial problems of the age – the sanction for moral judgement in a Lockean psychology, and the

83. Stephen, *History of English Thought*, I, pp. 301–6.
84. J. B. Bury, *The Idea of Progress: An Inquiry into its Origin and Growth* (Dover paperback ed., New York, 1955), pp. 92–7; Ernest L. Tuveson, *Millennium and Utopia: A Study in the Background of the Idea of Progress* (Berkeley, 1949), pp. 130 ff, 168–83, 201; Ronald S. Crane, 'Anglican Apologetics and the Idea of Progress, 1699–1745', *Modern Philology*, XXXI (February 1934), pp. 281–93.

meaning of evil in a Newtonian universe – by merging natural benevolence with a theology of historical progress.[85] By the 1780s the
Reverend James Ramsay, who had done much to promote the cause
of anti-slavery, could write that human nature had progressed so
far that the average peasant was morally superior to the ancient
Greek philosophers. This progress, moreover, had been largely due to
the abolition of European slavery. And when Negroes in the colonies
were finally emancipated, the way would be open to 'the fabulous
golden age, when mutual wants and mutual good, will & shall bind all
mankind in one common-interest'.[86]

It is hardly conceivable that anti-slavery could have become a
powerful international force had it not been preceded by a revolutionary shift in attitudes towards sin, human nature and progress. And for
England and the English colonies it was of the utmost importance
that these new values and attitudes had religious origins, and were
linked with a reformulation of Christian belief in the face of science
and scepticism.

Humanitarian reform provided a means of avoiding doubt and the
fear of meaninglessness. To an abstract and lifeless theology it
brought fresh symbols and the opportunity for dedicated action. In an
era of sterile controversy over the nature of evil, one might well ask,
'if slavery is not evil, what is?' In an era of fruitless debate over virtue
and self-interest, one might prove that benevolent affections and
social utility were not incompatible. Even self-approving joy must be
disinterested if the object of philanthropy was the distant and alien
Negro. And as the cultivation of sensibility moved from the literary
realm to the promotion of human happiness, man's capacity for feeling lost its subjective, private character, and became a basis for social
communication and consensus. Men of different faiths in distant
parts of the world could share hopes and emotions, and feel united in

85. Crane, 'Anglican Apologetics', pp. 299, 349–67; Lovejoy, *Great Chain
of Being*, p. 268.

86. James Ramsay, 'A MS Volume, Entirely in Ramsay's Hand, Mainly
concerned with his Activities Towards the Abolition of the Slave Trade'
(Phillipps MS 17780, Rhodes House, Oxford), fols. 69–71, 95. Roughly
similar ideas can be found in Thomas Clarkson, *The History of the Rise,
Progress and Accomplishment of the Abolition of the African Slave-Trade
by the British Parliament* (London, 1808), I, p. 87–8, and *passim*.

an ennobling cause. They could transform an abstract belief in progress into a plan for action, and at the same time reconcile the ideal of primitive simplicity with the ideal of civilized refinement. The Negro's enslavement, unlike legitimate restraints of society, was not occasional by sin or necessity. It was wholy undeserved. The Negro represented innocent nature, and hence corresponded, psychologically, with the natural and spontaneous impulses of the reformer. Accordingly, the key to progress lay in the controlled emancipation of innocent nature as found both in the objective slave and in the subjective affections of the reformer. The latter's compassion would evoke compassion in the slave, and the reciprocal love would slowly free the world from corruption and self-seeking. Above all, this regenerative process would not endanger piety or social order; there would be no vengeful assault of nature upon civilization. The slave would simply be lifted to the level of independent action and social obligation. The reformer would achieve freedom from the tyranny of self-interest by merging his soul in a transcendent cause. Philanthropy, as the abolitionist William Allen was to write, made religion meaningful to ordinary people, gave proof through human action of God's benevolent purposes, and conveyed deep joys which were a foretaste of paradise.[87]

87. William Allen, 'On the Duty and Pleasure of Cultivating Benevolent Dispositions', *The Philanthropist, or Repository for Hints and Suggestions Calculated to Promote the Comfort and Happiness of Man,* I (London, 1811), pp. 1–7.

12

Religious Sources of Anti-Slavery Thought:
Collective Guilt, Private Opinion
and Commitment

IN this chapter we shall trace some of the effects of latitudinarian theology in New England, and examine the special conditions in America that favoured or inhibited the application of ideals of universal benevolence and human happiness to the problem of slavery. Then we may turn to explicit discussions of slavery by a number of British writers who illustrate the changing trends in Protestant thought which we have outlined thus far. Finally, after emphasizing the limitations of rationalistic theology as a source of reform, we shall consider the relevance of eighteenth-century evangelicalism as a stimulus to individual commitment and decision.

Latitudinarian theology had a delayed impact in the American colonies, and its implications were greatly altered by local circumstance and tradition. In America there had been no Hobbes, no Mandeville, no corps of deists bent on proving the superfluity of revelation. Even by the mid eighteenth century many New Englanders detected atheism in rational apologies for revealed religion, and regarded such devout writers as Tillotson and Samuel Clarke as purveyors of infidelity. But as Yale or William and Mary acquired miscellaneous collections of sermons, tracts and moral philosophies, the lines of intellectual faction became obscure. Dangerous books carried no stamp of warning, and a young Calvinist like Ezra Stiles could read Shaftesbury with enthusiasm, not realizing that he was a deist. The great problem for colonial intellectuals was to digest a mass of free-floating ideas, and reconcile them, if possible, with provincial traditions.[1]

1. Conrad Wright, *The Beginnings of Unitarianism in America* (Boston, 1955), pp. 5–6, 22; Edmund S. Morgan, *The Gentle Puritan: A Life of Ezra Stiles, 1727–1795* (New Haven, 1962), pp. 47–57, 63–77; Herbert M.

There were two reasons why liberal theology had the profoundest effects in New England. The descendants of the Puritans possessed, of course, a coherent and well-established intellectual tradition. And within this tradition were rationalistic and humanistic tendencies which had never been nourished by a Hobbes or by the fanaticism of civil war, but which became fully manifest in the reaction to the Great Awakening of the 1740s. It was then that segments of the New England clergy discovered and assimilated the English Enlightenment. In opposing the claim that revivals were marks of God's special providence, they saw the relevance of the self-governing Newtonian world. In opposing the emotional orgies of itinerant preachers, they found solace in the calm rationalism of Locke, Tillotson and Samuel Clarke. In opposing the revivalists' emphasis on man's utter depravity, they drew support from Daniel Whitby, John Taylor, James Foster and Francis Hutcheson.[2]

The New England Arminians by no means abandoned belief in revelation or in the supernatural. In the beginning, they thought of themselves as simply defending the established order of churches and communities against ranting subversives who disparaged good character, depreciated moral conduct, and imparted delusions of superior sanctity to their converts from the lower classes. But Arminianism became essentially a moral protest against the *principle* of slavery in the doctrine of original sin. This doctrine lay at the very heart of both the Awakening and Jonathan Edwards's remarkable theology. Edwards's disciple, Samuel Hopkins, declared that he could not give up original sin without abandoning belief in Christianity. Edwards's theory of 'moral necessity' – that is, that man must choose what he

Morais, *Deism in Eighteenth-Century America* (reprint ed., New York, 1960), pp. 29–30, 54–5, 61, 77–80; Dumas Malone, *Jefferson the Virginian* (Boston, 1948), pp. 98–109.

2. Alice M. Baldwin, *The New England Clergy and the American Revolution* (reprint ed., New York, 1958), pp. 8–18; Joseph Haroutunian, *Piety Versus Moralism: The Passing of the New England Theology* (New York, 1932), pp. 9–14; Wright, *Beginnings of Unitarianism*, pp. 57, 78–80, 136–9, 142–4. John Taylor, a Dissenter who had moved from Calvinism to Arminianism, was particularly influential in New England. Jonathan Mayhew corresponded with James Foster, whose views on slavery we shall soon discuss.

most desires – amounted to moral slavery only if natural man were deemed totally incapable of desiring virtue. And to such Arminians as Charles Chauncy, Samuel Webster and Jonathan Mayhew, this doctrine was outrageous on two grounds. To say that unconverted men were incapable of choosing true virtue was to obliterate vital distinctions between right and wrong, justice and injustice, and hence to strike at the foundation of law and moral order. Furthermore, the entire covenant theology had rested on the assumption that God was a constitutional sovereign who acted in rational and predictable ways; and while the original Puritans had insisted that God was not subject to human standards of justice, the Arminians were confident that no benevolent ruler would condemn unborn generations to sin and eternal suffering. Samuel Webster was particularly concerned about infants who died before they had a chance to be regenerated. As John Taylor had shown, no one could justly be blamed for the fault of another, when his own personal choice was not involved. If electors were not responsible for the crimes of their representatives, how could it be claimed that men were responsible for what Adam, their legal representative, had done so long ago? And even if one granted that men had inherited Adam's mortal flesh, it did not follow that his moral failings could be passed on by physical generation. The absurdity of the idea could be seen in Jonathan Edwards's vain attempt to find another argument, and to rest his case for collective sin on obscure metaphysics.[3]

As Arminian thought crystallized in the 1750s, two points received particular emphasis: benevolence was God's dominant characteristic; human happiness was God's ultimate concern. And the Deity promoted human happiness not by coercion but by allowing men a freedom of choice and an ability to distinguish right from wrong. Even those who made the wrong choice could be punished only according to the degree of their sin. In time Charles Chauncy would conclude that no human failings could warrant perpetual suffering and that God's infinite benevolence would lead ultimately to the liberation of

3. Wright, *Beginnings of Unitarianism*, pp. 58–114; Perry Miller, *Jonathan Edwards* (New York, 1949), *passim*; H. Shelton Smith, *Changing Conceptions of Original Sin: A Study in American Theology Since 1750* (New York, 1955), pp. 10–85.

all the sinners in hell.[4] Such an altered view of the moral government of creation had an obvious bearing on the institution of slavery. The principle of inherited and perpetual servitude was clearly repugnant to an expanded belief in personal moral responsibility, in the benevolence of the Creator, and in the primacy of human happiness. Since these ideas filtered into the southern and middle colonies, as well as New England, we might expect to find a direct connexion between liberal theology and a widespread conviction that slavery was an intolerable evil. There was, however, a very great difference between holding beliefs which would make it difficult to justify slavery, and feeling a personal commitment to do something about the problem. Nor was the difference simply a matter of personality.

First of all, American colonists could not consider Negro slavery as a remote and exotic institution. They could not use it as a symbol of man's inhumanity to man, or of the abuse of innocent nature, without endangering accepted rationalizations and questioning the integrity of highly respected men. Religious liberalism made greatest headway among a mercantile elite who saw private property as the very cornerstone of a free and righteous society; and such men were acutely conscious that slaves were property. Enlightened New Englanders like Ezra Stiles and Moses Brown owned slaves as a matter of course; and while in the 1770s both men would give up their human property and later become abolitionist leaders, they took slavery as much for granted, prior to the Revolution, as did Thomas Jefferson.[5] Then, too, beliefs in God's benevolence and man's capacity for virtue were often linked with the philosophy of 'whatever is, is right'. Charles Chauncy, for example, accepted King's theory that apparent evils were essential parts of the harmony and continuity of being. Even pain and suffering, he felt, served a 'medicinal' function, and were accordingly part of the general good.[6] If American readers of *Pamela*

4. Wright, *Beginnings of Unitarianism*, pp. 161–6; Haroutunian, *Piety versus Moralism*, pp. 51, 136, 145.

5. Morgan, *Gentle Puritan*, pp. 2, 125, 277, 309–10, 452; Mack Thompson, *Moses Brown, Reluctant Reformer* (Chapel Hill, 1962), pp. 6, 12, 23, 72, 92–6, 202, 296.

6. Wright, *Beginnings of Unitarianism*, pp. 178–83; Stow Persons, 'The Cyclical Theory of History in Eighteenth-Century America', *American*

agreed that one should not disdain the lowliest slave – 'He's equally a link of nature's chain' – they might conclude, with another English writer, that 'Ev'n partial Ills, when wisely understood,/And well improv'd, become a general Good.'[7] Since human institutions were the products of uniform laws which promoted the maximum degree of happiness and reflected the wisdom and goodness of the Creator, it was inconceivable that the defects of slavery could be more than temporary maladjustments in a perfectly ordered and self-correcting universe. The attack on original sin undoubtedly weakened the view of slavery as a righteous punishment; but without a sense of the infinitude of sin and the absolute opposition between the depraved world and the City of God, it would be difficult to see any institution as an unmitigated evil.

But in America the problem of slavery had still another dimension. Colonists even outside New England tended to think of themselves as parties in covenant with God. They interpreted prosperity as the collective reward for faithfulness, which helped to cleanse wealth of the stain of self-seeking; national calamities were deserved rebukes for laxity in fulfilling the covenant's terms. In times of crisis American colonists shared the ritual, which was most highly developed in New England, of setting aside days for humiliation, self-condemnation and pleading for forgiveness. Far from being a mere formality, this tradition of confession and re-dedication provided a sense of unified purpose and gave moral coherence to the vicissitudes of colonial experience.[8] The very separateness of the American colonists

---

Quarterly, VI (Summer 1954), pp. 150–54. It should be noted, however, that theodicy was not confined to liberals; Joseph Bellamy, one of Edward's disciples, argued that God permits sin and that 'of all possible plans, this is the best'. Hopkins took a similar view (Haroutunian, *Piety versus Moralism*, p. 31).

7. Quoted in Arthur O. Lovejoy, *The Great Chain of Being; Study of the History of an Idea* (Harper Torchbook ed., New York, 1960), p. 207, and Hoxie N. Fairchild, *Religious Trends in English Poetry* (New York, 1939–49), II: *Religious Sentimentalism in the Age of Johnson, 1740–1780*, p. 285. For an imaginative treatment of the effect of such ideas in America, see Persons, 'Cyclical Theory', pp. 147–58.

8. Perry Miller, 'From Covenant to the Revival', in *The Shaping of American Religion* (ed. by James Ward Smith and A. Leland Jamison, Princeton, 1961), pp. 322–68.

revitalized the Old Testament idea of a people charged with a special mission; and this, in turn, tempered the moral reassurance of a Pope, and provided a bulwark against the dark pessimism that Voltaire felt when contemplating a mere earthquake.

The French and Indian War, for example, was obviously a punishment for decades of moral degeneration, to which Americans had been blinded by their pride in material growth. We have already seen how the war led Quakers to withdrawal and self-purgation, and to a decision to rid their sect of slavery. The New England clergy were equally intent on self-reformation, but much of their energy was directed towards arousing a will to fight to the death. Countless sermons made it clear that the penalty for continuing sins and for laxness in resisting the popish enemy would be absolute and perpetual slavery.[9]

The war with France had scarcely ended when some colonists perceived a threat of enslavement from another source. The New England clergy, particularly the Arminians, had played an important role in introducing and disseminating the political theory of the Enlightenment. What is not sufficiently appreciated is that the ideas of natural rights, limited power and dutiful resistance to tyranny, were incorporated within the traditional covenant theology. The high-handed measures of the British government were therefore not only violations of a sacred compact, but were clear evidence of America's national guilt and urgent need for reformation. The erosion of belief in original sin opened the way for an assertion of natural rights and an insistence on defining limitations of sovereignty; and yet the covenant psychology preserved a sense of unity in collective guilt, punishment and destiny. The crisis with Britain in the 1760s gave the Arminian clergy a dedication of soul which their theology had nearly made impossible; they now discovered new ways of describing sin, moral duty and the meaning of God's judgements. At the same time the heirs of revivalism found ways of accepting notions of natural liberty and natural rights without abandoning their apocalyptic vision.[10]

9. Baldwin, *New England Clergy*, pp. 85–7.

10. Miller, 'From Covenant to Revival', pp. 322–68; Baldwin, *New England Clergy*, pp. 65–8, 92–104; Moses Coit Tyler, *The Literary History of the American Revolution, 1763–1783* (reprint ed., New York, 1957), I, pp. 121–40.

It was for this reason that ministers of opposing persuasions could join in denouncing the Stamp Act, in portraying resistance as a sacred duty, and in calling for national humiliation and self-denial. The claim that compliance with British regulations would lead to certain slavery – which was repeated incessantly by Jonathan Mayhew, by his friend James Otis and by numerous others – was far more than rhetoric. Not only was freedom dependent on a contractual limitation of power, but bondage was obviously the punishment designed by God for those who failed to meet their obligations. When Samuel Webster and James Otis turned to attack Negro slavery in the 1760s, it was not a simple matter of perceiving the inconsistency between perpetual servitude and a liberalism which had already undermined belief in original sin.[11] No doubt religious liberalism had prepared the way, but the heirs of the Great Awakening, such as Samuel Hopkins, Levi Hart and Jonathan Edwards, Jr, would become at least as ardent as the Arminians in the anti-slavery cause. What had happened by the 1760s was that a complex convergence of forces had led a few Americans to see that, however free and virtuous individuals might be, the sins of a nation would be repaid in kind. And just as the punishment of taxes and commercial restraints pointed to the sins of greed and luxury, so the threat of political bondage revealed the source of the colonists' deepest guilt.

Having discussed certain broad trends in British Protestant thought, we may turn to a number of writers whose response to slavery illuminates the more general shift in values. Although he died in 1703, Thomas Tryon anticipated many concerns of later critics, and represents a different world from that of Baxter, Godwyn or Sewall. Like John Wesley, he was profoundly influenced by the mysticism of Jakob Boehme; as a youth he was kindled by the spark of An-

---

11. Haroutunian, *Piety versus Moralism*, p. 12; William Tudor, *Life of James Otis of Massachusetts* (Boston, 1823), pp. 143–4; Baldwin, *New England Clergy*, pp. 117, 119, 128; George H. Moore, *Notes on the History of Slavery in Massachusetts* (New York, 1866), pp. 124–8; Milton Cantor, 'The Image of the Negro in Colonial Literature', *New England Quarterly*, XXXVI (December 1962), pp. 473–4. None of the above authors draws this conclusion. The idea was suggested to me by Perry Miller's interpretation of the covenant.

abaptism. A primitivist, an astrologer and a dietary faddist, he wrote an immensely popular tract called *The Way to Health*, which gave inspiration to Franklin's Poor Richard. Aphra Behn, who contributed to the literay vogue of primitivism and sensibility, addressed some lines to Thomas Tryon. In the 1660s he spent some time in Barbados, and accordingly had first-hand knowledge of Negro Slavery.

As 'Philotheos Physiologus', Tryon published in 1684 *Friendly Advice to the Gentlemen-Planters of the East and West Indies*. A large portion of this work consists of information on herbs and fruits and the proper means of preserving one's health in the tropics. The sections on Negro slavery appear to be a confusing jumble of inconsistencies. By adopting the literary device of having Negroes voice their own complaints and outdo their masters in logical debate, Tryon foreshadowed both the cult of sensibility and primitivist attacks on the pretensions of Christian civilization. When English divines were just beginning to talk of tender passions and the moral sensitivity of uncorrupted man, Tryon portrayed a loving African mother being snatched from her helpless children, the anguish of violent separation of a young husband and wife, the dreadful sufferings of the Middle Passage, and the sadistic torture and grinding labour in islands where there was no charity, but only '*poysonous Tobacco* and *furious Pride, sweet Sugar* and most *bitter ill nature*'[12] In all this, according to Tryon, there was not a shred of right or justice. Without American receivers there would be no man-stealing in Africa or trade in slaves. And yet we are astonished to discover that Tryon's 'Sambo' becomes reconciled with his master, and promises to tell his fellows to 'be obedient, humble, just and respective to all their Masters'. So long as Negro slaves are treated like men, they will enjoy an 'unspeakable happiness'.[13]

A closer look shows that, while Tryon was genuinely concerned with the Negroes' welfare, he saw no inherent conflict between slaveholding and a good conscience. He was also much impressed by the increased profit which American slavery brought the world. To

12. [Thomas Tryon], *Friendly Advice to the Gentlemen-Planters of the East and West Indies* (London, 1684), pp. 77, 81–3, 103, 111.
13. ibid., pp. 220–22.

understand these inconsistencies we must ask what human bondage meant to a man who thought of sin and salvation in terms of sickness and health. For the starting-point in Tryon's philosophy was a pristine and mystical harmony between nature and spirit, the terrestrial and celestial. Whenever this original balance was broken, nature began secreting certain inner poisons which, 'by a secret and sympathetical Power', excited corresponding malignant forces in the celestial sphere. Sin, then, was a disease which brought its own retribution. The consumption of spiritous liquor or any unnatural diet would lead inevitably to the release of lustful passions, the corruption of nature, and final decay in the forms of plagues and disasters. And while labour was essential to health and virtue, its misuse amounted to a 'perpetual plague' which ate away at the life-giving forces of nature. It was to illustrate this truth that Tryon fastened upon the dreadful excesses of Negro slavery.[14]

Tryon's obsession with 'Pythagorean' mysticism should not blind us to the fact that he identified virtue with the balance and adjustment of nature. Through the voice of his imaginary Negro he was able to express considerable hostility towards the values and manners of his own civilization. He could even use slavery as a powerful symbol of class exploitation. One Christian, the Negro points out, squanders in a day to gratify his lusts what hundreds of slaves have produced by sweat and toil. Freed from the healthful discipline of work, the planter grows fat and gluttonous; and after debauching a pretty slave girl, he guzzles rum or brandy on his soft bed. But the Negroes dig and hoe under a scorching sun, driven by the lashes of fiends. At the sugar mills they work over copper cauldrons, inhaling the sulphurous fumes, until some, in whom nature has been overcome, fall into the boiling syrup.[15] America had often stimulated hope for an earthly paradise, but it could also stand for a terrestrial hell.

The contrast between indolent planters and exploited slaves carried radical implications for a society which had by no means accepted labour and temperance as the duties of all men. And Tryon's Sambo, who was significantly the son of an African priest, made trenchant comments on the religion which permitted such violations of natural

14. ibid., pp. 141, 177.
15. ibid., pp. 96, 123–7, 164.

law. Christians, he says, are fond of making new martyrs while honouring those of the past, and of using religion to justify hatred, wrangling, killing and persecution. Africans, he confesses, are ignorant of Latin and Greek, and have not learned to chop logic or construct ingenious syllogisms. Their only book was man himself, in whom could be found the true nature and properties of all being. From this source Negroes had learned all that man needs to know – to do as he would be done by – and they suspected that the more paint glass had on it, the more it would keep out the light. Sambo might well have been a student of the Cambridge Platonists.

To the charge that Africans were naked savages, it could be said that men had felt no need for garments as long as they remained in an innocent state. To cover their shame Europeans robbed thousands of animals of coats, and then adorned themselves with lace and finery that were more the mark of pride than virtue. And even so, they neither entered nor left the world with more ornament than the humble African. Negro women, unlike the lascivious ladies of Europe, were modest even in their nakedness. If Africans were polygamous, this was merely a custom and not a violation of nature like the adultery and whoredom which were everywhere countenanced in Europe. Africa, to be sure, could not boast of playhouses, of luxurious palaces, of cunning lawyers, or of tables loaded with rich and unnatural foods. But this was hardly evidence of depravity.[16]

In the end, Tryon recoiled from the implication that Negro slaves represented sinless nature exploited and corrupted by civilized Europe. Sambo says, without explanation, that if his people had not violated the pristine law of nature, they would never have been subjugated by Europeans. Nevertheless, Tryon made it clear that the sins of Africa did not justify the sins of Europe. 'The Cup of Wrath', he warned, 'is almost full.'[17]

In the late 1730s, when Francis Hutcheson was working on his *System of Moral Philosophy*, arguments against slavery appeared in the *London Magazine* and in a poem by Richard Savage; Benjamin Lay published his blistering attack on slaveholders; and the Darien Scots

16. ibid., pp. 118–19, 186, 194.
17. ibid., pp. 203, 208.

sent their famous anti-slavery petition to the Georgia Trustees. Hutcheson may have been influenced by the growing knowledge of the brutalities of Negro slavery, which came in part from the published travel accounts of such men as Sir Hans Sloane and John Atkins. But his views on slavery were also a logical application of his moral philosophy, which was a culmination of many of the trends we have already discussed.

The son and grandson of Presbyterian ministers, Hutcheson was early infected by the Arminianism of one of Samuel Clarke's disciples, and was then profoundly stirred by Shaftesbury's philosophy of benevolence, which became for him the very core of religion. As a professor at the University of Glasgow, he was a prime agent of the Scottish Enlightenment, and the founder of a school of moral philosophy which included his pupil and successor, Adam Smith. The Scottish moralists strove to construct a theory of ethics which would be compatible with Lockean psychology and Newtonian physics. Yet early in his career Hutcheson had directed attacks against Hobbes and Mandeville; and he and his followers, who were deeply stung by the probings of their countryman, David Hume, knew all too well that if ideas were derived from simple sensation, morality might be reducible to such non-moral sources as habit, association and self-interest. Their chief aim, therefore, was to derive from self-evident intuitions principles which would preserve faith in individual responsibility and in the moral order of the world. In one form or another, the ideas of the Scottish moralists would become a vital part of the anti-slavery creed, and would leave a deep imprint on French and German philosophy, as well as on American Protestantism.[18]

From self-analysis Hutcheson concluded that man is a skilfully

18. Gladys Bryson, *Man and Society: The Scottish Inquiry of the Eighteenth Century* (Princeton, 1945), p. 2; Caroline Robbins, *The Eighteenth-Century Commonwealthman; Studies in the Transmission, Development and Circumstance of English Liberal Thought from the Restoration of Charles II until the War with the Thirteen Colonies* (Cambridge, Mass., 1959), pp. 185–90.; Fairchild, *Religious Trends in English Poetry*, III (*Romantic Faith, 1780–1830*), pp. 25–9; Leslie Stephen, *History of English Thought in the Eighteenth Century* (3rd ed., New York, 1949), II, pp. 56–63; Sydney E. Ahlstrom, 'The Scottish Philosophy and American Theology', *Church History*, XXIV (September 1955), pp. 257–72.

balanced mechanism of senses and passions. The internal sense of sympathy enables us to feel the suffering of others, and to desire to relieve their distress without any 'artful views of advantage'. Since this propensity is particularly evident in women and small children, it cannot be the result of education. The internal moral sense perceives virtue as the eye perceives light, and after first giving approval to our own benevolent passions, it teaches us to approve the actions of others which stem from similar motives. Our delight in benevolence is an instinctive reflex; it is not dependent on reason or an anticipation of pleasure. And yet we have been so artfully contrived by our Creator that our subjective feelings correspond perfectly with an external and general good. For the benevolent passions we most approve are precisely those that promote the greatest happiness of the greatest number of people. And it is from our unqualified approbation of 'calm, stable, universal good-will to all, or the most extensive benevolence' – a social force analogous to gravitation – that we derive our 'most distinct notion' of the Deity.[19]

Hutcheson attempted, then, to link the innate moral sense with an objective principle of social utility. Man's natural tastes and inclinations served the public good; his vices arose not from sin but from erroneous judgement or mistaken self-love. For as long as reason sifted out correct data to which the senses could respond, self-love would be balanced by benevolence and would serve its proper function.

But suppose someone argued that slavery was necessary for the public welfare of a particular society? Compassionate men might very well sympathize with the slaves' plight, but if moral action were not seen as conformity to an eternal law willed by God, or to a system of rational principles inherent in nature, then social utility must be the ultimate standard. And, indeed, Hutcheson accused certain nations of being so 'immoderately' addicted to liberty and so blind to the public welfare that they failed to accept perpetual servitude as a highly 'useful punishment'. Since nothing was so 'effectual' as

19. Francis Hutcheson, *An Inquiry Concerning Moral Good and Evil*, in *British Moralists* (ed. by L. A. Selby-Bigge, Oxford, 1897), I, pp. 69–177; Hutcheson, *A System of Moral Philosophy* (London, 1755), I, pp. 19–20, 69, 238–41, 273, 281.

slavery in promoting industry and restraining sloth, especially in the 'lower conditions' of society, it should be the 'ordinary punishment of such idle vagrants as, after proper admonitions and tryals of temporary servitude, cannot be engaged to support themselves and their families by any useful labours'.[20]

How, then, could Hutcheson preserve the connexion between our instinctive benevolence and a utilitarianism that justified individual suffering in the interest of the general good? Was it the function of the moral sense, when properly tuned by reason, to give automatic approval to the most efficient social system, which according to Hutcheson's friend, William King, was much like the system then in being? The answer is partly revealed in Hutcheson's arguments against Aristotle's theory of the natural slave.

No men, he pointed out, were devoid of a moral sense, or of desires for liberty, property and happiness. These universal capacities and desires gave men the natural rights to defend their lives and persons, to follow the dictates of their own consciences, and to pursue happiness. Such rights were 'perfect' and 'unalienable', because their violation could never be compatible with the general welfare. Differences in wisdom or talents were never so well-defined that the public good would be served by making some men totally subordinate to others. If Hutcheson rejected natural law as something deducible from the eternal essences of being, he discovered it again in universal principles which were necessary for human happiness. And as natural law became less abstract and absolute, it could be applied more flexibly to human institutions.[21]

Armed with the cross-cut teeth of benevolence and utility, Hutcheson easily sawed through the conventional rationalizations for slavery. Nothing could be more absurd than the claim that sparing a life subjects the recipient and his offspring to the absolute will of the benefactor. Altruism is a sufficient motive for doctors, midwives and soldiers, who save our lives without the bribe of our perpetual service. And yet Hutcheson's doctrine of utility leaves a somewhat ragged edge. Self-love may not be necessary for the saving of lives, but men will not work voluntarily without the reward of property. It is only

20. Hutcheson, *System of Moral Philosophy*, II, p. 202.
21. ibid., I, pp. 273, 281, 293–303.

just, therefore, that an African whose life has been saved pay back in service (with reasonable interest) the expenses incurred in his maintenance and transportation to America. And this he should be able to do in ten or twelve years, providing, as Hutcheson added, he is not among the one-third of his fellows who die.[22] The enslavement of prisoners of war revolts the moral sense and is equally repugnant to the general interests of mankind. Even within an aggressor nation a relatively small number of men are guilty of crime. The majority of soldiers have no choice but to fight, and under no circumstances are their children deserving of punishment. The burden of proving just title lies always with the owner of slaves, and this is particularly true when the origins of captivity are distant and obscure. Yet here, again, utility has its backlash. In war the important thing is to achieve specific objectives, and these may require reprisals and even the enslavement of innocent people. But while Hutcheson at times justified perpetual servitude on the ground of public welfare, he took pains to stress its limited character. The greatest happiness of the greatest number of people might be served by a lifetime of forced labour, but never by a violation of a person's freedom of conscience or right of self-defence.[23]

In substance Hutcheson said little about slavery that had not been said before. He was less radical than Albornoz or Bodin.[24] Although he attacked some of the ancient arguments for human bondage, he did not hold that the moral sense was subject to progressive improvement. His ethical system made no allowance for a compelling obligation to combat evil. And yet he suggested the seminal idea that absolute bondage might be contrary to the general principles that promote human happiness. This insight would be developed by Adam Smith and the Physiocrats. He preached the universality of benevolence, and held that our sympathy for the most remote members of our species was proof of our disinterested virtue. Above all, he

22. ibid., II, pp. 84–5, 202–3.
23. ibid., II, pp. 203–11.
24. In stressing the importance of Hutcheson's 'sentimentalism' for later anti-slavery thought, Wylie Sypher overlooks this significant point ('Hutcheson and the "Classical" Theory of Slavery', *Journal of Negro History*, XXIV [July 1939], pp. 263–80).

popularized the view that the essence of morality lies in man's instinctive and unpremeditated compassion for his fellow creatures.

James Foster was a famous dissenting preacher who propagated many of Hutcheson's ideas. His *Discourses on All the Principal Branches of Natural Religion and Social Virtue*, which appeared between 1749 and 1752, was widely admired in Britain and America. By that time latitudinarian religion had become so infused with nature and reason that the Bible could be treated as a useful supplement. Mankind formed a great system 'linked together by inviolable bonds of reason, instinct, interest'. And, Foster cautioned, 'if the *Gospel*, instead of confirming, had abrogated the common ties of human nature it would be both impiety, and inhumanity, to embrace it'.[25] Foster differed little from Hutcheson on the natural rights of all men, or on the usefulness of self-love, when balanced by benevolence. He gave particular attention to the reciprocal duties of the various ranks and orders of men, and justified social inequality on the ultimate grounds of utility and happiness. 'Whatever tends to mischief, upon the whole,' he wrote, 'is an unnatural relation; and ought to be for ever abolished.' Hutcheson could have said the same, but Foster carried the doctrine of universal tendency to a point that anticipated Kant; the single rule for judging morality was this: 'If *all* men acted, as *one vicious* man . . . thinks himself at liberty to act; what would be the *result* upon the whole?'[26]

Since servitude arose from the same purposeful causes that produced inequality, it could not be an 'unnatural relation'. Yet here Foster confronted a dilemma. Even more than Hutcheson he favoured limited power and government by consent; perpetual servitude in any form appeared to be a deviation from the divine scheme in which individuals were free in order to be rational, and were allowed 'to exert the capacities of their nature without *reserve*'. But Foster hesitated to restrict the principle of utility by declaring that slavery must always be incompatible with the general good. He agreed with Hutcheson that extreme measures were sometimes

25. James Foster, *Discourses on All the Principal Branches of Natural Religion and Social Virtue* (London, 1749–52), II, pp. 4–7.
26. ibid., II, pp. 11, 17–18.

necessary in achieving the aims of war, although from a personal standpoint the freeing of a captive would give us much more 'sublime and exquisite pleasure' than keeping him in degrading bondage. Foster went on to say that whereas commerce should extend benevolence and 'a more *universal sense* of morality', the African slave trade was an 'outrageous violation of natural *rights*'. If we should read of such cruelty and tyranny in accounts of the ancient Greeks and Romans, we would 'despise all their *pretended* refinements of morality'. But this, Foster admitted, was only a personal opinion, a 'private protest'.[27] The moral sense had not yet found a social outlet.

Nevertheless, within the next two decades the private protest against slavery increasingly became a test of religious sincerity. James Beattie, a Scottish philosopher who won immense fame for supposedly demolishing the arguments of Hume, saw the defence of slavery as one of the consequences of religious scepticism. In defending the 'immutability of moral sentiment' against the spreading poisons of doubt and disbelief, he took time to show that perpetual bondage was contrary to the British love of liberty and to the sacred rights of mankind. But though Beattie gathered material for a more specific indictment, he decided to confine his opinions to the classroom; and when Parliament finally took up the question of the slave trade, he favoured the utmost caution.[28]

In 1766, the year before Beattie finished his celebrated *Essay on Truth*, Bishop William Warburton told the Society for the Propagation of the Gospel that the great idol of American colonists was 'the GOD OF GAIN'. These 'sincere Worshippers of Mammon' claimed that Negroes were a species of property. 'Gracious God!' the good bishop exclaimed, 'to talk (as in herds of Cattle) of Property in rational Creatures!'[29] Although Warburton was somewhat latitudi-

27. ibid., II, pp. 152–8.
28. Stephen, *History of English Thought*, I, pp. 381–3; James Beattie, *An Essay on the Nature and Immutability of Truth, In Opposition to Sophistry and Scepticism* (7th ed., London, 1807), pp. ix, xi, 6, 428; William Forbes, *An Account of the Life and Writings of James Beattie* (Edinburgh, 1807), III, pp. 36–8, 42–4, 54–5, 60–61.
29. William Warburton, *A Sermon Preached before the Incorporated Society for the Propagation of the Gospel in Foreign Parts . . .* (London, 1766), pp. 25–6.

narian in his beliefs and was an intimate friend of Pope, he had an arrogant contempt for deists as well as Methodists. Like Morgan Godwyn, he associated American slavery with luxury, declining faith and infidelity. Like Richard Baxter, he feared that Catholics were winning in the struggle for heathens' souls. He attacked the injustice of slavery in terms reminiscent of Albornoz: 'Did your Slaves ever complain to you of their *unhappiness* amidst their native woods and desarts?'[30] And yet Warburton offered no specific proposals; his final suggestion was that Colonel Codrington's gift of the Barbadian plantations showed that God intended the SPG to be the instrument to produce good from so much evil.

No one went further than William Paley, the Archdeacon of Carlisle, in demonstrating how good comes from apparent evil. With Paley, Hutcheson's utilitarianism triumphs over sentiment. Every bone, tendon and impulse shows the wisdom of our Creator who, Paley assures us, would have won first prize had there been a competitive examination for the best model of a reptile. Even heaven and hell perform the vital function of balancing human desires, and hence of promoting the greatest possible happiness.[31] Now in such a delicately contrived world, as Paley acknowledges, there can be no basis for claiming that human slavery is illegal. So long as it serves a purpose, such as being a proportionate penalty for a given crime, there can be no objection. Early Christians accepted even harmful kinds of slavery, for to have done otherwise would have been inexpedient, and might have endangered the spread of the faith. Yet no one had proved the usefulness of modern slavery, which unquestionably brought war and anarchy to Africa, and a tyrannical system to America. Paley's doctrine of utility acquires its cutting edge from the forward motion of history:

The great revolution which seems preparing in the western world, may probably conduce, and who knows, but that it is designed to accelerate the fall of this abominable tyranny: and when this contest, and the

30. ibid., pp. 5–6, 12–13, 17–18, 26–30; Arthur W. Evans, *Warburton and the Warburtonians; A Study in Some Eighteenth-Century Controversies* (London, 1932), *passim*. Warburton said that the Church should take some lessons from the Jesuits on converting the heathen.

31. Stephen, *History of English Thought*, I, pp. 410–11; II, pp. 122–3.

passions that attend it are no more, there will succeed a season for reflecting, whether a legislature, which had so long lent its assistance to the support of an institution replete with human misery, was fit to be trusted with an empire, the most extensive that ever obtained in any age or quarter of the world.[32]

By 1785, when these words were published, anti-slavery already provided a meeting ground for men whose beliefs ranged from orthodox to Quaker and Unitarian. Because British Protestantism had absorbed so much rationalism, and had rested its case against scepticism on man's benevolence and capacity for progress, British abolitionists could sound like radical *philosophes* and yet think of themselves as vindicators of religion. As we have suggested, however, the very latitudinarianism which gave man a more favourable picture of himself and the world, furnished little basis for more than a private protest against evils that had lost the infinite horror of sin. A fully developed anti-slavery movement could hardly arise from a subjective sentimentalism or a frigid utilitarianism without the stimulus of a new apocalypse.

In the early 1770s John Wesley read a good bit of moral philosophy, and was deeply troubled by what he discovered. He could not even enjoy Captain Cook's *Voyages*, which he started to read with 'huge expectation'. The stories were absolutely incredible: 'Men and women coupling together in the face of the sun, and in the sight of scores of people! . . . Hume or Voltaire might believe this, but I cannot.'[33] Wesley was not so incredulous, however, when he came upon a pamphlet by Anthony Benezet, 'an honest Quaker',

on that execrable sum of all villanies commonly called the Slave Trade. I read of nothing like it in the heathen world, whether ancient or modern. And it infinitely exceeds, in every instance of barbarity, what ever Christian slaves suffer in Mahometan countries.[34]

32. William Paley, *The Principles of Moral and Political Philosophy* (London, 1785), introduction, pp. 196–8.

33. John Wesley, *The Journal of the Revd. John Wesley ...* (London, 1836), pp. 286, 686–7.

34. ibid., p. 656.

When Wesley turned in 1774 to write his own tract on Negro slavery, he quoted descriptions of Africa which gave an 'image of pure nature', and which revived 'the idea of our first parents . . . the world in its primitive state'. These native Africans did not couple together in the face of the sun, but rather behaved like potential Methodists. If they spent perhaps too much time reclining at ease in their lovely paradise, they punished adultery with proper severity, and worshipped God regularly. They were capable of that moral sensibility which Wesley failed to find in the captains of slave ships:

Do you never *feel* another's pain? Have you no sympathy? . . . No pity for the miserable? When you saw the flowing eyes, the heaving breasts, or the bleeding sides or tortured limbs of your fellow-creatures, was you a stone, or a brute? . . . Did not one tear drop from your eye?[35]

Even after the most unspeakable hardships the slaves retained an acute degree of human feeling, and in America one might see 'mothers hanging over their daughters, bedewing their naked breasts with tears, and daughters clinging to their parents, till the whipper soon obliges them to part'.[36]

To primitivism and sensibility, Wesley added an idea derived from deductive science: since the same causes always produce similar effects, 'the dreadful consequence of slavery is the same amongst every people and in every nation where it prevails'. No argument of utility could justify debasing a rational creature to the level of a brute. Like the Abbé Raynal, Wesley would prefer that the West Indies remained uncultivated, or be 'sunk in the depth of the sea, than that they should be cultivated at so high a price, as the violation of justice, mercy and truth',[37] But Wesley's most compelling thoughts had nothing to do with reason or nature. His ultimate message was that the sins of this world would soon be judged. Every merchant,

35. John Wesley, *Thoughts upon Slavery* (Philadelphia, 1772), pp. 10–14, 52.

36. ibid., p. 23.

37. ibid., pp. 39–40, 56, 58 ff. But Wesley also argued, on the basis of his own observations in Georgia, that free white labour was feasible in semi-tropical climates (p. 42).

every investor, every owner of American property was deeply involved in guilt: 'Thy hands, thy bed, thy furniture, thy house, thy
lands are at present stained with blood.' The time for repentance was
at hand, and repentance could only be shown by emancipating the
Negro slaves.[38]

While Wesley's pamphlet was no less a part of the anti-slavery
movement than earlier works of Woolman, Sharp and Benezet, we
have included it here because it represents a religious source of abolitionism that we have not yet discussed. On the surface, it would
appear that the Methodist and Evangelical[39] movements had nothing
to contribute to secular reform. The trend towards natural religion,
which did so much to enlarge views of human rights and capabilities,
was one of the chief targets of the revivalists. They were revolting not
only against moral decay and the laxness of a worldly and self-con-
tented clergy, but also against the entire drift of British thought from
Locke and Tillotson to Shaftesbury, Bolingbroke and Hutcheson.
When it became difficult to distinguish supposedly orthodox divines
from the most disreputable deists, it was clear that old doctrines had
been drained of all meaning, and that theology had become a lifeless
exercise in abstract speculation.[40]

38. ibid., pp. 51–5. Wesley's tolerance is shown by the fact that he reprinted Bishop Warburton's sermon of 1766, although Warburton had
bitterly attacked Wesley as a fanatic. Wesley's anti-slavery stand was
approved by many who were unsympathetic towards Methodism, and was
highly praised by the Gentleman's Magazine (XLV [March 1775], p. 137).

39. For clarity I shall follow the custom of using 'Evangelical' for the
non-Methodist movement within the Church of England, and 'evangelical'
for the revivalist movements as a whole. Hence John Venn and John Newton
would be Evangelicals, but Jonathan Edwards an evangelical. Yet as John
Henry Overton remarked, all Methodists would have wished to be called
Evangelical, and all Evangelicals, despite their wishes, were called Methodists (The Evangelical Revival in the Eighteenth Century [London, 1891], p.
45).

40. Stephen, History of English Thought, II, pp. 381–3, 413–16, 423–4;
James Stephen, Essays in Ecclesiastical Biography (4th ed., London, 1849),
pp. 378–9, 399; Leonard E. Elliott-Binns, The Early Evangelicals: A Religious and Social Study (London, 1953), pp. 83–115; Haroutunian, Piety
versus Moralism, pp. 10 ff.; Overton, Evangelical Revival, pp. 1–7; Leslie
Stephen, Hours in a Library, Second Series (London, 1876), pp. 108,
117–19, 149.

But in another sense, the revivalists' attempt to reinvigorate traditional beliefs, and to find new symbols and methods to express human emotions, was closely related to certain trends in natural religion. Methodists were not the only men of their age to be wracked with doubt and fear of meaninglessness; to turn inwards, to their nonrational experience, in search of moral certainty; or to place great value in sincerity, earnestness, and a life of useful service. But with the revivalists these impulses were raised to a heightened pitch, and proceeded from what Sir James Stephen called a 'tension of the soul which admitted neither lassitude nor relaxation'.[41] And, of course, they interpreted man's predicament within the old framework of sin and grace, and consequently spoke a language which was meaningful to those who had never heard of Locke or David Hume.

If the philosophy of benevolence was associated with an expanded view of man's capacity for virtue, the very core of evangelicalism was a renewed conviction of original sin. One of the reasons why early Methodists shocked their contemporaries, and were accused of being Puritan zealots was that they really believed in a doctrine which had long been smothered by sweet reassurances.[42] To some extent, this rediscovery of man's utter alienation from the sources of righteousness fortified traditional sanctions for slavery. But now sin was not conceived primarily as a metaphysical corruption, or even as a judicial punishment. William Law, who left so deep an impression on Wesley's generation, spoke of the shallowness and insufficiency of what most men considered a devout life. For Wesley sin was above all a psychological fact which one discovered as he became discontented with himself and began to struggle against evil inclinations.[43] It by no means diminished personal responsibility or prevented even natural men, thanks to the mercy of 'prevenient grace', from knowing

41. Stephen, *Essays in Ecclesiastical Biography*, p. 399.

42. Arthur C. McGiffert, *Protestant Thought before Kant* (New York, 1961), pp. 159–64; Fairchild, *Religious Trends*, II, pp. 118–19; Stephen, *Essays in Ecclesiastical Biography*, p. 399.

43. William Law, *A Serious Call to a Devout and Holy Life* (London, 1893), pp. 13–18, 26–8; A. Skevington Wood, *Thomas Haweis, 1734–1820* (London, 1957), pp. 6–7; Stephen, *History of English Thought*, II, pp. 396–407; Harald Lindström, *Wesley and Sanctification: A Study in the Docrine of Salvation* (Stockholm, 1946), pp. 20–35.

the spirit of the law or seeking repentance and justification. As an Arminian, Wesley held that Christ had died for all men, and that only those who wilfully resisted salvation would be condemned to eternal bondage in hell.[44] George Whitefield, who accepted the institution of Negro slavery, thought that man's sin was so vile that God saved only a predestined few. Yet Whitefield used dramatic preaching to change men's dispositions, and the Calvinistic followers of Jonathan Edwards increasingly defined sin as selfishness.[45] While some philosophers were coming to see self-interest as a positive and calculable force which turned the wheels of society, for many evangelicals it became the very essence of sin. And men who thought that self-interest was a source of indeterminate evil could hardly believe that a planter's concern for his property was an adequate protection for his slaves.

When sin was interpreted as self-centredness, true virtue was to be found in a transcendence of the self or, in Edwards's terms, in a disposition to love 'Being in general'. In effect, therefore, the reaffirmation of original sin did not necessarily mean a repudiation of the philosophy of benevolence. In Edwards's account of regenerate man, Hutcheson's moral sense is simply spiritualized and raised to a higher level; the saint automatically delights in benevolence and holy beauty, and recoils from sin.[46] Although Edwards did his utmost to keep holiness distinct from human notions of morality, his so-called New Divinity was slowly permeated with the ideas of its Arminian opponents. For Edwards's son, the ultimate purpose of creation was human happiness; for Samuel Hopkins, true virtue lay in disinterested benevolence towards mankind.[47]

44. Lindström, *Wesley and Sanctification*, pp. 30–36, 44–5; Abel Stevens, *The History of the Religious Movement of the Eighteenth Century Called Methodism* (New York, 1858–9), I, pp. 148–9.

45. Smith, *Changing Conceptions of Original Sin*, pp. 10–85.

46. Haroutunian, *Piety versus Moralism*, p. 43; Jonathan Edwards, *The Nature of True Virtue* (ed. by William K. Frankena, Ann Arbor paperback ed., Ann Arbor, Mich., 1960), *passim*.

47. Haroutunian, *Piety versus Moralism*, pp. 58–66, 82–7, 92–5, 151–2; Wright, *Beginnings of Unitarianism*, pp. 115–16; Oliver Wendell Elsbree, 'Samuel Hopkins and His Doctrine of Benevolence', *New England Quarterly*, VIII (December 1935), pp. 534 ff.

Benevolence, or a habitual disposition of love, was also the ultimate ideal of Methodism. Wesley described New Birth as an instantaneous transformation of the soul. He distinguished, however, a number of logical and temporal stages in the drama of salvation. Grace was free and boundless, which meant that any man, regardless of his sins or station in life, was potentially capable of holiness. After a period of contrition and inner struggle, he might suddenly be liberated from the guilt of his sins. This external justification brought profound inner changes, which for Wesley were the vital heart of religion. Sanctification meant the restoration of the soul to its 'primitive health', to its original freedom for growth towards perfection. This New Birth did not result in a complete eradication of sin, or in a freedom from moral law. A man might be assured of his own sanctity, but he might also fall from the state of grace. There was an obligation, then, to strive towards perfect love and holiness, and good works were both signs and conditions of this gradual progress.[48]

The conviction that man might actually achieve a sanctified life was the power which lay behind the Methodists' remarkable organizational activity, the love feasts and watch nights that gave social expression to the converts' deepest yearnings, the joyful hymn-singing, the outpouring of printed tracts, and the open-air preaching which brought tears to the sooty eyes of thousands of British miners. Most of the Evangelicals within the Church of England did not share Wesley's faith in perfectionism. The aristocrats who clustered around Lady Huntingdon, and listened to Whitefield at her invitation, were unsympathetic to the idea that any collier might be a saint. Even the clergy who had begun independently to preach of sin and the forgiveness of Christ were troubled by the Methodists' invasion of local parishes and by their challenge to Church discipline and order. But despite differences in doctrine and policy, Methodists, Evangelicals

48. Lindström, *Wesley and Sanctification*, pp. 19, 44–5, 59, 76–84, 100–115, 116–18, 145–54, 205; Overton, *Evangelical Revival*, pp. 23–5; McGiffert, *Protestant Thought*, p. 160; Wade C. Barclay, *History of Methodist Missions*, pt 1 (New York, 1949–50), I, pp. xxii–xxiii; Robert Southey, *The Life of Wesley, and the Rise and Progress of Methodism* (New York, 1855), II, pp. 69–70. One may note that the nineteenth-century abolitionist, A. A. Phelps, said that carrying out the decision for immediate emancipation was like acquiring sanctification after conversion.

and American revivalists were engaged in a similar revolt against abstract and ossified theology; they strove to awaken men to the inadequacy of a worldly life, and to make the quest for true holiness a constant concern; they held up a common ideal of piety, typified by such saintly men as David Brainerd, the American missionary and associate of Jonathan Edwards; and they associated sanctity with a selfless effort to save the millions who lived in darkness and poverty. Because eighteenth century revivalism was international and was pre-occupied with similar problems of religious apathy and social upheaval, it produced complex patterns of influence and reaction which no historian has yet unravelled.[49]

But even if we should conclude that there were certain similar tendencies in evangelicalism, the philosophy of benevolence, and the literary quest for sensibility and the sublime, what has this to do with Negro slavery? Revivalism did not lead automatically to pleas for emancipation. Religious conviction did not keep Whitefield or Jonathan Edwards from owning slaves, nor did it alter the views of the Evangelical president of the Board of Trade, Lord Dartmouth. John Newton did not abandon his 'genteel employment' as captain of a slave ship when he became a pious Christian; he simply ran a tighter ship and had divine communion on deck, while the Negroes groaned in their chains below.

In America, to be sure, the Great Awakening reinvigorated the

49. Stevens, *History of Religious Movement*, I, pp. 167–217; Overton, *Evangelical Revival*, pp. 40–44; Stephen, *Essays in Ecclesiastical Biography*, pp. 440–45; Stephen, *History of English Thought*, II, pp. 138–43; Wood, *Thomas Haweis*, pp. 10–21, 91–7; Lodwick Hartley, *William Cowper: The Continuing Revaluation* (Chapel Hill, 1960), pp. 14–16, 23–34; Frederick C. Gill, *The Romantic Movement and Methodism: A Study of English Romanticism and the Evangelical Revival* (London, 1937), pp. 14–33, 56–7, 130–34; Michael Kraus, *The Atlantic Civilization: Eighteenth-Century Origins* (Ithaca, N.Y., 1949), pp. 45, 63; Maldwyn Edwards, *John Wesley and the Eighteenth Century; A Study of His Social and Political Influence* (London, 1955), pp. 13, 23; Michael Hennell, *John Venn and the Clapham Sect* (London, 1958), pp. 14, 105–6, 138; Rufus M. Jones, *The Later Periods of Quakerism* (London, 1921), I, pp. 265–87; E. R. Taylor, *Methodism and Politics, 1791–1851* (Cambridge, 1935), pp. 15–27. I am also indebted to John D. Walsh for furnishing me with a copy of his study of 'The Magdalene Evangelicals'.

belief in spiritual equality and increased the number of Negro slaves in Christian fellowship. Preachers like Samuel Davies, the leader of the Presbyterian revival in Virginia, made a special effort to convert slaves, but never doubted the compatibility of servitude with Christian liberty.[50] By the time of the Revolution a master might have various motives for freeing his slaves; it would appear that a few Methodists were persuaded by Wesley's uncompromising stand. Yet Thomas Coke discovered that his life would be in constant peril during his American missions unless he moderated Wesley's antislavery principles. And other Methodist leaders would soon find that the issue was far too delicate for a church which was primarily concerned with conversion and expansion. The main thrust of eighteenth century revivalism ended with the missionary, not the abolitionist.[51]

There was an important connexion between evangelical religion and anti-slavery, but it was generally blurred, as in the case of Wesley, by an intermixture of mild rationalism, primitivism and sensibility.[52] Early abolitionist leaders tended to be men who had absorbed many of the latitudinarian values, but who were emotionally inspired by the evangelical revivals. Even Quakers and Uni-

50. Wesley M. Gewehr, *The Great Awakening in Virginia, 1740–1790* (Durham, N.C., 1930), pp. 235–8. Winthrop D. Jordan, in his forthcoming book on attitudes towards the Negro in colonial America, suggests that the Great Awakening re-emphasized the spiritual equality of whites and Negroes, provided a new ground for acculturation and a sharing of religious experience, and promoted a self-scrutiny which led many white Americans to recognize the racial problem for the first time (chs 5 and 7).

51. Barclay, *History of Methodist Missions*, I, pp. 100–109, 144, 268–9; II, pp. 7–8, 50–57; Southey, *Life of Wesley*, II, p. 258; Kenneth L. Caroll, 'Religious Influences on the Manumission of Slaves in Caroline, Dorchester, and Talbot Counties', *Maryland Historical Magazine*, LVI (June 1961), pp. 187–93; Wood, *Thomas Haweis*, pp. 195–207; Donald G. Mathews, *Slavery and Methodism: A Chapter in American Morality, 1780–1845* (Princeton, 1965), pp. 3–29. On many reform issues American Methodists were far more compromising than their British brethren.

52. It is perhaps significant that Wesley's interest in slavery followed a sudden renewal of the internecine conflict between Methodists and Calvinistic Evangelicals (Stevens, *History of Religious Movement*, II, pp. 31–2).

tarians could not help but be impressed by the astonishing success of Methodist organization and publicity; by groups of 'earnest Christians' who were united by the highest ideals of purity and benevolence; and by the thought that, if the lives of so many people could be transformed in so short a time, the millennium might indeed be at hand.

But above all, revivalism provided a model of personal decision and commitment. When John Newton finally chose to denounce the slave trade, it was not to express a private opinion or even to enlighten the general public. No other Evangelical minister had established such a record of ascent from depravity. Early in life Newton had been corrupted by reading Shaftesbury, and had become a freethinker who made sport of God. As a sailor he had been toughened by merciless flogging and by being cast in chains. He had been, by his own confession, the 'willing slave' of every evil, which included sexual indulgence on the coast of Africa. But after reading Young's *Night Thoughts*, and surviving a terrifying storm at sea, Newton became increasingly devout. Illness required him to leave the slave trade, and his inclination towards the ministry was reinforced by hearing Whitefield preach. But while Newton used his experiences in the Guinea trade to symbolize his early depravity, his upward climb was no more complete than was that of his country. He still considered the slave trade to have been 'the line of life which Divine Providence had allotted me'. He had been in African villages, and knew that the people were thoroughly human. He knew how slaves were obtained. He had seen the branding, the flogging, the use of thumbscrews, the division of Negro girls among the sailors. He had seen enough of West Indian plantations to conclude that they were worse than the slave ships. But Newton had never had the least scruple about the justice of the trade, nor had any friend suggested that it was not a legitimate employment. 'Inattention and interest', he later wrote, simply prevented the evil from being perceived. No one realized that not even highway robbery had 'a more direct tendency to efface the moral sense, to rob the heart of every gentle and humane disposition, and to harden it, like steel, against all impressions of sensibility'. Newton's contribution to anti-slavery was, therefore, a public confession, a decision to speak when he knew that further silence would be 'criminal'.[53] And his uncertain progress towards this decision was virtually an allegory of the progress of Great Britain.

53. Bernard Martin, *John Newton: A Biography* (London, 1950), *passim*; Stephen, *Essays in Ecclesiastical Biography*, pp. 400–411; John Newton, *Thoughts upon the African Slave Trade* (2nd ed., London, 1788), pp. 1–4, 7, 14–16, 20–24.

13

The Enlightenment as a
Source of Anti-Slavery Thought:
The Ambivalence of Rationalism

WE have often been told that the Enlightenment emancipated the European mind from a slavish subservience to authority, tradition and superstition; that it marked an age when reason unveiled the truths of nature, vindicated the rights of man, and pointed the way to human perfectibility and happiness. We might well assume that such revolutionary tendencies would lead directly to militant abolitionism. Yet the traditional justifications for slavery had survived the scrutiny of Humanists and seventeenth-century rationalists. Famous philosophers had shown that a defence of slavery could be reconciled with belief in abstract natural law and natural rights. Hobbes and Locke, who established much of the framework for future social thought, also openly sanctioned human bondage. And one must remember that it was in the Age of Enlightenment that the African slave trade and West Indian plantation enjoyed their golden years.

No intellectual movement is free from imprints of the past, and the process of secularization, as we have already seen, does not always lead to reform. Anti-slavery writers sometimes complained that even the *philosophes* who boldly attacked most injustices were curiously blind to Negro slavery.[1] Still more disturbing was the fact that many of the key ideas of the Enlightenment could easily be turned against pleas for the abolition of slavery. If human bondage was, as Voltaire said, 'as ancient as war, and war as human nature', then the insti-

1. 'Extracts from the Voyages of a French Officer', *Gentleman's Magazine*, XLV (1775), p. 168; Mercer Cook, 'Jean-Jacques Rousseau and the Negro', *Journal of Negro History*, XXI (July 1936), p. 294; Guillaume-Thomas Raynal, *Histoire philosophique et politique des établissemens et du commerce des Européens dans les deux Indes* (Genève, 1781), VI, pp. 105–6.

tution might be justified by the doctrine of sufficient reason, or be seen as a part of the natural economy of forces.[2] Gordon Turnbull, who drew heavily on Hume and Montesquieu and who pictured his abolitionist opponents as religious fanatics, condensed in a single passage the conservative side of the Enlightenment:

Negro slavery appears, then, to be, as far as reason can judge, one of those indispensable and necessary links, in the great chain of causes and events, which cannot and indeed ought not to be broken; or, in other words, a *part* of the stupendous, admirable, and perfect *whole,* which, if taken away, would leave a chasm, not [to] be filled up by all the wit or the wisdom of erring and presumptuous man.[3]

Repudiation of original sin did not necessarily lead to a sanguine view of human nature or to an abandonment of the ancient distinction between absolute natural law, under which all men were free and equal, and relative natural law, which justified slavery and other forms of subordination. According to Voltaire, domination would be 'a mere chimera, an absurdity which no one would think of', in an ideal world that supplied an easy and certain subsistence for every man. But unfortunately, 'the human race, constituted as it is, cannot subsist unless there be an infinite number of useful individuals possessed of no property at all'. If equality was in one sense 'natural', in the actual world there must always be a class who command and a class who obey.[4] Unlike other animals, said the Marquis de Mirabeau, man projects his greed into the future, where it encounters no

2. Voltaire, *Philosophical Dictionary* (London, 1824), VI, p. 104. Although Voltaire notes that the extremes of slavery and liberty have often coexisted, and that the institution was accepted by early Christians, he adds caustically, 'Those who call themselves whites and Christians proceed to purchase Negroes at a good market, in order to sell them dear in America' (ibid., p. 106). His own position, however, was equivocal; and he was accused of believing in the inferiority of Negroes, and of writing a letter in support of the slave trade (see Edward D. Seeber, *Anti-Slavery Opinion in France during the Second Half of the Eighteenth Century* [Baltimore, 1937], pp. 65–6).

3. Gordon Turnbull, *An Apology for Negro Slavery, or the West-Indian Planters Vindicated from the Charge of Inhumanity* (2nd ed., London, 1786), pp. 34–5.

4. Voltaire, *Philosophical Dictionary,* III, pp. 107–11.

limits: 'Il est avide de tout.' It was to be expected that fratricidal conflict should have divided the first two men of equal age and rank; and while it was true that man possessed an instinct for sociability and brotherhood, his cupidity made it necessary that the first laws of society bring a division of goods and hence of power.[5] J. Bellon de Saint-Quentin held to a more traditional view of sin, but his picture of man's nature echoed common themes of the Enlightenment: 'He has become a slave not only of sin, the Devil, and the world, but also of his own mind, of his body, of his senses, and generally of all the objects which surround him.' For this reason he concluded, servitude was not only a necessary modification of absolute natural law, but a useful instrument for promoting the public welfare.[6]

When the most rigid social stratification prevailed through all of Europe, one had to be careful about holding that slavery violated the Golden Rule or the law of nature. Most of the *philosophes* followed the example of Aquinas, and argued that if equality was the first intention of nature, inequality was natural in a secondary sense of being necessary for the order and well-being of society.[7] D'Alembert flatly said equality was a delusion; Diderot was not so sure, but thought the question could not be safely examined in a monarchy.[8] Yet it was monarchs like Joseph II of Austria who tried to extend to the lowest serfs the protections of a centralized state; and throughout much of Europe it was the landed nobility who said that the central government had no right to interfere in the relation between lord and

5. Victor Riqueti de Mirabeau, *L'Ami des hommes, ou traité de la population* (5th ed., Hamburg, 1760), I, pp. 2–4; III, pp. 333–4.

6. J. Bellon de Saint-Quentin, *Dissertation sur la traité et le commerce des nègres* (Paris, 1764), pp. 18–19. Saint-Quentin repeated the ancient argument that since slavery was authorized by *jus gentium*, it could not be repugnant to *jus naturale*.

7. This was true, for example, of D'Holbach, though not of Morelly, Mably or, of course, Rousseau (see Paul Hazard, *European Thought in the Eighteenth Century, from Montesquieu to Lessing* [tr. by J. Lewis May, Meridian paperback ed., Cleveland, 1963], pp. 176–7; and John Herman Randall, Jr, *The Career of Philosophy: From the Middle Ages to the Enlightenment* [New York, 1962], pp. 962–3).

8. Arthur M. Wilson, 'The Development and Scope of Diderot's Political Thought', in *Studies on Voltaire and the Eighteenth Century*, XXIV/XXVII (Geneva, 1963), p. 1874.

peasant, that the peasants would be content were it not for outside agitators, that unless peasants were coerced to work they would become idle, drunken and dangerous. During the eighteenth century the European nobility did much to popularize arguments that would soon be used in defence of colonial slavery. And their powerful counter-offensive to protect and extend their ancient privileges was justified by appeals to traditional liberties, constitutional rights and the virtues of self-government.[9] In America similar appeals from provincial legislatures would be fused with the radical philosophy of natural rights; but precisely because equality in America was not a delusion, and there was no need to associate liberal reform with centralized authority, any localized oppression was peculiarly invulnerable. It was an unfortunate fact that Negro slavery was guarded not only by ancient theories of inequality, but also by the rights of private property and the traditional liberties of colonies and states.

Local varieties of subordination might also find positive sanction in a philosophy that emphasized empirical facts, the determining influence of environment, and the utility and inter-relationship of established institutions. Although Montesquieu attacked the traditional justifications for slavery, he conceded that the institution would have a rational basis in a despotic state, whose subjects would have nothing to lose by selling themselves into bondage. And if slavery would serve no useful function in Europe, where there were sufficient inducements for voluntary labour, Montesquieu thought it might be founded on natural reason in tropical countries, where the heat made men slothful and unwilling to do heavy work except for the fear of punishment.[10]

Insofar as European thought moved from abstract, universal principles towards an appreciation of the concrete, the variable and the useful, it furnished new weapons for the defenders of colonial sla-

9. Robert R. Palmer, *The Age of the Democratic Revolution: A Political History of Europe and America, 1760–1800* (Princeton, 1959), pp. 387–96, and *passim.*

10. Charles Louis de Secondat de Montesquieu, *Oeuvres complètes de Montesquieu* (publiées sous la direction de M. André Masson, Paris, 1950), I (tome i), pp. 287, 331–3.

very.[11] From Montesquieu such apologists learned that there was really no need to reconcile involuntary labour with natural law or the social compact.[12] They pointed out that one could not apply European notions of liberty and justice to Negro bondage without resorting to fanciful metaphysics. It was simply an objective fact that the Negroes purchased in Africa were slaves; no one could possibly know the hidden motives behind each African war and every act of enslavement. As in any commercial transaction, much had to be assumed on faith. In any event, Africa was so despotic that Negroes had nothing to lose by becoming slaves and everything to gain by being shipped to America. Having no understanding of true liberty, they would be content so long as proper discipline kept them in their place. As Montesquieu had suggested, coercion was a necessary inducement to labour in tropical climates, but in actual fact there was a nicely tuned balance between the master's self-interest and the slave's aspirations for happiness. Indeed, 'slavery' was a mere word that had misleading connotations; the actuality was a reciprocal relationship between human beings similar to that between lord and peasant or master and apprentice, except, of course, that slaves lived in luxurious abundance compared to European peasants and workers.[13]

11. For a searching discussion of the origin of ideas that were used against the natural rights philosophy, see Elie Halévy, *The Growth of Philosophic Radicalism* (tr. by Mary Morris, Beacon paperback ed., Boston, 1955), pp. 3–155.

12. For the ambivalent nature of Montesquieu's influence on the slavery controversy, see F. T. H. Fletcher, 'Montesquieu's Influence on Anti-Slavery Opinion in England', *Journal of Negro History*, XVIII (October 1933), pp. 414–26; Russell P. Jameson, *Montesquieu et l'esclavage: étude sur les origines de l'opinion antiesclavagiste en France au XVIII siècle* (Paris, 1911), pp. 306–7, 340–47. For typical pro-slavery uses of Montesquieu, see Turnbull, *Apology for Negro Slavery*, pp. 7–8; [Edward Long], *The History of Jamaica, or, General Survey of the Antient and Modern State of that Island* (London, 1774), II, pp. 476–7; Thomas R. R. Cobb, *Inquiry into the Law of Negro Slavery* (Philadelphia, 1858), p. 13.

13. *Gentleman's Magazine*, V (February 1735), pp . 91–2; [Arthur Lee], *An Essay in Vindication of the Continental Colonies of America* (London, 1764), p. 25; Turnbull, *Apology for Negro Slavery*, pp. 5–8; [Long], *History of Jamaica*, II, pp. 401–3; 'The African Slave Trade Defended: And CORRUPTION the Worst of Slaveries', *London Magazine*, IX (October

Even writers who expressed sympathy for the Negro slave and who agreed that the institution was wrong in the abstract were apt to conclude that a necessary evil is not unmixed with blessings. One could take the hard-boiled approach of Edward Bancroft:

In this state there is no medium; either the minds of slaves must be depressed by abject slavery, or the lives of their masters are in imminent danger. ... Many things ... which are repugnant to humanity, may be excused, on account of their necessity for self-preservation.

But more common was the plea offered in 1746 by the *London Magazine*:

But allowing some Justice in, or, at least, a great deal of Necessity for, making Slaves of this sable Part of the Species; surely, I think, Christianity, Gratitude, or, at least, good Policy, is concern'd in using them well, and in abridging them ... of several brutal and scandalous Customs.[14]

The attitudes of Edmund Burke are important because they were partly an extension of the ideas of Montesquieu and also represented a turning-point in the philosophy of the Enlightenment. Nothing could have been more repugnant to Burke's thought than militant abolitionism. Anyone who regarded abstract reasoning on natural rights as 'the great Serbonian bog', who worshipped stability and continuity, who looked on existing institutions as the products of purposeful experience and the unconscious wisdom of past gener-

1740), pp. 493–4; [Robert Norris], *A Short Account of the African Slave Trade* (Liverpool, 1787), *passim*; Lord Rodney to Lord Hawkesbury, March 1788, British Museum Add. MSS, 38,416, fols. 72–6; [Anon.], *Considerations upon the Fatal Consequences of Abolishing the Slave Trade* (London, 1789), *passim*; Saint-Quentin, *Dissertation sur la traité et le commerce des nègres*, pp. 19–21, 63–6, 70–80; [Chambon], *Le commerce de l'Amérique par Marseille* (Avignon, 1764), II, pp. 195–8. This last work also presented anti-slavery arguments, leaving it to the reader to decide the justice of slavery for himself.

14. Edward Bancroft, *An Essay on the Natural History of Guiana, in South America* (London, 1769), pp. 367–8; 'Observations in Several Voyages and Travels in America', *London Magazine*, XV (July 1746), pp. 324–5.

ations, and who feared the 'inconveniences' of sudden change far more than the persistence of injustice, could not help but find a certain prescriptive sanction for slavery. Yet the American colonies clearly lacked that large number of 'low and middling men of a free condition, and that beautiful gradation from the highest to the lowest, where the transitions all the way are almost imperceptible', which were necessary conditions for a secure and prosperous society. And, as Burke noted as early as 1757, nothing could justify a trade 'which must depend for its support upon the annual murder of several thousands of innocent men . . . but the necessity we are under of peopling our colonies, and the consideration that the slaves we buy were in the same condition in Africa'.[15]

For a time Burke looked upon Negro slavery as an empirical fact, as part of the unique institutional structure of the colonies. Its victims suffered more than 'any people in their condition . . . in any other part of the world . . . in any other period of time'. But Burke realized that Negroes were 'stubborn and intractable for the most part, and that they must be ruled with the rod of iron. I would have them ruled, but not crushed with it.' Severe oppression was both dangerous and uneconomical. In time of war the slave colonies were particularly vulnerable to insurrection; and an improvement in the Negroes' condition

15. Leslie Stephen, *History of English Thought in the Eighteenth Century* (reprint ed., New York, 1949), II, pp. 224–33; Alfred Cobban, *Edmund Burke and the Revolt against the Eighteenth Century* (London, 1929), *passim*; C. P. Courtney, *Montesquieu and Burke* (Oxford, 1963), pp. 96–7 ; [Edmund Burke?], *An Account of the European Settlements in America*, II (London, 1757), pp. 118, 128–9. I am aware that modern scholarship attributes the last-named work to William Burke, a friend and kinsman of Edmund. There seems to be agreement, however, that Edmund probably wrote parts of the original manuscript and doubtless had a hand in revising it. Contemporaries like Arthur Lee assumed the book reflected Burke's opinions on slavery; I see no reason for not making the same assumption. One may note that in the 1770s Burke was defending the interests of Bristol slave traders in Parliament (see Thomas H. D. Mahoney, 'Edmund Burke as Historian', *The Burke Newsletter*, III [Winter and Spring 1961–2], p. 85; Carl B. Cone, *Burke and the Nature of Politics* [Lexington, Ky, 1957], pp. 29–30, 267; D. Bryant, *Edmund Burke and his Literary Friends* [St Louis, 1939], p. 104; *The Correspondence of Edmund Burke* [ed. by John A. Woods, Chicago, 1963], IV, pp. 60–62; [Lee], *Essay in Vindication of the Continental Colonies*, pp. 15, 21).

would not only increase security but lessen costs of production and enlarge the American market for British goods. Such reforms, however, would have to be made slowly and in accordance with what Montesquieu called the 'esprit général' of the colonies, which included climate, laws, manners and established usages. If some day slavery were to be abolished, it should be done by the Americans themselves; yet even that was probably not desirable, since 'slaves are often much attached to their masters. A general wild offer of liberty would not always be accepted.'[16] As late as 1792 Burke thought 'the cause of humanity would be far more benefited by the continuance of the trade and servitude, regulated and reformed, than by the total destruction of both or either'. Some twelve years earlier, however, he had drafted an elaborate plan to make both the African trade and colonial slavery humane, moral and antiseptic.[17] Under ideal circumstances, Burke's concern for details of regulation and his views on the flexible use of sovereign power might have fulfilled his new objective of eradicating slavery through gradual amelioration. But as Burke knew, circumstances were never ideal; and, eventually, time alone would give a presumption of legitimacy to the worst injustices. It would seem, in view of later events, that a power and determination sufficient to carry out Burke's long-range plan could more easily have abolished in a few years what he termed an 'incurable evil', and with probably far less 'inconvenience' for both masters and slaves.[18]

16. [Burke?], *Account of European Settlements*, II, pp. 119–20, 124–8, 130–32; Courtney, *Montesquieu and Burke*, pp. 96–7. A somewhat exaggerated impression of Burke's contribution to the anti-slavery cause is given in James Prior, *Memoir of the Life & Character of the Right Hon. Edmund Burke . . .* (London, 1826), I, pp. 368–9; II, pp. 33, 191. Burke's position was always governed by Montesquieu's assumption that, whatever the evils of slavery, civil law could prevent its worst abuses and dangers (Montesquieu, *Oeuvres*, I, pp. 336, 342, 345). This was, it must be stressed, the assumption which defenders of colonial slavery did their most to foster.

17. Edmund Burke, 'A Letter to the Right Hon. Henry Dundas, One of His Majesty's Principal Secretaries of State; with the Sketch of a Negro Code', in *The Works of the Right Honourable Edmund Burke* (Boston, 1866), pp. 257–89.

18. This was, in effect, the main lesson learned by British abolitionists over a period of forty years. See my articles, 'The Emergence of Immediatism in

Yet it would be misleading to conclude that the attitudes expressed by Burke were confined to a small group of conservatives. The ideal of social equilibrium, the belief in the interrelationship and slow evolution of institutions, and the assumption that practical ethics were governed by utility and environment – were all part of the eighteenth-century climate of opinion. They were worked into justifications for American slavery, but also permeated the thought of reformers. Even the radical *Amis des Noirs* feared immediate emancipation, and searched for a scheme that would slowly transform the slave into a free labourer.[19] Had not the great Montesquieu warned against sudden or large-scale emancipations, recalling that when Volsinien slaves had won both liberty and political power, they had voted themselves the right to sleep with the brides of freeborn men?[20] The most enlightened of men agreed that benevolence and moral sensibility were all very well but could not be allowed to bring sudden changes that might break the delicate adjustment of natural and historical forces. Humanitarian zeal must be balanced by a respect for solid facts and for the testimony of calm and sensible men. Above all, one must preserve a sense of proportion and an expedient regard for the public interest. There were many forms of evil and oppression in even the most advanced nations; it would be sheer hypocrisy to blame

British and American Anti-Slavery Thought', *Mississippi Valley Historical Review*, XLIX (September 1962), pp. 209–30; 'James Cropper and the British Anti-Slavery Movement, 1821–1823', *Journal of Negro History*, XLV (October 1960), pp. 241–58; 'James Cropper and the British Anti-Slavery Movement, 1823–1833', *Journal of Negro History*, XLVI (July 1961), pp. 154–73.

19. Benjamn Frossard, *La cause des esclaves nègres et des habitans de la Guinée, portée au tribunal de la justice, de la religion, de la politique …*. (Lyon, 1789), I, pp. 17–20; J. P. Brissot de Warville, *An Oration upon the Necessity of Establishing at Paris a Society to Promote the Abolition of the Trade and Slavery of the Negroes* (Philadelphia, 1788), p. 142; Mitchell B. Garrett, *The French Colonial Question, 1789–1791* (Ann Arbor, 1916), p. 33; Léon Cahen, 'La Société des Amis des Noirs, et Condorcet', *La révolution française*, L (1906), pp. 481–97; Charles O. Hardy, *The Negro Question in the French Revolution* (Menasha, Wisc., 1919), pp. 56–7.

20. Montesquieu, *Oeuvres*, I (tome i), p. 345.

one class of property holders for the excesses of a few individuals or for desiring the valid goals of profit and public security.[21] Perhaps the enlightened mind's most typical response to the problem of slavery was to devise a plan like Burke's for the inspection and regulation of all phases of the system, from the African market to the daily life of the plantation; or to inaugurate administrative reforms in the manner of the Marquis de Pombal of Portugal and Charles III of Spain. Even the more dedicated abolitionists assumed that they could work towards their goal indirectly and without infringing on legitimate rights and interests; a single act, such as outlawing the slave trade, would set in motion a chain of forces that would lead irresistibly to freedom.[22]

There was, however, a far more explosive side to the ideas and tendencies of the Enlightenment. In 1748 a Jamaican physician named James Smith decided to experiment with the popular eighteenth-century device of satire. A believer in down-to-earth practicality and good sense, he was much disturbed by a proposed bill which would have allowed free Negroes and mulattoes to give evidence in court against members of their own class. To dramatize the danger of such an injudicious move, he wrote a petition that purported to come from 'Cudjoe', and to represent the sentiments of 160,000 slaves, 'unjustly and inhumanly detained in thraldom and bondage, in the island of Jamaica'. Thinking that the new law would give *them* the right to testify in all cases, the slaves looked forward to the vindication of 'our natural rights as men'. Soon they would imprison their 'Egyptian taskmasters', exterminate the Jews, and take possession of the promised land. James Smith may have thought it witty to sport with such ideas as a means of deflating do-goodery; but for the Jamaican assembly it was no laughing matter. After solemnly resolving that the petition was a false, scandalous, seditious libel, which could only excite mutiny and insurrection,

21. See, for example, the letter written for the London *Public Advertiser*, in all probability by Benjamin Franklin, and reprinted by Verner Crane, 'Benjamin Franklin on Slavery and American Liberties', *Pennsylvania Magazine of History and Biography*, LXII (January 1938), pp. 1–11.

22. I have documented this point in my article, 'Emergence of Immediatism', pp. 215–18.

they asked the governor to prosecute the good doctor without delay.[23]

For all its respect for utility, moderation and rational order, the Enlightenment was a challenge to traditional authority. Like the Protestant Reformation, it was based on a conviction that history had somehow polluted the sources of truth and virtue. But where the Protestant Reformers had searched for authentic standards in the revealed word of God, the men of the Enlightenment looked to an uncorrupted human nature.[24] The transition was epitomized in an argument in the *Gentleman's Magazine* in 1735: because 'Reason and Virtue are *natural* to the Mind of Man', the true explanation 'of our ancient Bigotry, and of our Ancestors being *Slaves to Principle or Faith*, was because they were *Slaves by Law and Power*.'[25]

We have already said that seventeenth-century British Protestantism announced many of the themes of the secular Enlightenment. In France, where the new philosophy had to fight for survival against an absolutist Church and State, its doctrines became at once more anticlerical and revolutionary. After the Glorious Revolution and the rise of latitudinarian religion, Englishmen had less need of picturing God as an abritrary tyrant whose authority and very existence must be denied. Their respect for historic liberties made them fundamentally unsympathetic to Voltaire's pronouncement that 'past times are as if they had never been. It is always necessary to start at the point at which one already stands, and at which nations have arrived.' Nevertheless, the *philosophes* bore a heavy debt to British deism and to the rational theology of men like Locke and Samuel Clarke; if their thought continued to carry the imprint of Cartesian rationalism, they were inspired by British books and they looked to England for examples of tolerance, public enlightenment and free institutions. It

23. *Journals of the Assembly of Jamaica*, IV (London, 1827), pp. 120–27.

24. Franklin L. Baumer, *Religion and the Rise of Scepticism* (New York, 1960), pp. 45–56, 67, 71; Ernst Cassirer, *The Philosophy of the Enlightenment* (tr. by Fritz Koelln and James P. Pettegrove, Beacon paperback ed., Boston, 1951), pp. 136, 141, 164–5.

25. 'Remarks on our Ancient Ecclesiastical Constitution' [reprinted from the *Daily Gazetteer*], *Gentleman's Magazine*, V (1735), p. 656.

was Voltaire who inaugurated the convention of using British and American Quakers as models of a simple and heart-warming virtue that stood in sharp contrast to the inhumanity of orthodox Christians.[26]

And there were ideas shared by *philosophes* and liberal British Protestants which directly challenged the traditional Christian view of slavery. God was a benevolent and constitutional ruler who desired the happiness of his subjects; He would not think of sanctioning perpetual and unmerited punishment of any kind. Because men possessed a natural capacity for virtue, their mistakes arose from superficial troubles, and could be better controlled by education and psychological adjustment than by coercive discipline. There was no sharp dualism between the material and spiritual realms; true freedom and harmony were not to be found in resignation and faith, but in gradual illumination of the mind, in eradication of error and superstition, and in leading a useful life. The test of a religion or philosophy was its tendency to promote virtue and happiness. If the patriarchs of the Old Testament possessed slaves, that was simply another crime to be added to their acts of incest, treachery, adultery and murder.

Although Montesquieu believed that the spirit of Christianity had eliminated bondage in Europe, Voltaire accumulated evidence to show that the Church had always accepted slavery, which was further proof of its contempt for human nature.[27] Ironically, pro-slavery writers like Saint-Quentin presented similar evidence to establish the legitimacy of perpetual servitude.[28] Since most British and American abolitionists would be devout Christians, they would meet this

26. Hazard, *European Thought in Eighteenth Century*, pp. 44–73; Preserved Smith, *A History of Modern Culture* (reprint ed., Gloucester, Mass., 1957), II, pp. 479–505, and *passim*; Henri Sée, *Les idées politiques en France au XVIIᵉ siècle* (Paris, 1923), *passim*; Sée, *L'Evolution de la pensée politique en France au XVIIIᵉ siècle* (Paris, 1925), pp. 33–51, 203–5; Cassirer, *Philosophy of the Enlightenment*, pp. 168, 174–5; George R. Havens, *The Age of Ideas: From Reaction to Revolution in Eighteenth-Century France* (New York, 1955), p. 165; Arthur M. Wilson, *Diderot: The Testing Years, 1713–1759* (New York, 1957), pp. 49–50.

27. Voltaire, *Philosophical Dictionary*, VI, pp. 105–11.

28. Saint-Quentin, *Dissertation sur la traité et le commerce des nègres,*

problem by resorting to the doctrine of moral progress, or by devising
elaborate anti-slavery interpretations of Scripture and early Church
history. But Voltaire prepared the way for more secular critics who
would dismiss religious sanctions as irrelevant. And, above all, he
stood for a questioning frame of mind which could say, with respect
to a war captive's right to escape, 'Nature decides against
Grotius.'[29]

It was, however, the more conservative Montesquieu who did the
most to undermine the pro-slavery authority of Aristotle, the Justinian Code and the seventeenth-century philosophers. This was not
because he developed a clear and forthright position against slavery.
Montesquieu's profound respect for institutions, for stability and balance, for the established orders of society, and for the concrete varieties of human laws and customs, made his political philosophy less
conducive to abolitionism than was that of Locke, whose social compact was too abstract and inflexible to allow for slavery. As we have
seen, Montesquieu's emphasis on environmental differences played
into the hands of pro-slavery apologists. His suggested legislative
reforms fell short of the more enlightened slave codes, to say nothing
of Burke's sweeping plan. Since his sharpest critical remarks were in
the dangerous form of satire, they were easily misinterpreted.[30] Even
in an age of sparkling wit, there was risk in saying that Negroes had

pp. 22–51; Philippe Fermin, *Description générale, historique, géographique
et physique de la colonie de Surinam* ... (Amsterdam, 1769), I, pp. 109–12.
Voltaire was able to cite a Christian apology for slavery, Linguet's *Théorie
des lois civiles*, which had been directed against Montesquieu (*Philosophical
Dictionary*, VI, p. 107).

29. Voltaire, *Philosophical Dictionary*, VI, p. 109.

30. Frossard, *Cause des esclaves nègres*, I, p. 65; Jameson, *Montesquieu et
l'esclavage*, pp. 315–18, 340–41; Fletcher, 'Montesquieu's Influence on
Anti-Slavery Opinion in England', pp. 415–16. Montesquieu failed to discuss limits on amount of work, compensation in the form of a plot of land or
peculium, the right of transfer to a more humane master, the means of
detecting and punishing the abuse of slaves, or specific procedures for en-
suring regular manumissions. His uncertainty in writing the satirical passages is seen in his repeated revisions (Robert Shackleton, *Montesquieu: A
Critical Biography* [Oxford, 1961], p. 237; Montesquieu, *Oeuvres*, III, p.
592).

such black skins and squashed noses that it was almost impossible to pity them; or that it was hardly to be believed that God, in His infinite wisdom, should place a soul, 'surtout une ame bonne, dans un corps tout noir'. To be sure, Montesquieu made his purpose more obvious by adding that Egyptians, who were the best philosophers in the world, killed all red-haired men who fell into their hands. He pointed to the Negroes' preference for glass necklaces, over ones of gold, as certain proof of intellectual inferiority. He concluded that 'it is impossible for us to suppose that these beings should be men; because if we supposed them to be men, one would begin to believe that we ourselves were not Christians'. But these passages were later used to support the doctrine of Negro inferiority, and even in 1900 the editor of an English translation of *L'Esprit des lois* could solemnly say, 'The above arguments form a striking instance of the prejudice under which even a liberal mind can labour.'[31]

The key to Montesquieu's remarkable influence on anti-slavery thought lies in the fact that he was the first important philosopher to subject the problem to the critical tools of the Enlightenment. And in an age of emergent literacy, when knowledge of the most fashionable writers was an indispensable mark of status, the opinions of so great a figure were bound to be reprinted in magazines, quoted by statesmen and philosophers, and embodied in the works of men like William Blackstone. If the Enlightenment impeached all the old authorities, it provided new ones in their place.[32]

The intellectual context and background of Montesquieu's views on slavery have been meticulously analysed by Russell P. Jameson, and therefore require only the briefest summary. By the mid 1730s, when Montesquieu decided to write *L'Esprit des lois*, a growing

31. Montesquieu, *Oeuvres*, I (tome i), pp. 330–31; Montesquieu, *The Spirit of the Laws* (tr. by Thomas Nugent, rev. by J. V. Prichard, New York, 1900), p. 286 n.

32. Hazard, *European Thought in Eighteenth Century*, pp. 259–62; *Gentleman's Magazine*, XXXIX (1769), p. 85; The *Weekly Magazine, or Edinburgh Amusement*, VI (30 November 1769), p. 85; Jameson, *Montesquieu et l'esclavage*, pp. 339–47; Fletcher, 'Montesquieu's Influence', pp. 416–23; F. T. H. Fletcher, *Montesquieu and English Politics, 1750–1800* (London, 1939), pp. 12–53.

interest in Africa and the West Indies had been excited by the travel accounts of men like William Bosman, Pierre Labat and Pierre Charlevoix; and the Academy of Bordeaux, of which Montesquieu was a member, was sponsoring an inquiry into the reasons for the Negro's physical characteristics. As president of the Parlement of Bordeaux, Montesquieu not only spent much of his time in the slave-trading port, but was a close friend of Jean Melon, the economist who defended slavery in 1734 on principles of utility and public welfare. Montesquieu was an extraordinarily erudite jurist and scholar; he was well aware of the anti-slavery arguments of Bodin and of the embarrassing questions which Germain Fromageau had raised in the 1690s concerning legitimacy of title. He probably knew that a few Protestants, such as Jacques Bernard and Johann Buddeus, had held that slavery was repugnant to the spirit of Christian love and that consent was a prerequisite to legitimate servitude. Given this background, one might have expected Montesquieu to consider the relations of Negro bondage to the precepts of divine and natural law, to the rules of war, to the principles of labour, commerce and national wealth. One might have looked for speculations on the meaning of racial differences, and for detailed discussion of the modes of enslavement in Africa, the character of the slave trade, and the management of Negroes under American law and custom. But none of this is to be found in *L'Esprit de lois*.[33] Montesquieu did not include slavery in his chapters on war, government, liberty or commerce; he turned to the subject immediately after his famous Book XIV on the influence of climate on mankind. And Book XV was not really addressed to slavery as such, but to the ways in which the laws of civil slavery relate to 'the nature of the climate'. The odd thing is that Book XV has little to say about climate, but rather considers slavery at once in terms of universal principles and of specific consequences in different societies. And this is what gives the analysis its subtle importance.

Future anti-slavery movements would be absolutely dependent upon the ancient doctrine of an immutable, higher law, whose authority would nullify the prescriptive sanction of a local institution. But historically, this higher law had tended to be so transcendent that it

33. Jameson, *Montesquieu et l'esclavage*, pp. 167–70, 180–81, 186–7, 198–205, 249–51, 263–87; Shackleton, *Montesquieu*, pp. 21, 194–224, 238.

had little bearing on existing institutions; or, as *jus gentium*, it was identified with the immemorial experience of mankind, and hence gave support to certain forms of human bondage. The abolition of slavery would also require a theory of law as the positive will of the sovereign, whose commands would be guided by a sense of social utility and public welfare. But without the standard of a higher and universal law, a sovereign might agree with Hobbes or Melon that slavery served the best interests of the State.

Montesquieu had the genius to find a compromise that was not unlike the Church's synthesis of spiritual power and objective institutions. There was, he insisted, an eternal, uniform and rational system of law, which limited even the will of God. But this higher law was not a set of abstract rules. It consisted of certain inherent and necessary relationships which could be understood only in concrete situations. In other words, to grasp the underlying principles of a form of government, one had to study specific governments; natural law as a norm for future action was to be derived from an empirical examination of social relationships. The wise sovereign would try above all to preserve the integrity of the general principles which gave form to his particular society. Fully cognizant of the limiting forces of climate, soil and geography, he would still be an instrument of moral influence and, so far as possible, would shape and adjust institutions in conformity with natural law.[34] We have already seen how Francis Hutcheson, who was writing at about the same time as Montesquieu, worked from the subjective moral sense to the principle of social utility. Montesquieu, in effect, worked from social utility towards general laws which would guide the enlightened sovereign. When brought together, these two approaches would provide a theoretical basis for effective anti-slavery action. The private moral judgement of individuals would find a 'useful' outlet in the demonstration that slavery was contrary to the public good, and hence to natural law; and the sovereign power, with an eye on both expediency and principle, would take positive action to eliminate the evil.

Unfortunately, Montesquieu's attempt to apply his method to slavery was curiously uncertain and disjointed. In *Les lettres persanes*

34. Shackleton, *Montesquieu*, pp. 244, 248, 251–2; Cassirer, *Philosophy of the Enlightenment*, pp. 205–14, 243.

his approach had been purely utilitarian and relativistic. Usbek, one of the Persian travellers, takes a sceptical view of all American colonization, and regards the slave trade as an extravagant waste of men which has brought no benefit to Europe, Africa or America. In Persia, slaves are mostly used for the protection of harems, and thus the State is deprived of potential fathers and workers. But Usbek notes that it was otherwise in ancient Rome, where slaves contributed to the wealth, population and general good of the Republic.[35] Yet in his *Pensées*, Montesquieu refuted the justifications for slavery in Roman law; he asserted that 'l'esclavage est contre le Droit naturel, par lequel tous les hommes naissant libre & indépendans'; and eloquently concluded 'En vain des loix civiles forment des chaînes; la Loi naturelle les rompra toujours.'[36] His task, then, in *L'Esprit des lois*, was to reconcile this view of natural law with his profound respect for the differing needs of various forms of government and society. And he confessed that he was unsure whether his pen had been guided by his heart or his understanding.

When it came to the question of a man's selling himself into slavery, Montesquieu fell back upon an abstract syllogism: a sale presupposed a price; by definition slavery meant that one man had absolute dominion over the life and fortune of another; therefore the slave could receive nothing and the sale was void. Put positively, liberty was a priceless blessing to its possessor.[37] But then Montesquieu came down from the lofty realm of formal logic, and extracted a normative rule from a description of the actual behaviour of

35. Montesquieu, *Oeuvres*, I (tome i), pp. 229–30, 236–7, 240. Edward Seeber sees *Les lettres persanes* as more definitely anti-slavery, but this is partly because he misinterprets Letter CXV, in which Usbek compares slavery in ancient Rome with that in Persia, and not, as Seeber implies, with modern slavery in general (*Anti-Slavery Opinion*, p. 30).

36. Montesquieu, *Oeuvres*, II, pp. 57–9. The problem of determining the chronological development of Montesquieu's views is extremely complex and not really relevant to this study. Some light is shed on the subject by Jameson, *Montesquieu et l'esclavage*, pp. 324–30; and Shackleton, *Montesquieu*, pp. 236–8.

37. Montesquieu, *Oeuvres*, I (tome i), p. 327. Montesquieu elaborated upon this judgement in his letter to Grosley of 8 April 1750, replying to specific criticisms of Book XV (*Oeuvres*, III, pp. 1293–4).

men. All nations rejected the idea of killing prisoners of war in cold blood. And since there was no necessity of killing an enemy if it was possible to capture him, there could be no ground for arguing that slavery was a necessary means of saving life. In any event, it was not compassion to substitute one inhumane act for another, even if it meant a lessening of cruelty.[38] On a still more specific level, Montesquieu tried to show that slavery violated the underlying principles of monarchy, aristocracy and democracy. And if this demonstration was not particularly convincing, it gave a more universal cast to important themes which the philosopher had touched upon in *Les lettres persanes*: slavery retarded the growth of population; debased one class, to the detriment of public virtue; and corrupted another with luxury and excessive power. Finally, the institution was to be gauged by examining its tangible effects as a reciprocal relation between two men. According to Montesquieu even the murderer benefited from the law that condemned him to death, since his life had always been protected by it. But no such utility, however dubious, could be found in slavery. The institution prevented the slave from acting virtuously, and imparted to the master a cruel and choleric spirit.[39] Empirical evidence, then, confirmed the deductions of logic; utility coincided with natural law.

There were, of course, those disturbing questions about despotic states and debilitating climates. But Montesquieu had done much to discredit the classical justifications for slavery, and he had struck off any number of quotable epigrams, such as 'La liberté de chaque citoyen est une partie de la liberté publique'.[40] And it was this sense of the public good, as distinct from any private or partial interest, which was perhaps his most significant contribution to anti-slavery thought. The slave, by the very nature of his condition, was beyond the reach of civil law and hence of civic obligation. His subordination, unlike that of a subject to his sovereign, could not serve the general good.[41]

38. ibid., I (tome i), p. 326; III, p. 1293.
39. ibid., I (tome i), pp. 326–8.
40. ibid., I (tome i), p. 327.
41. As Jameson has remarked, this view seemed to put Montesquieu in the position of saying that the civil law could not intervene to protect the slave (*Montesquieu et l'esclavage*, pp. 311–12).

The partiality of the defenders of slavery could be exposed, Montesquieu said, by watching their reaction to a plan for a national lottery that would make nine-tenths of the population the absolute slaves of the remaining tenth. This would prove, he wrote to Grosley, that 'le cri pour l'esclavage est donc le cri des richesses & de la volupté & non pas celui du bien général des hommes ou celui des sociétés particulières'.[42]

These conclusions set the tone for much of the Enlightenment's response to Negro slavery. Montesquieu showed first of all that the subject involved momentous issues which invited rational analysis and debate. In an age when universities and scientific academies promoted essay and debating contests on the most controversial topics, it was only natural that the legality of slavery should preoccupy the students at Edinburgh in 1764, at the College of Philadelphia in 1768, and at Harvard in 1773. The following year even a Jamaican debating society considered whether the slave trade was consistent with morality, sound policy and the laws of nature, and the negative side won.[43] It was such an essay contest at Cambridge University that first aroused the zeal of Thomas Clarkson.

Montesquieu also popularized assumptions and methods that would be highly useful for later anti-slavery writers. Through an analysis of concrete facts, one could reconstruct the general principles which governed the growth and social consequences of a particular institution. Such analysis and synthesis proved that, underlying superficial differences in government and religion, men revealed the same basic needs and weaknesses, a desire for the same pleasures and aversion for the same pains.[44] But the dramatization of this point required imaginative devices that would expose self-centred prejudice and, for a startling moment, thrust the complacent European into another man's role. This was the motive behind Montesquieu's

42. Montesquieu, *Oeuvres*, III, p. 1294. This letter was added to later editions of *L'Esprit des lois*.

43. Lowell Joseph Ragatz, *The Fall of the Planter Class in the British Caribbean, 1763–1833* (New York, 1928), p. 242.

44. Diderot, 'Fragments échappés du portefeuille d'un philosophe', in Diderot, *Oeuvres complètes* (ed. by Jules Assézat and Maurice Tourneux, Paris, 1875–7), VI, pp. 444–57.

Les lettres persanes, his proposed 'lottery' and his satirical treatment of racial prejudice. The discovery of a new level of objectivity and self-scrutiny was the goal of much eighteenth-century writing.[45]

In 1725 Pierre Marivaux wrote a popular one-act comedy, *L'Île des esclaves*, in which two Athenian aristocrats are forced to exchange roles with their slaves for three years, and are accordingly cured of prejudice and inhumanity.[46] If Negroes, said a writer in the *Weekly Miscellany*, were to seize men on the coast of England, one could imagine the screams of 'Unjust!' that would arise.[47] Voltaire enlarged upon the notion, and pictured an outraged European captain, whose ship and crew have been captured by Negroes. What right, the captain asks, have the Negroes to violate the law of nations and enslave innocent men? The Negro chieftain, who presumably has been reading *L'Esprit des lois*, explains 'your nose is long, and ours is flat; your hair is straight, and our wool is curled; you are white, and we are black; consequently we ought, according to the sacred and unalterable laws of nature, to be ever enemies.' And after being reminded of the treatment of Negroes on the Guinea coast, the Europeans 'had nothing to say against so wise a discourse'. In 1766 the Physiocratic journal, *Ephémérides du citoyen*, asked its readers to imagine what would have happened if African slave dealers had landed in France during the days of feudal anarchy. Would the tyrants and sanguinary judges who had been responsible for so much evil have refrained from selling their countrymen as slaves? Even now who could say there could be no price high enough to tempt Frenchmen to sell their neighbours or even their relatives?[48]

Such a reversal of roles exposed the hypocrisy of a double standard, and the pretence of saying that some men were happiest in a

45. Hazard, *European Thought in Eighteenth Century*, pp. 1–13.

46. Pierre Carlet de Chamblain de Marivaux, 'L'île des esclaves', in *Oeuvres complètes de Marivaux*, IV (Paris, 1830).

47. 'Some Reflections on the Trade of Buying and Selling Negroes' [reprinted from *Weekly Miscellany*], *London Magazine*, VII (March 1738), p. 129.

48. Voltaire, 'The History of the Travels of Scarmentado', reprinted in *Gentleman's Magazine*, XXVIII (May 1758), pp. 221–4; *Ephémérides du citoyen, ou chronique de l'esprit national*, VI (1766), pp. 189–90.

state of slavery.[49] 'What in a *European*,' said a letter writer of 1745, 'would be called a glorious Struggling for Liberty, we call in them Rebellion, Treachery.' For a freedom-loving people, such as the English, it was 'doubly criminal' to sacrifice human beings to the idol of avarice. One day even the roles of nations might be reversed, since the progressing revolution in science and the arts might enable Africa or America to seek revenge upon Europe.[50] By the 1760s, the inconsistency had become a favourite target of those who would prove their own intellectual emancipation from the ethno-centrism of European culture. In the disgusted words of Diderot, 'Nous les avons réduits, je ne dis pas à la condition d'esclaves, mais à celles de bêtes de somme; & nous sommes raisonnables! & nous sommes chrétiens!'[51]

Marivaux's comedy of 1725 did not question the right of men to hold slaves. In the end Arlequin and Cléanthis, the slaves who become masters, voluntarily relinquish power to their true owners. But a half-century later, in Marmontel's melodramatic *Les Incas*, Las Casas speaks the following words: 'Mon frère, tu es mon esclave, est une absurdité dans la bouche d'un homme, un parjure et un blasphème dans la bouche d'un chrétien.'[52] The difference illustrates a major passage of intellectual history, the central theme of which is the dignity and happiness of the individual man.

One of the sources of this heightened concern for individual happiness was the cult of moral sensibility which emerged from British Protestantism in the late seventeenth century. While the tender passions were first celebrated as a defence against materialism and

49. 'Some Reflections on the Negro Trade' [reprinted from the *London Gazetteer*], *London Magazine*, XXI (October 1752), p. 472.

50. *London Magazine*, XIV (October 1745), p. 496. This idea had also been suggested in 1737 by Richard Savage, in his poem 'Of Public Spirit in Regard to Public Works', *The Works of Richard Savage*, II (London, 1777), p. 141.

51. Quoted by Wilson, 'Development and Scope of Diderot's Political Thought', p. 1883, from the *Encyclopédie* article, 'Humaine espèce', probably written by Diderot about 1762.

52. Quoted in Gilbert Chinard, *L'Amérique et le rêve exotique dans la littérature française au XVIIᵉ et au XVIIIᵉ siècle* (Paris, 1913), pp. 388–9.

scepticism, they soon became the common property of philosophers who sought to improve the world and to vindicate human nature from the stigma of original sin. In 1725, the year of *L'Île des esclaves*, the Abbé de Saint-Pierre coined the word 'bienfaisance' to describe man's disinterested impulse to promote the happiness of his fellow creatures.[53] On the eve of the French Revolution, Benjamin Frossard could say that 'bienfaisance' was the spirit of the age, that it had sanctified wealth by providing a channel for aiding the unfortunate, and that it must now redress the crime of past generations who had enslaved the innocent Africans.[54] And as he hid from Robespierre's police, a victim of the Reign of Terror, the Marquis de Condorcet gave perhaps the most eloquent definition to the humanitarian ideal:

The feeling of humanity, that is, a feeling of tender, active compassion for all the evils afflicting mankind, or horror for everything arising either from public institutions or from governmental decrees or from individual acts, which added new torments to Nature's inherent ills ...[55]

The Age of Reason was also an age of compassion for afflicted humanity. Diderot, who had written a French translation of Shaftesbury, could weep over the relatively minor sufferings of Pamela and Clarissa.[56] Candide shed tears as he entered Surinam, for he had just conversed with a young Negro who, in accordance with the custom of the country, had had an arm and leg cut off, and who had shattered Candide's philosophic optimism by saying that this was the price for the sugar Europeans enjoyed.[57] The hero of *La nouvelle Héloïse* had a similar encounter with slaves. In eighteenth-century literature a

53. Hazard, *European Thought in Eighteenth Century*, pp. 170–71.

54. Frossard, *Cause des esclaves nègres*, I, pp. 1–13.

55. Marie Jean de Condorcet, *Esquisse d'un tableau historique des progrès de l'esprit humain* (texte revu et présenté par O. H. Prior) (Paris, n.d.), pp. 164–5.

56. Hazard, *European Thought in Eighteenth Century*, p. 386; Cassirer, *Philosophy of Enlightenment*, pp. 105–7; Wilson, *Diderot*, pp. 49–50.

57. Voltaire, *Candide* (New York, 1936), pp. 62–3. By the 1770s the idea that sugar, a symbol of European luxury, was stained with blood and tears of slaves, had become a commonplace in French and British literature. See, for example, *Gentleman's Magazine*, XLV (1775), p. 168.

feeling of shock and indignation at the physical cruelties of Negro slavery increasingly became a test of sensibility, just as the cruelties themselves became a symbol of man's inhumanity to man.[58]

But an even more significant source of the new interest in individual happiness was the Lockean belief that society is composed of discrete, self-governing individuals, whose true humanity lies in their proprietorship of their own persons.[59] The disciples of Locke found moral freedom not in self-denial and transcendence of worldly condition, but in a lack of dependence upon the will of others, in the natural exercise of the human faculties, and in the unfettered pursuit of enlightened self-interest. Instead of assuming that this kind of freedom would lead to total anarchy, they held that nature and society could be made compatible only if individuals retained a certain inviolable core of autonomy and self-direction. These ideas, which did so much to shape subsequent political and economic thought, were obviously of the highest importance in discrediting the traditional view of slavery. For in the Lockean philosophy a slave, so long as he is deemed to be human, must either be classed as a criminal who is beyond the pale of the social contract, or be considered a freeman who has been forcefully and unnaturally suppressed.

In England the doctrine of a higher law that supports the rights of individuals lived on through the eighteenth century, despite a growing respect for utility, the authority of statute law, and the omnipotence of Parliament. It sometimes found sanction in courts and was championed by a few theorists like Granville Sharp.[60] As early as the 1730s an occasional essay or letter to a periodical made the momentous observation that, because all men were born free and equal, Negro slavery was a violation of the natural rights of man.[61] This

58. Typical examples are: Voltaire, *Essai sur les moeurs,* in *Oeuvres de Voltaire* (Paris, 1817), XII, p. 417; *London Magazine,* VII (March 1738), pp. 130–31; Savage, 'Of Public Spirit in Regard to Public Works', p. 141.

59. Crawford B. Macpherson, *The Political Theory of Possessive Individualism: Hobbes to Locke* (Oxford, 1962), pp. 263, 270.

60. J. W. Gough, *Fundamental Law in English Constitutional History* (Oxford, 1955), pp. 185–200.

61. *London Magazine,* VII (March 1738), p. 129; *Gentleman's Magazine,* X (July 1740), p. 341; *Monthly Review,* XXXI (July–December

essentially Lockean argument appeared infrequently, but it was endorsed by no less a conservative than Samuel Johnson, who said that the Negro slave was 'certainly subject by no law, but that of violence, to his present master', and who was reported to have given a toast at Oxford to the next insurrection in the West Indies.[62]

But if Lockean ideas could be turned against the institution of slavery, they also supported private property and hereditary inequality. And as Rousseau shrewdly observed, Pufendorf had argued that a man might alienate his liberty just as he transferred his property by contract; and Grotius had said that since individuals could alienate their liberty by becoming slaves, a whole people could do the same, and become the subjects of a king.[63] Here, then, was the fatal flaw in the traditional theories of natural rights. Nature could not create masters or slaves, princes or subjects, the rich or the poor; therefore, asked the socialist, Bonnot de Mably, 'how can laws decreed by the body politic, and meant to be but the extension of natural laws, establish with impunity such a shocking and cruel difference between men?'[64]

Rousseau was interested in larger issues than Negro slavery, but because slavery had conventionally been linked with justifications for the existing social order, he saw that an attack on the principle of involuntary servitude might unravel the network of sanctions for every species of injustice. Hence he repeated Montesquieu's arguments on the invalidity of any contract for self-sale, and on the dis-

---

1764), p. 116; The *Weekly Magazine, or Edinburgh Amusement*, VI (30 November 1769), p. 258.

62. James Boswell, *The Life of Samuel Johnson* (Modern Library ed., New York, n.d.), pp. 747–8. While Johnson had long shown a great distaste for slavery, Boswell accused him of 'zeal without knowledge', and saw fit to include many of the conventional pro-slavery arguments in his great biography.

63. Jean-Jacques Rousseau, *The Social Contract and Discourses* (tr. by G. D. H. Cole, Everyman's Library ed., London, 1930), pp. 9, 227.

64. Quoted in Elizabeth L. Hickman, 'Anti-Slavery Agitation in France during the Latter Half of the Eighteenth Century' (Cornell University Ph.D. dissertation, June 1930), p. 21. But according to Vincent Confer, Mably had no objections to Negro slavery ('French Colonial Ideas before 1789', *French Historical Studies*, III [Spring 1964], p. 346).

crepancy between the lawful objectives of war and the enslavement of captives. But Rousseau went on to a far more radical set of conclusions. Men were born free and equal; the renunciation of liberty meant the renunciation of being a man. Since slavery always rested on brute force, which was but thinly disguised by meaningless conventions, bondsmen had no duties or obligations to their masters. The words 'slave' and 'right' were contradictory and mutually exclusive. Even the Lockean notion of a continuing private war between slave and master was without foundation; for in the true state of nature, where there was no private property to defend, there could be no war of dominion; and once within the social compact, all men were subject to its laws. The master, then, could appeal to no principle or right to justify his power. And, in Rousseau's eyes, the same was true of all the authorities and powers in Europe. For the loss of natural equality necessarily brought the loss of liberty; and because the development of agriculture and technology had led to widening inequalities, the great mass of mankind had become enslaved by either force or fraud. All Rousseau's arguments against empty conventions, prescriptive rights and the alienation of liberty were as applicable to society in general as to the most tyrannical forms of servitude.[65]

Except for such radical sectarians as the Ranters and Taborites, no one had condemned the principle of slavery so uncompromisingly; but Rousseau's very extremism led to certain paradoxes. He regarded the subordination of one individual to another as an act of dehumanization to which only a madman could consent. Like the orthodox idea of sin, slavery was so vile and corrupting a state that its victims lost even their natural love for liberty. Men born into slavery were as content with their condition as were the swine who had once been the companions of Ulysses.[66] Rousseau assures us that Aristotle mistook effects for causes when he concluded that some men must be born *to be* slaves. But this distinction would seem academic to many future apologists for the institution, who could ask, quite plausibly, why the condition of happy and contented men should be changed? Baron D'Holbach brought out the more disturbing implications of the environmentalist argument when he claimed that it was possible

65. Rousseau, *Social Contract and Discourses*, pp. 5, 9–13, 215, 227–8.
66. ibid., pp. 6–7.

for entire nations to be beaten down by fear, superstition and habits of thought, until they became indifferent to the charms of liberty.[67] If this were so, why should the detention of such men be more tyrannical than the detention of men who were slaves by nature? Of course a man whose personality had been shaped for slavery by the environment would be potentially capable of being moulded back into a free man. But if one agreed with John Millar that bondage often made a man 'worthy of that contempt with which he is treated',[68] it would appear that, whatever the origins of slavery, the obstacles to emancipation remained very great.

Emancipation involved another paradox. In a Lockean view it would simply mean a severing of artificial bonds and restoration of natural liberties. Condorcet, though fully aware of the corrupting effects of bondage, put his faith in the restorative power of nature: 'Give them their freedom; and because they are closer to Nature, they will be better men than you.'[69] But because Rousseau addressed himself to the emancipation of all mankind, and because he had no faith in either gradual progress or a return to the state of nature, he was convinced that true freedom could be achieved only through subjection to the General Will. Whether one regards his theory as democratic or totalitarian, it is clear he had revived the ancient idea that the only genuine liberation lies in a higher form of servitude. Rousseau's citizen would find his identity in the General Will much as Aristotle's slave found his identity in his master.

The final paradox is that Rousseau, by associating slavery with all forms of authority and subordination, reinforced the traditional claim of pro-slavery theorists. In effect, he may have made conservatives more convinced that an attack on even a remote and somewhat distasteful institution would be a very dangerous thing.

67. Paul Henri Thiry D'Holbach, *La politique naturelle, ou, discours sur les vrais principes du gouvernement, par un ancien magistrat* (London, 1774), II, p. 88. D'Holbach was, however, strongly opposed to slavery.

68. John Millar, *The Origin of the Distinction of Ranks; or, An Inquiry into the Circumstances which Give Rise to Influence and Authority in the Different Members of Society* (3rd ed., London, 1781), pp. 349–50.

69. Marie Jean de Condorcet, *Remarques sur les Pensées de Pascal,* in *Oeuvres,* III (Paris, 1847–9), p. 650.

In 1755, the year of Rousseau's *Discours sur l'inégalité*, the death of Montesquieu evoked an introductory eulogy in Volume V of the *Encyclopédie*. The great jurist was specifically credited with having exposed the illegality of human bondage; and in a long article on 'Esclavage', which fell within the alphabetical range of the same volume, the Chevalier de Jaucourt developed and strengthened Montesquieu's anti-slavery arguments.[70] Next to *L'Esprit des lois*, the *Encyclopédie* was without doubt the most important agent in making anti-slavery a part of the Enlightenment's overriding concern for the happiness and well-being of mankind. It was not until 1765, however, when the editors arrived at 'Traite des Nègres', that de Jaucourt was able to rise above the qualifications engendered by Montesquieu's tolerance for institutional differences.[71] The encyclopedist's verdict was now unclouded by historical examples and question of climate and government; his conclusions carried a note of extraordinary simplicity and directness:

Thus there is not a single one of these hapless souls – who, we maintain, are but slaves – who does not have the right to be declared free, since he has never lost his freedom; since it was impossible for him to lose it; and since neither his ruler nor his father nor anyone else had the right to dispose of his freedom; consequently, the sale of his person is null and void in and of itself: this Negro does not divest himself, indeed cannot under any condition divest himself of his natural rights; he carries them everywhere with him, and he has the right to demand that others allow him to enjoy those rights. Therefore, it is a clear case of inhumanity on the part of the judges in those free countries to which

70. *Encyclopédie, ou dictionnaire raisonné des sciences, des arts et des métiers* . . ., V (Paris, 1755), xi, pp. 934–9. De Jaucourt defined slavery in broad enough terms to include political bondage. He followed Montesquieu on the reasonableness of civil slavery in a despotic state. It should be noted that the article 'Esclave' in Volume V provided a wealth of factual detail on West Indan slavery and the *Code Noir*.

71. De Jaucourt was something of a workhorse for Diderot's project; he was of the upper nobility, was a Protestant of latitudinarian views, and as a youth had spent three years at Cambridge (Wilson, *Diderot,* pp. 201–2). The most exhaustive study of the *Encyclopédie,* including problems of authorship, is Jacques Proust, *Diderot et l'Encyclopédie* (Paris, 1962).

the slave is shipped, not to free the slave instantly by legal declaration, since he is their brother, having a soul like theirs.[72]

This passage has seemed worth quoting at some length, since it is one of the earliest and most lucid applications to slavery of the natural rights philosophy, and succeeds in stating a basic principle which was to guide the more radical abolitionists of the nineteenth century. De Jaucourt was repelled by the idea that local civil law could establish a condition which infringed upon basic human rights. If there were no supreme and eternal law which applied equally to all men, then any kind of banditry might be cloaked with legal forms.[73] De Jaucourt did not say with Rousseau that the entire social order was in fact banditry cloaked with legal forms; but with respect to slavery, at least, his version of natural law had something of the uncompromising absolutism of Rousseau's General Will. A slave was not really a slave but a man grievously wronged. His right to escape was as certain as that of a man cornered by highwaymen. Any court refusing to grant a slave his immediate liberty was flouting eternal justice and was, by implication, no longer a valid court. Furthermore, since the sources of natural law were to be found in man's own nature, in his common physical and spiritual needs, the dictates of such law could never be inconsistent with public utility. If the eradication of colonial slavery brought temporary strains of commercial readjustment, in the long run it could not fail to promote the growth of industry, population and happiness.[74]

By 1765, then, a radical anti-slavery manifesto had been embodied in the great summa of the French Enlightenment. And beginning in 1770, the subject moved more directly into the foreground with the Abbé Raynal's *Histoire des deux Indes*. If this work turned out to be an ill-planned hodgepodge of miscellaneous facts and turgid prose, it was also the chief medium for popularizing the enlightened mind's mixed attitudes towards America; and as such, it was to exert a

72. *Encyclopédie*, XVI (Neuchâtel, 1765), p. 532.

73. ibid. The basis for this secularized view of natural law can be found in Volume V in the articles 'Egalité naturelle' and 'Droit naturel'.

74. ibid., pp. 532–3. De Jaucourt's fusion of utility and humanitarianism was also characteristic of Diderot, on a more theoretical level (see Wilson, 'Development and Scope of Diderot's Political Thought', pp. 1873, 1887–8).

profound influence on humanitiarian thought, especially in Great Britain, where in 1777 it appeared in translation.[75] We have already discussed Raynal's view of the relevance of slavery to America's meaning in history. But as the work brought together many of the anti-slavery ideas which had been developing during the half-century since Montesquieu's *Les lettres persanes*, it may also be considered as a culmination of the trends we have just been examining.

Like the *Encyclopédie*, the *Histoire des deux Indes* was a collaborative enterprise in which Diderot played an important role. In 1772, in his *Fragments échappés du portefeuille d'un philosophe*, Diderot attacked the legality of slavery much as de Jaucourt had done, and even defended the right of bondsmen to use any possible means to regain their freedom.[76] But though some of Diderot's writings were apparently spliced into the sections on slavery in the *Histoire des deux Indes*, the most inflammatory passages were the work of Jean de Pechméja, a young tutor and future socialist, who was reported to have said, 'I am as pale as death, and as sad as life.'[77] Pechméja's boldest lines were deleted from the third edition: 'Whoever justifies so odious a system deserves scornful silence from the philosopher and a stab with a poniard from the Negro.' But despite such textual changes there is reason to believe that Raynal, Diderot and the other collaborators shared a militant hatred for Negro slavery, and that the ambivalent attitudes of the *Histoire des deux Indes* were largely the result of changing stylistic preferences and, one suspects, of underlying tensions in the mind of the Enlightenment.[78]

75. Irvine D. Dallas, 'The Abbé Raynal and British Humanitarianism', *Journal of Modern History*, III (December 1931), pp. 564–77.

76. Diderot, *Oeuvres complètes*, VI, pp. 444–57.

77. Michèle Duchet, 'Diderot collaborateur de Raynal: à propos des "Fragments imprimés" du Fonds Vandeul', *Revue d'histoire littéraire de la France*, LX (1960), pp. 531–56; Anatole Feugère, 'Raynal, Diderot et quelques autres "Historiens des deux Indes" ', *Revue d'histoire littéraire de la France*, XX (1913), pp. 343–78; Hans Wolpe, *Raynal et sa machine de guerre* (Stanford, Calif., 1957), pp. 178–89, 250–52. After teaching rhetoric at La Flèche, Pechméja became closely associated with Necker and Dr Dubreuil. In a long poem of 1784 he attacked private property and inheritance; he died the following year at the age of forty-four.

78. Wolpe, *Raynal et sa machine de guerre*, pp. 178–81. Herbert Dieckmann has published a letter in which Jacques Naigeon complained about

There was, first of all, the sense of living in an age of revelation when all the frauds and errors of the past were being unmasked, and when nothing could be taken for granted, except, of course, man's capacity to know and choose his true good. In words that echoed Rousseau, Raynal (and for convenience we shall call him the author) said that what distinguished man from the beasts was not reason but freedom of will – the power to say 'je veux' or 'je ne veux pas', which even God could not take away.[79] The early Hebrews and Christians had often spoken of themselves as the willing slaves of God; but to Raynal this was an absurdity, since man could not be human if he were God's slave. And how could one give a power to another man which was denied even to God? To be sure, religion might inculcate a spirit of subservience. But if there was a religion, Raynal wrote, which tolerated the horrors of the African trade, which failed to thunder constantly against the agents of such tyranny, which condemned the slave who broke his chains, and which embraced the judge who sentenced him to death, then its ministers deserved to smother under the debris of their altars.[80] Raynal agreed with Voltaire that Christianity had never lightened the burden of slaves; and in a passage which foreshadowed William Lloyd Garrison's denunciations of the American churches, he declared: 'If the Christian faith did thus sanction the greed of empires, it would be necessary to proscribe for all time to come its bloodthirsty doctrines.'[81]

Nor was prescriptive authority less fallible than religion. The fact that servitude had been accepted through the ages was no proof that it was right: 'If the universality of a practice was proof of its validity, the case for usurpation, for conquest, for all manner of oppression

---

the deletion of Pechméja's lines, which he considered the boldest and most eloquent in the section on slavery. Hans Wolpe is persuasive, however, when he argues that the edition of 1781 is at least as militant as the one of 1774, in which Pechméja's lines appeared. He offers considerable evidence to show that textual changes were dictated by stylistic considerations.

79. Raynal, *Histoire des deux Indes*, VI, pp. 105, 126–7. For convenience I have used the 1781 edition, though I have consulted several of the others and have profited greatly from Hans Wolpe's detailed analysis of textual changes.

80. ibid., VI, pp. 126–7.

81. ibid., VI, p. 134.

would be made.' Human history, as Rousseau had said, had been a movement from natural freedom and simplicity to a dependence based on force and convention. In most nations, including Europe, the mass of people were in chains, their natural liberty sacrificed to passions of their oppressors. But where Rousseau became wholly pre-occupied with this discovery, Raynal was quick to draw distinctions. In an age of light and prosperity, Europe would assuredly progress towards greater liberty; and, in fact, the condition of the most un-fortunate serf was not like that of the Negro slave. It was in America that greed and power and arrogant pride had corrupted an entire class; and it was in America that another class had become so dis-pirited and degraded in soul that its members almost considered themselves an inferior species. The Old World might still suffer from the decaying vestiges of former tyrannies; but in the New World, where there were no limits to either power or subjugation, one might see the spectre of what most threatened the progress of mankind.[82]

With this recognition of a fundamental difference between the two hemispheres, Raynal found that he must descend from the abstract level of universal justice. Like Montesquieu, he saw that character and institutions were shaped by environment. Like Rousseau, he saw that slaves had been so dehumanized that they appeared to have been created for no higher condition. And like Burke, he concluded that if such men were given freedom, they could only lead lives of indolence and crime. Raynal's plan for meeting this problem was similar to Burke's, except that it was less legalistic and moved towards liberty more swiftly and through an explicit series of phases. Most of the present generation of slaves could not be freed, but their physical sufferings would be alleviated and their morale improved by music, games and dances. Emancipation would be a reward for mothers of large families, and would eventually be given to those Negroes who, at the age of twenty-five, had earned the cost of their upbringing and had been well-behaved during a five-year apprenticeship. Raynal was more generous than most governments proved to be. He insisted that the public treasury provide each freedman with a cabin and a small plot of land.[83]

82. ibid., VI, pp. 105, 117–18, 128–9, 133–4, 170.
83. ibid., VI, pp. 110–16, 130–36.

This was the kind of rational scheme that appealed to the enlightened mind. It required, of course, a strong and enlightened sovereign, and hence Raynal addressed his appeal to the kings of Europe. In a poem of 1775, Claude de Sacy put his hopes in the King of France:

> Oh you, young Louis, whose calm youth
> Promises serene days to the French citizen who reveres you,
> You must set an example to a hundred different peoples.
> See that our laws are respected in the New World:
> Their sublime equity has no place for slavery.
> Break, break the chains which bind the Negro and Indian. . . .[84]

But young Louis could not have cared less, and Raynal himself was well aware that the sovereigns of Europe might be blinded by self-interest. He seemed suddenly to sense the inconsistency of saying that slaves were the innocent victims of tyranny, and then relying on kings to inaugurate a plan which would perpetuate the tyranny for at least a generation. To that part of the enlightened mind which prized stability and order, the debased Negro might not seen fit for freeom. But in Raynal's eyes the American slaves were not like Circe's swine. Contented beasts did not revolt, flee to the wilderness, or try to poison their owners. Nature, Raynal concluded, owed her oppressed children a leader, a strong man who would vindicate the honour of the human race, and seek vengeance for three centuries of oppression. And if the black heroes followed the law of reprisal, their 'code blanc' would rightfully be a code of terror.[85]

This sympathy for outright violence was more than mere sensationalism. It arose from a division in the mind of the Enlightenment, from a tension between the ideal of individual liberty and the quest for a rationally balanced society. It was all very well to speak of 'bienfaisance' as the spirit of the age, and to construct plans

84. Claude de Sacy, *L'Esclavage des Américains et les nègres; pièce qui a concouru pour le prix de l'Académie Françoise, en 1775* (Paris, 1775), p. 11.

85. Raynal, *Histoire des deux Indes*, VI, pp. 132–3, 138–9. According to Wolpe, this passage was taken from Sebastien Mercier's utopian novel, *L'an 2440 (Raynal et sa machine de guerre*, p. 177).

for the elimination of human misery. But still, as Raynal said, 'The slaves are tyrannized, mutilated, burnt and stabbed; and we receive the news of their torture coldly and with indifference.' Condorcet came to the same bitter thought: 'Only a few "philosophes" have from time to time dared raise a cry in favour of humanity, a cry which the Establishment has not heeded, and which a superficial society has soon forgotten.' And in the words of de Jaucourt: 'Sensitive and generous souls will doubtless second these reasons which favour humanity; but avarice and greed, which rule the earth, will never heed their plea.'[86]

In the last analysis, therefore, the oppressors must either be crushed by a superior force, or be persuaded that humanity coincided with their own self-interest.

86. Raynal, *Historie des deux Indes*, VI, p. 105; Condorcet, *Remarques sur les Pensées de Pascal, Oeuvres*, III, p. 649; De Jaucourt, 'Traite des Nègres', *Encyclopédie*, XVI, p. 533.

14

The Enlightenment as a
Source of Anti-Slavery Thought:
Utility and Natural Law

SUCH a narrowing of alternatives suggests increasing moral uncertainty in the mind of the Enlightenment. When poets like Doigny du Ponceau celebrated the impending insurrection of the slaves, they were really endorsing a Hobbesian view that power justifies itself.[1] D'Holbach bluntly conceded there must be a perpetual conflict between man's will to freedom and his will to dominate. Diderot concluded that it was only the individual's natural impulse to free himself from external authority that prevented all humanity from becoming slaves in a meaningless stream of generations.[2]

But what was the relation between individual liberty and the stream of generations? Was history no more than a cyclical fluctuation between D'Holbach's principles of freedom and domination? There had been other periods of relative liberty and enlightenment, but they had not endured. Were decadence and enslavement the ultimate price for human progress?[3] This possibility haunted even the

1. Edward D. Seeber, *Anti-Slavery Opinion in France During the Second Half of the Eighteenth Century* (Baltimore, 1937), pp. 72–3. For a broad study of the eighteenth-century crisis in ethics and moral philosophy, see Lester G. Crocker, *An Age of Crisis: Man and the World in Eighteenth-Century French Thought* (Baltimore, 1959), *passim*.

2. Paul Henri Thiry D'Holbach, *La politique naturelle, ou discours sur les vrais principes du gouvernement, par un ancien magistrat* (London, 1774), II, p. 8; Paul Hazard, *European Thought in the Eighteenth Century, from Montesquieu to Lessing* (tr. by J. Lewis May, Meridian paperback ed., Cleveland, 1963), pp. 388–9.

3. A study which balances the oversimplified view of the eighteenth century as an age of optimism is Henry Vyverberg, *Historical Pessimism in the French Enlightenment* (Cambridge, Mass., 1958); see esp. pp. 229–30. For French anti-colonial thought, see Vincent Confer, 'French Colonial Ideas before 1789', *French Historical Studies*, III (Spring 1964), pp. 338–59.

optimists who congratulated themselves on living in the eighteenth century; their uncertainty helps to account for a growing ambivalence towards the New World. There could be no doubt that the expansion and economic progress of Europe had been closely connected with the discovery of America. The very existence of a New World had helped to disintegrate old assumptions in a solvent of unlimited possibilities. The great question, however, was whether this dissolution of traditional limitations had increased the cumulative happiness of the human race.

For all their faith in individual freedom, the *philosophes* were often obsessed by the ancient fear of moral decay as the inevitable result of luxury and a pursuit of wealth.[4] The most striking modern example, as British Protestants had long insisted, was the degeneration of the Iberians following their orgy of greed and cruelty in the New World. The 'black legend' of the Spanish conquest could be used by either Protestants or *philosophes* to illustrate the depravity of the old Catholic order. But then the entire history of American colonization seemed to show what extremes of waste, suffering and tyranny one could expect when man's self-interest went unrestrained. Through the writings of Montesquieu, Diderot, Raynal and Condorcet the sense of shock deepened: after enslaving and exterminating the innocent Indians, the Europeans had turned to depopulate Africa. 'The New World', wrote de Sacy, 'does not have enough slaves; our need, our desires are greater than the continent itself.'[5] This meant, said Jean François de Saint-Lambert, that the discovery of America had been a lethal event for three-quarters of the world's

4. Guillaume-Thomas Raynal, *Histoire philosophique et politique des établissemens et du commerce des Européens dans les deux Indes* (Genève, 1781), IV, pp. 213–16; Marie Jean de Condorcet, *Remarques sur les Pensées de Pascal,* in *Oeuvres,* III (Paris, 1847–9), pp. 647, 651; Vyverberg, *Historical Pessimism,* p. 193; Michèle Duchet, 'Diderot collaborateur de Raynal: àpropos des "Fragments imprimés" du Fonds Vandeul', *Revue d'histoire littéraire de la France,* LX (1960), p. 545. For classical influences on anti-colonial thought, see Léon Deschamps, *Histoire de la question coloniale en France* (Paris, 1891), pp. 213–17.

5. Claude de Sacy, *L'Esclavage des Américains et des nègres; pièce qui a concouru pour le prix de l'Académie Françoise, en 1775* (Paris, 1775), p. 7.

inhabitants. And what, asked numerous *philosophes*, were the end-products that justified such misery? The ladies of Europe had brighter dyes for their dresses; they had more rouge for their cheeks; they had chocolate to eat and sugar to sweeten their tea.[6]

When earlier writers like Morgan Godwyn and Thomas Tryon had commented on the same irony, they could assume that avarice and luxury were marks of man's sinful nature, and that a righteous society required a tight reining of individual self-interest. But without the Christian framework of sin and redemption, how was one to interpret the relation between oppression and self-indulgence? According to Bernard Mandeville, whose views were influential in France as well as England, the wasteful follies and luxuries of the rich were an indispensable stimulus to industry; rational analysis, when freed from superstitious asceticism, showed that civilization rested on the individual's pursuit of pleasure. But according to Rousseau, who was also convinced that superstitions distorted men's view of reality, civilization was itself a sham. Only a total reconstruction of society could end the vicious system which enslaved the mass of humanity to the selfish interests of a privileged few. These were, in a sense, the polar extremes of the divided mind of the Enlightenment. In one view, norms were to be derived from an empirical description of human experience; society was regulated by immanent laws which were as unalterable as the laws of the physical universe. In the other view there was an absolute gulf between society as it existed and the transcendent laws of nature. Neither position provided the basis for perceiving a single institution as an unmitigated evil.

Even by the mid eighteenth century, however, philosophers had discovered a middle way which appeared to synthesize empirical reality with the rational ideal. Turgot agreed with Mandeville that man's selfish passions, his greed and his injustices, all served useful functions. But the ultimate end, to which all human experience contributed, was a utopia of reason and love. From the beginning of history man had staggered blindly forward, unaware that his movements were always in the right direction, that his sins were redeemed by time. Such an idea of inevitable progress was an antidote for both

6. Seeber, *Anti-Slavery Opinion*, pp. 43–4, 90–93.

complacency and discontent. It provided, by the last third of the eighteenth century, a meeting-ground for devout Christians and secular philosophers who were equally in need of believing that the sufferings of the past had prepared the way for an age of reason and benevolence.[7]

A faith in inevitable progress could, of course, be as stifling to reform as was the theodicy which showed that this was the best of all possible worlds. In making notations in his copy of Lord Kames's *Principles of Morality and Natural Religion*, Thomas Jefferson drew from history an example of the progressive development of man's moral sense. The enslavement of prisoners of war had surely been a marked improvement over their brutal slaughter. Enlightenment had now progressed so far that Montesquieu had shown that even enslavement was no longer a humane necessity. Some day, no doubt, nations would look with horror on the ransoming of captives.[8] Jefferson clearly felt that each custom had served a progressive function in its particular stage of moral evolution. And while he earnestly desired to see an end to Negro slavery, his faith in progress smothered the sense of urgency he felt when he was calling for the abolition of entail or the separation of Church and State.

It all depended on whether the past was seen as the seedbed of the future, or as a rotting husk that threatened to impede healthy growth. The belief that history moved through a logical succession of ascending stages did not preclude the possibility of conflict between the forces of progress and retrogression. If the promotion of human happiness was ultimately to become a science, it was the business of the legislator to ask whether existing institutions were the most effective

7. J. B. Bury, *The Idea of Progress; An Inquiry into its Origin and Growth* (Dover paperback ed., New York, 1955), pp. 52–158; Frank E. Manuel, *The Prophets of Paris* (Cambridge, Mass., 1962, pp. 22, 38–49; Lois Whitney, *Primitivism and the Idea of Progress in English Popular Literature of the Eighteenth Century* (Baltimore, 1934), pp. 153, 179–80, and *passim*; Ernst Cassirer, *The Philosophy of the Enlightenment* (tr. by Fritz Koelln and James P. Pettegrove, Beacon paperback ed., Boston, 1951), pp. 174–96.

8. Adrienne Koch, *The Philosophy of Thomas Jefferson* (reprint ed., Gloucester, Mass., 1957), p. 18.

means of harmonizing private interests with the public good.[9] And for men who strove for scientific objectivity, such a question could best be met by quantative standards. In the eyes of early utilitarians, for example, it was unlikely that an institution could be contrary to the public interest if it encouraged a steady growth in population.

David Hume was anything but an abolitionist, but in 1752 he helped to put the slavery controversy in a new perspective by demolishing the traditional belief that, owing to the great fertility of slaves, Europe's population had been vastly larger in antiquity than in modern times. For our purposes the most significant points Hume made were these: he maintained that the rate of population growth is dependent upon economic and social institutions; he argued that neither slaves nor livestock could profitably be bred where costs were high, as in large cities, which explained why Romans had relied on an influx of bondsmen from the provinces; he observed that where the ratio of slaves to freemen was disproportionately large, as in the American colonies, the result must be an insecurity and a severity of discipline which would retard the growth of population. The implication was that the institution was a kind of economic aberration which consumed itself the more it grew.[10]

A year before Hume's essay appeared, Benjamin Franklin had recorded similar thoughts on slavery in his *Observations Concerning the Increase of Mankind*. Franklin had owned Negro servants as late as 1750, and it would appear that his desire to get rid of them was more a product of racial prejudice than humanitarianism.[11] But while his moral concern over slavery arose only late in life, Franklin was per-

9. Elie Halévy, *The Growth of Philosophic Radicalism* (tr. by Mary Morris, Beacon paperback ed., Boston, 1955), pp. 17–18; Bury, *Idea of Progress*, pp. 172–4; Henri Sée, *L'Évolution de la pensée politique en France au XVIIIᵉ siècle* (Paris, 1925), pp. 203–13.

10. David Hume, *Essays, Moral, Political, and Literary* (Edinburgh, 1817), pp. 377–419.

11. Carl Van Doren, *Benjamin Franklin* (New York, 1938), pp. 197–8. Van Doren does not draw this conclusion, but prejudice seems to be implied in the letter he quotes, and is more explicit in Franklin's *Observations Concerning the Increase of Mankind*. One may note that Franklin hardly took notice of Negro slavery, except for this one essay, until he came into contact with the Physiocrats in the late 1760s.

haps the first modern man to subject the institution to a book-keeping analysis. In an age when people were easily impressed by any statistical evidence, he calculated the cost of American slave labour in terms of original investment, risk, lack of interest on capital, and maintenance and discovered that it was more expensive than free labour in England. This, he claimed, put the colonies at a disadvantage in trade. And not only was the mortality of slaves greater than their natural increase, but the institution impeded the growth of white population by depriving the poor of employment and enfeebling the rich with luxury. Then why did Americans continue to buy Negroes? There was, Franklin conceded, a shortage of white labour, and hired workers soon left their jobs to acquire land of their own.[12]

In 1756, the year after Franklin's figures were published, the Marquis de Mirabeau presented the world with a systematic treatise on population growth, economic laws and human happiness. If a nation were a tree, he said, the leaves would be commerce, the branches would be industry, the roots would be agriculture and the trunk, population. As a skilled horticulturist, the wise sovereign should encourage healthy growth by removing all impediments to the free operation of natural laws. He should realize that commerce and industry, while vulnerable to passing storms, would prosper if population continued to grow; and that this, in turn, would be assured by a healthy state of agriculture. He should pursue the utilitarian ideal of increasing the total happiness of the human race by looking to nature for the secrets of fecundity and abundance. For Mirabeau, as for Quesnay and the later Physiocrats, progress could not be economically and morally secure unless harmonized with a primitivistic ideal of the land as the source of all goodness.

Given these assumptions, Mirabeau could only conclude that the American colonies were blighted by a disease that threatened the progress of Europe. Instead of nourishing liberty, prosperity and happiness, colonial agriculture destroyed population and depleted the soil. Mirabeau was as indignant as a Christian moralist over the arguments of men like Hume and Melon, who justified luxury on

12. *The Papers of Benjamin Franklin* (ed. by Leonard W. Labaree *et al.*, New Haven, 1959–19—), IV, pp. 229–31.

grounds of social utility. True progress required freedom of trade and a wider distribution of goods; yet colonization had led to a form of commercial exploitation that allowed the avarice and over-consumption of a small group to choke the sources of healthy growth. The principle of slavery had infected colonial commerce as well as colonial labour.

It might seem that Mirabeau would have had reform begin at the roots, with a transformation of American agriculture. But he was a fervent believer in the rights of private property and the beneficent effects of individual self-interest, when unrestrained by artificial bar-riers. He showed little interest in the plight of the Negro, and feared the dangers of miscegenation. His remedy, therefore, was to open America to the free trade of the world. As soon as economic laws were allowed to operate without obstruction, the colonists would see the unprofitableness of Negro slavery; free labour would be attracted to those employments most useful to humanity; and there would emerge a great commercial commonwealth which would distribute the benefits of technology and civilization to all mankind.[13]

It must be emphasized that Negro slavery was a matter of small concern to such writers as Franklin, Hume and Mirabeau, and that their brief comments on the subject can hardly be taken as evidence of an upswell of anti-slavery sentiment. But the deepening imperial conflicts of the mid eighteenth century gave a new importance to even such casual attempts to judge colonial slavery by the laws of economic and historical development. In the Seven Years' War prized sugar lands were devastated and captured, fears of slave insur-rection rose to a heightened pitch, European governments sagged from the pressure of mounting debts, and France lost the greater part of her colonial empire. So sudden a transformation in the balance of power brought a growing awareness of the instability and inefficiency

13. Victor Riqueti de Mirabeau, *L'Ami des hommes, ou traité de la popu-lation* (5th ed., Hamburg, 1760), I, pp. 2–8; III, pp. 235–88, 324–36, 400–410. Victor de Mirabeau was a friend of Montesquieu and the father of the revolutionary. His brother was governor of Guadeloupe and was appar-ently opposed to slavery. Mirabeau said that any imperial power would be highly fortunate if its colonists demanded their independence.

of the old colonial system. We have noted how Malachy Postlethwayt praised the slave trade as 'an inexhaustible Fund of Wealth and Naval Power', and then concluded, by 1757, that since France was winning economic dominance in the Caribbean, Britain's interests lay in developing Africa. In 1756 the Abbé Coyer thought it was essential for France to expand the slave trade; a decade later he favoured its abandonment.[14]

In 1765 one of Mirabeau's disciples, the Abbé Baudeau, founded a journal which championed agrarianism and free trade, rustic simplicity and economic progress, natural rights and social utility. As a vehicle for Physiocratic ideas, *Ephémérides du citoyen* was highly critical of the wastefulness of the old colonial system, and looked upon the recent loss of Canada as a blessing in disguise. For Baudeau the key to America's future, and to the future of Western civilization, lay in the immense regions of virgin land that stretched westward from the Mississippi. Reviving the old dream of La Salle, he described the great agrarian empire that would arise one day in Louisiana. And since Spain had no means of settling so vast an area, he proposed that colonization be undertaken as a joint enterprise by France, Spain and Sicily, with each nation pooling her resources in an international company. Settlers could be recruited from Germany and central Europe, but Baudeau assumed that the project would also require large numbers of Negroes from the coast of Africa. And thirty-seven years before the Louisiana Purchase, fifty-four years before the Missouri Compromise, the editor of *Ephémérides du citoyen* raised the momentous question whether slavery should be permitted on the prairies of North America.[15]

Baudeau showed great concern for the sensitivity of French planters in the Caribbean, who, he said, had been reconciled to slavery by long custom and perhaps by necessity. Since Europeans only bought men who had already been enslaved, and since the practice

14. Seeber, *Anti-Slavery Opinion*, pp. 97, 100. For the relation of slavery to the great eighteenth-century debate over the value of colonies, see Deschamps, *Histoire de la question coloniale*, pp. 259–331.

15. *Ephémérides du citoyen, ou chronique de l'esprit national*, I (1765), pp. 49–50, 113–28; II (1765), pp. 33–64; V (1766), pp. 17–67. Although originally modelled on the *Spectator*, the journal soon became absorbed with economic issues.

had been sanctioned by the government, one must refrain from moral judgement. And yet Baudeau considered slavery a barbarous evil. In words that echoed Rousseau, he condemned the pride and cupidity of the first man who pretended that another was his slave. Nothing could be more inhumane and self-defeating than to fasten slavery on a new colony whose very basis was human liberty and progress. European settlers would live in freedom and simplicity, relieved of all dues and obligations except for a general tax consisting of one-eleventh of their produce. If Negro slaves were purchased in Africa, transported to Louisiana, and transformed into free citizens, the company could still make a profit by charging a perpetual rent of one-sixth or one-fifth of all their produce. The Africans would not mind such discrimination, since their condition would have been improved, and, in any event, they had been 'façonnés à l'esclavage'.[16]

Even this cautious free-soil proposal drew an angry retort from a French correspondent, who said he had been born in a colony whose very existence depended on slavery. The writer demanded that Baudeau retract his aspersions on the morality of colonists, admit the inferiority of Negroes, and recognize slavery as a positive good. This provided the editor with an opportunity to develop a philosophic basis for opposing slavery. For Baudeau the first principle of knowledge and judgement was the universal accord between natural law and the true self-interest of all men. By nature man was endowed with the animal instinct to search for good and to seize and consume what he could find. This instinct was the source of man's first labour and of his first ideas of goodness and natural right. Unlike other animals, his reason enabled him to mitigate the pains and anxieties of the struggle for survival by respecting the right of his fellow creatures to consume the products of their labour. This sense of trust and mutual interest was anterior to all social conventions, and was founded on each man's proprietorship of his own person. The social compact, while entailing certain duties for the common interest, did not alter primitive liberties; and between men of different societies the law of nature was the only governing force. To deprive a man of his elemental freedom to work and enjoy the fruits of his effort was therefore the primal sin

16. ibid., V (1766), pp. 39, 66–7.

against both nature and the interests of mankind. It was inevitable that wherever slavery existed 'tout est désordre, injustice & mal, passion, colère, combats, vengeance, crainte & horreurs de toute espèce'. Baudeau admitted that his argument would have no force if it could be shown that Negroes were not true men. But despite the corrupting effects of slavery the laws and behaviour of white colonists gave eloquent proof that the Negro, no matter how degraded, was a man.[17]

By 1768 Du Pont de Nemours had succeeded Bandeau as editor of *Ephémérides du citoyen,* and in the next few years the journal became the leading organ for economic arguments against slavery. In 1771 Du Pont drew upon Franklin's now famous essay (when he had visited Paris in 1767, the Philadelphian had been lionized by the Physiocrats, and had even contributed to *Ephémérides*), and printed detailed calculations to show the unprofitableness of slave labour.[18] When the Academy of Bordeaux offered a prize for the best plan for making the slave trade more humane, Du Pont exposed the fatal flaw in all such thinking: to improve the condition or reduce the number of Negroes on each ship would make an already precarious trade intolerably costly and dangerous. Long before Burke proposed his own scheme, Du Pont insisted that in such a trade profit and humanity were incompatible. The only solution was to abolish the trade and, by diversifying crops and providing new incentives, transform the colonial labour system.[19]

Du Pont showed particular enthusiasm for an idea which had been suggested in 1762 by the Abbé Roubaud, which had been promoted in England by the Quaker physician, John Fothergill, and which ultimately inspired Henry Thornton, Granville Sharp and other philanthropists to found Sierra Leone. As an alternative to the expensive system of slave trade and American colonies, why not use free labour for the cultivation of tropical staples on the coast of Africa? Du Pont was encouraged by a travel account of Pierre Poivré, published in 1768, which reported that sugar cane was grown by free

17. ibid., VI (1766), pp. 129–30.
18. *Ephémérides du citoyen, ou bibliothèque raisonnée des sciences morales et politiques,* VI (1771), pp. 218–40.
19. ibid., XI (1771), pp. 211–26.

labourers in Cochin China. Poivré, who was president of the Royal Society of Agriculture at Lyon, also blamed slavery for the low level of African civilization. A comparison of the world's nations proved that civilization depended upon a healthy state of agriculture, and that agriculture could flourish only where there was freedom and justice.[20] It followed, then, that science offered Europe a second chance at colonization. With a single stroke she might redeem the mistakes she had made in America, assure herself a cheap supply of tropical produce, and bring freedom and civilization to the Dark Continent. The dream would fire the imagination of William Pitt and endure for at least a century.

There were those, however, who thought that economists should stick to hard facts. This was the approach of Turgot, whose *Réflexions sur la formation et la distribution des richesses* became one of the classics of Physiocracy. Turgot agreed with his *philosophe* friends that slavery violated the laws of humanity; but this did not mean that the institution was exempt from the laws of economics. All wealth was derived from the land. When there was much land in relation to labour, proprietors often resorted to coercions. But slave labour was a temporary expedient, since it was uneconomical in the long run. The cost of slaves was certain to rise as the supply diminished; proprietors would discover there was greater profit in hiring free labour or in charging rent.[21]

Du Pont was a close friend of Turgot, and felt at liberty to revise the text of *Réflexions* in 1769, when he began reprinting the book in his journal. Turgot had used slaves and cattle as examples of fluid capital. Du Pont deleted 'slaves' from this discussion, and added arguments to show that slavery was always unprofitable as well as being a crime against humanity. Turgot, intensely annoyed by these unauthorized changes, defended his position in a series of letters. He acknowledged that Franklin had shown slave labour to be more ex-

20. ibid., VI (1771), pp. 240–46; Pierre Poivré, *Travels of a Philosopher, or, Observations on the Manners and Arts of Various Nations in Africa and Asia* (Augusta, 1797), pp. 7–8, 46, 90–92.

21. Anne Robert Jacques Turgot, *Oeuvres de Turgot et documents le concernant, avec biographie et notes par Gustave Schell* (Paris, 1913–23), II, pp. 544–8, and *passim*.

pensive than one might think. But this did not prove that it was unprofitable for individual proprietors, especially those who wanted to make quick fortunes from commodities of high commercial value. Moreover, slavery might serve the interests of a country that valued wealth and commerce more than an increase in population. Turgot was sympathetic with Du Pont's moral objections, but unfortunately, he said, men did not always suffer for their injustices. Utility and righteousness coincided only in the long sweep of history.[22]

Although the Physiocrats helped to encourage anti-slavery opinion, the division between Du Pont and Turgot was symptomatic of fundamental problems that would long haunt economic liberalism. Given the facts of history, how could it be shown that slavery was not a natural expression of individual self-interest, and thus in accordance with economic laws? Was there not a contradiction in arguing that slavery was always unprofitable, and then condemning slave holders for avarice, as if one still believed Mammonism to be a sin? How could one say that the worst thing about perpetual bondage was its crushing effect on incentive and ambition, and then denounce the incentive and ambition of slave traders? Finally, the Physiocrats would substitute purely economic relations for those based on privilege and prescriptive power. But without intervention by a power independent of economic interest, how was the Negro to be protected and helped? And as West Indian planters would continually ask, what disciplinary force would keep the Negro at work in a tropical climate where food could easily be grown or even picked from trees?

In the mid-1760s Turgot and other Physiocrats entertained a brilliant Scottish philosopher whose ideas had much in common with their own. Adam Smith had already developed an ingenious world view from the ideas of his mentor, Francis Hutcheson. According to Smith, the laws of social relations promoted benevolence and happiness because there was perfect harmony between morality, which arose from our spontaneous inclination to identify ourselves with others; and utility, which was the product of our self-interested de-

22. ibid., II, pp. 544–8, 565; III, pp. 373–5, 378; *Ephémérides du citoyen*, XI (1769), pp. 41 ff.

cisions as economic men. In 1759, in his *Theory of Moral Sentiments*, Smith had found that the Golden Rule was grounded in a psychology of sympathetic association.[23] This provided a moral basis for condemning slavery. It was, however, with *The Wealth of Nations*, which owed something to his Physiocratic friends, that Smith made his significant contribution to the anti-slavery cause.

As everyone knows, Smith attacked the entire network of laws, customs and usages which stifled initiative and kept individual self-interest from advancing the public good. Slavery was simply part of this disharmonious system of monopoly and special privilege. Indeed, the relations between slave and master epitomized those artificial restraints that prevented self-interest from being harnessed to the general good. For if a man had no chance of obtaining property, it was clearly in his interest to work as little as possible. This self-evident deduction was confirmed by experience, which, as Du Pont had said, universally showed that slavery was the most costly and least productive form of labour.[24] Like Turgot, Smith was certain that economic causes explained the abolition of bondage in Western Europe. Landowners simply came to realize that their profits would increase by giving labour a share of the produce.[25]

But even in the early 1760s, in his lectures at the University of Glasgow, Smith had acknowledged that a small part of Western Europe was the only portion of the globe free from slavery. Why, then, were so many men blind to their own self-interest? Smith's answer was that they were corrupted by pride. They loved domination and found it distasteful to persuade their inferiors to work.

23. Adam Smith, *The Theory of Moral Sentiments*. . . . (6th ed., London, 1790), *passim*.

24. The superiority of free labour was a popular theme in eighteenth-century English literature; however, it was often linked with a fear of over-population and social disorder in England, and with proposals for sending indigent children to the American plantations (see Richard Savage, *The Works of Richard Savage*, II [London, 1777], p. 132; *London Magazine*, XXVII [December 1758], p. 624).

25. Adam Smith, *An Inquiry into the Nature and Causes of the Wealth of Nations* (ed. by Edwin Cannan, Modern Library ed., New York, 1937), pp. 365–9.

Consequently, they preferred slave labour when it was permitted by law and by the nature of the work.[26]

If this distinction between the love of power and economic self-interest appeared to solve the problem, it did not remove a number of paradoxes. Smith took note of the report that American Quakers had resolved to free their slaves. He agreed with the Abbé Raynal, however, that this would have been impossible if slaves had formed a major part of the Quakers' property. Pride might distort the judgements of economic man, but philanthropy was evidently not a sufficient motive for the sacrifice of wealth.

A second puzzle was that slave labour, being highly expensive, could not be afforded by the growers of the less lucrative crops; but this meant that the institution was linked with the most profitable kinds of agriculture. And Smith also associated wealth with lax and careless management of labour. Where the rich planter was inattentive to high costs of maintenance, the manager of free labour, being frugal, parsimonious and efficient, kept wages as low as possible. Yet this might well imply that wage-earners received less return for their labour than did slaves.

Finally, Smith held that involuntary servitude was more humane and profitable under despotic governments, which allowed magistrates to interfere with the management of private property. In a free country, where the rights of property were protected and masters had a voice in the government, there was little chance of elevating slaves to a higher level of intelligence and usefulness.[27] One might conclude that nothing could be worse for American Negroes than Smith's entire programme of economic reform. But such a conclusion would mean that the institution was unnatural in a double sense. It reversed the law which said individual self-interest must advance the public good. And its improvement required the strong hand of a despotic government. Before abandoning mankind to the invisible hand of nature, perhaps it was necessary that there be one last act of arbitrary power.

In 1771, five years before the appearance of *The Wealth of Nations*, one of Smith's students and protégés had published a socio-

26. ibid., p. 365.
27. ibid., pp. 80–81, 365–6, 553–4.

logical study which must be rated as one of the most imaginative products of the Scottish Enlightenment. Although he has long been overshadowed by better-known men, John Millar, who was Professor of Civil Law at the University of Glasgow, anticipated many themes that would preoccupy social scientists in the eras of Darwin, Marx and Freud.[28] For Millar, property relationships were the key to the various stages of social evolution, which he defined as hunting, pastoral, agricultural, commercial and manufacturing. Closely related to forms of property-holding were distinctive institutions which regulated authority and sexual relations. Economic activity, the authority of fathers, the position of women, social rank, laws, customs and uses of leisure – all formed a pattern of functional relationships. And in judging cultural and historical variations, Millar was a strict relativist. Primitive men appeared to be free and independent only because they lived in wretched want; as soon as the need arose, they quickly submitted to the most absolute authority. Sexual freedom was appropriate to the simplest societies where its consequences could not be injurious. Refined tastes and humanitarian sentiments could serve no useful purpose in the rough life of the barbarian. Yet man's evolution moved irresistibly, though at differing rates of speed, from a state of freedom, coarseness, ignorance and poverty, through a stage of authority and restraint to a high level of wealth, liberty, science and sexual equality.[29]

In Millar's eyes no revolution in history had advanced human happiness as much as the abolition of slavery in Europe. Nevertheless, this momentous progress had been the result of purely utilitarian causes. After the barbarian invasions of the Roman Empire, populations had been dispersed over such vast areas of land that slave labour could no longer be supervised. As a consequence of this problem of labour discipline, and of political struggles between kings and

28. Millar may win more appreciation as a result of William C. Lehman's helpful study, *John Millar of Glasgow, 1735–1801: His Life and Thought and Contributions to Sociological Analysis* (New York, 1960).

29. John Millar, *The Origin of the Distinction of Ranks; or, an Inquiry into the Circumstances which Give Rise to Influence and Authority in the Different Members of Society* (3rd ed., London, 1781), pp. 4–13, 67–71, 112, 123, 133–69, 295–6.

barons, the *servi* gradually acquired rights and privileges. Finally, a change in laws and customs, particularly in the nature of warfare and in the punishment of criminals, removed any legal basis for personal slavery. When the institution was revived in the American colonies, Europeans had been forced to pay the expense of purchasing and transporting men from primitive nations. This reversion to an earlier stage of development had not been simply the result of pride and lust for power, but had been encouraged by that 'blind prepossession which is commonly acquired in favour of ancient usages'. In spite of the fact that slavery was uneconomical, and became more oppressive as society progressed, public opinion either remained indifferent or regarded any proposed innovation as dangerous.[30]

Millar encountered certain difficulties in explaining cultural lag. He assumed that slavery in America violated the same laws of utility which had brought its gradual disappearance in Europe. Yet he admitted two important qualifications: there was no conclusive evidence to show that whites could replace Negro labourers in the hotter climates; and because a concentrated labour force was required for the cultivation of such staples as sugar, there was less need to substitute individual incentive for external discipline. In fact, slavery had persisted even in Scotland among the colliers and salters, some of whom wore collars bearing their owners' names.[31] Men would not suffer such degradation, Millar thought, unless they received more sustenance than they would as free workers. The system, then, was uneconomical for the mine owners, whose labour costs were artificially high. Such waste was possible only because mining demanded the collection and supervision of labour in one place.

But in the early 1770s one might well ask whether the labour system of the Scottish mines and American plantations was an anachronistic as Millar suggested. It is an intriguing fact that the decade from 1763 to 1773, which brought such widespread interest in the economics of slavery, also saw the portentous impact of the spinning jenny and the water frame. The sudden leap forward in the quantity

---

30. ibid., pp. 297–312, 320–44.

31. ibid., pp. 341, 354–9. For a description of Scottish slavery, see Paul Mantoux, *The Industrial Revolution in the Eighteenth Century* (rev. ed., tr. by Marjorie Vernon, New York, 1929), pp. 74–5.

and quality of yarn production would bring an unprecedented demand for raw cotton, and prepare the way for Eli Whitney's simple invention and all its woeful consequences. And there were those who would see certain similarities between the colonial plantation and the textile factories which emerged from Richard Arkwright's Derby workshops where, even by 1773, women and children were producing pure cotton calicoes.[32]

But it was this very context of stirring economic change that gave force to Millar's central point. He wrote after a decade of unparalleled innovation in British Transportation, agriculture, mining and iron production; he admired and represented the spirit of men like John Roebuck, Richard Arkwright, Matthew Boulton and Josiah Wedgwood. Human progress, he maintained, meant a widening influence of utility and efficiency; it meant an accelerating growth of new techniques and inventions, an increase in skill and disciplined concentration, and above all, expanded production of cheaper and improved commodities. In the last analysis, therefore, colonial slavery was a crime against humanity because it epitomized those forces of barbarism, ignorance and wastefulness which blocked the way to a material happiness almost within the reach of man.

The Enlightenment disseminated ideas that could serve the defender of slavery as well as the abolitionist. If the main current of secular thought ran against any institution that arbitrarily deprived men of liberty and happiness, discussions of servitude, prior to the 1760s, tended to be cautiously abstract and hedged with qualifications. But Arthur O. Lovejoy has observed that a term or set of phrases which gain acceptance because one meaning meets the needs of a particular age, may help to alter beliefs as other meanings are gradually seen.[33] There is evidence of this phenomenon in the changing connotations of such words as 'slavery', 'bondage' and 'emancipation'.

In the 1760s the Physiocrats called for emancipation from the economic slavery of monopoly and special privilege. And despite

32. For the economic revolution of the 1760s and early 1770s, see Mantoux, *Industrial Revolution*, pp. 118–19, 124 ff., 220–29, 310.

33. Arthur O. Lovejoy, *The Great Chain of Being; A Study of the History of an Idea* (Torchbook paperback ed., New York, 1960), p. 14.

their agrarian bias, their rhetoric was congenial to the aspirations of budding industrialists. Radicals like D'Holbach repeatedly used the terms of personal slavery to describe any legal or political system which subordinated public welfare to the whims of a favoured few.[34] In 1769 the *Gentleman's Magazine* attacked the policy of sending troops to America, reminding Britons that all continental Europe had been enslaved by taxes and standing armies.[35] In the eyes of French and American republicans, all Englishmen were slaves. In the eyes of patriotic Englishmen, the French were the slaves of a Bourbon despot. And Bernardin de Saint-Pierre, an engineer who had seen Negro slavery in Île de France, perceived an ominous connexion between the various meanings of servitude. He warned the rulers of France that they could not remain free unless their people were free; the intolerant always reaped the harvest of their own intolerance. Tyrannical ideas were like a plague. If allowed to spread in the colonies, they would soon infect the entire realm. Already the wealthy colonial slaveholders had allied with the most conservative nobility, and had begun to treat the people of France like American Negroes. If colonial slavery was not abolished, the liberties of France could not survive.[36]

Few writers made the connexion so explicit. But the political and constitutional crises beginning in the 1760s evoked a contagious fear that traditional authorities could no longer be trusted, that traditional liberties were no longer secure. As Robert R. Palmer has pointed out, the Seven Years' War intensified strains between central governments and various 'constituted bodies', which ranged from aristocratic councils to the relatively democratic assemblies of some colonies. Burdened by mountainous debts, central governments inaugurated administrative reforms and searched for more effective means of raising revenue. The constituted bodies interpreted all encroachments on their corporate rights as moves towards slavery. From Geneva to Boston these bitter conflicts undermined fundamental ideas of sovereignty. And as various elites dug in to defend

34. D'Holbach, *Politique naturelle*, pp. 29–37.
35. *Gentleman's Magazine*, XXXIX (1769), pp. 85–6.
36. Bernardin de Saint-Pierre, *Voeux d'un solitaire*, in *Oeuvres complètes*, XI (Paris, 1818), pp. 136–40.

their traditional prerogatives, they were also challenged by middle-class groups who sought more direct access to sources of power. Partly as a result of rapid economic changes, class divisions seemed to widen and to lose much of their aura of prescriptive or providential sanction. When it became obvious that aristocratic rank was a purchasable commodity, there was a growing suspicion that most authority was without legitimate title.[37] And there was no more perfect symbol of untitled power than the colonial planter.

America was the stage on which a Hamlet-like Europe witnessed the play within the play. The New World was where the fears and aspirations of the 1760s were first dramatized, where extra-legal associations of common citizens defied acts of a sovereign power, where abstract ideals of political philosophy were substantiated in the actions of ordinary men. After 1760 Europe absorbed a swelling stream of books and articles that assessed the meaning of this new spirit of freedom. And with few exceptions, the literature focused particular attention on the anomaly of Negro slavery.[38]

There were various ways in which Negro slavery became entangled with colonial grievances. When young Arthur Lee was studying in Britain in the 1760s, for example, he was shocked and outraged to discover the following passage in Adam Smith's *Theory of Moral Sentiments*:

There is not a negro from the coast of Africa who does not ... possess a degree of magnanimity which the soul of his sordid master is too often scarce capable of conceiving. Fortune never exerted more cruelly her empire over mankind, than when she subjected those nations of heroes to the refuse of the jails of Europe.[39]

37. Robert R. Palmer, *The Age of the Democratic Revolution: A Political History of Europe and America, 1760–1800* (Princeton, 1959), pp. 21–3, 79–86, 450.

38. Most of the books mentioned by Palmer (ibid., pp. 243–4) deal with Negro slavery. For the 'discovery' of British North America by the French *philosophes* in the period 1767–70, see Durand Echeverria, *Mirage in the West: A History of the French Image of American Society to 1815* (Princeton, 1957), pp. 3–25.

39. Smith, *Theory of Moral Sentiments*, II, p. 37; [Arthur Lee], *An Essay in Vindication of the Continental Colonies of America* (London, 1764). p. 9.

In 1764, the year he received a medical degree from the University of Edinburgh, Lee published an essay which told the renowned Adam Smith that Virginians, at least, were not descended from the scum of Europe, but from some of the finest families in England. And Negroes, far from being a nation of heroes, were 'a race the most detestable and vile that ever the earth produced'.[40] Lee assured his readers that he was a man of the Enlightenment and was sensitive to the liberal spirit of his age. He piously quoted the anti-slavery arguments of Hutcheson and Montesquieu, and took their side against Pufendorf and Grotius (the latter's views on killing prisoners of war, Lee said, were more worthy of an African savage than a European philosopher). But writers like Smith failed to appreciate that American slaves lived in palaces, compared with the peasants of Scotland; and worst of all, they displayed a total ignorance of the Negro's character. Even Aristotle, who had said slaves could have no virtue, 'knew not of any who were so utterly devoid of any semblance of virtue as are the Africans'. If men like Smith were sincerely interested in the question, they should do something to end the slave trade, which was a European crime, rather than slander poor Americans who had made the best of a burdensome and unfortunate institution. Lee hinted that calumnies against American slaveholders were part of a growing spirit of contempt for the rights and feelings of colonists; already British merchants had secured the enactment of arbitrary restrictions and impositions which threatened to enslave all Americans.[41]

In 1764 these same measures provoked another and better-known assertion of colonial rights. James Otis also saw certain connexions between Negro slavery and the infringement of colonial liberties; but Otis's vantage-point was different from that of Lee. Curiously enough, he also attacked Grotius and Pufendorf for accepting ancient abuses as the law of nations. But unlike Arthur Lee, he quoted Rousseau as the modern authority on natural rights and liberties.[42] He

40. [Lee], *Essay in Vindication of the Continental Colonies*, p. 34.
41. ibid., pp. 11–15, 20–22, 25, 33–46.
42. James Otis, *The Rights of the British Colonists Asserted and Proved* ... (Boston, 1764), p. 38. In general, of course, Otis followed Locke on the defence of property rights and on the people's right to alter an oppressive government.

argued that Americans, after separating themselves from European society, had actually passed through a state of nature before founding societies of their own. Their knowledge that all men were born free was based on more than theory. And after reaching this conclusion, Otis turned abruptly to Negro slavery, which 'threatens one day to reduce both Europe and America to the ignorance and barbarity of the darkest ages'.[43]

Otis did not expand upon the point, except to ridicule those who defended servitude on racial grounds. His purpose was to warn his fellow colonists that slavery would be their own certain fate if they allowed the British government to take their property without consent. There was, however, a more subtle connexion between bondage and economic oppression. New Englanders saw the Sugar Act as part of a conspiracy engineered by British West Indian interests. Otis suggested that while the continental colonists had fought bravely in the war against France, and were now accused of paying too little for imperial defence, the West Indians, who had done nothing to win the war, were using political influence to increase their riches and impoverish their patriotic brethren of the north. How was one to account for such depravity? Dealing in slaves, Otis remarked, 'has a direct tendency to diminish the idea of the inestimable value of liberty, and makes every dealer in it a tyrant. . . . It is a clear truth, that those who every day barter away other men's liberty, will soon care little for their own.' The only idea Creole planters had of government was of an overseer coercing tens of thousands of men. For a little gain, the Creole would betray British ideals of liberty and make slaves of even his own posterity.[44]

Less than two years after Otis's pamphlet, John Adams heard that the West Indies had not stood with the continental colonies resisting the Stamp Act, and he recorded these bitter words in his diary:

But can no Punishment be devised for Barbadoes and Port Royal in Jamaica? For their base Desertion of the Cause of Liberty? . . . Their mean, timid Resignation to slavery? . . . They deserve to be made Slaves to their own Negroes. But they live under the scortching Sun, which melts them, dissipates their Spirits and relaxes their Nerves. Yet their

43. ibid., pp. 42–3.
44. ibid., pp. 34–5, 44–6, 57, 87.

Negroes seem to have more of the Spirit of Liberty, than they. .... I could wish that some of their Blacks had been appointed Distributors and Inspectors &c. over their Masters. This would have but a little aggravated the Indignity.[45]

Imperial conflict had suddenly given ideological force to the theories of Montesquieu and to analogies and verbal associations which had become commonplace in eighteenth-century literature. And since ideology demands self-discipline and conformity, it is not surprising that in 1766 the citizens of Boston instructed their representatives, including Otis and Samuel Adams, to purify Massachusetts by moving for a prohibition on the importation and purchase of slaves.[46]

Because the American and French Revolutions had a profound influence on the early history of anti-slavery movements, they fall beyond the scope of this volume. We may note the obvious fact that political instability is seldom conducive to long-range plans for reform. Assertions of the right to self-government, which were to be heard in Jamaica and Saint Domingue as well as in Massachusetts, blocked the way to abolitionist schemes that depended on centralized power. In time of war attitudes towards slavery were dominated by questions of security. A serious paper shortage reduced the number of all publications, including anti-slavery tracts. Yet it would be a mistake to think that the eruption of revolutionary forces diverted attention from Negro slavery. The crises of the 1760s and 1770s left a sense of expectancy, of an approaching fulfilment, which would be an essential catalyst in transforming abstract ideals into militant anti-slavery protest.

This international mood of change, the expectation of an impending age of liberty or bondage, provided a matrix in which religious, philosophical, literary and economic trends could converge. The developing pattern can perhaps best be seen in the pages of *Ephémérides du citoyen*. In 1769 Du Pont demonstrated his keen interest in the cause of the American colonists by reprinting John

45. *The Adams Papers: Diary and Autobiography* (ed. by L. H. Butterfield, Atheneum paperback ed., New York, 1964), I, p. 285.
46. Benjamin Quarles, *The Negro in the American Revolution* (Chapel Hill, 1961), p. 40. The legislature did not pass a bill against the slave trade until 1771, and then Governor Hutchinson refused to sign it.

Dickinson's *Letters from a Pennsylvania Farmer* and by making some highly significant remarks on a letter which Benjamin Rush had sent from Philadelphia to Jacques Barbeu Dubourg, a physician, botanist and friend of Benjamin Franklin. There could be no doubt, Du Pont said, that the British colonies of North America would develop into an empire of greater extent and power than all of Europe, if only their inhabitants could keep from making discriminatory distinctions between Pennsylvanians and Virginians, Europeans and savages, blacks and whites. This was what gave such overwhelming importance to Dr Rush's report that 'our Quakers' had held a great meeting in which they had agreed unanimously to set their Negroes free, and that the majority of Pennsylvania Friends had already complied with the decision. While Rush was guilty of considerable exaggeration, he did not fail to draw a timely moral from the story: 'It would be useless for us to denounce the servitude to which the *Parliament of Great Britain* wishes to reduce us, while we continue to keep our fellow creatures in slavery just because their colour is different from ours.'[47] Du Pont was certain that the example of the honest Quakers would soon inspire all Pennsylvanians to free their slaves, and that the benefits would then be so apparent that the other colonies would rapidly follow suit. Nor would the consequences stop there. Through much of Europe the people still suffered from the stifling effects of serfdom. Even the proprietors, who were neither very free nor wealthy, were beginning to see the need for reform. While it would hurt Europe's vanity, Du Pont concluded, she might have much to learn from the New World.[48]

Two years later Du Pont showed that the slavery issue could be used as a means of synthesizing an even wider range of values, and of articulating a more unlimited faith in man's spiritual and material progress. The occasion was a review of the third edition of Jean-

47. *Ephémérides du citoyen*, IX (1769), pp. 172–4. While Philadelphia Quakers were attempting to rid themselves of the taint of slavery, they had not yet made slaveholding or even slave-buying a disownable offence. The letter which Du Pont reprinted is not included in Lyman H. Butterfield's *Letters of Benjamin Rush* (Princeton, 1951).

48. *Ephémérides du citoyen*, IX, pp. 174–5. To prove that Europe had her own sources of reform and *bienfaisance*, Du Pont went on to describe the social experiments of Count Oginski in Poland.

François de Saint-Lambert's *Les saisons*, a work which copied James Thomson in more than title, and which exploited all the devices of literary sensibility and primitivism. After expressing contempt for frivolous verse which merely amused, the editor praised Saint-Lambert as 'un Poète sublime', which meant not only that he aroused emotions of love, pity, horror and hatred, but that the emotions were objectively related to the best interests of mankind. Du Pont was almost wholly concerned with a tale called *Ziméo*, which the poet had appended to his work. *Ziméo* was the story of a young Apollo from Benin who tells of the happy innocence of Africa and the grisly horrors of the Middle Passage; who prays to 'Orissa', god of both blacks and whites, for deliverance; and who leads the armed *marons* in the hills of Jamaica. 'George Filmer', the English narrator, concludes with an eloquent attack on avarice and the mercantile spirit, the principles of Hobbes and Machiavelli, theories of racial inferiority, and all violators of natural law. But what most excited Du Pont was the realization that this moral passion and poetic sublimity could now be confirmed by the rigorously practical science of economics; it could now be proved that injustice earned no profit, that 'l'homme n'est point né pour mal faire'. It was Saint-Lambert's noble savage with all his overtones of righteous retribution, who served as a springboard for Du Pont's elaboration of Franklin's statistics, for his most detailed calculations on the unprofitability of slave labour, and for his confident prediction that the slave system would be doomed as soon as the first nation saw the advantage of buying sugar from free labourers on the coast of Africa.[49]

Despite their wide differences in every other realm of thought, a growing number of evangelicals and *philosophes*, of Quakers and revolutionaries, were coming to sense that American slavery might symbolize all the forces that threatened the true destiny of man.

49. ibid., VI (1771), pp. 163–246.

15

The Changing Image of the Negro

WE have suggested that by the 1760s broad changes in cultural values had undermined traditional religious and philosophic justifications for slavery. Yet the very trends of thought which weakened Biblical and historical sanctions also magnified the importance of man's mental and physical characteristics. Insofar as the Enlightenment divorced anthropology and comparative anatomy from theological assumptions, it opened the way for theories of racial inferiority.[1] In the eighteenth century such theories won little acceptance from scientists, who generally held to the Christian belief in the common nature and origin of mankind. Nevertheless, the Negro character increasingly became a subject of interest for natural philosophy as well as for drama and poetry, and the changing image of the African would have profound effects on the future controversies over slavery. To complete our understanding of the cultural background of anti-slavery thought, we need to know what traditions writers could exploit, what beliefs they could assume as common knowledge, and what prejudices they would have to overcome.

For reasons that can perhaps never be fully explained, it was the African's colour of skin that became his defining characteristic, and aroused the deepest response in Europeans. Though often designated as a 'Moor' or 'Ethiopian', he was also a 'negro' to the Spanish and Portuguese, a 'noir' to the French, and a 'black' to the English; and in

1. This point is also made by Winthrop D. Jordan, whose 'White Over Black: Development of American Attitudes Towards the Negro', is the most systematic and imaginative study I have seen of racial relations and attitudes in the colonial period. While Professor Jordan and I have approached the subject of this chapter from different directions and for different purposes, we have used many of the same sources and have independently arrived at many similar conclusions.

all four languages the word carried connotations of gloom, evil, baseness, wretchedness and misfortune. Early in the seventeenth century a
French traveller remarked: 'It might be properly said, that these Men
came out of Hell, they were so burnt, and dreadful to look upon.' A
century later John Atkins agreed that 'The Black Colour and woolly
Tegument of these *Guineans*, is what first obtrudes itself on our
Observations, and distinguishes them from the rest of Mankind.'
'This gloomy race of mankind', said Oliver Goldsmith, 'is found to
blacken all the southern parts of Africa, from eighteen degrees north
of the line.' And after stating his preference for 'the lovely White and
Red', Benjamin Franklin admitted 'perhaps I am partial to the Complexion of my Country, for such Kind of Partiality is natural to
Mankind'. Franklin did not think it necessary to explain the grounds
on which he classed red and white as the complexions of his
country.[2]

Harry Levin has shown how the moral and aesthetic 'power of
blackness' pervades a host of cultures and mythologies. God brought
light into the dark void and divided day from night; there were the
forces of Ormazd and the forces of Ahriman, the Children of Light
and the Children of Darkness. Black was the colour of death, of the
River Styx, of the devil; it was the colour of bad magic and melancholy, of poison, mourning, forsaken love and the lowest pit of hell.
There were black arts and black humours, blackmail and blacklists,
blackguards and black knights, the Black Death and 'souls as blak as
pykke'.[3] Borrowing the theme from Ovid, Gower and Chaucer had
Phoebus punish the crow by depriving him of his song and feathers

2. Jean Mocquet, *Travels and Voyages into Africa, Asia, and America, the
East and West-Indies, Syria, Jerusalem, and the Holy-Land* (tr. by Nath-
aniel Pullen, London, 1696), pp. 44–5. [Mocquet departed from Europe in
1601]; John Atkins, *A Voyage to Guinea, Brasil, and the West-Indies* ...
(London, 1735), p. 39; Oliver Goldsmith, *An History of the Earth, and
Animated Nature* (London, 1774), II, p. 226; *The Papers of Benjamin
Franklin* (ed. by Leonard W. Labaree *et al.*, New Haven, 1959–19—), IV, p.
234.

3. Harry Levin, *The Power of Blackness* (New York, 1958), pp. 35–8;
Don C. Allen, 'Symbolic Colour in the Literature of the English Re-
naissance', *Philological Quarterly*, XV (January 1936), pp. 83–4; P. J.
Heather. 'Colour Symbolism', *Folk Lore*, LIX (1948), pp. 165–83, 214.

'Welmore whyt than eny Swan'; henceforth, said Phoebus to Corvus, 'Thou and thyn of-spring ever shul be blake'. Before the discovery of America, Saracens were said to be 'Blac and blac als led', and there were countless legends of men turning black from sin and of black races sprung from hell.[4]

White, Herman Melville tells us, is the colour of purity and justice, of joy and sovereignty and holiness; it gave the European 'ideal mastership over every dusky tribe'. Yet there 'lurks an elusive something in the innermost idea of this hue, which strikes more panic to the soul than that redness which affrights in blood'.[5] Only the most unimaginative minds could fail to see the moral ambiguities of colour. A black whale or white Othello would lose all meaning. Through the ages men prized the darkest jet and ebony; Shakespeare's Proteus repeats 'the old saying' that 'black men are pearls in beauteous ladies' eyes', though Julia replies, ' 'Tis true, such pearls as put out ladies' eyes; For I had rather wink than look on them'.[6] According to Edmund Burke, blackness was a prime source of the sublime. Any dark object had the effect of relaxing the pupil of the eye, which then recovered by a kind of 'convulsive spring'. This optical shock evoked emotions of pain and terror. Burke told of a blind boy who had suddenly acquired vision as a result of surgery: 'The first time the boy saw a black object, it gave him great uneasiness. . . . Some time after, upon accidentally seeing a negro woman, he was struck with great horror at the sight.' Custom, however, 'reconciles us to every thing', and we learn to transmute our fear of dark things into feelings of awe, melancholy and fascination.[7]

Despite the sinister connotations of blackness, and despite the esteem which painters and poets showed for the fairest complexions, it was the opinion of Sir Thomas Browne, of Sir Joshua Reynolds and of Lord Kames that standards of beauty were a matter of custom. The African, no doubt, was happy with his own colour, and con-

4. Heather, 'Colour Symbolism', pp. 208–15.

5. Herman Melville, *Moby-Dick, or the Whale*, ch. xli.

6. *The Two Gentlemen of Verona*, V, 2.

7. Edmund Burke, *A Philosophical Enquiry into the Origin of our Ideas of the Sublime and Beautiful* (ed. by J. T. Boulton, London, 1958), pp. 59, 143–9. Burke was attempting to refute Locke's argument that man's terror of darkness was simply a product of association.

sidered the European's less attractive.[8] And Europeans were by no means blind to the physical beauty of Negroes. Velazquez's 'The Servant' portrays the warm flesh tones of a Negro woman whose resigned expression only heightens her great beauty and dignity.[9] Nor was such appreciation confined to Spain. Richard Ligon, writing in London in 1653, recalled that the Negro men he had seen were shaped exactly in accordance with Albrecht Dürer's rules on proportion. Even a Titian could not have captured the softness of muscle and the perfect movements of the young virgins. 'The young Maids', he went on, 'have ordinarily very large breasts, which stand strutting out so hard and firm, as no leaping, jumping, or stirring, will cause them to shake any more, than the brawns of their arms.' Ligon remembered meeting the black mistress of the Governor of St Jago:

Of the greatest beauty and majesty together: that ever I saw in one woman. Her stature large, and excellently shap'd, well favour'd, full ey'd, and admirably grac'd, she wore on her head a roll of green Taffaty, strip'd with white and Philiamort. ... On her body next her Linnen, a Peticoat of Orange Tawny and Sky colour ... and upon that a mantle of purple silk. ... In her ears, she wore large Pendants, about her neck, and on her arms, fair Pearls. But her eyes were her richest Jewels, for they were the largest and most oriental that I have ever seen.

Desperate to speak to this queenly beauty, Ligon presented her with a gift, whereupon he received the most lovely smile he had ever beheld, and 'such a look, as was a sufficient return for a far greater present'.[10]

European travellers, even the slave-ship captains, commented

8. Sir Thomas Browne, *Pseudodoxia Epidemica*, III, in *The Works of Sir Thomas Browne* (ed. by Geoffrey Keynes, London, 1928), pp. 246–7; Wylie Sypher, *Guinea's Captive Kings: British Anti-Slavery Literature of the Eighteenth Century* (Chapel Hill, 1942), pp. 50–51.

9. This painting may be seen in the Chicago Art Insititute. Carl N. Degler has called my attention to a similar subject painted by Rubens.

10. Richard Ligon, *A True and Exact History of the Island of Barbadoes* (London, 1673), pp. 12, 15–16, 51. Like many writers, Ligon much preferred the inhabitants of the Cape Verde Islands and other northern regions to those from the south. However, he wrote warmly human descriptions of the Negroes in Barbados, without making distinctions on point of origin.

with wonder on the agility, the gracefulness and the physical beauty of many Africans. Unused to the sight of whole populations in partial nakedness, they were often revolted by the sagging flesh of ageing women, but looked admiringly at the athletic forms of youths and maidens.[11] Moreover, to European writers of the seventeenth and eighteenth centuries, the Negroes were remarkable for the great beauty of their teeth and for general neatness and cleanliness. Again and again we find amazement expressed over the Africans' custom of daily baths. And Samuel Purchas was not the only chronicler to make the blunt confession that, although the Africans were totally unashamed of nakedness, 'yet it is holden shame with them to let a fart, which they wondered at in the Hollanders, esteeming it a contempt'.[12]

There was, however, the problem of the Negro's colour. Greeks said that when Phaeton's chariot had brought the sun too close to earth, the heat had blackened the Ethiopians' skin by rapidly forcing the blood to the surface. Onesicritus insisted that the cause was not the hot sun, as Theodectes claimed, but rather a different kind of water. This failed to convince Strabo, who observed that, while the sun might be equidistant from all parts of the earth, it certainly felt hotter

11. John Ogilby, *Africa: Being an Accurate Description of the Regions of . . . the Land of the Negroes . . .* (London, 1670), pp. 318–19; John Barbot, *A Description of the Coasts of North and South Guinea. . .*, in John Churchill, *A Collection of Voyages and Travels* (London, 1732), V, pp. 33–4, 235, 238; M. Adanson, *A Voyage to Senegal, the Isle of Goree, and the River Gambia,* in John Pinkerton, *A General Collection of the Best and Most Interesting Voyages . . .*, XVI (London, 1814), p. 608; William Bosman, *A New and Accurate Description of the Coast of Guinea . . .*, in Pinkerton, *General Collection,* XVI, p. 388; Thomas Astley, *A New General Collection of Voyages and Travels . . .* (London, 1745–47), I, pp. 152, 629, and *passim*; II, pp. 256, 263; *The Voyages of Cadamosto and Other Documents on Western Africa in the Second Half of the Fifteenth Century* (tr. and ed. by G. R. Crone, London, 1937), p. 14. It should be noted that many accounts of Africa borrowed from preceding ones.

12. Samuel Purchas, *Purchas his Pilgrimes in Five Bookes* (London, 1625), V, p. 718; Barbot, *Description of the Coasts of North and South Guinea,* pp. 235, 238; Ogilby, *Africa,* p. 318; Astley, *New General Collection,* II, p. 630, and *passim*; *Voyages of Cadamosto,* pp. 32–3.

in some regions, and probably darkened men's colour by reducing the amount of moisture on the surface of the skin.[13] The Koran affirmed that hell-fire blackens the skin. Negroes, said the Babylonian Talmud, were the children of Ham, who, according to varying legends, was cursed with blackness because he had castrated his father, or because he had had sexual relations on the Ark, in violation of God's command.[14]

These ancient beliefs were hardly improved upon as Europe entered the modern era. Early in the seventeenth century, Samuel Purchas subjected 'the varietie of answeres' he had heard to the tests of reason and religion. In a marginal note he mentioned the theory that Negroes bore the curse of Ham, who had been punished for knowing his wife in the Ark; Purchas apparently considered this plausible. But it was absurd to attribute blackness to the heat of the sun, since there were no black natives in the American tropics. Nor could one rely on the dryness of earth or air, 'as though the Libyan Dessarts are not more drie, (and yet the People no Negro's) and as though Niger were here dried vp'. Besides, the descendants of the early Portuguese remained white in Africa. If the colour of Negroes was due to the blackness of their parents' seed, as some affirmed, why were they reddish at birth and yellowish at age? It was, then, one of God's supreme mysteries, and simply demonstrated the divine pattern of substance and accident, of unity and diversity. And in an eloquent expression of Christian faith, Purchas concluded that God had infinitely multiplied mankind,

exceedingly varried in accidents, that we also might serue that *One-most* God: that the tawnie Moore, blacke Negro, duskie Libyan, ash-coloured Indian, oliue-coloured American, should, with the whiter Europaean become *one sheepe-fold*, vnder *one Great Sheepheard*, till *this mortalitie being swallowed up of life*, we may all *be one, as He and the*

13. Thomas Bulfinch, *Bulfinch's Mythology* (Modern Library ed., New York, n.d.), p. 40; Strabo, *Geography*, xv, 1, 24.

14. *The Koran* (tr. by J. M. Rodwell, London, 1957), p. 22; Thomas F. Gossett, *Race: The History of an Idea in America* (Dallas, 1963), p. 5. We have already discussed ambiguities in the Biblical account of Canaan's curse. The fact that the curse was laid on Canaan, and not Ham, his erring father, caused considerable confusion through the ages.

Father are one ... filling Heauen and earth with their *euerlasting Halleluiahs*, without any more distinction of Colour, Nation, Language, Sexe, Condition, all may bee *One* in him that is ONE, *and only blessed for euer. Amen.*[15]

This was the very heart of Christian belief and the basis for all attempts at conversion. Scholars might continue to ponder the origins of the African's colour. Sir Thomas Browne, for example, rejected the heat of the sun and the curse of Canaan, and suggested that the cause of the original mutation might have been the use of certain oils on the skin, the power of imagination, or some chemical substance or 'black Jaundise'.[16] But good Christians knew that all men were created in God's image and that all were black, as Samuel Bowden wrote, in the darkness of the tomb.[17] The theory that Negroes were descended from apes or at least had a separate origin from the rest of mankind was first associated with freethinkers and innovators like the German physician, Paracelsus, and the Italian philosophers, Lucilio Vanini and Giordano Bruno.[18]

Yet many writers magnified the physical or mental differences between whites and Negroes, and sought to explain them by ancient legends. Richard Jobson, who traded along the African coast in 1621, refused to buy slaves on grounds of moral principle. But he took 'the enormous Size of the virile Member among the Negroes' as 'an infallible Proof, that they are sprung from *Canaan*, who, for uncovering his Father's Nakedness, had (according to the Schoolmen) a

15. The quotations are from the 3rd ed. of Purchas's *Pilgrimes* (London, 1617), pp. 821–2. The marginal note is in vol. V of the 1625 ed., p. 723. Winthrop Jordan points out that as early as 1516, Peter Martyr remarked on the differences between Negroes and Indians living at the same degrees of latitude.

16. Browne, *Pseudodoxia Epidemica*, pp. 232–46; Sypher, *Guinea's Captive Kings*, pp. 50–51. Browne devoted considerable effort to refuting the theory of Canaan's curse. The curse of Canaan had long been used to justify even the servitude of Europeans, and was part of Portuguese and Spanish rationalizations for Negro slavery.

17. Hoxie Neale Fairchild, *Religious Trends in English Poetry* (New York, 1939–49), II: *Religious Sentimentalism in the Age of Johnson, 1740–1780*, p. 56.

18. Gossett, *Race*, p. 15.

Curse laid upon that Part'.[19] Although Peter Heylyn was presumably a good Christian, since he was a 'high-flying' Anglican and a friend of Archbishop Laud, he described Negroes as lacking 'the use of Reason which is peculiar unto man; of little Wit, and destitute of all Arts and Sciences; prone to Luxury, and for the greatest part Idolaters'. They had a bad smell and were so in love with their own complexions that they painted the devil white! Heylyn at first agreed with Purchas that the origin of their colour was one of God's mysteries, but by the 1660s he was inclined to give some credit to the theory of Ham's curse. As late as 1704 an English letter-writer cited him as an authority for this view.[20]

With the growth of the international slave trade in the last quarter of the seventeenth century, theories of Negro inferiority apparently gained in popularity. In 1680 Morgan Godwyn shrewdly observed that it was in the interests of planters and traders to propagate the belief that Africans were not really men; and the character of his rebuttal gives some clue to the shifting trends of opinion. The legend of Ham was respectable enough to deserve an outflanking movement; even if a black skin were the mark of Ham's curse, Godwyn said, this failed to prove that Negroes were not human. Planters would hardly use brutes to oversee the work of other brutes. Like Sir Thomas Browne, Godwyn emphasized the relativity of colour, which may be taken as evidence of a common prejudice towards blackness.[21] He also felt it necessary to counter the claim that Negroes were monsters whose unions with human beings produced only sterile offspring. And even Godwyn was prepared to believe reports that Africans had 'unnatural conjunctions' with apes and drills.[22]

Winthrop Jordan has commented on the tragic consequences of

19. Astley, *New General Collection*, II, p. 268.

20. Peter Heylyn, ΜΙΚΡΟΚΟΣΜΟΣ, *A Little Description of the Great World* (5th ed., Oxford, 1631), p. 719; Heylyn, *Cosmographie in Foure Books Contayning the Chorographie and Historie of the Whole World* ... (3rd ed., London, 1667), pp. 44–5, 87; *The Athenian Oracle: Being an Entire Collection of All the Valuable Questions and Answers in the Old Athenian Mercuries*, III (London, 1704), pp. 380–81.

21. Morgan Godwyn, *The Negro's and Indian's Advocate, Suing for their Admission into the Church* ... (London, 1680), pp. 12, 19–22.

22. ibid., pp. 12, 23.

the entirely fortuitous fact that Negroes and the most human-appearing apes were found living in proximity in the same part of the world.[23] European folklore was filled with ape men, were-animals, and the monstrous products of every kind of bestiality; the variety and grotesqueness of such creatures had been greatly increased by the fantasies of early explorers and chroniclers. Despite the European's view of himself as a god-like being, his mythology had always acknowledged an uneasy awareness of kinship with the lower animals. And despite the ancient belief in the fixed distinctiveness of species, the equally ancient belief in continuity suggested the likelihood of infinite gradations between each form of animal life.[24] In the late seventeenth century one such link between man and the apes was supposedly found in the Hottentots, whose brutish appearance and bestial customs became stereotyped in the literature of the following century.[25] Then in 1699 Dr Edward Tyson published the results of his dissection of a chimpanzee, *Orang-Outang, sive Homo Sylvestris*, which proved the anatomical similarities between man and ape. Anton Leeuwenhoek claimed that the blood of Negroes was different from that of whites. Marcello Malpighi located the Negro's colour in a layer of mucous membrane between the scarf and true skin. All these discoveries were employed by writers, particularly in France, who argued that the Africans were a separate species and constituted a link between man and the beasts. While the theory of Ham's curse continued to be defended and refuted through the eighteenth century, the *Journal des Savants* concluded as early as 1684 that Negroes must be a different species from the rest of mankind.

23. Jordan, 'White Over Black', chs. 1 and 6.

24. Arthur O. Lovejoy, *The Great Chain of Being: A Study of the History of an Idea* (Torchbook paperback ed., New York, 1960), pp. 183, 194–203, 227–34.

25. Isaac Schapera, *The Early Cape Hottentots, Described in the Writings of Olfert Dapper (1668), Willen ten Rhyne (1686) and Johannes Gulielmus de Grevenbraek* (1695) (Capetown, 1935), p. 127, and *passim*; Katherine George, 'The Civilized West Looks at Primitive Africa, 1400–1800; A Study in Ethnocentrism', *Isis*, XLIX (1958), pp. 66–72; Paul Hazard, *European Thought in the Eighteenth Century, from Montesquieu to Lessing* (Meridian paperback ed., tr. by J. Lewis May, Cleveland, 1963), pp. 367–8.

Thomas Astley pointed out that such a 'heterodox' view threatened to undermine the entire Biblical view of man's creation. But precisely for this reason, the belief in Negro inferiority became an anti-religious weapon in the hands of French philosophers, the most notable of whom was Voltaire.[26]

For our purposes it is unnecessary to discuss the complex history of biological theory or the controversies over the objectivity of 'species'. It is sufficient to note that the eighteenth century witnessed the initial breakthrough in biological science. And as systems of classification were refined by Linnaeus and Buffon, it became ever more apparent that man was part of the animal kingdom, and was structurally and functionally so much like the ape that no sharp distinctions could be made. The discoveries of biologists seemed to confirm the ancient idea of the chain of being as an infinitely graded continuum from the lowest to the highest forms. The classification of mankind by colour and physical type, which was initiated by François Bernier in 1684, did not necessarily imply a ranking within the species by relative superiority. Yet Bernier referred to the Lapps as 'villains animaux', and Linnaeus, who resisted all theories of racial inferiority, described the Africans as 'phlegmatic ... indolent and negligent ... [and] governed by caprice'. Various writers, such as Charles Bonnet and Soame Jenyns, expressed belief in an unbroken scale of beings from the ape through the Hottentot to a final pinnacle of genius usually symbolized by Sir Isaac Newton. Such a ranking by individual intelligence was not the same as relegating an entire race to a subordinate position. Nevertheless, the Negro continued to suffer by his repeated association with the 'orang-outang', or chimpanzee. Even Buffon said the orang-outang was 'ardent' for Negro women. Lord Monboddo, who had an obsessive interest in feral men and who claimed that he could prove there had been a mathematics teacher at Inverness with a

26. Gladys Bryson, *Man and Society: The Scottish Inquiry of the Eighteenth Century* (Princeton, 1945), p. 57; Russell P. Jameson, *Montesquieu et l'esclavage: étude sur les origines de l'opinion antiesclavagiste en France au XVIIIᵉ siècle* (Paris, 1911), pp. 174–82; Edward D. Seeber, *Anti-Slavery Opinion in France during the Second Half of the Eighteenth Century* (Baltimore, 1937), pp. 14–15; *Gentleman's Magazine*, XII (1742), p. 279; Astley, *New General Collection*, p. 270; Charles Leslie, *A New History of Jamaica* ... (London, 1740), p. 312; Gossett, *Race*, p. 45.

foot-and-a-half long tail, insisted that orang-outangs were rational men who happened to live in a primitive state of nature.[27]

Such blurring of the traditional line between man and the beasts was encouraged by eighteenth-century environmentalism. One of the most extreme environmentalists, Julien de La Mettrie, held that if a monkey were only taught the art of speech, he would be the equal of Louis XV! On one level, this faith in the teachability of all primates blocked the way to theories of racial inferiority. Montesquieu pointed to the importance of climate as a shaping influence, and the Abbé Raynal confidently asserted that Negroes became whiter the longer they lived away from Africa. According to Adam Smith, the philosopher and common street-porter had been much alike as children; individual differences could generally be explained by education, custom and habit. Similarly, the differences between societies were the result of economic conditions and opportunities. Africa had simply been handicapped by geographic isolation and by a lack of navigable rivers.[28] Men were so plastic that their physical and cultural variations were merely the temporary products of environmental pressures.

But on another level, environmentalism severely strained the belief in man's natural equality. We have seen how Rousseau suspected that certain oppressive conditions might dehumanize men by depriving them of their love for liberty. Oliver Goldsmith could attribute the Negro's differences to climate, and yet refer to the entire race as

27. Bryson, *Man and Society*, pp. 58–73; Jordan, 'White Over Black', ch. 6; George Louis Leclerc Buffon, *Natural History, Containing a Theory of the Earth, a General History of Man, of the Brute Creation . . .* (London, 1797–1807), IV, pp. 277–333, 351–2; Gossett, *Race*, pp. 32–6; Leslie Stephen, *History of English Thought in the Eighteenth Century* (reprint ed., New York, 1949), I, pp. 68–9; [Jean F. Dauxion-Lavaysse], *A Statistical, Commercial, and Political Description of Venezuela, Trinidad, Margarita, and Tobago* (tr. by E. Blaquière, London, 1820), pp. 366–9.

28. John Herman Randall, *The Career of Philosophy: From the Middle Ages to the Enlightenment* (New York, 1962), p. 897; Guillaume-Thomas Raynal, *Histoire philosophique et politique . . . des Européens dans les deux Indes* (Genéve, 1781), VI, pp. 39–40; Adam Smith, *An Inquiry into the Nature and Causes of the Wealth of Nations* (Modern Library ed., New York, 1937), pp. 15–16, 20–21. *Gentleman's Magazine* told of a Negro maid in Maryland who supposedly turned white (XXX [1760], p. 361).

'stupid, indolent and mischievous'.[29] Even sympathetic writers often implied that, while the African's differences arose from his environment, he had become in some way inferior to the European. This conclusion was actually reinforced by the theories of scientists like Buffon and Pierre de Maupertuis, who none the less believed in the unity of the human race. Negroes and Europeans had the same origin and were members of the same species. But for Buffon, as indeed for most theorists of the eighteenth century, the white man was the human norm, the Negro the deviation. This ethnocentric assumption seemed to be confirmed by African albinos and by the relative whiteness of Negroes at birth. Blackness was therefore a kind of aberration or disease – some said it came from a vitriolic substance that had been trapped and had fermented between the layers of skin; and as a result of climatic and chemical causes, the Africans had 'degenerated', to use Buffon's term, from their white ancestral type.[30] This was, in a sense, a secular version of Ham's curse, the climate taking the place of God's judgement.

Environmentalists repeatedly associated cultural traits with the Negro's supposed physical deformity. And the one eighteenth-century writer who had some understanding of the relation of character to cultural and situational environment failed to extend his insights to the Negro. Even before Montesquieu had made it a fashion to exaggerate the influence of climate, David Hume had written a brilliant analysis of the ways cultural environment and social role affect human character. He gave no thought to race as a product of biological inheritance. A coxcomb, he said, might beget a philosopher. But in 1754, some twelve years after the first appearance of the work, Hume appended a long note to his essay, 'Of National Characters'. The extremes of climate in the polar and tropical latitudes 'perhaps' accounted for the apparent inferiority of 'nations' in those areas. Yet like Thomas Jefferson a generation later, Hume suspected Negroes 'to be naturally inferior to the whites'. This was because they had produced no civilized nations, no eminent individuals in the arts and sciences, in government or war. Hume now seemed to doubt his original suggestion about climate: 'Such a uniform and constant dif-

29. Goldsmith, *History of the Earth*, pp. 228, 239–40.
30. Buffon, *Natural History*, IV, pp. 324, 351–2; Gossett, *Race*, p. 36.

ference could not happen, in so many countries and ages, if nature had not made an original distinction betwixt these breeds of men.' There had been reports, it was true, of a learned Negro in Jamaica, but Hume thought it likely his accomplishments had been much like those of a parrot.[31]

Here was an assertion of racial inferiority cloaked in the cautious, reasoned language of science. Yet Hume's reputation as a notorious atheist gave the theory a strong flavour of infidelity. Chambon accused Voltaire of using the same idea to undermine revealed religion, and tried to check the subtle strategy with a battery of arguments ranging from biology to Newtonian optics. James Beattie, who led the assault against Hume, warned that the inferiority of Negroes had become a favourite topic for writers whose real target was the authority of Scripture. Beattie was quite beyond his depth when he challenged Hume in such subjects as epistemology; but he was able to show that the philosopher had no evidence to support his claim of 'a uniform and constant difference'. Hume knew nothing of the history of Africa. He compared primitive and civilized societies without regard for the relativity of customs, the crimes and vices of Europe, and the fact that civilization had been contingent upon a few accidental inventions, for which the bulk of Europeans could claim no credit. Above all, he offered no proof that Africans could not be educated and improved. About 1730 a Negro had attended meetings of the Royal Society and had been rejected for membership only because of his colour. The trouble was that Negroes had been universally treated as inferiors, and had never been given a chance.[32] In effect, Beattie showed that apparent racial inferiority could be explained by Hume's own theories of character formation. But by quoting Hume at such length, he also helped disseminate the very idea he sought to refute.

31. David Hume, *Essays Moral, Political, and Literary* (ed. by T. H. Green and T. H. Grose, London, 1889), I, pp. 244–52.

32. [Chambon], *Le commerce de l'Amérique par Marseille* . . . (Avignon, 1764), II, avertissement, pp. 346–400, 436–43; *Gentleman's Magazine*, XLI (1771), pp. 594–6; James Beattie, *An Essay on the Nature and Immutability of Truth, in Opposition to Sophistry and Scepticism* (7th ed., London, 1807), pp. 56–7, 424–8.

In the eyes of John Wesley, Hume was 'the most insolent despiser of truth and virtue that ever appeared in the world'. And while Wesley in general thought of primitive men as bestial idolators, who would be too much honoured if compared with horses, he looked upon the Africans, as we have seen, in an altogether different light. For most orthodox Christians, indeed, the barbarity of primitive peoples was empirical proof of man's degeneration from an uncorrupted state. But Hume had helped to make a defence of the African a defence of religion itself. Accordingly, early anti-slavery writers like James Ramsay and Granville Sharp tried to vindicate human nature with all the fervour and caustic wit of the first anti-Darwinists. If Hume were a West Indian slave, Ramsay said, he would no doubt be a conjurer, and would be rightfully flogged for imposing on the credulity of his fellows.[33] By repeatedly identifying the theory of racial inferiority with Hume, Voltaire and materialistic philosophy in general, anti-slavery writers undoubtedly made the idea less palatable. Unfortunately, this alignment also had the effect of tying racism to secular science, which by the late eighteenth century was beginning to show an increasing sensitivity to human differences. Some of the most eminent investigators, such as J. F. Blumenbach, continued to maintain that racial types were only varieties of a single species. But at the very end of the century it was possible for a famous English physiologist to oppose slavery, observing that laws should give no greater freedom to the Newtons than to other men, and yet hold that the Negro's place on the chain of being was closer to the ape than to man.[34]

Few eighteenth-century writers could equal Edward Long in gross racial prejudice, and because Long's most outrageous slanders have

33. Margaret T. Hodgen, 'The Negro in the Anthropology of John Wesley', *Journal of Negro History*, XIX (July 1934), pp. 308–23; James Ramsay, *An Essay on the Treatment and Conversion of African Slaves in the British Sugar Colonies* (London, 1784), pp. 198–245 ; Granville Sharp to William Dilwyn, 25 July 1774 (Sharp Papers, British and Foreign Bible Society); Prince Hoare, *Memoirs of Granville Sharp* ... (London, 1820), pp. ix–xi.

34. Gossett, *Race*, pp. 47–50; Frank E. Manuel, *The Prophets of Paris* (Cambridge, Mass., 1962), pp. 125–7.

often been quoted, it is easy to overlook the fact that he assumed the mantle of the scientific philosopher, and expressed opinions which were not only public ideology in Jamaica and South Carolina, but were apparently acceptable to an influential minority in Europe. A number of random examples may help substantiate the latter point. C. R. Boxer has translated a pamphlet published in Lisbon in 1764, which, he says, accurately reflects Portuguese racial attitudes of that time. The work is in the form of a dialogue between a Portuguese lawyer and a miner who has recently been in Brazil. The lawyer accepts slavery and even the need for corporal punishment; his arguments are all in defence of charitable treatment. The miner at first thinks the lawyer must be joking. Since he was a boy he has heard that Negroes were descended from Cain; in any event they are black and cannot be true men like the Europeans. In Brazil they are treated worse than animals and yet endure all their suffering. An owner has a perfect right to do as he pleases with his own property; he may break his word or even kill his slaves, and no one cares. The miner speaks from his own observations. He insists that the lawyer does not know what Negroes are like, and he is indignant to think that any white man would defend Negroes. Although this pamphlet was obviously written to encourage more humane treatment, it also reveals the existence of widespread racial prejudice.[35]

In 1765, when Arthur Lee was enlightening Englishmen on the Negro character, Rousselot de Surgy was spreading similar views in France. The following year a critic of *Ephémérides du citoyen* triumphantly quoted from a work of natural history which asserted that Negroes' souls were as black as their skins, and that their intelligence appeared inferior to that which had been admired in elephants: 'Leur naturel est pervers, toutes leurs inclinations sont vicieuses.' And since there was not a Negro from the highest king to the lowliest slave who would not sell his wife and children for some alcohol, it was obvious that fear alone would make them perform their duties.[36] In 1775 the argument that Negroes were by nature incapable of freedom received

35. C. R. Boxer, 'Negro Slavery in Brazil', *Race* (January 1964), pp. 38–47.

36. Seeber, *Anti-Slavery Opinion in France*, p. 52; *Ephémérides du citoyen, ou chronique de l'esprit national*, VI (1766), pp. 139–40.

strong support from Pierre Victor Malouet, who had been a high official in Guiana and Saint Domingue; and in 1777 a royal declaration prohibited the entry of Negroes into France on grounds of public security and because 'les maisons publiques en sont infecées; les couleurs se mêlent, le sang s'altère'.[37]

In 1774, the year when Long's *History of Jamaica* was published, Oliver Goldsmith described the Negroes' physiognomy and 'insupportable' smell in terms as derogatory as Long's; and in the same year Janet Schaw, a British 'lady of quality', visited Antigua and mistook the Negro children for monkeys. Though shocked at first by the scars from brutal floggings, she was comforted to find 'when one comes to be better acquainted with the nature of the Negroes, the horrour of it must wear off'. The Africans were 'brutes' whose 'natures seem made to bear it, and whose sufferings are not attended with shame or pain beyond the present moment'. The slaves remained indifferent even to the division of their own families in public sales. At least such was the opinion of a cultivated lady who was well versed in the works of the Scottish Enlightenment.[38]

We must not presume, therefore, that Edward Long lacked a sympathetic audience, or was totally unrepresentative of his time. For credentials he could offer twelve years of residence in Jamaica, which included service with the lieutenant-governor, who was his brother-in-law, and experience as a vice-admiralty judge. He could make a show of familiarity with all the leading authorities on race and servitude, and lost no chance of enlisting in his cause such names as Hume and Franklin. He compared the theory that Negroes were a separate species to the Copernican system, which had also appeared heretical at first, but which proved to be the only means of accounting for observable phenomena. And Long couched the most vicious falsehoods in the language of cautious inquiry: examples might possibly

37. Leon Deschamps, *Histoire de la question coloniale en France* (Paris, 1891), pp. 327–8; Charles Verlinden, *L'Esclavage dans l'Europe médiévale, I: Péninsule Ibérique, France* (Brugge, 1955), p. 853.

38. Evangeline W. Andrews and Charles M. Andrews (eds.) *Journal of a Lady of Quality: Being a Narrative of a Journey from Scotland to the West Indies, North Carolina, and Portugal, in the Years 1774 to 1776* (New Haven, 1921), pp. 87, 127–8.

have occurred, he admitted, of living offspring being produced from the union of two mulattoes. He had never heard of such a case, however (and he implied that he had given the matter serious study); and he strongly suspected that whenever an apparently fruitful match had been found, the 'lady' had been intriguing with a white man or Negro. Long made it clear that he stood for freedom of thought and healthy scepticism, as apposed to bigotry, credulity and superstition.[39]

He claimed, nevertheless, to be a pious man. Instead of degrading human nature, the theory of racial inferiority should confirm our belief in the rationality, the fecundity and the perfection of our Creator. What could be better testimony of the omnipotence of God than a beautifully complete chain of being, a 'series and progression from a lump of dirt to a perfect man', which displayed an infinite number of variations on a simple design or model? Long did not explain why one link in this harmonious chain should be so loathsome. But he made no effort to conceal his disgust for the 'bestial fleece', the 'tumid nostrils', the 'bestial or fetid smell, which they all have in a greater or less degree'. Even the Negroes' lice were black and presumably inferior.[40]

When he turned to the field of psychology, Long did not have to bother with the ancient assumption that all men were endowed with a rational soul. It was sufficient to say that Negroes were incapable of combining or reflecting upon the simple ideas received through their senses. They also lacked the inherent moral sense which was a prerequisite to virtue. Consequently, they could desire no more than food, drink, sex and idleness, and would pursue these ends without restraint. Regardless of what might be said of the Africans in ancient times – and Long stated that there had been no sign of progresss for two thousand years – they were now 'a brutish, ignorant, idle, crafty, treacherous, bloody, thievish, mistrustful, and superstitious people'. And there was even a proverb to the effect that all the world's people possessed some good qualities, except for the Africans.[41]

39. [Edward Long], *The History of Jamaica, or, General Survey of the Antient and Modern State of that Island* . . . (London, 1774), II, 335–7, 376, 533.
40. ibid., II, pp. 337, 352–8.
41. ibid., II, pp. 353–4, 377.

As might be expected, the good judge took a more favourable view of the 'orang-outang'. Just as Negroes appeared to become less human as one moved southwards from the region of the Moors and Jaloffs to the Hottentots, so there were many gradations of apes. Buffon and other writers had described chimpanzees who showed feelings of shame and sensibility, and who had been taught to eat at a table with knives and forks. It was probable that they could learn a degree of speech and could 'perform a variety of menial domestic services'; with 'a little pains', Long thought, they might be taught as much of the 'mechanic arts' as any Negro. There were reports of apes in Africa who lived in fabricated huts, to which they sometimes carried Negro women.

And for this subject Long showed a fantastic obsession. The chimpanzee would covet Negro women 'from a natural impulse of desire, such as inclines one animal towards another of the same species, or which has a conformity in the organs of generation'. Presumably the latter principle could be extended to all mankind. But with Negroes the sexual act was as 'libidinous and shameless' as with monkeys and baboons. And since 'both races' shared such a 'lasciviousness of disposition', Long did not think 'that an orang-outang husband would be any dishonour to a Hottentot female'. Indeed, there was reason to believe that Negro women frequently admitted such animals to their embraces. Such a union had reportedly occurred in the refined atmosphere of England itself; thus 'how freely may it not operate in the more genial soil of Africa, that parent of every thing that is monstrous in nature, where . . . the passions rage without any controul; and the retired wilderness presents opportunity to gratify them without fear of detection'![42] Obviously the West Indies presented a similar opportunity to men like Edward Long, and we may suspect, without indulging in long-distance psychoanalysis, that his obsession with the animality of sex was in some way coloured with guilt. And yet he had merely developed universal themes of folk mythology to their most extreme and grotesque conclusions.

There were two obvious ways of disproving Long's contention that Negroes were a separate species, inferior to men and closely related to apes. One might find individual Negroes whose attainments met

42. ibid., II, pp. 355, 359–74, 382–3.

the tests of European refinement. This would become a major preoccupation with anti-slavery writers, and Long did his best to head off the strategy. He recited the history of Francis Williams, who was the 'parrot' referred to by Hume. As an experiment, the Duke of Montague had had Williams educated in England, where he had attended Cambridge University and had progressed in mathematics. After returning to Jamaica, he had written Latin poems and had run a school in Spanish Town. But according to Long, he had 'looked down with sovereign contempt on his fellow Blacks, entertained the highest opinion of his own knowledge, treated his parents with much disdain, and behaved towards his children and his slaves with a severity bordering upon cruelty'. This could be dismissed as a prejudiced judgement, although such overcompensations are by no means unusual in individuals who have been subject to rapid acculturation. But then Long printed some of Williams's celebrated poetry, and laid down a highly exacting principle. Such specimens must be judged with absolute impartiality, 'for if we regard it as an extraordinary production, merely because it came from a *Negroe*, we admit at once that *inequality* of genius which has been before supposed, and admire it only as a rare phaenomenon'.[43] So far as one accepted the premise that Negroes must prove their equality by meeting the standards of European culture, Long's point could not be denied. The problem would continue to plague the opponents of slavery. But another line of attack would be to demonstrate that the inhabitants of Africa were by no means so destitute of culture as Long maintained. And here, both sides of the racial controversy would be dependent on the accounts of captains and traders who had mostly gone to the African coast in search of slaves.

Historians have sometimes exaggerated Europe's long ignorance of the Dark Continent. It is true that the most informed pictures of Africa were usually blurred by mists of exotic fantasy. So much of Europe's original knowledge had been filtered through the Arab world that even eighteenth-century accounts of Negro culture often had a strongly 'Moorish' flavour.[44] Before 1796, when Mungo Park

43. ibid., II, pp. 475–84.
44. Sypher, *Guinea's Captive Kings*, pp. 25–30.

made his great exploration of the Niger, apparently no European had journeyed with a slave caravan. Except for the Portuguese in Angola, European contact with African tribes was limited to a narrow belt along the coast. On the other hand, the men who wrote reports of their African travels were generally curious, practical-minded and highly skilled in observation. As virtual business partners of the Negro traders they asked questions, watched the societies around them, and recorded a vast amount of detailed information. And if one may judge by the number of travel books and the massive collections of 'voyages', often lavishly adorned with maps, charts and illustrations, there was an astonishing market for comparative anthropology in eighteenth-century England and France. Nor did the readers of this literature receive only a fanciful impression of the Negro as a generalized type. Anyone with a casual exposure to the subject would know that differences in character and custom distinguished even neighbouring groups like the 'Koromantees' of the Gold Coast and the 'Papaws' of Whidah.[45] The newest authors were quick to expose the misconceptions of their predecessors, and editors claimed to present the true versions of old texts that had previously appeared in garbled form. Abolitionists like William Smith subjected dozens of accounts to the most conscientious analysis, and found a high degree of consistency in descriptions of African customs.[46]

Indeed, one of the most comprehensive modern studies of a West African culture presents a picture strikingly similar to that of eighteenth-century accounts.[47] It was known two centuries ago that

45. Astley, *New General Collection*, I, preface; II, preface; Basil Davidson, *Black Mother: The Years of the African Slave Trade* (Boston, 1961), p. 10. This point receives support from Philip D. Curtin's *The Image of Africa: British Ideas and Action, 1780–1850* (Madison, Wisc., 1964), pp. 10–13, which appeared too late to be of use.

46. In William Smith's papers (Duke University Library) there are detailed charts summarizing information about Africa and the slave trade.

47. I have compared historical accounts of Dahomey and neighbouring areas with Melville J. Herskovits, *Dahomey: An Ancient West African Kingdom* (New York, 1938), and Melville J. and Frances S. Herskovits, *Dahomean Narrative: A Cross-Cultural Analysis* (Evanston, Ill., 1958). It should be noted that Dahomey, or Whidah, was a key area for the slave

Negroes lived in settled, agricultural societies; that they cultivated a variety of crops, raised large herds of cattle, and planted groves of shade trees. It was known that they were highly skilled in the use of iron and copper, in the making of jewellery and pottery, and in the weaving of fine cotton textiles. As early as 1670 John Ogilby commented on their handsome clothing, and various writers admired what they termed a blue-glazed linen.

It was known that Africans lived in neat and spacious villages, which allowed privacy to the individual while preserving an intricate system of class and family distinctions. It was known that Negro children were particularly close to their mothers, and were seldom punished or made to work, which was a fact that shocked Europeans. Numerous books told of the Negroes' polite manners, their well-established patterns of trade, their knowledge of the planets and con-stellations (Michel Adanson thought they would make excellent as-tronomers), and their skilful but 'lascivious' dances.[48] Few Europeans could appreciate African music; but in Barbados, Richard Ligon be-came fascinated by the drum rhythms of the newly arrived slaves. Though their music had no tune, 'so strangely they varie their time, as 'tis a pleasure to the most curious ears. . . . If they had the variety of tune, which gives the greater scope in Musick, as they have of time, they would do wonders in that Art.' If this seemed to be a forecast of jazz, Ligon was even more impressed when he began instructing a slave named Macow. Macow instantly grasped the significance of sharps and flats, and proceeded to invent a kind of xylophone.[49] We can only guess what sounds must have emerged from this seven-teenth-century experiment in musicology!

But today, when so much of the world has been Westernized, and when the Western world has come to value primitive styles in art and

---

trade, and that many of the cultural patterns found by the Herskovitses were common to other West African tribes.

48. Ogilby, *Africa*, pp. 320–23; *Voyages of Cadamosto*, pp. 31–2; Ad-anson, *Voyage to Senegal*, p. 654; Astley, *New General Collection*, II, pp. 275, 632; III, pp. 11–14; Philippe Fermin, *Déscription générale, historique, géographique et physique de la colonie de Surinam* . . . (Amsterdam, 1769), I, pp. 133–40; II, pp. 263–5.

49. Ligon, *True and Exact History*, pp. 48–9.

music, it is difficult to imagine the cultural gap that separated eighteenth-century Europe and Africa. John Atkins probably spoke for most travellers when he said that the Africans seemed like the people one might expect to find on another planet.[50] Observers searched for categories with which to explain the astounding fact that creatures could be so obviously human and yet so different. Adanson, in a passage later borrowed by John Wesley and other anti-slavery writers, compared West Africa to the Garden of Eden, and the inhabitants to man's first parents. The garden image extended from the world primeval to Jean Labat's description of Sierra Leone as an idyllic Arcadia, with orchards, grazing flocks, and many rivers watering the fertile soil.[51] But in Western culture primitivism had always been balanced by anti-primitivism; if somewhere there were noble savages whose simple virtue and happiness had never been infected by civilization's sins, then there must also be nasty savages who delighted in the most bestial acts of cruelty and indecency. The two types of savagery, which were projections of civilized man's deepest wishes and fears, screened off the reality of Africa.

The Negro was either an idolator who lacked any sense of piety, or he worshipped one Creator and grasped the essential truths of natural religion. Even the most perceptive observers were incapable of appreciating the African's highly complex picture of the supernatural world, the significance of his rituals, the richness of his mythology and artistic forms; nor did they understand the pervading influence of the African's ancestors, the meaning of his extended family and social groupings, or his intricate rules on property holding and inheritance.[52] Ironically, it was his business dealings with the European

50. Atkins, *Voyage to Guinea*, p. 34; William Smith, *Nouveau Voyage de Guinée* (Paris, 1751), pp. 29–31.

51. Adanson, *Voyage to Senegal*, p. 612; Astley, *New General Collection*, II, pp. 322–3; III, pp. 7–8. One may note that travellers often associated the parasitic diseases of West Africa with the climate, which is actually temperate and healthful (see W. E. F. Ward, *A History of Ghana* [London, 1958], pp. 30–31).

52. Herskovits, *Dahomey*, I, pp. iv, 29–30, 80–96, 157–94, 207–10, 239, 242–4; II, pp. 101–3, 288–94; Herskovits and Herskovits, *Dahomean Narrative*, pp. 91–4.

that provided the most convincing glimpses of the Negro's humanity and high level of sophistication; and this was information which anti-slavery writers declined to use. Anthony Benezet, for example, does not tell us about the beautiful and witty Negro courtesan who spoke fluent English, French and Portuguese, who lived in a well-furnished house equipped with many slaves, and who served Sieur Brüe a magnificent dinner on fine table linen, and even gave him English punch. The travel books make it clear that Europeans in West Africa were dominated politically by powerful natives. The king of Dahomey prevented forts from being built along his coast, and for two years held an Englishman for ransom. The shrewd Negro merchants who dealt with Europeans on equal terms and kept a tight control over the interior trade were anything but 'natural slaves'. But the power and disciplined organization which evidenced a high level of cultural development also proved that Negroes played a larger part in the slave trade than abolitionists wished to believe.[53]

It takes unusual objectivity to see that an alien society is neither more innocent nor more wicked than one's own. And since African culture permitted the open expression of many impulses that had long been sublimated in Europe, it presented something of the shock and challenge of defiant criminality. Negroes did practice human sacrifice, and since large numbers of slaves were sometimes killed at religious ceremonies, there was a shred of truth to the argument that the slave trade saved lives. Cruelty was closely related to the African's ideal of stoic courage. Melville J. Herskovits has noted the absence of tragic themes in the ancient oral narratives of Dahomey. The Dahomean assumed a mask of insensitivity in the face of trials, thinking that self-pity in any form would only invite further trouble. To the European, however, this cultural trait often appeared as evidence of unfeeling animality, although few animals are notable for their resignation to pain. The impression was reinforced, however, by the Africans' judicial ordeals of torture and their cosmetic devices of bored lips and cicatrization. The most memorable images that emerged from the travel literature were not of industrious farmers and wea-

53. Barbot, *Description of the Coasts of North and South Guinea,* p. 34; Astley, *New General Collection,* II, p. 83; Ward, *History of Ghana,* pp. 88, 142–3; Smith, *Nouveau Voyage de Guinée, passim.*

vers, but of a people who mutilated their bodies and drank human blood, and of kings who lived in palaces decorated by thousands of human skulls.[54]

The latter picture was furnished by Bullfinch Lambe, the English prisoner of the king of Dahomey. Lambe also reported that the king had two thousand wives, and was eager to obtain a white mistress. Hoping to win his freedom, Lambe wrote to Governor Tinker and asked whether he knew of some cast-off woman who could be persuaded she would have little to fear from a king with two thousand wives.[55] This incident, which was repeatedly used to document the Negroes' barbarity, brings us to the greatest irony in the conflict between European and African cultures. For if sex obviously provided a medium for very human relationships, it was also the major obstacle to an acceptance of the Negro as an equal being.

Long before the discovery of America, Europeans associated the Negro with sexual indulgence. We have already mentioned some of the legends which gave a sexual colouring to the curse of Ham. In 1447 Antonio Malfante learned from the caravan gossip of the Sahara that the people to the south lived in cities, committed all forms of incest, and were as carnal as the beasts. Through the seventeenth and eighteenth centuries the accounts of French, Dutch and English travellers were virtually unanimous: Africans were shamelessly licentious; the women were incredibly hot and lascivious, and would prostitute themselves for a trifling quantity of European goods. Jean Barbot was one of the few writers to observe that Europeans had been a corrupting influence; the women of the interior, he had heard, were not so lewd.[56]

54. Herskovits, *Dahomey*, I, pp. 99–103; II, pp. 16–19, 53–4; Herskovits and Herskovits, *Dahomean Narrative*, pp. 44–5; Astley, *New General Collection*, I, pp. 148–9; II, p. 630; Purchas, *Pilgrimes*, V, pp. 710–16; Bosman, *New and Accurate Description*, p. 349; Barbot, *Description of the Coasts of North and South Guinea*, pp. 235–6; *Gentleman's Magazine*, VIII (1738), pp. 472–3; *London Magazine*, IX (1740), pp. 493–4.

55. Elizabeth Donnan (ed.), *Documents Illustrative of the History of the Slave Trade to America* (Washington, 1930–35), II, pp. 342–61; Astley, *New General Collection*, II, pp. 482–505.

56. *Voyages of Cadamosto*, p. 89; Barbot, *Description of the Coasts of North and South Guinea*, pp. 34–6, 239; Ogilby, *Africa*, p. 347.

The arrival of Europeans on the West African coast clearly disrupted the pattern of native laws and mores governing sexual behaviour. All reports indicate, for example, that Negroes took adultery to be an extremely serious offence. Unfaithful wives were often sold as slaves, and if married to a king, were tortured and killed. Yet jealous husbands were apparently appeased by the promise of goods that could revolutionize a family's way of life.[57]

But wholly apart from European influence, there can be no doubt that many African cultures made sex a prominent and publicly acknowledged part of life. The mythology of sib groups traced their origin to the union of a woman with some animal, a fact which may have nourished European legends of bestiality. The most popular god in several West African cultures was a fun-loving prankster and wanderer who was free to take any woman, and whose erotic impersonations in dances shocked and fascinated Europeans. Negro girls received from older women a well-planned sexual education, which included elaborate exercises and prolonged stimulation of the appropriate organs. Princesses, or women descended from royalty, enjoyed an unrestricted love life, and could divorce a husband at will. At least some African societies accorded high status to public prostitutes, who were required to satisfy the desires of any man. On the other hand, sexual relations were regulated by a highly structured body of customs. Boys remained shy and innocent of sexual matters until well into puberty, and were then initiated into certain forms of play by the more experienced girls. Despite their dominant role, girls were expected to be virgins until the consummation of marriage, which was presided over by the mothers of the wedded couple. Though families were generally polygynous, wives possessed various rights and prerogatives, and were exempt from most duties for a considerable period after childbirth. Precise rules defined the limits of decency; it was forbidden, for example, to make sexual jokes with certain relatives.[58]

Such a mixture of freedom and restraint was, of course, incom-

57. Astley, *New General Collection*, II, pp. 273–4, 436, 644; Ligon, *True and Exact History*, p. 47.

58. Herskovits, *Dahomey*, I, pp. 153, 165, 277–339; II, pp. 38, 45; Herskovits and Herskovits, *Dahomean Narrative*, p. 46.

prehensible to Europeans. It was inconceivable that nakedness should be taken as a sign of virginity in a girl, or that purity could coexist with what seemed the most obscene rites and ceremonies. Travellers faithfully reported that Negroes valued chastity and punished adultery; but this information could not be reconciled with the obvious and shocking fact that Africans enjoyed sex and were unashamed. On occasion, European writers failed to conceal their envy; the Negroes, it was claimed, were free from the crime of rape and from the sneaking hypocrisy of Europeans. But the challenge to conventional standards was too great for such an argument to win widespread acceptance.[59] Hostile writers were able to exploit the most sensational details of African sexual customs, and convey the impression that Negroes were governed by an animal lust that could never be sanctified by the tender emotions of love. This idea served to justify the sexual exploitation of slaves. And it could repeatedly be said that the low birth rate of West Indian slaves was due to the licentiousness of Negro women, though no one explained why a presumably equal licentiousness had opposite results in Africa. The entire subject obviously embarrassed anti-slavery writers, who either ignored it as best they could, or attributed sexual indulgence to the degrading influence of bondage.[60]

But for all their bizarre contrasts of primitive simplicity and primitive carnality, the travel books made one incalculable contribution to anti-slavery opinion. The attempt to justify the slave trade by portraying Africa as a sinkhole of sin could easily boomerang: for if Africa were utterly bereft of law and virtue, then the

59. Astley, *New General Collection*, II, pp. 276, 296; III, pp. 17–20; Sir Hans Sloane, *A Voyage to the Islands of Madera, Barbados, Nieves, S. Christophers and Jamaica* ... (London, 1707), I, pp. xlvii–xlviii; Bryan Edwards, *The History, Civil and Commercial, of the British Colonies in the West Indies* (Philadelphia, 1806), II, pp. 359–60; Sypher, *Guinea's Captive Kings*, p. 33.

60. An important exception was the Abbé Raynal (*Histoire des deux Indes*, VI, p. 116), who tended to romanticize the Negroes' passion. Though the supposedly free sexuality of South Sea islanders appealed to English poets in the 1770s, John Millar argued that primitive people had too little leisure and independence to place much value on sex (*The Origin of the Distinction of Ranks* ... [3rd ed., London, 1781], pp. 18–19, 34–49).

European trader could hardly escape the stain of guilt. According to the popular poet, Edward Young, trade enhanced the power and nobility of 'Tartar Grand' and 'Mogul Great',

> While Afric's black lascivious, slothful breed,
> To clasp their ruin, fly from toil;
>
> That meanest product of their soil,
> Their people, sell; one half on t'other feed. . . .
> 'Mid citron forests and pomegranate groves
> (Cursed in a Paradise!) she pines. . . .[61]

Even Francis Moore, a factor for the Royal African Company, admitted that African chieftains sold their subjects into slavery for the pettiest offences. Numerous French and British accounts revealed that kidnapping and trepanning were common practices among the Negroes, and were far from unusual among European captains and traders who needed a few extra slaves to make up a cargo. Given the constant demand, people sold themselves and their relatives in time of famine, parents sold their children and, as John Atkins put it, the man who sold you slaves today might be sold himself a few days later. Nor were princes and princesses immune from the deadly machine which sucked endless lines of people towards the coastal forts and deposited them between the decks of ships. Traders who did their best to justify the grim business told nevertheless of the wars and slaving raids in the interior, the haggling with African merchants over bars of iron and rifles, the branding and inspection, and the dreadful mortality at sea. Travel books sometimes completed the story with pictures of Negro women being driven to work in the West Indian fields or of recalcitrant men hanging in iron collars from trees.[62] Sir Hans Sloane, who succeeded Newton as president of the Royal Society, and who gave England the collections that formed the

61. Edward Young, 'Imperium Pelagi', in *The Poetical Works of Edward Young* (London, 1866), II, p. 367.

62. Astley, *New General Collection*, II, pp. 35, 242; Barbot, *Description of the Coasts of North and South Guinea*, pp. 47, 110, 270–72; Herskovits, *Dahomey*, II, p. 32; Atkins, *Voyage to Guinea*, pp. 41–2, 61, 151–9, 176–8; Leslie, *New History of Jamaica*, pp. 305–6; François Froger, *Relation of a Voyage Made in the Years 1695, 1696, 1697* (London, 1698), pp. 118–20.

nucleus of the British Museum, also bequeathed the most notorious description of West Indian slavery. Like Pierre Charlevoix and other travellers who left similar accounts, Sloane was not a champion of the Negro. He said that they sometimes merited their worst punishments, and even more. But he told of slaves being gelded, of having spurs jammed into their mouths, of salt and pepper being ground into their wounds, and of their having half a foot chopped off. And he told of Negroes being nailed to the ground and slowly burned with fire.[63] If these scenes had not particularly troubled the good doctor, they troubled some of his readers. And when abolitionists finally began to comb through the travel literature, systematically recording the evidence, they were able to show that the cruelties and barbarities of the most depraved Africans could not begin to match the horrors for which Europe and America were directly responsible.[64]

In Surinam the Governor's Council wanted to make an example of Oroonoko, who had led a slaves' revolt. But when he was tied to a stake, the white men granted his request for a pipe filled with lighted tobacco:

And the Executioner came, and first cut off his Members, and threw them into the Fire; after that, with an ill-favour'd Knife, they cut off his Ears and his Nose, and burn'd them; he still smoak'd on, as if nothing had touch'd him; then they hack'd off one of his Arms, and still he bore up and held his Pipe; but at the cutting off the other Arm, His Head sunk, and his Pipe dropt. ... Thus died this great Man, worthy of a better Fate, and a more sublime Wit than mine to write his Praise: Yet, I hope, the Reputation of my Pen is considerable enough to make his glorious Name to survive to all Ages, with that of the brave, the beautiful and the constant *Imoinda*.[65]

The reputation of Aphra Behn was not so secure as she thought, but indirectly, her hope was fulfilled. Her novelette, *Oroonoko, or the History of the Royal Slave*, was published in 1688, the year of the first definite anti-slavery protest in America. Through the stage

63. Sloane, *Voyage*, I, p. lvii.
64. Seeber, *Anti-Slavery Opinion in France*, pp. 27, 49–51; lists and charts in William Smith papers (Duke University Library).
65. Aphra Behn, *Oroonoko, or, the Royal Slave*, V, *The Works of Aphra Behn* (ed. by Montague Summers, London, 1915), pp. 207–8.

adaptations of Thomas Southerne and John Hawkesworth, and translations by Antoine de Laplace and the Abbé le Blanc, the tale of Oroonoko became one of the most internationally popular stories of the eighteenth century, and served as the prototype for a vast literature depicting noble African slaves.[66]

In order to appreciate the significance of this literature it must be realized that descriptions of cruelty, such as those of Sir Hans Sloane, made little impact so long as the Negro was regarded as merely an object in the colonial system. For example, Daniel Defoe's 'Colonel Jack' realizes that Negroes are human beings and even shows Virginia planters the profitableness of lenient treatment. But Jack's success at labour management, which enables him to rise from indentured servant to wealthy tobacco planter, is based on efficient discipline: first he makes the erring Negro expect the worst imaginable punishment; then he grants a reprieve, accompanied by a lecture designed to leave a 'lasting impression'; and while Jack's technique might have broken even the spirit of an Oroonoko, he admits that a few 'intractable' slaves had to be dealt with more severely.[67] When the Negro was categorized simply as a black, a heathen or a savage, he could be no more than an impersonal object that men manipulated for certain purposes. The growth of anti-slavery opinion would require a shift in focus from the Negro's generalized qualities to specific actions and capabilities that would at once reveal his individuality and his true humanity.

Defenders of slavery could rely on the Christian's traditional horror of paganism and idolatry: how fortunate was the African who was rescued from savagery and given the wholesome discipline of a Christian country! Apologists also affirmed that Negroes would work only under compulsion and were virtually insensitive to pain. These arguments would remain convincing unless Europeans came to think of the African as a man of feeling whose desire for liberty and capacity

66. Edward D. Seeber, ' "Oroonoko" in France in the Eighteenth Century', *Publications of the Modern Language Association*, LI (1936), pp. 953–9; Seeber, *Anti-Slavery Opinion in France*, p. 28; Hoxie Neale Fairchild, *The Noble Savage; A Study in Romantic Naturalism* (New York, 1928), pp. 402–5; Sypher, *Guinea's Captive Kings*, pp. 108–16.

67. Daniel Defoe, *Life, Adventures, and Piracies of Captain Singleton, and Life of Colonel Jack* (London, 1882), pp. 377–93.

for a moral life could not be extinguished by the most oppressive environment. The great question, then, was whether the literary imagination could build a bridge of sympathy and understanding across the enormous gulf that divided primitive and civilized cultures. And if modern taste finds the Negroes of eighteenth-century literature ridiculously contrived and their speech loaded with fustian or obsequiousness, this is really beside the point. Europeans could conceptualize the meaning of enslavement only in the familiar terms that increasingly aroused a sensitive response from the middle class: the separation of young lovers; the heartless betrayal of an innocent girl; the unjust punishment of a faithful servant. And no matter how stylized the literary Negro was to become, his great prototype, Oroonoko, was more realistic than critics have imagined.

Our knowledge of Aphra Behn is distressingly vague. Experts disagree on whether she spent her youth in Surinam, but there can be no doubt that she had some knowledge of colonial slavery. In 1666, when still in her twenties, she travelled to Holland as a British secret agent; her code name was 'Astrea'. Though she served her country well as a spy, she was in a debtor's prison the following year. Her first play, which exposed the evils of forced marriage, was performed on the London stage in 1670. Mrs Behn was celebrated for her great beauty, her brilliant conversation and her love affairs. Known as 'the lewd widow', she wrote some poetry that might have come from the hand of Fanny Hill. But she was also apparently the first Englishwoman to make a living as a professional writer. She was close to Dryden and to a galaxy of Restoration wits, poets and dramatists; she translated La Rochefoucauld and Fontenelle; and Charles II admired some of her plays.[68]

Mrs Behn presented *Oroonoko* as a true story, part of which she had witnessed herself in Surinam. From the outset she made no effort to hide her unconventional primitivism. The South American Indians live in innocent nakedness, instructed by Nature alone: 'Religion would here but destroy that Tranquillity they possess by Ignorance; and Laws would but teach 'em to know Offences, of which now they

68. George Woodcock, *The Incomparable Aphra* (London, 1948), *passim*; Aphra Behn, *Selected Writings of the Ingenious Mrs Aphra Behn* (ed. by Robert Phelps, New York, 1950), *passim*.

have no Notion.' But in sheer beauty and natural dignity the Indians were hardly in a class with Oroonoko and Imoinda, whom Mrs Behn claimed to have known. The African prince had a Roman nose, the body of a Greek god, and a face of 'perfect Ebony, or polished Jet'. Aphra had seen one hundred white men sigh after his 'fair Queen of Night'. And while Oroonoko had been educated by a French tutor as well as by English traders, it was his capacity for 'the highest Passions of Love and Gallantry' that reflected his true greatness of soul. In one of her plays Mrs Behn proclaims that love is a 'divine passion of the soul ... to which we may justly attribute all the real satisfactions of life'.[69]

Oroonoko came from the 'Coramantien' country, where love was uncorrupted by vice or hypocrisy and where, despite the practice of polygamy, the only known crime against a woman was abandonment. As a young prince he led armies into battle and sold his captives to European traders, for which Mrs Behn has no word of reproach. His troubles began when he fell in love with Imoinda, who was also coveted by his grandfather, the king. Though most Coramantien girls thought it the highest honour to be chosen for the king's harem, Imoinda vowed to preserve her chastity for the prince. She could not, however, refuse the king's summons, and Mrs Behn makes it clear that even a Negro girl could have the deepest feelings of shame, modesty and fear. Oroonoko was able to slip into the forbidden sanctum, and consummate his love with Imoinda; but the couple were then betrayed by a guard. Fortunately the old king was not a ruthless man. Believing Imoinda's story that she had been ravished, he refused to kill her. Yet custom forbade his taking her for himself, or allowing another man to marry a woman who had received the royal veil. He had no choice but to sell her into slavery. And because the king's conscience was troubled, he pardoned Oroonoko, after telling him that his lover had been killed.[70]

Some time later, an English captain captured Oroonoko by sheer treachery. Shipped as a slave to Surinam, he was purchased by a man who appreciated his heroic qualities and who granted him unusual liberties. Of course the kindly master also owned Imoinda, whom he

69. Behn, *Oroonoko*, pp. 129–37; Behn, *Selected Writings*, p. 72.
70. Behn, *Oroonoko*, pp. 154–7.

had tried unsuccessfully to seduce. Deeply touched by the couple's remarkable story, the master allowed them to live together, but refused to accept Oroonoko's offers for ransom. Oroonoko, who was now known as Caesar, began brooding over books of Roman history, which nourished his contempt for Christianity. As Imoinda was soon expecting a child, his impatience for freedom grew ever stronger. He began to see that his fellow slaves were treated like senseless brutes, that 'they suffer'd not like Men, who might find a Glory and Fortitude in Oppression; but like Dogs, that lov'd the Whip and Bell, and fawn'd the more they were beaten'.[71]

From the very beginning, the field slaves had looked upon Caesar as a divine leader. And now, fired by long-festering desires for vengeance, he rose up to deliver what must have been the first call for a slave revolt in modern literature. He reminded them of their incredible sufferings, and then asked:

And why . . . my dear Friends and Fellow-sufferers, should we be Slaves to an unknown People? Have they vanquished us nobly in Fight? . . . No, but we are bought and sold like Apes or Monkeys, to be the Sport of Women, Fools and Cowards; and the Support of Rogues and Runagades [sic], that have abandoned their own Countries for Rapine, Murders, Thefts, and Villanies.

Caesar's plan was for the slaves to fight their way, if necessary, to the coast, where they could either found a colony or capture a ship. The party was pursued, however, and the mass of slaves surrendered after their women intervened in the fight. While Caesar denounced the cowardice of his followers, even saying they were fit to be slaves, his greatest scorn was reserved for the Christian religion: 'They wanted only to be whipped into the Knowledge of the Christian Gods, to be the vilest of all creeping Things; to learn to worship such Deities as had not Power to make them just, brave or honest.' Caesar and his chief lieutenant gave themselves up only in response to pleas from his master and a promise of pardon from the governor. But as soon as the two men fell into the hands of the Christians, they were brutally whipped and tortured. Knowing that Imoinda would be raped by every white brute and receive a shameful death, Caesar

71. ibid., pp. 160–72, 190.

managed to escape with her to the woods. There he tenderly embraced her, and then killed her, hiding her body beneath the leaves. Caesar tried to kill himself by disembowelment, but was still alive when the English came. He fought savagely, but was finally captured and dragged to the stake.[72]

This remarkable tale obviously drew on the neo-classic traditions of the French and English stage, but it also contained some significant points of authenticity. Cormantines (the spelling varied considerably) came from the Gold Coast, and were widely esteemed for their bravery, spirit and physical beauty. No less an expert than Christopher Codrington told the Board of Trade that Cormantines 'are really all born Heroes. . . . There never was a raskal or coward of that nation. . . . Not a man of them but will stand to be cut to pieces without a sigh or groan, grateful and obedient to a kind master, but implacably revengeful when ill-treated.'[73] None of the important details of Oroonoko's rivalry with his grandfather, including the significance attached to Imoinda's virginity, seem to conflict with what is known of West African cultures. Some Negro princes did receive instruction from Europeans. Some independent traders did kidnap princes and other important personages, which was a subject of complaint by the Royal African Company eight years before Aphra Behn wrote her story.[74] Indeed in 1749 two such princes created a tremendous sensation when, after being betrayed by an English captain, sold as slaves in the West Indies, ransomed by the British government, and presented to King George himself, they attended Covent Garden to see *Oroonoko*. The audience received them, according to the *Gentleman's Magazine*, with a loud clap of applause, and one prince was so overcome by the play that he had to leave at the end of the fourth act. His companion stayed to the bitter end, shedding tears over the plight of Oroonoko and Imoinda.[75] One may add

72. ibid., pp. 166–9, 191–208.

73. Edwards, *History Civil and Commercial*, II, pp. 252–3; Donnan (ed.), *Documents*, I, p. 398.

74. Barbot, *Description of the Coasts of North and South Guinea*, p. 297; Donnan (ed.), *Documents*, I, pp. 156–7, 267–71.

75. *Gentleman's Magazine*, XIX (1749), pp. 89–90; *London Magazine*, XVIII (1749), p. 94. See also Benjamin Franklin's tale of an African's honour in *Gentleman's Magazine*, XXXIV (1764), p. 177.

that Mrs Behn was accurate in her description of selling slaves by lot. Her pictures of Surinam are convincing. And as late as 1767 it was reported that Jamaican slaves smiled contemptuously while being burned alive.[76]

But the story's significance went beyond its verisimilitude. Despite the fact that Mrs Behn made no explicit attack on the slave trade, she succeeded in portraying a Negro bondsman who was admirable, heroic, full of sex appeal, and passionately in love with freedom. Moreover, he defiantly challenged the entire ideology of Christian obedience and subservience: his own master was a kindly Christian gentleman, and still Oroonoko rebelled. If the prince was set off in sharp relief from the mass of cowardly slaves, he spoke to them of their common degradation and urged them to fight for liberty. Above all, he was not merely part of an undifferentiated species called 'Negro'; he was a Negro who was an individual man.

This message endured even in Thomas Southerne's watered-down play, which was enacted at Drury Lane in 1696 and was then performed nearly every season for a century. Southerne cut out the grisly torture and Oroonoko's violent attacks on Christianity. His Negroes are more wooden and genteel, and their pious love is juxtaposed with the licentious schemings of Europeans, who are bad not because they are white men but because they are not faithful to the white man's creed. Oroonoko's sexuality is refined by his concern for Imoinda's honour in face of the lustful designs of the governor. And the true rebel is Aboan, who tells Oroonoko that the slaves should cut their masters' throats. The prince, however, is now so virtuous that he repeats favourite pro-slavery arguments: these planters, he says, did not make us slaves, but bought us 'in an honest way of trade'! Nevertheless Oroonoko is finally persuaded to revolt, and no audience could mistake the fact that the Negroes are the heroes, and the whites the villains. When Hawkesworth's version appeared on the stage, Oroonoko was played by the great Garrick himself, and Imoinda by Mrs Cibber.[77]

Oroonoko's speech to his fellow slaves must have been the model

76. *London Magazine*, XXXVI (1767), p. 258.

77. Thomas Southerne, *Oroonoko, a Tragedy* (London, 1776), pp. 14–28, 34–49; Montague Summers, introduction to Behn, *Oroonoko*, pp. 127–8.

for the inflammatory harangue of Moses Bom Saam, which appeared in 1735 in both the *Gentleman's Magazine* and the Abbé Prévost's *Pour et Contre*. While the fictional Moses lived in Jamaica and had received full freedom as a reward for courageous service, he studied the white man's civilization in the manner of Oroonoko. Realizing that ignorance kept his fellow Negroes from reflecting upon their wrongs, he saw that he could not enjoy his own liberty while they continued to suffer. He addressed the slaves as brothers-in-misfortune, as fellow sufferers and victims of the white man's tyranny. He informed them that these oppressors, who were so proud of their 'sickly *Whiteness*', were neither wiser nor braver than other men; their apparent superiority was due to mere artifice and education. If the Negroes were to save their children and descendants from endless degradation, they must rise in arms and strike for the mountains, where they could become invincible. Oroonoko was a new Caesar who found inspiration by reading Roman history. The Jamaican leader had steeped himself in the Old Testament, and was a new Moses who would lead his children out of Egypt.[78]

Even before the living example of Toussaint L'Ouverture, the image of a Negro Moses or Caesar was a bit too strong. In 1734 the *Gentleman's Magazine* had reported several slave rebellions in Jamaica; masters had been murdered, plantations burned and Negroes had escaped to the mountains. In the following year the journal printed an outraged reply to the speech of Moses Bom Saam, which included one of the most fully developed defences of colonial slavery yet to appear.[79] But the Oroonoko tradition lived on, even if increasingly softened by sentimentality. It left its mark on Saint-Lambert's

78. *Gentleman's Magazine*, V (1735), pp. 21–2. In 1734 there had been much excitement in England over Job Ben Solomon, a Moslem, and apparently a member of the Jaloff tribe, who had been kidnapped and sent as a slave to Maryland. After writing a letter in Arabic which fell into the hands of James Oglethorpe, Solomon was freed and taken to England, where he was patronized by the queen and nobility, while subscriptions were raised for his return to Africa. The Royal African Company eventually took him home. While the incident undoubtedly increased sympathy for Africans in general, Solomon himself had dealt in slaves and offered no criticisms of the slave system (Donnan [ed.], *Documents*, II, pp. 414–27).

79. *Gentleman's Magazine*, IV (1734), pp. 48, 277; V, pp. 91–2.

Ziméo, which portrayed a noble Negro rebel in Jamaica; it gave a heroic cast to Thomas Day's *The Dying Negro*; it came to full fruition in the multitude of poems and dramas that celebrated Toussaint L'Ouverture.[80]

In chapter 1 we discussed the legend of Inkle and Yarico, which began as a tale of European avarice and Indian innocence, and then served to incorporate the Negro slave within the literary cult of primitivism. This story of natural love and heartless abandonment became a second mode of empathizing with a people otherwise cut off by insurmountable barriers of culture. Originally, as we have seen, Africa was excluded from the primitivism that endowed Indians with pristine natural virtues. Defoe, for example, took pains to show that his Friday was not a Negro. But the increasing interchangeability of Indians and Negroes was perhaps less a sign of racial ignorance than of a gradual extension of the primitivistic ideal.[81] After the mid eighteenth century Africa became less a symbol of monstrous barbarism, and more like the earthly paradises which moved always from the more familiar regions to the more remote. In 1775, the year after London's craze over Omai of the South Seas, the *Gentleman's Magazine* could find primitive virtues in even the Hottentots: 'But what signifies the mind's being vacant, if the heart be full, and the sweet emotions of nature agitate it?'[82]

It was the agitations of the heart that defined the final literary image of the Negro, which reached its apotheosis in Harriet Beecher Stowe's *Uncle Tom*. Wylie Sypher has commented on the great inconsistency between the noble savage and the suffering slave who arouses only sympathy and tears.[83] Yet both figures played essential

80. *Ephémérides du citoyen, ou bibliothèque raisonée des sciences morales et politiques,* VI (1771), pp. 182–207; Thomas Day and John Bicknell, *The Dying Negro, a Poetical Epistle, from a Black, Who Shot Himself on Board a Vessel in the River Thames, to His Intended Wife* (2nd ed., London, 1774).

81. Wylie Sypher discusses the confusion of Indians and Negroes, but does not make this point (*Guinea's Captive Kings,* pp. 105–7). See also R. M. Kain, 'The Problem of Civilization in English Abolition Literature, 1772–1808', *Philological Quarterly,* XV (October 1936), pp. 103–25.

82. Kain, 'Problem of Civilization', p. 109.

83. Sypher, *Guinea's Captive Kings,* pp. 9, 103–5.

roles in conditioning anti-slavery opinion. If the Negro was a terrifying avenger, returning blow for blow, demanding as many drops
of blood as he had shed through centuries of oppression, he struck a
response in one part of the white man's nature. This would be how
the European should want to act if he were a slave. But if the Negro
patiently accepted flagellation and torture; if he cut his own throat,
like Raynal's 'Quazy', rather than resist his master's unjust punishment; if he hung in a cage, like the slave described by Crèvecoeur
appealing pathetically for water, his eyes pecked out by birds – he
struck an equally important response of pity and fascination.[84] This
was, after all, the way Christians were supposed to behave. In both
postures the Negro was unmistakably a sensitive man, and not a
brute. In both postures he challenged the traditional ideal of Christian servitude as a relationship of reciprocal love and obligation. And
if there was a note of artificial sentimentality to the pining, agoniz-
ing slaves who became stock characters in the literature of the late
eighteenth century, they gave a directness and emotional intensity to
rational arguments that had long been ignored. Beginning in 1768,
British playgoers confronted 'Mungo', in Isaac Bickerstaffe's *The
Padlock*; who asked: 'Comes freedom then from colour? blush with
shame,/ And let strong nature's crimson mark your blame![85] Even
Germans became familiar with the slave's lament:

> Far from my fatherland
> Must I here languish and waste away,
> Without comfort, in toil and shame;
> Oh the white men! Wise and handsome!
> And I haven't harmed the merciless whites.
> Oh Lord in Heaven,
> Help this poor black soul![86]

84. Raynal, *Histoire des deux Indes*, VII, pp. 254–5; Michel-Guillaume
Jean de Crèvecoeur, *Letters From an American Farmer* (Dutton paperback
ed., New York, 1957), pp. 166–8.

85. Sypher, *Guinea's Captive Kings*, pp. 236–7.

86. Quoted in German by Anna Christie Cronholm, *Die Nordameri-
kanische Sklavenfrage im Deutschen Schrifttum des 19. Jahrhunderts*
(Ph.D. thesis, Free University of Berlin, 1958), pp. 5–16.

By the 1770s and 1780s the plight of the Negro had become a major theme in French poetry. In England the subject would attract a host of forgotten scribblers, along with Blake, Cowper, Burns, Coleridge, Southey and Wordsworth.

One may easily take a critical view of these literary fashions. Englishmen and even West Indians wrote of sable Venuses, dusky swains, tear-bedewed daughters of 'injur'd Afric', and yet defended the slave trade as a vital part of the Empire.[87] In 1844 a critic pointed out to the British and Foreign Anti-Slavery Society that some of the sympathy for Negroes was like 'that sensibility which sheds floods over the feigned distresses of the stage, and looks unmoved upon the miseries of the world'.[88] But it is sometimes necessary to act out moral problems upon the stage before grappling with the worst miseries of the world. For a variety of reasons the Negro had been cut off from the normal mechanisms of sympathy and identification. He was burdened by the weight of ancient fears associated with his colour; he suffered from the consequences of an immense cultural barrier, which was heightened by the European's sensitivity to unrepressed sexuality; he carried the stigma of all the vices which slavery had thrust upon him; and the very spirit of secular science which brought emancipation to the European mind tended to relegate him to a position of natural inferiority. There is no precise way of knowing how much the changing literary image of the Negro counteracted these obstacles. We do know, however, that by the 1770s anti-slavery writers as diverse as Raynal and Wesley were able to exploit a whole range of themes and conventions which portrayed the Negro slave as a man of natural virtue and sensitivity who was at once oppressed by the worst vices of civilization and yet capable of receiving its greatest benefits.

87. Edwards, *History Civil and Commercial*, II, pp. 227–33, 294–5; James Grainger, 'The Sugar Cane', in *The Works of the English Poets, from Chaucer to Cowper*, XIV (London, 1810), pp. 504–8; Sypher, *Guinea's Captive Kings*, p. 169.

88. George R. Mellor, *British Imperial Trusteeship, 1783–1850* (London, 1951), pp. 161–2.

Epilogue

John Woolman's Prophecy

In 1746 a young West Jersey tailor named John Woolman felt a 'concern' in his mind to visit fellow Quakers in Virginia and North Carolina. Woolman's urge to travel may have been influenced by the fact that his employer's retirement had left him without a job at a time when living costs were being elevated by the prosperity of Neighbouring Quaker merchants, who were making fortunes in the West India trade.[1] And yet ascetic travel had long been accepted by Quakers as a means of self-discipline and social purification. John Pemberton, whose family was deeply involved in West Indian rum and sugar, would soon be travelling as a missionary in Great Britain, denouncing worldliness and corruption, and warning sinners of the impending Day of Judgement. Samuel Fothergill, brother of the cosmopolitan London physician, would soon be telling Maryland Quakers that slavery was corroding their religious purity.[2]

Woolman had long felt a poignant fear of the vanities, luxuries and selfish interests of the world. Having steeped himself in the writings of English and French mystics, he had come to see the sufferings and rewards of this life as a succession of tests through which man must seek eternity.[3] But although his religious exercises had helped him

1. Janet Whitney, *John Woolman: American Quaker* (Boston, 1942), pp. 100, 109; John Woolman, *The Journal of John Woolman* (Introduction by Frederick B. Tolles, Corinth paperback ed., New York, 1961), pp. 19–22.

2. Journal of John Pemberton, 1752 (Pemberton Papers, Pennsylvania Historical Society); Sydney V. James, *A People Among Peoples: Quaker Benevolence in Eighteenth-Century America* (Cambridge, Mass., 1963), pp. 159–61.

3. W. Forrest Altman, 'John Woolman's Reading of the Mystics', *Bulletin of the Friends' Historical Association*, XLVIII (Autumn 1959), pp. 103–15; Amelia Mott Gummere, introduction to John Woolman, *The Journal and Essays of John Woolman* (New York, 1922), pp. 14–15.

overcome youthful frivolity and wantonness, he was troubled by the memory of one crucial failure. When his master had asked him to write a bill of sale for a Negro woman, he had complied against the promptings of his conscience. In the South he was similarly uneasy over accepting food and lodging from Quaker slave-owners, especially as he saw how the white youth, relieved from the healthful discipline of work, were led to idleness and worldly vice. The depraving effects of slavery became deeply impressed on Woolman's mind as he travelled through Virginia, where the institution appeared 'as a dark gloominess hanging over the land'. Soon after returning to Burlington County, he gave expression to his anxieties by writing *Some Considerations on the Keeping of Negroes*. But though encouraged by his dying father to consult leading Friends on the advisability of publishing the tract, Woolman kept his opinions to himself until 1754.[4]

The mid eighteenth century was not an auspicious time to launch an anti-slavery crusade. When Woolman made his first Southern trip, officials in Georgia had virtually abandoned efforts to impede the importation of slaves, and in four years an act of Parliament would officially end the single experiment to exclude Negroes from an American colony. Nearly a decade before Woolman's journey, Benjamin Lay had published his blistering indictment of slaveholders, but in 1746 Lay was a forgotten eccentric who lived in isolation, disowned and ostracized by the Society of Friends. The most admired and envied of Woolman's Quaker acquaintances – the Pembertons, the Logans, the Smiths – owned slaves. The most advanced position that could win acceptance from the Quaker elite was probably epitomized by a printed epistle of 1741 from John Bell, an English Friend. The essence of Bell's message was the necessity of spreading the Gospel light after a long night of apostasy. True Christians must 'be as Lights to those who yet remain in Darkness'. They should treat their slaves with compassion, and convert servitude into an agency of conversion. But Bell's interpretation of the Golden Rule assumed that slavery was not incompatible with Christian duty. His exhortation was no more than the conventional attempt to apply the dualisms of

4. Woolman, *Journal* (this and subsequent references to the *Journal* are to the 1961 ed.), pp. 14–15, 22–32; Whitney, *John Woolman*, p. 187.

Saint Paul to an exploitive and speculative economic institution.[5]

And yet the eight years that intervened between Woolman's Southern trip and the publication of his first anti-slavery tract represented a turning point in the history of Western culture. To both religious and secular writers the period brought an almost explosive consciousness of man's freedom to shape the world in accordance with his own will and reason. And as the dogmas and restraints of the past lost their compelling force, there was a heightened concern for discovering laws and principles that would enable human society to be something more than an endless contest of greed and power. This quest for moral assurance led inevitably to examinations of inequality, sovereignty and servitude. Two years after Woolman's trip, Montesquieu's *L'Esprit des lois* demolished the traditional justifications for slavery, and placed the subject on the agenda of the French Enlightenment. In 1752 James Foster's *Discourses* judged the institution by the ethics of latitudinarian theology, and David Hume focused attention on the relation of slavery to population growth. The year 1775 saw the appearance of Hutcheson's *System of Moral Philosophy*, Rousseau's *Discours sur l'inégalité*, de Jaucourt's first anti-slavery article in the *Encyclopédie*, and Franklin's calculations on the economic wastefulness of slave labour.

One may also note that the publication of Woolman's *Considerations* coincided with the outbreak of hostilities on the Pennsylvania frontier, and hence with the beginning of a war which soon involved English, Spanish and French colonies from Grenada to Gorée, and from Cuba to Bengal. The loss by France of most of her colonial empire, and the acquisition of Canada by Britain, quite naturally stimulated a searching reassessment of all aspects of imperial economics and administration. And the post-war inquiries of economists and statesmen came at a time when the British sugar islands were suffering from the effects of exhausted soil and antiquated methods of production, and were increasingly dependent on an artificially protected market; when French and Spanish sugar was

5. Whitney, *John Woolman*, pp. 82–3: [John Bell], *An Epistle to Friends in Maryland, Virginia, Barbados, and the Other Colonies, and Islands in the West-Indies, Where Any Friends Are* (Bromley near London, 1741), pp. 1–3.

glutting the European market and depressing prices; when the cost of African slaves was rising; when debts and depleted soil in the North American tobacco colonies were forcing planters to turn to crop diversification and westward expansion. Such conditions provided a favourable context for questioning slavery on economic and political grounds. And if this was not enough, the Seven Years' War gave added force to the feelings of physical insecurity which had long plagued colonists who lived among vast populations of slaves. Since the war proved that whole empires were vulnerable to military conquest, colonists had new reason to fear the unlimited importation of men who might someday look to an invader for liberation.

Given this convergence of cultural, intellectual, economic and strategic developments, it is not surprising that the climate of opinion on slavery should have changed by 1769, when John Woolman felt obliged to make a missionary trip to the West Indies. In this study we have not been concerned with events which led directly to the international anti-slavery movements of the late eighteenth century. We should not conclude our inquiry, however, without taking note of certain patterns of communication and influence that were developing on the eve of the American Revolution.

Benjamin Rush was one of the focal points of converging intellectual currents. A member of an old Pennsylvania family which had originally been Quaker and which had connexions with the Keithian anti-slavery schismatics, Rush was educated and deeply influenced by the 'New Light' Presbyterian, Samuel Finley. A friend of the revivalists George Whitefield and Samuel Davies, he was also close to Benjamin Franklin and, as a student at Edinburgh, to David Hume and William Robertson. With Arthur Lee he visited John Wilkes in prison. In Paris, thanks to Franklin's introductions, he became acquainted with the Physiocrats, the elder Mirabeau and Diderot, the latter entrusting him with correspondence to deliver to Hume. As we have seen, it was in 1769 that Rush's letter to Barbeu Dubourg prompted Du Pont de Nemours to link the Quaker's manumission of their slaves with the hope of universal emancipation, the rise of an American empire, and the economic reformation of Europe. In 1773 Rush was encouraged by his friend Anthony Benezet to initiate a long and fruitful correspondence with Granville Sharp and to write an anti-slavery pamphlet which drew on the recently published theories of John Millar.[6]

In 1769 the *Weekly Magazine or Edinburgh Amusement* printed one of the strongest indictments of slavery yet to appear in a British journal. The author's arguments were chiefly derived from Montesquieu. In the same year Granville Sharp, who had become involved in a legal battle to free a Negro in London, published *A Representation of the Injustice and Dangerous Tendency of Tolerating Slavery in England*. This work, which was also indebted to Montesquieu, was thought by later abolitionists to have signalled the beginning of the British anti-slavery crusade. By 1769 Sharp had become so convinced that slavery was an innovation which violated fundamental rights that he was addressing appeals to everyone from William Blackstone to the Archbishop of Canterbury, and was warning his erring land of the certainty of God's judgements. In 1767 he had been browsing in a bookstall and had stumbled upon Anthony Benezet's *A Short Account of That Part of Africa, Inhabited by the Negroes*. Sharp was so impressed by the pamphlet that he had it reprinted right away. Originally published in Philadelphia in 1762, the work presented favourable descriptions of Africa extracted from some of the travel literature we have already discussed, and quoted anti-slavery passages from Hutchinson, Foster, Richard Savage, J. Philmore and George Wallace, none of whom were American. Even before Sharp had reprinted Benezet's tract in England, it had been translated into French.

In 1772, just as John Woolman was beginning the travels in England which resulted in his death, Sharp learned of his own victory in the celebrated Somerset case, in which Chief Justice Mansfield ruled that the power claimed by a slaveholder had never been acknowledged in English law. At almost the same moment, Sharp received his first letter from Anthony Benezet, who had already

6. Benjamin Rush, *The Autobiography of Benjamin Rush* (ed. by George W. Corner, Princeton, 1948), *passim*; *Letters of Benjamin Rush* (ed. by L. H. Butterfield, Princeton, 1951), I and II, *passim*; [Benjamin Rush], *An Address to the Inhabitants of the British Settlements in America, upon Slave-Keeping* (Philadelphia, 1773). I am much indebted to John A. Woods for letting me see his transcripts of Rush's letters to Sharp, which are not included in the above collection.

reprinted an abridgement of *A Representation of the Injustice and Dangerous Tendency of Tolerating Slavery in England*, along with William Warburton's sermon of 1766 to the SPG. Though Sharp regarded Benezet as 'unhappily involved in the errors of Quakerism', this letter initiated a highly significant correspondence which was to touch leaders of the Church of England as well as Benjamin Franklin.[7]

While the Quakers provided a striking model of humanitarianism and were praised by John Wesley as well as by Turgot and Voltaire, the Society of Friends was hardly in advance of enlightened opinion on both sides of the Atlantic. In 1767, when one of Benezet's pamphlets was being reprinted and distributed by the London Meeting for Sufferings, the author himself was sending out copies of an anti-slavery address which had just appeared in *The Virginia Gazette*. Only a few years later there was a flurry of anti-slavery agitation in New England, where Arminians, revivalists, Quakers and revolutionaries seemed to have found a common cause. It was in 1771 that the Massachusetts legislature passed a bill to outlaw the importation of slaves, and that Du Pont de Nemours, after trying to synthesize an anti-slavery philosophy of utility and sensibility, vowed to employ all his powers to break the Negro's chains. Two years later Thomas Day of Birmingham, an intimate of Erasmus Darwin, Matthew Boulton, Josiah Wedgwood and Joseph Priestley, wrote his immensely popular *The Dying Negro*, a poem which cited Montesquieu, Hutcheson and Adam Smith, and the second edition of which was dedicated to Rousseau.[8]

Illustrations could easily be multiplied, but the central point should now be clear. By the early 1770s a large number of moralists, poets, intellectuals and reformers had come to regard American sla-

7. *Weekly Magazine or Edinburgh Amusement*, 31 October 1769; *Prince Hoare, Memoirs of Granville Sharp . . .* (London, 1820), *passim*.

8. Lorenzo J. Greene, 'Slave-Holding New England and its Awakening', *Journal of Negro History*, XIII (October 1928), pp. 525–7; George Warren Gignilliat, *The Author of 'Sanford and Merton': A Life of Thomas Day* (New York, 1932), pp. 71–9; Thomas Day and John Bicknell, *The Dying Negro, a Poetical Epistle, from a Black, Who Shot Himself on Board a Vessel in the River Thames, to His Intended Wife* (London, 1773); the same (2nd ed., London, 1774).

very as an unmitigated evil. In Britain, France and the North American colonies there were forces in motion that would lead to organized movements to abolish the African trade and the entire institutional framework which permitted human beings to be treated as things. Although slavery was nearly as old as human history, this was something new to the world. By now we should have some understanding of the cultural and intellectual changes which made possible so dramatic a shift in perception. We might schematize what we have learned as a great equation. On one side were the classical and Christian theories of servitude, which tended to rationalize the brute fact that forced labour had been an integral part of the American experience. On the other side were increasing strains in the traditional system of values, the emergence of new modes of thought and feeling, and a growing faith in the possibility of moral progress which was to some extent associated with the symbolic meaning of the New World. But in the last analysis, such trends and contexts and backgrounds are only abstractions. No matter how 'ripe' the time, there would be no coalescing of anti-slavery opinion until specific decisions and commitments were taken by individual men.

This is not to say that a John Woolman or Anthony Benezet single-handedly awakened the world. One can easily exaggerate the importance of the fact that Granville Sharp, John Wesley and Thomas Clarkson were all inspired by Benezet's words. The ideas, as we have seen, were in the air. Yet when all allowances are made for cultural trends and climates of opinion, one must ultimately come down to the men who precipitated change. If the Western world became more receptive to anti-slavery thought between the time when Woolman left for North Carolina in 1746 and when he arrived in England in 1772, the self-effacing Quaker was a major instrument of the transformation.

At first sight it is difficult to understand why Woolman should have been so revered by later anti-slavery historians. He was not a fearless castigator of sin like Benjamin Lay. He was not a compiler and publicist like Anthony Benezet. He was not an anti-slavery theorist like George Keith, Francis Hutcheson and Montesquieu. His enduring contribution to anti-slavery literature was not an inflammatory tract or an eloquent manifesto, but rather the journal of his own life. For the secret of Woolman's influence was his sense of personal involvement, his ability to see Negro slavery as something more than an abstract institution, his conviction that he shared the profound guilt of all America.

His *Journal* has too often been read as the expression of a man at peace with himself and the world, of a man who has found perfect serenity of soul. It is actually the inner record of a soul tormented by a ceaseless conflict between yearnings for peace and purity. John Woolman was acutely sensitive to the opinions of others and valued consensus and accord. He was familiar with all the self-righteous disguises of his own ego. And yet few men have been so aware of the subtle ways in which society accommodates the individual conscience to self-interest. So far as slavery was concerned, he was too devout to be contemptuous of Biblical sanctions, or of the traditional ideal of the paternalistic master and humble servant. He knew pious men whose consciences were apparently not troubled by the ownership of Negroes. But as a shopkeeper and scrivener, Woolman had to make decisions which either supported or questioned the rightness of slave-holding. In 1753 he began refusing to write wills that bequeathed slave property. The following year, in executing the will of a deceased Quaker, he sold a small Negro boy for a term of service that would end at the age of thirty, and applied the money to the estate. The transaction haunted Woolman's conscience, and in later years he sought to make restitution for the sin. His sense of guilt was augmented by the fact that he had long sold West Indian sugar and molasses. These were the pressures behind Woolman's plan of 1769 to make a pilgrimage to the Caribbean. He would apply the profits he had made from slave-grown produce to a holy cause.[9]

He was troubled, however, by the thought of travelling on a ship engaged in the deadly trade which nourished the slave system. Recalling how David could not bring himself to drink water for which men had risked their lives, merely to satisfy his 'delicacy of taste', Woolman had for some years declined to eat sugar. He was willing to face the charge of eccentricity by wearing clothes and even a hat untainted by dyes. But how could one go to minister to the un-

9. Woolman, *Journal*, pp. 14–15, 30, 36–7, 174–5, 179.

righteous without partaking of their unrighteousness? On his second journey through the South, in 1757, Woolman had left money for the slaves who served him in each house where he stayed, so that he might be free from all association with unrequited labour. He felt he should pay more than the usual passage money to the West Indies, on the assumption that the low fare was the result of an unnatural trade. He thought of hiring a ship to sail in ballast. He acknowledged, however, that if trade with the West Indies were to be suddenly stopped, 'many there would suffer for want of bread'. In the end, the burden of decision proved too great, and after vacillating in his plans, Woolman became seriously ill. He was thus spared the sight of field gangs on a West India plantation.[10]

By 1769 Woolman was showing signs of mental strain and personal oddity which were only partly related to his continuing testimony against slavery. By that time he no longer stood virtually alone, as he had at mid-century. In 1761 London Yearly Meeting had ruled that dealing in slaves merited disownment. For eleven years Philadelphia Yearly Meeting had been excluding Friends who bought or sold slaves from participation in the business affairs of the society. The rule of 1758 was being used as a weapon by local visiting committees, who made it clear to slaveholders that total disownment would be the penalty for a continuing refusal to prepare their Negroes for eventual emancipation. The evolution of these policies owed much to the stimulus of the Seven Years' War, to the general reform movement within the Society of Friends, and to the activities of such men as the Fothergills, John Churchman and Anthony Benezet. And yet Woolman had written the influential epistle sent out by Philadelphia Yearly Meeting in 1754, which expressed concern over the Quakers' growing involvement in slavery, and which announced the new ideal of educating Negroes for ultimate freedom. He had been instrumental in securing official approval for the rule of 1758; and in the face of stiffening resistance, he had led the way in visiting and exhorting slaveholders to cleanse themselves of corruption. On a tour of New England he had urged prominent Quakers to petition their assemblies to prohibit further importation of slaves. Travelling through Delaware he had given encouragement to the followers

10. ibid., pp. 52, 132, 180–84.

of Joseph Nichols, who in 1768 decided to free their slaves.[11]

While John Woolman's chief influence lay in his face-to-face confrontation with slaveholders, we may assume that the substance of his thought can be found in *Some Considerations on the Keeping of Negroes*, the second part of which appeared in 1762. These essays are infused with a calm and charitable spirit that reinforces the simplicity and moral earnestness of the author's message. Woolman is always careful to refrain from judging slave-owners as a group. He does not demand immediate and universal emancipation. But he writes in the language of an Old Testament prophet, and his judgements have the authority of man's universal conscience.

There are two great themes in Woolman's work. To those who held to the ancient dualisms of body and soul, who maintained that external condition had no effect on internal freedom and purity, Woolman replied with devastating candour. Theoretically, a master might retain his slave for only the highest motives. But could any slaveholder affirm that his perception had not been distorted by custom, self-love and racial prejudice? Could he honestly imagine himself in his

---

11. James, *People Among Peoples*, pp. 130–40, 159–61, 216–71; 'Letters Which Passed Betwixt the Meeting for Sufferings in London, and the Meeting for Sufferings in Philadelphia . . .' (Bound MSS, Friends House, London), esp. London to Philadelphia, 1 February 1759; [Nathan Kite], *A Brief Statement of the Rise and Progress of the Testimony of the Religious Society of Friends, against Slavery and the Slave Trade* (Philadelphia, 1843), pp. 43–4; Anne T. Gary, 'The Political and Economic Relations of the English and American Quakers' (D. Phil. thesis, Oxford, 1935), pp. 191–2, 200–201; Society of Friends, Philadephia Yearly Meeting, *An Epistle of Caution and Advice, concerning the Buying and Keeping of Slaves* (Philadelphia, 1754), pp. 1–7; Whitney, *John Woolman*, pp. 191–5, 261–7; Woolman, *Journal*, pp. 53–5, 84–5, 92–3, 113; Kenneth L. Carroll, 'Religious Influences on the Manumission of Slaves in Carolina, Dorchester, and Talbot Counties', *Maryland History Magazine*, LVI (June 1961), pp. 184–6. Joseph Nichols founded a schismatic Nicholite Society, which was in advance of other Quakers in anti-slavery principles. He should not be confused with Thomas Nicholson, a North Carolina Quaker, who in an open letter of 1 June 1767 pointed to the corrupting effects of slavery on true religion, called on Quakers to abandon the 'Babylonish' practice, and offered a plan for getting around North Carolina laws restricting manumissions (Pennsylvania Historical Society, Misc. Collec., Negroes, Box 11-A & B).

bondsman's place, and think that he would still approve a system which led to wars and kidnapping in Africa, to the Middle Passage, and to the subjugation of one race for the benefit of another? In Woolman's view human beings were not saintly enough to make Negro slavery conform to the Christian ideal. The degradation of Negroes was so complete that even the most humane masters were misled by a false association of ideas. The notion of racial inferiority blocked the flow of natural affections and opened the flood gates to self-love and aggression. Bit by bit the evils fed upon themselves and the darkness thickened and became fastened upon the land.[12]

The full meaning of self-delusion and personal guilt could be understood only when one remembered that the God of our fathers 'furnished a table for us in the wilderness, and made the deserts and solitary places to rejoice'. The Lord had opened a New World to mankind, and as with Israel of old, had blessed His chosen people with freedom and material plenty. And instead of being humbled by such success, and being content with the satisfaction of simple wants, the people had succumbed to greed. They had become absorbed in the pursuit of luxury, which they sought to pass on to their children, instead of 'an inheritance incorruptible'.[13] God's displeasure was already manifest in a succession of wars and calamities. And it was the prophecy of John Woolman that if Americans continued to be unfaithful to their high destiny, their descendants would face the awful retribution of God's justice.

12. Woolman, *Journal and Essays*, pp. 337–40, 352–81.
13. ibid., pp. 340–45, 381.

Index

Slavery – *contd*

economic meanings of, 365–6, 408–9, 424–6, 460–62, 464–70, 471–3; image of in antislavery literature, 211, 390, 403–6, 413–15, 444–5, 506–17; in China, 50, 67, 100–101; in Cyprus, 57–8; in England, 53, 54–5, 233–4, 235–6; in French Canada, 145–6, 201–2; in India, 62–3, 67–8; in Italy, 53, 58–60, 71–2, 119–20; in Latin America, 22, 147–51, 214–20, 252–4, 255–7, 258–69, 289–90, 291–6; in Ptolomaic Egypt, 100–101; in Russia, 49–50, 56–8; in Scotland, 471–2; in the ancient world, 47–8, 50–52, 62–6, 70–71, 76–7; in the Bible, 62–4, 79–82, 101–3; in the British West Indies, 179, 180–83, 184–5, 243–7, 307–9; in the French West Indies, 184, 230–32; in the Iberian peninsula, 56–7, 58–60, 68–9, 120–22, 264–5; in the Northern colonies, 155–7, 221–2, 398–9; in the Southern colonies, 156–8; in the Southern states, 73–4, 296–301; inherent contradiction of, 74–6, 77–8, 84, 187–8, 274; institutional continuity of, 46, 52, 60–61; legal characteristics of in the British and French colonies, 274–88; metaphorical meanings of, 50, 101; philosophical meanings of, 79, 83, 92–8, 135–6, 391–3, 424–5, 456–7, 472–3; political meanings of, 81, 83–5, 87–8, 136–9, 401–2, 424–7, 432–3, 440–41, 446–7, 448–9, 451–3, 472–4, 475–6; profitability of, 152–4, 176–9, 461, 465–8, 468–9, 471–2; racial basis of, 45, 61–2, 64–5, 67–9, 119–20, 197–8, 200, 224, 246–7, 271–3; religious meanings of, 80–82, 94–5, 101–8, 187–8, 215–18, 228–30, 339–40,

396–8, 417–18, 420–22, 433–4, 452–3; role of in development of America, 22–4, 29–31, 147–51, 175–7, 179–81, 186; status of inherited from mother, 53, 55–6, 114–5, 304–6; *see also* Antislavery thought, Authority, Emancipation, Enslavement, Freedmen, Luxury, Natural law, Negroes, Original sin, Proslavery thought, Sin, Slave trade, Slaves, *and* Wealth: problem of

Slaves: baptism of, 116–20, 227–32, 233–6, 239–40, 243–5, 260–61, 278–9, 377–9; branding of, 64–5, 244–5, 265–6, 286–7; demand for, 145–6, 152–8, 162–3, 168–9, 170–71; differentiated from freemen, 62–70; foreign origin of, 62–3, 67–9, 118–20, 198–203; fugitive, 72–3; holidays for, 262–3, 278–9; humanity of recognized by courts in the Southern States, 274, 282–4, 296–301; insurrections of, 51, 72, 149, 158–60, 265–6, 454–6, 511, 514–5; legal protection of, 73–4, 76–7, 120–22, 256–8, 259–61, 264–5, 277–8, 280–88; legitimacy of sale of, 211–13, 219–21, 427, 439–40, 449–50; manumission of, 70–74, 102, 110–11, 265–6, 289–301, 305–8, 313–15; marriage of, 53, 62–3, 74, 122–5, 244–5, 278–9; mistreatment of, 76–7, 219–20, 261–2, 263–4; mortality of, 245–6, 257–8; natural inferiority of, 82–3, 86–7, 114–16, 225, 227, 447–9, 474–5; occupations of, 51, 75; origin of word, 68; privileges accorded to in the Southern states, 254–5, 296; property of, 74–5, 280–81; punishment of, 76–7, 121–2, 262–3, 512; separation of families of, 256–7, 260–61; social control of, 242–3,

MORE ABOUT PENGUINS
AND PELICANS

Penguinews, which appears every month, contains details of all the new books issued by Penguins as they are published. From time to time it is supplemented by *Penguins in Print*, which is a complete list of all books published by Penguins which are in print. (There are well over three thousand of these.)

A specimen copy of *Penguinews* will be sent to you free on request, and you can become a subscriber for the price of the postage. For a year's issues (including the complete lists) please send 25p if you live in the United Kingdom, or 50p if you live elsewhere. Just write to Dept EP, Penguin Books Ltd, Harmondsworth, Middlesex, enclosing a cheque or postal order, and your name will be added to the mailing list.

Note: *Penguinews* and *Penguins in Print* are not available in the U.S.A. or Canada